INTERNATIONAL HISTORY OF THE TWENTIETH CENTURY AND BEYOND

'The best single volume study now available ... admirably suited to under-graduate survey courses.'

Michael F. Hopkins, *Contemporary British History*

This major global history of the twentieth century is written by four prominent international historians for first-year undergraduate level and upward. Using their thematic and regional expertise, the authors have produced an authoritative yet accessible account of the history of international relations in the last century and beyond, covering events in Europe, Asia, the Middle East, Africa and the Americas. They focus on the history of relations between states and on the broad ideological, economic and cultural forces that have influenced the evolution of international politics over the past one hundred years and more. Among the areas this book covers are:

- the decline of European hegemony over the international order
- the diffusion of power to the two superpowers
- the rise of newly independent states in Asia and Africa
- the course and consequences of the three major global conflicts of the twentieth century: the First World War, the Second World War and the Cold War.

New features of the second edition include:

- a new chapter on European integration and the rise of supra-governmental organizations
- a new chapter overview on the state of the world with an emphasis on events post-9/11 and the 'global war on terror'
- a new textbook design with margins for glossary terms and cross-references, chapter introductions and conclusions, debates boxes, bibliographical essays and documents
- a support website with links to primary source sites, discussion questions for each chapter and downloadable debates boxes and maps at www.routledge.com/textbooks/9780415438964

Antony Best is Senior Lecturer in International History at the London School of Economics. **Jussi M. Hanhimäki** is Professor of International History and Politics at the Graduate Institute of International Studies, Geneva. **Joseph A. Maiolo** is Senior Lecturer in International History at the Department of War Studies, King's College London. **Kirsten E. Schulze** is Senior Lecturer in International History at the London School of Economics.

INTERNATIONAL HISTORY OF THE TWENTIETH CENTURY AND BEYOND

SECOND EDITION

Antony Best

Jussi M. Hanhimäki

Joseph A. Maiolo

Kirsten E. Schulze

Routledge
Taylor & Francis Group

LONDON AND NEW YORK

First published 2004

Reprinted 2004, 2005 (twice), 2006, 2007 (three times), 2008, 2009
Reprinted 2010

This edition published 2008
by Routledge
2 Park Square, Milton Park, Abingdon, Oxon OX14 4RN

Simultaneously published in the USA and Canada
by Routledge
270 Madison Ave, New York, NY 10016

Routledge is an imprint of the Taylor & Francis Group, an informa business

Typeset in Adobe Garamond and Parasine by
Keystroke, 28 High Street, Tettenhall, Wolverhampton
Printed and bound in Great Britain by
the MPG Books Group, Bodmin

British Library Cataloguing in Publication Data
A catalogue record for this book is available from the British Library

Library of Congress Cataloging-in-Publication Data
International history of the twentieth century and beyond/Antony Best . . .
[et al.]. — 2nd ed.
     p. cm.
   Revision of: International history of the twentieth century. 2004.
      Includes bibliographical references and index.
   1. World politics–20th century.   2. World politics–21st century.
   I. Best, Antony, 1964–   II. International history of the twentieth
century.
   D443.I57 2008
   909.82–dc22   2007051679

ISBN10: 0–415–43895–0 (hbk)
ISBN10: 0–415–43896–9 (pbk)
ISBN10: 0–203–88986–X (ebk)

ISBN13: 978–0–415–43895–7 (hbk)
ISBN13: 978–0–415–43896–4 (pbk)
ISBN13: 978–0–203–88986–2 (ebk)

FOR OUR PARENTS

Contents

CONTENTS

ILLUSTRATIONS

Maps

Figure

Tables

Boxes

Debates and controversies

Documents

Plates

AUTHORS

Antony Best is Senior Lecturer in International History at the London School of Economics. He is the author of *Britain, Japan and Pearl Harbor: Avoiding War in East Asia, 1936–41* (1995), *British Intelligence and the Japanese Challenge in Asia, 1914–1941* (2002) and a number of articles on Anglo-Japanese relations in the inter-war period. He is currently working on a study of race, mutual perceptions and images in Anglo-Japanese relations.

Jussi M. Hanhimäki is Professor of International History and Politics at the Graduate Institute of International Studies, Geneva, Switzerland, and Finland Distinguished Professor at the Academy of Finland and Tampere University. He is the author (with Odd Arne Westad) of *The Cold War: A History in Documents and Eye-Witness Accounts* (2003), *The Flawed Architect: Henry Kissinger and American Foreign Policy* (2004), and *United Nations: A Very Short Introduction* (2008).

Joseph A. Maiolo is Senior Lecturer in International History in the Department of War Studies at King's College London. He is the author of *The Royal Navy and Nazi Germany: A Study in Appeasement and the Origins of the Second World War* (1998), editor, with Robert Boyce, of *The Origins of World War Two: The Debate Continues* (2003), and assistant editor of *The Journal of Strategic Studies*. He is currently working on a study of the global arms race and the origins of the Second World War.

Kirsten E. Schulze is Senior Lecturer in International History at the London School of Economics. She is the author of *Israel's Covert Diplomacy in Lebanon* (1998), *The Arab–Israeli Conflict* (1999), *The Jews of Lebanon: Between Conflict and Coexistence* (2001), *The Free Aceh Movement (GAM): Anatomy of a Separatist Organization* (2004) and the co-editor of *Nationalisms, Minorities and Diasporas: Identities and Rights and the Middle East* (1996). She has also published numerous articles on the Aceh conflict, radical Islam in Indonesia, the Arab–Israeli conflict, negotiations and reform in the Middle East, and the Northern Ireland peace process.

ACKNOWLEDGEMENTS

This book began to struggle its way into the world about eight years ago when we were all teachers in the Department of International History at the London School of Economics. Since then we have become more dispersed, one of us going over the road to King's College London, via Leicester and Leeds, and another to the Graduate Institute of International Studies, Geneva. Sadly this has meant that the second edition could not be hammered out at Pu's Brasserie over their rightly celebrated Thai duck curry. Instead, it was the product of frequent telephone communications and email. However, the original idea that we had, namely that the best way to produce a comprehensive international history of the twentieth century is to collect together four regional and chronological specialists, still holds true and has proved itself as we transformed the book into a history of the twentieth century and beyond.

Many people have helped in the writing of this book. In particular, we would like to thank those colleagues in Britain and the United States who read and commented on the chapters. Thus we express our gratitude to Ernest Bolt, Sylvia Ellis, David Fieldhouse, Patrick Hagopian, Akram Khater, Robert A. Mortimer, David S. Painter, David Reynolds, Jackie Sheehan, Avi Shlaim, Sue Townsend, David Welch, Arne Westad, Keith Wilson and Chris Wrigley. Above all, we would like to honour our debt to Akira Iriye, who took on the unenviable task of reading each chapter as it was completed. We hope that he is satisfied with the way in which we have taken his perceptive advice and criticisms on board.

Among those who have assisted at Routledge we would like to thank Heather McCallum, who first mentioned the need for a new history of the twentieth century, Victoria Peters who commissioned the second edition, Eve Setch who took over from her when Victoria went on maternity leave, Moira Taylor for pre-proposal and post-proposal development and helping with the pictures, but above all for her superhuman patience, understanding and unflagging support throughout both editions, Carol Fellingham-Webb for copyediting the expanded and updated book and Anna Hines for its production. At the London School of Economics we would like to thank Mina Moshkeri of the Cartography section, who did wonders for us with the maps and was patient with our muddle-headed requests for revisions.

Our individual acknowledgements are as follows. Antony Best would like to thank Saho for her patience and understanding as the 'monster' was completed, the late Jasper the Dog for walking inspiration, and his parents for their usual kind assistance. Jussi would like to thank Jari for placing international history into its proper perspective by sharing his extended knowledge of the intergalactic adventures depicted in *Star Wars*. Joe would like to thank Catherine for her patience and support. And Kirsten would like to thank Hannah for inspiration and long mid-day naps which allowed her to work. Jussi, Joe and Kirsten would like to thank Antony for putting the final manuscript together despite his also having to attend to extended paperclip duties at the Department of International History.

The authors and publisher would like to thank the following for permission to reprint maps in print and electronic form:

Map 7.1 German expansion, 1935–39. From *A Map of History of the Modern World*, by Brian Catchpole. Reprinted by permission of Pearson Education.

Map 8.1 German expansion in Europe, 1939–40. From *A Map of History of the Modern World*, by Brian Catchpole. Reprinted by permission of Pearson Education.

Map 8.2 Japanese expansion in Asia, 1940–42. From *A Map of History of the Modern World*, by Brian Catchpole. Reprinted by permission of Pearson Education.

Map 10.2 The Korean War. After Leffler, 1992.

Map 16.1 The United States and Latin America since 1945. After Paterson et al., *American Foreign Relations*, fourth edition. Copyright © 1995 by Houghton Mifflin Company. Used with permission.

NOTE ON THE TEXT

In this book the following styles have been used for the romanization of foreign words and names. Japanese names have been converted into the Western style, whereby the family name comes last. Chinese words and names have been rendered in Pinyin, with the sometimes more familiar Wade-Giles transliteration appearing in brackets for well-known figures. Where countries changed names during the course of the twentieth century we have used the old name when it was in contemporary use with the new name following it in brackets.

Abbreviations

ACC	Allied Control Commission
ANC	African National Congress
ANZUS	Australian–New Zealand–United States Pact
APEC	Asia-Pacific Economic Co-operation
ARF	ASEAN Regional Forum
ARVN	Army of the Republic of Vietnam
ASA	Association of South-East Asia
ASEAN	Association of South-East Asian Nations
CAP	Common Agricultural Policy
CCP	Chinese Communist Party
CENTO	Central Treaty Organization
CFSP	Common Foreign and Security Policy
CIA	Central Intelligence Agency
CoCom	Co-ordinating Committee
COMECON	Council for Mutual Economic Assistance
Cominform	Communist Information Bureau
Comintern	Communist International
CPSU	Communist Party of the Soviet Union
CSCE	Conference on Security and Co-operation in Europe
DFLP	Democratic Front for the Liberation of Palestine
DOP	Declaration of Principles
DPRK	Democratic People's Republic of Korea
DRC	Democratic Republic of Congo
DRV	Democratic Republic of Vietnam
EC	European Community
ECOMOG	Economic Community of West African States Monitoring Group
ECSC	European Coal and Steel Community
ECU	European Currency Unit
EDC	European Defence Community
EEC	European Economic Community
EFTA	European Free Trade Association
EMS	European Monetary System
EP	European Parliament
EPC	European Political Co-operation
ERP	European Recovery Programme
EU	European Union

EURATOM	European Atomic Energy Community
FIDES	*Fonds d'Investissement et de Développement Economique et Social des Territoires d'Outre-Mer*
FLN	*Front de Libération National*
FMLN	Farabundo Marti National Liberation Front
FNLA	National Front of Liberation of Angola
FRELIMO	Liberation Front of Mozambique
FRG	Federal Republic of Germany
G-7	Group of Seven
G-8	Group of Eight
G-77	Group of Seventy-Seven
GATT	General Agreement on Tariffs and Trade
GDR	German Democratic Republic
GMD	Guomindang
GNP	gross national product
IAEA	International Atomic Energy Agency
ICBM	inter-continental ballistic missile
IDF	Israel Defence Forces
IMF	International Monetary Fund
INF	Intermediate Nuclear Forces
ISI	Inter-Services Intelligence
ITT	International Telephone and Telegraph
JCA	Jewish Colonial Association
JI	Jemaah Islamiyya
JNF	Jewish National Fund
JSP	Japanese Socialist Party
KWP	Korean Workers Party
LDP	Liberal Democratic Party
MAD	mutually assured destruction
MFN	most favoured nation
MIRV	multiple independently targetable re-entry vehicle
MITI	Ministry of International Trade and Industry
MPLA	Popular Movement for the Liberation of Angola
NAFTA	North American Free Trade Agreement
NATO	North Atlantic Treaty Organization
NEPAD	New Partnership for African Development
NIEO	New International Economic Order
NLF	National Libération Front
NPT	Nuclear Non-Proliferation Treaty
NSC	National Security Council
OAS	Organization of American States
OAU	Organization of African Unity
ODA	overseas development aid
OPEC	Organization of Petroleum Exporting Countries
PA	Palestinian Authority
PDPA	People's Democratic Party of Afghanistan

PFLP	Popular Front for the Liberation of Palestine
PfP	Partnership for Peace
PKI	Communist Party of Indonesia
PLA	People's Liberation Army
PLO	Palestine Liberation Organization
PPS	Polish Peasants Party
PRC	People's Republic of China
PRI	Institutional Revolutionary Party
ROC	Republic of China
ROK	Republic of Korea
RPF	Rwandese Patriotic Front
RVN	Republic of Vietnam
SALT	Strategic Arms Limitation Talks
SCAP	Supreme Commander Allied Powers
SDF	Self-Defence Force
SEA	Single European Act
SEATO	South-East Asia Treaty Organization
SED	Socialist Unity Party
SEZ	Special Economic Zone
SHP	Smallholders Party
SLA	South Lebanese Army
SLBM	submarine-launched ballistic missile
SMR	South Manchurian Railway
START	Strategic Arms Reduction Treaty
TEU	Treaty on European Union
UFCO	United Fruit Company
UGCC	United Gold Coast Convention
UN	United Nations
UNCTAD	United Nations Conference on Trade and Development
UNEF	United Nations Emergency Force
UNESCO	United Nations Educational, Scientific and Cultural Organization
UNGA	United Nations General Assembly
UNITA	National Union for the Total Independence of Angola
UNPROFOR	UN Protection Force
UNSCOP	United Nations Special Commission on Palestine
VNQDD	Vietnamese Nationalist Party
WHFTA	Western Hemisphere Free Trade Area
WMD	weapons of mass destruction
ZANU	Zimbabwe African National Union
ZAPU	Zimbabwe African People's Union

Introduction

The second edition

Since publication of the first edition of *International History of the Twentieth Century* in 2004, world events have evolved rapidly. The search for al-Qaeda leader Osama Bin Laden and the efforts to destroy his power base and cut off his finances led to the US and its Allies attacking Afghanistan in 2001 and Iraq in 2003. However, they failed to destroy, or even contain, al-Qaeda; instead, al-Qaeda-inspired terror spread. In 2002 suicide bombers targeted Bali, in 2003 Jakarta, in 2004 Madrid, and in 2005 London. As unsuccessful as the global war on terror were efforts to resolve the Arab–Israeli conflict. The second Palestinian *intifada* continued unabated and after the death of Yasser Arafat the already existing rivalry between different Palestinian factions descended into internecine fighting. In 2007 Hamas took over the Gaza Strip while the Palestinian Authority continued to govern the West Bank. The situation along Israel's northern border also heated up, culminating in Israel's Second Lebanon War in 2006, which like the first one was a complete failure. In South-East Asia Indonesia consolidated its democracy and ended the conflict in Aceh in 2005 while in Thailand Prime Minister Thaksin Shinawatra was ousted in a bloodless military coup in 2006; and in 2007 Buddhist monks in Burma tried to achieve regime change in what became dubbed the Saffron Revolution.

In order to incorporate all these new events it was necessary to change the title to bring the book into the twenty-first century. Like the first edition, the second edition offers the benefits of a cohesive view of world history by four specialists with regional expertise. It also offers the benefit of having received considerable feedback from lecturers and students using the book on their courses. In light of their excellent suggestions we have updated all chapters, reorganized some, and added two new chapters: one on European integration and the other on the global war on terror. We have expanded the material on the Middle East to include a more detailed discussion of the second *intifada*, the 2006 Lebanon War and post-2000 attempts at resolving the Arab–Israeli conflict. We have also added illustrations to each chapter and included additional web links to primary resource sites which students can link to from the support website at www. routledge.com/textbooks/9780415438964.

Introduction to the twentieth century

globalization
The cultural, social and economic changes caused by the growth of international trade, the rapid transfer of investment capital and the development of high-speed global communications.

Great Powers
Traditionally those states that were held capable of shared responsibility for the management of the international order by virtue of their military and economic influence.

In the twentieth century the history of international relations revealed four powerful trends. The first, and the one that received the greatest attention at the end of the century, was that the years between 1900 and 2000 witnessed a shrinking world in which the rapid growth of trade and finance created a truly global economy, while advances in communications and transport radically reduced the boundaries of time and space. Moreover, this trend towards **globalization** was reinforced by the fact that closer contacts and interdependence between political communities spurred on the formation of permanent inter-governmental institutions as well as a mushrooming of non-governmental organizations. Linked to this trend was a second major theme, which is that the twentieth century was a period defined by the quest for modernization and the perfection of modernity. Accordingly, more than any previous century, its course was shaped by ideological innovations and confrontation, ranging from the progressive utopianism of communism to the outwardly nostalgic visions of political Islam. Another major trend was that the century saw the steady diffusion of power away from Europe, which had dominated the world in 1900. At the level of **Great Power** politics, Europe was eclipsed by the rise of the United States and the Soviet Union, but this change to the international order also had another vital element, the proliferation of new nation-states in Asia and Africa, which acquired sovereignty as the European colonial empires broke up. These dramatic transformations in the world led to the fourth trend, the century's all-too-frequent tendency to descend into conflict, fed by ideology, nationalism, and advances in technology and institutional administration. No previous century can claim the violent death toll of the twentieth, in which lives were lost not just in war, but also in barbarous acts of organized state violence.

Our purpose is to offer students a single-volume, clear and wide-ranging account of the twentieth century and to explain why world politics followed this complex and often violent course. Such an exercise contains the danger that, in explaining long-term historical developments, the historian can, if not careful, erase the fundamental variable in all human affairs – contingency. There was no overriding reason why the past century had to be plagued by war, economic upheaval and political turmoil, for other routes to the future were open as the nineteenth century gave way to the twentieth. Indeed, many on the cusp of that transition, such as Norman Angell in his 1910 book, *The Great Illusion*, foresaw a new age of perpetual inter-state harmony ushered in by the rise of industrial economies and new technologies. Unfortunately, however, these prophets of peace proved to be wrong, and thus the history that we have to account for is defined by the violent dissolution of the old order dominated by Europe and the emergence of a titanic struggle between two hostile coalitions that possessed enough firepower to extinguish all human life completely.

In approaching our task, we have emphasized the international politics and the ideological doctrines of the past century. This approach may strike some as old-fashioned, especially as the historical discipline now considers the ways in which cultural, gender, social, economic and scientific factors, as well as the actions of non-governmental bodies, have influenced international affairs. We do not dismiss the influence of these factors on the structure and character of international politics, but nevertheless we had to make choices about what should be included in a single-volume book designed to cover the whole of the century and much of the globe. As this book is aimed at history, international relations and politics undergraduates, we agreed that it should provide a solid foundation in international politics, for it is only by understanding such a framework that students can make sense of the diversity and complexity of the twentieth century.

Our intended audience also influenced the choices we made about structure. We rejected a thematic approach on the grounds that in our experience students find the study of events over time the most rewarding way to learn history. Hence the book is divided into twenty-two chapters arranged in a roughly chronological manner, with the origins and course of the world wars and the Cold War providing the core of the book. This overall structure introduces the tricky issue of periodization. It has recently been common in history texts to talk of the artificiality of centuries as objects of study; for example, historians of eighteenth-century Europe tend to end their studies in either 1789 or 1815. Similar objections can be made to analysis of the twentieth century. Arguably the century really began in terms of its broad themes not in 1900 but in 1914, when the outbreak of the First World War destroyed the **Concert of Europe** that had arisen in the nineteenth century, and did not end in 2000 but with the resolution of the Cold War in 1991. However, the authors felt that the distinct period of hyper-competitive inter-state relations between 1914 and 1991 could not be comprehended clearly unless our study included some discussion of the years both before and after. Moreover, while the core of the book deals with the major international conflicts of the century, more than half of the chapters examine developments in Latin America, Asia, Africa and the Middle East and raise questions about how far and in what ways the Great Powers have shaped the destinies of these areas.

Concert of Europe
The nineteenth-century European system of regulation of international affairs by the Great Powers. Although much of the historical literature argues that the system was successful in keeping the general peace of Europe because it was based on a 'balance of power', more recent work has stressed the importance of shared rules of conduct, values, goals and diplomatic practices in relations between the Great Powers.

How should this book be used? All the chapters relate to each other in a coherent and chronological manner, and we encourage students to read the book from beginning to end, but each chapter may also be read independently as background before lectures and seminars. Indeed, course organizers may wish to design a full introductory course around this compact text. The book incorporates special features with both beginners and their teachers in mind. Since history is about arguments over causation, continuity and change, structure and agency, values, definition and the limits of historical knowledge, each chapter contains a 'debates and controversies' section that discusses historiographical disputes or issues. Our aim in highlighting historiography in this way is to show students that they must learn to identify the main points of contention between different historical perspectives and to locate historians' arguments within one of the conflicting perspectives. Students fresh to the topic of twentieth-century international history will encounter many key names and terms that will be unfamiliar to them. Certain important names and terms are therefore highlighted in bold the first time they appear in a chapter and a definition also appears in the margin. So, for instance, in this Introduction, as we are sure you noticed earlier, globalization, the Concert of Europe and Great Powers were rendered in bold with a definition in the margin. We have also included a glossary of key names and terms at the end of this book.

While encountering many of the terms contained in this volume for the first time may be bewildering enough, locating all the places, nation-states and shifting frontiers discussed on the pages that follow would be impossible without a healthy supply of maps. Accordingly, you will find twenty-four maps in this book dealing with all parts of the globe. Finally, because no single book, no matter how lengthy or thorough, could cover every aspect of every topic in twentieth-century international relations, readers will find an annotated list of further reading at the end of each chapter. A book of this size covering such a wide expanse of time and range of issues is ultimately a work of synthesis. When writing this book, we have endeavoured to use the latest scholarship and to include up-to-date secondary sources. However, in order not to clutter up the text, we decided not to use footnotes or the Chicago form of citation. Instead, the recommended reading sections may be taken as indicative of the sources that we have used. We strongly urge students to make use of the recommended readings, for a textbook can never be more than a general introduction.

CHAPTER ONE

Great Power rivalry and the World War, 1900–17

Contents

Introduction

Europeans lived in relative peace in the nineteenth century, although the recent upheavals that had racked the continent loomed large. After the revolution of 1789, France had exploded with a seemingly unbounded potential for ideological war and after 1804 Napoleon had harnessed this power to destroy the independence and security of the **Great Powers** and to make France the master of all continental Europe. Undisputedly Napoleon possessed a genius for war, but eventually he overreached himself both militarily and politically, and Britain, Austria, Prussia and Russia prevailed on the battlefield. The Congress of Vienna of 1814–15 founded a lasting peace based on Great Power management of international politics and moderation in the pursuit of self-interest. This management was not perfect, for national antagonism and egotism did not evaporate and war remained an instrument of policy. The general peace was broken by the Crimean War of 1853–56, and then by the three wars of Italian and German unification between 1859 and 1871. Yet these Great Power conflicts were limited in scope and fought for limited objectives, and once these objectives were achieved, order was restored. After the 'long' peace of 1815–54 came that of 1871–1914.

As a consequence, by the end of the century, Europe dominated the globe. Of course other factors played an essential part: Europe possessed the population size, the machine power and a massive organizational and technological edge over

Great Powers
Traditionally those states that were held capable of shared responsibility for the management of the international order by virtue of their military and economic influence.

its rivals. But stability at home permitted the impulses of the so-called 'new imperialism' to translate steam engines, machine guns and administration into supremacy abroad. In the 1880s and 1890s, these impulses ushered in not only the 'scramble for Africa', but also competition to extend empire in Persia, South-East Asia and the Pacific. Europe's commercial, intellectual and cultural influence also spread. Under this corrosive pressure, the last great non-European empires, Qing China and Ottoman Turkey, crumbled, while Europeans planned partition. Afghanistan and Siam remained in part independent because they served as useful buffers between the Russian and British and the British and French imperial spheres of influence. Japan escaped European domination through modernization: after 1868 Japan was transformed into a quasi-European power – through the adoption of modern Western financial, military and industrial methods. Even so, the European Great Powers called the shots. When Japan defeated China in 1894–95, the Europeans intervened to rein the Japanese in and to take for themselves some of the spoils at China's expense.

Unfortunately, the legacy of one century proved to be short lived in the next. If 1815–54 and 1871–1914 are the conspicuous features of the nineteenth century, then the two world wars and the Cold War blot the twentieth. Europe lost its capacity to contain inter-state violence just when the process of modernization handed Europeans an unprecedented capacity to wage **total war**. The killing machine of 1914–18 was the result. Between the wars, the European system lurched forward slowly, as political **isolationism** and revolution preoccupied America and Russia. The coming of Hitler's war finally extinguished the European system, and with it European world primacy. The Soviet Union and the United States emerged as superpowers. Their ideological, strategic and economic rivalry began in Central Europe but quickly spread beyond, drawing in revolutionary China and the newly independent states of Africa, Asia and the Middle East. The German question disturbed the peace intermittently, but only as one front in a global Cold War. Until 1989, Germany, like the European continent as a whole, remained split between the two hostile coalitions. Europe enjoyed another 'long peace', but not on its own terms. Only after the USSR collapsed did Europeans begin to reshape the political landscape without the boundaries drawn by the world wars.

To understand why the European era of international politics came to an end requires an answer to why the nineteenth-century states system broke down in the first decade and a half of the twentieth. Before addressing this question, however, it will be helpful to set out some of the terms and concepts essential to an understanding of the history of Great Power relations.

The Great Powers, power politics and the states system

see Map 1.1

Only five European states undisputedly held Great Power status when the twentieth century opened – Britain, France, Germany, Austria-Hungary and Russia. The statesmen of 1815 would have recognized this arrangement, although Germany

total war
A war that uses all resources at a state's disposal including the complete mobilization of both the economy and society.

isolationism
The policy or doctrine of isolating one's country by avoiding foreign entanglements and responsibilities. Popular in the United States during the inter-war years.

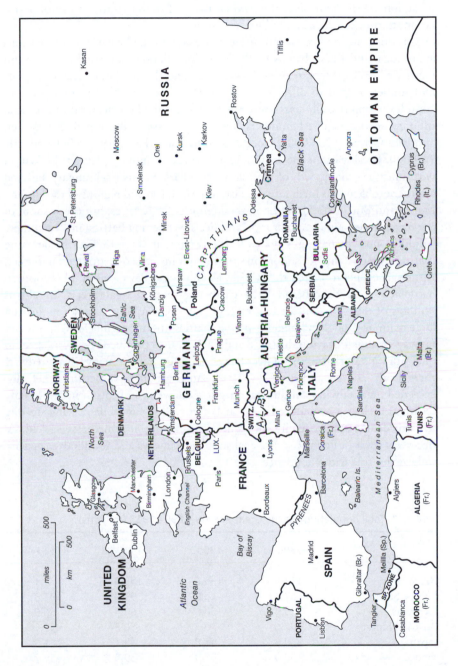

Map 1.1 Europe in 1914

Source: After Rich (1992)

(then Prussia) had greatly expanded its power and that of Austria (Austria-Hungary after 1867) had shrunk just as swiftly. At the crudest level, the term 'Great Power' applied to those states with the greatest capacity for war. Here, in the calculations of diplomats and strategists, the *hard* currency of power counted: size of population, territory, finance and industrial output.

On this scale the five did not measure up equally, and clear-cut comparisons are problematic. Russia had by far the largest population, but Britain, France and Germany had large literate urban populations and this pool of educated workers and soldiers helped to offset numbers in the era of machine production and complex weapons. Still, mass conscript armies recruited on the basis of universal military service required numbers: by 1900, Russia called up 335,000 men annually, Germany 280,000, France 250,000, Austria-Hungary 103,000 and Italy 100,000. Because of the low birth rate in France, its military planners looked on with unease at the growth of Germany's population. Austria-Hungary suffered another problem – its birth rate was fastest in the backward regions of the empire. France and Britain could call upon their empires for reserves, but the wisdom of the day assumed rapid mobilization and decisive opening battles, in which there would be no time to train colonial levies. Britain, at any rate, with its far-flung maritime empire, did not adopt conscription but instead concentrated on its fleet. Although unable to match the British, all the Great Powers assembled modern battle fleets in the years before 1914, partly in response to real threats, but also as symbols of their place in the first rank of states. Great Power armies required a large manpower pool and high birth rates; battleships, modern field weapons and railways required heavy industry. Britain and France produced coal and steel in quantities appropriate to their Great Power status, even if Germany began to dwarf them both, as well as Russia, by 1914. Austria-Hungary, Berlin's chief ally, exceeded only Italy in its industrial output. Following unification in 1861, Italy regarded itself as a contender for Great Power status, but while moving steadily towards demographic equality with a declining France, it nonetheless lacked the necessary levels of literacy, secure coal supplies, railways and productive capacity to bear this title with confidence.

see Table 1.1

Table 1.1 Total populations of the Great Powers, 1890–1913 (millions)

	1890	1900	1910	1913
Russia	116.8	135.6	159.3	175.1
United States	62.6	75.9	91.9	97.3
Germany	49.2	56.0	64.5	66.9
Austria-Hungary	42.6	46.7	50.8	52.1
Japan	39.9	43.8	49.1	51.3
France	38.3	38.9	39.5	39.7
Britain	37.4	41.1	44.9	45.6
Italy	30.0	32.2	34.4	35.1

Source: Adapted from Kennedy (1988, p. 255)

The ability to generate revenue in order to purchase armaments, train soldiers and build railways was another important power indicator. Once again, clear-cut comparisons are problematic. A look at defence spending in the decade before 1914 indicates that all five Great Powers had the financial strength to enter into an arms race. Germany and Russia, in terms of absolute outlay, outpaced the rest, with Britain and France holding their own. Austria-Hungary stayed ahead of Italy, but could not keep up with the big players. Britain spent far more than any other Great

see Figure 1.1

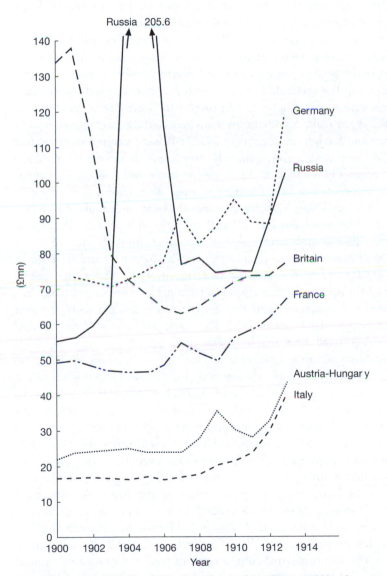

Figure 1.1 Defence expenditure of the European Great Powers, 1900–13

Source: D. Stevenson (1996)
Note: The high levels of defence expenditure in 1900–02 for Britain reflect the costs of the Boer War, while the high levels in 1904–05 for Russia reflect those of the Russo-Japanese War.

Power on warships, while on land Russia, Germany and France ('a poor third') not surprisingly dominated. Other important differences existed. Britain, France and Germany, the states with the highest per capita income, spent much more of their national wealth on defence than Russia (though it was in absolute terms still a giant) and Italy, which could not bear a similar burden. Although France did not spend as much as Germany, the financial assistance it extended to St Petersburg proved significant in speeding up Russia's economic and military development after 1905. Indeed, paradoxically enough, despite the impressive steel output and undisputed wealth in the years before 1914, the German government had reached the limits of what its fiscal and political structure could raise for defence.

However, *formal* recognition of Great Power status resulted not just from statistical reckoning but also from inclusion in the inner circle of diplomacy, especially the drafting of the general peace treaties and territorial adjustments. Normally the rights of Great Powers could not be neglected in international affairs, while smaller states were routinely ignored and subject to Great Power management. Like the rules of any club, diplomatic etiquette reflected the 'pecking order'. The heads of state and foreign ministers of the Great Powers met at congresses (the last in 1878), not conferences; generally only they exchanged ambassadors (diplomatic officials of the highest rank), not ministers. Nonetheless, diplomatic practice also accommodated the fuzziness of these distinctions. One might be invited into the Great Power club even without the hard credentials of membership. Italy was a 'courtesy' Great Power. The Powers treated Italy like a Great Power in an effort to entice Rome into one alliance or another. Similarly, after 1892, the Great Powers upgraded their representatives in Washington to ambassadors. In 1895, Britain deferred to the **Monroe Doctrine** over the Venezuelan border dispute. By 1900 the United States also had a formidable industrial economy. Yet, though treated as a 'courtesy' Great Power – the Americans participated in the conference on equatorial Africa in 1884–85 – even Italy carried more political weight where it counted most, that is, in Europe.

Notwithstanding the importance of armed strength, military success alone was not enough to allow a state to join the top rank. In 1898 the United States forced the Spanish out of Cuba and the Philippines. Spain, however, with little industrial and financial muscle, pulled no weight in Europe. At best, the victory only confirmed the United States as a regional power in the Western Hemisphere. Even so, in 1902–03, when Britain, Germany and Italy sent warships to force Venezuela to make good on debt payments, the Americans discovered that they lacked the military, economic or diplomatic means to forestall European gunboat diplomacy. In Italy's case its humiliating defeat in Africa at the hands of Abyssinian (Ethiopian) tribesmen at Adowa in 1896 confirmed its reputation as 'the least of the Great Powers', and the conquest of Libya in 1911 from the Ottomans did little to overturn this impression. The Russo-Japanese war of 1904–05 illustrates another case. The war originated from a clash of rival ambitions to dominate Manchuria and Korea. Japan struck first, with a surprise attack on the Russians at Port Arthur, followed up by a series of rapid victories over the inefficient Russian armies along the Yalu River and in Manchuria. In May 1905, with superior gunnery, the Japanese navy annihilated the Russians at the Battle of Tsushima.

Monroe Doctrine
The doctrine declared by President James Monroe in 1823 in which he announced that the United States would not tolerate intervention by the European Powers in the affairs of the Western Hemisphere.

Europe saw the Japanese triumph and the resulting revolution in Russia as degrading Russian power and causing an elevation of Japan's standing. Yet St Petersburg was down but not out. Given Russia's *reputation* as a first-rate power, everyone understood that with time Russia would again exercise its strength.

The inexact relationship between military potential and international status can in part be explained by the elusive nature of power. Statesmen form perceptions of the relative strength of other states based on multiple sources of information, everything from newspapers and personal experiences to secret intelligence. This information is compiled and filtered through complex bureaucracies which are no less subject to human error and bias. Statesmen may strive to form concrete judgements about the realities of international power, but these judgements are frequently inconclusive or wrong. For example, apart from Japan's ally, Britain, European governments generally underestimated Japanese power before the 1904–05 war. What changed afterwards was not the *reality* of Japanese power (military efficiency, population and armaments) but European *perceptions* of it. Even if the problem of perception could be overcome, power would remain a slippery concept. It is not reducible to 'military capacity', measured by plotting industrial output, manpower and finance. All forms of power must be weighed in relation to potential challenges. It must operate within a geographical, political, intellectual and even cultural context, and must be projected over time and space.

Take, for instance, the security situation of Austria-Hungary, a multinational state encompassing Germans, Magyars, Romanians, Italians, Slovaks, Croatians, Czechs, Serbs, Slovenes, Ruthenians and Poles, all united under the Habsburg monarchy. It had survived the Napoleonic Wars as a Great Power and thereafter acted as a key enforcer of the European order. It also united much of Central and South-Eastern Europe under one dynasty, thus providing a useful check to Russian ambitions in the region. Indeed, the empire's survival can be partly explained by the fact that the other Powers had recognized that its collapse would spark a crisis fatal to European stability and peace. In the latter half of the nineteenth century, the rise of nationalism and national **self-determination** – exemplified by German and Italian unification – placed strains on the empire's precarious political and economic ties. In an effort to solve the problem, the *Ausgleich* (compromise) of 1867 reconstituted the empire into two autonomous states under Emperor Franz Josef – in Austria, Germans would dominate the subject nationalities, while in Hungary Magyars would do the same. The *Ausgleich* appeased the Hungarians, but also made it difficult to co-ordinate security policy because each half of the empire had its own government, parliament and budget. Not only were resources scarce, but, as was the case with Germany's fiscal problems, *translating* resources into armed strength proved difficult. The size and quality of the army suffered – in 1866 it was one of the largest armies, by 1914 it was one of the smallest – while challenges to security and internal cohesion multiplied. The decline of the Ottoman Empire in the Balkans, the rise of Balkan nationalism – including Serbia's drive to unite the Slavs – and the breakdown of relations with Serbia's Slavic patron, Russia, over what should replace the Ottoman order in the Balkans, all generated an unfavourable balance between capabilities and vulnerabilities with far-reaching consequences.

self-determination
The idea that each national group has the right to establish its own national state. It is most often associated with the tenets of Wilsonian internationalism and became a key driving force in the struggle to end imperialism.

Further complicating the problem of measuring power is that intangible elements, such as the quality of political and military leadership and diplomatic skill, also count. In the negotiations leading to the renewal of the 1905 Anglo-Japanese Alliance, for instance, the outcome was determined not by raw power, but by diplomatic skill. The Japanese not only dodged a commitment to send troops to fight with the British army against Russia in India, but they secured in 1907 a British commitment to ship Japanese troops to Manchuria in the event of war with Russia. To put the problem another way, power is not an *object* – something one possesses – but a *relationship*. It might be helpful to think about power in the abstract: A exercises power over B when A gets B to do something it would *not* otherwise do. The Japanese influenced the British to accommodate their needs. Austria-Hungary increasingly found it lacked both the levers to compel its troublesome nationalities to live happily under the Habsburg Monarchy and the military means to deter Serbia, Russia, Romania, Greece and Italy from exploiting that weakness. Accordingly, whether A imposes its will by force or persuasion, the pull of an idea or even through deceit, does not matter. All represent the exercise of power. Another example might be useful here. In 1904, France and Britain concluded an *Entente* (flexible agreement), settling their long-standing overseas rivalry. After 1905, when Germany appeared more threatening, the two Powers also co-ordinated military plans. Although the *Entente* and the military talks did not commit Britain to go to war in 1914 alongside France in the way a formal alliance certainly would have, the connection (or even the sense of obligation) made itself felt in London. As Sir Edward Grey, the British foreign secretary, wrote: 'The Entente and still more the constant and emphatic demonstrations of affection . . . have created in France a belief that we shall support them. . . . If this expectation is disappointed, the French will never forgive us.' Britain made its decision in 1914 on strategic grounds, but the moral pull of the *Entente* did have a real impact.

Another reason why it is misleading to focus exclusively on the hard components of power is that the instruments of power in one political, geographical or strategic *context* do not necessarily work in another. The Boer War (1899–1902) provides a telling example. Britain, the world's greatest seapower, with over-whelming military, financial and industrial resources at its disposal, found itself humiliated when two tiny and backward Afrikaner republics resisted British annexation. Two years of brutal and bitter guerrilla warfare exacted a dispro-portionate toll on the British, who finally achieved their victory in 1902. Battleships, factories, manpower and money, the assets of a global giant, deterred the other Great Powers from directly assisting the Boers, but could not be *converted* into a swift victory over a small yet determined guerrilla army in southern Africa. Nevertheless, this ability to resist did not make the Boers more powerful than the British even for a short time. The Boer War (like the American war in Vietnam decades later) only underscored the limits of the instruments of power when moved from one context to another. Depending on the international situation, Britain's overseas empire, the source of British prestige and strength, could also be a source of weakness. For much of the nineteenth century, British maritime supremacy made the empire invulnerable, but by the turn of the century the upsurge in overseas expansion and naval building, combined with Britain's lack of European allies, left parts of the empire vulnerable to encroachments, especially by France and Russia. Britain's alliance with Japan and the *ententes* with France and Russia were thus a political response to an increasingly threatening global environment.

Naturally, what preoccupied statesmen most of all was how to exercise power in the European states system. Since there was no common sovereignty – that is, one great monarch or one coercive government to decide things – states had to influence the behaviour of other states. In this anarchy of states, war (state-led violence for political purposes) was the ultimate means by which states imposed their will or defended their independence, but war among the Great Powers had never been constant. Indeed, one scholar called the states system the 'anarchical society' because war and the pursuit of order through co-operation have both been constant facts of international life. The cost of general war forced statesmen to turn to methods of achieving political goals through consensus building and mutual security rather than war. This was, for instance, the chief consequence of the Napoleonic Wars. Tactically superior and zealously patriotic revolutionary armies had marched from one decisive victory to another to install French imperialism and Napoleon as Europe's common sovereign. Lessons were learned. A letter from the British prime minister to the Russian tsar in 1805 captures the essence of the consensus or system-building drive that Bonapartist ambitions had inspired. The wartime allies, he wrote, should found the peace on 'a general Agreement and Guarantee for the mutual protection and security of different Powers, and for re-establishing a General system of Public Law in Europe'. What emerged after 1815 was a system of collective Great Power supremacy and security designed to contain international violence and to prevent another hegemonic threat – the so-called **Concert of Europe**.

To understand why this Concert broke down in the twentieth century requires an insight into why it worked in the first place, and continued to do so despite the 1848 revolutions and mid-century wars. Historians disagree, but the typical answer is that after Napoleon's defeat the balance of power was restored. The balance metaphor suggests a self-adjusting alliance mechanism: when any one state gains inordinate power and drives towards supremacy, the others close ranks to form a blocking coalition, thus restoring the equilibrium. According to this view, the wars of 1914–45 can be explained as two failed bids by Germany to impose its mastery over Europe. To be sure, the web of roughly counteracting military capabilities helped to check national ambitions, but the balance of power should be viewed not solely as a system of mutual military deterrence, but also as one of co-operation. The Vienna settlement was founded on a series of interlocking treaties binding the Great Powers into a co-operative balance, expressed in a set of rules or customary law, designed to safeguard Great Power rights (security and independence) and to regulate changes in the European order. Co-operation made for containment. The makers of the Vienna settlement had not lost sight of the fact that France still possessed the raw resources to play a fundamental role. French *participation* in the inner circle after 1818 signalled its place among the Great Powers. Inclusion carried with it rights and responsibilities: the right to participate in the management of the system and the responsibility to manage it well. Although later governments voiced pretensions of Napoleonic

Concert of Europe
The nineteenth-century European system of regulation of international affairs by the Great Powers. Although much of the historical literature argues that the system was successful in keeping the general peace of Europe because it was based on a 'balance of power', more recent work has stressed the importance of shared rules of conduct, values, goals and diplomatic practices in relations between the Great Powers.

grandeur, France, like the other Powers, became contained within and, for the most part, *content* with the European balance.

Despite mid-century setbacks, the system lasted because it satisfied the vital interests of the only states with the potential capacity to upset it – the Great Powers. The treaties in the main were upheld, and the Powers co-operated among themselves to make adjustments and distribute compensation at ad hoc conferences or congresses. Crucially, states did not view their own security as requiring the *elimination* of another Great Power or the end of the balance as a whole. Moderate aims were pursued with a willingness to work with others to achieve them. Statesmen understood that overly ambitious goals at the expense of the other Great Powers or of the status quo would be regarded as a breach of the 'Public Law in Europe' and thus might provoke a self-defeating backlash. Yet the rules were not followed because of mutual deterrence alone. Adherence brought concrete and lasting benefits: security, status and control.

Otto von Bismarck's policy of a rapid revolution in the international status quo followed by renewed co-operation illustrates this point. German unification was completed by cunning diplomacy and Prussian military efficiency in wars against Austria in 1866 and France in 1870. Rather than allow the upheaval caused by these wars to destroy the Concert, the German chancellor took the lead after 1871 in rebuilding co-operation in order to safeguard the newly unified Germany. At the Congress of Berlin in 1878, the Great Powers compelled Russia to moderate its excessive claims against the Turks after the 1877 Russo-Turkish war. At the Berlin conference of 1884–85, rules designed to isolate Europe from Great Power rivalry over the partition of Africa were agreed. Thus while much changed after 1815, Concert diplomacy remained 'a habit of mind' and statesmen and diplomats continued to pursue their national interests and short-term gains without deliberately jeopardizing *long-range* stability. These generalizations, admittedly more true of 1815–48 than 1871–1900, require qualification and explanation beyond the space available. What should be stressed is that the international system (and peace) endured because the Great Powers had far more to gain by upholding it than by destroying it.

Broadly, what had changed by 1900? The rapid pace of modernization after 1870 is most striking. Modernization flowed as a consequence of the scientific, French and industrial revolutions, characterized by rationalization, secularization, urbanization and industrialization. Political, social and economic life moved from the control of a narrow elite to become subject to wider influences; the movement of people from rural areas to large urban, industrial communities structured along class lines promoted a rise in population; and mechanized production displaced the primacy of agriculture. One estimate that exemplifies this change holds that the value of international trade over the period from 1800 to 1913 may have risen from one-thirtieth to one-third of world production. Modernization wore away old institutions and the fabric of traditional social, cultural and economic life. At the political level, publics began to exert influence through parliaments, political parties, pressure groups and the press. Elites everywhere struggled to moderate calls for changes at home, and the most outspoken groups called for expansion abroad. This political tension must be set against the background of a much wider intellectual revolt: Nietzsche declared God dead, Darwin proved Genesis a myth, Freud unearthed the subconscious and Einstein swept away traditional thinking about time and space. Uncertainty, disorientation and the myth of a decaying civilization rushing towards disaster also expressed itself in the arts. Technology at the same time inflated the destructiveness and speed of modern warfare. Mass armies could be transported by rail to deliver knockout blows. Mobilization required general staffs and detailed plans. War plans and the arms race altered the character of foreign policy: the instinct or habit for co-operation and moderation gave way to fear and excess. In the minds of statesmen, dark images of the future military balance mixed with unease about whether the states system would continue to grant safety, status, influence and, indeed, even survival, to all the Great Powers for much longer.

However, caution is required when applying terms such as modernization. Its impact should not be exaggerated. After all, in 1900 two-thirds of Europe's inhabitants were still peasants. Old practices and methods always co-existed alongside emerging modern ones. Armies mobilized by railway but marched to move beyond the railhead and used horses to draw artillery and supplies. Modernization was uneven: north-west Europe modernized faster than the south and east. Some considered it a liberating and progressive force, while others despaired at the loss of traditional cultural and social practices. Most important of all, the term 'modernization' is only the historian's shorthand for a complex process of change, not an independent force in history.

Moreover, the relationship between modernization and international relations is ambiguous. At the turn of the century, many believed that it worked to inhibit Great Power conflicts. Ivan Bloch wrote in *War in the Future* (1898) that the destructiveness of modern weapons made their use pointless, while Norman Angell argued in *The Great Illusion* (1910) that the ever-closer integration of advanced trading economies rendered war futile. In the same year that Bloch's book appeared, diplomats gathered for the first Hague Peace Conference to consider disarmament and to promote the judicial arbitration of international disputes. In 1907, the second Hague Conference drafted rules to limit the horrors of modern warfare. Seven years later, war came. In retrospect, modernization explains the scale, intensity and cost of the fighting in 1914–18, but *not* why war broke out in the first place. To answer that question, we need to turn to the factor of causation.

The long-term causes of the First World War

The study of international history is dominated by controversies surrounding the causes of great wars. Many explanations have been offered. Some assert that great wars arise from economic and imperial rivalry. Others hold that world wars coincide with inevitable shifts in the distribution of international power. Still others look to miscalculation, misperception, accident, fear or simply the lust for conquest. Whatever approach they may select, scholars often examine the interaction between two sets of causes: long-term causes (or conditions) which made a war *probable* and the immediate causes and decisions which *triggered* a particular war at a particular moment. What follows is divided between a discussion of some long-term causes and then a look at how events moved to spark war in the summer of 1914.

One important condition was the system of Great Power alliances and alignments. Overly rigid alliances prevented the 'proper' functioning of the balance of power, so the usual argument goes, and ensured that what might have been an isolated crisis in the Balkans became a general war. Certainly, from 1900 onwards, Europe was increasingly split into two coalitions: Germany and Austria-Hungary (the Central Powers) were bound by the 1879 Dual Alliance to support each other 'with the whole strength of their empires' if Russia attacked, and Italy joined in 1882 to form the Triple Alliance; France and Russia closed ranks in 1891–94 to counter the German–Austrian alliance, and Britain settled its imperial disputes with France in 1904 and with Russia in 1907. However, it is easy to exaggerate the point, for these alliances remained flexible enough to permit the Powers to withhold diplomatic and military support in order to exert a *restraining* influence on a partner, especially, as was so often the case, if no common interests were at stake. Britain remained the least committed. Italy remained neutral in 1914 and went to war on the side of the *Entente* Powers in 1915. Up until 1912–13, Berlin withheld its support for Austria in the Balkans and advised caution.

The real importance of the alliance system was the way in which the alliances and alignments were transformed into something very different from what their makers had intended. Bismarck's Dual Alliance was intended to stabilize the European status quo. It handed him a lever over Austrian policy, especially vis-à-vis the South Slavs. In 1887 he persuaded Russia to sign a 'Reinsurance Treaty' with Germany in order to prevent a hostile Franco-Russian combination emerging. Italy was likewise drawn in so as to prevent it from aligning with France. Bismarck's successors failed to renew the Russian treaty in 1890, but the resulting Franco-Russian alliance of 1894 was one of *restraint* rather than *aggression*: St Petersburg would not back a French war to recover the provinces lost to Germany in 1871 (Alsace and Lorraine), and Paris would not support Russia in Central or East Asia against Britain. The alliance did give Russia more freedom of action in the Balkans, but from 1897 to 1908 St Petersburg and Vienna agreed not to challenge each other's interests in the region. However, the original stabilizing character of these alliances eroded. The turning point came in 1904–05: Britain settled its overseas quarrels with France and Russia by concluding *ententes*, while Germany became increasingly isolated. From 1905 onwards, Great Power statesmen found that they could no longer afford the risk of restraining allies for fear of *undermining* alliances – as the Great Powers increasingly looked to violent solutions to security problems, allies became more important.

Germany's fear of isolation was only partly responsible for this transformation. With the 1904 *Entente Cordiale*, Paris dropped its claims on Egypt, and London offered support to the plans of the French foreign minister, Théophile Delcassé, to extend French domination in Morocco. Twice – in 1905 and again in 1911 (the Agadir crisis) – clumsy German efforts to frustrate French ambitions and divide

Entente Cordiale
A phrase coined to describe the Anglo-French rapprochement that took place in 1904. Subsequently used as a shorthand for the Anglo-French relationship in the twentieth century.

the British from the French pulled the *Entente* tighter. Equally, if not more important, than the clumsy German diplomacy over Morocco was the retreat of the Ottoman Empire from 1908 onwards. Russia saw Ottoman decline as an opportunity to assert its traditional role as protector of the Balkan Slavs in order to secure more influence over the Black Sea Straits and Constantinople, while Austria-Hungary feared that the consequence of Ottoman decline and Serb expansion would be the dissolution of its own multinational empire. Moreover, German statesmen could not afford to lose their principal ally, and therefore Austria's Balkan problem became Germany's as well. Similarly, since the Russian alliance was central to French security and hopes of regaining Alsace-Lorraine, France had little choice but to close ranks with Russia.

The transformation of the alliances after 1905 is also connected to another important condition leading to war in 1914: the arms race. These words usually conjure up an image of the tit-for-tat battleship building of the Anglo-German rivalry. Indeed, the rise of 'military-industrial complexes', and the stirring up of popular agitation for more warships, exemplifies much about the military buildup generally. The German challenge was the brainchild of Admiral Alfred von Tirpitz, who became state secretary for the navy in 1897. Tirpitz's plan revolved around building a 'risk fleet'. This was one so large that even if the British attacked and won, German ships would inflict enough damage to leave Britain and its empire vulnerable to the other Powers. By threatening London with a 'risk fleet', so Tirpitz believed, German statesmen could force the British into an alliance or at least compel them to cut a favourable deal on overseas issues. The German Naval Laws of 1898 and 1900 authorized ship construction at a rate that would over twenty years reach the required 2:3 ratio. But Tirpitz's thinking was flawed, for it assumed that Britain would do nothing to frustrate his plan. However, the British simply out-spent and out-built the Germans. In 1905–06, the First Sea Lord, Admiral Sir John Fisher, introduced the first all-big-gun battleship, the *Dreadnought*, and another faster class of all-big-gun vessel, the battle-cruiser. These technical innovations forced the Germans to reply in kind. In 1908 Tirpitz increased the rate of expansion with another Naval Law, but the British, determined to keep ahead at every stage, replied in 1909 by laying down twice as many dreadnoughts. By 1912, it was clear that Tirpitz had failed, and London and Berlin began to search for agreement. Although not a direct cause of the war, the normal arms race, along with the Moroccan crises, helped to turn British political opinion against Germany and led Britain to consider whether it ought to land an army on the continent to assist France in the event of war.

The developing arms race on the continent between the Franco-Russian and German–Austrian blocs was much more significant. The reasons for this are more political than technological. In the last decades of the nineteenth century, weapons innovations – quick-firing artillery, machine-guns and repeating rifles – were the cutting edge of the 'new imperialism' abroad. In Europe, the first decade of the new century saw slow change as armies integrated these new weapons into their existing force structures. German spending focused on naval rather than land armaments. More crucially, Russia's military and political collapse in 1904–05 left Germany in a position to overawe France, and Austria-Hungary relatively secure in the Balkans. After the 1908–09 crisis in the Balkans, with substantial financial assistance from France, Russia's remarkable economic recovery upset the military equilibrium. Not only did spending on arms increase, but also steps were taken to restructure the army radically and to improve the rail network for faster and more efficient mobilization. St Petersburg did not launch these initiatives in order to menace Berlin and Vienna, but in both capitals the image of a more powerful Russia generated unease.

In 1912–13, war in the Balkans accelerated the arms race. A complex action–reaction cycle of arms programmes set in. In Germany, naval spending was cut. The Army Law of May 1913 increased the army's peacetime strength (515,000 to 544,000) and more artillery and machine-gun units were raised. The Austrians followed suit, but the growing threat from Serbia meant that a large proportion of the army would be pointed southwards, limiting Vienna's capacity to assist Germany against Russia. Indeed, the Germans put forward the 1913 Army Law to make up for the weakness of Austria-Hungary and the ground lost to the Franco-Russian bloc. Foreign observers saw something different. They concluded that the German increase in peacetime army strength was designed to enhance German striking power. News of the German buildup paved the way for a French reply. In August 1913, the French National Assembly extended compulsory military service from two to three years (initiating a change from 545,000 to 690,000 men) and authorized more arms spending. The following year, the French (who needed Russia to mobilize faster in order to threaten Germany with ready forces on two fronts) offered a 2,500 million franc loan to St Petersburg to build 5,000 kilometres of strategic railways by 1918. Russia's 1.5 billion rouble 'Great Programme' of 1913, which Tsar Nicholas II regarded as a necessary step to prepare for the 'unavoidable' war with Germany and Austria-Hungary, was the most striking measure. By 1918, the peacetime strength of the army was to be increased to 800,000 and armed with impressive quantities of artillery and machine-guns. Worse still for Berlin, the Russians did not feel any financial strain. Paradoxically, Germany – an economic powerhouse – was in danger of being out-spent. The problem was political rather than economic, for it was due to the fact that the German leadership found it nearly impossible to persuade the **Reichstag** to raise sufficient revenue. The implication for Berlin and Vienna was clear: the Central Powers could not win an arms race against the Franco-Russian bloc.

The destabilizing influence of the continental race and the general trend towards violent solutions to security problems become apparent when placed in the context of war plans. Before 1910, all general staffs drew up war plans, but only Germany, with the notorious **Schlieffen Plan**, intended to go on the offensive at the outbreak of war. After 1910, France, Russia and Austria all considered attack to be the best form of defence: the Austrians planned to smash Serbia; the French to launch an offensive into the lost provinces of Alsace-Lorraine and the Russians likewise into East Prussia. Historians have concluded that this pre-1914 'cult of the offensive' was based on the apparent lessons of Bismarck's wars of unification, when, exploiting the potential of railways and telegraphs to mobilize a large conscript army swiftly, the Prussian general staff had executed a series of crushing

Reichstag
The lower house of the German parliament during the Wilhelmine and Weimar periods.

Schlieffen Plan
The German pre-1914 plan for a pre-emptive military offensive against France, which would involve troops passing through neutral Belgium. It is named after the German army chief of staff, General Alfred von Schlieffen.

blows against Austria and France. Stunned by this exercise in military-political finesse, all Powers soon followed the Prussian example by adopting conscription and setting up planning staffs. By doing so, they ensured that the earlier Prussian successes could not be repeated. Moreover, as the industrial killing of 1914–18 would show, the development of magazine-feed rifles, quick-firing artillery, the machine-gun and barbed wire now handed the advantage from the attacker to the defender. Few saw this change coming. Before the war, most informed observers believed that armies could obtain quick victory and decisive outcomes. This 'short war illusion' bred aggressive foreign policies, brinkmanship and a sense of premonition at all levels – war was coming and the sooner the better.

Even if the trend towards offensive plans was a general one, the influence of the Schlieffen Plan remains fundamental to understanding how war came. The plan, inspired by Alfred von Schlieffen, the chief of the German general staff from 1891 to 1906, and adopted by his successor, General Helmuth von Moltke, provided Germany with a military solution to the problem of war on two fronts. The main body of the army would plunge through neutral Belgium to deliver a series of blows against the French, while Germany's eastern frontier remained on the defensive to meet the more slowly mobilizing Russians: with France defeated, the combined German and Austro-Hungarian forces would then concentrate in the east to deal with Russia. Success depended on two premises: a healthy military superiority over France and Russia mobilizing slowly. The development of the inter-bloc arms race undermined these two premises. The Russian economic and military recovery and the diversion of Austrian forces to the Balkans meant it was very risky to leave the eastern frontier exposed. Improvements to the French and Belgian armies called into question the feasibility of a western knockout blow. By 1913–14, the combination of the French Three-Year Law, the Russian Great Programme and the Franco-Russian railway agreement cast a shadow over the German war plan. Moltke modified it to account for greater resistance in the west and faster Russian mobilization. Nonetheless, the long-term trend was clear: the German–Austrian bloc would lose the continental arms race and the Schlieffen Plan would be rendered unworkable in a matter of three years. In 1914, this approaching military inferiority generated a powerful incentive in the minds of German decision-makers to strike pre-emptively.

The Schlieffen Plan therefore strengthens the case for historians who wish to place the burden of responsibility for war on Berlin. They also add to this case the consequences of Germany's world policy (*Weltpolitik*). There is some substance here. *Weltpolitik* raised suspicion and hostility abroad: what Germany saw as 'encirclement' by the *Entente* Powers was in reality partly of its own making. *Weltpolitik* emerged in the 1890s as a result of Germany's deep unease about its future place among the Powers. Before *Weltpolitik*, Bismarck had rejected colonies on the grounds that German interests lay in upholding the European status quo. The men who replaced him, especially the new emperor, Wilhelm II, feared that Germany would sink into second-class status unless it acquired a great overseas empire like Britain. Enthusiasm for overseas expansion fed that for naval building. The emperor, convinced by the equation that navies equal empires – he had read Mahan's celebrated *The Influence of Seapower on History* (1890) – embraced

Aus großer Zeit

v. Mackensen   v. Moltke   Kronprinz Wilhelm   v. François   v. Falkenhayn   v. Beseler   v. Bethmann-Hollweg
v. Preussen   v. Einem
v. Bülow   Kronprinz Rupprecht   Herzog Albrecht   v. Kluck   v. Emmich   v. Haeseler   v. Hindenburg   v. Heeringen
v. Bayern   v. Württemberg   Kaiser Wilhelm II.   v. Tirpitz   509

Plate 1.1 Kaiser Wilhelm II and his chief military, naval and political advisers, 1910. (Photo: General Photographic Agency/Getty Images)

Tirpitz's 'risk fleet' strategy: to acquire an empire, Germany had to compel Britain to conciliate or give way. Imperialism through naval coercion failed spectacularly. Germany's gains in south-west Africa and the Pacific were small and economically burdensome. The German leadership had defined the goals of *Weltpolitik* only vaguely and pursued them in an erratic way. Historians put this down to the volatile personality of Wilhelm II and the ineptitude of his ministers. In reality, Germany simply could not make real advances abroad without plunging the whole European states system into conflict – in other words, not without jeopardizing German security.

Certainly, once war had broken out in Europe for reasons *other* than *Weltpolitik*, the pent-up aspirations for world power would come to the surface in German war aims – but only *after* the European states system had collapsed. If Berlin had really been bent on world power at all costs, then 1905 – when Russia was reeling from humiliation in Asia and Germany had military superiority over France – was the year to act. This course of action, proposed by Schlieffen in May that year, was rejected by Wilhelm II. To be sure, there are good reasons for focusing on Berlin, but this can be misleading. *Weltpolitik* was an expression of a much wider trend: 'to remain a great nation or to become one,' as one French statesmen put it, 'you must colonize.' France, Britain and Russia had been the winners of nineteenth-century expansion; Germany and Italy were latecomers scrambling to catch up. Indeed, the only link between imperialist rivalries and the coming of war can be found in the way in which the Europeans greeted the decline of the Ottoman Empire as an opportunity to be exploited rather than as a threat to Balkan, and therefore European, stability. More broadly, the significance of European imperialism before 1914 lies in the way in which the neo-Darwinian impulses which drove the scramble for colonial expansion poisoned the European states system with the same struggle-or-die logic of excessive competition and inevitable war.

The same line can be taken with the view that German foreign policy was determined by domestic politics. This school sees *Weltpolitik* as manipulation. It was a cause around which Wilhelm II and his advisers hoped to rally the middle and industrial working classes behind the autocracy. Confronted by steadily rising socialism – the Social Democratic Party had won a landslide victory in the 1912 elections – German conservatives sought war in 1914 to stave off domestic political change. Once again, there is some substance here. In 1898, Chancellor Bülow justified *Weltpolitik* in these terms: 'We must unswervingly wrestle the souls of our workers; [we] must try to regain the sympathies of the Social Democrat workers for the state and the monarchy.' Nonetheless, while domestic politics may help to explain *Weltpolitik*, historians now agree that domestic factors did *not* play a crucial role in 1914. Moreover, comparative history shows that the German situation was not unique. On the eve of war, all the Powers had to cope with internal pressures and relate them to external circumstances. Austria-Hungary is the most telling case: aggressive action against Serbia, it was thought, would arrest the nationalist forces pulling the empire apart. In Russia, military defeat at the hands of the Japanese in 1904–05 had resulted in revolution and concessions to the Duma (parliament). Nicholas II and his advisers were therefore apprehensive, fearing that another humiliation abroad, especially in the Balkans, might shatter the tsarist regime, while a great victory in support of the South Slavs might strengthen it. France and Britain, the two liberal parliamentary Powers, also were not immune to political turmoil and industrial unrest. In 1914, the British prime minister, H.H. Asquith, feared civil war in Ireland over Home Rule more than a European conflict. Generally speaking, across Europe, the Powers had to contend with the social and political challenges arising from modernization. The most that can be concluded from this is that internal factors played a background role in 1914.

From one crisis to the next, 1905–13

Making judgements about the connection between long-term causes, which made war *probable*, and the immediate events and decisions, which *triggered* war, presents historians with complex problems. Some maintain that the broad factors determined events. 'Things have got out of control', wrote the German chancellor in July 1914, 'and the stone has begun to roll.' Recent scholarship, however, tends to reject theories of inadvertent war or 'war by timetable'. Statesmen in fact understood the potentially cataclysmic consequences of their decisions. In 1914 they deliberately cast aside the habits of nineteenth-century diplomacy. In particular, faith in the European Concert eroded over the period 1905–14. It is in this process of erosion that the connection between conditions and triggers is made. The breakdown of peace, as David Stevenson has argued, must be seen as a 'cumulative' process, in which the Great Powers steadily rejected co-operation and moderation in the pursuit of national interests and turned towards armed diplomacy and violent solutions to their security problems.

In examining the period from 1905 to 1914, one must focus on how the Great Powers responded diplomatically and militarily, and what consequences flowed from one crisis to the next. Significantly, the Moroccan crisis of 1905–06 was the first *militarized* confrontation between the Powers since the 1880s. Britain, Belgium and France made defensive preparations – the French reinforced units, trained reservists and procured arms – to signal their determination. Germany only took similar limited steps late in the crisis. Despite these moves, neither side desired war. The French knew that they were weak and did not wish to provoke the Germans, and Delcassé, the foreign minister, who alone advocated firmness, was forced to resign from the cabinet. Bülow, the German chancellor, alive to the danger of escalation, had no intention of risking a European war over African concessions. Accordingly, the Powers turned to conference diplomacy at Algeciras in January 1906 to end the dispute. At Algeciras, close Anglo-French collaboration forced Berlin to accept a diplomatic defeat. This not only confirmed Berlin's isolation – only Austria-Hungary offered support – but more importantly France and Britain strengthened the *Entente* with secret military staff talks.

In the next three crises – Bosnia in 1908–09, Morocco in 1911 and the Balkans in 1912–13 – the destabilizing trend of armed diplomacy continued. The first resulted from an attempt by the new government in Turkey, led by a group of officers known as the **Young Turks**, to assert sovereignty over the province of Bosnia-Herzegovina. At the Congress of Berlin in 1878, the Great Powers had agreed that the province should *formally* remain part of the Ottoman Empire but that Austria-Hungary should occupy and administer it. Vienna therefore reacted to the assertive policies of the Young Turks by annexing the province. The Austrian foreign minister, Alois Leza von Aehrenthal, hoped that this could be done peacefully. To his surprise, Serbia and Montenegro mobilized to object to the annexation of fellow Slavs among Bosnia's population, forcing the Austrians to mobilize in their turn. The Russians proposed a Great Power conference to deal with the annexation. After all Austria had *challenged* the authority of the European Concert by unilaterally overturning the decisions of the Congress of Berlin. However, armed diplomacy won the day. Germany stood beside Austria with a veiled threat of force. Of course, Bülow knew that the threat could be made safely. The Russians were too weak to intervene and made this clear. Russia and Serbia gave way. The crisis ended peacefully but not without serious consequences. Armed diplomacy had worked. The machinery of Great Power management had been sidelined. Accordingly, once it had the benefit of its military reforms in place, Russia resolved to show firmness next time. Meanwhile, in Berlin, it was clear that without support Austria-Hungary could not hold its position in the Balkans for long.

The second Moroccan crisis outwardly followed the pattern of the first. France moved to consolidate its claims in North Africa and Germany challenged it by sending the gunboat *Panther* to Morocco. In fact, the crisis took the inter-bloc confrontation a stage further, partly owing to blundering German diplomacy. Although France had acted in violation of the Algeciras agreement, Germany

Young Turks
Name given to a group of young army officers who in 1908 pushed the Ottoman Empire towards reformist policies and a more overtly Turkish nationalist stance.

failed to communicate its limited goals. At one point, the German foreign minister claimed the entire French Congo in compensation for its control of Morocco. As a result, the *Entente* Powers closed ranks. Unlike in 1905–06, however, the two alliance blocs were now more evenly matched in armaments, and the *Entente* took yet more extensive, though still defensive, military measures in a display of determination. London, alarmed that it had lost track of the German fleet for a time, brought the Royal Navy to a high state of alert. German restraint again made for a peaceful outcome: the Germans avoided provocative military moves and accepted an unfavourable compromise. The legacy of the crisis was more important than the outcome. Germany, now perceived to be the chief antagonist by officials in London, was once again isolated by *Entente* firmness. Another victory for armed diplomacy reinforced the trend to security through military strength. Faced with what they perceived to be *Entente* 'encirclement', German decision-makers were now determined to swing the military balance back in Germany's favour.

The next stage in the breakdown of peace contributed greatly to the atmosphere of near-permanent crisis. The Franco-Russian response to the 1913 German Army Law convinced German decision-makers that they could not win the arms race. As the Bosnian crisis had shown, Austria-Hungary – Germany's principal ally – needed Germany in a contest with Russia. Since 1897, co-operation between Vienna and St Petersburg had helped to keep the Balkans 'on ice'. After 1909, the Russians were no longer content to do so. Confident in the French alliance and its own growing strength, Russia helped to form a league of Balkan states (Serbia, Bulgaria, Montenegro and Greece) to promote its interests when the time was right. However, much to St Petersburg's chagrin, the small Powers took the initiative. In the winter of 1912–13, with the Ottoman Empire still reeling from Italy's successful attack in 1911, the Balkan League went on the offensive and succeeded in driving the Turks back to the Bosphorus in the First Balkan War of October 1912 to May 1913. The defeat of one of the region's two multinational empires placed a question mark beside the viability of the other. The Balkan League partners later fought among themselves over the spoils in the Second Balkan War of June–July 1913, and Serbia made additional territorial gains and drove westward to the Adriatic Sea. Austria-Hungary in reply increased its troop strength and demanded a halt to Serbian expansion. Germany promised support. Russia backed the Serbs. Britain announced that it would assist France. And France backed Russia. In the end, though, the Great Powers steered away from war. The ambassadors of the Great Powers met in London and hammered out a joint solution. Outwardly, the Concert had worked successfully once again.

However, the formalities of Great Power co-operation did not add up to much when set against the consequences of the Balkan wars. The crisis in the Balkans had sparked unprecedented levels of militarization and, moreover, tipped the strategic balance against Germany and Austria-Hungary, for Vienna's south-eastern enemies were now becoming more powerful just as Russia entered the game of armed diplomacy. In contrast to 1909, when the Russians had been forced to acquiesce, they had now flexed their muscles with a display of menacing military activity. Britain and France had also prepared for war. Germany had neither pressed

Austria to back down, nor taken threatening measures. His behaviour would change in 1914, but during this crisis Theobald von Bethmann Hollweg, the German chancellor, had resisted pressure from his soldiers to act. Indeed, when Serbia had defied Vienna's warnings against the capture of an outlet to the Adriatic, and in response to Britain's warning about a German attack on France, the German military leadership had assembled in the absence of the chancellor for the so-called 'War Council' of 8 December 1912. Wilhelm had favoured an Austrian war with Serbia. Moltke had agreed and pointed out that a European war was inevitable and 'the sooner the better'. The German historian Fritz Fischer has portrayed the meeting as a German decision to delay aggression until 1914. The judgement of one participant is closer to the mark: the result was 'pretty much nil'. As an indication of the changing mood in Berlin, though, Moltke's words tell us much. The mood in Vienna, now utterly disillusioned with the Great Power co-operation, was not much better. Furthermore, although the Conference of Ambassadors agreed to set up an Albanian state as a barrier to Serb expansion, Serbia had still doubled in size in two years and only complied with the London decisions when Vienna threatened force. In sum, this last gasp of the Concert and Great Power management succeeded only in containing the Balkan wars, not the general crisis in the states system. Viewed from Berlin and Vienna, the future no longer promised co-operation and moderation, but increasing isolation and inferiority. Instead of guaranteeing the security and independence of all the Great Powers, which had been the bedrock of nineteenth-century international stability, the system now appeared to be jeopardizing the survival of the Central Powers.

1914: decisions for war

The series of decisions leading to the outbreak of war in the summer of 1914 was triggered by the murders of the Austrian Archduke Franz Ferdinand and his wife in Sarajevo, the capital of Bosnia, on 28 June 1914. To understand why, we must describe how another Balkan crisis became connected with the general crisis in the states system. Although the terrorists who carried out the murder had been aided by Serbian intelligence without the sanction of the Serbian prime minister, Belgrade's lack of direct responsibility counted for little in Vienna, for the assassinations provided the opportunity for the violent solution to the South Slav problem that Austro-Hungarian officials now craved. On 23 July Vienna issued an ultimatum. Serbia accepted all but one of the ultimatum's demands, but this did not make any difference to Austrian thinking. 'The Monarch must take an energetic decision to show its power of survival', the Hungarian premier remarked, 'and to put an end to intolerable conditions in the south-east.' Austria declared war on 28 July. The decision was a reckless leap into the dark since no one in Vienna could have overlooked that war with Serbia was war with Russia. The decision originated from desperation in the face of irreversible decline, but, in retrospect, there is every reason to conclude that Vienna would not have been so reckless had Berlin not issued the so-called 'blank cheque' in support of Austria's Balkan war.

The 'blank cheque' was issued by Bethmann Hollweg on 6 July. Many of the long-term causes of war set out above converge here. The European alliance system had solidified into two blocs. German efforts to break up the *Entente* had only resulted in further isolation. Austria-Hungary, Germany's principal ally, might abandon it or, worse, crumble without German backing. The Franco-Russian armaments programmes, combined with Russia's willingness to flex its muscles, meant that the Central Powers would come under the shadow of *Entente* power. It was against this background that in Berlin military and civilian opinion agreed on the 'blank cheque'. A limited war in the Balkans would crush Serbia, humiliate Russia and perhaps even break up the *Entente*, which was a gross misjudgement of the Russian commitment to Belgrade. The next step was an easy one. If a European war came as the result of a local one, so went the reasoning in Berlin, then this would be the time to fight. The barriers to running such a calculated risk had long since been worn away. At the prompting of Wilhelm II, Bethmann Hollweg made at the end of July a half-hearted attempt to restrain Austria. By this stage, Russia's military preparations had reached alarming proportions. Intelligence also reported French and Belgian war preparations. Time was running out for a successful execution of the Schlieffen Plan. Berlin issued warnings to St Petersburg and Paris and then ultimatums on 31 July, neither of which was accepted. The German war plan continued to move ahead.

The Austro-Serbian war confronted Nicholas II and his advisers with a stark choice on 24 July. As the Russian foreign minister, Sergei Sazonov, put it, if Russia did nothing except protest, then its influence in the Balkans would 'collapse utterly'. The alternative was to act. The lessons of 1908–09 and 1912–13 made pressure to do so immense. Diplomatic avenues would be explored, but mobilization preparations were planned for 26 July. Over the next four days, as the crisis escalated, decisions were taken to order first partial and then full mobilization. Russian mobilization cut across Berlin's calculation that the Austro-Serbian war could be localized and so triggered activation of the Schlieffen Plan. The warning from Berlin on 29 July had little impact in St Petersburg, where war was now thought to be unavoidable. Once again confidence in the French alliance and Russia's strength combined to propel Russia's leaders forward. By coincidence, the French president, Raymond Poincaré, and René Viviani, the prime minister, were on a return voyage by sea from a state visit to St Petersburg early in the crisis and, consequently, out of contact with Paris. Regardless, the French ambassador, Maurice Paléologue, spoke unequivocally: 'France would not only give Russia strong diplomatic support,' he told Sazonov, 'but would, if necessary, fulfil all the obligations imposed on her by the alliance.' Perhaps if France had advised restraint, Russia might not have acted alone. Yet such a course would have destroyed the cornerstone of French security – the Franco-Russian alliance.

Once the German plan went into operation on 1 August, war between four of the Great Powers was certain, and two now had to choose. Italy, financially weak, vulnerable to blockade and fearful of domination by a victorious German–Austro-Hungarian bloc, opted for neutrality first and then joined with the *Entente* Powers in 1915. Britain was less committed by treaty than Italy. Certainly Britain was a signatory to the 1839 Treaty of London that guaranteed Belgium's independence

– not to mention the *ententes* of 1904 and 1907. However, the *ententes* and the staff talks with the French did not add up to military alliances. The British cabinet had decided that any decision to help Belgium had to be 'rather one of policy than legal obligation'. The Germans were optimistic and on 29 July Bethmann Hollweg offered the British a promise not to annex Belgian territory in exchange for neutrality. As late as 1 August the British had no plans to land an army in France; rather, the latest storm over Irish Home Rule preoccupied London.

German optimism proved to be wishful thinking. On 2 August, the cabinet resolved to defend the French coast and fleet and to protect Belgium against a 'substantial' violation of its neutrality. The German invasion of Belgium followed and Britain declared war on 4 August. Unquestionably the invasion tipped the scales in the cabinet. Safeguarding Belgium and Holland from the control of a hostile power had been a strategic interest for centuries. Equally important was the legacy of the Anglo-German naval antagonism. The German violation persuaded liberals who saw upholding the rights of small nations and the rule of law against aggressors as a moral duty. Germany was believed to be set on conquest of Napoleonic proportions. Britain's own safety would be jeopardized if Germany won. Yet containing Germany was not Britain's *only* strategic concern in 1914. What if Britain opted for neutrality and the Franco-Russian alliance won? The *ententes* had been intended to secure the British Empire from these two once hostile Powers, both well positioned to menace it. If they won, Russia and France would be dominant in Europe and in no way friendly to Britain, which had left them to face the Central Powers alone.

The triple stalemate

In the summer of 1914, the call to arms was greeted with widespread (though not universal) enthusiasm and relief. The international Left and pacifists were sidelined. Despite decades of hostility from the ruling elites, opposition parties united behind the national war efforts in a show of patriotic solidarity. Few grasped what kind of war it would be and still fewer could have foreseen its far-reaching consequences. The Schlieffen Plan, like the other pre-war plans, failed: the 'short war illusion' evaporated. Fronts stabilized, east and west. Barbed wire, artillery shells and machine-guns brought home the brutal realities of trench warfare.

Indeed, the First World War left deep scars in European life precisely because it became a full-scale four-year struggle between armies, economies and societies. Without it, the Bolshevik Revolution and the Second World War are unimaginable. This is why, having examined how war came, we also need to consider briefly why it lasted so long. The answers are connected. Each step towards 1914 and each step afterwards was an 'incremental' and 'sequential' one. As always, the interplay between what leaders chose to do and the circumstances in which they confronted each choice is key to understanding why a return to the pre-war status quo was impossible. Over time, options narrowed. Every new offensive plan or diplomatic initiative held out the promise of success. Not only did it become easier to lose

50,000 soldiers after losing the first 50,000, but the victory required to justify such sacrifice had to be all the more complete. Until 1917 a triple stalemate reigned: diplomatically, a compromise peace did not emerge; militarily, decisive breakthrough was unrealizable; and, on the home fronts, national solidarity held firm.

The incompatibility of war aims highlights why compromise proved to be impossible. Given the circumstances of its outbreak, none of the Powers entered the war with well-defined aims. As they developed afterwards, maximum war aims illustrated the degree to which the European Concert and moderation in the pursuit of security had disappeared. In September 1914 Bethmann Hollweg set out Germany's aim as 'security for the German Reich in west and east for all imaginable time'. This programme included the end of France as an independent Power and the erection of an economic sphere in Central Europe and Africa. However, Germany, like all the Powers, moderated its war aims in order to woo allies or to drive wedges into the opposing camp. All hoped to win over the Poles with promises of an independent state of some sort, and territorial pledges of large areas of Austrian territory were likewise extended by the *Entente* to Italy, Romania and Serbia. In Vienna, opinion swung towards eliminating Serbia altogether, unless a separate peace with Russia could be bought in exchange for a nominally independent Serbia. Apart from punishing German aggression, Britain wished to eliminate Germany as a naval and colonial rival, restore Belgium and expand overseas. France sought the return of Alsace-Lorraine and to cripple Germany for a generation by exacting indemnities and occupying the left bank of the Rhine. Russia supported France in the west and sought limited annexations in the east – including what was required for Poland and an independent Hanover. Russian officials also toyed with the idea of supporting greater autonomy for the Czechs, but on the whole the *Entente* Powers steered away from the breakup of Austria-Hungary in an effort to draw Vienna away from Berlin. Against the Ottomans, however, who had entered the war on the side of the Central Powers in October 1914, no such restraint operated: Russia looked to acquire the Black Sea Straits and Constantinople, while Britain prized the Persian Gulf region, Egypt and Palestine, and France likewise eyed Syria and Lebanon.

The drive towards annexations and war aims premised on stripping foes of their independence and security also helps to explain why, as we shall see in Chapter 2, no compromise peace emerged until December 1917, when the **Bolsheviks** signed an armistice. In the eight months before, Austria-Hungary and Russia, the faltering members of each coalition, explored the prospects for a compromise, but both initiatives fell flat for the same reasons: territorial issues and alliance cohesion. Britain and France could not break the secret pledge to Italy to support its territorial ambitions against Austria without jeopardizing not only Italian support, but also that of Serbia, Romania and possibly Russia. Vienna would not break with Berlin, nor did it have the power to moderate German war aims. After the abdication of Tsar Nicholas II in March 1917, moreover, both the provisional government and the revolutionary Petrograd Soviet, the two rival centres of political authority that succeeded the tsar, sent out peace feelers, but to find a general peace, not a separate one. Russia continued to adhere to the September 1914 Pact of London that committed the *Entente* Powers to refrain from separate peace talks. At the same

Bolsheviks

Originally in 1903 a faction led by Lenin within the Russian Social Democratic Party, over time the Bolsheviks became a separate party and led the October 1917 revolution in Russia. After this 'Bolsheviks' was used as a shorthand to refer to the Soviet government and communists in general.

time, Russia did not have the strength or single-mindedness to reshape Allied war aims to permit a compromise. Finally, unofficial contacts between France, Britain and Germany initiated by the Vatican peace note of August 1917 also came to nothing because both sides regarded their core war aims – Alsace-Lorraine and Belgium – as too important to abandon. Moreover, neither Britain nor France was willing to cut a deal with the Germans at the other's expense.

The diplomatic deadlock would not have mattered had one coalition managed to convert its strength into a decisive military victory, but the preponderance of defensive fire made such a breakthrough impossible. Tanks, motor transport and close-support aircraft, married with 'infiltration tactics', would restore mobility on the battlefield by 1939, but once the armies of 1914 marched away from the railheads, they became bogged down in trench warfare owing to the superiority of the defence. With offensive ideas running dry, the goal simply became, as General Ludendorff put it, to last 'ten minutes longer' than the enemy. The war thus resembled a titanic siege between mass armies, societies and economies. Which Great Power would give in or collapse first? Both sides hoped to manipulate neutrals and to recruit allies to tip the scales. Turkey and Bulgaria (October 1915) joined the Central Powers. The *Entente* assembled a global coalition of twenty-two states, including Japan and America. Britain and France struck at the Ottomans at Gallipoli and in the Middle East. The war expanded into Africa and Asia as well. The *Entente* blockaded the Central Powers, and the Germans launched a counter-blockade with **U-boats**. However, victory was to be found only in Europe, where the preponderance of men and fire counted. At the outbreak of war, the total French stockpile of artillery shells was five million. Two years later they were lobbing this many shells at the Germans per month. By 1918, the figure had reached ten million per month. Supplying these storms of steel and manning the trenches required an unprecedented level of state intervention in economic and social life. Large ministries responsible for the efficient management of munitions, fuel, labour, transport and food became crucial for survival. Twentieth-century total war had arrived.

If not militarily or diplomatically, the only other way in which the war could have come to an early end was by the domestic collapse of one of the Great Powers. What is striking, especially given pre-war fears about social revolution, is how resilient even the multinational empires of the east proved to be under the strain of total war. In both coalitions, the circumstances of 1914 permitted governments to present the war as a life-and-death struggle of defence in the face of unprovoked aggression. The domestic political truces of 1914 thus held firm, and the crises caused by 'shell shortages' pulled together strong alliances between business, labour and government. The capacity of governments to finance a protracted war by borrowing defied the pre-war assumption that wars would be short because no state could afford to fight them for very long. Overall, the internal political situation remained in favour of those committed to victory, and thus sustained the war. At the top, the real fear of the ruling elites was disappointing the high (even hyper) state of public expectations. Across Europe, therefore, successive civilian governments gave way to politicians or (in Germany) generals promising a decisive outcome – not peace at any price.

U-boat (English abbreviation of *Unterseeboot*) A German submarine.

Conclusion

The triple stalemate explains why the war continued for fifty-two months, and why the decisions of July–August 1914 were so momentous in their consequences. The men of 1914 must bear a heavy burden of responsibility, even if they could not foresee what would flow from their individual decisions, and even if at times their choices appeared to be predestined. As we saw, the choices they made to cross over the long-established thresholds of Concert diplomacy were deliberate ones, calculated in the full knowledge that European civilization was on the brink. And so it was. In addition to the horrific loss of life and wealth, the struggle accelerated Europe's decline in world affairs, and initiated the changes that culminated in Europeans losing the capacity to shape their own affairs. As we shall see in Chapter 2, the turning point arrived in 1917, when pressure for peace became significant and cracks first began to show. The French armies mutinied and the tsarist regime fell apart. Though Austria-Hungary and Italy were also on the brink, it was the Bolshevik take-over that knocked Russia out of the war. Berlin could now seek victory in the west. The entry of the United States, however, in the short term probably rescued the *Entente* from bankruptcy, and in the long term turned the contest against the Central Powers. The advent of the Russian Revolution and America's entry into the fray also brought to the forefront men with fresh ideas on how to create lasting peace. These ideas would help shape the course of twentieth-century international relations.

Debating the origins of the First World War

The debate about the outbreak of the First World War is divided between those who place the burden of responsibility on Germany and those who locate German policy within a much broader explanation for the breakdown of international relations. Of the first viewpoint, the case put forward by Fritz Fischer of Hamburg University in *Germany's Aims in the First World War* (London, 1967) is the most important. Fischer argued that Germany was aggressively expansionist. Its ruling elite believed that conquest abroad would secure imperial Germany's autocratic political and social order at home. For Fischer, German decisions in 1914 were the culmination of a premeditated 'grab for world power' (*Griff nach der Weltmacht*). Adversaries of the Fischer thesis attacked the parallels he drew between Bethmann Hollweg in 1914 and Hitler in 1939. They questioned the primacy he attached to domestic factors. And, most of all, historians have recently illustrated how Germany's 'calculated risk' in 1914 sprang from a deteriorating position within a states system in crisis.

Recommended reading

The best general introductions to European history in the period covered by this chapter are Felix Gilbert and David C. Large, *The End of the European Era, 1890 to the Present*, 4th edn (New York, 1991), Christopher J. Bartlett, *The Global Conflict: The International Rivalry of the Great Powers, 1880–1990* (London, 1994), Norman Stone, *Europe Transformed, 1878–1919* (Oxford, 1999) and James Joll, *Europe since 1870*, 4th edn (London, 1990). Students without a background in the history of nineteenth-century diplomacy will find Christopher J. Bartlett, *Peace, War and the European Powers, 1814–1914* (Basingstoke, 1996) and F. R. Bridge and Roger Bullen, *The Great Powers and the European State System, 1815–1914*, second edition (London, 2004) indispensable.

On the subject of the Great Powers and the states system, Bartlett, Bridge and Bullen (cited above) and A. J. P. Taylor, *Struggle for the Mastery of Europe, 1848–1914* (Oxford, 1954) are superb texts. Matthew Anderson, *The Rise of Modern Diplomacy* (London, 1993) and Paul Kennedy, *The Rise and Fall of the Great Powers: Economic Change and Military Conflict from 1500 to 2000* (London, 1988) provide a broad perspective. Kennedy's thesis on the long-term patterns of Great Power ascendancy and decay has been criticized by David Reynolds, 'Power and Wealth in the Modern World', *Historical Journal* (1989), vol. 32, pp. 475–87, and Gordon Martel, 'The Meaning of Power: Rethinking the Decline and Fall of Great Britain', *International History Review* (1991), vol. 13, pp. 662–94.

For studies of international politics and the search for order, see F. H. Hinsley, *Power and the Pursuit of Peace* (Cambridge, 1963) and Hedley Bull, *The Anarchical Society: A Study of Order in World Politics* (London, 1977). On the nineteenth-century balance of power, see Paul W. Schroeder, 'Did the Vienna Settlement Rest on a Balance of Power?', *American Historical Review* (1992), vol. 97, pp. 683–706, and his 'The 19th-Century International System: Changes in Structure', *World Politics* (1986), vol. 39, pp. 1–26.

On the Venezuela Blockade and the Anglo-Japanese Alliance negotiations, see N. Mitchell, 'The Venezuela Blockade, 1902–3', *Diplomatic History* (1996), vol. 20, pp. 185–209, and Keith Wilson, 'The Anglo-Japanese Alliance of August 1905 and Defending India: A Case of the Worst Scenario', *Journal of Imperial and Commonwealth History* (1994), vol. 21, pp. 334–56.

For a survey of the breakdown of the nineteenth-century states system, see Richard Langhorne, *The Collapse of the Concert of Europe: International Politics, 1890–1914* (London, 1981). The best general introduction to the origins of the war is James Joll, *The Origins of the First World War*, 2nd edn (London, 1992). The essays in H. W. Koch, *The Origins of the First World War*, 2nd edn (London, 1984) and Richard Evans and Harmut Pogge von Strandmann, *The Coming of the First World War* (Oxford, 1988) are also excellent. On the Balkan wars, see Richard C. Hall, *The Balkan Wars 1912–13: Prelude to the First World War* (London, 2000). For two books which explore the intellectual and cultural background to 1914, see Daniel Pick, *War Machine: The Rationalisation of Slaughter in the Modern Age* (New Haven, CT, 1993) and Robert Wohl, *The Generation of 1914* (London, 1980).

On European alliances and alignments, see Paul W. Schroeder, 'Alliances, 1815–1945: Weapons of Power and Tools of Management', in K. Knorr, *Historical Problems of National Security* (Lawrence, KS, 1976). For background on the arms race and war plans, see Geoffrey Wawro, *Warfare and Society in Europe, 1792–1914* (London, 2000). David Stevenson has written the most detailed study in *Armaments and the Coming of War: Europe, 1904–1914* (Oxford, 1996). See also S. Van Evera, 'The Cult of the Offensive and the Origins of the First World War' and Jack Snyder, 'Civil–Military Relations and the Cult of the Offensive, 1914 and 1984', both in *International Security* (1984), vol. 9, pp. 58–146. For the argument that, despite its apparent wealth, Germany was losing the arms race because its federal political structure and taxation system prevented the necessary levels of defence spending, see Niall Ferguson, *The Pity of War* (London, 1998), Chapters 4 and 5. On the European crises of 1905–14 and the militarization of diplomacy, see David Stevenson, 'Militarization and Diplomacy in Europe before 1914', *International Security* (1997), vol. 22, pp. 125–61.

David Stevenson has supplied the most cogent and up-to-date study of 1914 in *The Outbreak of the First World War: 1914 in Perspective* (London, 1997), including a survey of the debate in Chapter 5. For fascinating and detailed studies of individual capitals, see Keith Wilson's *Decisions for War, 1914* (London, 1995). Works critical of 'inadvertent war' are J. S. Levy, T. J. Christensen and M. Trachtenberg, 'Mobilisation and Inadvertence in the July Crisis', *International Security* (1991), vol. 16, pp. 189–203 and Marc Trachtenberg, 'The Coming of the First World War: A Reassessment', in his *History and Strategy* (Princeton, NJ, 1991).

For a revisionist account of the war's course, conduct and outcome, see Ferguson, *The Pity of War* and the first volume of Hew Strachan's *The First World War: To Arms* (Oxford, 2001). The account of why the war continued for as long as it did is based on David Stevenson, *The First World War and International Politics* (Oxford, 1991). The best single-volume treatment of the origins, conduct and consequences of the war is David Stevenson's *1914–18: The History of the First World War* (London, 2004) (published in the United States under the title *Cataclysm: The First World War as Political Tragedy*).

The search for European stability, 1917–29

Introduction

Peace is not merely the absence of war. An end to the fighting does not necessarily mean that the antagonisms that originally provoked war and the new ones thrown up by war are resolved. An armistice signifies that an absolute resolution by force is unnecessary because one belligerent has attained undisputed military dominance, but translating battlefield verdicts into political settlements is the task of diplomacy. Bridging the gap between an armistice and peace has proved one of the greatest challenges of modern statesmanship. There is no ultimate recipe for peace. Peace may be founded on hegemony and deterrence or it may come with the formation of a stable security community of states which share common values and goals. Most stable international systems combine these features.

For much of the nineteenth century, the **Concert of Europe** resembled the latter form of peace. The outbreak of the First World War, however, discredited the 'old' diplomatic instruments for maintaining international order: military alliances, secret treaties and balance-of-power politics. Some concluded that order needed stronger international laws and a world court to enforce them, while others demanded an end to the system of international competition and sovereign states altogether. The radical solution was nothing less than a transformation of old social, economic and political structures to found a global brotherhood of working

Concert of Europe
The nineteenth-century European system of regulation of international affairs by the Great Powers. Although much of the historical literature argues that the system was successful in keeping the general peace of Europe because it was based on a 'balance of power', more recent work has stressed the importance of shared rules of conduct, values, goals and diplomatic practices in relations between the Great Powers.

people. Precisely because the triple deadlock on the military, diplomatic and home fronts propelled the engine of war forward, and because the Europeans could not bring the war to a decisive end, the advocates of 'new diplomacy' found millions of ready converts to their cause in 1917. The voices of change came from the great continental powers, the United States and Russia. After the October 1917 Revolution, Lenin, the leader of the minority revolutionary wing of the Russian Communist Party known as the **Bolsheviks**, became the chief proponent of the revolutionary solution to international anarchy. President Woodrow Wilson shared with Lenin the conviction that the ill effects of inter-state competition had to be alleviated. Old diplomacy had been the practice of autocrats and exclusive ruling elites who suppressed their own peoples as well as minority national groups. The American president therefore advocated a more open diplomatic system, based on the rule of law, composed of free and independent nation-states and guided by the 'organized moral force of mankind'.

The aim of this chapter is to examine the process of peacemaking and European reconstruction from the armistice in 1918 to the end of 1929. It considers the influence of Lenin and especially Wilson on the resolution of the First World War. Broadly, it attempts to answer the question of why the Paris peace settlement failed to lay down the foundations for a lasting European peace. Did responsibility rest on the shoulders of the Paris peacemakers, or with those who later attempted to operate the European system they created? Why did the Allied coalition that had won the war in 1918 fall apart so quickly after victory? What does the period from the French occupation of the Rhineland in 1923 to the Locarno treaties of 1925 tell us about the *structural* problems associated with peacemaking? Was the European détente of 1925–29 a tragically brief but stable start on the road to peace, or a false dawn?

Bolsheviks
Originally in 1903 a faction led by Lenin within the Russian Social Democratic Party, over time the Bolsheviks became a separate party and led the October 1917 revolution in Russia. After this 'Bolsheviks' was used as a shorthand to refer to the Soviet government and communists in general.

The 'new diplomacy'

The starting point for this analysis is the breakdown of the diplomatic, military and domestic political stalemate in 1917, and the coming of the western armistice in November 1918. The first break in the triple stalemate came on the home front in war-exhausted tsarist Russia. The refusal in March 1917 of the Petrograd (St Petersburg) garrison to fire on strikers and food demonstrators triggered the abdication of Nicholas II. A 'dual' authority replaced the tsarist regime, shared between the Provisional Government and the Petrograd Soviet of workers' and soldiers' deputies. Both centres of political power remained committed to the war, but not equally so. The Provisional Government hoped to remobilize Russia's demoralized armies in order to pursue imperial Russia's original war aims. The Petrograd Soviet, in contrast, expressed the longing on the streets, in factories and on the front line for peace – though not peace at any price. In April 1917, when the Provisional Government reaffirmed Russia's interest in Constantinople and the Straits, the Petrograd Soviet called for peace without annexations

self-determination
The idea that each national group has the right to establish its own national state. It is most often associated with the tenets of Wilsonian internationalism and became a key driving force in the struggle to end imperialism.

or indemnities, and a frontier settlement based on the principle of national **self-determination**. Although the Petrograd Soviet's call for a non-imperialist peace energized Europe's socialist and left-wing opposition parties, the official war aims of the leading Powers in both coalitions remained unchanged. An attempt by the international socialist movement to revive itself by holding an international conference on peace in Stockholm was thwarted by the Allies. Worse still for Russia, the offensives launched in June and July in the name of the new head of the Provisional Government, Alexander Kerensky, ended in utter disaster. Russia desperately needed peace.

The Bolshevik seizure of power in November 1917 with the slogan of 'peace, land and bread' initiated Russia's exit from the war. According to Lenin, the expansionist impulses of monopoly capitalism had caused the war and these inherently self-destructive forces would lead to the ruin of capitalism itself. A great wave of workers' revolutions, so the Bolsheviks believed, would sweep away the bourgeois ruling classes, thus creating an enduring peace within a new international solidarity of workers' states that would replace the pre-1914 world of imperial competition. In the same way that war had destroyed tsardom, it was hoped that the war would soon spark more proletarian revolutions across Europe. To ignite the revolutionary spark, the Bolsheviks issued a Decree on Peace in November 1917, which called for a general three-month armistice and a final peace settlement without annexations or indemnities. At the same time, in a bid to mobilize public opinion, they exposed the annexationist war aims of the *Entente* by publishing secret inter-Allied agreements on war aims. This appeal to the streets for revolutions fell flat. After the armistice on the eastern front was concluded, the Bolsheviks presented the Central Powers with a six-point peace plan, once again rejecting annexations and indemnities and now calling for the application of national self-determination inside and outside Europe. The Central Powers accepted on condition that the Allies concurred too. As they anticipated, the Allies refused. When negotiations resumed in January 1918, the Central Powers made clear their resolve to impose a punitive peace by force. The first blow to the Bolsheviks was the treaty of 9 February 1918 between the Central Powers and now-independent Ukraine. L. D. Trotsky, Lenin's commissar for foreign affairs, stalled brilliantly, walking away from the talks declaring 'no war, no peace', but the Germans called his bluff and resumed their advance. Confronted with a choice between the survival of his regime and total defeat, Lenin chose survival.

see Map 2.1

The resulting Treaty of Brest-Litovsk (3 March 1918) stripped Russia of its Great Power assets. The Bolsheviks surrendered Poland, the Baltic States, Ukraine, Finland and the Caucasus, nominally as 'independent' states, but in fact as German satellites. Russia lost sovereignty over a third of the former empire's population, a third of its agricultural land and nearly 80 per cent of its iron and coal industry. These terms represented a triumph for the German high command and the fulfilment of the dreams of German imperialists. Lenin, however, regarded the treaty as a temporary measure. Once Russia had recovered, the Treaty of Brest-Litovsk would be reversed. In the meantime, peace with the Central Powers caused tension with Russia's former Allies. As war developed inside Russia between

Map 2.1 Territorial changes in Europe after the First World War

Source: After Keylor (1998)

counter-revolutionaries and the Bolsheviks, the Allies dispatched forces to inter-vene, at first to prevent stockpiles of *Entente* arms falling into German hands, and later to help bring down the Bolsheviks.

Lenin's was not the only ideological voice to be heard. The American entry into the war in 1917 had a similar impact. The Russian Revolution and the American entry sharpened the distinction between liberal and autocratic Powers. A common anti-imperialist streak ran through Lenin's 'Decree on Peace' and President Wilson's cry of 'peace without victory'. However, Lenin pulled out of the war first to save his regime and then later to reshape world politics through workers' revolutions from below; Wilson aimed to reform the international system through the exercise of American power at the top. Wilson's 'new diplomacy' combined realism and idealism (though, as we shall see, not always in equal measures). According to the president, the war had been caused by an anarchical and lawless system of states, which had brought about a frantic search for security through the stockpiling of armaments. As the war progressed, American economic policies had steadily favoured the *Entente*, while Wilson had labelled Germany an almost irremediably militaristic state. If Germany and its allies won, he had reasoned, the United States would be forced to transform itself into a heavily armed garrison state in which liberties would be crushed by militarization. The need to defeat Germany and the American ambition to build a better world thus drove Washington into the *Entente* coalition.

The US declaration of war on 6 April 1917 was not immediately decisive. To be sure, American maritime power and finance rescued Britain and France from Germany's **U-boats** and probable economic collapse, but the Americans had only 80,000 troops in Europe by October 1917. By 1919, the number would rise to two million. In the meantime, Wilson played a waiting game. He affirmed his self-appointed role of mediator – America was an 'associated' Power, not an *Entente* ally – and hoped that with Germany defeated and France and Britain reliant on American men, *matériel* and money, he would be able to impose a liberal peace on all the belligerents. His vision was embodied in his famous **fourteen points** of 8 January 1918. The fourteen points were a reformist reply to the Bolsheviks' peace manifesto and a notice to the *Entente* that their secret agreements on war aims and spoils would have to be revised. **Collective security** and self-determination were Wilson's binding themes. He called for 'open covenants openly arrived at', 'freedom of the seas', the removal of economic barriers, the reduction of armaments and the foundation of a **League of Nations**. Belgium would be restored; Poland made independent; Alsace-Lorraine returned to France; and Italy's frontiers redrawn along national lines. German forces would also have to withdraw from Russia, and the Austro-Hungarian and Ottoman empires would be forced to grant autonomy to their subject peoples.

Wilson's 'new diplomacy' confounded the battle-scarred British and French as much as Lenin's; the difference was that the Western Europeans now needed 'Uncle Sam' to win the war. The disasters they had suffered in 1917 had driven this point home. Russia had been knocked out of the war. Romania was reduced to a German satellite. French and British offensives were halted with horrific casualties. French troops had even mutinied. The Italians were routed at Caporetto. German U-boats played havoc with Allied shipping. In fact, the need for troops, supplies and credit from the United States very quickly raised questions about the potential impact of American dominance. One French statesman worried

> that before Germany has been thoroughly beaten she may propose terms which President Wilson may consider acceptable, but which would not be acceptable at all to France and England, and President Wilson may put pressure on the *Entente* Allies to accept them.

At the end of 1917, a co-ordinating conference initiated close inter-Allied co-operation on the strategic and economic matters, but, inauspiciously, a joint political response to the Bolshevik Decree on Peace could not be hammered out. Wilson's insistence that Americans would not fight for 'selfish aims', 'with the possible exception of Alsace-Lorraine', offered Georges Clemenceau, the French

U-boat (English abbreviation of *Unterseeboot*)
A German submarine.

fourteen points
A speech made by the American president Woodrow Wilson on 8 January 1918 in which he set out his vision of the post-war world. It included references to open diplomacy, self-determination and a post-war international organization.

collective security
The principle of maintaining peace between states by mobilizing international opinion to condemn aggression. Commonly seen as one of the chief purposes of international organizations such as the League of Nations and the United Nations.

League of Nations
An international organization established in 1919 by the peace treaties that ended the First World War. Its purpose was to promote international peace through collective security and to organize conferences on economic and disarmament issues. It was formally dissolved in 1946.

premier, very cold comfort. Moreover, Wilson's reference to 'freedom of the seas', 'impartial adjustment of all colonial claims' and the removal of economic barriers caused David Lloyd George, Britain's prime minister, equal unease. The *Entente*, of course, was not a perfect alliance. Paris and London bickered over Eastern Europe and their designs on the Ottoman Empire clashed. But, judging from Wilson's public statements, what united them was the craving for peace *with* victory. Wisely, before the Central Powers capitulated, the Europeans played down their differences with the president to ensure unity.

In Germany and Austria-Hungary, Wilson's fourteen points helped to spark strikes and demands from the opposition parties for a non-annexationist peace. Yet, despite desperate war-weariness, labour strife and food shortages, the domestic balance against a negotiated settlement held firm. In Berlin, the ascendancy of Generals Paul von Hindenburg and Erich von Ludendorff over the civilian leadership was confirmed by Bethmann Hollweg's replacement by an uninspiring civil servant, George Michaelis, who was amenable to the high command's wishes. When in July 1917 the liberal-left majority in the **Reichstag** called for political reform and a 'peace of understanding', the new chancellor replied that he accepted the Reichstag's Peace Resolution 'as I understand it'. Austria-Hungary grew ever more reliant on Germany as the empire fell to its knees under the burden of war. Its leadership considered a negotiated settlement, but its contacts with Britain and France made no headway, for Italy's plans to make gains at Austria's expense blocked any deal. In any case, Vienna really wanted a *general* peace, not a *separate* one. This could come only if Berlin moderated its war aims – something beyond Vienna's power to achieve. In the end, the opportunity presented by Russia's collapse locked the Central Powers into one last desperate gamble on battlefield victory, while the Treaty of Brest-Litovsk hardened Allied attitudes towards their foes.

Reichstag
The lower house of the German parliament during the Wilhelmine and Weimar periods.

The armistice

In 1917, the German army in the west remained on the defensive. Attacking British and French divisions suffered severe casualties, but help from across the Atlantic was on its way. With the reserves now freed from the Russian front, Ludendorff launched offensives in spring 1918 aimed at punching a series of holes in the Allied front lines, in one last desperate attempt to force the *Entente* to the peace table before American troops arrived in strength and tilted the balance. His reinforced mobile storm divisions achieved some operational successes, but a war-winning breakthrough was beyond their reach. From July 1918 onwards, Allied counter-attacks and the growing American army reversed the military situation. Germany's armies retreated. In October, the smallest of the Central Powers, Bulgaria, requested an armistice. Germany, Austria-Hungary and Turkey soon followed the Bulgarian lead.

The German request for an armistice meant that the political struggle over the coming peace now began in earnest. In an attempt to split their foes and obtain moderate peace terms based on the fourteen points, the German government approached President Wilson directly for an armistice. The president, as the Germans had calculated, excluded his Allies from the armistice talks. 'Have you ever been asked by President Wilson whether you accept the fourteen points?' Clemenceau inquired: 'I have not been asked.' Lloyd George replied no. Disagreements about the shape of the post-war settlement, suppressed before for the sake of Allied unity, now surfaced. The British and the Americans quarrelled over 'freedom of the seas', and the Allies split on reparations. Wilson wanted Germany to make 'restoration' for civilian damage caused by the aggression of German forces on land, air and sea; Clemenceau and Lloyd George wished to make it clear that Germany was responsible for the wider costs of waging war. Fortunately for Allied unity, the president's peace programme remained ambiguous enough to be open to future interpretation and negotiation. Unfortunately for post-war stability, the reparations question and exactly what Germany had agreed to in the pre-armistice agreement also remained ambiguous and was later reinterpreted. In the meantime, while Washington insisted that the fourteen points should set the agenda for the peace conference, Paris and London seized the initiative in setting out the military and naval clauses of the armistice, which left Germany militarily helpless. On 11 November 1918 the armistice was finally concluded.

Victory caught the Allies by surprise. Military planners had expected another year of war in the west. Consequently, French and British policies on war termination were as fluid as American ones. As a result, the Europeans may have accepted peace far too soon. Arguably, the psychological impact of an Allied invasion of German soil would have made the German people more agreeable to the Versailles settlement. Did the politicians make the wrong strategic choice? While the retrospective case for a 'missed opportunity' has great merit, we need to see the situation as it appeared to the policy-makers of 1918. Certainly, the Republicans in the US Congress had called for Germany's unconditional surrender, but European statesmen were wise to place a huge question mark beside President Wilson's readiness to storm the German frontier. More importantly, Lloyd George and Clemenceau believed that they could get what they wanted from their enemies without more bloodshed. Nonetheless, a tantalizing 'might have been' lingers. If the British and French intelligence services had known just how close Germany was to disintegration, then the politicians in London and Paris might have made the decision to ignore the Americans and advanced into Germany. As David French has speculated, 'that might have had incalculable results for the subsequent history of Europe'.

One of the results might have been a more stable German democracy. To stamp out 'Prussian militarism', the Allies agreed that German constitutional reform was a precondition for peace. This was well understood in Berlin. When Ludendorff recognized that defeat was imminent, a new government, supported by the centre-left, was formed to negotiate the peace under the moderate-liberal Chancellor Prince Max. Of course, the German high command did not have a sudden conversion to the merits of democratic reform, but instead turned to constitutional change as a ploy to win a moderate, Wilsonian peace from the Allies, and also to saddle the civilian politicians who would follow them with the responsibility for Germany's defeat and humiliation. Unfortunately, the ploy worked rather well. To many Germans, it appeared that internal revolution had preceded the military collapse. A mutiny of German sailors started the process that finally led to the abdication of the kaiser and the foundation of a republic. Its first chancellor, Friedrich Ebert, arrived at an accommodation with the generals, whom he needed to safeguard the republic from revolutionaries. Obligingly, Ebert greeted returning German soldiers as 'unconquered' heroes. Of course, the legend that the army was defeated not on the western front but at home by socialists, pacifists and Jews (the so-called stab-in-the-back legend), which right-wing propagandists later exploited to vilify the **Weimar Republic**, did not 'doom' German democracy. Of greater significance was the close connection in the minds of many between democracy, defeat and the Paris peace.

Weimar Republic
The German parliamentary democracy that existed between November 1918 and January 1933. Attacked from both the Right and the Left of the political spectrum, it never won the loyalty of the majority of Germans.

The Paris peace settlement

In January 1919, when the representatives of more than thirty Allied and associated nations assembled for the start of the Paris Peace Conference, the First World War had claimed ten million combatant deaths and twice that number maimed. The destruction in Europe and beyond, not to mention the spent wealth, lost trade and squandered production, defied definitive calculation. Meanwhile, along the borderlands of the Habsburg, tsarist and Ottoman empires, formerly subject peoples took up arms, while the Bolsheviks fought counter-revolutionaries (half-heartedly backed by the Western Powers) and Allied intervention forces. Despite the enormity and urgency of the task, and a great deal of preparation, the opening proceedings of the Paris Conference were marked by administrative chaos and organizational improvisation. A functioning decision-making process, supported by expert committees and commissions, took some time to develop. At first, the Council of Ten dominated. It was composed of two members each from the major Allied Powers (Britain, France, Italy, Japan and the United States). The Council of Ten, however, proved unwieldy. From March to June 1919, the Council of Four (consisting of Wilson, Lloyd George, Clemenceau and, with the least influence, the Italian Premier Vittorio Orlando) dominated and made the key decisions concerning the peace treaty with Germany (signed at Versailles on 28 June 1919). From July 1919 to 1923, the lesser peace treaties with Austria, Hungary, Bulgaria and Turkey were left to government officials and inter-Allied agencies to negotiate through regular diplomatic channels.

Critics at the time and since have charged that the Paris peace fell well short of the just settlement promised by Wilson's magnificent slogans 'peace without victory' and 'a war to make the world safe for democracy'. The 'Big Three' – Wilson, Clemenceau and Lloyd George – missed an opportunity to fashion a new

Plate 2.1 Versailles Peace Conference attendees, France, 1919. Seated left to right: Italian Premier Vittorio Orlando, British Prime Minister David Lloyd George, French Premier Georges Clemenceau, and US President Woodrow Wilson. (Photo by US Army Signal Corps/Time & Life Pictures/Getty Images)

and legitimate order, so the usual argument runs, because the Europeans pursued narrow selfish interests, and because Clemenceau and Lloyd George either bamboozled Wilson or the whole exercise was one of supreme cynicism. In reality, it was much easier for a few men in 1914 to destroy the world than for their successors to replace it with something better. After the most destructive war in history, there were limits to the peacemakers' capacity to refashion Europe. They had little real power to control the pace of events in Central and Eastern Europe. Moreover, Wilson, Lloyd George and Clemenceau did not share a *common* vision of the post-war order. The Paris settlement represented a series of trade-offs and compromises between the victorious Allies (most notably in the application of the principle of self-determination). More difficult still, the growing threat of anarchy and revolution in 1919–20 placed a premium on timely rather than optimal solutions. Each solution needs to be examined in its own context to be fully understood.

Take, for example, the foundation of the League of Nations. To achieve his great mission of international reform, Wilson made this task his top priority. Many agreed with the president that unbridled military competition and balance-of-power politics had made war in 1914 inevitable. Some suggested that had a permanent machinery for 'crisis management' and arbitration existed, then the First World War might have been prevented. Opinions varied, but a standing organization for Great Power co-operation and consultation was seen as the key innovation for future international politics. Radicals demanded the democratic control of foreign policy and a powerful world government; conservatives looked to some refinement of the old Concert of Europe. Wilson publicly championed the radicals, who took his promises of 'open covenants openly arrived at' more religiously than he did. Revelling in the role of Europe's saviour, the president personally took the chair of the conference's commission on the question of a new international organization in order to see his vision of a league to enforce peace through the exercise of world opinion come into being. The French, in contrast, wanted a *Société des Nations*, backed by its own troops, to perpetuate the wartime alliance against Germany. Not only was there enthusiasm for a League of Nations inside and outside British officialdom, but Lloyd George also calculated that by backing the president he would ease American pressure on more contentious points, such as freedom of the seas.

The strategy worked. The Covenant (or constitution) of the League of Nations was based on an Anglo-American draft. It described a system of Great Power management and made gestures towards Wilson's ideals. To promote open diplomacy, the League, based in Geneva, would consist of a Council and an Assembly, supported by a permanent secretariat. The Covenant obliged signatories to observe the rule of law in international affairs, to reduce armaments and to preserve the territorial integrity and independence of member states. Members undertook to consider collective action against covenant-breakers. To prevent another 1914, international disputes would be subject to a three-month period of arbitration. This would allow time for cool-headed diplomacy and for 'the public opinion of the world' to mobilize for peace. War-weary people everywhere regarded the League as a break from the unscrupulous practices of the 'old diplomacy'. In reality, it was a workable compromise between the aspirations of liberal internationalists like Wilson and the inescapable limitations of any voluntary association of sovereign states. It was not a world government, nor did any of its makers wish it to be one. As a result, the Covenant contained ambiguities and contradictions: the League would deter war by threatening covenant-breakers with *universal* war; all members were equal, but the Great Powers would call the shots; and, to function, the League required member states to abide by the Covenant without any binding obligation on them to do so, especially in disputes between the Great Powers.

If the League was the idealistic dimension of the peace, the German settlement was the punitive one. Germany was not dismembered – and so remained a potential Great Power – but it did lose some 27,000 square miles of territory, 6.5–7 million inhabitants and 13.5 per cent of its economic potential. In the west, *see Map 2.1* France gained Alsace-Lorraine, a small border district (Eupen-Malmédy) was handed over to Belgium, and Denmark took northern Schleswig. To compensate France for the sabotage of its coal mines by the retreating German troops, the Saar valley was placed under League administration for fifteen years and its mines under French ownership for at least that period. The Saar's fate would ultimately be decided by plebiscite. The Rhineland would also be demilitarized and occupied by the Allies, who would also control the Rhine bridges. The eventual three-stage, fifteen-year evacuation of occupation forces was tied to Germany's treaty

Danzig, Free City of (Polish: Gdansk)
A historically and commercially important port city on the Baltic Sea. In 1919, the Paris peacemakers made Danzig politically independent as a 'free city' under the League of Nations in order to give the new state of Poland free access to the sea. However, the vast majority of the city's inhabitants were Germans. The return of Danzig to German sovereignty was thus a key issue for German nationalists between the wars. Hitler exploited the Danzig question as a pretext for his attack on Poland in 1939.

see Document 2.1

Versailles Treaty
The treaty that ended the Allied state of hostilities with Germany in 1919. It included German territorial losses, disarmament, a so-called war guilt clause and a demand that reparations be paid to the victors.

compliance. In the east, Germany ceded Posen and much of West Prussia to Poland (the 'Polish corridor'), and the German port of **Danzig** was designated a free city under the League, though under Polish customs and foreign policy control. Lithuania seized the German port of Memel. Berlin also surrendered its colonies, overseas investments and much of its merchant fleet. The German navy was allowed a few obsolete ships; the army was denied heavy weapons and aircraft, and its official strength was limited to only 100,000 men.

On reparations, the peacemakers deferred the difficult decisions. Everyone agreed that Germany should pay something. The real questions were: how much should Germany pay; how much could it pay; what form should payment take (money, goods or both); and over how long a period should the instalments be scheduled? The Council of Four recognized that there was an enormous gap between the entire cost of the war and Germany's capacity to pay reparations. Indeed, what constituted the 'entire cost of the war' was a major issue. There were also serious technical limitations on transferring wealth from one nation to another. Consequently, in order to address Germany's *theoretical* responsibility for the entire cost of the war while *in practice* limiting its financial liability, the peacemakers inserted two Articles, 231 and 232. In the first, later misleadingly dubbed the 'war guilt' clause, Germany and its allies accepted responsibility for the 'aggression' of 1914 and its consequences, while the second required Germany to provide compensation for specified civilian damages. Ironically, therefore, the original purpose of Articles 231 and 232 was to *protect* Germany from the economic ruin of making good on war costs. Finally, instead of fixing a final figure in 1919, the **Versailles Treaty** only demanded an interim payment of 20 billion gold marks before 1 May 1921 (to pay for the Allied occupation), the date by which the inter-Allied Reparations Commission was to determine a total.

Document 2.1

Extracts from the Treaty of Versailles

Article 231
The Allied and Associated Governments affirm and Germany accepts the responsibility of Germany and her allies for causing all the loss and damage to which the Allied and Associated Governments and their nationals have been subjected as a consequence of the war imposed upon them by the aggression of Germany and her allies.

Article 232
The Allied and Associated Governments recognise that the resources of Germany are not adequate, after taking into account permanent diminutions of such resources which will result from other provisions of the present Treaty, to make complete reparation for all such loss and damage.

The severity of Versailles cannot be blamed on any one Power. All the peacemakers combined policies of conciliation and punishment. For Clemenceau, French security was paramount, and that could only come in one of three ways.

The first was by permanently weakening Germany. The second was by seeking a lasting and mutually beneficial Franco-German accommodation. The third was by way of a security alliance with the United States and Britain. The French tried all three without much success. Despite secret overtures to Berlin proposing a German commitment to treaty compliance in return for a promise of future treaty revision, there was no chance of such a deal flourishing in the poisonous air of 1919. It was feared in French circles that the Treaty of Versailles would only *temporarily* strengthen France and cripple Germany. General Foch, the Allied supreme commander, therefore proposed a more permanent solution: France should hold on to the Rhineland as a strategic buffer. Fearful of creating 'an Alsace-Lorraine in reverse' and mindful of self-determination, Lloyd George and Wilson refused. Instead of a detached Rhineland, France was offered Anglo-American Treaties of Guarantee against unprovoked German aggression. Clemenceau, who would not have otherwise relented, regarded the guarantees as the 'keystone of European peace'. Unfortunately, the guarantees fell through when the American Senate rejected the Treaty of Versailles in November 1919, and British adherence was conditional on American.

The collapse of the Anglo-American guarantees epitomized France's frustration at the hands of its wartime Allies. It was typical of Lloyd George's opportunism that the British treaty would only come into force if the American one did. His double-dealing would not have mattered had London not pursued a balance-of-power policy – that is, with France cast in the role as the next European hegemon. With Germany's navy sunk and its overseas possessions confiscated, the British cabinet could safely regard its former enemy as the counterweight to what it wrongly perceived as an aggressive France bent on mastery of the European continent. Britain should stand back from Europe, and allow the free play of inter-state rivalry to give rise to a new equilibrium. Balance-of-power calculations such as this blocked British strategic empathy with France. British officials could not see that French security and Franco-German reconciliation were essential to peace, and that France *needed* Britain in order to feel secure against Germany. Lloyd George's handling of reparations was also questionable. Because Britain had suffered little direct civilian damage from the war, the prime minister insisted that *pensions* payable to servicemen and their dependants should be included to increase Britain's share of reparations. Even if this blatant violation of the pre-armistice agreement had little impact on the total sum claimed by the Allies, there is no doubt that it helped to undermine the moral authority of the whole settlement. Moreover, fearing a backlash in Parliament if the total for reparations was too moderate, Lloyd George pressed his fellow peacemakers to postpone the painful decisions for two years. Ironically, French officials, who are often portrayed as the villains on reparations, at first proposed very moderate sums based on *civilian war damages* in accordance with the pre-armistice agreement. They also considered partnership with Germany on iron and steel production as an alternative means of taming the economic might of their former enemy.

Wilson, like Lloyd George, must also take responsibility for the post-war blight of reparations. Although the United States emerged in 1919 as the world's largest creditor nation, the American government refused to combine inter-Allied war debts, reparations and reconstruction into one big package. According to Marc Trachtenberg, an American cancellation of war debts and a contribution to reconstruction would have resulted in moderation on reparations. In striking contrast to the generosity of the **Marshall Plan** in 1947, American 'tight-fistedness' in 1919 ensured that the Allies burdened the Weimar Republic with reparations. American policy stemmed more from Wilson's moralistic approach to international politics than from any narrow American financial interests. Germany had started the war and so the Germans must pay as an act of penance. Until justice had been done, Wilson reasoned, Germany must be treated as a moral inferior and barred from the League of Nations. The conviction that Germany had to be punished before it could be rehabilitated, however, could not be squared with Wilson's reluctance to commit the American might to peace enforcement. For precisely the opposite reason to Lloyd George – namely, the president's *hostility* to balance-of-power politics – Wilson in like manner failed to understand the French position. What France needed was American and British backing to promote a sense of security and reconciliation with Germany; instead, France was largely stranded with an inherently more powerful neighbour, whose hostility was compounded by an indemnity and 'war guilt', both of which were contained in a treaty that presupposed Germany's voluntary compliance.

The Paris peace settlement in Central and Eastern Europe

The Treaty of Versailles, of course, preoccupied the Big Three – Wilson, Clemenceau and Lloyd George – but the Paris peace settlement entailed more than the German problem. 'All the races of Central Europe and the Balkans', wrote one American delegate, 'are actually fighting or about to fight with one another . . . the Great War seems to have split up into a lot of little wars.' The peacemakers knew that stamping out these little wars and preventing the spread of Lenin's revolution (which at moments threatened to take hold in Berlin, Vienna, Munich and, especially, in Budapest, under the Bolshevik Béla Kun) was essential to peace. During the war, all the belligerents had courted subject nationalities with promises of greater post-war autonomy in order to destabilize the opposing camp. The collapse of the three eastern empires propelled the nation-founding process forward in 1918, as the Allies quickly adjusted their policies to the new map. The Americans and the British, after all, had supported the principle of self-determination, while the French looked to the new Czechoslovakia, Poland and Yugoslavia as future allies in the containment of Germany and as a *cordon sanitaire* against Soviet Russia.

Consequently, the Poles, Czechs and the *Entente* Allies – Serbia, Romania and Greece – were all beneficiaries; the losers were Germany, Austria-Hungary, Turkey and Bulgaria. Four treaties modelled on Versailles, including similar clauses on disarmament, reparations and 'war guilt', confirmed the new territorial

Marshall Plan
Officially known as the European Recovery Programme (ERP). Initiated by American Secretary of State George C. Marshall's 5 June 1947 speech and administered by the Economic Co-operation Administration (ECA). Under the ERP the participating countries (Austria, Belgium, Denmark, France, Great Britain, Greece, Iceland, Italy, Luxembourg, the Netherlands, Norway, Sweden, Switzerland, Turkey and West Germany) received more than $12 billion between 1948 and 1951.

see Map 2.1

arrangement: the Treaty of Saint-Germain with Austria (10 September 1919), the Treaty of Trianon with Hungary (4 June 1920), the Treaty of Neuilly with Bulgaria (27 November 1919) and the Treaty of Sèvres with Turkey (10 August 1920). Significantly, in contrast to Versailles, each of these lesser treaties included provisions for the protection of ethnic, linguistic and religious minorities. The Treaty of Saint-Germain also prohibited the union (*Anschluss*) of Austria and Germany. In Poland's case, its western frontier was drawn at Germany's expense, and then, after defeating the Red Army in 1920, it agreed its eastern border with Russia in the 1921 Treaty of Riga. Czechoslovakia, which like Poland benefited from astute lobbying and well-placed sympathizers among the peacemakers, declared its independence in October 1918. To make the Czech-dominated union with the Slovaks economically and strategically viable, the **Sudetenland** (the border area between the historic kingdom of Bohemia and Germany, which included three million German-speaking inhabitants) was incorporated into it. Yugoslavia emerged as a voluntary amalgamation of former Austro-Hungarian territories around the pre-war Serbia. Romania more than doubled its territory and population, taking Russian Bessarabia and Austrian Bukovina. Greece obtained Eastern Thrace from Turkey and, in April 1920, Western Thrace from Bulgaria. Soviet Russia, free of Brest-Litovsk, now lost control over much of what it had turned over to the Central Powers in 1918, including Poland, the Baltic States and Finland.

Despite reducing by half the number of people living under alien rule, self-determination, as put into practice by the Paris Peace Conference, generated yet more ethnic strife and national conflict – but it is impossible to see how this might have been otherwise. No matter how sharp the pencil or small scale the map, the peacemakers' careful lines cut across the ethnographic patchwork of Eastern Europe, leaving about thirty million people on the wrong side of contestable frontiers. Even natural status quo allies such as Poland and Czechoslovakia fell out over their mutual borders. Rather than seeing it as a tool for peaceful national integration, the small Powers regarded minority protection arbitrated by the League of Nations as a Great Power imposition on their newly won national sovereignty. In the German case, self-determination had to give way to strategic considerations: the victors could not reinforce their one-time enemy by permitting an *Anschluss*, nor would they enfeeble Poland by denying the small state 'secure access to the sea' or cripple Czechoslovakia by withholding the Sudetenland. At the same time, because they conflicted with self-determination, some of the promises made to Italy in 1915 went unfulfilled. Thus, while Italy absorbed part of the frontier with Austria (South Tyrol), Wilson stubbornly resisted Orlando's claim to territory along the coast of the Adriatic. The Italian premier stormed out of the Council of Four to force concessions from his fellow peacemakers, but caved in upon his humiliating return. Even so, the small Adriatic port of Fiume remained a source of tension between Italians and Yugoslavs, and Rome sulked about what many Italians regarded as their 'mutilated peace'.

Anschluss
The political union of Germany and Austria. *Anschluss* was specifically prohibited under the Versailles Treaty, but was carried out by Hitler in March 1938 without any resistance from the victors of the First World War.

Sudetenland
The geographical area in Bohemia mainly inhabited by ethnic Germans. In 1919 it was placed on the Czech side of the German–Czech border and in 1938 led to an international crisis ending in the infamous Munich Agreement.

The implementation of the peace

For all its flaws, the Paris peace does not deserve the often-cited verdict that it amounted only to 'an armistice for twenty years'. To be sure, the imperfect solutions to the German problem and Europe as a whole certainly set out the battle lines for the future. Too many important states were left dissatisfied and looked to the future for the revision rather than the defence of the status quo. Germany and Russia, still potential Great Powers, would revive and the fate of Eastern Europe would depend on whether they regarded the successor states as useful buffers or potential spoils. Nevertheless, historians must not draw straight lines between 1919 and 1939. Diplomacy is an open-ended process. Adjustments to the settlement – at first on the margins, later in some of the essentials – were inevitable. Whether this process would end in another general European war or smaller-scale conflicts depended on what followed. In David Stevenson's view, the failures of the 1930s might have been averted by a combination of leniency over reparations and the strict enforcement of the security clauses of the Versailles Treaty. This approach required continuing co-operation among the Allies and the survival of moderate revisionism in Germany.

Unfortunately, the first victim of the peace was inter-Allied solidarity. America's withdrawal from the settlement, occasioned by the Senate's rejection of the Treaty of Versailles in November 1919 and again in March 1920, was the most tragic. Wilson had raised expectations for a new era of world politics so high that he was bound to disappoint (disillusioned Wilsonians rushed to print stinging criticisms of their former hero). As in most tragic plots, this downfall was of the protagonist's own making. Although Wilson worked to the point of exhaustion and suffered a stroke during the treaty fight, he obstinately refused to placate the Republican majority to win ratification of the German peace. Wilson had also ensured the rejection of the League of Nations by his earlier insistence that the League's Covenant form an integral part of the Versailles Treaty. In 1921, the Americans signed a separate peace with Germany, but remained outside the League of Nations – the centrepiece of Wilson's peace project. The great American mission to liberalize the world had come to an end, at least for now. Indeed, American public opinion in the late 1920s and 1930s became even more averse to entanglements abroad. Of course, the Americans did not entirely retreat from the international stage; for example, in 1921–22 Washington hosted a multilateral conference on naval disarmament and East Asia. Moreover, America's economic status as the world's largest creditor meant that it could not entirely cut itself off from the outside world. Even the most 'isolationist' Republican administrations of the 1920s did not shy away from pulling the financial levers to promote stability in Europe. However, the exercise of financial muscle could not compensate for the lack of a concrete American security commitment to the post-war peace.

The Soviet Union likewise remained isolated. Despite some sparks in Germany and Hungary, Lenin's world revolution failed to materialize. Moreover, the experience of civil war, Allied intervention, the Red Army's defeat at the hands of the Poles, and the loss of Finland, Bessarabia and the Baltic States all warned of

see Chapter 3

isolationism
The policy or doctrine of isolating one's country by avoiding foreign entanglements and responsibilities. Popular in the United States during the inter-war years.

the dangers of survival in a world system dominated by the twin forces of capitalism and imperialism. Soviet Russia was vulnerable. The tension between the need to spread revolution (the source of the regime's legitimacy and identity) and the need to strengthen the regime generated a dual-track policy: the Soviet Union would promote the overthrow of capitalism by supporting the international communist movement and, at the same time, build 'socialism in one country' in order to provide itself with security. Thus, Georgi Chicherin, the Soviet foreign minister, plotted a careful course between hostility to the status quo and peaceful co-existence with it. Moscow renounced its debts, denounced the 1919 settlement and the League of Nations, but at the same time turned to diplomacy and trade agreements to forestall any anti-Soviet coalition. The result of this diplomatic posture was a rapprochement with the other potential Great Power alienated from the Paris peace: Weimar Germany. In April 1922 the two pariah states agreed at Rapallo to establish diplomatic contact and expand economic co-operation. Secret military co-operation increased: Russia helped Germany evade disarmament and Germany provided Russia with technical know-how. The great bogey of a revisionist alignment (reaffirmed in the 1926 Treaty of Berlin), and, moreover, the spread of communism in China and to the European empires, reinforced the deep antipathy felt in London and Paris towards the Soviets. The French took the ideological transformation of their one-time eastern ally very hard indeed. French officials had clamoured the loudest to turn the limited Allied intervention in civil-war Russia into a crusade to topple Lenin's regime, and when this failed, Poland became the obvious substitute eastern ally.

When the Anglo-American security guarantees fell through, Clemenceau hoped Lloyd George would make good his promise anyway. Negotiations towards a security pact in 1921–22, however, made no progress. Some British officials recognized the French need for British reassurance. Many more, especially the British foreign secretary, Lord Curzon, believed that the French harboured ambitions of Napoleonic proportions. Balance-of-power rhetoric provided a high-sounding rationale for what was really a turning away by Britain from Europe's problems, motivated by a deep and understandable aversion to another military commitment on the scale of 1914–18. At the same time, J. M. Keynes, in his best-selling study of the peace, *The Economic Consequences of the Peace* (1919), undermined the legitimacy of Versailles in British (and American) minds by attacking reparations as both vindictive and ruinous. The more Britain backed away from Europe, the more France sought to convert its temporary supremacy on the continent into a lasting one. By doing so, they confirmed British misconceptions and prejudices. Friction in the Middle East between the two empires compounded the mistrust. A successful Turkish challenge to the Treaty of Sèvres precipitated the most spectacular rupture. In October 1921, the French made a deal with Kemal Atatürk, the nationalist president who had modernized the army and state, under which the Allies would withdraw from Anatolia. The pact nullified Sèvres and salvaged French interests at the expense of Greece, Italy and Britain. At the Dardanelles town of Chanak a year later, the French once again dealt bilaterally with the Turks and deserted the British.

Just like the Treaty of Sèvres, the Treaty of Versailles was not self-enforcing. The split in the *Entente* provided Germany with the opportunity to challenge the peace in the same fashion as the Turks. Indeed, any defeated Power faced with such a coalition would have done so. France after the Napoleonic Wars and Russia after the Crimean War had sought to reverse their defeats. What was different about Germany between the wars was the intensity of hatred towards the 'Versailles *Diktat*'. The explanation for this lay in the mismatch between what was expected from a peace based on Wilson's fourteen points and the terms the Weimar's socialist coalition was forced to accept unconditionally in June 1919. The Allies, fearful that their unity would unravel if talks with the Germans were opened, refused to bargain, leaving the German delegates indignant, humiliated and scornful. In Germany, an overpowering sense that a great injustice had been done and the popular myth that the German army had not been defeated on the battlefield made for a heady cocktail and a widespread determination to undermine Versailles took hold. In the 1920s, the publication of pre-1914 German diplomatic documents provided German scholars and liberal revisionists in the English-speaking world with ammunition to dispute the official Allied doctrine that Germany and its allies were responsible for 1914. To drive wedges between the Allies, Weimar foreign policy swung between shades of defiance and fulfilment. By defiance, possibly in alliance with the Soviet Union, some hoped to alienate Britain from France by confronting both with the unpleasant realities of treaty enforcement. With compliance, others hoped to play on British guilt over Versailles and prove that the treaty's economic terms were impossible to fulfil.

The principal battlefield was reparations. As Sally Marks has argued, nothing less than the verdict of 1918 was at stake. The danger for the Europeans, especially France, was that the cost of reconstruction would ruin their economies and leave Germany, which had suffered less physical damage, economically dominant. American debt forgiveness would have eliminated this prospect and might have encouraged a Franco-German economic reconciliation. Instead, the Europeans were left to choose between ruining themselves or their former foe. The electorates had been promised that it would be Germany. On 27 April 1921, the Reparations Commission set payments at 132 billion gold marks in cash and goods. This sum was set to appease public expectations and as a bargaining chip in debt negotiations with the Americans. German politicians pleaded that 132 billion gold marks was impossible to pay and (arguably) they plunged the German economy into an inflationary spiral to prove it. The real figure of 50 billion gold marks over thirty-six years, buried in the complex technical details, though still substantial and burdensome, probably fell within Germany's capacity to pay, had it tried. Indeed, the way both sides exploited the 132 billion figure to send different messages to their electorates instead of facing the unpalatable truths (for the Germans, defeat; for the Allies, the pitfalls of a settlement premised in Germany's voluntary compliance) illustrates that the struggle over reparations was primarily a political one.

As Berlin anticipated, the battle over reparations generated friction within the *Entente*. The British began to regret their decisions over reparations, and vented their frustration at what they saw as French vindictiveness. French officials, in turn, were exasperated by the British, who had no compunction about taking possession of 1,653,000 tons of German shipping, but dragged their feet over the coal, timber and cash due to France. Paris insisted on enforcement before leniency; London pressed for leniency in the hope that a German economic recovery would fuel a European one and revive British markets. In the winter of 1921–22, security talks between Lloyd George and the French premier, Aristide Briand, ran up against the usual obstacle: Briand asked for a military alliance to deter Germany, Lloyd George offered only a one-sided guarantee against 'unprovoked' attack. The way to break the impasse was to erect a comprehensive international security and economic structure within which the European antagonists could be reconciled, and concerted action to promote economic prosperity could take place. Lloyd George had something like this in mind when he called for an economic conference at Genoa in 1922. The countries invited included Soviet Russia and the United States, but the conference failed for the same reasons that had hampered diplomacy ever since 1919. The Americans stayed home. Without British backing, the new French premier, Raymond Poincaré, who was less amenable than Briand, declined to attend and refused to agree to reparations being on the agenda, while Chicherin and Rathenau, the Russian and German foreign ministers, left for Rapallo to cut their own bilateral deal.

So the disputes over reparations continued. British willingness to grant Germany a six-month moratorium ran up against the French condition that Berlin turn over its Ruhr mines as 'productive guarantees' in exchange for the suspension of payments. At this point, the French were ready to try their own solution. On 26 December 1922, the Reparations Commission in a three (France, Belgium and Italy) to one (Britain) vote declared Germany in default of reparation payments. On 11 January 1923 French and Belgian troops occupied the Rhineland. As Lloyd George had been forced to resign in October 1922, this crisis in Anglo-French relations fell on the shoulders of the new prime minister, Andrew Bonar Law. Any German hopes that the British might block or obstruct the French were quickly dashed. Bonar Law's cabinet issued only diplomatic protests. The British would wait and see. On the question of what Poincaré hoped to achieve, historians are divided and the evidence is ambiguous. Some believe that the occupation was really a bid to support Rhenish separatism and detach the Rhineland. Others criticize the French premier for the lack of any clear strategy at all. Perhaps in his own mind he lurched back and forth from a policy of straightforward treaty enforcement to one of initiating Germany's breakup? Whatever Poincaré's goals, pursuing them proved a grim task. Occupation troops met with widespread passive resistance that sometimes had to be overcome with bayonets. In Berlin, Chancellor Cuno printed marks to pay striking workers. Hyper-inflation was the result. By the end of 1923, however, the French had successfully imposed their will. The mines produced coal and freight trains moved across the frontier. In September, the new chancellor, Gustav Stresemann, called an end to resistance.

French victory came at a very great price. The occupation further alienated Anglo-American opinion. Anyone who had previously entertained suspicions of a Napoleonic thirst for mastery now appeared to have had their suspicions confirmed. Britain from this point onwards firmly planted itself between France and Germany as a mediator, and not as a French ally. Poincaré, who should have first explored the possibility of a bilateral deal with Germany, instead turned to the Anglo-American Powers to rescue the German mark and the rapidly falling French franc. In 1924, as a result of the plan devised by an expert committee headed by the American banker Charles Dawes, reparations were scaled down and the *Reichsbank* was reorganized. An American loan financed German reparations payments on a new, lighter schedule. American and British loans to France were conditional on the acceptance of the Dawes Plan and the evacuation of the Rhineland. The powers of the French-dominated Reparations Commission were also curtailed. Independent treaty enforcement, which in any case had been beyond France's reach, was no longer an option.

The Locarno era

The Dawes Plan signalled American willingness to resort to using financial power to promote continental stability; the task of building a fresh European security structure and making it work was left to the Europeans themselves – that is, Europe minus the Russians. The outlines of the structure came into focus in 1924–25 in talks between London and Paris. A Franco-German détente was the centrepiece. France would end the 1923 occupation and slowly surrender other controls over German sovereignty. Germany would be integrated into the states system and fulfil its obligations under the Dawes Plan. Britain would play the honest broker and offer some sort of pledge to French security, but only as part of a larger overarching guarantee of Western Europe's frontiers.

At the small Swiss resort of Locarno in October 1925, the outlines of this basic structure became concrete agreements. The most important, signed by France, Germany and Belgium, and guaranteed by Britain and Italy, was the Rhineland Pact. It affirmed the inviolability of the Franco-German and Belgo-German frontiers and the demilitarization of the Rhineland. Arbitration treaties between Germany and France, Belgium, Poland and Czechoslovakia were also concluded, and France handed out new security promises to its Central and East European allies. The **Locarno treaties** marked a turning point in international affairs. One British statesman wrote that 'the Great War ended in November 1918. The Great Peace did not begin until October 1925.' Its makers, Briand, Stresemann and the new British foreign secretary, Austen Chamberlain, shared the Nobel Peace Prize for their achievement.

Historians, with the benefit of hindsight, frequently deride the so-called 'Spirit of Locarno' or 'Locarno honeymoon' as just one among many other illusions of inter-war international security. There is substance to this view. Locarno was more the product of a French policy defeat rather than a change of heart; German nationalists of all shades had not given up the goal of overturning the Paris peace settlement. If anything, the British Locarno 'guarantee' was more

Locarno treaties
The series of treaties concluded at Locarno in Switzerland in October 1925. The most important was the Rhineland Pact, signed by France, Germany and Belgium and guaranteed by Britain and Italy, which affirmed the inviolability of the Franco-German and Belgo-German borders and the demilitarization of the Rhineland. In addition, Germany signed arbitration treaties with France, Belgium, Poland and Czechoslovakia.

limited than anything offered previously to France by successive British cabinets, and confirmed Britain's detachment from the continent. Germany offered no assurances about fulfilling its disarmament commitments, and Stresemann did not conceal his ambition to revise the settlement of Germany's eastern frontiers. The weaknesses of the security structures erected in the mid-1920s, however, did not determine the course of the 1930s. The three foreign ministers, Briand, Chamberlain and Stresemann, each saw Locarno as a first step towards a more distant and difficult transformation of the status quo – although all three hoped for different yet not incompatible foreign policy outcomes. Chamberlain, who would have readily offered France the sort of guarantee Briand had wanted in 1922 had he been able to persuade his isolationist colleagues, hoped that the limited guarantee of Locarno would be enough to extinguish the most serious threat to peace, the Franco-German antagonism, and later permit peaceful change in Central and Eastern Europe. Briand likewise hoped that the guarantee would provide France with some security and restore a measure of Anglo-French unity. After the defeat of 1923, Briand understood that France's temporary advantage over the inherently more powerful Germany could not be frozen. France would now have to seek salvation within the constraints of a dysfunctional coalition of victorious Powers and Berlin's unwillingness to comply with Versailles. Instead of strict enforcement of reparations, now the way forward economically appeared to be formal Franco-German industrial and commercial co-operation to meet the needs of French reconstruction and recovery.

Because the victors of 1919 would not (and France alone could not) enforce the verdict of 1918, the success of European détente rested on German behaviour. To see the possibilities here, we need to understand the rationale of German policy under Weimar's longest-serving foreign minister, Stresemann. He has been portrayed as both an unscrupulous nationalist working for the destruction of the post-war order and as a good European working for political stabilization and economic integration. Both images are caricatures. Although Stresemann was a vociferous liberal-nationalist before 1914, Germany's defeat in 1918 and the disaster of 1923 had profoundly altered his outlook. This should not be surprising. From his vantage point as chancellor in 1923 he saw how the Ruhr occupation had nearly plunged Germany into civil war and delivered the republic into the hands of the military, while France had come close to detaching the Rhineland. According to Stresemann's British biographer, Jonathan Wright, after 1923 the German foreign minister aimed at peaceful change in Europe and the construction of a broad nationalist consensus at home, which would be robust enough to keep the extreme right and left at bay. He accepted the Dawes Plan because it broke Germany's diplomatic isolation, enlisted Anglo-American sympathy to check France, and set the stage for an economic recovery that would elevate Germany once again to the rank of a Great Power. To extreme nationalists at home, he spoke of buying time before Germany could rearm and follow the path of the sword – but these words were only intended to appease his hard-line listeners. A consummate realist, Stresemann believed that the only way ahead was through the exercise of political and economic leverage *within* the states system.

For Stresemann's revisionist programme to succeed, Weimar first needed to be accepted as an equal among the Great Powers. In early 1925, fearing that Britain might offer France a security pledge and that the League of Nations might tighten the supervision of German disarmament, Stresemann seized the initiative. To forestall Germany's isolation, he launched a bold 'peace offensive' that ultimately resulted in the Locarno treaties. The treaties were his triumph. Stresemann's goal was to get French troops out of the Ruhr and to secure the Rhineland in exchange for a voluntary renunciation of Alsace-Lorraine, which he considered lost anyway. Locarno would encourage private American investment and give Washington a stake in German prosperity. An intricate balance had to be struck between *immediate* pacification in the west and *future* revision in the east. Stresemann refused to recognize Germany's eastern frontiers as final, but the French had military conventions with Poland and Czechoslovakia, and London and Washington would not countenance violent change. Frontier revision would have to come with the co-operation of the Western Allies. Yet the danger of courting the West was the alienation of Germany's Rapallo partner, the USSR. Though utterly repelled by Bolshevism, Stresemann needed Moscow to pressure Warsaw and to exploit any future crisis in Eastern Europe. In the event of a Russo-Polish war or some other great upheaval, Germany could bridge the ideological gulf between the Powers, and act as the chief broker of a new settlement. Indeed, Stresemann imagined that at some future Great Power conference assembled to redraw Central and Eastern Europe's frontiers, Germany would benefit from the support of the West and the acquiescence of Moscow.

In 1926–29, such calculations did not appear unrealistic. Certainly, nothing could erase the scars of 1914–18 or ease the deep fears and antagonisms that the war had engendered among political elites and electorates alike. Yet the trajectory of events in these years permits us to see a stable but fragile international structure taking shape. European economies emerged from the dislocation and destruction of 1914–18. The influx of American short-term loans into Germany and American capital investments generally promoted European recovery. Talks on inter-Allied war debts made progress and the burden of payment was reduced by lower interest rates. A bargain encompassing Germany, France, Belgium, the Saar and Luxembourg on steel production quotas was struck. Currencies stabilized and a general return to the gold standard signalled confidence. In May 1927, the first steps were taken at the World Economic Conference in Geneva to lower trade barriers. Of course the economic recovery was uneven and fitful. Industrial production remained below pre-war levels, and the agrarian economies of Eastern Europe were vulnerable to fluctuations in food prices and extra-European competition. But at this stage the world economic crisis that began with the New York stock market crash in 1929 was still over the horizon, and the short-lived economic revival of 1925–28 buttressed the emerging truce between the Western Great Powers.

In September 1926, Briand and Stresemann agreed on troop withdrawals from the Rhineland and an end to inter-Allied inspection of German disarmament. On 8 September 1926, Germany joined the League of Nations with a place on the Permanent Council. Unquestionably, the League of Nations in action disappointed one-world idealists everywhere. There was no break between the 'old' and 'new' diplomacy. The 1928 'International Treaty for the Renunciation of War as an Instrument of National Policy' (the so-called **Kellogg–Briand Pact**) expressed an aspiration, not a reality. Important diplomatic activity took place outside the League. In 1923, for instance, the crisis between Italy and Greece over Corfu was resolved by Great Power diplomacy. Measures to strengthen the legal mechanism of collective security and arbitration likewise ran up against the hierarchical nature of international politics: the League of Nations was for regulating the small states; the Great Powers turned to the League only if it suited their purposes. The ideological war between the West and the Bolsheviks engendered bitter hostility and fear. An Anglo-Soviet dispute over espionage triggered a Russian 'war scare' in 1927. Quarrels between the Allies were also common. A spectacular row over the construction of cruisers split Washington and London at the 1927 Geneva Naval Conference. Yet international disputes were as much a feature of the late 1920s as they are in any other post-war period. The question is whether the structures of peace and stability were strengthened or eroded by these disputes. Despite the limited powers of the League, the breakup of the wartime coalition against Germany and its allies, and the precarious balance between revisionists and status quo powers, a political equilibrium was emerging.

As before, the European system suffered from the disengagement of the two peripheral Great Powers. Washington was content with dollar diplomacy, while Moscow, fearful of a capitalist crusade against socialism, concentrated on industrialization and rearmament. Italy was an important prop of the European system but not a critical one. In fact, one success of the Locarno system was the way in which Italian revision in the 1920s was contained by the concerted action of the Powers. To be sure, Benito Mussolini, Italy's Fascist head of government (of whom more in Chapter 7), had designs on the Danube Basin and the Balkans. He encouraged Croatian separatism and intrigued with the Hungarians. Nonetheless, so long as Germany sought peaceful territorial revision inside the states system, there was little scope for a serious Italian challenge. And, at this phase in his career, the Fascist leader's craving to be accepted as a fellow player in the circle of Great Power statesmen suppressed his appetite for military adventures. Ultimately, the Locarno equilibrium rested on the relationship between the Western Europeans. Locarno's architects understood this, as well as the need to reinforce the Franco-German détente and to facilitate change. Serious obstacles remained. Disarmament foundered on France's refusal to see Germany rearm and Germany's demand to be treated as an equal. But there were signs that revision could take place and be successfully absorbed. In 1929, a committee of experts under another American, Owen D. Young, once again scaled down German reparations. The final evacuation of Allied occupation forces from the Rhineland was scheduled. Moreover, in an effort to contain Germany's economic revival with a mutually beneficial economic alliance – foreshadowing the later success of the Schuman Plan that led to the **European Coal and Steel Community** of 1950–51 – Briand proposed a 'United States of Europe' in an address to the League of Nations in September 1929. Unfortunately for Briand and the era of Locarno peace, time had run out for European solutions.

Kellogg–Briand Pact
Or more formally the 'International Treaty for the Renunciation of War as an Instrument of National Policy', 27 August 1928. It arose from a suggestion by the French prime minister, Aristide Briand, to the US secretary of state, Frank Kellogg, that the two states should agree to renounce war. At Kellogg's suggestion, other states were invited to join France and the United States in signing an agreement. In total, sixty-five did so. Manifestly a failure, the pact is often ridiculed as an empty gesture indicative of the idealistic internationalism of the inter-war years. In fact, Briand saw the treaty as a way to obtain some sort of moral American commitment to the preservation of the status quo.

see Chapter 7

European Coal and Steel Community (ECSC)
Established by the Treaty of Paris (1952) and also known as the Schuman Plan, after the French foreign minister, Robert Schuman, who proposed it in 1950. The member nations of the ECSC – Belgium, France, Italy, Luxembourg, the Netherlands and West Germany – pledged to pool their coal and steel resources by providing a unified market, lifting restrictions on imports and exports, and creating a unified labour market.

Conclusion

The onset of the global economic crisis after October 1929 wrecked the Locarno equilibrium. It functioned briefly because Stresemann pursued moderate revisionist goals from within the system. He died of overwork weeks before the start of the 'great crash'. In any case, Germany's precarious domestic political balance was coming under severe strain long before Weimar lost its foreign minister. Germans were impatient with the slow pace of revision. Right-wing agitation against acceptance of the **Young Plan** helped to legitimize the **Nazi Party** in the eyes of the German electorate. Not just in Weimar Germany, but across Eastern Europe, where recently established democratic institutions were linked closely with the imposition of the post-war order, the crisis in capitalism seemed to herald the end of democracy and the Paris peace. It is not surprising that this revisionist trend found one form of expression in the vilification of minorities, especially Jews, and the desire to recast Europe into exclusive national communities. In 1919, Woodrow Wilson had placed a great deal of faith in the rationality of humankind and the moderating force of public opinion. As the Depression deepened, Clemenceau's riposte – 'the voice of the people is the voice of the devil' – now seemed much more prophetic.

As the domestic supports of stability crumbled, governments desperately sought to shelter their economies from the global slump. Rather than taking joint action to lessen its impact, the Western Powers turned to **protectionism**, imperial preference and competitive devaluation. The bitter recriminations that followed this failure to co-ordinate policies further divided the war-winning coalition of 1918, just when Western unity to enforce the status quo was needed most. The pattern of the 1920s continued into the 1930s. Finally, when the crisis that Stresemann had anticipated over Poland came, Eastern Europe's frontiers were not redrawn at a summit of Great Powers, at which Germany benefited from the goodwill it had engendered by behaving as a responsible member of the states system. Instead, Nazi and Soviet revisionism conspired in the summer of 1939 to destroy Poland.

Young Plan
Name given to a financial scheme, worked out in 1929 by a committee chaired by the American businessman Owen D. Young, to reduce German reparations and arrange fresh credit for Germany. It was *informally* agreed by German, French and British delegates that reparations would be scaled back further if the former European Allies secured a reduction in debt repayments to the United States.

Nazis (or Nazi Party)
The abbreviation for the National Socialist German Workers Party (*Nationalsozialistische Deutsche Arbeiterpartei* (NSDAP)). It was founded in October 1918 as the German Workers Party by the German politician Anton Drexler to oppose both capitalism and Marxism. It took on its more notorious title in February 1920. One year later Hitler became the Nazi Party Führer (German: leader).

protectionism
The practice of regulating imports through high tariffs with the purpose of shielding domestic industries from foreign competition.

Recommended reading

On the end of the war and the coming of the armistice, this chapter has relied on David Stevenson, *The First World War and International Politics* (Oxford, 1991). For the illusory strategy of the Central Powers in 1918, see Holger H. Herwig, *The First World War: Germany and Austria-Hungary, 1914–1918* (London, 1998). Students should also consult Bullitt Lowry, *Armistice 1918* (Kent, OH, 1996), Arno J. Mayer, *Wilson vs. Lenin: Political Origins of the New Diplomacy, 1917–18* (New Haven, CT, 1964) and the excellent set of chapters by Stevenson, David French, Thomas Knock and Alan Sharp in Manfred F. Boemeke, Gerald D. Feldman and Elisabeth Glaser (eds), *The Treaty of Versailles: A Reassessment after*

Debating peacemaking in 1919

The opening phase of the debate on the 1919 settlement was dominated by the memoirs of former members of the British and American delegations to the Peace Conference. John Maynard Keynes's *The Economic Consequences of the Peace* and Harold Nicolson's *Peacemaking, 1919* are foremost among the British, and Ray Stannard Baker's *Woodrow Wilson and the World Settlement* among the American. Keynes denounced the Paris peace as both vindictive and ruinous, Nicolson blamed the chaotic organization for what he described as a botched peace, while Baker defended Wilson as the champion of a moderate peace and criticized the selfish Europeans, especially the vindictive French, for what became a punitive one. Between the two world wars, these criticisms by disillusioned 'insiders' resonated powerfully with revisionist scholarship on the causes of war and the 'war guilt' question. For many, the coming of the Second World War confirmed that the Paris peacemakers had blundered. Few now took issue with Jacques Bainville's 1919 verdict that the Versailles Treaty was 'too gentle for all that is in it which is harsh'.

After a period of some scholarly neglect, the ideological polarization and the political turmoil of 1960s' America gave rise to a fresh interpretation. In *Politics and Diplomacy of Peacemaking: Containment and Counterrevolution at Versailles* (London, 1968), Arno Mayer argued that the peacemakers, alarmed by the spectre of Lenin and the threat of Bolshevism, were more concerned about reversing the revolutionary tide in Europe than about founding a truly just social, economic and political order. Although many took issue with Mayer's portrayal of peacemaking after 1918 as a contest between the 'forces of order' and the 'forces of movement', the historiographical debate benefited from his shift in focus away from the German question to the broader ideological and domestic political influences working on the minds of the peacemakers.

In the early 1970s, the French archives opened for research. The new sources initiated not only a positive reassessment of French policy, but also a full challenge to the negative verdicts of the inter-war writers. Several historians argued, for example, that the French were more moderate and flexible in their peace aims, for instance on German reparations, and, conversely, that the Americans and the British were more punitive and inflexible in theirs, than had been previously supposed. The long-held assumption that reparations were an impossible burden beyond Germany's capacity to pay was widely questioned. Historians now see the Paris settlement as a workable compromise, and perhaps the best one possible under such difficult circumstances. Mistakes of course were made, so the revisionists admit, but the peacemakers did not pave the way for Hitler, nor did they condemn Europe to another great war.

75 Years (Washington, DC, 1998). This impressive collection of essays is essential reading on the Paris peace and marks the culmination of the revisionism of the 1970s and 1980s.

The best introductory text on peacemaking in 1919 is Alan Sharp, *The Versailles Settlement: Peacemaking in Paris 1919* (Basingstoke, 1991). William Keylor (ed.), *The Legacy of the Great War: Peacemaking, 1919* (New York, 1998) reprints useful essays and Keylor's introduction provides an excellent overview of the historical debate. On the policies of the 'Big Three', students should read David Stevenson, *French War Aims against Germany, 1914–1919* (Oxford, 1982), Michael L. Dockrill and J. Douglas Goold, *Peace without Promise: Britain and the Peace Conferences, 1919–1923* (London, 1981), Anthony Lentin, *Lloyd George and the Pre-history of Appeasement* (London, 1984), Arthur S. Link, *Woodrow Wilson: Revolution, War and Peace* (1979), Lloyd E. Ambrosius, *Wilsonian Statecraft: Theory and Practice of Liberal Internationalism during World War I* (Wilmington, DE, 1991) and Klaus Schwabe, *Woodrow Wilson, Revolutionary Germany and Peacemaking, 1918–1919* (Chapel Hill, NC, 1985). For an excellent recent reassessment of Wilson's diplomacy, see Ross Kennedy, 'Woodrow Wilson, World War I and the American Conception of National Security', *Diplomatic History* (2001), vol. 25, pp. 1–31. On the origins and development of the League of Nations, apart from the texts already cited, consult the two chapters in David Armstrong, Lorna Lloyd and John Redmond, *From Versailles to Maastricht: International Organisation in the Twentieth Century* (1982) and J. P. Dunbabin, 'The League of Nations' Place in the International System', *History* (1993), vol. 78, pp. 421–42.

The opening up of the French archives in the 1970s inspired a wholesale revision of our understanding of French foreign policy and the reparations question: for a review of the literature, see Jon Jacobson's 'Strategies of French Foreign Policy after World War I', *Journal of Modern History* (1983), vol. 55, pp. 78–95. For a statement of Marc Trachtenberg's views, see his 'Versailles after Sixty Years', *Journal of Contemporary History* (1982), vol. 17, pp. 487–506 and his *Reparations in World Politics: France and European Economic Diplomacy, 1916–1923* (New York, 1980). See also Stephen Schuker, *American 'Reparations' to Germany, 1919–1933* (Princeton, NJ, 1988) and Walter McDougall, *France's Rhineland Diplomacy, 1914–1924: The Last Bid for a Balance of Power in Europe* (Princeton, NJ, 1978). Anthony Adamthwaite, *Grandeur and Misery: France's Bid for Power in Europe, 1914–1940* (London, 1995) offers a cogent counter-argument to the revisionists. For a vigorous defence of the reparations settlement, which also serves as a succinct guide to the complexities of the post-war financial settlement, see Sally Marks, 'The Myth of Reparations', *Central European History* (1978), vol. 18, pp. 231–55 [reprinted in Keylor's collection] and her contribution to Boemeke *et al.*, *The Treaty of Versailles: A Reassessment after 75 Years*.

On the 1920s, the best short survey on Europe is Sally Marks, *The Illusion of Peace: International Relations in Europe, 1918–1933*, 2nd edn (Basingstoke, 2003) and the best comprehensive survey of international relations overall is Zara Steiner's *The Lights that Failed: European International History 1919–1933* (Oxford, 2005). For a look at the 1920s and 1930s as a clash of ideas and ideologies, see the relevant chapters in Mark Mazower's superb volume, *Dark Continent: Europe's Twentieth Century* (London, 1998). On attempts to initiate a European economic and political recovery, see the essays in Carole Fink *et al.* (eds), *Genoa, Rapallo, and European Reconstruction in 1922* (Cambridge, 1991) and her *The Genoa Conference: European Diplomacy 1921–22* (Cambridge, 1984). For a revisionist account of attempts at political and economic stabilization in Europe, see Patrick O. Cohrs, *The Unfinished Peace after World War I: America, Britain and the Stabilisation of Europe, 1919–1932* (Cambridge, 2006). On the European economic recovery and collapse, see Patricia Clavin, *The Great Depression in Europe, 1929–39* (Basingstoke, 2000).

On Franco-British relations, see Philip M. H. Bell, *France and Britain, 1900–1940: Entente and Estrangement* (London, 1996) and Alan Sharp and Glyn Stone (eds), *Anglo-French Relations in the Twentieth Century: Rivalry and Co-operation* (London, 2000). Also read Brian J. McKercher, 'Austen Chamberlain's Control of British Foreign Policy, 1924–29', *International History Review* (1984), vol. 6, pp. 570–91 and E. Keeton, 'Politics and Economics in Briand's German Policy, 1925–31', in Carol Fink (ed.), *German Nationalism and the European Response* (Norman, OK, 1985). On the diplomacy and policies of the United States and the Soviet Union, see Melvyn Leffler, *The Elusive Quest: America's Pursuit of European Stability and French Security, 1919–1933* (Chapel Hill, NC, 1979) and Teddy J. Uldricks, 'Russia and Europe: Diplomacy, Revolution and Economic Development in the 1920s', *International History Review* (1979), vol. 1, pp. 55–83. For two broad studies of the Weimar Republic, which include chapters on foreign policy, see E. Kolb, *The Weimar Republic* (London, 1988) and Detlev Peukert, *The Weimar Republic: The Crisis of Classical Modernity* (London, 1992). The best comprehensive study of Locarno is Jon Jacobson, *Locarno Diplomacy: Germany and the West, 1925–1929* (Princeton, NJ, 1972). For an entirely convincing and positive reassessment of Stresemann's diplomacy, see Jonathan Wright, 'Stresemann and Locarno', *Contemporary European History* (1995), vol. 4, pp. 109–31.

CHAPTER THREE

Japan, China and the origins of the Pacific War, 1900 – 41

Introduction

Manchuria
The three north-eastern provinces of China and home of the Manchu people. From 1932 to 1945, with the addition of Jehol province, it became the Japanese puppet state of Manchukuo.

Great Powers
Traditionally those states that were held capable of shared responsibility for the management of the international order by virtue of their military and economic influence.

Pacific War
The phrase usually used to refer to the Allied war against Japan from 1941 to 1945.

The history of the twentieth century is in part the story of the relative decline of Europe and the rise of non-Europeans to a position of equality within the international system; the first step in this process began in East Asia with the rise of Japan. In 1904–05 Japan, which had only opened up to the world in 1853, defeated tsarist Russia in a war over control of Korea and South **Manchuria** – the first occasion in modern times that an Asian state had vanquished one of the **Great Powers**. It was a victory that prompted fear and admiration in Europe and the United States and which reverberated around Asia, inspiring nationalists in China, India and elsewhere to work against Western rule. Over the next forty years the Japanese challenge to the status quo continued as it strove to create a hegemonic position for itself in East Asia, until finally in the **Pacific War** of 1941–45 it fatally undermined the European order in the region while temporarily destroying itself in the process.

The motives behind the Japanese challenge to the West in the inter-war period have been the subject of much debate. In the wake of its defeat in 1945, Japan's expansionism was largely seen as the result of the hijacking of the state in the 1930s by a militarist clique that had sought power for its own sake both at home and abroad. Simultaneously much emphasis was put on American–Japanese relations as the fundamental dynamic within the region. This perspective has gradually been modified. Studies of Japan itself have questioned whether the imperial Japanese army should be seen as solely responsible by emphasizing the rivalries within the Japanese elite and by demonstrating that an internal battle for power continued even into the Pacific War. More broadly, analysis of the nature of inter-war Japan has led to interest in the significance of the political, social and economic imperatives generated by modernization and by its position as a late imperial power. In addition, a recent development has been the study of the ideological and cultural roots of Japanese foreign policy. This, in turn, has raised the issue of the degree to which **pan-Asianism** and ideas about Japan's predestined leadership role in Asia influenced its actions. Meanwhile, works on the international history of East Asia have demonstrated that many actors influenced the history of the region. In particular, access to archives in Taipei, Beijing and Moscow has helped to stress the centrality of China's own modernization process as a force in regional history and the importance of the triangular relationship between Russia, China and Japan. The simple answers provided in the aftermath of the war have thus been replaced by a complex series of interlocking interpretations.

pan-Asianism
The idea that Asia should free itself from Western imperialism and unite in a common effort to modernize. Espoused chiefly by Japan before 1945, but some Indian and Chinese nationalists were also attracted to the concept.

The First World War in East Asia

In trying to understand the origins of the Pacific War, it is important to see that Japan's desire for regional hegemony and the West's attempts at containment did not begin in the 1930s. Indeed, it could be said that the seeds of war went back to the breakdown in the mid- to late nineteenth century of the traditional China-centred international system that had dominated East Asia. The steady erosion of imperial China's authority under the weight of both external challenges from the West and internal challenges from a series of large-scale rebellions led Japan into a fundamental reassessment of its own relationship with the outside world. In one sense China's plight posed a grave danger, for there was the possibility that the resulting power vacuum might be filled by hostile Western powers, particularly Russia, which would seek to gain not just economic but also political control over the region. However, at the same time, Chinese decline also provided Japan with the opportunity to fill this power vacuum itself and to create a new East Asian international order in its own image. Thus, concerned for its security and desiring to raise its status, Japan from the 1870s onwards moved to increase its influence in East Asia. Its fears and ambitions eventually led it into war, first with China in 1894–95 and then with Russia in 1904–05, and conquest, most notably of Taiwan (1894), South Manchuria (1905) and Korea (1910). In addition, its growing prestige led it in 1902 to acquire Britain as an ally, for the latter too had misgivings about Russian ambitions in the region.

see Map 3.1

For countries such as the United States that were interested chiefly in trade with East Asia, Japan's expansion became a matter of some concern. It was feared that Japan's pursuit of security might prejudice the right of other countries to trade

open door

The maintenance in a certain territory of equal commercial and industrial rights for the nationals of all countries. As a specific policy, it was first advanced by the United States in the late nineteenth century as a way of safeguarding American economic interests in China.

freely in the region, and in particular that it might limit their access to the Chinese market, thus compromising what the United States referred to as the '**open door**' to China. Their apprehension might not have been so great had China been in a position to resist Japanese pressure, but this was not the case. By the start of the twentieth century the Qing dynasty that ruled China was in terminal decline, its authority so compromised that it was not able to persuade the provinces to finance the reforms that it needed to redeem itself. In 1912, due to a rebellion that had

Map 3.1 Japanese expansion in East Asia until 1939

Source: After Iriye (1987)

begun the previous year, the Qing abdicated and a Chinese Republic was established, ending thousands of years of imperial rule. The republic proved, however, to be no stronger than its predecessor, for it soon found itself mired in controversies about its political direction and was no more able to control the provinces than the Qing had been. As China could not protect itself, Japan was kept in check largely by the presence of the Western Powers, but this situation changed with the start of the First World War.

The First World War was for Japan an unprecedented opportunity to strengthen itself and expand its power in the region. As the Western Powers turned their attention to the conflagration in Europe, Japan took advantage of their absence in a number of ways. In the economic sphere, the drying up of European trade with the region meant that it was in a position to fill the vacuum and its exports flourished. In addition, the absence of imports from Europe of iron, steel and chemicals encouraged the development of Japan's own heavy industrial base. Japan was thus able to emerge from the war richer than ever before and with a modernized economy. Above and beyond this, however, the circumstances were ripe for a further expansion of Japan's political power in the Asian continent.

Japan entered the First World War in August 1914 when it honoured its alliance with Britain by declaring war on Germany and attacking the latter's Jiaozhou lease in China's Shandong peninsula. In January 1915 it then attempted to acquire a predominant position for itself in China by issuing the Twenty-One Demands, which called for recognition of the secession of Jiaozhou to Japan and for a variety of economic and political concessions that would dramatically increase Japan's influence in Manchuria, the Yangtze valley and Fujian. Owing to Chinese intransigence and diplomatic pressure from Britain and the United States, Japan gained only some of its objectives. Undaunted by this opposition, it turned between 1916 and 1918 to a new strategy, which involved utilizing its new financial power in the form of loans to China to gain by largess what it could not seize through coercion.

Japan's activities in China and its commercial penetration into the hitherto European-dominated markets in India and South-East Asia did not endear it to its *Entente* partners, and in particular alienated its ally Britain. However, as long as the war dragged on and there was still a need for Japanese naval assistance against Germany, particularly in the Mediterranean, little could be done to restrain Tokyo. As well as irritating Britain, Japan also strained its relations with the United States. To the Wilson administration, Japan's China policy was a flagrant violation of the principle of the 'open door'. Added to this was naval rivalry, as Japan sought to keep pace with the large-scale expansion of the United States navy announced in 1916. Moreover, the decision by the United States and Japan in July 1918 to intervene to restore order in Siberia, while, on the surface, a demonstration of solidarity, in reality only added another bone of contention, as each suspected the other of desiring a monopoly over the region's economic resources.

The Paris Peace Conference of 1919 did little to dissipate these tensions. Japan attended with three main aims: first, to formalize its control over the Jiaozhou lease; second, to acquire the German islands in the west Pacific; and third, to insert

League of Nations
An international organization
established in 1919 by the
peace treaties that ended the
First World War. Its purpose
was to promote international
peace through collective
security and to organize
conferences on economic and
disarmament issues. It was
formally dissolved in 1946.

mandates
The colonial territories of
Germany and the Ottoman
Empire that were entrusted to
Britain, France, Japan,
Australia and South Africa
under the supervision of a
League of Nations
Commission.

a clause opposing racial discrimination into the Covenant of the **League of Nations**. It thus sought to expand its empire and to seal its position as the equal of the other Great Powers. It met with only partial success. The United States initially opposed the transfer of Jiaozhou to Japan, and only relented after the latter had indicated its intention to ensure the eventual retrocession of the lease to China. Meanwhile the racial equality clause fell prey to Australia's absolute refusal to make concessions over its immigration policy, while Japan gained the former German Pacific islands only as League of Nations **mandates** rather than outright possessions. Japan thus left the conference only half-satisfied, while the United States and Britain sought new means to curb Japanese power.

The Washington Conference

From 1919 to 1921 American–Japanese relations remained tense and fears grew of an all-out naval arms race. In the end, however, the spiral of escalation was controlled. In November 1921 a conference of the Powers with interests in the western Pacific convened in Washington to discuss international co-operation in the region, particularly in regard to China, and how to establish a framework for naval arms limitation. The conference proved, at least in the short term, to be a marked success, for by February 1922 it had led to the return of the Jiaozhou lease to China and the conclusion of three new treaties. These were the Five-Power Treaty on naval arms limitation, the Four-Power Pact to preserve the status quo in the Pacific (which allowed for the abrogation of the Anglo-Japanese alliance), and the Nine-Power Treaty to uphold the open door policy in China.

The obvious question that arises is: why at Washington did Japan abandon its former policy of single-minded expansion and accept the need for a new international order in East Asia? One could, of course, rely on a purely *realpolitik* explanation, and state that the end of the First World War and the apparent formation of an Anglo-American bloc forced Japan to accept its relative powerlessness. To an extent this is true, for Japan clearly realized that its diplomacy at Paris had failed and that it could not win a naval race with the United States. However, it is also possible to see its acceptance of the Washington treaties as symbolic of a new spirit in the country, reflecting the worldwide trend towards greater idealism in both foreign and domestic policy. Certainly some elements in the foreign policy elite welcomed Wilsonian 'new diplomacy', for they realized that Japan could benefit from multilateral co-operation as this would both guarantee its security and allow expansion of its economic stake in China. The most notable proponent of this view was Kijurō Shidehara, the ambassador to the United States at the time of the conference, and later foreign minister in 1924–27 and 1929–31.

In addition, Japan was at this time shifting from oligarchical rule towards government by party politicians: the so-called period of 'Taishō democracy'. In 1918 Takashi Hara, the head of the Seiyūkai Party, became the first commoner to

Plate 3.1 Washington Conference, USA, November 1921. From left to right: British ambassador, Sir Auckland Campbell Geddes, Sir Maurice Hankey, Arthur Balfour and Arthur Lee in Washington, DC for the International Conference on Naval Limitation. (Photo by Topical Press Agency/Getty Images)

be made prime minister, and from 1919, as in many other states at the time, the political agenda came to be dominated by debates about universal suffrage and labour issues. This shift towards a new mass politics was aided by the relatively high rate of literacy in Japan, which meant that the new ideas emanating from the West about issues such as morality in international affairs, unionization and women's rights received a wide audience. Indeed, by 1925 Japan would introduce universal male suffrage and in 1928 socialist parties would stand in a general election. This change in the nature of Japanese politics had implications for foreign policy, for the rise of the parties saw a growth of anti-militarist sentiment, as the military were perceived to be the last bastions of oligarchic government. This in turn meant that plans for international co-operation, including naval arms limitation, found a ready constituency in Japan, for such measures would clearly help to curb the military's political power.

The treaties signed in 1921–22 helped to shape the nature of international relations in East Asia for the next twenty years. Indeed, some historians have described them as constituting a 'Washington system', in that they established a new overarching framework for international co-operation in the region. Linked to this concept is the idea that the Powers agreed to take a 'gradualist' approach towards China, in which they would slowly shed their privileges as the latter became more politically stable. This can be seen in the terms of the Nine-Power Treaty, which committed its signatories to respect China's sovereignty and territorial integrity, and to consider in the near future the raising of its external tariffs and in the longer term the abolition of extra-territoriality. It is possible, however, to overstate this case, for in practice little was done to assist China; indeed, continued economic competition between the Powers seemed to be the order of the day. For example, at the tariff reform conference of 1925, each of the Powers viewed assistance to China solely in terms of trade advantages to themselves. It is therefore possible to exaggerate the degree of Great Power co-operation engendered by the Washington Conference and the extent to which the Powers were committed to end China's inferior status. In practice, the main focus of the conference was to contain Japan and to restrict international competition in China to the economic field.

Chinese nationalism and the Northern Expedition

In retrospect, the Washington Conference's relative indifference to the demands of Chinese nationalism can be seen as its chief failing, for its achievements relied on China remaining a passive arena for Great Power economic activity. The problem was that the Chinese were not willing to play this quiescent role. China, like Japan, was influenced by the internationalist, democratic and socialist ideas that arose at the end of the First World War. Within the former, however, they had an even more profound effect, for they helped to turn what had initially been a largely intellectual nationalist cause into a mass movement. The main spark came in May 1919, when the hopes among students that Wilsonian ideas of **self-determination** would be applied to China were dashed by the decision under the **Versailles Treaty** to transfer the Jiaozhou lease to Japan. This insult to Chinese prestige led to anti-Japanese demonstrations by students in Beijing and Shanghai which soon developed into a nationwide protest involving strikes by industrial workers and a boycott of Japanese goods. This campaign, dubbed the May Fourth Movement, can now be seen to be a seminal event in Chinese history, for it showed that the Chinese were willing to take coherent political action against the imperialists. In the short term, however, while it had a profound influence on political thought, it had little impact on international politics, for in the turmoil of the warlord years there was no central force capable of tapping its potential. What China needed if it was to turn its nationalism into an effective weapon against imperialism was a modern political and military organization and greater ideological coherence. The construction of both was, however, to require co-operation from another state – the Soviet Union.

The **Bolsheviks**, who were notable by their absence from the Washington Conference, had decided by the early 1920s that the **Comintern** should become active in the colonized parts of the world. The aim, however, was not to create

self-determination
The idea that each national group has the right to establish its own national state. It is most often associated with the tenets of Wilsonian internationalism and became a key driving force in the struggle to end imperialism.

Versailles Treaty
The treaty that ended the Allied state of hostilities with Germany in 1919. It included German territorial losses, disarmament, a so-called war guilt clause and a demand that reparations be paid to the victors.

Bolsheviks
Originally in 1903 a faction led by Lenin within the Russian Social Democratic Party, over time the Bolsheviks became a separate party and led the October 1917 revolution in Russia. After this 'Bolsheviks' was used as a shorthand to refer to the Soviet government and communists in general.

Comintern
The Communist or Third International founded in Moscow in 1919 as an organization to direct and support the activities of communist parties outside Russia. It was abolished in 1943 in a short-lived effort by Stalin to reassure Britain and the United States that the Soviet Union no longer sought to export Marxism-Leninism.

proletarian revolutions in the colonized countries, for they clearly lacked the economic conditions for such ventures, but primarily to support nationalist parties in order to undermine Western imperialism. However, at the same time the Comintern sought to encourage the growth of indigenous communist movements in an effort to assist the mobilization of the masses and to prepare for the future. As a result, the Comintern's interest in Asia, added to Lenin's musings on the nature of imperialism, had a profound effect, for, by stressing that socialism and nationalism were fighting against the same common enemy, Lenin helped to radicalize a new generation of Asian nationalists. Moreover, Marxism-Leninism appealed to figures such as the young Mao Zedong, Zhou Enlai and Ho Chi Minh, because it made clear why traditional society had failed to resist foreign encroachment and provided a blueprint for future modernization and social equality. The virulently nationalist Asian Marxist hybrid that was to thwart the superpowers in the Cold War thus had its origins in this era.

China in the early 1920s appeared to Moscow to be a viable field for Comintern activities and, in particular, the **Guomindang (GMD)** party created by the veteran nationalist Sun Yatsen, which espoused anti-imperial ideas mixed with a vaguely socialist domestic agenda, emerged as an attractive potential partner. In January 1923 a Comintern agent, Alfred Joffe, met Sun in Shanghai where they agreed on a framework for Soviet support for the GMD. This included the promise of advisers, arms and the establishment of a 'United Front' between the GMD and the infant Chinese Communist Party (CCP), which had only been established in 1921. The following autumn the first Comintern advisers arrived at Sun's political base in Guangzhou in southern China.

Over the next three years Soviet assistance helped to turn the GMD into a formidable political and military machine. As early as 1925, shortly after Sun's death, the GMD, taking advantage of Britain's heavy-handed treatment of a Chinese demonstration in Shanghai, organized a sixteen-month strike that paralysed British trade in Hong Kong and Guangzhou. At the same time its armed forces expanded its area of direct control over Guangdong and Guangxi provinces. Its very success, however, raised questions about its future direction. Should the GMD seek to spread the nationalist cause merely through political actions such as strikes and boycotts or should it unite China militarily under its own rule? The answer was provided by Sun's successor as the dominant figure within the party, Jiang Jieshi (Chiang Kaishek), who in July 1926 launched the Northern Expedition, a military offensive to unify the country.

The Northern Expedition was an event of great significance for, as well as leading to Chinese unification under the GMD, it forced the Great Powers to review their policies towards China. Britain and the United States after careful deliberation came to the view that they should reconcile themselves to the rise of Chinese nationalism, on the grounds that concessions over its territorial privileges now could safeguard their positions in the Chinese market later. This approach meant that once tensions dissipated, particularly after Jiang abruptly broke with the Comintern in April 1927 and purged the GMD of Soviet and CCP influence, they were well placed to enter into a new relationship with nationalist China. Thus, from 1928, when Jiang set up his Nationalist government in Nanjing, both

Guomindang (GMD)
The Chinese Nationalist party founded in 1913 by Sun Yatsen. Under the control of Jiang Jieshi, it came to power in China in 1928 and initiated a modernization programme before leading the country into war against Japan in 1937. It lost control over mainland China in 1949 as a result of the communist victory in the civil war. From 1949 it controlled Taiwan, overseeing the island's 'economic miracle', until its electoral defeat in 2000.

of these Powers proved willing to enter into negotiations about returning tariff autonomy to China and getting rid of extra-territoriality. Japan, however, took a different view, for although willing to make concessions about its commercial interests, it could not accede to China's demands for the return of all territories that had been leased to foreign powers. The sticking point was the Kwantung lease in South Manchuria that Japan had gained in 1905 as one of the fruits of the Russo-Japanese War. For economic, military and political reasons, Japan could not afford to make concessions about this leased territory or about its ownership of the South Manchurian Railway (SMR). Equally, the Nanjing government could not compromise its 'rights recovery' policy by opting not to raise the issue of the future of the Kwantung lease. Japan and China were therefore on a collision course.

The Manchurian Crisis

From 1928 tensions in Manchuria steadily escalated, largely because the pro-Jiang warlord who controlled the region, Zhang Xueliang, tried to challenge Japanese influence by building railways in parallel to those owned by the SMR. Zhang's provocative behaviour appeared to the Kwantung Army, the Japanese military force in the region, to be an ample justification for Japanese annexation of Manchuria. On 18 September 1931, after a tense summer, middle-ranking officers of the Kwantung Army, without prior approval from Shidehara, now foreign minister, or even the army general staff in Tokyo, staged an incident on the SMR outside Shenyang which they used as a pretext for military action. Over the next six months the Kwantung Army brought the whole of Manchuria under its control and established the new state of Manchukuo, and in so doing permanently undermined 'Shidehara diplomacy' and set East Asia on the road to a wider conflagration.

Various reasons have been postulated to explain why the Kwantung Army precipitated the Manchurian Crisis in defiance of the civilian government in Tokyo and how it succeeded in redefining Japan's national agenda. In part, its actions can be seen as a reaction to Chinese provocations and a revival of Russian power in the region, and the fear that, over the long term, Japan's position in Manchuria would be steadily undermined. However, it is important to recognize that the seizure of Manchuria was just as much an act of expansion as one of defence.

One important motive behind the Kwantung Army's actions was the desire to seize the economic resources of the area in order to enhance Japan's ability to mobilize for **total war**. Following the First World War, some army officers, such as Tetsuzan Nagata and Kanji Ishiwara, believed that Germany's defeat was largely the result of the Allied blockade. This had important ramifications for Japan because, as a resource-poor island nation, it was itself open to such economic pressure. The answer therefore was a 'drive for **autarky**' which would give Japan

total war
A war that uses all resources at a state's disposal including the complete mobilization of both the economy and society.

autarky
A policy that aims at achieving national economic self-sufficiency. It is commonly associated with the economic programmes espoused by Germany, Italy and Japan in the 1930s and 1940s.

the industrial and military capability to defeat its major potential enemies, the Soviet Union and the United States. In this the seizure of Manchuria with its coal and iron ore resources and its potential to become a major industrial producer was a vital preliminary step.

Events in Manchuria were also conditioned by domestic instability within Japan. One aspect of this was the growing division between the services and the government over the size of the armed forces. In 1930 the government made the imperial Japanese navy agree to the terms of the London Naval Treaty concerning quantitative limitation for cruisers. This led the army, which already in 1925 had suffered a cut of four divisions, to fear that at the forthcoming Geneva disarmament conference it would be asked to accept further reductions in its strength. The army's actions in Manchuria can thus be seen as an attempt to justify its own existence and to use a sense of national crisis to increase its power over civilians.

Despite the Kwantung Army's considerable autonomy in military matters, it still did not in itself have the ability to defy the government and completely reconfigure Japanese external policy; that could only take place if its actions attracted broad domestic support. However, the economic conditions that existed in the early 1930s were such that the public was generally supportive of the Manchurian adventure. By 1931 Japan was feeling the full force of the world depression, which, owing to falling prices for rice and raw silk, hit rural areas particularly hard. Matters were not helped by the government's decision in January 1930 to return the yen to the gold standard in the hope that the discipline of exchange into gold would encourage long-term growth and competitiveness. Unfortunately this move had exactly the opposite effect, for the high interest rates required to support parity caused a decline in domestic demand and investment, while at the same time the high value of the yen hit Japan's exports.

The economic distress naturally poisoned the political climate. Already the popularity of the political parties had been eroded as a result of a series of corruption scandals and the impression that the politicians only served the interests of the large Japanese industrial and trading combines, the *zaibatsu*. The Depression heightened this animosity, and led to 'ultra-nationalists' rejecting the whole concept of party government and to a proliferation of nationalist societies offering solutions to the pressures engendered by modernization. To some of these groups, the answer to Japan's problems lay in a complete rejection of Western ideas and a return to national unity based upon traditional Japanese values. Others were drawn to the fascist model of development emanating from Italy and later Germany, showing how to use state planning and corporatism to achieve social stability and economic progress.

In this heated atmosphere, the actions of the Kwantung Army clearly struck a resonant chord, for the attempt to construct a new Manchuria at least seemed to provide a possible solution to Japan's economic crisis. To many in Japan the supposedly 'virgin land' of Manchuria appeared as a 'lifeline' which would rescue them from the trough of the Depression. To the business community it appeared as a new market for trade and investment, to the struggling agricultural community it offered new fertile pastures, and to intellectuals a laboratory for putting state planning into practice. The media, in their desire for increased circulation, fuelled this wave of enthusiasm by lauding the achievements of the army and the idealism of the 'Manchukuo' experiment. Faced with this outpouring of emotion, the two major political parties, together with many other groups within Japan, including some of the socialist parties, trade unions and even women's societies, were forced to accept the position of patriotic supporters of expansion.

Another aspect of the crisis that made it difficult for the 'internationalists' in Japan to control the situation was the reaction of China and the Powers to events in Manchuria. In 1931 the Nanjing government was still comparatively weak and had only nominal control over large areas of the country. It faced challenges to its authority from the remaining warlords, from discontented elements within the GMD, and most of all from the CCP, which controlled some rural areas in China, notably the Jiangxi Soviet. As China could not hope to win a war in this condition, Jiang decided to make internal reconstruction his priority, and therefore to follow a policy of 'non-resistance' towards Japan and to appeal to the League of Nations and the United States for assistance.

This did little to assist China, as the League's ability to influence Japan was strictly limited. The problem was that, while the smaller states in the League engaged in enthusiastic rhetoric supporting China's cause, the organization could only provide assistance in the shape of military or economic sanctions if the Great Power members, such as Britain, and non-members, such as the United States, were willing to act. This level of support was not, however, forthcoming. Both Britain and the United States were unprepared militarily, and the idea of introducing sanctions in the midst of a depression was not a viable political option. The League and the United States therefore did little more than register their disquiet. In January 1932 Washington announced that it would not recognize Japan's fruits of aggression, while in February 1933 the League of Nations Assembly voted to adopt the Lytton Report, which, although criticizing Chinese provocations, declared that Japan's actions were illegitimate and that the new state of Manchukuo was not an expression of popular self-determination.

The high level of criticism but lack of firm action by the international community played into the hands of the hard-liners in Tokyo, for it suggested that Japan could not rely on the outside world for a 'just' hearing. It was also easy to link this chorus of disapproval to earlier acts of perceived discrimination against Japan, such as the defeat of the racial discrimination clause in 1919 and the anti-Japanese nature of the US Immigration Act of 1924, and thus claim that the latest criticisms fitted into a pattern of racist ill-treatment. Moreover, this image was reinforced by the belief that, as Britain and France were turning their own empires into protectionist blocs and the United States dominated trade in Latin America, it was unfair of them to criticize Japan for constructing its own empire. Japan thus perceived itself as a 'have-not' country hemmed in by a hypocritical Anglo-American status quo, which, if not resisted, would assign Japan to perpetual poverty and desperation. In this feverish atmosphere the hitherto largely marginalized radical pan-Asianists, who had ever since the late nineteenth century decried the West and called on Japan to liberate Asia from European oppression, at last found an audience and exerted influence on foreign policy as never before.

The 'internationalist' party politicians and diplomats in Japan proved to be unable to counter or resist the arguments of the ultra-nationalists and, as a result, their influence began to be eclipsed. As a result of Manchuria and its own failed economic policies, in December 1931 the Minseitō government, with Shidehara as foreign minister, fell from power and was replaced by a Seiyūkai administration led by Tsuyoshi Inukai. However, in an atmosphere of increasing political violence, Inukai also failed to appease the Right, and on 15 May 1932 was assassinated by a group of ultra-nationalist naval cadets. After Inukai's death the emperor's advisers judged that the political parties could no longer ensure stability and he therefore appointed a 'national unity' administration under Admiral Makoto Saitō. From this point until 1945, although the Diet would continue to scrutinize legislation, there were to be no party governments. With the reduction of the influence of the party politicians, the army asserted itself as the dominant voice in government, and Japan moved towards an explicit rejection of the post-war order, including withdrawal from the League of Nations in March 1933 and the rejection of arms control.

Japan's 'Monroe Doctrine' for East Asia

The most important result of Japan's new policy was that from 1933 it shifted towards espousing the idea that it should establish its own '**Monroe Doctrine**' for East Asia. This arose out of the belief that the foundation of China's antagonism towards Japan was its reliance upon and manipulation by the Western Powers. It was therefore held that if Japan limited Western activities in the region, China could be persuaded to co-operate, and that this would pave the way for the development of regional prosperity under Japanese leadership. The clearest exposition of this view came in the Amau statement of 18 April 1934, when the spokesman of the Japanese Foreign Ministry, Eiji Amau, expounded these ideas to the press. There was, of course, a sizeable pan-Asian element in these sentiments, but in addition there was a clear economic rationale. In a world in which the major Powers were retreating into their own economic blocs, and where Japanese exports, such as cotton textile goods, were the subject of economic discrimination, Japan was keen to establish its own trade bloc in East Asia. The increasing trade rivalry between Japan and the European colonial Powers in South and South-East Asia from 1932 to 1936, which was caused by the increased competitiveness of Japanese goods after the devaluation of the yen in late 1931, only helped to fuel this sentiment.

The problem, however, for Foreign Minister Koki Hirota was that he was not allowed to pursue this policy unhindered, for the army had its own rationale for supporting a bloc economy, which differed from that of the Foreign Ministry. The army saw China as a vital source of raw materials for the achievement of autarky, which was now considered more desirable than ever as a result of the rising tensions with the Soviet Union along Manchuria's borders with Outer Mongolia

Monroe Doctrine
The doctrine declared by President James Monroe in 1823 in which he announced that the United States would not tolerate intervention by the European Powers in the affairs of the Western Hemisphere.

and Siberia. Indeed, such was the level of hostility within Japan that as early as 1932 the army minister, General Sadao Araki, began to talk openly of a 'year of crisis' coming in 1936, when preparations for war with the Soviets would be completed. In this situation the army soon grew impatient with the slow progress made by Hirota in weaning the Nanjing government away from its reliance on the West. In addition, it had serious doubts about whether such a policy stood any chance of success, for it believed that Jiang Jieshi was not negotiating with Japan sincerely, but only in order to gain time. The army therefore pursued its own China policy, which often conflicted with that of Hirota. As early as 1933–34 the Kwantung Army, in order to expand Japanese influence and pre-empt the Soviets, supported forces in Inner Mongolia seeking independence from China. In 1935 it went much further and took measures in the summer and autumn to establish autonomy for the five provinces of northern China, thus undermining Hirota's efforts and heightening Sino-Japanese tensions.

Still fearing the prospect of war and concentrating on the extinction of the CCP, Jiang reluctantly acquiesced to the Japanese army's demands, but this was to be the last act of his 'non-resistance' policy, which had only ever been designed to appease the Japanese for as long as his domestic position remained weak and there was no chance of foreign support. In 1935–36 conditions began to change and make resistance possible. One key development was the strengthening of the Nanjing government. In 1934 Jiang's German-trained army drove the CCP out of its Jiangxi stronghold, forcing it to engage in the Long March to Shaanxi province. While the fortitude shown in this event by the CCP would become part of party mythology, in the short term its main effect was to cripple the party and thus reduce its challenge to Nanjing's authority. In addition, it appeared that the modernization policies that the GMD had pursued since taking power were finally paying off. For example, the Nanjing government began to grow financially stronger, particularly after the successful introduction of a new currency in the autumn of 1935. This change in political and economic fortunes meant that when, in 1935–36, the humiliation in north China led to a 'National Salvation Movement' clamouring for an end to appeasement and for resistance against Japanese aggression, Jiang was able to risk toughening his policy towards Japan, even though he felt these calls to be premature.

In addition, Jiang's fortunes were changing on the international front. In August 1935, owing to the Soviet Union's fear of Japanese attack, the Seventh Congress of the Comintern called for a united front in China to resist Japan. Against the will of the CCP, within which Mao had now emerged as the dominant figure, the Comintern announced that Jiang had to be included in this 'united front' as he was the only truly national figure in the country, and therefore resistance against Japan could not work without him. To reinforce this policy, the Soviet Union promised its support if the Nanjing government found itself at war with Japan. At the same time, Britain and the United States also appeared to be taking a greater interest in China, seeing its market as a valuable spur to their own economic recovery. Jiang therefore could take comfort from the hope that, if resistance did provoke Japan, he might be able to garner support from some of the major Powers.

Jiang's tougher stance first manifested itself in the autumn of 1936 when, after a number of incidents involving attacks on Japanese nationals and property, he rejected the usual litany of demands that issued from Tokyo. However, he still wished for the eradication of the CCP before engaging upon a policy of full resistance, and in early December 1936 flew to Xi'an to goad Zhang Xueliang, now the commander in Shaanxi, to pursue the campaign against the still weak CCP. Zhang, however, believed that full resistance against Japan was long over-due. He therefore responded to these exhortations by taking Jiang prisoner and, with Soviet and CCP backing, refused to release him until he had undertaken to resist Japan and end the civil war in China. Jiang had no choice but to comply. The Xi'an incident marked the point of no return for Jiang, for now he was publicly committed to resist Japan. All it would take would be another incident and a conflict with Japan was assured.

At first, however, it appeared that the clouds of war were receding, for major changes were under way in Japan. After a failed coup by a group of disaffected officers in February 1936, those within the army who sought to build a 'national defence state', such as Ishiwara Kanji, the head of the operations section of the army general staff, became more powerful. This group had come to believe that the confrontational policy towards China practised by the Kwantung Army was counter-productive and that it distracted Japan from preparing to meet the Soviet challenge. They therefore sought to rebuild Sino-Japanese relations, while endeavouring at home to promote greater state control over industry. In June 1937 the prospects for this new direction appeared favourable with the appointment of Prince Fumimaro Konoe as prime minister. Konoe sympathized with the army, but at the same time was well placed to reconcile Japan's financial and industrial elite to further rearmament.

The Sino-Japanese War

On 7 July 1937, less than a month after Konoe took office, an incident took place at the Marco Polo Bridge outside Beijing. There is no evidence in this case to suggest that the incident was staged or deliberately provoked by the local Japanese forces. In addition, it is clear that, at least initially, the authorities in Tokyo did not desire any escalation of the fighting, as Ishiwara and others feared the derailing of their long-term plans for the building of a war economy. However, once fighting began, it proved very difficult to contain as neither side wished to be the first to make a concession. In late July the Japanese government decided to punish Jiang's intransigence by launching a full-scale offensive in north China. The war soon spread to central China, for Jiang's reaction to the hostilities in the north was to open a new front in Shanghai. This had the advantage of bringing the conflict into an area of Western interest, thus hopefully precipitating British and American support for China. In addition, this was the region where GMD control was greatest and where Jiang's German-trained army divisions were stationed. Thus, by mid-August, a Sino-Japanese war was well under way.

The Japanese believed that they could inflict a rapid defeat upon China, which would pave the way for a negotiated solution of the problems in Sino-Japanese relations and a return to the construction of a defence state at home. In order to bring about a swift conclusion to the conflict, the Japanese pursued peace talks while fighting continued around Shanghai. However, although the Chinese suffered a series of setbacks, such as the fall of Shanghai in November and of Nanjing in December, they refused to make peace on Japan's terms. The problem for Japan was that Jiang was not in a mood or position to compromise. On 21 August 1937 a Sino-Soviet non-aggression pact was signed which led the Russians to start a policy of large-scale military aid and assistance to China in the hope that its resistance would prevent any Japanese offensive against Siberia. Soviet support paved the way for a new 'united front' agreement between the Nanjing government and the CCP, in which, in the interests of co-operation against Japanese imperialism, the latter recognized the former's political authority in return for considerable political and military autonomy. Once the 'united front' was established, Jiang's range of options narrowed even further, for it was clear that if he appeased Japan, this would only increase support for the CCP, which would claim for itself the mantle of being China's only true 'nationalist' party.

In addition, moves within the Western democracies encouraged Jiang's resistance. The revival of Japanese aggression led to a wave of sympathy for China in the West, particularly after newspapers and newsreels carried stories of the Japanese bombing of civilians in Shanghai, Nanjing and Guangzhou. The result was that in both government and public circles there was talk of unleashing economic sanctions against Japan. On 5 October Roosevelt made his 'quarantine' speech, in which he hinted at the need for a naval blockade of Japan, and a day later the League of Nations called for a conference of the signatories of the Nine-Power Treaty to be convened in Brussels. In the short term, this anti-Japanese sentiment led to nothing substantial, for Britain was too preoccupied by events in Europe to send its fleet to East Asia, while Roosevelt remained hemmed in by isolationist opinion. Even Japanese attacks on both American and British gunboats on the Yangtze in December 1937 only led to a brief call for united action before the moment passed. However, the Western democracies did take some measures to bolster China's resistance. In February 1938, for example, the British agreed to the construction of a road linking Yunnan province to Burma, while the Americans in the summer introduced a 'moral embargo' on aircraft exports to Japan.

see Chapter 7

Such moves encouraged Jiang in his belief that there must be a limit to the West's patience, and thus he remained impervious to Japan's calls on him to surrender. Frustrated by Jiang's recalcitrance in January 1938 the Japanese called off the peace talks that they had established through German channels and announced that they no longer recognized the GMD government. Instead they now concentrated on achieving a military victory and building a 'national defence state' through such measures as the General Mobilization Law of April 1938.

Even after a year of war, however, Japan found itself as far from victory as ever. To a considerable extent it blamed this on Western support for China. From the autumn of 1938 it therefore sought to isolate China from the West. One of the major planks of Japanese policy was to appeal to China by emphasizing, as it had done before in the Amau statement, that it sought no more than to bring about co-operation between and prosperity for the peoples of East Asia. Accordingly, in the 'New Order in East Asia' statement of 3 November 1938, Konoe called for a union between Japan, Manchukuo and China. These pan-Asian sentiments were, however, too far from the reality of Japanese practice to persuade many Chinese. By this stage in the war Japan had engaged in a number of atrocities against Chinese civilians, such as the Nanjing massacre in December 1937, which made its words about brotherly co-operation sound decidedly unconvincing. Still, the 'New Order' did lead to the defection of one leading GMD figure, Wang Jingwei, from Jiang's camp and after much delay he established a puppet regime in Nanjing in April 1940.

In addition, Japan sought to apply pressure on the Western Powers. Within China it began a policy of harassment towards their territorial concessions, particularly at Tianjin in north China, in order to try to force them to become more strictly neutral. In addition to this, in the autumn/winter of 1938–39 it expanded its influence over south China and the South China Sea, thus beginning to encroach on the European possessions in South-East Asia. Another weapon in the Japanese arsenal was to strengthen its ties with the **Axis** Powers in Europe. Even before the Sino-Japanese War, the army had pressed for links with Germany in order to contain the Soviet threat and this had led on 25 November 1936 to the conclusion of the Anti-Comintern Pact. This agreement provided for an exchange of information on Comintern activities as well as a guarantee that if Russia attacked either signatory, the other would not assist the Soviets in any way. With the start of the Sino-Japanese War, Japan soon recognized that its links with the Axis could be used as a diplomatic weapon against the Western democracies. This led it to welcome the accession of Italy to the Anti-Comintern Pact on 5 November 1937, and in late 1938 to engage in military alliance talks with the Axis Powers. Japan, however, found that it could not go as far as the Axis Powers desired and the latter concluded the Pact of Steel in May 1939 without Japanese involvement.

Japan's prevarication was the result of a key weakness in its position, which was that, although it greatly resented the West's attitude, it still needed to trade with the democracies. In particular, Japan depended for most of its raw materials, such as oil, rubber, wool and tin, on the United States and the British Empire, and this reliance had grown rapidly as a result of the economic demands of the war with China. To come out in open opposition to them thus raised the danger that Japan might become the victim of economic sanctions. The precariousness of its position was underlined in July 1939, when the Roosevelt administration, in the light of domestic pressures and the recent Japanese confrontation with Britain over Tianjin, announced the abrogation of its commercial treaty with Japan. Japan's difficulties became even greater with the start of the European war, for the British and French empires now became war economies which limited Japan's ability to

Axis
A term coined originally by Mussolini in November 1936 to describe the relationship between Fascist Italy and Nazi Germany. The German–Italian Axis was reinforced by the so-called Pact of Steel signed by Rome and Berlin in May 1939. More broadly speaking, the term is often used (as in Chapter 8 of this book) to refer to the relationship between Germany, Italy and Japan. These three Powers were formally linked by the German–Japanese Anti-Comintern Pact of November 1936, which Italy signed one year later, and the Tripartite Pact of September 1940.

acquire raw materials from these sources. Thus, despite its efforts to use coercion to bring about the end of Western support for China, Japan found itself no nearer a successful conclusion to the war and faced new threats to the economic foundations of its war effort.

Towards the Pacific War

A possible way out of its dilemma was provided by news from Europe. In May and June 1940 Germany seized control of Holland, forced France to surrender, and threatened to extinguish British resistance. The weakening of these European Powers suddenly meant that the colonies of South-East Asia, such as French Indochina, the Dutch East Indies, and British Malaya, Borneo and Burma, were very susceptible to Japanese pressure. This raised the possibility that Japan could bring pressure to bear on the colonial authorities in order to stop trade with China and increase its own access to raw materials from the region. Germany's new ascendancy in Europe thus provided a 'once in a lifetime' opportunity. In the consequent mood of national enthusiasm, Konoe, who had resigned as prime minister in January 1939, was recalled to the premiership in July 1940 with the task of forming a 'new order' at home and increasing Japan's influence abroad.

Konoe chose as his foreign minister the controversial figure of Yosuke Matsuoka. Matsuoka acted quickly to increase Japan's influence in South-East Asia. On 1 August he announced that Japan intended to construct a Greater East Asian Co-Prosperity Sphere. This was rapidly followed by the sending of an economic mission to the Dutch East Indies and an agreement with the **Vichy** French regime in Indochina to allow the stationing of Japanese troops in Tonkin. In addition, in autumn 1940 and into early 1941 he attempted to increase Japan's influence in South-East Asia by mediating in a border dispute between Thailand and French Indochina. On the global scale he signed a Tripartite Pact with the Axis Powers on 27 September, which was designed to keep America from intervening either in Europe or in Asia by threatening it with the possibility of having to fight a two-front war. Matsuoka's hope was that this would force Washington, and by inference London, to agree to Japanese penetration into South-East Asia.

This new assertiveness did not, however, have the intended effect on the United States and Britain, for not only did they refuse to acquiesce, they also began to take retaliatory action. The cause was not only the provocative nature of Japanese actions, but also the fact that South-East Asia's raw materials were vital for the British war effort against Germany and for American rearmament, and thus had to be protected. On 26 September Washington retaliated against the move into North Indochina by announcing a ban on the export of scrap metal and petroleum capable of conversion into aviation fuel. Britain followed suit and over the next months pressed the Americans to go further and jointly introduce a concerted policy of economic warfare against Japan. Finally, in February 1941, after rumours

Vichy France
The regime led by Marshal Pétain that surrendered to Hitler's Germany in June 1940 and subsequently controlled France until liberation in 1944.

that Japan was about to negotiate control over military bases in South Indochina and Thailand, the United States responded to British pressure. Over the next few months an economic noose was constructed around Japan, which involved limiting its ability to trade with not only the British Empire and the United States, but also Latin America and the Middle East. The only major commodity that remained untouched was oil. In addition, regional defence talks began between the British Empire, the Americans and the Dutch, along with collaboration over intelligence and propaganda issues.

The situation by the spring of 1941 was therefore that, although Japan had managed to strengthen its position, it had not removed the obstacles to its expansion. Two further gambits were in store. First, in March 1941 talks were begun in Washington by Ambassador Kichisaburō Nomura with Secretary of State Cordell Hull in order to try to find a solution to American–Japanese differences. Second, on his way back from a visit to Europe to meet with Hitler and Mussolini, Matsuoka stopped in Moscow to sign a Neutrality Pact with the Soviet Union, which in theory freed Japan to concentrate upon southern expansion. Further problems, however, emerged, for Hull took an unexpectedly tough line in the negotiations, while on 22 June Hitler upset Japan's calculations by declaring war upon the Soviet Union. Japan was now torn between taking advantage of the USSR's predicament and launching an assault on Siberia or taking further moves in the south. On 2 July at an Imperial Conference it avoided this stark choice by deciding to make preparations for a northern war, while at the same time improving its position in South-East Asia by placing troops in South Indochina. This attempt to maintain strategic flexibility soon, however, met an obstacle.

As a result of the American ability to read the Japanese diplomatic code, Washington was aware of the decisions taken at the Imperial Conference. Fearing that either an advance south against British interests or an attack north on the Soviet Union would assist the German war effort, Roosevelt decided that the occupation of South Indochina should be used as a justification for the introduction of restrictions on oil exports to Japan. Whether Roosevelt intended to introduce a complete embargo or whether one was implemented by bureaucratic error is still a matter of debate, but what is clear is that after the Japanese move into South Indochina in late July, its oil imports dried up. Japan was now faced with a grave dilemma: before its oil supplies ran dry, it had to make a choice between trying to find an acceptable diplomatic settlement with the United States or seizing the raw materials of South-East Asia, including the oil of the Dutch East Indies, which would involve war with both America and Britain.

Typically Japan pursued both goals; it prepared for war while simultaneously attempting to find a way out through negotiations. The problem with this strategy was that the bellicosity of Japan's military movements naturally contradicted its avowed belief that a diplomatic solution could be achieved. Further undermining the diplomatic route was the fact that Western faith in Japan's sincerity was already limited, owing to the fact that the latter remained allied to Nazi Germany, and was collaborating with the Axis over intelligence, propaganda and trade issues. If this were not enough, the talks were also doomed by another factor, namely that, while Japan became increasingly desperate to reach a settlement, American policy rested on extending the Hull–Nomura talks for as long as possible. Washington's hope was that, while the negotiations were in progress, the United States and Britain could use their economic and military power to tip the balance of power in the Pacific against Japan and thus deter it from going to war.

The Western belief in the efficacy of this policy rested on two false assumptions derived largely from a faulty interpretation of intelligence. First, there was a conviction that the Japanese armed forces were of indifferent quality. They had, after all, failed to win the war in China and appeared to possess technologically backward weapons compared with those available in the West. The second factor was that it was held that the Japanese were aware of their relative weakness and that this heightened their innate cautiousness. Thus while Japan might threaten to take dire action, it was believed that, in all likelihood, this was bluff. Consequently it was held that the current Anglo-American military presence in the region, along with the promise of gradual reinforcements in the shape of American bombers and British capital ships, was a sufficient deterrent to Japanese aggression.

In these circumstances the Hull–Nomura talks stood little chance of success. The West felt that it had little reason to compromise because of its misreading of the military balance, while Japan was not prepared to make satisfactory concessions to the United States, particularly in regard to the conclusion of the war in China. Faced with the lack of a diplomatic escape route, the government of General Hideki Tōjō, which had taken office in October 1941, felt that it had no choice but to go to war and hope that a series of rapid victories, allied with German successes in Europe, would force the democracies into a compromise peace in the Pacific. This proved to be a fatal miscalculation.

Conclusion

The origins of the war that began on 7/8 December 1941 with the Japanese invasion of Malaya and the attack on the American naval base at Pearl Harbor can be seen from a number of perspectives. In regard to the immediate origins, it is probably safest to see the conflict as part of a global conflagration in which Japan sided with Germany and Italy against the Anglo-American world order. The essential issue that led to rising tensions in 1941 was the future of South-East Asia, whose resources were vital for both blocs in their pursuit of victory. Once a battle for influence in that region began, war could not be avoided.

It is also possible, however, to say that the war had long-term roots and that a clash between Japan and the Western democracies was always likely and perhaps increasingly inevitable. The fundamental point is that tectonic forces were at work; that from the turn of the century Japan was a rapidly modernizing power and that this naturally alarmed the West, which feared for its trading interests. This therefore led to Western suspicion of Japan, which in turn engendered feelings of insecurity in the latter.

Debating the intelligence failure at Pearl Harbor

While there are many areas of debate about the origins of the Pacific War, public attention has been concentrated upon one issue above all others – whether President Franklin Roosevelt and Prime Minister Winston Churchill had foreknowledge of the Japanese attack on Pearl Harbor, but failed to do anything to prevent the assault in order to provide an opportunity for American entry into the Second World War. The controversy about this issue began in the immediate post-war era when a number of books by critics of the late president accused him of deliberate subterfuge over Pearl Harbor. They argued that the intelligence information available to the president, which was revealed by the Congressional investigation into the Pearl Harbor attack in 1945–46, meant that he must have known a Japanese attack was imminent. These politically motivated attacks on Roosevelt were effectively parried by Roberta Wohlstetter's excellent book, *Pearl Harbor: Warning and Decision* (Stanford, CA, 1962), which demonstrated the folly of imagining that the intelligence pinpointing an air raid on Hawaii would necessarily have stood out amid the wealth of intelligence material available to Washington. Gordon Prange's monumental study, *At Dawn We Slept: The Untold Story of Pearl Harbor* (New York, 1981), took a similar view.

However, reminiscences by intelligence officers and confusion about whether the United States and Britain were able to read Japanese naval codes meant that the conspiracy theories have re-emerged with a vengeance over the past decade or so, particularly in the contentious arguments used by James Rusbridger and Eric Nave, *Betrayal at Pearl Harbor: How Churchill Lured Roosevelt into War* (London, 1991) and Robert Stinnett, *Day of Deceit: The Truth about FDR and Pearl Harbor* (New York, 2000). These books have, however, failed to provide conclusive evidence that any intelligence reports indicating Japan's intentions reached those at the highest level of government; indeed, contemporary diaries and records of meetings suggest that the attention of those in authority was focused on a possible Japanese thrust into South-East Asia rather than an attack on Hawaii. The Pearl Harbor controversy is a classic example of a historical conspiracy that can be neither proved nor disproved and as such invites endless speculation. In doing so, however, it detracts from a true understanding of the origins of the Pacific War to the detriment of real history.

Heightening this atmosphere of mutual unease were a number of phenomena in the inter-war period that exacerbated Japan's desire for hegemony and security. The most obvious example is the Depression. The severity of the slump between 1929 and 1931 caused a crisis in Japan, which led it to reject the pro-Western orientation of the 1920s in domestic politics and foreign policy and to seek a new order at home and expansion overseas in order to overcome the problems of modernization. Japan's subsequent military adventures in East Asia and, in addition, its export of cheap consumer goods to the European colonial empires directly challenged Western interests and provoked substantial hostility which was reined in only by the fact that there were even more pressing security problems in Europe. Thus, well before 1941, Japan was already identified in the United States and Britain as a pariah state. The West's criticisms, however, failed to restrain Japan and, if anything, only contributed to its desire for expansion, for it exacerbated pan-Asian sentiments and calls for Japanese 'liberation' of Asia.

The other vital factor in the inter-war period was the change in Japan's geopolitical position as a result of the rise of nationalism in China and the growing strength of the Soviet Union. The inter-war period saw a marked shift in China's role in the international system from being little more than a canvas for international competition to becoming a modern nation-state determined to rid itself of all vestiges of foreign imperialism. As such, nationalist China naturally rejected Japan's pretensions to regional leadership. Meanwhile, Japan pursued a policy that brought it into direct conflict with this new nationalist China. Failing to understand both China's pride and its animosity towards Japan, the Japanese authorities sought to force the Nanjing government to accept co-operation. For Japan, this co-operation was essential, for it feared the military and ideological threat posed by Russia, and knew that without China's raw materials, it could not achieve autarky and thus resist the Soviet threat. Reinforcing its concern was the danger that, if Japan left China to itself, the latter might be susceptible to communist influence. Japan was thus determined that China should accept its guidance and the construction of a 'New Order in East Asia' and believed that, as the Nanjing government was still militarily and politically weak, it could be bent to Tokyo's will. In such circumstances, war between these Asian neighbours was more or less unavoidable and this in turn added further strain to Japan's relations with the West.

Japan's path to war was thus the result of both internal and external forces. It sought expansion in order to overcome the problems engendered by modernization and to guarantee its security through the achievement of autarky. However, it never developed any coherent plan of action and found that its striving for hegemony only worsened rather than improved its strategic position. Its activities united China against it, leading to a war that brought Japan no benefits. Then, desperate to find a way out of this quagmire, it sided with Hitler's Germany against the Western democracies and brought destruction upon itself.

Recommended reading

The best introductions to this subject are Akira Iriye, *The Origins of the Second World War in Asia and the Pacific* (London, 1987) and Peter Calvocoressi, Guy Wint and John Pritchard, *Total War: The Causes and Course of the Second World*

War, vol. II (London, 1989). For general histories of Japan, see Michael Barnhart, *Japan and the World since 1868* (London, 1995), W. G. Beasley, *Japanese Imperialism, 1894–1945* (Oxford, 1987), Christopher Howe, *The Origins of Japanese Trade Supremacy: Development and Technology in Asia from 1540 to the Pacific War* (London, 1996) and Akira Iriye, *Japan and the Wider World: From the Mid-Nineteenth Century to the Present* (London, 1997) and the essays by T. Mitani, G. Berger and I. Hata in P. Duus (ed.), *The Cambridge History of Japan*, vol. VI: *The Twentieth Century* (Cambridge, 1988). For China in this period, the best books are Lloyd Eastman, *The Abortive Revolution: China under Nationalist Rule, 1927–1937* (Cambridge, MA, 1974) and John Fairbank (ed.), *The Cambridge History of China*, vols XII and XIII: *The Republican Era, 1912–1949* (Cambridge, 1983 and 1986).

On the First World War in East Asia, see Frederick Dickinson, *War and National Reinvention: Japan in the Great War, 1914–1919* (Cambridge, MA, 1999), Ian Nish, *Alliance in Decline: A Study in Anglo-Japanese Relations, 1908–1923* (London, 1972) and G. Xu, *China and the Great War: China's Pursuit of a New National Identity and Internationalization* (Cambridge, 2005). The best recent study of the Paris Peace Conference from an Asian perspective is Naoko Shimazu, *Japan, Race and Equality: The Racial Equality Proposal of 1919* (London, 1998). The 1920s are a comparatively neglected decade, but Edmund Fung, *The Diplomacy of Imperial Retreat: Britain's South China Policy, 1924–31* (Oxford, 1991), Akira Iriye, *After Imperialism: The Search for a New Order in the Far East, 1921–1931* (Cambridge, MA, 1965), William F. Morton, *Tanaka Giichi and Japan's China Policy* (New York, 1980) and J. Martin Wilbur, *The Nationalist Revolution in China, 1923–1928* (Cambridge, 1984) are useful.

There are a number of books on the origins and course of the Manchurian crisis, the best of which are James W. Morley (ed.), *Japan Erupts: The London Naval Conference and the Manchurian Incident, 1928–32* (New York, 1984), Ian Nish, *Japan's Struggle with Internationalism: Japan, China and the League of Nations, 1931–3* (London, 1993) and Christopher Thorne, *The Limits of Foreign Policy: The West, the League, and the Far Eastern Crisis of 1931–1933* (London, 1972). An important study that emphasizes the reaction of the Japanese people to the Manchurian Crisis is Louise Young, *Japan's Total Empire: Manchuria and the Culture of Wartime Imperialism* (Berkeley, CA, 1997), but see also Sandra Wilson, *The Manchurian Crisis and Japanese Society, 1931–33* (London, 2001), which qualifies some of Young's observations. For pan-Asianism and the ideological roots of Japanese foreign policy, see the following very useful edited collections: Dick Stegewerns (ed.), *Nationalism and Internationalism in Imperial Japan: Autonomy, Asian Brotherhood, or World Citizenship?* (London, 2003), Narangoa Li and Robert Cribb (eds), *Imperial Japan and National Identities in Asia, 1895–1945* (London, 2003) and Sven Saaler and J. Victor Koschmann (eds), *Pan-Asianism in Modern Japanese History: Colonialism, Regionalism and Borders* (London, 2007).

On Japanese foreign policy in the 1930s, see Michael Barnhart, *Japan Prepares for Total War: The Search for Economic Security, 1919–1941* (Ithaca, NY, 1987), James B. Crowley, *Japan's Quest for Autonomy: National Security and Foreign Policy, 1930–38* (Princeton, NJ, 1966) and James W. Morley (ed.), *The China Quagmire:*

Japan's Expansion on the Asian Continent, 1933–1941 (New York, 1983). The Chinese reaction to Japanese imperialism is covered in Parks Coble, *Facing Japan: Chinese Politics and Japanese Imperialism, 1931–1937* (Cambridge, MA, 1991) and Youli Sun, *China and the Origins of the Pacific War, 1931–1941* (New York, 1993). For the Soviet angle, see Jonathan Haslam, *The Soviet Union and the Threat from the East, 1933–41* (Basingstoke, 1992), John Garver, *Chinese–Soviet Relations 1937–1945: The Diplomacy of Chinese Nationalism* (New York, 1988), James W. Morley (ed.), *Deterrent Diplomacy: Japan, Germany and the USSR, 1935–1940* (New York, 1976) and Michael Sheng, *Battling Imperialism: Mao, Stalin and the United States* (Princeton, NJ, 1997).

The growing rift between Japan and the Anglo-Saxon powers can be studied in Antony Best, *Britain, Japan and Pearl Harbor: Avoiding War in East Asia, 1936–41* (London, 1995), Antony Best, *British Intelligence and the Japanese Challenge in Asia, 1914–1941* (Basingstoke, 2002), Dorothy Borg and Shumpei Okamoto (eds), *Pearl Harbor as History: Japanese–American Relations, 1931–1941* (New York, 1973), Peter Lowe, *Great Britain and the Origins of the Pacific War: A Study of British Policy in East Asia, 1937–1941* (Oxford, 1977), Ann Trotter, *Britain and East Asia, 1933–1937* (Cambridge, 1975) and Jonathan Utley, *Going to War with Japan, 1937–1941* (Knoxville, TN, 1985). The immediate origins of the Pacific War are best covered in Robert Butow, *The John Doe Associates: Backdoor Diplomacy for Peace, 1941* (Stanford, CA, 1974), Waldo Heinrichs, *Threshold of War: Franklin D. Roosevelt and American Entry into World War Two* (New York, 1988), James W. Morley (ed.), *The Fateful Choice: Japan's Advance into Southeast Asia, 1939–1941* (New York, 1980) and James W. Morley (ed.), *The Final Confrontation: Japan's Negotiations with the United States, 1941* (New York, 1994).

Finally, there are some good bibliographical essays on the period, notably Michael Barnhart, 'The Origins of the Second World War in Asia and the Pacific: Synthesis Impossible?', *Diplomatic History* (1996), vol. 2, pp. 241–60, Louise Young, 'Japan at War: History Writing on the Crisis of the 1930s', in Gordon Martel (ed.), *The Origins of the Second World War Reconsidered* (London, 1999), and the relevant chapters in Warren Cohen (ed.), *Pacific Passage: The Study of American–East Asian Relations on the Eve of the Twenty-First Century* (New York, 1996) and Robert Boyce and Joseph A. Maiolo (eds), *The Origins of World War Two: The Debate Continues* (Basingstoke, 2003).

The European colonial empires, 1900–45

Introduction

The rise of Japan to **Great Power** status was by no means the only challenge to European predominance, for the rise of nationalism more broadly in Asia, Africa and the Middle East brought about one of the most remarkable features of the twentieth century, the collapse of European colonial rule. The scale of this transformation can be seen in the fact that in 1913 very few countries in Asia and Africa had escaped colonial subjugation, and even those that retained their sovereignty, such as Siam (Thailand), Persia (Iran), Abyssinia (Ethiopia) and Liberia, found their freedom of manoeuvre constrained by European financial and strategic interests. Within less than seventy years the situation had changed dramatically. Between 1945 and 1980 newly independent states swelled the ranks of the **United Nations (UN)** while the British, French, Dutch and Portuguese empires were either dead and buried or wizened mockeries of their former glory. While one might debate to what degree these new states were now free from unwelcome outside intervention, this transformation clearly demonstrates that **decolonization** was one of the century's main themes.

The rapidity of the decolonization process after 1945 has meant that much of the writing on the European empires has dwelt on the immediate post-war period down to the mid-1960s. The result has been that, until recently, historical accounts have tended to portray the empires as being largely static in the pre-1939

Great Powers
Traditionally those states that were held capable of shared responsibility for the management of the international order by virtue of their military and economic influence.

United Nations (UN)
An international organization established after the Second World War to replace the League of Nations. Since its establishment in 1945, its membership has grown to 192 countries.

decolonization
The process whereby an imperial power gives up its formal authority over its colonies.

period and then entering into a rapid decline precipitated by the Second World War and the Cold War. This, however, is a skewed and over-generalized view of a very complex phenomenon. Such an interpretation fails to take into account the many battles that took place between nationalism and imperialism in the inter-war period, and overlooks the fact that after 1945 the European Powers made strenuous efforts to revitalize certain parts of their empires in what is known as 'the second colonial occupation'. Thus, in order to understand the decolonization process and the nature of the post-colonial states, it is vital to look at the roots as well as the immediate origins of the shift towards independence, and to study the factors that over time led to the erosion of European colonial rule.

Empires and power

Dominion
A completely self-governing colony which is freely associated with the mother country. Within the British Empire, the Dominions were Australia, Canada, the Irish Free State (1922–49), New Zealand and South Africa.

see Map 4.1

Before studying the political and economic evolution of the colonial world in the period up to 1945, it is important to examine the state of the European overseas empires at the start of the twentieth century. In 1913 the British Empire extended across more than 12 million square miles, some 24 per cent of the world's land mass, taking in the **Dominions** of Canada, Australia, New Zealand and South Africa, the Indian subcontinent and large stretches of South-East Asia, Africa and the West Indies. The second largest empire belonged to France, which controlled just less than 5 million square miles, about 9 per cent of the world's land mass, including Indochina and much of North, Central and West Africa. Meanwhile, the lesser imperial Powers, Germany, Portugal, Belgium, Italy, Spain, Holland, Japan and the United States, controlled a range of overseas colonies extending across the globe.

Some colonial possessions had already been in the hands of the European Powers for more than four centuries, but the nineteenth century brought a great transformation in the European empires. While declining Powers, such as Spain and Portugal, lost control over South America, the industrializing countries, and in particular Britain and France, rapidly extended their possessions, particularly in the latter part of the century. Thus in Asia, Britain gained control over Malaya and Burma, France seized Indochina, and the Dutch moved out from their established bases in Java and Ambon to exercise control over the Indonesian archipelago. In addition, and perhaps most famously, this period saw the 'scramble for Africa' in which the vast majority of that continent was divided up between the Powers within the space of two decades.

The motives for this sudden expansion of empire have been much discussed by historians, leading to great disagreement over whether strategic or economic gain was the primary objective. What is clear, however, is that once the colonies had been subjugated, they provided the imperial Powers with many material advantages. The fact that empires could add to a nation's power was ably demonstrated in the First World War. During this conflict the British Dominions contributed just over one million troops to the struggle, India provided another

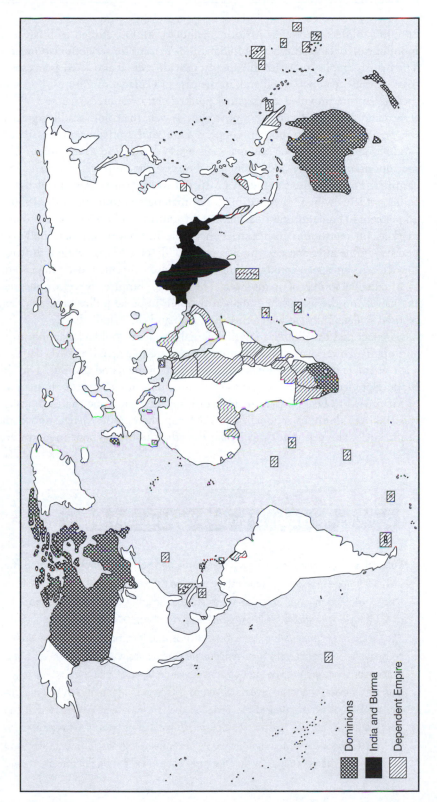

Map 4.1 The British Empire in 1922

Source: After Brown and Louis (1999)

Dominions

India and Burma

Dependent Empire

800,000 soldiers, and West Africa contributed 80,000. Added to this was the mobilization of large numbers of Indians and Africans for service in labour corps. The British Empire, however, did not just provide men; it also acted as an essential source of raw materials, food and, in the case of Canada, munitions. For France too, its empire provided an essential pool of extra resources, namely 600,000 troops and 200,000 labourers. In peacetime as well, the colonies added greatly to the power of the metropolitan country. One vital contribution was that the production and export of raw materials assisted with the development of the metropolitan economy and, moreover, boosted the empire's foreign currency earnings. For example, the Dutch prospered from their possession of the East Indies, which, owing to their wealth of raw materials, accounted by the 1930s for 14 per cent of Holland's national income. In addition, colonies could act as useful markets for metropolitan industries that were no longer internationally competitive; in the inter-war era, this was particularly true of the textile industries in the Western European countries. The colonies also continued to act in peacetime as a valuable source of manpower. The British Empire, for example, relied extensively on the use of the Indian army as an imperial police force that could be used to defend interests in South-East Asia and the Middle East.

The fact that the mobilization of colonial resources could add significantly to an imperial Power's strength and international prestige meant that the latter had a considerable interest in modernizing and developing its possessions. This drive for development became one of the key themes in twentieth-century imperialism, but it proved to be a double-edged sword, for one can argue that, ironically, it was this very desire to rationalize and develop the empires that sounded their death-knell. The reason for this is that the effort to bring about modernization

Debating the origins of modern Western imperialism

Political thinkers and historians have been divided about the motives behind the drive for empire in the late nineteenth century ever since this wave of expansion took place. Various competing explanations exist. One idea that can be seen in the works of A. J. P. Taylor, *The Struggle for Mastery in Europe* (Oxford, 1954) and William L. Langer, *The Diplomacy of Imperialism* (New York, 1951) is that imperialism was an inevitable consequence of the tensions that were building up in Europe during that period, and that imperialist expansion became a zero-sum game, in which one country's strategic gain was inevitably another's loss. Linked to this is the argument that colonialism can be seen as a reflection of the belief in the late nineteenth century that the possession of empire was a symbol of Great Power status. However, such interpretations raise serious problems. For example, if strategic imperatives and prestige were so important, why did this great wave of expansion not provoke a war?

After all, scholars of the origins of the First World War largely agree that the reasons for this conflict lay in Europe, not in competition in Africa.

In contrast to the explanations that dwell on strategy and prestige, a number of contemporary critics of empire, such as J. A. Hobson and V. I. Lenin, argued that imperialism was caused by economic factors, such as the desire to capture new markets for trade and investment. This theory has been countered by the observation that industrialists stood to gain far more from markets in Europe, the United States and Latin America than from Africa, thus demonstrating that the argument that imperialism is a product of capitalism is a chimera. However, in recent years Peter Cain and Anthony Hopkins have forcefully restated the case for economic factors, at least in Britain's case. In their book *British Imperialism 1688 – 2000* (London, 2002), Cain and Hopkins argue that British imperialism came about to serve the interests of a 'gentlemanly capitalist' elite that dominated both the City of London and Whitehall, and that it consisted of both a formal empire, that is the possession of colonies, and an informal empire, in other words economic spheres of influence. This is at first glance a persuasive argument, but, once one begins to think about the anomalies, it raises as many questions as it solves, particularly again in the case of Africa.

Another interpretation of imperialism, which has been put forward by, among others, Ronald Robinson (1972) and David Fieldhouse (1973), is that far too much stress has been put on decision-making in Europe rather than on events on the periphery. They have emphasized in their work on informal and formal empire that the shift towards formal control was often as a result of local factors and the interactions between indigenous elites and European communities. While this view has some validity, it also fails to provide a complete explanation, for if peripheral problems were the main cause of expansion, why is it that they all occurred around the same time in the late nineteenth century? Surely the only answer to this lies in the rising European pressure on these societies, which then takes us back to looking at European economic and strategic motives.

As with most areas of study, all these arguments have some elements of truth in them, and thus it is wise to conclude in the end that strategic, economic and local factors were important. However, it is also vital not to overlook the fact that the military technology and administrative innovations of late nineteenth-century Europe provided the imperialists with a marked superiority over those they sought to conquer. Nor should one ignore the fact that the idea of a 'civilizing mission', as exemplified by the evangelical Christianity of both Protestant and Catholic missionaries, provided an ideological justification for imperial gain. The drive for empire was therefore a complicated process, and to attempt to describe it by referring to a mono-causal explanation is to fail to do it justice.

necessitated heightened intervention in colonial societies, and that the resultant destruction of the status quo unleashed the forces of indigenous nationalism.

In order to understand the drive towards modernization and why it proved so problematical, it is important to see that at the start of the twentieth century the controls that the European Powers exercised over their colonial possessions varied greatly in terms of both their nature and efficiency. The most advanced form of imperial governance existed in the British settler colonies, Canada, Australia, New Zealand and South Africa, which had achieved a substantial degree of self-government as Dominions within the empire. The vast majority of colonies, however, were either ruled directly by the imperial government through the appointment of viceroys and governors, or controlled as **protectorates**, where a native ruler was left to exercise power over domestic affairs, but only on the advice of representatives from the imperial Power. Protectorates had the advantage that they made imperial control relatively cheap by keeping power over many domestic matters in local hands, but at the same time this devolution of authority created problems, for it weakened the ability of the colonial power to bring about the profound economic and social changes required for modernization.

Complicating the situation even further was that different types of colonial rule could exist within what we now think of as one colony. In India, a sizeable area of the subcontinent remained under the nominal control of local rulers; these **Princely States** included such substantial areas as Hyderabad and Kashmir. In Senegal, the French practice of encouraging assimilation meant that from the 1870s the four original *communes* were allowed to return one Senegalese representative to the National Assembly in France, but the newer additions to the colony had no representation. A particularly bewildering mixture existed in Malaya, where three different types of state existed: the directly governed Straits Settlements, the partially directly ruled Federated Malay States and various indirectly ruled non-federated protectorates.

Another important fact that made utilization of imperial resources difficult was that most of the colonies were comparatively recent acquisitions. Even as late as the 1900s the European Powers were still expanding their existing colonies and adding new territories to their imperial portfolio. For example, Britain merged the Ashante kingdom into its Gold Coast colony only in 1902, the Dutch conquest of the sultanate of Aceh in northern Sumatra was completed in 1903, and France gained its protectorate over Morocco in 1912. All these colonies had to be digested, made to pay for their own upkeep and then readied to contribute to the wider imperial cause.

The complex mixture of self-government, direct rule and indirect rule that existed within the barely suppressed territories that constituted the empires clearly complicated the task of colonial administration and acted as an obstacle to economic development. It was therefore only natural that the imperial Powers sought in the early twentieth century to simplify and improve colonial governance in Asia and Africa so that power could be exercised with more authority. However, as the imperial Power believed that the colonies should be largely self-supporting, modernization was to be brought about mainly through the mobilization of indigenous resources. Development therefore involved two key things: first, higher

protectorates
Territories administered by an imperial state without full annexation taking place, and where delegated powers typically remain in the hands of a local ruler or rulers. Examples include French Morocco and the unfederated states in Malaya.

Princely States
The states in British India that remained formally under the control of local rulers rather than direct British administration. They included states such as Hyderabad and Kashmir.

taxation within the colony to pay for economic and social improvements, and, second, the employment by the colonial state of greater numbers of indigenous bureaucrats, police, lawyers and doctors. These requirements led in turn to major changes in colonial rule, namely the introduction of representative government, which was necessary to legitimize higher taxation, and increased education provision, which was needed to train the indigenous population to assist in the development process.

The difficulty with the reforms that were designed to underpin the drive towards modernization was that they unintentionally raised expectations that could not be fulfilled. Once representative government had been conceded in cities, towns and provinces, there was clearly going to be a desire for this to be extended to the national level. Meanwhile, Western-style education led to the new urban elite being exposed to Western notions of political rights, such as universal suffrage and **self-determination**, which could not be satisfied by the colonial state. The result, not surprisingly, was that liberal education frequently led to the appearance of nationalist dissatisfaction, which then posed a political challenge to empire. Moreover, these changes also created the problem that they threatened the position of the traditional collaborators, such as the chiefs, sultans and kings, who benefited from indirect rule, and inevitably led to resistance from these groups. The desire to rationalize thus led to cries of discontent from two constituencies: first, from the traditional elites, who had little to gain from political change, and second, from the nascent nationalist movements, who felt frustrated that the reforms did not go far enough.

Reinforcing these problems in the early twentieth century were outside pressures, for the wars between the Great Powers, the rise of new ideologies and the workings of modern capitalism also buffeted the colonial system. The major external influence prior to 1939 was the First World War, which for many reasons had a deleterious impact on the future of empire. The key effects can be broken down into three problem areas. The first was that the sheer magnitude of the mobilization of imperial resources, both economic and military, stimulated discontent within the empires, and that this could be satisfied only by political concessions. The second problem was that by the end of the war, the Allied Powers ostensibly sought the defeat of Germany in order to promote the principle of self-determination and to bring an end to unwarranted territorial aggrandizement. Accordingly, it was decided at the Paris Peace Conference that the former Ottoman territories in the Middle East and the German colonies in Africa and Oceania should be transferred to the victors not as colonial possessions but as trusteeships in the form of **League of Nations mandates**. These mandates were to be ruled in the interests of the inhabitants with self-determination as the eventual goal. This clearly had broad implications for the future of all European colonial possessions, for it implied that trusteeship should be the fundamental principle guiding imperial rule. Accordingly, it helped to incite the rise of nationalist agitation for greater self-government. The third problem, again connected to the collapse of the Ottoman Empire, was that the harsh treatment meted out to the Ottoman sultan, who as Caliph acted as one of the leading Islamic spiritual leaders, led to outrage in the Muslim world. The reaction, from Morocco to the

self-determination
The idea that each national group has the right to establish its own national state. It is most often associated with the tenets of Wilsonian internationalism and became a key driving force in the struggle to end imperialism.

League of Nations
An international organization established in 1919 by the peace treaties that ended the First World War. Its purpose was to promote international peace through collective security and to organize conferences on economic and disarmament issues. It was formally dissolved in 1946.

mandates
The colonial territories of Germany and the Ottoman Empire that were entrusted to Britain, France, Japan, Australia and South Africa under the supervision of a League of Nations Commission.

see Chapter 19

Khalifat Movement
The protest movement that swept through the Islamic world from 1919 to 23 in opposition to the harsh treatment meted out by the Christian powers to the Ottoman sultan, who as Caliph was one of the protectors of the faith.

Dutch East Indies, was the rise of the *Khalifat* Movement, which marked the beginning of Islamic resurgence, but which also played an important part in the development of nationalism and anti-imperial sentiment.

Other international factors also created difficulties for the imperial Powers. As early as 1905 Japan showed in its war in Russia that non-Europeans could resist Western encroachment, and in the inter-war era this impression was reinforced by Kemalist Turkey's defiance of Britain in the early 1920s and by the rise of Chinese nationalism later in that decade. In addition, the establishment of the Soviet Union and its espousal of a virulently anti-imperial ideology inspired resistance, while the Great Depression brought ruin to many colonial economies, thus provoking an interest in political salvation.

Under the influence of the drive for development and the changed international environment, the inter-war years were to prove an important transitory period in the history of the colonial empires. In those colonies, such as India and Indonesia, where the development process was already well advanced, imperial rule now entered into a running battle with indigenous nationalism, while in others, such as those in Africa, where political and economic transformation was only beginning, the storm clouds started to gather. Moreover, instability was sparked by the fact that the rise of print and broadcast media and the spread of literacy meant that reports of unrest or even imperial retreat in one part of the European empires could inspire disturbances elsewhere. However, in order to understand events in the key imperial possessions in Asia and Africa, it is necessary to look first at the highly volatile conditions in Ireland and the Middle East.

Ireland and the British Dominions

The new challenge to empire in the post-1918 period was demonstrated most emphatically by the fact that the early 1920s witnessed the first major act of decolonization – the independence of Ireland. While Ireland was a very idiosyncratic case owing to its long and complex relationship with Britain, its example was very important because its efforts to free itself from British shackles demonstrated that it was possible for colonies to fight to achieve national liberation.

Since before the Middle Ages Ireland's proximity to England and its strategic importance had made it an integral part of British life. Ireland was therefore never formally conceived as part of the British Empire but seen as part of the kingdom itself – the United Kingdom of Britain and Ireland. Yet the English attitude towards Ireland was undoubtedly colonial. Ireland contained a clear settler element and there had been extensive dispossession of 'native' land. The Westminster government had the right of veto over Irish legislation, the key positions in the Irish executive were more often than not filled by Englishmen, Catholics were only enfranchised by the Emancipation Act of 1829 and the

Presbyterian community, while possessing the franchise, was in practice not represented at all.

As a result of this treatment of Ireland as a British dependency, at least one, and arguably two, distinct Irish nationalisms – Irish (Catholic) republicanism and Ulster (Protestant, specifically Presbyterian) unionism – emerged in the nineteenth century. Both drew upon the same sources of inspiration, the American and French revolutions and the United Irishmen Rebellion of 1779, and upon the same grievances – political, economic and social discrimination by an Anglican ascendancy which had almost as much contempt for the Presbyterians as it did for the Catholics. While Irish Catholics embraced republicanism in pursuit of self-determination, Ulster Protestants sought equality rather than secession. Thus the beginning of the Home Rule movement in 1870 ultimately pitted the predominantly Presbyterian north-eastern counties of the island, who saw 'Home Rule as Rome rule', against the rest of the island, who saw Home Rule as the first step towards independence. British–Irish dynamics were dramatically changed by the outbreak of the First World War, which reinforced both Ulster loyalism and Irish republican militancy. Representing the Presbyterian community, the newly formed Ulster Volunteer Force set aside its own battle to keep Ulster British and enlisted as a whole in the British army. By thus showing its loyalty to the flag, it ultimately ensured that Ulster could opt out of Home Rule and that Ireland would be partitioned instead.

Although almost as many Irishmen as Ulstermen enlisted in the British army, in the end it was the actions of a couple of hundred Irish republican 'volunteers' which went down in Irish history and sent shock waves around the world. Seeing Britain's preoccupation with war in Europe as Ireland's opportunity, on Easter Monday, 24 April 1916, this group proclaimed the Provisional Government of the Irish Republic from the steps of the General Post Office in Dublin. What came to be known as the Easter Rising was quickly and brutally suppressed; an estimated 3,500 suspected revolutionaries were detained, of whom 170 were tried and convicted, and 16 executed. Despite, or perhaps because of, the heavy-handed British attempts to restore order, the idea of Irish independence now flourished as never before. In 1919 the Irish Republican Army unleashed a guerrilla war that lasted for two and a half bitter years. In the end, both sides compromised, for in 1921 they agreed that southern Ireland would be given Dominion status as the Irish Free State, while the north-east counties would remain part of the United Kingdom. There was, however, no hiding the fact that this was a substantial defeat for Britain which had broad implications for the future of empire as a whole. Across the empire nationalists could now take heart from the knowledge that when faced with a crisis Britain might retreat rather than fight to the bitter end.

Ireland's new status as a Dominion also provided little consolation for the British, for Britain's relations with the Dominions were undergoing considerable change in the post-First World War era. The problems that Britain had with the Dominions can be seen as symptomatic of the general difficulties that the metropolitan Powers faced, for, while the government in London sought to use the Dominions to supplement its own power, the latter sought greater independence. Even before the First World War some thinkers in Britain, such as

autarky
A policy that aims at achieving national economic self-sufficiency. It is commonly associated with the economic programmes espoused by Germany, Italy and Japan in the 1930s and 1940s.

Joseph Chamberlain, Lord Milner and their acolytes, had espoused the idea that the constituent parts of the empire should draw closer together to form an **autarkic** bloc. The apparent imperial unity during the First World War stimulated further interest in this concept, with Milner proposing the need for some kind of imperial federation that would see a pooling of defence resources, preferential trade terms and perhaps even an imperial parliament. However, the Dominions, and in particular Canada, South Africa and Ireland, had very different ideas for the future. Instead of greater assimilation with Britain, they sought to gain more autonomy for themselves within the empire and to be treated as equals by the metropolitan government. After the First World War they accordingly made it clear that they were not prepared to see their armed forces subsumed into an imperial army and navy. In addition, when the Lloyd George government was on the verge of hostilities against Kemalist Turkey in the Chanak incident of 1922, Canada and South Africa indicated that they would not feel bound to go to war as their interests were unaffected. After some debate the pendulum swung in the Dominions' favour. In 1926 the Balfour Report confirmed the equal constitutional status of the Dominions with Britain, which was then given legal sanction by the Statute of Westminster in 1931.

A chance to reverse this process, at least in the field of economic co-operation, was offered by the Depression. The decision by the National Government of Ramsay MacDonald in 1931–32 to end Britain's traditional policy of free trade raised the prospect, long cherished by imperialists, of the empire forming a protectionist economic bloc. Accordingly, at the Ottawa Conference in 1932, Britain and the Dominions discussed the introduction of a system of imperial preference, whereby goods produced within the empire were to be subject to preferential tariffs compared with goods produced outside. The end result was less favourable than the followers of Joseph Chamberlain and Milner had anticipated, for the Dominions were not willing to sacrifice the growth of their own nascent industries for the sake of Britain, and thus made only restricted concessions to British products. The imperial preference system, though, did lead to one important achievement, which was that it laid the basis for financial co-operation in the form of the Sterling Area. At least here the Dominions proved to be very useful to Britain, for the recovery of sterling after the tribulations of 1931, when it had been forced to forgo its parity with gold, was of vital importance to British power.

Empire and nationalism in the Middle East

see Map 4.2

The other major new challenge to empire was the extension of British and French influence into the Middle East. Here too, the European imperial Powers faced the task of dealing with an upsurge of nationalist sentiment. This might seem surprising when one considers that much of the region had only recently been conquered by Britain and France from the Ottomans. However, the unfortunate

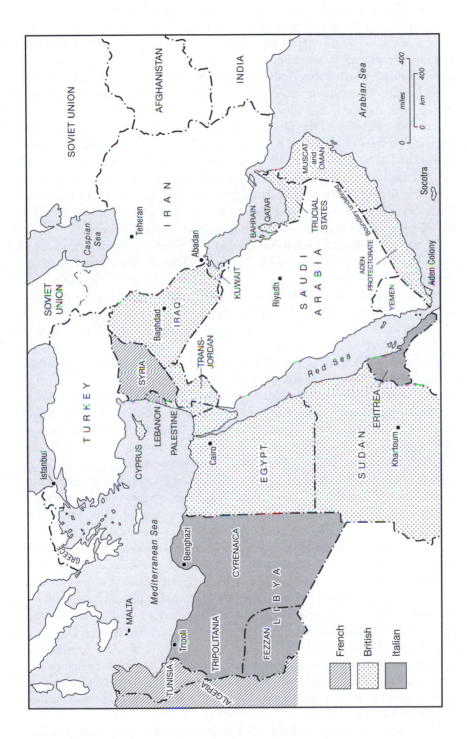

Map 4.2 The Middle East in 1922

fact was that, by taking control of this area, they inherited the anti-colonial dynamic that had already risen in opposition to Turkish control.

By the turn of the twentieth century the Ottoman Empire was in its last throes. This gave rise to two distinct developments: first, increased European interest in Ottoman territories in the Middle East and, second, the emergence of local nationalisms, most notably **Arab nationalism**. The European interest in the declining Ottoman Empire was driven by colonial and hegemonic competition dating back to Napoleon's abortive occupation of Egypt, which had clearly revealed the inability of the Ottoman army to protect its own territory. This triggered further European intervention, such as the French occupation of Algeria, Tunisia and Morocco from the 1830s onwards, the British occupation of Egypt in 1882, and the Italian invasion of Libya in 1911. This scramble for territory was propelled by the power imbalance between the Ottoman Empire and the European states but, at the same time, it was regulated by the intra-European balance of power in what came to be known as the Eastern Question.

The combination of Ottoman weakness and steady European penetration created the environment for the rise of Arab nationalism, the belief that all Arabic-speakers form a nation that should be independent and united. The movement has its origins in the nineteenth century. It started among intellectuals in different geographic centres such as Cairo, Beirut and Damascus, drawing upon a variety of intellectual traditions, secular and religious, but also a shared history dating back to the Arab conquests following the death of the Prophet Muhammad in 632. Muslim intellectuals such as Rifaa Rafi Tahtawi, Jamal al-Din al-Afghani and Muhammed Abdu saw the Arab national revival through Islam. In fact, the latter two emerge as the 'fathers' of modernist or reformist Islam. Many Christian intellectuals such as Butrus al-Bustani, Shibli Shumayyil and Farah Antun promoted secular nationalism, focusing on the Arab language and culture. Another facet of the emerging nationalist debate was the territorial unit. For example, Ahmed Lufti al-Sayid advocated a distinctly Egyptian nationalism while Muhammed Rashid Rida promoted **pan-Arabism**. Until the First World War notions of Arab autonomy within an Ottoman framework competed with notions of independence.

Ottoman centralism and European colonialism influenced Arab nationalism in no uncertain terms. The relationship between European colonialism and Arab nationalism can best be described as one of love and hate in that Arab nationalism embraced some European ideas passionately while, at the same time, fervently opposing European domination. Ultimately European colonialism strengthened the sense of Arab national identity. No matter how much progress and modernization were introduced by the colonial administrations, self-government was still preferable to foreign rule. However, the European portrayal of Islam as backward also planted the seeds of self-doubt. Ironically, this resulted in the retarding of social transformations, as nationalists often felt compelled to defend religious and cultural traditions they would otherwise have reformed on the sole basis that they were indigenous and non-European. However, it also resulted in the rejuvenation of Islamic thought.

In the same way that Arab nationalism adopted anti-European characteristics, it also developed anti-Turkish ones. In fact, it could be argued that the Arab

Arab nationalism
The belief that all Arabic-speakers form a nation that should be independent and united.

see Chapter 19

pan-Arabism
Movement for Arab unity as manifested in the Fertile Crescent and Greater Syria schemes as well as attempted unification of Egypt, Syria and Libya.

nationalist debate began with the demand for greater autonomy for the Arabic-speaking provinces of the Ottoman Empire rather than in reaction to contact with the West. This becomes clear when examining the institutional origins of the Arab nationalist movement, which lie in a number of small and often secret societies formed in opposition to the Turkification policies of the Ottoman central government from 1875 onwards. They sought Arab autonomy, the recognition of Arabic as the official language and the restoration of Arab pride, and even went as far as rejecting the sultan's claim to be Caliph as a usurpation of Arab rights.

One event which had a profound impact on Arab nationalism was the 1908 **Young Turk** revolution. The reorientation from the Ottoman dynasty to the Turkish nation in the long run strengthened those Arab nationalists who sought independence rather than autonomy, for it encouraged many Arabs to think about their future in their own nationalist terms. This also had implications for the intellectual direction of Arab nationalism in the sense that, just as the Turks rewrote their history books, toning down the Ottoman characteristics, Arab nationalists reached back to the pre-Ottoman days of the Arab **Caliphate**, when the Middle East had flourished under Arab-Islamic civilization. Finally, the Young Turk revolution also marked the point when Arab nationalist ideas ceased being the property of a few intellectuals and started to spread to the general population, truly becoming a mass movement. A key example of this was the convening of the first Arab Congress in Paris in 1913, which brought together Arab nationalists from different intellectual traditions ranging from Egypt to Iraq.

Thus, when the First World War led to the final disintegration of the Ottoman Empire, the victorious European states found that Arab nationalism was already a potent force. This was to cause great problems, for Britain and France had hoped that their increased influence in the Middle East would provide both strategic and economic benefits, and their initial intention was to exert close control over both their existing colonies and protectorates and the new mandates. The strength of Arab nationalism was, however, to force them to tailor their ambitions to local circumstances.

Under the League of Nations' mandate system, France added the Levantine states of Syria and Lebanon to its existing North African possessions of Morocco, Algeria and Tunisia, while Britain increased its sphere of influence, hitherto limited to Egypt, Aden and the Gulf states, by receiving responsibility for Palestine, Transjordan and Iraq. The mandate system involved an interesting contradiction. On the one hand, in a spirit of *realpolitik*, it stipulated that the Ottoman Empire, as the losing party, should lose its 'overseas' territory to the victors, thus reducing it to the 'rump' state of Turkey. It then divided the mandates between Britain and France in line with the secret Sykes–Picot Agreement of 1916, a treaty that was as cynical an exercise in balance of power politics as could be imagined. And, finally, the League, by deeming that the Ottoman territories were not ready for independence, gave credence to beliefs in some European quarters that empire rather than independence was the 'natural' condition in the Middle East. Yet, on the other hand, the League also endorsed Wilson's **fourteen points**, which included the right to self-determination, and made it clear that it was the duty of the mandate powers to prepare the population for independence

Young Turks
Name given to a group of young army officers who in 1908 pushed the Ottoman Empire towards reformist policies and a more overtly Turkish nationalist stance.

Caliphate
The office of the successor to the Prophet Muhammad in his political and social functions. The Caliphate was abolished by the Turkish president Mustafa Kemal Atatürk in 1924 after the dismemberment of the Ottoman Empire and the establishment of the Turkish Republic.

fourteen points
A speech made by the American president Woodrow Wilson on 8 January 1918 in which he set out his vision of the post-war world. It included references to open diplomacy, self-determination and a post-war international organization.

and to aid with institution- and state-building. It therefore set the mandate Powers on a collision course with the indigenous populations.

Empire might still have been the natural state of affairs in European thinking, but as far as the Arabs were concerned, they had just been cheated out of independence. After all, they too had joined the fight against the Ottomans, and had received promises of independence, in writing, in the 1915–16 Hussein–McMahon correspondence. Britain and France were therefore faced with a difficult challenge for, in acquiring the mandates, they were put in charge of territories which had been on the verge of independence and had established nationalist movements, and where the inhabitants saw themselves as equals not subjects. Not surprisingly, friction quickly emerged between the European administrators and the Arab populations. The worst case was Palestine, where both Arabs and Jews believed that their aspirations for statehood had been sacrificed at the altar of British imperial interests. This sense of betrayal was shared by the Kurds, who had been promised a state of their own at the Lausanne Conference only to find that it did not serve British interests to fragment the Iraqi mandate, especially if it threatened the disputed oil-rich area of Mosul.

see Chapter 5

Influenced by their strategic and economic interests, Britain and France attempted to find local collaborators with whom to share power. In the French mandates and Palestine, France and Britain used partition as a tool to assure the dominance of key allies. In its territories France carved Greater Lebanon out of Ottoman Syria, transforming it into a multi-ethnic and multi-religious republic under Maronite Christian hegemony, while, even before the mandates had been granted, Britain partitioned Ottoman Palestine along the Jordan River to create a wholly new entity, Transjordan. This was placed under the rule of Emir Abdullah, the son of the **Hashemite** Sharif Hussein of the Hejaz on the Arabian peninsula. Meanwhile Britain put Abdullah's brother, King Faisal, on the throne of Iraq, which in 1932 became the first of the mandates to become an independent state.

Hashemites
The family of the Sharifs of Mecca who trace their descent to the Prophet Muhammad.

The effort to assert control over the newly acquired mandates was further complicated by the parallel struggle for independence in the 'old' colonial possessions such as Egypt, Algeria and Tunisia. Egypt had come under formal British occupation in 1882 and was a colony in all but name until the First World War. With the Ottoman entry into the war, Britain severed Egypt's formal ties to the Ottoman Empire and transformed it into a British protectorate. During the war, British administrators attempted to reform Egypt by establishing a bicameral legislature in which the British effectively constituted the upper house. Not surprisingly, this met with resistance from the elites upon whom the British traditionally relied. This fuelled Egyptian nationalism, with the result that, at the end of the war, British authority was challenged by the Wafd Party and by rioting in the major cities. As in Ireland, Britain was forced to concede and in 1922 Egypt became a 'sovereign' independent country, although it was forced to sign an Anglo-Egyptian agreement to cover the protection of British imperial communications in Egypt, Egypt's defence against foreign aggression, protection of foreign interests and minorities in the country, and control of the Sudan. Apart from these reserved points, Egypt embarked upon reform, drawing up a constitution based on that of Belgium, setting up democratic institutions and, in 1923, holding its first free elections. However, the continued British presence remained a thorn in Egypt's side. Relations were renegotiated in 1936 and, again, in 1954, two years after the Egyptian monarchy had been overthrown and an Arab nationalist regime had taken power. But it was not until the 1956 **Suez Crisis** that Egypt was finally to rid itself of the last colonial vestiges.

The French experience in Algeria and Tunisia was similar, in that the elites of these two colonial possessions started to turn from co-operation with the colonial power to rallying against it in the name of nationalism and independence. Before the First World War both Algeria and Tunisia had seen outbreaks of violence against French rule. They were popular in nature, were often sparked by religious incidents, and placed the *ulama* in leadership positions. In the inter-war period the nature of the challenge changed with the appearance of distinctly nationalist political parties led by the intellectual elites, who were inspired by acts such as the Turkish resistance to the European Powers. In Algeria a number of small political groups emerged but at this stage posed little threat to French rule. In Tunisia resistance to the French was embodied by the Destour ('Constitution') Party which pursued independence from a combined Tunisian nationalist-Islamic platform in the 1920s, and then by the Neo-Destour Party with a secular-nationalist agenda from 1934.

The situation in the Middle East in the inter-war period was therefore one of lingering unrest and instability. Rather than adding unconditionally to the power of the European empires, their commitments in the region proved to be expensive and time-consuming. Moreover, the virulence of Arab nationalism proved, as with Ireland, to be an inspiration to other ethnic and religious groups elsewhere in the empires who were seeking independence from imperial rule.

India in crisis

One of the chief concerns for the British was that the changing international environment and the instability in Ireland and the Middle East might affect the most important colony of all – India. In the period before 1914 Britain had already begun to liberalize the political system in India. For example, in the wake of the great revolt of 1857 the government established representative bodies, such as the viceroy's advisory council, provincial legislatures and municipal councils. Such bodies were necessary in order to legitimize the higher taxation that followed from the increased cost of policing and administering India. In addition, by allowing Indians limited power at the local level, the British sought to win over the political elite, thus turning them into collaborators. To a degree this latter aim worked, for the leading voice of Indian nationalism, the Indian National Congress (hereafter **Congress**), which was established in 1885, tended to pursue a moderate agenda. However, the British policy also created problems for the future, for, in an effort to conciliate the Muslim community, it was given votes for its own

see Chapter 18

Suez Crisis
The failed attempt by Britain and France in 1956 to take advantage of a war between Israel and Egypt by seizing control of the Suez Canal and bringing down the government of Gamal Abdel Nasser. It is often taken as a symbol of the collapse of European imperialism and the rise of the Third World.

ulama
Clerics or Islamic scholars who are learned in theology and the *shari'a*.

Congress
Shorthand for the Indian National Congress, a nationalist party first formed in India in 1885. Congress played the most important role in bringing about Indian independence in 1947 and since then has been one of the major political parties in Indian politics.

reserved seats. By such actions the British exacerbated the growing sense of religious communalism within India. This was dangerous, because already factors such as the activities of Christian missionaries had helped to stimulate a Hindu revival and interest among Muslims in the Islamic resurgence. The result was that radical politicians, such as Bal Gangadhar Tilak, began to use Hindu imagery in their efforts to construct a more assertive form of Indian nationalism. Meanwhile, in response, Muslim leaders created their own national organization, the Muslim League, in order to counter Congress, which was already largely Hindu dominated, and to create a common identity for India's many disparate Islamic communities.

The first stage in India's political evolution culminated in the Morley–Minto reforms of 1909, which allowed for Indian majorities in the provincial legislatures. But if Britain had hoped that this would be enough to quieten India, then the First World War and the general imperial instability precipitated by that conflict proved it wrong. As noted above, India played a substantial role in the fighting, and the government was forced to raise income tax and tariffs to meet its defence expenditure. The heavy burden placed on the Indian people naturally led to unrest. The degree of discontent was demonstrated in 1916 when the Muslim League and Congress overcame their antipathy and signed the Lucknow Pact, in which they agreed to push forward a common reform programme. In order to appease this latest wave of agitation, the British government in 1917 declared its intention to steer India towards responsible 'self-government' within the empire. Accordingly, in 1919 the Montagu–Chelmsford reforms were introduced which devolved more powers to, and increased Indian representation at, the provincial level. Britain's largess was, however, not enough to satisfy Congress. Inspired by the unrest in Egypt and Ireland, and in association with Indian Muslims affected by the *Khalifat* Movement, Congress in 1919, under the leadership of the British-trained lawyer Mohandas Gandhi, launched the first of its non-cooperation campaigns calling for an end to British rule.

The first non-cooperation campaign witnessed the start of the struggle for Indian independence that would end in 1947. However, in the period before 1939, although the Indian issue proved to be a heavy burden for the British government, neither side proved strong enough to vanquish the other. The British attempted to control the situation through a dual policy of concession and repression. In the field of political reform it continued to try to assuage moderate Indian opinion by incrementally making moves towards full representative government at the provincial level, while at the same time maintaining its own strict control over military and financial matters at the political centre. In particular, it hoped that, by allowing Indians to exercise power at the provincial level, it could tame local politicians and divide them from the national-level leaders, such as Gandhi and Jawaharlal Nehru. At the same time, whenever it was necessary, it used repressive legislation to break up outbreaks of non-cooperation, and periodically detained tens of thousands of Congress members. However, aware of the potential for criticism from the Left in Britain and from anti-imperial opinion elsewhere in the world, and fearful of provoking even greater dissent within India, the government was careful to act within the letter of the law. The

Plate 4.1 Indian nationalist leader and organizer of the Indian National Congress's campaign of passive non-cooperation, Mahatma Gandhi, with his wife, shortly before his arrest for conspiracy, January 1922.

result of these policies was that they were enough to slow down Congress's progress but not to defeat it.

Meanwhile, Congress similarly proved unable to defeat the British. Given Britain's hesitation about using excessive force, it might be argued that Congress should simply have tried to make India ungovernable by organizing a mass insurrection. The problem here, however, was that Congress was not an organization capable of mounting such a challenge. In part, this can be seen as a moral problem, in that the sort of protest necessary to dislodge Britain would require violence, which was unacceptable in principle to Gandhi and his supporters. However, there were other motives at play. As with many other nationalist organizations in the decolonization period, the ideas espoused by Congress primarily reflected the interests of the educated urban bourgeoisie and the rural landlords. Accordingly, it backed away from the potential dangers of mobilizing the whole population for revolution. Indeed, it is noticeable that when, during the 1930s, socialists within Congress called for the construction of a mass party that would take up class issues, this was decisively rejected in favour of an all-nation approach. Also important in this respect was that Congress was financed by Indian industrialists, who clearly had little interest in seeing a mobilized proletariat. Another problem was that Congress saw itself as the sole legitimate voice of Indian nationalism. It was therefore temperamentally disinclined to co-operate with other political parties, such as those representing Muslims or the 'untouchables', and thus found it difficult to construct a coalition of forces opposed to British rule. It is, for example, noticeable that there was very little Muslim involvement in the second non-cooperation campaign of 1930–34.

The competition between Britain and Congress was not, however, a complete stalemate, for over time the need to appease Indian opinion led to a steady weakening of ties between Britain and India. Apart from reasons of imperial prestige, India was important to Britain for two reasons – its economic value to the British economy and as a source of military manpower. However, the need to assuage Indian opinion steadily eroded India's contribution in these two areas. The problem was that as the British gradually allowed Indians to take a role in provincial government and to be consulted about central government matters, this led to greater Indian interest in both revenue collection and expenditure. Accordingly, the government in India found itself forced to raise duties on imports, even on goods from Britain, to finance its rule, as this was preferable to causing problems by raising taxation. This naturally had a deleterious effect on the export to India of British goods, in particular the cotton textile products of Lancashire. Further exacerbating this problem was that the customs duties provided a wall behind which India could establish **import substitution** industries. The British and Indian economies thus began to diverge. In addition, Indian opinion was increasingly vocal in its criticism of Britain's widespread use of the Indian army to police the empire in Asia at India's expense. The situation therefore was that, while Britain engaged in its trial of strength with Congress, the foundations of British rule were already eroding.

import substitution
The process whereby a state attempts to achieve economic growth by raising protective tariffs to keep out imports and replacing them with indigenously produced goods.

Rationalization and resistance in South-East Asia

Just as British rule in India was weakened over the long term by the confrontation with nationalism, so this phenomenon also existed elsewhere in the British, French and Dutch empires. In South-East Asia a good example of the problems faced by the Europeans can be seen in the Dutch East Indies. At the start of the twentieth century, the Dutch introduced what it termed an 'ethical policy', advocating greater education provision and centralizing political reforms in order to provide the foundations for the economic development of the Indonesian archipelago. This policy culminated in 1918 with the formation of the *Volksraad*, a central representative assembly with limited political powers. However, these reforms in turn unleashed forces that the Dutch found increasingly difficult to control, particularly when allied to a number of disturbing influences from outside.

The first major problem came with the formation in 1912 of the *Sarekat Islam* movement, which, as its name suggests, was an organization that sought greater political rights for Muslims. It was in part inspired by the Islamic resurgence that occurred throughout the Muslim world, but it also represented local concerns, and, in particular, the fear that the **overseas Chinese** population in Java was benefiting disproportionately from the improving economy. Within a short space of time *Sarekat Islam* developed into a mass movement that the Dutch could not ignore, although, like the British in India, they did try to disarm its effectiveness by pushing it into local politics rather than dealing with its claims at the national level. Economic reforms complicated the problem further by stimulating the growth of a trade union movement and interest in socialism. The result was that in the period following the First World War, the combination of an economic recession, the *Khalifat* Movement and increased activities by socialists culminating in the appearance of the Communist Party of Indonesia, the PKI, led to fifteen years of unrest. Indeed, in 1926 and 1927 the PKI engaged in abortive insurrections in Java and Sumatra. Fortunately for the Dutch, the indigenous opposition to their rule by secular nationalists, Islamic parties and socialists was hopelessly disunited. Nevertheless, the authorities were forced to bring in severe measures, such as increasing powers of arrest, curbing union power and sending into internal exile the leading secular nationalists Ahmed Sukarno and Mohammed Hatta. Thus, by the 1930s the 'ethical policy' had been abandoned and Dutch rule had been forced to become increasingly strict. It is therefore no surprise that the Indonesian nationalist movement should have been so violently opposed to the Dutch returning after the Second World War.

The revolutionary activities of the PKI were but one manifestation of a phenomenon that more broadly affected South-East Asia in the inter-war period and within which lay the roots of many future conflicts, namely the influence on the region of political events in China. From the first, the rise of Chinese nationalism in the early twentieth century struck a resonant chord with the overseas Chinese population in South-East Asia, who became major financial backers of Sun Yatsen's **Guomindang (GMD)** party and began to organize their own political associations, particularly in Malaya. However, the influence of the GMD's strident nationalism and modernization policies went beyond Chinese circles, providing, for example, a model for one of the major nationalist parties in Indochina in the 1920s, the VNQDD (Vietnamese National Party). Also important was that the strong **Comintern** presence in China helped to foster communist activity in the region. Mirroring the actions of the PKI, in 1931 the Indochinese Communist Party launched a short-lived insurrection in Vietnam, which was suppressed with great ferocity by the French authorities. Meanwhile, in Malaya the local communist party inspired a series of labour disputes, culminating in a general strike in 1940.

Thus, by end of the 1930s, on the surface South-East Asia was no nearer independence than it had been twenty years earlier, for colonial rule remained

overseas Chinese
The descendants of the Chinese who immigrated to South-East Asia in the nineteenth and early twentieth centuries. They have tended to act as a merchant class and as such have stirred up a good deal of resentment among the indigenous people who envy their wealth and doubt their loyalty to their adopted countries.

Guomindang (GMD)
The Chinese Nationalist party founded in 1913 by Sun Yatsen. Under the control of Jiang Jieshi, it came to power in China in 1928 and initiated a modernization programme before leading the country into war against Japan in 1937. It lost control over mainland China in 1949 as a result of the communist victory in the civil war. From 1949 it controlled Taiwan, overseeing the island's 'economic miracle', until its electoral defeat in 2000.

Comintern
The Communist or Third International founded in Moscow in 1919 as an organization to direct and support the activities of communist parties outside Russia. It was abolished in 1943 in a short-lived effort by Stalin to reassure Britain and the United States that the Soviet Union no longer sought to export Marxism-Leninism.

intact and had in some areas become more authoritarian than ever. However, this apparent stability was merely a veneer. In reality, sophisticated nationalist movements that drew on a variety of political affiliations, including communism, were waiting in the wings for the opportunity to deliver a deathblow to European colonialism. They would not have to wait long.

The colonial empires in Africa

At first glance Sub-Saharan Africa seems to have been far more stable than the Middle East, India and South-East Asia, but in fact here too important changes were taking place as the development imperative began to exercise its influence. Initially, as the European Powers digested their recent conquests in Africa, they decided that, owing to the scarcity of administrators and the vast geographical distances involved, the most efficient type of political control was 'indirect rule'. This involved allowing tribal chiefs to exercise power at the local level and the use of customary law to settle disputes and regulate society. An intellectual justification for devolving power to chiefs was provided by anthropologists, who argued that ordinary Africans should be allowed to evolve politically and socially at their own pace and be protected from the tempest of modernity. In reality, however, indirect rule did not always involve a simple perpetuation of tradition. For example, in areas such as south-eastern Nigeria, where no strong tradition of chiefs exercising power existed, leaders were imposed on the local population and in Bechuanaland (Botswana) long-exercised restraints on the abuse of power by chiefs were removed. All the European Powers engaged in such practices, even the French, who in public espoused the idea of assimilation, but it was the British who, inspired by the activities of Lord Lugard as governor of Nigeria from 1912 to 1919, turned 'indirect rule' into a doctrine.

see Map 4.3

In contrast to the position in much of the world, colonial control over Sub-Saharan Africa was not greatly disturbed by the First World War, but during the inter-war period a series of factors led to the undermining and revision of the 'indirect rule' system. One of the most important was that in some areas of Africa the development of industrial-scale commodity production either began or accelerated. These industrial commodities included the gold and diamond mines of South Africa, the copper mines of Northern Rhodesia (Zambia) and the Belgian Congo, and the tin mines of northern Nigeria. This led to a number of consequences, such as urbanization, unionization of workers and a vast increase in migrant labour, all of which undermined the traditional forms of control. In addition, the development of these products and cash crops, such as cocoa, for the world market meant that Africa was increasingly susceptible to fluctuations in commodity prices. The result was that in the 1930s the Depression had a marked effect on a number of colonies, causing discontent with colonial rule and sometimes violent strike movements, such as that in the Northern Rhodesian copper-belt in 1935.

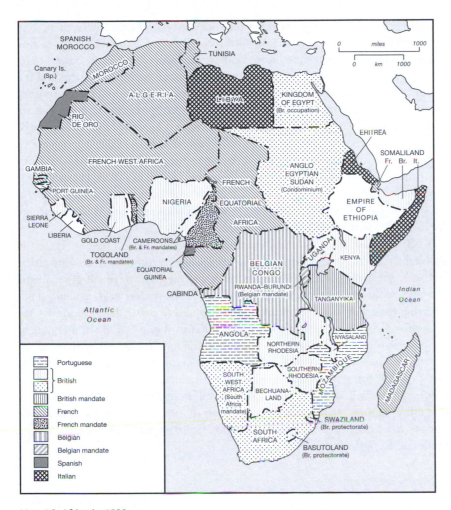

Map 4.3 Africa in 1922

Source: After Holland (1985)

The unrest that emerged in the 1930s was not nearly as serious as the problems that Britain had to face in India, but there was fear for the future unless reforms were introduced. This led both Britain and France to consider, particularly in regard to West Africa, plans for encouraging development through improved agricultural methods and increased welfare provision. Furthermore, the serious disturbances that racked the West Indies between 1934 and 1938 reinforced this British interest in reform, for they demonstrated what could happen if colonies were neglected. The intended reforms did not, however, sit comfortably with the continuation of 'indirect rule', but rather mirrored the efforts elsewhere in the empires to make colonial administration more rational and efficient. Thus, on the eve of the Second World War, ideas about empire in Africa were beginning to come into line with practice elsewhere.

In addition to the changes arising from increased economic activity, there were other challenges to the reliance on 'indirect rule'. In British West Africa one important factor was that the educated indigenous bourgeoisie in the coastal cities were beginning to organize political movements against colonial control and the 'indirect rule' system. Before the scramble for colonies in the nineteenth century this group, which was heavily influenced by Western political thought, culture and religion, had played an important role in the civil society of the trading ports. However, as European rule expanded, they had been marginalized in favour of the chiefs and had found that a colour bar increasingly blocked their entry into the professions or, if they were employed by the state, their prospects for promotion. This naturally led to discontent and gradually, in areas such as Sierra Leone, the Gold Coast and Nigeria, local urban-based political organizations appeared that were critical of British rule.

In British East and Central Africa conditions were very different. Here the problems that emerged centred on the existence of white settler communities. Influenced by white control over South Africa and the granting of self-government to white-dominated Southern Rhodesia in 1923, the settlers in Kenya, although a small minority of the total population, attempted to persuade London to agree to devolve power to themselves, and to form Kenya, Uganda and the mandate of Tanganyika into a union. Concerned about unrest and influenced by the concept of trusteeship, the British government was reluctant to concede to the settlers, but this did not prevent fear among the African elite that the latter might eventually get their way. The result of this, and problems over land pressure, was that ethnic groups, such as the Kikuyu, began to form their own political organizations to represent their interests. The stage in Africa was thus being set for the battles of the post-1945 period.

The Second World War and empire

Just as the First World War stimulated profound change and a marked acceleration of existing political and economic trends within the European empires, so too did the war of 1939–45. As before, one of the main reasons for this was the need to mobilize imperial resources in the pursuit of victory, which had profound consequences for the economic and social life of the colonies. In addition, however, this conflict raised new problems owing to the inability of Britain, France and Holland to defend their imperial possessions. This was most apparent in 1941–42 when their colonies in South-East Asia were either conquered or occupied by the Japanese. The fact that the British and Dutch lost militarily to an Asian power and that France meekly accepted Japanese occupation of Indochina constituted crushing blows that destroyed the aura of European power. The ability of the imperialists to govern vast areas of the world with relatively few forces had, after all, always relied on an image of racial invincibility. With the fall of the fortress of Singapore and other symbols of empire, this image was now shattered, which naturally raised the question as to whether the indigenous populations would permit the colonial Powers to reclaim their South-East Asian colonies in the event of a Japanese defeat.

The effects of the events in South-East Asia were felt not just in the region itself but all over the colonized world. In particular, they exacerbated an already tense situation in India. In September 1939 Britain had compromised its professed stance of steering India towards self-government when, without consulting Indian opinion, the viceroy declared war on behalf of the country. Outraged by this act, Congress withdrew its members from provincial governments in protest. The need to obtain support from Congress for the war effort soon, however, forced Britain to return to its reforming agenda and in fact to go further than ever before in its promises of constitutional reform. In March 1942, following the setbacks in South-East Asia, the Cripps mission proposed self-government once the war was over and greater involvement in government while the conflict was in progress. This was not enough to satisfy Gandhi and Nehru. Indeed, the former, in the light of recent British defeats, famously described the offer as 'a post-dated cheque on a failing bank'. Accordingly, in August 1942 Congress launched the 'Quit India' movement, a broad non-cooperation campaign that soon descended into violence. The government reacted by arresting the Congress leadership and using the Indian army to suppress the public disorder. This crackdown did not mean that the offer of Dominion status was withdrawn, but rather that India's future was put on hold until the war was over. The unity of the British Empire was also affected in another way by the events of 1941–42, for Britain's inability to defend South-East Asia led Australia, which previously had been one of the most loyal Dominions, to look increasingly to the United States to guarantee its security. With Canada and South Africa already acting autonomously and Ireland declaring its neutrality, the seal was thus set for a further loosening of Empire–Commonwealth ties.

Another important aspect of the war that had repercussions for the future of empire was that American entry into the conflict on the side of the colonial Powers led to increased pressure on the latter to divest themselves of their imperial possessions. The **Atlantic Charter** signed by Roosevelt and Churchill in August 1941 revitalized the idea that self-determination was a right, while the UN looked set to be more searching in its policy towards mandates and colonies than its predecessor had been. Thus, the international environment was changing, with the emphasis once again being placed on ideas of responsible trusteeship and progress towards self-government.

At one level, therefore, the Second World War provided a dramatic shock which starkly revealed the fallibility of the Europeans and led to new anti-colonial pressures. However, it should not be imagined that this necessarily led to a loss of will on the part of the imperialists. Indeed, the defeat in South-East Asia, with its attendant loss of vital raw materials such as rubber and tin, only helped to persuade Britain and the **Free French**, who controlled French Equatorial Africa from 1940 and West Africa from 1944, to devote considerable resources to the development of Africa's economic potential. Thus what had been discussed in the abstract in the 1930s now became practical policy and major efforts were made

Atlantic Charter
A document signed by Franklin Roosevelt and Winston Churchill in August 1941 which committed the United States and Britain to support democracy, self-determination and the liberalization of international trade.

Free French Forces
General Charles de Gaulle commanded an armoured division in the battle of France and then, briefly, held a junior post in Paul Reynaud's cabinet on the eve of France's defeat. In June 1940, in radio broadcasts from London, he called upon French people everywhere to join him in the struggle to free France from the Nazi occupation and, later, Marshal Pétain's Vichy regime. At first, the general's calls went largely unanswered. His abrasive, overbearing personality and his lack of diplomatic finesse ensured that his relationship with Roosevelt and Churchill was always rocky at best. By 1943, however, he had become the undisputed leader of the Free French movement, whose growing volunteer forces participated in Allied military operations in North Africa and the Middle East. In 1944, Free French Forces triumphantly participated in the liberation of France. The Allies recognized his administration as the French provisional government in October 1944, and de Gaulle, a national hero, was elected president in November 1945. He resigned shortly thereafter when the National Assembly refused to grant him American-style executive powers. He again served his country as president from 1958 to 1969.

to boost raw material and cash-crop production. This in turn set the path for European policy towards their African colonies in the immediate post-war period.

The end result of the pressures exerted by the war was that by 1945 the imperial Powers were being drawn towards a bifurcated approach to empire. On the one hand, all too aware of their weakness, they were willing to allow some territories to move towards independence. These tended to be those colonies or mandates, such as India and Palestine, where the economic benefits of empire appeared to be outweighed by the potential security costs. In the Middle East this led to independence being granted to Lebanon in 1943, and to Syria and Transjordan in 1946, although with a mixed record for the future. However, on the other hand, while independence came relatively quickly to South Asia and most of the Middle East, policy was very different towards those colonies in South-East Asia and Africa that were considered to be vital for post-war reconstruction. Here the imperial Powers aimed to re-establish their authority and to develop the colonial economic potential for the good of their own damaged industrial and financial bases. This was, however, to prove a naive goal, for in much of South-East Asia it was impossible to re-establish imperial rule, while in Africa the efforts at rationalization paved the way towards independence just as they done previously in India.

see Chapters 10 and 17

Conclusion

During the first half of the twentieth century the European empires underwent significant change. To a large degree this was owing to the effects of the two world wars. Between them these two conflicts forced the imperial Powers to derive as great an advantage as possible from the human and commodity resources at their command, but in so doing helped to lay the foundations for the erosion of the imperial order. Of these two conflicts, the Second World War had the most immediate and dramatic effects, but it is wise not to underestimate the significance of the First World War. As a result of the destruction of the Ottoman Empire, the establishment of the mandate system and the espousal of self-determination, this conflict contributed significantly to the rise of imperial problems in the inter-war period. For example, without the First World War, India would not have made demands for self-government so quickly, nor would Britain have made the concessions it did.

However, while some of the events that took place during these two wars posed new problems, it is possible to argue that in the end these conflicts were most important for accelerating already existing trends within the empires. After all, colonies existed to be exploited, and not just in wartime. But the mere act of exploitation was enough to generate indigenous resistance and to require the colonial Power to make concessions to whatever collaborating elite existed. Wars only served to heighten the intensity of this process. Moreover, the situation was not helped by the fact that so many colonies were of such recent origin and that in these areas colonial power was comparatively untested. Thus the European empires always rested on a fragile foundation and the conflicts of the early twentieth century only sealed their fate quicker than might otherwise have been the case.

Recommended reading

The best place to begin when looking at the roots of the decolonization process is Robert Holland, *European Decolonization 1918–1981: An Introductory Survey* (Basingstoke, 1985). Specifically on the British Empire, see Bernard Porter, *The Lion's Share: A Short History of British Imperialism 1850–1995* (London, 1996) and Judith M. Brown and W. Roger Louis (eds), *The Oxford History of the British Empire*, vol. IV: *The Twentieth Century* (Oxford, 1999). In addition, a provocative overview is provided in John Gallagher, *The Decline, Revival and Fall of the British Empire* (Cambridge, 1982). On the French Empire, see Robert Betts, *France and Decolonization, 1900–1960* (Basingstoke, 1991). For the effect of the Second World War on empire, see W. Roger Louis, *Imperialism at Bay: The United States and the Decolonization of the British Empire* (Oxford, 1977).

On the relationship between Britain and the Dominions in the inter-war period, see Philip G. Wigley, *Canada and the Transition to Commonwealth: British Canadian Relations, 1917–26* (Cambridge, 1977) and Peter Cain and Anthony Hopkins, *British Imperialism, 1688–2000* (London, 2002). On Ireland, see Alvin Jackson, *Ireland 1798–1998* (Oxford, 1999), Jonathan Bardon, *A History of Ulster* (Belfast, 1992), F. S. L. Lyons, *Ireland since the Famine* (London, 1973), Paul Bew, *Ideology and the Irish Question: Ulster Unionism and Irish Nationalism, 1912–1916* (Oxford, 1994), D. George Boyce, *Ireland 1828–1923: From Ascendancy to Democracy* (Oxford, 1992), Michael Laffan, *The Partition of Ireland, 1911–25* (Dundalk, 1983), Alan O'Day, *Irish Home Rule, 1867–1921* (Manchester, 1998), Eunan O'Halpin, *The Decline of the Union: British Government in Ireland, 1892–1920* (Dublin, 1987), Brendan Sexton, *Ireland and the Crown, 1922–36: The Governor Generalship of the Irish Free State* (Dublin, 1989), David Fitzpatrick, *The Two Irelands, 1912–1939* (Oxford, 1998) and Dermot Keogh, *Twentieth Century Ireland: Nation and State* (Dublin, 1994).

For the collapse of the Ottoman Empire, see Justin McCarthy, *The Ottoman Peoples and the End of Empire* (London, 2000), Turfan M. Naim, *Rise of the Young Turks: Politics, the Military and the Ottoman Collapse* (London, 2000), Alec L. Macfie, *The End of the Ottoman Empire, 1908–1923* (New York, 1998) and L. Carl Brown, *Imperial Legacy: The Ottoman Imprint on the Balkans and the Middle East* (New York, 1996). British imperial policy in the Middle East is examined in Elizabeth Monroe, *Britain's Moment in the Middle East 1914–1971* (London, 1981) and Bruce Westrate, *The Arab Bureau: British Policy in the Middle East, 1916–20* (University Park, PA, 1992), and French imperial policy in the Middle East and North Africa is discussed in Moshe Gershovich, *French Military Rule in*

Morocco: Colonialism and its Consequences (London, 2000) and Peter Shambrook, *French Imperialism in Syria* (Reading, 1998). The seminal works on Arab nationalism are Albert Hourani, *Arabic Thought in the Liberal Age, 1798–1939* (Cambridge, 1993) and George Antonius, *The Arab Awakening: The Story of the Arab National Movement* (London, 1938). Other useful works include Rashid Khalidi *et al.* (eds), *The Origins of Arab Nationalism* (New York, 1991), Bassam Tibi, *Arab Nationalism: Between Islam and the Nation-State* (London, 1997), Hilal Khashan, *Arabs at the Crossroads: Political Identity and Nationalism* (Gainesville, VA, 2000) and James Jankowski and I. Gershoni (eds), *Rethinking Nationalism in the Arab Middle East* (New York, 1997).

On India, good overviews are provided by Sugata Bose and Ayesha Jalal, *Modern South Asia: History, Culture, Political Economy* (London, 1998), Barbara D. Metcalf and Thomas R. Metcalf, *A Concise History of India* (Cambridge, 2002) and Peter Robb, *A History of India* (Basingstoke, 2002). For more specific texts, see Judith Brown, *Gandhi: Prisoner of Hope* (New Haven, CT, 1989), R. J. Moore, *The Crisis of Indian Unity, 1917–40* (Oxford, 1974), Anil Seal, *The Emergence of Indian Nationalism: Competition and Collaboration in the Later Nineteenth Century* (Cambridge, 1968) and Brian Tomlinson, *The Political Economy of the Raj, 1914–1947: The Economics of Decolonization in India* (London, 1979). Some very useful essays are contained in John Gallagher, Gordon Johnson and Anil Seal (eds), *Locality, Province and Nation: Essays on Indian Politics, 1870–1940* (Cambridge, 1973) and Christopher Baker, Gordon Johnson and Anil Seal (eds), *Power, Profit and Politics: Essays on Imperialism, Nationalism and Change in Twentieth-Century India* (Cambridge, 1981).

On South-East Asia, see Clive J. Christie, *A Modern History of Southeast Asia: Decolonization, Nationalism and Separatism* (London, 1996) and Nicholas Tarling (ed.), *The Cambridge History of Southeast Asia*, vol. II (Cambridge, 1992). For more detailed accounts, see H. W. Brands, *Bound to Empire: The United States and the Philippines 1890–1990* (New York, 1992), William Duiker, *The Communist Road to Power in Vietnam* (Boulder, CO, 1981), David Marr, *Vietnamese Tradition on Trial, 1920–1945* (Berkeley, CA, 1981), Anthony Milner, *The Invention of Politics in Colonial Malaya* (Cambridge, 1994), Michael Ricklefs, *A History of Modern Indonesia* (London, 1999) and Takashi Shiraishi, *An Age in Motion: Popular Radicalism in Java 1912–1926* (Ithaca, NY, 1990).

For Africa in the period up to 1945, useful overviews can be found in Bill Freund, *The Making of Contemporary Africa* (Basingstoke, 1998), J. D. Fage, *A History of Africa* (London, 1995), John Hargreaves, *Decolonization in Africa* (London, 1996) and John Iliffe, *Africans: The History of a Continent* (Cambridge, 1995). For more detailed information, see Bruce Berman and John Lonsdale, *Unhappy Valley: Conflict in Kenya and Africa* (London, 1992), Martin Chanock, *Unconsummated Union: Britain, Rhodesia and South Africa, 1900–45* (London, 1977), John Iliffe, *A Modern History of Tanganyika* (Cambridge, 1979), Anne Phillips, *The Enigma of Colonialism: British Policy in West Africa* (London, 1989) and Jean Suret-Canale, *French Colonialism in Tropical Africa, 1900–1945* (London, 1971).

The origins of the Arab – Israeli conflict, 1900 – 48

Introduction

The origins and causes of the Arab–Israeli conflict have been the subject of much debate. Some have argued that religion is at its heart, seeing the contest for Palestine as an extension of the religious wars over Jerusalem in previous centuries and the Arab–Israeli wars as a continuation of the dispute between the Prophet Muhammad and the Jews of Medina. Others have asserted that it was the result of Western colonialism, which denied Arabs **self-determination** while at the same time favouring Zionism as an essentially European colonialist movement. Others still have claimed that it was the intransigent and irrational, if not fanatical, behaviour of Arabs or Zionists or both which provoked inter-communal violence.

While there is some validity to all these arguments, this chapter will argue that the causes of the conflict were the product of distinct historical developments in the late nineteenth and early twentieth centuries: European **anti-Semitism** and the rise of Zionism, the emergence of **Arab nationalism** and the quest for Arab independence, the Ottoman defeat in the First World War, the British **mandate** in Palestine, and the Second World War and the **Holocaust**. Thus it was not religious antagonism, fanaticism or colonial policy which pitted Arabs and Jews against each other, but, above all, competing national projects, laying claim to the same territory and resources. Arab nationalism and **Zionism** almost inevitably

self-determination
The idea that each national group has the right to establish its own national state. It is most often associated with the tenets of Wilsonian internationalism and became a key driving force in the struggle to end imperialism.

anti-Semitism
A word which appeared in Europe around 1860. With it, the attack on Jews was based no longer on grounds of creed but on those of race. Its manifestations include pogroms in nineteenth-century Eastern Europe and the systematic murder of an estimated six million Jews by Nazi Germany between 1939 and 1945.

found themselves embroiled in a bitter struggle for land and self-determination which came to be known as the Arab–Israeli conflict.

The origins and development of Zionism

In order to understand the competition between Jews and Arabs over Palestine it is necessary to take a closer look at their respective national claims and underlying ideas and ideologies. Modern Zionism – the belief that the Jews are one people and should have a state of their own – dates back to the second half of the nineteenth century. Like other European nationalisms, it was inspired by the French Revolution and the Enlightenment's secular and rationalistic traditions, notions of social contract, and principles of equality and citizenship. More importantly, however, it was a direct response to the continuing prevalence of anti-Semitism in Eastern and Western European society. The idea of a Jewish home or state as the solution to the so-called Jewish problem arose both in the Eastern European environment of segregation, persecution and oppression and in the freer Western European environment of legal equality and assimilation. The result was that Zionism as a national movement was the product of a number of thinkers, who drew upon different personal experiences and intellectual traditions.

In 1881, a series of pogroms swept through southern Russia. As the first extensive anti-Jewish disturbances since the slaughter of the Jews in Poland in 1648–49, they had a profound impact on the local Jewish community. They dashed any hopes the Eastern European Jewish intelligentsia had nurtured for reform and assimilation, sparking a wave of emigration, mainly to the United States. But they also triggered aspirations for the renewal of Jewish national life in the biblical Land of Israel – *Eretz Israel* – and thus gave birth to the Zionist movement.

It was in response to these pogroms that Leo Pinsker, a Jewish doctor from Odessa, published his pamphlet *Auto-Emancipation* in 1882 which saw a territory for Jews as the answer to the burden of life as a Jewish minority among Gentiles and as the means to regain lost dignity and self-respect. In fact, his focus on honour was more important to him than the actual location of the territory and consequently Pinsker was willing to consider countries other than Palestine for the Jewish home. This willingness, however, was not shared by many of his Zionist contemporaries, most of whom had come from a traditional religious background steeped in the longing for Zion. Drawing upon Pinsker's ideas, these Zionists formed *Hibbat Zion* (Lovers of Zion), an organization which channelled small groups of idealist settlers to Palestine. They were part of what became known as the first *Aliyah* (immigration wave) which lasted from 1882 to 1903.

This small number of Eastern European idealists founded the first Jewish settlements of Rishon LeZion, Petah Tikva, Rehovot and Rosh Pina. It was not, however, their commitment that fired the imagination of European Jews who knew little about the early Zionist endeavours in Palestine, but the writings of a

Western European assimilated Jew by the name of Theodor Herzl. A Viennese playwright and journalist, Herzl made one of the most important contributions to Zionism by providing it with a practical and institutional framework. Following the 1894 trial of the French Jewish officer Alfred Dreyfus, who had been falsely accused and convicted of treason, in 1896 Herzl wrote a book entitled *Der Judenstaat* (The Jewish State). In it Herzl called for the creation of a Jewish state as assimilation had not produced the hoped-for end to anti-Semitism. Only a state of their own could provide a rational solution to the Jewish experience of rejection, humiliation and shame. Herzl's notion of the state was firmly based on the principles of the French Revolution in the sense that it was an essentially artificial construct, rather than a mystical rebirth of a primordial entity. Herzl's utopian novel *Altneuland* (Old New Land), which is generally considered to have been his blueprint for the Jewish state, in fact described it as a thoroughly Western European upper-middle-class paradigm of civility, cleanliness, charm, theatre and opera – an idealized version of Herzl's Vienna, grounded in religious tolerance, mutual respect and brotherhood. It was devoid of any distinctly Jewish qualities, so much so that Herzl, like Pinsker, was in principle prepared to accept land in Argentina or, as later suggested by the British colonial secretary, Joseph Chamberlain, in British East Africa rather than Palestine.

In 1897, Herzl convened the first Zionist congress in Basle, Switzerland, bringing together Eastern and Western European Zionists for the first time. It led to the establishment of the World Zionist Organization for the 'creation of a home for the Jewish people in Palestine to be secured by public law'. This stated aim revealed two important issues: first, that the Eastern European Zionists' preference for Palestine had resolved the territorial question, and, second, that this Jewish state was to be achieved incrementally through the purchase and settlement of land, on the one hand, and through diplomacy and the blessing of the Great Powers on the other.

Herzl's approach soon came under fire from a number of different sources. Intellectually, his rational nationalism, which saw Zionism as the result of the external pressures of anti-Semitism, was challenged by romantic nationalists, such as Ahad Ha Am and Micha Joseph Berdichevsky, who asserted that Jewish nationalism was the product of the innate Jewish instinct for national survival and the eternal spirit of the nation. According to this school of thought, the Land of Israel was crucial to national revival as it represented continuation with the biblical past. Only through a return to the land would the Jewish people be liberated from the weakness and degeneration of exile. Herzl's bourgeois vision was also challenged by the budding socialist movement in Eastern Europe, whose quest for social equality had attracted a number of Jewish intellectuals. These intellectuals, in turn, introduced socialist principles into Zionism. It was not, however, these principles but the pogroms that followed the aborted Russian Revolution in 1905 that provided the stagnating Zionist movement with new momentum. It gave rise to the second *Aliyah* from 1904 to 1914 which is conventionally credited with laying the institutional foundations for the Jewish state in Palestine.

By the time Zionism collided head on with Arab nationalism in Palestine it had moved away from Herzl's rational Enlightenment basis. Instead it had become a romantic-exclusivistic brand of nationalism based on a precarious mixture of unifying ethnic-cultural bonds and mytho-historical spirit which organically linked Jewish nationalism to Palestine alongside socialist revolutionary principles of restructuring society. Not only did this transformation of Zionism exclude the indigenous Arab population from the Jewish state-building project, as exemplified by the slogan of 'a land without a people for a people without a land', the centrality of land as an essential prerequisite for redemption for both the romantic nationalist and agricultural socialist also placed the Zionist settlers in a zero-sum competition with the Arab peasants – the Palestinians.

Palestinian nationalism

see Chapter 4

The growth and development of Zionism was paralleled by that of Arab nationalism and it was over the territory of Palestine that these two national movements competed and ultimately came into direct conflict. One question that is often raised with respect to Arab nationalism and Palestine is whether a distinctly Palestinian nationalism existed or whether it developed later purely in reaction to Zionism. Apart from the obvious political implications, this question is particularly pertinent as historians, until the second half of the twentieth century, seem to have answered this question in the negative in the sense that Palestinians are indeed marginal to the mainstream narratives. The first point that needs to be taken into account is that few of these narratives were, in fact, written by Arabs, never mind Palestinians. Second, European historiography on Palestine in the nineteenth and much of the twentieth centuries focused on issues of European interest – Jerusalem, biblical Palestine and Crusader Palestine – thus writing about Palestine without Palestinians. Third, traditional Zionist historiography, as the only other main source of writings on Palestine, has denied any meaningful Palestinian existence, thus aiding Jewish settlement in the same way that the notion of the 'virgin territories' had aided European pioneer settlement of the Americas and Africa.

Given these historiographical problems, it is necessary to take a closer look at what kind of national identity did exist in Palestine. At the turn of the century, the majority of Arabs in Palestine did not define themselves in national terms, but rather by family, tribe, village or religious affiliation. Among intellectuals, however, the process of nationalist self-definition can be traced back to the Ottoman reforms of 1872, which established the independent *sanjak* (sub-province) of Jerusalem as well as giving rise to the local urban notables. However, it took another five decades for this to develop into a more cohesive discourse. This delay can be explained by a number of factors: Arabs generally considered Palestine as the southern part of Greater Syria; the local political culture was highly fragmented; territorial nationalism was generally less developed in the Arab Middle East; and last, but not least, any emerging ideas of Palestinian nationalism were in direct competition with the more encompassing ideas of Arab nationalism.

Only when the European Powers carved up the Middle East following the First World War, drawing artificial boundaries, did local territorial nationalisms, including Palestinian nationalism, start to assert themselves against the ideological pull of **pan-Arabism**. While Arab and Palestinian nationalisms emerged irrespective of Zionism, their development was profoundly affected by the emerging conflict in Palestine just as it had been by Arab resistance to Turkish rule and the region's encounter with the colonial Powers.

pan-Arabism
Movement for Arab unity as manifested in the Fertile Crescent and Greater Syria schemes as well as attempted unification of Egypt, Syria and Libya.

The twice-promised land

The First World War had a profound impact on Palestine. Economically, it almost destroyed the agricultural sector through the Ottoman army's confiscation of food, the conscription of the *fellaheen* (peasants), and a European blockade on the ports, which prohibited the import of grain. As a result, the population was on the brink of starvation. Politically, Palestine's competing nationalist movements were both harshly suppressed through sweeping arrests, the expulsions of foreign Jews and the execution of some Arab nationalists. Yet, while the population in Palestine suffered greatly, Arab nationalist and Zionist leaders outside Palestine were able to strengthen their respective territorial claims as a result of British alliance policy.

The Ottomans' entry into the war in November 1914 on the side of Germany resulted in two independent yet inextricably linked developments. First, it provided an opportunity for both Arabs throughout the Middle East and the Zionists in Palestine to shake off Ottoman control. Second, it pitted Britain against the Ottomans in the Middle East, initiating a British search for allies. This search culminated in a number of secret agreements with the Russians, Italians and French on the future of the Ottoman territories in the event of an *Entente* victory. The most important such agreement was the 1916 Sykes–Picot Agreement which mapped out British and French zones of control. It also resulted in agreements with the Arabs and with the Zionists, known as the Hussein–McMahon correspondence and the Balfour Declaration.

see Documents 5.1 and 5.2

The Hussein–McMahon correspondence consisted of a set of letters in 1915 and 1916 between the British high commissioner in Cairo, Sir Henry McMahon, and Sharif Hussein, head of the **Hashemites** and the guardian of the holy places in Mecca and Medina on the Arabian peninsula. Sharif Hussein's requests for British military aid to help the Arabs rid themselves of the Turks preceded the outbreak of the war, but had then been rejected as the Ottomans were still considered a friendly power and necessary for maintaining the European balance. Britain's interests in Hussein's plans, however, changed once it declared war on Turkey. The British now believed that Hussein might be able to inspire an Arab revolt which would undermine the Turks, stretch their resources and divert them from threatening Britain's link to the rest of its empire, the Suez Canal. This change of interest laid the foundation for the Hussein–McMahon correspondence, which ultimately contained the British promise of Arab independence

Hashemites
The family of the Sharifs of Mecca who trace their descent to the Prophet Muhammad.

in return for their support against the Ottomans. The Hussein–McMahon corres-pondence was not a formal treaty in any sense. Its lack of formality, however, was not the main problem. Rather, it was the territorial ambiguity and its implicit definition of 'Arabness'.

Document 5.1

Letter from McMahon to Sharif Hussein, 24 October 1915

. . . it is with great pleasure that I communicate to you on their [HMG's] behalf the following statement, which I am confident you will receive with satisfaction:

> The two districts of Mersina and Alexandretta and the portions of Syria lying to the west of the districts of Damascus, Homs, Hama and Aleppo cannot be said to be purely Arab, and should be excluded from the limits demanded.
> Subject to the above modifications, Great Britain is prepared to recognise and support the independence of the Arabs in all regions within the limits demanded by the Sharif of Mecca.
>
> Source: Reich (1995, pp. 19–25)

The territory to be given to the Arabs thus explicitly excluded portions of what became Lebanon and Syria but made no reference to either Palestine or Jerusalem. Thus it is not surprising that the Arabs believed Palestine would be part of their national territory. Consequently, when the British after the end of the war claimed that Palestine had been excluded, the Arabs felt bitterly betrayed. This was especially so as Hussein's campaign had contributed significantly to the British war effort – first, through the seizure of the Red Sea port of Aqaba, which opened the way for attacking Ottoman forces in Palestine from the south-east, and, second, through encouraging the Arab uprising in the northern provinces towards the end of the war. Hussein thus believed he had upheld his end of the deal honourably, while the British had not only failed to uphold theirs, but had also promised Palestine as a home to the Jews.

If the First World War provided the opportunity for Arab nationalists to push for independence through a military alliance with the British, it also provided the opportunity for the Zionists to obtain international recognition of their aspirations in Palestine. In 1917 the war in Europe started to go badly for the *Entente* and once again the British began to explore alliances to shift the balance of power in their favour. The Zionist movement had already been involved in the war through the Zion Mule Corps attached to the British forces at Gallipoli and several Jewish battalions attached to General Allenby's forces in Palestine, but up to this point it was considered a marginal player. This situation, however, was soon to change, for the British prime minister, David Lloyd George, and the foreign secretary, Arthur James Balfour, came to see support for the Zionist movement as a means of preventing Russia from exiting the war after the February Revolution, of undermining Germany from within and of galvanizing the American war effort.

The key Zionist player in the formation of this alliance was a chemistry lecturer at Manchester University by the name of Chaim Weizmann. A Russian-born British subject and an eloquent Zionist spokesman, Weizmann had already come into contact with and lobbied a number of British politicians prior to the war, including Arthur Balfour, whom he had first met during the 1906 general election campaign. The notion of a Jewish state pushed by Weizmann gained prominence among British politicians owing to his importance as a scientist involved in the synthesizing of acetone, which was essential for making explosives. Weizmann, through his diplomatic skills and his personal contacts, was able to obtain from the British what had eluded Herzl in all his years of futile diplomacy with the Ottomans: an international, in this case British, guarantee for a Jewish home in Palestine. This guarantee was embodied in a letter from Balfour to the prominent British Zionist Lord Rothschild and is commonly known as the Balfour Declaration.

Document 5.2

The Balfour Declaration, 2 November 1917

His Majesty's Government view with favour the establishment in Palestine of a national home for the Jewish people, and will use their best endeavours to facilitate the achievement of this object, it being clearly understood that nothing shall be done which may prejudice the civil and religious rights of the existing non-Jewish communities in Palestine, or the rights and political status of Jews in any other country.

Source: Reich (1995, p. 29)

As in the Arab case, the land promised to the Jews had no specified territorial boundaries and the notion of a 'national home' was also vague. Even more important for the development of the conflict in Palestine was the fact that the same land – Palestine – seemed to have been given to both Jews and Arabs for what by now had become mutually exclusive state-building projects.

The mandate and British policy

The end of the war raised expectations for independence among both Arabs and Jews. Their hopes were, however, dashed when Britain ended up as first *de facto* and later *de jure* in control of Palestine. Indeed, the Arab territories of the Ottoman Empire were divided up and placed under French and British mandates awarded at San Remo in 1920 and ratified by the **League of Nations** in 1922, a territorial division which bore a remarkable resemblance to the 1916 Sykes-Picot Agreement. Yet, while Britain, on the one hand, was clearly expanding its power in the Middle East, on the other, it continued to back Arab, Jewish and Armenian

League of Nations
An international organization established in 1919 by the peace treaties that ended the First World War. Its purpose was to promote international peace through collective security and to organize conferences on economic and disarmament issues. It was formally dissolved in 1946.

claims for independence, often as a means to undermine rival European Powers, particularly France. Indeed, British policy was more often than not driven by European factors or imperial considerations and this placed the British authorities in a rather awkward position in Palestine as the conflict between Arabs and Jews escalated.

Britain's position was further complicated by the divergence in views that emerged between its officials on the ground and those in London. British officials in Palestine tended to be more sympathetic to the Arabs. This tendency was further strengthened by the fact that the Zionists in pursuit of equal rights had on a number of occasions appealed over the head of the local administration to London. Moreover, the local administration believed that Zionists' aspirations for statehood threatened stability not only in Palestine but also in other parts of the British Empire, particularly those with Muslim populations. This view was not shared by British officials in London. They saw the Balfour Declaration as the main reason for the British presence in Palestine and backed Zionism, both domestically and internationally. Furthermore, they felt bound by the official incorporation of the Declaration into the Mandate Charter, which effectively transformed the achievement of a Jewish national home into an international obligation. The main result of this contradiction was that both Arabs and Zionists were wary of British intentions. Therefore rather than balancing the situation, British policy contributed to the tensions as the Zionists believed that Britain was pro-Arab and the Arabs believed it was pro-Zionist.

see Table 5.1

British policy under Sir Herbert Samuel, the first high commissioner of Palestine, was to uphold its pledge to assist the fulfilment of Zionist aims but also to ensure that the Arab population's civil and economic rights were safeguarded. In concrete terms, this meant that Samuel ensured that Arabs could not stop Jewish immigration and land purchases while at the same time he gave Arabs a part in the mandate's civil administration. He encouraged both Arabs and Jews to build institutions and made several attempts to reconcile the two communities as he did not believe that co-existence was impossible. His attempts, however, were undermined by an increasing cycle of inter-communal violence.

The 1921 Nebi Musa riots constituted the first outbreak of large-scale Arab–Jewish violence. The unrest, as well as the British response, laid down the

Table 5.1 British high commissioners for Palestine, 1920–48

Name	Dates of tenure
Sir Herbert Samuel	1920–25
Lord Plumer	1925–28
Sir John Chancellor	1928–31
Maj. Gen. Sir Arthur Wauchope	1931–37
Sir Harold MacMichael	1937–44
Lord Gort	1944–45
Sir Alan Cunningham	1945–48

pattern for the rest of the mandate period; it was characterized by urban clashes between the two groups, in this case in Tel Aviv and Jaffa, followed by Jewish and Arab reprisals and by Arabs attacking outlying Jewish settlements. The British response was an investigation into the causes of the disturbances and a subsequent temporary halting of Jewish immigration.

A similar pattern can be observed following the 1928–29 Wailing Wall riots, which were the result of Muslim and Jewish suspicions, each thinking that the other was planning to lay sole claim to the area which encompasses the remnants of the Jews' Second Temple as well as the Muslims' Al-Aqsa mosque and Dome of the Rock. Almost a year of tension finally descended into outright violence in Jerusalem, followed by Arab attacks on the Jewish quarters of Hebron and Safed, leaving an estimated 133 Jews and 116 Arabs dead. The British response was an investigation into the causes of the riots by the 1929 Shaw Commission which concluded that Arab feelings of hostility were caused by their landlessness and fear for their economic future as a result of Zionist land purchases and immigration. The 1930 Hope–Simpson Commission was then charged with formulating proposals to tackle these problems, with the result that recommendations to limit both Jewish immigration and land purchases became the basis of the 1930 Passfield White Paper. The White Paper blamed the Jews for inciting the riots and demanded that the Zionists make concessions in regard to their demand for a national home. Jewish protests in Palestine and London elicited a letter from the British prime minister, Ramsay MacDonald, repudiating the White Paper, which, in turn, angered the Arabs.

What is interesting when looking at the early investigations of the causes of the riots is that all of the commissions seemed to be aware of the growing impossibility of co-existence and the mutually exclusive national aspirations, yet it was not until the 1937 Peel Commission that partition was recommended and not until 1947 that partition and separation became the preferred choice of 'resolving' the conflict. Throughout the 1920s and, indeed, the 1930s and 1940s the British approach to regulating the conflict appeared to revolve solely around the issue of Jewish immigration and land purchases.

The effects of this policy in the 1920s become clear when looking at the 1930s. Inter-communal tension remained high and hopes harboured by Samuel for reconciliation faded. Both Zionists and Arabs felt betrayed by the British and felt they could not rely on the British to 'protect' them. While the Zionists established their own defence organizations in Palestine, their main political tool was exerting pressure on British policy in London. Diplomacy was lower on the Arab agenda for three key reasons. First, their representatives lacked access to high-level European decision-makers and the necessary language skills to argue their case eloquently. Second, European Orientalist attitudes towards Arabs and Muslims were ungenerous, to say the least. And, third, Arab leaders assumed that the British would always side with their fellow 'Europeans' – the Jews. They had, however, learnt one important lesson from the riots of the 1920s – that British policy-makers responded to the use and threat of violence – and this was drawn upon when the **Arab Revolt** erupted in 1936, catching both the Palestinian leadership and the British mandate authority by surprise.

Arab Revolt
Peasant uprising in Palestine between 1936 and 1939 characterized by strikes and civil disobedience during the first year and violence against the British and Zionists during the subsequent two years.

The Arab Revolt is significant for a number of reasons: it brought to the fore the land question, as the revolt predominantly drew upon Arab peasants; it signalled clearly that the Arabs were not going to accept quietly the Zionist state-building project; and it left no doubt that a distinctly Palestinian identity existed. With respect to the Palestinian leadership, on the one hand it showed a certain degree of unity among urban notables, but, on the other, reflected the clear dissatisfaction of the rural population with their urban leaders, with the exception of the *mufti* of Jerusalem, Hajj Amin al-Husayni. The British response to the outbreak of the revolt was brutal repression, followed by the 1937 Peel Commission which, following the pattern of previous commissions, concluded that co-existence was impossible but, unlike its predecessors, recommended partition. This recommendation, however, was not heeded. Over the next two years the revolt escalated from general strikes and civil disobedience, which had characterized much of 1936, to outright rebellion from 1937 to 1939. The possibility of Palestine becoming ungovernable at a time when Europe was sliding into another world war led the British authorities to rely on tried and tested methods of conflict regulation rather than experimenting with new approaches. Moreover, in 1938 the Woodhead Commission declared that partition was not feasible and the Foreign Office expressed concern that a pro-Zionist policy would drive the Arabs into the arms of the Axis Powers. All these dimensions were reflected in the 1939 MacDonald White Paper issued only a few months before the Second World War, which severely restricted Jewish immigration and land purchases, while seemingly guaranteeing the achievement of an Arab Palestinian state within ten years. The White Paper achieved the desired result in the sense that the Arab Revolt came to an end. The Arab Revolt had also achieved its desired result: a complete reversal of British policy, a clear step back from the Zionist state-building project while simultaneously supporting Arab independence. However, for the Jews faced with the unfolding events in Europe, the White Paper came to represent the deepest act of betrayal.

mufti

A government-appointed Muslim religious official who pronounces usually on spiritual and social matters. The exception is the *mufti* of Jerusalem who also played a political role.

Palestine and the Second World War

On 30 January 1933 Adolf Hitler was sworn in as Germany's new chancellor. In July 1935 Hitler's government passed the Nuremberg Laws on racial purity, laying the foundation for legal and institutionalized anti-Semitism. On 9 November 1938, in a night of terror, the Nazis destroyed synagogues, Jewish businesses and Jewish property throughout Germany in what became known as the *Kristallnacht*. On 30 January 1939, on the sixth anniversary of his rise to power, Hitler made a speech predicting the destruction of European Jewry should war be 'forced' upon him. On 1 September 1939, this war began.

The political changes in Germany and the outbreak of the Second World War profoundly influenced the dynamics of the conflict in Palestine. Between 1933 and 1936, 164,000 Jews, predominantly from Germany and Austria, immigrated

see Chapter 7

see Chapter 8

to Palestine, virtually doubling the Jewish population. Unlike the First *Aliyah* of Zionist idealists and the Second and Third *Aliyot* of socialist agriculturalists, this Fifth *Aliyah* was predominantly middle class, bourgeois and urban. The new immigrants did not flock to outlying settlements, but instead settled in the cities of Tel Aviv and Haifa, where they expanded the *yishuv*'s commercial and industrial sectors.

While these new immigrants strengthened the Zionist state-building project, they also presented a challenge to its homogeneity. Up until this point the *yishuv* had been composed of mainly Eastern Europeans from working-class backgrounds. Now Jewish society in Palestine saw its first class differences as well as the introduction of a different set of cultural values and references.

The need to take in the steady stream of refugees from Europe placed Zionist leaders in an awkward position once the 1939 White Paper had been issued. On the one hand, they had to do everything to help European Jews immigrate to Palestine, if need be illegally and in open defiance of the British. On the other hand, they had to do everything they could to support the British war effort against Germany. Indeed, with respect to the latter, an estimated 136,000 Palestinian Jews volunteered for service with the British during the course of the war, including some 4,000 women.

British policy in Palestine during the war was guided by broader strategic considerations. British troops were fighting Germany in Europe and in North Africa as well as having to keep an eye on Germany's **Vichy** French ally who had taken over the mandate in Lebanon and Syria. What they could not afford at this time was further troops being tied down in Palestine through an Arab uprising and the only way to prevent this was strictly to enforce the limits on Jewish immigration and land purchases.

Faced with concerted Jewish efforts to bring in refugees at all costs, this put the Zionists in a difficult situation, leading to incidents such as the sinking of the *Struma* in February 1941. The *Struma* was a decrepit cattle boat converted to bring Jewish refugees escaping the Holocaust to Palestine. It had been anchored off the Turkish coast while British and Zionist officials argued over its fate. Before any agreement could be reached, an unexplained explosion sank the boat, killing 768 Jewish refugees. This, however, did not deter the British from continuing their naval blockade, nor did it deter Jewish refugees from trying to enter Palestine.

In 1939 an average of 2,371 legal and illegal immigrants entered Palestine each month. The British reaction in October 1940 was to suspend even the quota allowed under the White Paper, to tighten the blockade, to confiscate ships, to prevent others from sailing or to divert them to ports in Cyprus and even to deport refugees who had entered illegally. As the Nazis extended their control, effectively closing the avenues of flight, the number of Jews escaping from Europe to Palestine dwindled to 500 per month in 1941 and 300 in 1942, but increased again towards the end of the war with the liberation of the concentration camps. In 1945, at the conclusion of the war, the population of the *yishuv* had increased to 554,000, including 115,000 Jewish refugees who had entered illegally.

While the Jews were trying to balance their position vis-à-vis the British, some Palestinian leaders saw the war as an opportunity to free themselves from British

yishuv (Hebrew: settlement)
The Jewish settlement in Palestine before the establishment of the State of Israel.

Vichy France
The regime led by Marshal Pétain that surrendered to Hitler's Germany in June 1940 and subsequently controlled France until liberation in 1944.

colonial control. For instance, the *mufti* of Jerusalem, Hajj Amin al-Husayni, who had already overplayed his hand with the British during the Arab Revolt, now made contacts with the Axis Powers from his exile in Iraq. He believed that a German victory would not only free Palestine from both the British and the Zionists, but also lead to independence. The Germans conversely saw the *mufti* as a vehicle for undermining Britain's position in the Middle East, particularly in Iraq, as well as for recruiting Bosnian Muslims into the SS. The British reaction to Hajj Amin's collaboration with the Nazis was as forceful as their attitude towards Jewish immigration. Failing to capture the *mufti* himself, the British mandate authorities in Palestine sentenced to death thirty-nine Palestinian nationalists between November 1939 and June 1940. Every single one of them was either a personal or family friend of the *mufti*.

The combined Arab and Zionist challenge to British policy, the latter of which increasingly included paramilitary attacks from the *Irgun* and Stern Gang, as well as the fact that Britain's priority lay in Europe, led to the loosening of British control over Palestine. This trend was reinforced by the end of the war and changes in the international balance of power, most notably the decline of the British Empire and the rise of the United States. At the same time American decision-makers had also started to become the target of Zionist lobbying. In May 1942, the American Zionist network issued the Biltmore Program which called for a Jewish state in Palestine. The programme did not find immediate support in the Roosevelt administration, which was preoccupied with the war in Europe and worried about Arab oil supplies. It was, however, eventually adopted by both key parties in the 1944 presidential elections owing to the first recorded lobbying pressure that directly linked Jewish votes to support for the Zionist project. Both Democrats and Republicans thus endorsed the quest for a Jewish state, laying the foundation for future American policy. The support of the United States was further strengthened through the wave of revulsion which swept the population upon the liberation of the concentration camps and the revelation of the full details of the Holocaust. The extermination of 5.6–6.9 million Jews not only made the Zionist movement more determined than ever to achieve its goal, but also engendered widespread international sympathy for its cause. Interestingly, the establishment of a Jewish state was not only seen as a morally just cause, but was also, in a more practical sense, perceived as a partial solution to the much broader European refugee problem and was recommended as such by the 1946 Anglo-American Commission of Inquiry.

Partition and the end of the mandate

From the end of the Second World War onwards Britain's hold on Palestine became increasingly tenuous as Arab and particularly Jewish violence increased in a last concerted push for independence. The final British decision to relinquish its mandate and withdraw from Palestine was the result of a combination of factors, the most important of which was the need to focus on domestic post-war reconstruction and economic recovery from a war that had cost Britain £7 billion.

Another factor that should not be underestimated was the series of concerted attacks on British targets in Palestine which started in 1944 and became known as the Jewish Revolt. The revolt was carried out by all of the *yishuv*'s paramilitary organizations, the mainstream *Haganah*, its strike force the *Palmah*, and the extremist *Irgun* and *Lehi*. It aimed at sabotaging British installations such as radar posts, police stations, airfields, railways and the British-owned Iraqi Oil Company pipeline. While the *Haganah* and *Palmah* limited their attacks to British property, the *Irgun* and *Lehi* also targeted British military personnel and civilians, as exemplified by the *Irgun*'s July 1946 bombing of the King David Hotel, a section of which was used as the British military headquarters. Ninety-one lives were lost, including many civilians, among them British, Jews and Arabs.

The need for additional troops, the growing number of casualties and the increased cost of maintaining the mandate under such circumstances at a time when the economy was failing and the public's tolerance for military conflict had dropped to an all-time low, resulted in domestic pressure on the British government to withdraw. Added to this was growing international pressure as a result of Britain's continuation of its naval blockade to prevent Jewish immigration to Palestine. The images of ships full of Holocaust survivors either being sent back to their port of origin or re-routed to Cyprus where their passengers were again interned in camps turned international opinion against Britain. Moreover, the end of the war saw expectations that colonialism was coming to an end and that a new age of independence and self-determination was beginning, as embodied by the newly formed **United Nations** (UN).

Thus it was not wholly surprising that on 14 February 1947 Britain decided to refer the Palestine problem to the UN. At the first special session of the General Assembly in May 1947 the United Nations Special Commission on Palestine (UNSCOP) was set up to investigate the causes of the conflict and to recommend solutions. For the next four months UNSCOP conducted hearings in New York, Jerusalem, Beirut and Geneva, virtually replicating the work of the previous commissions of inquiry. It also came to a similar conclusion: both Jewish and Arab claims to the land were of equal validity but their national aspirations were irreconcilable. The majority opinion in UNSCOP was that only partition of the territory would recognize these claims, allow both peoples self-determination and thus resolve the conflict. The minority considered partition unworkable and suggested a federal union of an Arab state and a Jewish state with a common foreign and defence policy under a central power-sharing government.

The Zionists rejected the minority proposal but accepted partition. The Arabs, who had earlier decided to boycott the UNSCOP inquiry, rejected both proposals. These decisions ultimately deprived the Palestinians of an opportunity to make their case and to influence the debate, as well as the subsequent vote, in the UN General Assembly. The combination of Arab non-cooperation, general sympathy for the Jews following the Holocaust and immense lobbying efforts by the Jewish Agency resulted in a vote of thirty-three in favour of partition, thirteen against and ten abstentions. The partition plan, drawn up by UNSCOP, divided Palestine

Haganah (Hebrew: Defence) Jewish underground organization established in 1920 following Arab riots and the British failure to defend the Jews. It became the core of the IDF in 1948.

United Nations (UN)
An international organization established after the Second World War to replace the League of Nations. Since its establishment in 1945, its membership has grown to 192 countries.

see Map 5.1

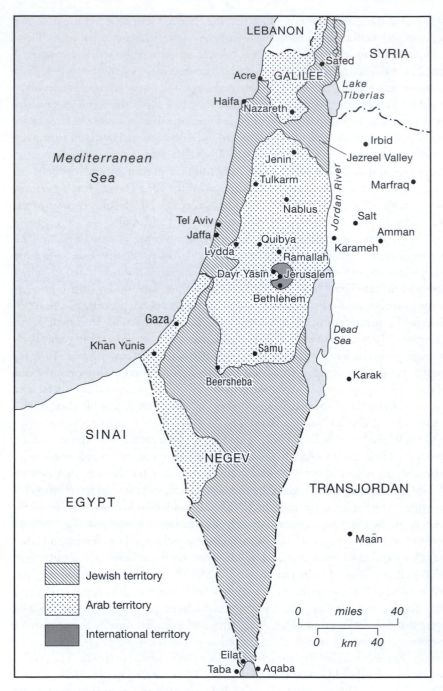

Map 5.1 UN partition plan for Palestine, 1947

Source: After Schulze (1999)

in accordance with existing settlement patterns, and meant that the proposed Arab state was to consist of the coastal strip of Gaza, Galilee in the north, and the area around Nablus, Hebron and Beersheba, while the proposed Jewish state would consist of the coastal area around Tel Aviv and Haifa, the Negev in the south, and the Jezreel and Huleh valleys. Jerusalem was to come under international control.

However, the lack of territorial contiguity for either state and the problem that small populations of either side were 'trapped' in the state of the other did not augur well. Added that the Palestinian Arabs held on to their rejectionist position and that neighbouring Arab countries vowed to destroy any Jewish state, this unsatisfactory compromise ensured that the partition resolution was not the end of the Palestine conflict but rather the beginning of years of Arab–Israeli war.

Arab and Zionist institution-building

One of the questions often asked is: why, following the partition of Palestine in November 1947, did only the Zionists end up with a state in 1948 while the Palestinians remained stateless? This can be partially explained by the differences in the Zionist and Palestinian institution-building processes over the preceding five decades and partially by the outcome of the 1948 war, Arab disunity and the Palestinian refugee problem. It is thus useful to take a closer look at institution-building before moving on to the war itself.

Jewish immigration, land purchases and self-sufficiency were vital to the Zionist state-building effort and that was reflected at the institutional level. The early institutions included the Jewish Colonial Association (JCA) which was established in Paris in 1891 and the Jewish National Fund (JNF) established in 1901. These bodies were responsible for acquiring land for collective use by the Jewish nation. In addition, there was the first Palestine Office of Herzl's Zionist Organization, opened in the port city of Jaffa in 1908, which, in turn, established the Palestine Land Development Company to train Jewish immigrants in agriculture with the aim of settling them on the land purchased by the JNF and the JCA.

The 1917 Balfour Declaration, followed by the arrival of the British in Palestine and the mandate, resulted in a proliferation of Zionist institutions encouraged by Sir Herbert Samuel as well as by the belief that the incorporation of the Balfour Declaration into the 1922 Mandate Charter amounted to international support for the Zionist state-building efforts.

The Zionist Commission arrived in April 1918 and, as it had been granted semi-independent status by the British Foreign Office, it was in a better position to extract concessions from the mandate authorities than were Arab institutions. For instance, its requests to give Hebrew equal language status to Arabic and appoint Jews as government officials were granted early on, providing the Zionists with a foundation from which to push for full equality, despite numerical inferiority.

The 1920s and 1930s saw the proliferation of Zionist institutions, including the main financial institution *Keren Hayesod* (Foundation Fund) and the *Histadrut* (General Federation of Jewish Labour), as well as the Palestine Worker Party *Mapai* and Zeev Jabotinsky's Zionist Revisionist Party which respectively formed the basis for today's centre-left Labour Bloc and centre-right Likud Bloc. The key political institution, however, was the Jewish Agency established in 1929, which served as the official representative body of the Jews vis-à-vis the British administration and the League of Nations. The basic aims of the Jewish Agency included the facilitation of immigration to Palestine, the advancement of the Hebrew language, the acquisition of land through the JNF, the development of agriculture and the fulfilment of Jewish religious needs. Moreover, the Jewish Agency effectively became the government of the emerging state with its executive not only assuming the role of a cabinet, but also providing the training ground for future Israeli politicians, including Israel's first prime minister, David Ben Gurion, and its first female prime minister, Golda Meir.

The last bodies that need to be discussed are the defence organizations, for these completed the transformation of the Zionist institutional network into a proto-state. The establishment of the *Haganah* (Defence) in 1920 with the aim of protecting Jewish community property was a reflection of the growing conflict with the Arabs and the declining trust in the British. It also paved the way for the 'victory' of the 'hawks' within Zionism over the 'doves'. The 1920–21 Nebi Musa riots and the 1928–29 Wailing Wall riots further increased the sense of Jewish insecurity, resulting in the 1931 foundation of a rival paramilitary organization, the *Irgun Zva'i Le'umi* (National Military Organization) and the 1939 formation of the *Lohamei Herut Israel* (Fighters for the Freedom of Israel) or *Lehi*, also referred to as the Stern Gang. While the *Haganah* was closely associated with the labour movement and advocated an official policy of restraint, the *Irgun* and *Lehi* were associated with the revisionist movement and pursued an aggressive policy. The latter included both attacks on and retaliation against Arab activists and the Arab population, as well as terrorism against the British mandate authority. These actions underlined the revisionist belief in 'redemption through force' and the inevitability of conflict with the Arabs who ultimately had to be destroyed or expelled if the Zionist state project was to succeed.

What is clear when looking at the institutions of the *yishuv* is not only that they organized virtually every aspect of Jewish life but also that they, in all but name, functioned as a state with its own domestic, economic, foreign and defence policy. It is thus not surprising that upon the end of the British mandate, these institutions were easily transformed, with the Zionist Executive becoming the Israeli government, the *Haganah* becoming the Israel Defence Forces (IDF) and so on.

What is equally clear when looking at Palestinian Arab institutions during the same period is that they lacked the strength, cohesiveness and comprehensiveness of their Zionist counterparts. It is thus no accident that they could not be that easily transformed into a Palestinian government in 1948, although it must be stressed that this was not the only obstacle to state formation. The question that consequently must be asked is why Palestinian Arab institutions developed so asymmetrically.

The Palestinian process of institution-building was inspired by the 1913 Arab Congress as well as the need to deal with the Zionist challenge. A number of organizations sprang up at this point, the most important of which included the Arab Palestinian Economic Company, the Arab Club – *al-Nadi al-Arabi* – and the Literary Club – *al-Muntada al-Adabi* – which, despite its name, was a political organization. They promoted a blend of local and Arab nationalism, were strongly anti-Zionist and concerned with countering the growing Zionist presence, particularly in the economic sphere. Like most other nationalist organizations before the 1930s, they were oriented towards Syria, seeing Palestine as Southern Syria and to some extent looking to the Hashemites for political leadership. In addition to the political agenda, the Literary Club also played an active role in education and culture, particularly in the Arab schools of Jerusalem.

By far the most significant organization in this period, however, was the Muslim–Christian Association – *al-Jamiyya al-Islamiyya al-Masihiyya* – which convened the First Palestinian Arab Congress, also known as the All Palestine Congress, in Jerusalem in February 1919. It served as the mainstay of the Palestinian nationalist movement with branches in all major cities and representing both Christians and Muslims. The Muslim–Christian Association's political platform advocated opposition to Zionist immigration and the creation of an independent and elected Palestinian legislature. But it also saw Palestine as a self-governing province within a Syrian federation rather than as a state of its own.

Just as Zionist institutions proliferated under Samuel's encouragement, so too did Arab institutions as Samuel aimed at creating fully parallel structures. Thus in December 1920, at the Third Palestinian Arab Congress, an executive was established to deal with the mandate authority. It was headed by Musa Kazim al-Husayni of the Husayni notable family. However, while the Arab Executive represented Palestinian nationalists, it also reflected the divisions in Palestinian society. The Husaynis' rivals, the Nashashibis, for instance, boycotted the Executive, and this weakened it as an institution. It also ensured that the Executive was associated with a particular person rather than representing the people as a whole and when Musa Kazim al-Husayni died in 1934, the Executive virtually ceased to function. The Supreme Muslim Council, established by Hajj Amin al-Husayni in 1922 to manage Muslim religious affairs, suffered from similar weaknesses. While it grew beyond its original remit and evolved into a political institution, it too was torn by factional struggles between the supporters of the nationalist leadership led by the Husaynis as well as being continuously challenged by the opposition led by the Nashashibis.

Palestinian factionalization and institutional weakness were also to a large degree a reflection of Palestinian traditional society which had been under Ottoman governance until 1919. Palestinian *fellaheen* approached politics on an intensely local and personal level. As a result, the idea of bureaucratic institutions was not easily embraced. This placed them at a distinct disadvantage compared with the Zionists who came from a European tradition of state-building.

The British divide-and-rule policy further exacerbated Palestinian divisions. For instance, in 1921 the British supported Hajj Amin al-Husayni for the position of *mufti* of Jerusalem. When they perceived him as too strong and too extreme, they shifted their support to the mayor of Jerusalem, Raghid al-Nashashibi. In 1927, the Nashashibis won the municipal elections and the Arab Executive temporarily closed its offices. It was not until 1928 that the Husaynis and Nashashibis agreed to push for representative institutions together, only to be undermined by the 1928–29 riots.

In the 1930s, to some extent mirroring Zionist developments but also those in other Arab countries, a number of Palestinian parties were formed. They included Awni Abdel Hadi's *Istiqlal* (Independence) Party which was founded in 1932, Hajj Amin al-Husayni's Palestine Arab Party, Raghid al-Nashashibi's National Defence Party, Hussein Khalidi's Reform Party, and Abdel Latif Salah's Nationalist Bloc. While all these parties advocated resistance to the Jewish national project and the maintenance of the Arab character of Palestine, and while all lobbied the mandate authorities to improve the socio-economic position of the Arabs, unity in aims was eroded by the continuing focus on personalities.

The 1930s also saw the rise of Arab civil disobedience and violence, culminating in the 1936–39 Arab Revolt. The revolt itself led to institutional change with its greatest success being the establishment of the Arab Higher Committee, which was composed of the leaders of all the main factions and thus provided Palestinian unity. Despite the July 1937 secession of the Nashashibis, its proscription in October 1937 and the dismissal and exile of Hajj Amin in an attempt by the British to break the revolt, the Committee became a symbol of Palestinian unity and an example for future generations to emulate. Thus it is not surprising that the Arab Revolt served as an inspiration for the 1987 *intifada*.

While the Palestinian nation-building process benefited from the revolt, the Palestinian state-building process did not. In contrast to the Jewish case, the proliferation of Arab guerrilla bands did not lead to the establishment of a united paramilitary organization or indeed a Palestinian army. Instead the rise in violence, which influenced British policy so effectively, also led to a forceful clamp-down on the emerging national movement, resulting in the suspension of Arab institutions and the exile of Arab leaders. Finally, the revolt caused severe damage to the Palestinian economy, ultimately speeding up the unravelling of a highly factionalized and increasingly leaderless Palestinian society.

This overview of the Arab institutions reveals a number of weaknesses, the first of which was that not only were they competing with Zionist institutions, but they were in themselves divided between those focusing on Palestine and those advocating a greater Arab or Syrian agenda. Another problem concerning, in particular, the early Palestinian institutions was that many of them emerged outside the existing structure of elite politics. On the one hand, this meant the politicization of new segments of society, but, on the other, it threatened the interests of the current leadership, which wanted to preserve the existing political and economic patterns. This leadership was composed of a small number of wealthy Muslim families, including the Husaynis, the Nashashibis, the Alamis and the Khalidis, who had their bases in and around Jerusalem, had fared well under the Ottomans, and were essentially feudal in their approach. While being sincere Arab and Palestinian nationalists, their nationalism remained conservative and fearful of any move that could spark social changes which would undermine the existing political order. The leadership's indifference, and indeed hostility, to new

see Chapter 18

intifada (Arabic: shaking off) Name given to the Palestinian uprising against Israeli occupation which began on 9 December 1987 and lasted until the signing of the 1993 Oslo Accords between the PLO and Israel.

nationalist institutions assured that many of these movements were weak and short lived.

While the disunity within the Palestinian leadership prevented the creation of strong institutions from above, the general erosion of the socio-economic foundation since the late Ottoman period undermined them from below. The combination of oppressive tax and land-tenure systems with the practices of the urban landowners led to the dispossession of the *fellaheen*, to rural–urban migration, and to unemployment, all of which were aggravated by Zionist land purchases, the exclusion of Arabs from the labour market and the Arab Revolt. By the 1940s the Arabs in Palestine were not only unable to compete with Zionist institution-building and proto-state formation, they were without credible leadership and on the verge of societal collapse. Thus, when Palestine was partitioned in November 1947, Arab nationalist dreams in Palestine lay in disarray. Palestine collapsed into civil strife and the Palestinian exodus began. The dispersal of a large part of the Palestinian population across refugee camps in neighbouring Arab states dealt Palestinian statehood the final blow.

The 1948 war

On 14 May 1948 the British mandate came to an end and the state of Israel was proclaimed in the territory allocated to the Jews by the UN partition plan. The following day, 15 May, the armies of Egypt, Jordan, Syria, Lebanon and Iraq started their attack on the newly established state of Israel. An estimated 6,000 to 7,000 Arab volunteers constituting the Arab Liberation Army crossed the border to liberate Palestine and to destroy Israel. During the early period of the war Israel was on the defensive, literally fighting for its survival. By far the biggest problem for Israel was the arms embargo imposed after the partition resolution, which made it difficult to procure sufficient weapons. This military weakness was further compounded by its numerical inferiority and the difficulties of streamlining a fighting force composed of well-trained local Jews and untrained, physically weak European Holocaust survivors, who often had no knowledge of Hebrew. Israel's weaknesses and the high morale of the Arab fighters, who had been promised a quick and easy war, explain the Arab successes during the first phase of the war, in which Palestinian irregulars or *fedayeen* effectively laid siege to the Jewish part of Jerusalem, while the Arab Liberation Army isolated a number of Jewish settlements in Galilee.

fedayeen (Arabic: guerrillas; suicide squads)
Originally associated with the Ismaili 'Assassins' in medieval history. After 1948 the term was used to describe Palestinian guerrilla groups.

The turning point in the war came with the UN-decreed cease-fire on 11 June 1948. While the UN mediator, Count Folke Bernadotte, explored the possibilities of a compromise solution, the Israelis and Arabs rearmed, regrouped and prepared for the next confrontation. It was at this point that Israel began to gain the upper hand, for while the Arab forces started to suffer from low morale, lack of co-ordination and logistical support, and, above all, a lack of unity caused by mutual suspicion of each other's political and territorial aims, the IDF steadily increased not only its manpower to 65,000, as opposed to the Arab force of 25,000, but also

Plate 5.1 Declaration of the State of Israel, Tel Aviv, Israel, 14 May 1948. The first Israeli prime minister, David Ben Gurion, stands under a huge portrait of Theodor Herzl, the founder of political Zionism, surrounded by members of the National Jewish Council to officially proclaim the state of Israel. On the same day Israel received *de facto* recognition from the United States, and the Arab states of Lebanon, Syria, Jordan, Egypt and Iraq invaded Israel with their regular armies. (Photo: AFP/Getty Images)

its firepower. Indeed, during the truce Israel imported a significant number of rifles, machine-guns, armoured cars, field-guns, tanks and ammunition, despite the UN embargo. Consequently when fighting resumed on 8 July, Israel started to make its first territorial gains, including seizing the town of Nazareth. By December Israel controlled most of Galilee, and its forces had crossed into Lebanon in the north and broken the Egyptian blockade in the Negev in the south.

In January 1949, when it became clear that the Arabs would not win the war, armistice negotiations began on the island of Rhodes under UN auspices. First Egypt, then Lebanon, Jordan and Syria concluded agreements with Israel. On the territorial side both Israel and the Arab states gained. Israel increased its territory by 21 per cent and gained a contiguous and defensible border. Egypt gained the Gaza Strip and Transjordan the West Bank. The Palestinians, in contrast, lost the territory that they had been allotted under the UN partition plan. An estimated 150,000 Palestinians came under Israeli rule, 450,000 under Transjordan and 200,000 under Egypt. Between 750,000 and 800,000 Palestinians had become refugees at the end of 1948, dispossessed and homeless. While the territorial gains were perceived as a clear benefit, the armistice agreements left the political situation unsettled in many ways. The Arabs had lost the war and with it a considerable amount of prestige. This blow to their legitimacy had a destabilizing effect, leading to military coups, social ferment and revolution. The victor, Israel, fared only marginally better. It had failed to gain what it needed most: recognition and legitimacy in the eyes of its neighbours. Thus it was only a matter of time before what was referred to as 'no-war no-peace' turned once again into war.

see Map 5.2

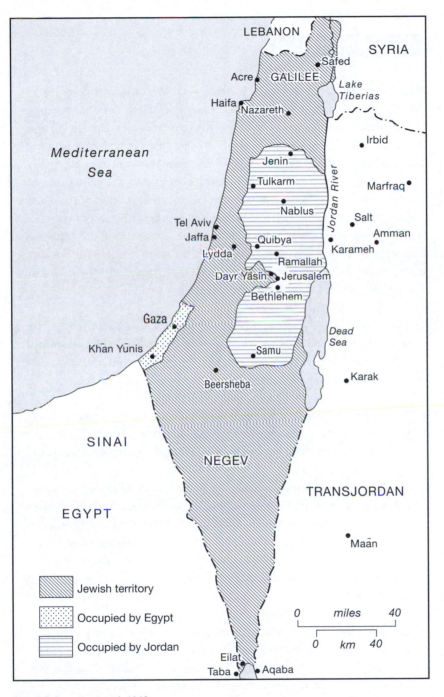

Map 5.2 Post-war Israel, 1948

Source: After Schulze (1999)

naqba (Arabic: disaster)
Term for the Palestinian
experience in the 1947–49
Arab–Israeli war, alluding to
the Arab defeat and the
Palestinian refugee situation.

Debating the 1948 war

The 1948 Arab – Israeli War, known by Israelis as the War of Independence and by Palestinians as *al-naqba* (the disaster), has become the subject of a heated historiographical debate. This war has been described in conventional Israeli historiography as the heroic struggle of a weak and embattled infant nation rising from the ashes of the Holocaust to fight against the overwhelming odds of Arab numeric superiority, British collusion with the Arabs, lack of international support, an unjustly imposed arms embargo and the blockade of Palestine. Like the biblical victory of David over Goliath, Israel's victory has been portrayed as a miracle, becoming part and parcel of Israel's national discourse. Since the opening of new archives in the late 1980s, this account of the 1948 war has been challenged by the so-called 'new historians' such as Avi Shlaim (1988), Benny Morris (1987), Ilan Pappé (1994 and 1999) and Simha Flapan (1987) with respect to six specific areas:

1 *The role of the United Kingdom*. Traditional historians have argued that the British were anti-Zionist and pro-Arab as evidenced by their handover of many of their military installations in Palestine to the Arab Legion. Revisionist historians assert that British policy was neither anti-Zionist nor pro-Palestinian but determined by their support for the Hashemite Kingdom of Transjordan.

2 *Israel's victory*. According to the new historians it was not a miracle but the result of a favourable military balance. With the exception of the first phase of the war, Israel's forces were better trained, better equipped, better motivated, better organized and better armed.

3 *The Palestinian refugee problem*. Israeli traditionalists claim that the Palestinians left of their own accord and thus Israel bears no responsibility for the refugee problem, while Arab historians have traditionally asserted that the Palestinians were expelled and consequently have the right to return. Israeli revisionists have added a further dimension to this politically charged debate, stating that there is no evidence of Arab broadcasts that encouraged the Palestinians to leave or of blanket expulsion orders. Instead, the refugee problem was the result of the war, of the protracted bitter fighting, and fear.

4 *Israeli – Jordanian relations*. These became the subject of controversy when 'new' historians maintained that the Zionists had colluded with King Abdullah between 1947 and 1949 by agreeing to divide Palestine between Israel and Jordan, thus depriving the Palestinians of a state. Such collusion, of course, challenges the image of Israel as a nation without allies and with only hostile Arab neighbours. It also shows that Abdullah had few qualms about betraying his fellow Arabs, in general, and the Palestinians, in particular, when he could expand Jordanian territory and influence.

5   *Arab war aims.* The traditional account of the Arab fighting against Israel has focused on the claim that the goal was to destroy the fledgling Jewish state totally. While this is supported by the rhetoric coming from the Arab camp, new research has shown that the Arabs were far less united than has been assumed. In fact, each of the Arab states was far more concerned with increasing its own influence and gaining control over the territory allotted to the Palestinians under the partition plan, so much so that the result was a general 'land grab' rather than the liberation of Palestine.

6   *The search for peace.* It has often been asserted that the lack of peace following the 1948 war was the result of Arab intransigence. Revisionists, however, have shown that Israel was equally intransigent when it came to making the compromises necessary for peace.

Conclusion

The origins and the causes of the Arab–Israeli conflict cannot be separated from the historical developments of the late nineteenth and early twentieth centuries. The emergence of modern nationalist movements based on the values of the Enlightenment, such as equality and citizenship, and the dismemberment of the Ottoman Empire after the First World War as part of the emerging process of **decolonization**, set in motion the quest for independence and statehood for both Arabs and Zionists. Developments in Europe added urgency to the Zionist project which, in turn, increased the need for an Arab response. The quest for statehood was further propelled by the introduction into the public discourse of the idea of self-determination with Wilson's **fourteen points**, the League of Nations and later the UN. In Palestine both nationalist movements started to compete with each other from the turn of the century onwards, eventually clashing over claims to the same territory. This competition gave rise to a distinctly Palestinian nationalism separate from Arab nationalism. However, compared with the Zionist movement, the Palestinian nationalist movement was clearly disadvantaged as it was highly factionalized and intensely personal and lacked the European tradition of state-building. As a result, when in May 1948 the Zionists established the state of Israel in the territory allocated to the Jews by the 1947 UN partition plan, the Palestinian quest for statehood remained tied to the hope that the Arabs would liberate them – only for this to be dashed by Arab disunity and the Israeli military victory.

decolonization
The process whereby an imperial power gives up its formal authority over its colonies.

fourteen points
A speech made by the American president Woodrow Wilson on 8 January 1918 in which he set out his vision of the post-war world. It included references to open diplomacy, self-determination and a post-war international organization.

Recommended reading

The best accounts of the early phase of the Arab–Zionist conflict over Palestine are generally found in books covering the whole of the Arab–Israeli conflict. By far the most comprehensive and objective history is Mark Tessler, *History of the Israeli–Palestinian Conflict* (Bloomington, IN, 1994). Shorter versions of the same material and useful particularly for newcomers to the subject include T. G. Fraser, *The Arab–Israeli Conflict* (New York, 1995), Charles D. Smith, *Palestine and the Arab–Israeli Conflict* (New York, 1996), Kirsten E. Schulze, *The Arab–Israeli Conflict* (London, 1999) and Don Peretz, *Library in a Book: The Arab–Israel Dispute* (New York, 1996).

The development towards a distinctly Palestinian nationalism is discussed by Yehoshua Porath in his books *The Emergence of the Palestinian Arab Nationalist Movement, 1918–1929* (London, 1974) and *The Palestinian Arab National Movement 1929–1939: From Riots to Rebellion* (London, 1977) as well as in Muhammad Y. Muslih, *The Origins of Palestinian Nationalism* (New York, 1988), while the effects of key personalities such as Hajj Amin al-Husayni and events such as the Arab Revolt upon Palestinian nationalism are extremely well analysed by Philip Matar, *The Mufti of Jerusalem: Al-Hajj Amin al-Husayni and the Palestinian National Movement* (New York, 1988). Two worthwhile books looking at the shortcomings of Palestinian leaders and society are Ann Mosely Lesch, *Arab Politics in Palestine, 1917–1939: The Frustration of a National Movement* (Ithaca, NY, 1979) and Issa Khalaf, *Politics in Palestine: Arab Factionalism and Social Disintegration, 1939–1948* (Albany, NY, 1991). Finally, useful sections on Palestinian identity and leaders can also be found in Joel S. Migdal, *Palestinian Society and Politics* (Princeton, NJ, 1980), Pamela Ann Smith, *Palestine and the Palestinians, 1876–1983* (London, 1984), Rashid Khalidi, *Palestinian Identity: The Construction of Modern National Consciousness* (New York, 1997) and Baruch Kimmerling and Joel S. Migdal, *The Palestinian People: A History* (Cambridge, MA, 2003).

While books on Palestinian nationalism are relatively few, books on Zionism are comparatively numerous. The better general histories of the intellectual roots and developments include Shlomo Avineri, *The Making of Modern Zionism: The Intellectual Origins of the Jewish State* (New York, 1981), Walter Lacqueur, *A History of Zionism: From the French Revolution to the Establishment of the State of Israel* (New York, 1972) and David Vital, *The Origins of Zionism* (Oxford, 1975), David Vital, *Zionism: The Formative Years* (Oxford, 1982) and also his *Zionism: The Critical Phase* (Oxford, 1987). Interesting additions to the general literature include Jehuda Reinharz and Anita Shapira (eds), *Essential Papers on Zionism* (London, 1996), which comprises a wide range of essays on specific turning points in Zionist history from different historiographical perspectives, Anita Shapira's in-depth analysis of the defensive ethos in Zionism in her book *Land and Power: The Zionist Resort to Force* (Stanford, CA, 1992) and Mitchell Cohen, *Zion and State: Nation, Class and the Shaping of Modern Israel* (Oxford, 1987), which looks at the struggle between the Zionist Left and Right. Further insightful works on Zionism and the history of the emerging Jewish state include Howard Sachar, *A History of Israel: From the Rise of Zionism to our Time* (New York, 1979), Bernard Reich, *Israel: Land of Tradition and Conflict* (Boulder, CO, 1985), Michael Wolffson, *Israel: Polity, Society and Economy, 1882–1986* (Atlantic Highlands, NJ, 1987) and Noah Lucas, *The Modern History of Israel* (New York, 1975).

Arab–Jewish relations are addressed in Neil Caplan, *Palestine Jewry and the Arab Question, 1917–1925* (London, 1978), *Futile Diplomacy*, vol. I: *Early Arab–Zionist Negotiation Attempts, 1913–1931* (London, 1983) and also his *Futile Diplomacy*, vol. II: *Arab–Zionist Negotiations and the End of Mandate* (London, 1986), Yosef Gorny, *Zionism and the Arabs, 1882–1948: A Study of Ideology* (New York, 1987) and Neville J. Mandel, *The Arabs and Zionism before World War I* (Berkeley, CA, 1976).

There are only a very small number of books that deal solely with the important issue of land acquisition, sales and ownership as well as rural development. The three books worth recommending in this category are Kenneth Stein, *The Land Question in Palestine, 1917–1939* (Chapel Hill, NC, 1984), Gershon Shapir's revisionist book, *Land, Labor and the Origins of the Israeli–Palestinian Conflict, 1882–1914* (Cambridge, 1989), and Warwick P. N. Taylor's book, *State, Lands and Rural Development in Mandate Palestine, 1920–1948* (Brighton, 2007).

British policy in Palestine is discussed by Nicholas Bethell, *The Palestine Triangle: The Struggle between the British, the Jews and the Arabs, 1935–1948* (London, 1979) and Bernard Wasserstein, *The British in Palestine: The Mandatory Government and the Arab–Jewish Conflict, 1917–1929* (London, 1978). A comprehensive analysis of British policy during the Second World War can be found in Ronald Zweig, *Britain and Palestine during the Second World War* (Suffolk, 1986) while Michael Cohen focuses on the final phase of the mandate in *Palestine – Retreat from the Mandate: The Making of British Policy, 1936–1945* (London, 1978). Two of the more interesting aspects of the British mandate are the Jewish Revolt and illegal Jewish immigration. A good book on the former is David A. Charters, *The British Army and Jewish Insurgency in Palestine, 1945–1947* (New York, 1989) while books on the Jewish paramilitary organizations include Munya M. Mardor, *Haganah* (New York, 1964) and J. Bowyer Bell, *Terror out of Zion: Irgun Zvai Leumi, LEHI and the Palestinian Underground, 1929–1949* (New York, 1977). For an insider's view, Menachem Begin, *Revolt: Story of the Irgun* (New York, 1951) is recommended. On the subject of illegal immigration, useful books include David Kimche's very readable account *The Secret Roads: The 'Illegal' Migration of a People, 1938–1948* (New York, 1955) as well as Ze'ev Venia Hadari, *Second Exodus: The Full Story of Jewish Illegal Immigration to Palestine, 1945–1948* (London, 1991). By far the most academic study of this subject which sets immigration in a broader context is Dina Porat, *The Blue and Yellow Stars of David: The Zionist Leadership in Palestine and the Holocaust, 1939–1945* (Cambridge, 1990).

The period of the end of the mandate has been attractive to both diplomatic and regionalist historians, most of whom have focused on Palestine as a reflection of the decline of Britain and the rise of the United States. Good works on this subject are Zvi Ganin, *Truman, American Jewry and Israel, 1945–1948* (New York,

1979), Evan M. Wilson, *Decision on Palestine: How the US Came to Recognize Israel* (Stanford, CA, 1979), Michael Cohen, *Palestine and the Great Powers, 1945–1948* (Princeton, NJ, 1982), W. Roger Louis, *The British Empire and the Middle East, 1945–1951: Arab Nationalism, the United States and Postwar Imperialism* (Oxford, 1984) and W. Roger Louis and Robert W. Stookey, *The End of the Palestine Mandate* (Austin, TX, 1986).

Finally, the emergence of the state of Israel and first Arab–Israeli war has become a battlefield among historians. Joseph Heller looks at the emergence of the Jewish state by focusing on its key architect, Ben Gurion, in *Birth of Israel, 1945–1949: Ben Gurion and his Critics* (Gainesville, FL, 2000). Good histories of the war are Uri Milstein, *History of Israel's War of Independence* (Lanham, MD, 1997) and David Tal, *War in Palestine, 1948: Strategy and Diplomacy* (London, 2004). Palestinian historians have focused on the loss of state and the refugee crisis. They include Walid Khalidi, *All that Remains: The Palestinian Villages Occupied and Depopulated by Israel in 1948* (Washington, DC, 1992) and Nur Masalha, *Expulsion of the Palestinians: The Concept of 'Transfer' in Zionist Political Thought, 1882–1948* (London, 1992). The period of 1947–48 has also been the target of Israeli revisionist historians. Important contributions are Benny Morris, *The Birth of the Palestinian Refugee Problem, 1947–1949* (Cambridge, 1987), Simha Flapan, *The Birth of Israel: Myths and Realities* (New York, 1987), Avi Shlaim, *Collusion across the Jordan: King Abdullah, the Zionist Movement, and the Partition of Palestine* (Oxford, 1988), Ilan Pappé, *The Making of the Arab–Israeli Conflict, 1947–1951* (London, 1994), Ilan Pappé (ed.), *The Israel/Palestine Question* (London, 1999), Eugene Rogan and Avi Shlaim (eds), *War for Palestine: Rewriting the History of 1948* (Cambridge, 2002) and Ilan Pappé, *Ethnic Cleansing of Palestine* (Oxford, 2006). Revisionism has not just been the domain of Israeli historians. Important Palestinian contributions include Issa Khalaf, *Politics in Palestine: Arab Factionalism and Social Disintegration, 1939–1948* (Albany, NY, 1991) and Salim Tamari and Elia Zureik, *Reinterpreting the Historical Record: The Uses of Palestinian Refugee Archives for Social Science Research and Policy Analysis* (Jerusalem, 2001).

CHAPTER SIX

'Good neighbors'? The United States and the Americas, 1900 – 45

Introduction

In the last quarter of the nineteenth century the Western Hemisphere appeared far removed from the centre of international relations. Having removed the yoke of European imperialism in the late eighteenth and early nineteenth centuries (with some exceptions, most notably Canada), the countries of North, Central and South America had played a minor role in the rivalries between the European Powers. Even the United States was too preoccupied with its own continental expansion and Civil War (1861–65) to pay much attention to the old continent, let alone Asia or Africa. Yet, as the century drew to a close, the United States emerged as an increasingly influential player in international affairs. During the first half of the twentieth century that role would be secured and enhanced to the point that, in 1945, the United States became the most powerful nation on earth.

In retrospect this seems hardly an accident. Already at the turn of the century the United States was, by any economic, geographic or population measure, one of the **Great Powers**. It had a population of more than 75 million in 1900, a domestic marketplace that stretched from the Atlantic to the Pacific (and north to Alaska), and an increasingly influential position in the world's financial markets. A key ingredient in the growth of American power was its ability to utilize, almost

Great Powers
Traditionally those states that were held capable of shared responsibility for the management of the international order by virtue of their military and economic influence.

at will, not only its own remarkable material resources but those of its southern neighbours as well. This unquestioned American dominance of the Western Hemisphere in the first half of the twentieth century is the central theme of this chapter. It will highlight the ways in which the United States penetrated deeply into Latin American, and particularly Central American and Caribbean, affairs.

This influence was obvious in two major ways. First, the United States was willing to use its military force – both the navy and the marines – to exercise its will upon, and even run a number of, Latin American countries. Second, the Americans dominated – and ultimately exploited – the Western Hemisphere economically through investment and ownership that effectively made American companies and individuals the key proprietors of Latin American resources.

A third aspect that this chapter will explore is the impact of world events and ideological debates on the specific means by which the United States exercised its dominance. In particular, the chapter will explore how American interventionism, while always present, needed to be justified and modified depending on the mood of the nation and the potential for alienating friends in the rest of the world. In short, while Americans dominated the Western Hemisphere, they would at times go to great pains to justify this dominance by invoking altruistic principles. This was particularly evident during the Democratic administrations of Woodrow Wilson and Franklin Roosevelt. For example, in the 1930s, when it was reluctant to intervene militarily, Washington looked to other means than 'gunboat diplomacy' to maintain its dominance, particularly after Roosevelt declared his **'Good Neighbor'** Policy in 1933. The result was a drive to develop joint decision-making under the rubric of **pan-Americanism**. Yet, as will be argued, the goals of the 'Good Neighbor' policy and pan-Americanism were ultimately not very different from those of, say, the overt American interventions that had been launched in the Caribbean during the 1920s.

The Monroe Doctrine and the imperial thrust

The **Monroe Doctrine** is undoubtedly the most hallowed – and longest lasting – of America's foreign policy doctrines. Pronounced initially by President James Monroe in a speech to Congress on 2 December 1823, the doctrine – mainly a product of Secretary of State (and later President) John Quincy Adams's thinking – had three key parts. First, Monroe stated that the various parts of the Western Hemisphere were no longer 'to be considered as subjects for further colonization by any European Powers'. Second, the Monroe Doctrine stressed the differences that existed between the political systems of Europe (monarchies) and the Western Hemisphere (democratic republics). Third, in return for the non-intervention of European Powers in the Western Hemisphere, the United States would not interfere in European affairs. Given the context of 1823 it was a bold statement; after all the United States, although it had recently acquired Florida from Spain, was militarily no match for the major Powers of Europe. While the Monroe

---

Good Neighbor Policy
A diplomatic policy introduced in 1933 by President Franklin D. Roosevelt, which was designed to encourage friendly relations and mutual defence among the nations of the Western Hemisphere after decades of American military interventionism.

pan-Americanism
The movement towards commercial, social, economic, military and political co-operation among the nations of North, Central and South America.

Monroe Doctrine
The doctrine declared by President James Monroe in 1823 in which he announced that the United States would not tolerate intervention by the European Powers in the affairs of the Western Hemisphere.

Doctrine remained, at the time of its proclamation, a doctrine that held little practical consequence, it did, however, emerge as a justification for growing American involvement in the affairs of its neighbours to the south. At the same time, the Monroe Doctrine lost much of its original 'democratic' message and became, in the eyes of many South and Central Americans, a smokescreen for a new kind of colonialism directed from Washington.

As the United States completed its westward expansion in the last decades of the nineteenth century and embarked on unprecedented economic growth, the debate about America's role in the world began to go beyond the confines of the Western Hemisphere. As the United States acquired bases in Hawaii, and as influential Americans pushed for Congress to support the financing of the Panama Canal, it became clear that the anti-imperialist and isolationist tradition was facing a growing challenge from those arguing for an expansionist foreign policy. By the 1890s disagreements between the so-called imperialists and anti-imperialists dominated the domestic debate about foreign policy.

The imperialists drew on some of the most popular ideas of their time. One influential historian, Brooks Adams, advanced the notion of **social Darwinism** by simply declaring that among nations, as among animals and plants, the principle of 'the survival of the fittest' applied. Hence, Adams maintained in his 1895 book *The Law of Civilization and Decay* that if the United States did not continue its expansion in the new century, it would enter a period of decline. This belief was reinforced by popular theories about racial inequality and the 'inherent superiority' of the English-speaking peoples; it was America's 'Manifest Destiny', John Fiske declared in the 1890s, to expand the 'blessings' of Anglo-Saxon civilization. Another historian, Frederick Jackson Turner, in 1893 warned about the negative impact that the loss of a continental frontier – a wilderness to be tamed – would have on the American character; the Americans needed future frontiers to conquer to set them apart from the rest of the world.

While such ideas undoubtedly had their impact, economic arguments were equally important in persuading many Americans of the need for overseas expansion. In the last quarter of the nineteenth century exports constituted about 7 per cent of the national output; when a sudden economic downturn hit the United States in 1893 the remedy, many industrialists argued, was to sell more abroad. Two problems stood in the way. First, in Europe **protectionism** reigned and threatened to cut the United States off from lucrative continental markets. Second, at the height of imperialism in the 1880s and 1890s, the Europeans transferred their protectionism to cover much of the rest of the world. Of particular interest to Americans was China, which was viewed, already in the 1890s, as holding the key to future prosperity. Thus, the United States needed, many argued, to make sure that it was not cut off from access to the Chinese market.

America's leading naval strategist, Alfred T. Mahan, presented another argument for overseas expansion. As early as 1890 Mahan argued that the United States had to look at the world's seas as being vital to America's prosperity and security; hence he advocated the building of a strong navy, additional investment in a vast merchant marine and, perhaps most significantly, the acquisition of

social Darwinism
A nineteenth-century theory, inspired by Charles Darwin's theory of evolution, which argued that the history of human society should be seen as 'the survival of the fittest'. Social Darwinism was the backbone of various theories of racial and especially 'white' supremacy.

protectionism
The practice of regulating imports through high tariffs with the purpose of shielding domestic industries from foreign competition.

overseas bases that could be used to protect American interests which, he argued, had become global.

Thus, the intellectual underpinnings of expansionism drew on numerous sources. At the time, in the 1890s, they still ran into strong opposition from those who viewed **isolationism** as a better way to protect American interests and democracy in a world that was still ruled mostly by imperialist monarchies. The anti-expansionist cause was, however, increasingly on the defensive and, to many, out of date. As the new century approached, the majority of influential Americans were ready to support US entry into world affairs. All they needed was a suitable pretext.

isolationism
The policy or doctrine of isolating one's country by avoiding foreign entanglements and responsibilities. Popular in the United States during the inter-war years.

The Spanish–American War

The event that most clearly thrust the United States into its new role as a Great Power was the Spanish–American War of 1898, which was fought mainly over the issue of who controlled the Philippines and Cuba, both long-standing Spanish colonies. By the late nineteenth century the ability of Spain to hold on to these possessions had become increasingly stretched as independence movements challenged its authority. In Cuba, an island whose close proximity to the United States made it a constant source of interest to Washington throughout the twentieth century, the Spanish had been able to put down a decade-long revolt in 1878. However, starting in 1895 the Cuban independence fighters, led by José Martí's Cuban Revolutionary Party, which had established its headquarters in New York in 1892, mounted a serious challenge. After a period of official neutrality, the United States eventually declared war on Spain in April 1898 following the explosion of an American battleship (*Maine*) in Havana harbour two months earlier.

Known as the 'Splendid Little War', the Spanish–American War lasted only four months. It clearly exposed the weakness of the Spanish Empire and resulted in the American acquisition of the Philippines (with a $20 million nominal payment to Spain), Puerto Rico and Guam. As a result, the United States became a major Pacific Power and acquired bases that satisfied both the navalists and those calling for it to gain a foothold in the Chinese market. In addition, the United States naturally strengthened its hold over the Caribbean region by effectively controlling the now nominally independent Cuba. After the Spanish–American War, comments about the Caribbean as 'an American lake' were not far from reality.

These imperial acquisitions did not come without a hefty price. Indeed, the Filipinos, under the leadership of Emilio Aguinaldo, rejected the transfer of their country from Spain to the United States, and a prolonged guerrilla war erupted in February 1899. Over the next three years, American forces fought in a far more ferocious campaign than the one they had just concluded against the Spaniards. Atrocities – including the torture of captured Filipino guerrillas – became commonplace in a conflict that cost the lives of 4,200 Americans and thousands of Filipinos. Eventually American forces were successful and William Howard Taft, the future president, took over as governor of America's largest colony.

The rise of an American empire at the turn of the century also prompted a debate in the United States about the nature of its foreign policy and how such moves as the acquisition of the Philippines could be justified. The so-called anti-imperialists, headed in the 1900 presidential campaign by the Democratic candidate William Jennings Bryan, protested against the acquisition of overseas territories as a betrayal of the nation's traditions. The imperialists, meanwhile, used a whole set of arguments to defend their position, ranging from invoking the 'white man's burden' to pointing to the need to prevent the European imperial Powers from stepping into the power vacuum left behind by Spain's decay. As William McKinley convincingly defeated Bryan in the 1900 presidential elections, it appeared that the imperialists had received a popular mandate for expansionism. And yet, as later events were to show, American imperialism in the twentieth century was to be very different from that of the Europeans. In fact, already in 1901 a special Congressional Commission recommended that the Philippines should be not formally absorbed into the United States, but granted independence after an undetermined period of American rule.

Theodore Roosevelt and the American empire

If any one man symbolized the new American imperial experiment it was Theodore Roosevelt. Thrust into the presidency in 1901 after McKinley's assassination, Roosevelt welcomed the possibility of exploiting the new opportunities created by the Spanish–American War. A firm believer in his nation's 'right' to play a major role in world affairs, Roosevelt considered it 'incumbent on all civilized and orderly powers to insist on the proper policing of the world'. As a follower of the doctrines of Mahan and a true social Darwinist, Roosevelt pursued policies destined to expand American influence in the Caribbean and the Pacific.

In practice, this meant that the Roosevelt administration took the Monroe Doctrine to another level. In late 1903 he engineered the independence of Panama from Colombia, which was followed by a treaty granting the United States the right to a perpetually renewable lease to build and operate the Panama Canal (officially opened in 1914). As a result, the United States acquired a preponderant strategic and commercial position in the Western Hemisphere, particularly in the Caribbean.

In Cuba, where troops remained until 1902, the Roosevelt administration made sure that American interests were guaranteed. In particular, the Cubans were compelled to include in their new constitution the so-called **Platt Amendment**, which gave Washington the right to intervene in Cuban affairs should its 'independence' be threatened from outside or its internal order be jeopardized. In addition, to facilitate potential intervention, the Americans established a

Platt Amendment
Introduced by Orville H. Platt, an American senator (1879–1905), the Platt Amendment to the Cuban Constitution stipulated the conditions for American intervention in Cuban affairs and permitted the United States to lease a naval base in Cuba (Guantanamo Bay). The United States subsequently intervened in Cuban affairs in 1906, 1912, 1917 and 1920. The Platt Amendment was abrogated in 1934, although the United States has retained its naval base in Guantanamo Bay.

protectorates
Territories administered by an imperial state without full annexation taking place, and where delegated powers typically remain in the hands of a local ruler or rulers. Examples include French Morocco and the unfederated states in Malaya.

Roosevelt Corollary (to the Monroe Doctrine)
Unveiled by President Theodore Roosevelt in 1904, the Roosevelt Corollary to the Monroe Doctrine asserted that the United States had the right to intervene in the affairs of an American republic threatened with seizure or intervention by a European country.

open door
The maintenance in a certain territory of equal commercial and industrial rights for the nationals of all countries. As a specific policy, it was first advanced by the United States in the late nineteenth century as a way of safeguarding American economic interests in China.

see Chapter 3

permanent base in Guantanamo Bay. Until Fidel Castro's successful revolution in the late 1950s Cuba effectively remained an American **protectorate**, despite its nominal independence.

In 1904 Roosevelt made the American dominance over, and right to intervene in, the Western Hemisphere open national policy by extending the Platt Amendment beyond Cuba. The so-called **Roosevelt Corollary** to the Monroe Doctrine stipulated that the United States would act as a 'policeman' in the Caribbean. American forces would intervene – 'however reluctantly' as Roosevelt, not devoid of a morbid sense of humour, put it – in cases where Caribbean states were threatened by internal or external dangers. The following year the United States put the Roosevelt Corollary into practice by taking over the finances of the Dominican Republic. In 1912 a similar intervention in Nicaragua was backed up – owing to internal Nicaraguan discontent – by the sending in of American marines. It was the beginning of two decades of American gunboat diplomacy in the Caribbean.

Roosevelt and his successors used two key arguments to justify the extension of direct American control over the Caribbean. First, Roosevelt in particular believed that the threat of German intervention in the Western Hemisphere was real and would jeopardize America's national interests as characterized in the Monroe Doctrine. Equally important, however, American intervention in the Caribbean was tied to its increasing investment in the region. For example, firms such as the United Fruit Company (UFCO) became extensive landowners in Central America while investment in the Cuban sugar plantations grew by about 400 per cent in the decade following the Platt Amendment. Indeed, as was to be the case throughout much of the twentieth century, American security and economic interests were closely tied together in Central America in the years preceding the First World War.

The United States also had strong economic and strategic interests in the Pacific. The American network of bases and acquisitions included – in addition to the Philippines and Hawaii – Samoa, Guam and Midway. However, in contrast to the position in the Caribbean, the United States found that its efforts to project its naval power into the west Pacific and China provoked opposition from a number of rivals, including Britain, Germany, France, Japan and Russia. In particular, the United States faced firm opposition to its attempt to secure a stake in the Chinese market. At the end of the nineteenth century China had been carved into spheres of influence by the rival imperial Powers. As a latecomer to this race and, at least in theory, a 'conscientious objector' to European-style imperialism, in 1899 Secretary of State John Hay circulated the first '**open door**' note, calling for equal access to the Chinese market. Unfortunately for the image of a 'different kind of imperialist', however, the United States joined the imperial Powers in suppressing the Chinese nationalists during the so-called Boxer Rebellion of 1900. To distinguish it from the pack, Hay now added a corollary to the 'open door' note, calling for all Powers to respect the integrity of independent China. Over the next few years the concept of the 'open door' exercised considerable influence over the imperial Powers' dealings with China, but it also led to a chasm opening up in Japanese–American relations with unfortunate consequences for the future.

By the start of the First World War, the United States was a strong regional and an emerging world power. To be sure, the lure of the Chinese market had proved elusive, and while the United States had experienced a series of triumphs in acquiring overseas bases, the profits from such ventures had been small and the liabilities more than a little onerous. At the same time, however, it had been able to secure its hold on the Western Hemisphere and effectively make the Caribbean into an American lake. On balance, as Europe descended into the madness of war, the Americans were powerful, secure and prosperous in their region of the globe. Nor did they have any intention of letting such a position evaporate.

Woodrow Wilson, the First World War and the Americas

If Theodore Roosevelt typified the hard-nosed *realpolitik* outlook in American foreign policy, Woodrow Wilson, who defeated Roosevelt in the 1912 presidential elections, exemplified the missionary and moralistic impulse that would resonate heavily in American rhetoric throughout the twentieth century. A well-known political scientist, former president of Princeton University, and the governor of New Jersey at the time of his election, Wilson was the first Democrat to assume the presidency in the twentieth century. His domestic programme, New Freedom – in contrast to Roosevelt's New Nationalism – was mainly aimed at solving domestic problems and included a strong states-rights (as opposed to strong federal government) agenda, low tariffs and an end to special privilege. A moralist to a fault, Wilson relished public speaking and was extremely intolerant of his critics. In contrast to his Republican predecessors, however, Wilson had little experience in foreign affairs. Yet it was foreign policy that presented Wilson with his toughest challenges as he tried to take his message of reform to the outside world. The problem was that the realities and pressures that Wilson had to contend with at home and abroad did not match his noble dreams. As a result, Wilson found himself engaging in a series of reversals during his eight-year presidency.

In Latin America, Wilson had the grand notion of abandoning the aggressive gunboat diplomacy that had, in the year of his election to the presidency, been symbolized by the dispatching of marines to Nicaragua. In a major speech in October 1913 Wilson captured his high-minded ideals by claiming that 'the United States will never again seek one additional foot of territory by conquest'. Instead, Wilson maintained, the United States

> will devote herself to showing that she knows how to make honorable and fruitful use of the territory she has, and she must regard it as one of the duties of friendship to see that from no quarter are material interests made superior to human liberty and national opportunity.

In short, the protection of American economic and strategic interests in Latin America by force seemed to have little room in Wilson's version of the Monroe Doctrine.

The reality turned out to be very different. At the time that Wilson delivered this speech, Mexico, the United States' closest neighbour to the south, was in a vortex of revolution that had begun in 1911 when the dictatorship of Porfirio Diaz had been overthrown. The new president, Francisco Madero, had, apparently, been a 'Wilsonian' believer in democracy and constitutional rights, but unfortunately he was killed a month prior to Wilson's inauguration. Victoriano Huerta, the new military dictator, thus became the target of Wilson's wrath and Mexico the first country where the United States intervened in the name of 'good government'. In practice, this meant that Wilson backed Venustiano Carranza's constitutionalist movement, which was based in the northern parts of Mexico. In 1913–14 the United States began selling arms to Carranza's movement and Wilson's secretary of state, William Jennings Bryan, worked to isolate Huerta diplomatically. When this did not work, American troops intervened in April 1914, causing Huerta's government to crumble. By August 1914 Carranza was in control of Mexico City.

The Mexican civil war was, however, far from over and dragged Wilson into a far more complex situation than he had envisioned. Carranza, for one, condemned the intervention as illegitimate and his troops came close to fighting against the Americans. Moreover, already by the end of 1914, Pancho Villa had split with Carranza and challenged his former boss's legitimacy in northern Mexico. As the infighting continued, Villa enraged the Americans by crossing the border into New Mexico in January 1916, prompting another American invasion to capture the illiterate but skilful guerrilla fighter. Despite Mexican demands and repeated engagements between American and Mexican troops, General John J. Pershing's troops remained in Mexico until early 1917. At that point Mexico held elections and ratified a new constitution, and consequently the United States officially recognized the Carranza government. The intervention, however, left behind a strong anti-American sentiment and did little to persuade the Mexicans that Wilson's election had meant an end to strong-arm tactics in America's dealings with its southern neighbours.

In fact, under the cloak of moral diplomacy, Woodrow Wilson intervened in the Caribbean even more than his Republican predecessors had done. In July 1915, after a series of revolutions and counter-revolutions, Wilson ordered the marines to Haiti to restore order. The Americans ended up supervising presidential elections and forcing the new Haitian government to sign a treaty that gave the United States control over the island's customs houses, finances and the military. In effect, the Platt Amendment was extended to Haiti, where the marines remained until 1934. In 1916 the marines landed in the Dominican Republic and remained there for the next eight years under similar terms as in Haiti. In the meantime, the United States continued its occupation of Nicaragua and engineered the election of the pro-American General Emiliano Chamorro to the presidency in 1916. Indeed, as the Europeans fought each other on the old continent, the United States secured its control over the 'American lake' (and over the access routes to the Panama Canal) in a way that hardly fitted the Wilsonian ideas of self-government and constitutionalism. Central Americans thus found their independence limited by the Wilsonian version of the Monroe Doctrine.

Plate 6.1 US marines are led by a guide to look for bandits in Haiti, 1919. (Photo: Time Life Pictures/US Marine Corps/National Archives/Time Life Pictures/Getty Images)

Wilsonian visions defeated

Woodrow Wilson's place in the history books is not, however, defined by his questionable forays into the Caribbean. Rather, it was the idealism and moralism that he tried to project back to the old continent as a result of America's belated intervention into the First World War that has made the term **Wilsonian internationalism** resonate loud in the history of twentieth-century international relations. As in the case of his efforts in Latin America, however, Wilson's high-minded ideals saw no immediate reflection in reality.

When Woodrow Wilson declared war on Germany on 2 April 1917, he committed the United States to a struggle that had started two-and-a-half years earlier. He did so – and Congress supported him – in large part because of the unrestricted German submarine war that had resulted in heavy losses to the merchant marine; on 16–18 March 1917 alone, three American ships were sunk on their way to Britain. Wilson was further prompted by allegations of German efforts to forge an alliance with Mexico in the spring of 1917 and domestic pressure from, among others, former President Theodore Roosevelt. America's entry helped to tilt the balance of the war against Germany, but unfortunately for

Wilsonian internationalism
Woodrow Wilson's notion, outlined in his so-called fourteen points, of trying to create a new world society, which would be governed by the self-determination of peoples, be free from secret diplomacy and wars, and have an association of nations to maintain international justice.

Wilson, it was an intervention that he had promised, during his re-election campaign of 1916, would never take place. Thus, Wilson – who wished to use America's role in Europe's war to dictate the conditions for peace – ultimately found himself fighting an uphill battle at home and abroad.

When Wilson returned home from the Paris Peace Conference with a treaty that had already been stripped of much of its Wilsonian idealism, the president faced another battle with his domestic opponents. Many Republicans objected to Wilson's attempt to get the United States to join a permanent international organization, the **League of Nations**, that Wilson hoped would become an agent of peaceful conflict resolution throughout the world. In a long and bitter fight that was clearly linked to the 1920 elections, the Republicans, headed by Senator Henry Cabot Lodge of Massachusetts, managed to block the ratification of the **Versailles Treaty** and American membership in the League. Wilson, unwilling to accept defeat, engaged in an extended speaking tour of the United States. It was too much for the 63-year-old, who collapsed in Colorado in September 1919 and suffered a severe stroke a few weeks later. While Wilson remained incapacitated throughout the rest of his second term, the Senate rejected the Versailles Treaty in November 1919. The following November, Republican Warren G. Harding – a man who could not be accused of an excess of idealism or a strong interest in foreign affairs – was elected president. The United States thus entered the 'roaring twenties' with Wilsonian internationalism defeated and overt entanglement with Europe rejected. In a sense, one could see the Monroe Doctrine behind Wilson's defeat: in return for European non-intervention in the Western Hemisphere the United States had, after all, guaranteed its non-intervention in the affairs of the old continent.

see Chapter 1

League of Nations
An international organization established in 1919 by the peace treaties that ended the First World War. Its purpose was to promote international peace through collective security and to organize conferences on economic and disarmament issues. It was formally dissolved in 1946.

Versailles Treaty
The treaty that ended the Allied state of hostilities with Germany in 1919. It included German territorial losses, disarmament, a so-called war guilt clause and a demand that reparations be paid to the victors.

From boom to bust

While Americans rejected permanent foreign entanglements in the form of the League of Nations, the United States continued to expand its economic influence throughout the globe. Statistics tell much of the story. In the 1920s the United States produced 70 per cent of the world's petroleum and 40 per cent of its coal, and accounted for 46 per cent of its industrial output. It was the largest exporter in the world (15 per cent of the world's total) and, for the first time, surpassed Britain as the major source of foreign investment. In the fifteen years between the start of the First World War and the beginning of the Great Depression in 1929, American exports doubled and its private investment grew by 500 per cent. According to such statistics, the United States was the world's most powerful nation.

Perhaps most impressive was the fact that this economic expansion was not restricted to any one region in the world. Rubber plantations in Malaya, copper mines in Chile, electric and car companies in Germany, oil companies in the

Middle East and financial investment in England were all part of the American economic expansion of the 1920s. Indeed, the prosperity that characterized the popular image of the 'roaring twenties' in the United States was in part made possible by this unprecedented economic thrust abroad.

Such economic influence did not come without its problems. For example, throughout the 1920s the United States found itself facing external resentment against its own selective use of the 'open door' policy. Effectively it meant that the United States was able to practise a 'closed door' policy in Latin America while preaching an 'open door' principle in Asia (where American companies faced stiff competition). Other countries retaliated by imposing higher tariffs on American products in the late 1920s and early 1930s. They could not have come at a worse time.

Because of its dominant position in the world economy in the 1920s, the Great Depression that hit the United States in 1929 wreaked havoc throughout the world. One often-cited barometer is the mere fact that between 1929 and 1933 the value of world trade declined by about 40 per cent. American exports alone went down from $5.4 billion to $2.1 billion in the same period, while annual external investment slumped by a quarter. This, as well as the political problems that the Depression caused or exacerbated in Europe and Asia, played a major role on the road towards the Second World War. In the United States itself, the Great Depression destroyed the credibility of the Republicans, and allowed Franklin Roosevelt to defeat Herbert Hoover in the 1932 presidential election.

see Chapters 3 and 7

During this boom-and-bust period Latin America was the region in which the economic influence of the United States was most apparent. In Honduras, for example, the United Fruit Company and Standard Fruit Company controlled most of the country's revenue. In Cuba, American companies accounted for approximately two-thirds of sugar production and hence held a stranglehold over the island's economic life, while in Venezuela they produced about half of the country's oil. Moreover, American firms could effectively shape the health of the Chilean economy as a result of their ability to determine the price of copper, Chile's chief export.

Such dominance was, in fact, commonplace throughout Latin America where American private investment almost tripled in the 1920s. In the same period Latin America accounted for about 20 per cent of the total of American exports, while Latin American export markets were far less diversified; Nicaragua, for example, shipped more than 90 per cent of its exports to the United States. In short, Latin America became increasingly dependent on the United States as a source of investment and markets. Unfortunately the profits from this economic activity rarely reached more than a small number of Latin Americans, causing heightened complaints about American domination and imperialism in the 1920s and 1930s. Indeed, with anti-Americanism on the rise, there was a need in Washington to reassess American policy in the Western Hemisphere. Yet there seemed to be no easy replacement for gunboat diplomacy and strict application of the Monroe Doctrine and its various amendments and corollaries.

From gunboat diplomacy to the 'Good Neighbor' Policy

In the anti-interventionist atmosphere of the early 1920s the Republican administrations of the 1920s showed some interest in curbing the American military presence in Nicaragua, the Dominican Republic and Haiti. The Harding (1921–23) and Coolidge (1923–29) administrations were concerned about the negative imperialist image of the United States that was feeding anti-Americanism throughout Latin America. Hence they tried to negotiate an orderly return of American troops from the Caribbean and, in 1924, the Dominican Republic became the first Caribbean nation to see the withdrawal of the marines (although the United States retained its control over the customs receivership of the former protectorate as a way of maintaining its influence). While a plan to bring back troops from Haiti was abandoned when it appeared that this would cause complete anarchy, the marines did leave Nicaragua in August 1925 after orderly national elections. The big stick of military intervention was seemingly being abandoned in favour of the soft stick of economic control.

In 1926, however, the United States reverted to its interventionist pattern in the Caribbean. Some 4,500 marines returned to Nicaragua in the midst of a bloody civil war to aid Adolfo Diaz's pro-American government in its defeat of Juan B. Sacasa's Mexican-supported rebels. Amid widespread criticism President Coolidge's special envoy, Henry Stimson, mediated the Truce of Tipitapa in 1927 leaving Diaz to head an interim coalition government until new elections were held (and supervised by the marines) in 1928. While the marines tried to maintain order and the State Department worked to promote the acceptance of democratic principles, one of Sacasa's generals, Augusto Sandino, continued to wage guerrilla war against the Americans. Unable to catch Sandino – who quickly became a symbol of resistance against American imperialism throughout Latin America – the administration of Herbert Hoover (1929–33) began to withdraw the marines in 1931, with the last contingent leaving Nicaragua in 1933. The following year Sandino was murdered after leaving a negotiating session with the American-supported Nicaraguan government. In 1936 the war-torn nation quickly succumbed to the military dictatorship of Anastasio Somoza, the head of the Nicaraguan National Guard (Guardia Nacional), whose family oligarchy would run the country until 1978.

The Nicaraguan events were symptomatic of the realization in Washington that direct rule in the Caribbean nations created more problems for American interests than it solved. Sandino's successful resistance and eventual murder also indicated that democracy could not be forced upon the Latin American countries and that overt American involvement in their internal affairs did little to support stability in the region. Furthermore, with the Japanese strengthening their position in East Asia and Nazi Germany making threatening noises in Europe, many American policy-makers now felt the need to secure American interests in the Western Hemisphere by supporting local strongmen, who often were, like Somoza, military men.

Indeed, even before Somoza had consolidated his rule over Nicaragua, the Dominican Republic had succumbed to the dictatorship of Raphael Trujillo. Since

see Chapters 3 and 7

1919 Trujillo had been close to the American military and after the marines withdrew in 1924 he played a major role in organizing the National Army under American tutelage. In 1930 he captured the presidency in a highly fraudulent election and, with the help of a strong and well-funded army, ruled the country with an iron grip and generous American support until his assassination in 1961.

In addition to Nicaragua and the Dominican Republic, the new 'strongman' policy found representatives in most countries in Central America and the Caribbean during the 1930s. In Cuba, for example, the United States ended up supporting Sergeant Fulgencio Batista who ruled Cuba from 1934, either as the president or from behind the scenes, until Fidel Castro's revolution forced him to flee the country in 1959. In Haiti, a nation the marines ran from 1915 to 1934, a succession of heavy-handed presidents were supported with generous loans even after President Franklin Roosevelt completed the withdrawal of American troops. Haiti's national finances, however, remained under American control until 1947.

It is perhaps ironic that such military dictators as Somoza, Trujillo and Batista were in the 1930s viewed as showcases of the so-called 'Good Neighbor' Policy that 'the other Roosevelt' – the first Democratic president since Wilson – proclaimed when he took over the White House in 1933. After all, as many American critics pointed out, it was hardly a great achievement of American foreign policy to be good neighbours with brutal rulers whose main accomplishment all too frequently was the ability to create vast personal fortunes while their countrymen lived in poverty. Raphael Trujillo, for one, amassed a fortune worth approximately $800 million while the Dominican Republic remained one of the poorest countries in Latin America. While dodging such embarrassing questions in public, Franklin Roosevelt's private opinion captured the thinking of many. 'He may be an S.O.B.,' Roosevelt reportedly agreed when Trujillo visited the United States in 1939, 'but', he added, 'he's our S.O.B.'

It was a fitting indication of how the theory and practice of Franklin Roosevelt's Latin American policy differed remarkably. Upon taking office Roosevelt had declared his intention to follow

the policy of the good neighbor – the neighbor who resolutely respects himself and, because he does so, respects the rights of others – the neighbor who respects his obligations and respects the sanctity of his agreements in and with a world of neighbors.

As the American experience in Haiti, the Dominican Republic, Nicaragua and elsewhere in Latin America during the 1930s shows, however, the Monroe Doctrine was far from dead, and the spirit of the Platt Amendment and the Roosevelt Corollary lived on. What the Roosevelt administration – and some of its predecessors – discovered was that there were willing opportunists in various Latin American countries who could be used to protect American interests without the physical presence of the marines. Hence the Somozas, the Batistas and the Trujillos could be viewed as the latest representatives of America's pervasive influence south of its border.

see Map 6.1

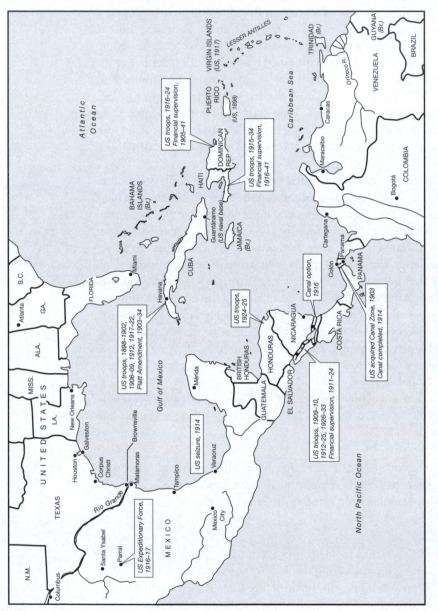

Map 6.1 US interventions in the Caribbean and Central America, 1898–1941

Source: After Paterson, Clifford and Hagan (1999)

The following labels appear on the map:

US Expeditionary Force, 1916–17

US seizure, 1914

US troops, 1898–1902, 1906–09, 1912, 1917–22, Platt Amendment, 1903–34

US troops, 1924–25

US troops, 1916–24 Financial supervision, 1905–41

US troops, 1915–34 Financial supervision, 1916–41

Canal option, 1916

US acquired Canal Zone, 1903 Canal completed, 1914

US troops, 1909–10, 1912–25, 1926–33 Financial supervision, 1911–24

One seeming exception to the indirect American dominance was the compromise reached with Mexico in the late 1930s. Following the American intervention in the 1910s, the most controversial issue that had plagued relations between the two countries was oil. The 1917 Mexican constitution effectively nationalized all mineral resources, including oil, which naturally alarmed companies such as Standard Oil. Only after extended negotiations in which the Mexican government agreed to recognize pre-1917 American property rights did the United States grant Mexico full diplomatic recognition in 1924. However, in 1938 the Mexican president, Lazaro Cardenas, nationalized all property held by foreign oil companies. Despite heavy lobbying from such companies as Standard Oil (which launched a major propaganda offensive in the United States branding Cardenas a communist), the Roosevelt administration did not revert to military intervention. Instead, after long negotiations, the United States in 1941 officially acknowledged Mexico's right to control its raw materials and the Mexican government agreed to pay restitution to those Americans whose property had been nationalized.

Mexico was in many ways a showcase of how far the United States had come from its earlier interventionist policies in Latin America. Indeed, it seemed that the 'Good Neighbor' Policy had clearly marked a turning point for inter-American relations. And yet the change hardly came about merely because non-interventionism seemed to be the right and just approach to take. Behind it lay the troublesome developments in Asia and Europe that – come 7 December 1941 – significantly increased the importance of having good neighbours with plenty of raw materials.

Debating the origins of American interventionism

Most historians would agree that the United States acted in an imperial manner towards Latin America. They disagree, though, on why this was the case. In broad terms, the explanations can be categorized into three groups, each stressing the pre-eminence of economic, security or ideological factors.

For those historians who emphasize economic considerations, the Monroe Doctrine and interventionism in Latin America are largely efforts to secure access to raw materials and markets to assure the growth of the American economy (for example, William A. Williams and Walter Lafeber). Others, like Lester D. Langley or David Healy, have stressed the primacy of national security considerations by pointing to American concerns over German expansionist designs. In the first decades of the twentieth century this new rivalry was particularly evident in the competition over the control of the Panama Canal and was heightened by the emphasis on naval power and the perceived need to establish bases to protect US interests. One should stress, though, that the two explanations often overlap: American economic interests were, often, perceived as central in national security strategy.

The third broad explanation for the growth and maintenance of US influence in Latin America stresses ideological factors. In this context, the debate and controversy – which extend throughout much of the history of American foreign policy – are about both the cause and impact of American policy. Originally, such historians as Samuel Bemis argued that the United States worked hard for the democratization of the Western Hemisphere; that much of American policy was driven by a missionary impulse; and, while the end results were not always what had been intended, the intentions were idealistic and well meaning.

Since the 1960s the 'democratization' school has been discredited. In explaining the persistent support for various dictatorial regimes, these historians point to the essentially racist outlook of much of American society and the assumption, held by many, that the people living in countries south of the United States were simply not ready for democracy. American dominance of the hemisphere was, thus, justified by a social Darwinist outlook that placed the 'Latinos' below the 'Whites' and was, by and large, reflected in the nature of American society (see Michael Hunt, *Ideology and American Foreign Policy*, New Haven, CT, 1987).

In short, the debate over the nature of inter-American relations – and US foreign policy in the Western Hemisphere in particular – offers an array of explanations and theories that touch upon the essence of American foreign policy. Exploring the debate will improve one's understanding not only of the inter-American relationship but also of the American role in the world throughout the twentieth century.

Pan-Americanism and the approach of war

Developments in Asia and Europe were another reason for the American reluctance to intervene directly in the Western Hemisphere in the 1930s. The Japanese attack on Manchuria in 1931 and the full-blown Sino-Japanese War that commenced in 1937 prompted increasing criticism of Japanese imperialism and interventionism throughout the 1930s. In such a climate it would have been supreme hypocrisy to dispatch the marines to protect American trade and strategic interests in Latin America. Equally importantly, though, the protracted crisis with Mexico over its oil resources raised the prospect that Mexico (and potentially other Latin American countries as well) might move towards Fascist Italy and Nazi Germany. Both the European Powers – as well as Japan – did actually increase their oil purchases from Mexico in the late 1930s and early 1940s. The need to improve relations with Latin America was thus intricately tied to the Roosevelt administration's policies towards the outbreak of the Second World War and the growing shift towards the anti-**Axis** cause.

As part of the 'Good Neighbor' Policy the Roosevelt administration thus sought to strengthen the pan-American movement. As early as 1889, an American initiative had led to the creation of the International Bureau of American Republics in Washington, which in 1910 was renamed the Pan-American Union, with its headquarters located near the State Department. While ostensibly designed to promote inter-American unity, in reality the Pan-American Union, chaired as it was by the American secretary of state, was a vehicle for promoting hemispheric trade. At the same time, however, Latin American representatives used its regular meetings as a forum within which to voice their discontent at the assumed right of the United States to intervene in their internal affairs. In the 1920s and 1930s, however, successive American administrations – including the Roosevelt administration at the 1933 Pan-American Conference in Uruguay – held on to this 'right' with a thinly veiled addendum to the various anti-interventionist resolutions. By the late 1930s, though, it was becoming increasingly clear that any American intervention would have to be through other than military means.

As Germans, Italians and even the Japanese increased their economic involvement in Latin America during the late 1930s, pan-Americanism became the latest vehicle for upholding the Monroe Doctrine. With Nazi activists working throughout Latin America (especially in Argentina, Brazil and Uruguay), the US government once again used the threat of an alien (non-democratic) political system to justify the need for hemispheric co-operation. In 1938 the Declaration of Lima endorsed a co-operative spirit of 'the American republics' to resist the influx of external influences. In 1939 the Declaration of Panama went even further by effectively creating a security perimeter around the Western Hemisphere and establishing an economic co-ordination committee. Although the conferees proclaimed their neutrality, the security perimeter was clearly designed to keep the Axis powers out of the American backyard, while the economic committee made it easier for the United States to block Latin American countries from trading with the future enemies.

Between the start of the Second World War in Europe in September 1939 and the American entry into the war in December 1941, the Roosevelt administration gradually inched closer to a partnership with Germany's main adversaries, Britain and (from June 1941) the Soviet Union. In 1940 the United States, in the so-called 'destroyers-for-bases' deal, began supplying Britain with military equipment. Because of strong isolationist sentiment, however, Roosevelt had to be careful about pushing the United States towards war lest he risk losing the 1940 presidential election. Thus, during the campaign, Roosevelt proclaimed that he would never send Americans to fight in a foreign war. However, after his re-election was secured, Roosevelt called upon the United States to become the 'arsenal of democracy', and in 1941 American aid shipments to Britain increased under the so-called **Lend-Lease** scheme; once Germany attacked the Soviet Union in the summer of 1941, this country – which the United States had only

Axis
A term coined originally by Mussolini in November 1936 to describe the relationship between Fascist Italy and Nazi Germany. The German–Italian Axis was reinforced by the so-called Pact of Steel signed by Rome and Berlin in May 1939. More broadly speaking, the term is often used (as in Chapter 8 of this book) to refer to the relationship between Germany, Italy and Japan. These three Powers were formally linked by the German–Japanese Anti-Comintern Pact of November 1936, which Italy signed one year later, and the Tripartite Pact of September 1940.

Lend-Lease
With the Lend-Lease Act of March 1941, the US Congress empowered the president to lease or lend arms and supplies to any foreign government whose defence the administration considered essential to US national security. The programme, originally intended to rescue Britain, was eventually extended to more than thirty-eight states fighting the Tripartite Pact Powers.

recognized less than a decade earlier – was added as another major recipient of American material support. In short, although it was ultimately the Japanese attack on Pearl Harbor on 7 December 1941 and Germany's subsequent declaration of war that formally pulled the United States into the conflict, it was already acting as a non-combatant ally and inevitably – through its strong commercial and political links – pulled its southern neighbours along.

The Second World War and the Monroe Doctrine

When the United States eventually entered the Second World War after the Japanese attack on Pearl Harbor in December 1941, there was, therefore, little question about which side the Latin American republics would join. Already in 1940, as German forces conquered France and the Netherlands, people in the Western Hemisphere had worried about the fate of the small French and Dutch colonies still in the Caribbean. Thus, Washington had invoked the original Monroe Doctrine by informing the Germans that the American government would not allow any transfer of territory in the Western Hemisphere from one European Power to another. The Act of Havana of July 1940 made this into a pan-American principle by declaring that the American republics would occupy any territory that was in danger of being transferred from one external Power to another (virtually unnoticed at the time was Argentina's reservation declaring the Malvinas, or the Falklands Islands, to be part of Argentina, not Britain).

The Germans, in 1940, effectively replied that such a principle would be respected, but only as long as the United States did not intervene in Europe. It was a 'trade-off' that was ignored in Washington at the time but would cause great embarrassment to American policy-makers in the decades to come as critics wondered how the United States could demand non-intervention in the Western Hemisphere while denying other powers the right to declare their 'Monroe Doctrines' in other parts of the world.

During the Second World War such concerns worried relatively few. Helped by its easy access to Latin American raw materials, the United States was able to act as the 'arsenal of democracy', as Roosevelt had called it already in 1940, and, as one of the 'Big Three', it eventually emerged as the most powerful country in the world in 1945. Its neighbours to the south – with the exception of Argentina, which refused to break completely with Germany until less than a month before the end of the European war – found themselves taken for granted as a resource base for the Allied war effort. Indeed, with the end of the war looming in 1945, the United States emerged in a stronger position than ever vis-à-vis the Western Hemisphere for two key reasons: first, the war had made trade with any other part of the world virtually impossible for the Latin Americans, and second, the war had either destroyed (Germany, Japan, Italy) or severely weakened (Britain) the power of those countries that could have presented any semblance of a challenge to American supremacy in the region.

see Chapters 8 and 9

Such obvious American dominance notwithstanding, it would have been difficult for the United States simply to revert to its old pattern of domination and intervention in 1945. One of Roosevelt's favourite themes in planning for a post-war world was the reshaping of the League of Nations into a more effective international organization in which the United States would play a key role. When it came down to translating such internationalism to the Western Hemisphere, however, a clash over internationalism and regionalism was inevitable. In 1919 the opponents of the League of Nations in the United States had insisted that American membership in the League contravened the principles of the Monroe Doctrine. In 1945 the Roosevelt administration was determined to avoid giving such an opposition a leg to stand on.

These issues and the future of inter-American relations in general were discussed in February 1945 at a pan-American conference in Chapultepec, Mexico. By declaring that any attack on any American state was an attack on them all, the Act of Chapultepec represented the first step towards a post-war military alliance in the Western Hemisphere. Indeed, the Act declared that such arrangements would be formalized after the war ended. Later in the year, in San Francisco, all Latin American countries – including Argentina, which had finally declared war on Germany in March 1945 – participated in the formation of the **United Nations (UN)**.

It was in San Francisco that the question over the seeming conflict between regionalism and internationalism – the Monroe Doctrine and the UN – was solved in a way that gave America's hallowed foreign policy doctrine a new lease of life. Originally, the UN and its Security Council were to have strong powers over regional issues. The problem with this for the Monroe Doctrine and American dominance over the Western Hemisphere was obvious. As one member of the American delegation in San Francisco, the future secretary of state John Foster Dulles, put it, having a UN with universal powers would mean that a non-American power such as the USSR or Britain would be given the ability 'to veto American regional action in the Western Hemisphere'. The counter-argument, however, reflected the growing concern over the post-war designs of one of America's key allies in the war. According to Leo Paslovsky, a Russian-born American who was a key adviser on UN matters to the State Department, weakening the UN's ability to play a role in regional affairs 'would be tantamount to throwing all Europe into the hands of the Soviet Union, and would break the world up into regional units'.

After much bargaining and brainstorming both within the delegation and with the other permanent members of the UN Security Council (China, France, Britain and the Soviet Union), the 'regionalists' got their wish. The approved UN Charter included four articles (51–54) that, while not explicitly mentioning Latin America or the Monroe Doctrine, effectively preserved the American ability to exercise preponderant influence in the Western Hemisphere without breaking the rules of the new world organization. That is, the four articles preserved the right of collective regional organizations to solve disputes and revert to individual or collective self-defence. By 1947, with the United States at its helm, the American republics concluded the **Rio Treaty**, a collective defence pact that became the

United Nations (UN)
An international organization established after the Second World War to replace the League of Nations. Since its establishment in 1945, its membership has grown to 192 countries.

Rio Treaty (Inter-American Treaty of Reciprocal Assistance)
Signed on 2 September 1947, and originally ratified by all twenty-one American republics. Under the treaty, an armed attack or threat of aggression against a signatory nation, whether by a member nation or some other power, will be considered an attack against all.

model for many other military alliances formed by the United States in the first decade of the Cold War.

Conclusion

As the Second World War drew to a close, the Western Hemisphere was firmly under the hegemony of the United States. In fact, notwithstanding the 'rebellious' attitude of some countries (e.g. Mexico in the 1930s and Argentina during the early 1940s), Washington had, throughout the five decades after the Spanish–American War, maintained and increased its influence over the affairs of its neighbours to the south. The virtual annexation of Cuba in 1899, the introduction of the Platt Amendment in 1904, the numerous military interventions during the 1910s and 1920s, and even the introduction of the 'Good Neighbor' Policy in the 1930s were all parts of a clear pattern in which north–south dependency was a constant feature. While the quality and style of American assertiveness changed, the reality did not. Hence, the talk of the Caribbean as an 'American lake' was not far from reality. If anything, the Second World War strengthened Latin America's economic dependency on the United States. Most remarkable, in contrast to the various European empires the United States had established its dominance with relatively minor expenditures and casualties. It was an empire on the cheap.

While this may have been the case, 1945 did signify the dawn of a new age in the Western Hemisphere. As the debates over regionalism and universalism showed, the United States was undergoing a fundamental change in its position vis-à-vis the rest of the world. This had important consequences for the structure and meaning of the US-dominated inter-American system. If at the end of the First World War the Monroe Doctrine had been one of the tools that Woodrow Wilson's opponents had used to defeat his aim of taking the United States into the League of Nations, at the end of the Second World War the Monroe Doctrine and the regionalism it represented were under serious threat of becoming a relic. Indeed, in the age of American universalism – a major aspect of the ensuing Cold War – holding on to a sphere of influence was ideologically questionable. As the Soviet Union established its sphere of influence in Eastern Europe, American criticism was easily branded as the height of hypocrisy.

In the midst of the debates over internationalism and regionalism – the UN versus the Monroe Doctrine – one aspect of inter-American relations was strangely absent: Latin American nationalism. Perhaps it was from force of habit, perhaps because Allied victory in the Second World War had seemingly dealt a death-blow to ultra-nationalism of the German, Italian and Japanese variety, but American planners seemed to have little time for considering the possibility that, say, Cuban, Guatemalan, Chilean or Argentinean nationalism could possibly emerge as a significant obstacle to its continued domination over the Western Hemisphere. But, as future events would show, it was just such nationalism, coupled with deep-rooted anti-Americanism, which was to forge the most significant changes in the Western Hemisphere and pose the toughest challenges yet to the colossus of the north after 1945.

Recommended reading

The best general work on American foreign policy during the twentieth century is Thomas G. Paterson, J. Garry Clifford and Kenneth J. Hagan, *American Foreign Policy: A History since 1900* (New York, 1999). For an even more general survey, see Walter LaFeber, *The American Age* (New York, 1989). For a general study on the early twentieth century, see Emily Rosenberg, *Spreading the American Dream* (New York, 1982). One of the most insightful studies of inter-war American foreign policy is Warren I. Cohen, *Empire without Tears* (New York, 1987).

The best general overview of the Western Hemisphere is Thomas E. Skidmore and Peter H. Smith, *Modern Latin America* (New York, 2002). For general works on the United States and Latin America, see Peter H. Smith, *Talons of the Eagle: Dynamics of US–Latin American Relations* (New York, 2000), John H. Coatsworth, *Central America and the United States: The Clients and the Colossus* (New York, 1994), R. H. Holden and E. Zolov, *Latin America and the United States* (New York, 2000), Lars Schoultz, *Beneath the United States: A History of US Policy toward Latin America* (Cambridge, MA, 1998), Lester D. Langley, *The United States and the Caribbean, 1900–1970* (Athens, GA, 1980), Walter LaFeber, *Inevitable Revolutions* (New York, 1983), David Healy, *Drive to Hegemony: The United States in the Caribbean* (Madison, WI, 1989) and Thomas Schoonover, *The United States in Central America, 1860–1911: Episodes in Social Imperialism and Imperial Rivalry in the World System* (Durham, NC, 1991).

Works on the Spanish–American War and the rise of the American empire include David F. Trask, *The War with Spain in 1898* (New York, 1981), David Healy, *US Expansionism* (Madison, WI, 1970), Walter LaFeber, *The New Empire* (Ithaca, NY, 1969), Ernest R. May, *The Imperial Democracy* (New York, 1961), Göran Rystad, *Ambiguous Imperialism* (Stockholm, 1982) and Robert L. Beisner, *From the Old Diplomacy to the New* (Arlington Heights, IL, 1986).

The classic account of Theodore Roosevelt's foreign policy is Howard K. Beale, *Theodore Roosevelt and the Rise of America to World Power* (Baltimore, MD, 1956); for different interpretations see Richard Collin, *Theodore Roosevelt, Culture, Diplomacy, and Expansion* (Baton Rouge, LA, 1985), Thomas Dyer, *Theodore Roosevelt and the Idea of Race* (Baton Rouge, LA, 1980) and William H. Brands, *TR: The Last Romantic* (New York, 1999). Roosevelt and Woodrow Wilson are contrasted in John M. Cooper's *The Warrior and the Priest* (Cambridge, MA, 1983), while Wilson himself is analysed in Arthur S. Link, *Woodrow Wilson, Revolution, War, and Peace* (Arlington Heights, IL, 1979), Lloyd Gardner, *Safe for Democracy* (New York, 1984) and Fredrick S. Calhoun, *Power and Principle: Armed Intervention in Wilsonian Foreign Policy* (Kent, OH, 1986). The Wilson administration's intervention in Mexico is detailed in Mark T. Gilderhus, *Diplomacy and Revolution* (Tucson, AZ, 1977), Friedrich Katz, *The Secret War in Mexico* (Chicago, 1981) and Ramon Ruiz, *The Great Rebellion* (New York, 1980). On Wilson's failed efforts to bring about a 'new world order', see Arthur Walworth, *Wilson and the Peacemakers* (New York, 1986) and Stuart I. Rochester, *American Liberal Disillusionment in the Wake of World War I* (University Park, PA, 1977). The myth of a German threat to US dominance in Central America is effectively exposed in Nancy Mitchell, *The Danger of Dreams: German and American Imperialism in Latin America* (Chapel Hill, NC, 1999).

Gunboat diplomacy and the 'Good Neighbor' Policy in the Caribbean are detailed in Irwin F. Gellman, *Good Neighbor Diplomacy* (Baltimore, MD, 1979), William Kamman, *A Search for Stability: United States Diplomacy toward Nicaragua* (Notre Dame, IN, 1968), Michael Grow, *The Good Neighbor Policy in Paraguay* (Lawrence, KS, 1981), Stephen J. Randall, *The Diplomacy of Modernization: Colombian–American Relations, 1920–1940* (Toronto, 1977), Dana G. Munro, *The United States and the Caribbean Republics, 1921–1933* (Princeton, NJ, 1974), G. Pope Atkins and Larman C. Wilson, *The United States and the Trujillo Regime* (New Brunswick, NJ, 1972) and Randall B. Woods, *The Roosevelt Foreign Policy Establishment and the 'Good Neighbor'* (Lawrence, KS, 1980).

Franklin Roosevelt and the Second World War are the subject of numerous accounts of which the most detailed are Robert Dallek, *Franklin D. Roosevelt and American Foreign Policy, 1932–1945* (New York, 1979), Robert A. Divine, *Roosevelt and World War II* (Baltimore, MD, 1969) and Warren Kimball, *The Juggler* (Princeton, NJ, 1992). For the role of Latin American countries in the Second World War and American policy, see Michael J. Francis, *The Limits of Hegemony* (Notre Dame, IN, 1977), Frank D. McCann, *The Brazilian–American Alliance* (Princeton, NJ, 1973) and Stanley Hilton, *Hitler's Secret War in South America, 1939–1945* (Baton Rouge, LA, 1981).

The path to European
war, 1930 – 39

Introduction

The coming of the Second World War in Europe is the classic morality tale of international politics. The *dramatis personae* are more than flesh-and-blood personalities buffeted by impersonal forces; the principal characters stand for good and evil, light and darkness, with few shades of grey in between. As theatrical conventions require, the stirring plot, which pits peace-loving democracies against war-hungry dictatorships, imparts a timeless lesson – that 'the malice of the wicked [is] reinforced by the weakness of the virtuous'. This quote from Winston Churchill, the figure most responsible for establishing this version of the 1930s, comes from *The Gathering Storm*, the opening volume of his history of *The Second World War*.

For Churchill, the prime mover in world affairs was human agency. The war occurred because statesmen made certain choices – either maliciously calculated or from naively optimistic motives. World war might have been prevented had alternative courses been taken. British and French leaders could have stopped Hitler had they armed more rapidly, stood firm in March 1936 over the Rhineland or in September 1938 over Czechoslovakia, and forged a coalition with Soviet Russia to deter war or, if deterrence failed, to wage it successfully from the start. What is compelling about Churchill's account is that it appeals to our urge to frame the past in the form of a clear-cut narrative that places human agency at the centre of the story.

Yet interpreting the 1930s as a morality tale obscures more than it illuminates. Singling out statesmanship as the key determinant in world politics neglects the way in which material and political circumstances restricted choices. Similarly, to see force as the only true instrument in inter-state relations erases the tangible role played by norms, ideas and values in shaping international structures and national strategies. Giving due weight to these fundamentals of political life throws into sharp relief the moral dimension of what was at stake in the 1930s, without turning the chief personalities into cardboard caricatures of abstract qualities. With these remarks in mind, this chapter will dispute Churchill's view that 'there was never a war more easy to stop' than the Second World War.

The dual crisis

The Depression was the turning point. The collapse of world trade and finance cannot be disentangled from the crisis in world politics. All the profound causes of the war are rooted in the length and severity of the slump: the rise of radical ideologies and exclusive nationalism, the formation of closed economic blocs, the Japanese and Italian challenges to the League of Nations, and the failure of the **Geneva disarmament talks** (1932–34). The mass psychological impact of unemployment, grinding poverty and unprecedented rates of financial, industrial and agricultural collapse defies quantification. The prevailing mood of pain and fear certainly persuaded those living at the time that civilization was on the brink of an epoch-defining change. The nineteenth-century order of free trade and liberal finance was breaking up into a few vast autarkic empires. Parliamentary democracy had also had its day. The modernizing ideologies of the totalitarian Right and Left would soon dominate the globe.

Some have suggested that the Depression would not have had such an impact had the major creditor Powers, the United States, Britain and France, co-operated to defend the global economy. Sadly, even if officials had recognized the scale and duration of the Depression early enough, the mutual recriminations over war debts, reparations and trade, which had typified their relations after 1919, intensified during the Great Depression. In the 1920s, the Europeans, reliant on dollar loans to feed the cycle of debt and reparations payments, resented the American practice of protecting their own producers while insisting that Europe open its markets to mass-produced American exports. Fears of American economic domination, particularly the domination of the growing markets for manufactured goods, were voiced in London and Paris. The Europeans also quarrelled among themselves. The French attributed their economic woes to the selfish practices of the Anglo-Saxons, and the British suspected that the French used monetary policy as a coercive instrument. At the outset of the slump, officials in Washington, London and Paris resorted first to tariff barriers, trade quotas, competitive currency devaluations and exchange controls to counter its effects. The rush to **protectionism** reduced the volume of world trade and confirmed the

Geneva disarmament talks
Article 8 of the Covenant of the League of Nations committed its signatories to the lowest level of armament consistent with national security and the fulfilment of international obligations. It also called for a Preparatory Commission to meet to draft a disarmament convention. The Preparatory Commission did not meet until 1926, and the disarmament talks did not begin at Geneva until 1932. Britain and France differed markedly over how to proceed, while the Weimar government refused to accept anything short of equality under the new convention. With Hitler's chancellorship, the chances for general disarmament evaporated. The Geneva disarmament talks were formally suspended in June 1934.

protectionism
The practice of regulating imports through high tariffs with the purpose of shielding domestic industries from foreign competition.

widespread belief that the true cause of one's own economic misery was the beggar-my-neighbour policies of the other Powers.

Since American trade, credit and foreign investments were fundamental to the functioning of the world economy, the American response to the New York stock market crash was of critical importance. Unfortunately, however, American markets were more important to Washington and New York than European ones. Indeed, for the American president, Herbert Hoover, economic nationalism was instinctive. Even before the economic crisis took shape, he had been hostile to the **Young Plan** of August 1929, which he regarded as yet another crooked scheme to permit the Europeans to dodge war debts by linking them to reparations. Therefore under Hoover's guidance, Washington raised tariff barriers in 1930 on almost all items entering American markets just when the Europeans were most anxious to export to the United States to earn dollars. Meanwhile, France introduced trade controls and preferential exchange agreements with Eastern European countries. Britain, the state most reliant on world trade and capital flows, was forced to raise import duties in late 1931, and, to the abiding enmity of American officials, negotiated at Ottawa in the summer of 1932 a preferential system of trade within the British Empire. Though much less vulnerable than Britain to the slowdown in world trade, the French followed suit in their own empire.

The collapse in economic confidence caused a run on the banks. Lenders called in loans. Borrowers lacked the securities and cash to service debts. Banks failed. Credit evaporated. In Europe and America, the banking crisis put pressure on currency exchanges and drained gold reserves. The gold standard began to fall apart. This had psychological and political repercussions. The restoration in the 1920s of the pre-1914 system of currency exchange rates fixed in relation to gold had symbolized the end of wartime monetary expedients. It would act as a check on inflation and promote prosperity. Britain returned to gold in 1925. France did so three years later. In September 1931, the pound was forced off gold. Fifteen other nations eventually suspended the gold standard. The world monetary system split apart into three main currency groups. The first consisted of countries, such as Britain, that had abandoned gold. The second group was the gold bloc. France, which had accumulated one of the world's largest gold reserves, led this small yet determined group of gold adherents until the *Banque de France* abandoned gold in 1936. The third group was made up of countries such as Germany, which emulated the Soviet practice of imposing exchange controls and negotiating barter agreements.

A banking crisis in Central Europe in the spring of 1931 showed just how politically divisive this breakdown process was. In May, the largest commercial lender of the Danube region, the Austrian *Credit-Anstalt*, became insolvent. The Austrian central bank and British lenders with investments in the region stepped in to help, but additional loans were required. The French government agreed to underwrite French commercial loans to Austria, but only if Vienna renounced plans for a customs union with Germany. Since the Germans had recently proposed just such an *Anschluss*, and talks along these lines between Berlin and Vienna had begun, the French demand was not unwarranted. Yet the British saw it as pointless French bullying, while the French believed that British financial

Young Plan
Name given to a financial scheme, worked out in 1929 by a committee chaired by the American businessman Owen D. Young, to reduce German reparations and arrange fresh credit for Germany. It was *informally* agreed by German, French and British delegates that reparations would be scaled back further if the former European Allies secured a reduction in debt repayments to the United States.

see Chapter 4

Anschluss
The political union of Germany and Austria. *Anschluss* was specifically prohibited under the Versailles Treaty, but was carried out by Hitler in March 1938 without any resistance from the victors of the First World War.

intervention in Central Europe was intended to undercut French influence. The focus of this Franco-British quarrel moved to Berlin as a run on the Reichsmark developed. In June, to relieve the pressure on German banks, Hoover proposed a one-year moratorium on all inter-governmental war debt and reparation payments. The French, who had not been consulted in advance, interpreted Hoover's standstill proposal as a strategy designed to rescue Anglo-American commercial interests in Germany at the expense of France's claims for reparations. It took two agonizing weeks to secure a consensus.

The Hoover moratorium was a breathing space. A solution to the debilitating problem of debts and reparations had to be found. Talks took place between the British chancellor of the exchequer, Neville Chamberlain, and the new centre-left premier in France, Édouard Herriot, at Lausanne in July 1932. A replacement for the Young Plan was agreed. Germany would make a final three billion Reichsmark payment (it was never paid). The deal, however, turned on a 'gentlemen's agreement'. Lausanne would not be ratified until the Europeans had concluded a 'satisfactory settlement' with their chief creditor, the United States. Details of the agreement leaked. Hoover was furious – but he was on his way out of the White House. In Europe, some officials speculated that the election of a Democrat to the presidency might transform American policy. Franklin D. Roosevelt, however, was as preoccupied and hamstrung by domestic concerns as anyone else, and shared some of the prejudices of his Republican predecessor. In April 1933, the dollar devalued against gold and a partial export upturn followed. This led to competitive currency devaluations elsewhere. Plans for interim exchange stabilization were put forward at the World Economic Conference in June–July, but Roosevelt denounced them. The last chance for a concerted response to the crash passed when the conference broke up.

The collapse of the Weimar Republic

In addition to dividing those Powers with a stake in the status quo, the crisis also affected the domestic politics of the revisionist states, especially Germany. The causal relationship between the slump and the **Nazi** regime was complex. Some argue that **Weimar** Germany's economy was in decline before the great crash, either as a structural consequence of the world war or as a result of the generous social policies of Weimar governments or both; the slump, according to this view, merely accelerated the descending spiral. We need not resolve the debate here to underscore a key point. The political emergency initiated by the downturn only made the collapse of German democracy the most *likely* outcome of the events of 1929–33; the crisis did not make the advent of the Nazi dictatorship a certainty.

To be sure, Germany was acutely vulnerable to the financial storms. Half of the deposits in German banks were foreign, mostly American and British. In Europe, German industry was the worst hit by the fall in demand. Moreover, the legiti-

Nazis (or Nazi Party)
The abbreviation for the National Socialist German Workers Party (*Nationalsozialistische Deutsche Arbeiterpartei* (NSDAP)). It was founded in October 1918 as the German Workers Party by the German politician Anton Drexler to oppose both capitalism and Marxism. It took on its more notorious title in February 1920. One year later Hitler became the Nazi Party Führer (German: leader).

Weimar Republic
The German parliamentary democracy that existed between November 1918 and January 1933. Attacked from both the Right and the Left of the political spectrum, it never won the loyalty of the majority of Germans.

macy of the Weimar Republic and its founding centre-left **Reichstag** coalition arose from a commitment to social reform and welfare. Modest unemployment insurance enacted in 1927 proved to be a major liability as the slump deepened. From 1929 to 1932, unemployment jumped from about 1.5 million to more than 6 million. Lengthening unemployment lines and declining tax revenue added up to a budget deficit. Bitter debates in the Reichstag over how to spend the shrinking budget shook the confidence of foreign investors and the domestic electorate. All across Europe this pattern of interlocking financial and political crises destabilized democracies. In Germany, where democracy was associated with defeat and humiliation, voters disavowed parliamentary politics in huge numbers. For salvation, they looked to the anti-democratic parties of the Left and Right. On the Right, a propaganda campaign waged against the Young Plan played on what many already believed: that Allied reparations and other sinister forces (**Bolsheviks**, Jews, etc.) were responsible for Germany's suffering.

In March 1930, unable to break the financial deadlock, Weimar's last social democratic coalition government resigned. From then on, until Hitler suspended the Reichstag altogether in March 1933, German chancellors no longer governed on the basis of a parliamentary majority, but instead enacted legislation through emergency powers of decree made available to them by the Reich president, Paul von Hindenburg. The 83-year-old field marshal hoped that this erosion of democratic checks on executive authority would eventually lead to an authoritarian regime drawn exclusively from the traditional ruling elites (army officers, the landed aristocracy and senior bureaucrats). While the anti-democratic motives of the Hindenburg circle are not in doubt, the personal aims of the first 'presidential' chancellor, Heinrich Brüning, remain a puzzle. Traditionally portrayed as leading the vanguard for the anti-democratic Right, some now suggest that Brüning had in fact hoped to preserve democracy with dictatorial expedients. Indeed, the only way his painful programme of tax hikes and budget cuts could be executed was through decrees. These measures had unmistakable internal and external purposes. First, austerity would demonstrate that Germany could no longer pay reparations (success on this front arrived with the Lausanne agreement). Second, Brüning believed that a balanced budget would ward off inflation until self-correcting market forces restored German economic growth. The unintended consequence of Brüning's strategy was that his use of presidential powers accustomed voters to the consolidation of power in the hands of a few, while the severe hardship of his austerity measures converted many to radical causes. In September 1930, the National Socialist German Workers Party – the Nazis – broke through to become the second largest Reichstag party with 107 seats; the communists won 77 seats. In the Reichstag, the Social Democrats, with 143 seats, provided Brüning's anti-socialist cabinet with passive support to prevent the Nazis from gaining a toehold in government.

Nonetheless, Brüning found it impossible to govern Germany in the midst of the crisis without, at the same time, antagonizing President Hindenburg. Ignoring the indispensable role that Brüning had played in the presidential election in April 1932 when Hindenburg had seen off a challenge from Hitler, the president lost confidence in the chancellor. Hindenburg disliked Brüning's flirtation with the

Reichstag
The lower house of the German parliament during the Wilhelmine and Weimar periods.

Bolsheviks
Originally in 1903 a faction led by Lenin within the Russian Social Democratic Party, over time the Bolsheviks became a separate party and led the October 1917 revolution in Russia. After this 'Bolsheviks' was used as a shorthand to refer to the Soviet government and communists in general.

socialists, and was outraged when he had the audacity to propose that landless peasants be settled on insolvent aristocratic estates. Accordingly, in May 1932, at the suggestion of the minister of defence, General Kurt von Schleicher, Hindenburg appointed Franz von Papen chancellor. The rise of this shallow mediocrity to high office was indicative of just how dangerous a game the conservative cabal around Hindenburg had begun to play. For General Schleicher, the redeeming attribute of the new German chancellor was his malleability. By controlling Papen, so Schleicher believed, he would control the German government. However, much to Schleicher's dismay, once in office, Papen asserted his independence. To make matters worse, the ambitious and conniving Papen began to ingratiate himself with Hindenburg. While the president's affection for Papen grew, in the country and the Reichstag his reputation plummeted. Reluctantly, in early December 1932, Hindenburg replaced Papen with Schleicher.

It is worth dwelling on the intrigue that followed Papen's downfall because, as Henry A. Turner argues, this was a moment 'when the fate of a great nation was contingent upon the actions of a handful of individuals'. The chief instigator was Papen. Allying himself with Hitler, Papen hatched a plot to return to office and to wreak revenge on his one-time sponsor, General Schleicher. Months earlier, both Schleicher and Papen had concluded that no conservative-dominated regime could be established without mass public support. Both men had made secret contacts with Hitler in order to harness his growing radical movement to achieve their own conservative political ends. In fact, to clear the way for a deal with the Nazis, one of Papen's first acts as chancellor was to lift Brüning's ban on Hitler's brown-shirted street thugs, the storm troopers. However, these negotiations always failed for the same reason: Hitler wished to be a 'presidential' chancellor, with full emergency powers, but Hindenburg, who distrusted the rabble-rousing former corporal, was only ever willing to appoint Hitler as a 'parliamentary' one. Some top-ranking Nazis criticized Hitler for refusing to take power in stages by entering into a political alliance with the conservatives. Hitler held out for all or nothing. He was fighting elections to destroy democracy, not to form a cabinet based on a right-wing coalition in the Reichstag.

In January 1933, Papen was ready to offer Hitler what he demanded. The two men agreed to form a new Hitler–Papen cabinet (Papen acting as deputy chancellor). Hitler had a sizeable presence in the Reichstag; Papen had the ear of the Reich president. Meanwhile, Schleicher, who never had any distinctive policies to offer, was embattled on all fronts. He had no firm base of support in the Reichstag and soon faced a vote of no-confidence. To remain in office, he needed Hindenburg, but the doddering field marshal shunned him. Not only had Papen turned Hindenburg against Schleicher, but the president now believed that Schleicher was planning a coup. Military government was a real possibility. Schleicher commanded loyal troops. Yet he backed away from using force to stay in power and resigned on 28 January. The next day, Papen deceived Hindenburg. He persuaded the president that the new Hitler–Papen cabinet would be supported by a majority right-wing alliance, and that Hitler would govern through the Reichstag; in reality, no such coalition had been formed. On 30 January, once Hitler had been sworn in, the promised Reichstag coalition failed to materialize and Hindenburg had little choice but to offer the new chancellor use of his emergency powers.

It was ultimately the woeful lack of judgement of Papen, Hindenburg and Schleicher that created Hitler's opportunity to seize power and to consolidate Nazi rule afterwards. By no means was this the *only* potential outcome of the first thirty days of 1933. Had Hitler been denied the chancellorship, his all-or-nothing quest for power might have backfired. His popularity among German voters was already on the decline. As frustration within the Nazi movement grew, the party might have fragmented. H. A. Turner argues that the most plausible alternative to the Hitler chancellorship was a military dictatorship under General Schleicher. This was what Hitler feared most. After all, the small but disciplined German army would have had little trouble controlling the streets. Hindenburg would have had to acquiesce. The prospective opposition to military dictatorship was too divided to mount a challenge. Furthermore, from 1933 onwards, General Schleicher's military dictatorship would have benefited from the same economic fortunes and easy foreign policy victories that the Nazis in fact benefited from.

Certainly Germany would have remained a revisionist state. Schleicher would have ordered early large-scale military growth. Such plans were under way under Brüning and, in December 1932, to salvage the world disarmament talks, the Western Powers had conceded to Germany the principle of equality of rights in armaments. Unlike Stresemann, who, as we saw in Chapter 2, sought to rebuild German power through diplomacy, Schleicher would have put force before diplomacy in the revision of the hated territorial settlement of 1919. Even so, Germany's top-ranking army officers were men of prudence. In all likelihood they would have fought rapid, localized conflicts against minor states such as Poland, but not risked another world war. The restoration of Germany to its place as a European **Great Power** was their long-range ambition. None of this of course happened. Instead, a few individuals, who had failed to appreciate the cunning and barbarity of the Nazi leader, betrayed everything that was civilized and humane in German life by turning over the state to Adolf Hitler.

Chapter 2

Great Powers
Traditionally those states that were held capable of shared responsibility for the management of the international order by virtue of their military and economic influence.

Revolution and expansion

The German ruling elites were not the last people to misjudge Hitler and his ideology. Many foreigners saw Nazism as just a more vulgar and brutal form of Prussian militarism. The National Socialists, with their goose-stepping para-military units, ubiquitous swastika banners and 'Heil Hitler' salutes, had much in common with other mass movements of the Left and Right. The Nazi message resonated with the anti-communism, anti-capitalism and anti-liberalism sweeping across Europe. In Germany, conservatives took comfort in Hitler's talk of national revival and anti-Bolshevism; radicals looked forward to the implementation of the socialism in National Socialism. Hitler played on public anxieties and used violence to secure Nazi rule. Political opponents were locked up and all other

Mein Kampf (German: *My Struggle*)

A semi-autobiographical book dictated by Adolf Hitler to his chauffeur and his personal secretary, Rudolf Hess, while he was serving a prison sentence for his part in the failed Munich beer hall *putsch* of 9 November 1923. It was published in 1925–26 in two volumes. Sales did not reach the hundreds of thousands until Hitler took power in 1933. It is a myth that the book was unread or ignored by foreign statesmen. It contained no detailed timetable for aggression; instead, *Mein Kampf* is a rambling exploration of Hitler's basic political and racial views.

League of Nations

An international organization established in 1919 by the peace treaties that ended the First World War. Its purpose was to promote international peace through collective security and to organize conferences on economic and disarmament issues. It was formally dissolved in 1946.

social Darwinism

A nineteenth-century theory, inspired by Charles Darwin's theory of evolution, which argued that the history of human society should be seen as 'the survival of the fittest'. Social Darwinism was the backbone of various theories of racial and especially 'white' supremacy.

anti-Semitism

A word which appeared in Europe around 1860. With it, the attack on Jews was based no longer on grounds of creed but on those of race. Its manifestations include pogroms in nineteenth-century Eastern Europe and the systematic murder of an estimated six million Jews by Nazi Germany between 1939 and 1945.

political parties were disbanded. Labour unions, the professions, churches and other public associations were 'co-ordinated' with Nazi practices. A parallel party structure was set up alongside that of the state, and, after Hindenburg's death on 2 August 1934, Hitler assumed the offices of both chancellor and president. Outside observers disapproved of Nazi criminality, but for diplomatic officials the real question was Hitler's foreign policy. From his campaign speeches and his book, *Mein Kampf*, there was no question that the new German chancellor would pursue revisionism with at least as much determination as his predecessors.

Hitler had something much more radical in mind. Before Germany was armed, though, he was careful not to provoke the European Powers. When he took Germany out of the **League of Nations** and disarmament talks in October 1933, he did so while proclaiming his love of peace. To maintain the pretence of policy continuity, he retained until 1938 the foreign and defence ministers appointed by President Hindenburg. Yet he despised the traditional ruling elites and their obsession with shifting frontiers and perpetual diplomacy. As a leader attuned to the new age of mass politics, he was determined to obliterate the old order. Even so, when Hitler assumed office, there was little in his past to suggest that he had the experience or talent to last one year as chancellor. After leaving school in 1907, this resentful son of a minor official employed by the Habsburg civil service eked out a dismal living as a landscape artist in Vienna. In the cosmopolitan capital of the Austro-Hungarian Empire Hitler absorbed the **social Darwinism**, radical nationalism and **anti-Semitism** that were later fundamental to Nazism. The defining experience in the young Hitler's life was the trench. He thrived on what he and many others held to be combat's purifying qualities. The Kaiser's army awarded him an Iron Cross for bravery. After recovering from the shock of Germany's defeat and blindness induced by poison gas, Hitler was recruited by the post-war German army as a political agitator. The soapbox demagogue then became an early member of a small nationalist German Workers Party. In November 1923, he earned national notoriety as the leader of the failed beer-hall *putsch* in Munich.

Sadly, Hitler's career did not end in obscurity. Instead, a decade later, he began to convert his vision into reality. Two concepts were fundamental to his world-view. One was race, the other space. Human history, according to Hitler, was a struggle between races. Superior races either flourished or perished. To grow, they had to preserve their biological purity and conquer ever more living space (*Lebensraum*). Destiny had ordained him as the saviour of the Germanic race from the folly of its aristocratic leaders. He intended to erase the disastrous 1919 settlement and to wage pitiless war against the most dangerous racial enemy, the Jews. In the eyes of Nazis, the Jews were a parasitic race that plotted to enslave some races with Bolshevism, such as the Slavs, and to destroy others, especially the Germanic (or Aryan) master race. Racism was commonplace in this era of European imperialism, but Nazism constituted a distinctly dogmatic and murderous form of state racism. Hitler did not distinguish between internal and external racial policy. To expand abroad, Germany needed a pure and vigorous racial core at home. The possibility of another 'stab in the back' (see Chapter 2) by internal enemies had to be removed. Race laws to isolate Jews, Gypsies and other 'alien' peoples were brutally enforced, while social measures were introduced to promote the birth rate of 'healthy' Germans and to sterilize, abort and later murder those who were deemed to be racially inferior or defective. Hitler's race revolution inside Germany, however, could not be consummated without a policy of ferocious and ceaseless expansion abroad. War would not only provide the *Lebensraum* essential for Germany's growth, but it would also permit the Nazis to sweep away the last remnants of the old conservative order.

Germany's initial military weakness dictated that Hitler's programme had to unfold in roughly defined stages. The first stage was Germany's return as a Great Power through large-scale rearmament and territorial expansion in Central and Eastern Europe. Stage two was the conquest of European Russia and the consolidation and ruthless economic exploitation of *Lebensraum* in the east. The final stage – one that Hitler was unsure he would live to see – would be the final battle for global supremacy against the United States. Achieving this long-term goal called for arms, **autarky** and allies. In *Mein Kampf*, Hitler had criticized the leaders of imperial Germany for gratuitously provoking Britain before 1914 with a naval armaments race. To secure a free hand on the European continent, Hitler hoped to strike a bargain on naval strength and spheres of influence with the British, and form a close alliance with Italy, thereby isolating Germany's arch-enemy, France. The precondition to world domination was, of course, military supremacy. As Hitler well knew, the First World War had taught military theorists everywhere that war preparations did not entail simply the buildup of large standing forces to fight the first battles (arms *in breadth*), but also the acquisition of huge arms industries and self-sufficiency in raw materials such as oil, rubber and iron ore to feed the voracious appetite of protracted modern war (arms *in depth*). From the very start of his chancellorship, Hitler aimed to build arms in depth by turning over the whole German economy to military preparations. At first, the Depression provided enough slack in the German economy to gain a swift head-start on rearmament, but when the scale of rearmament began to strain Germany's finances, Hitler rebuffed calls from the president of the *Reichsbank*, Hjalmar Schacht, to slow the pace and return Germany to the world economy through trade. Instead, Hitler raised the targets for arms growth and autarky. In September 1936, the Führer appointed Field Marshal Göring to head the Four Year Plan to accelerate the drive for a **total war** economy. Nonetheless, it would take until the mid-1940s for Germany to be ready to fight and win the wars of 'great proportions' that Hitler desired.

Relentless German aggression was one of the principal causes of the Second World War. Yet Hitler was not alone in his wish to overturn the status quo. Benito Mussolini dreamed of revolution too. The once-committed socialist broke with the Italian Left over its objection to Italy's entry into the European war in 1915. He fought, was wounded and then returned to civilian life as editor of a right-wing newspaper agitating for Italy to be rewarded for its part in the Allied victory. By 1921, he emerged as leader (Duce) of the Italian Fascist movement. A year later, in the midst of near civil war, King Victor Emmanuel III appointed Mussolini prime minister. Although these events were later mythologized as the 'March on Rome', Mussolini's premiership was in fact the product of an alliance

autarky
A policy that aims at achieving national economic self-sufficiency. It is commonly associated with the economic programmes espoused by Germany, Italy and Japan in the 1930s and 1940s.

total war
A war that uses all resources at a state's disposal including the complete mobilization of both the economy and society.

between Italy's new radical Right and traditional conservatism against the bogey of communism. In the 1920s, while he built up the power and prestige of his regime internally, Mussolini played the responsible statesman in Europe, a posture which also stemmed from Italian weakness as well as the limited scope for mischief-making in the era of Locarno.

see Chapter 2

Spanish Civil War
Began on 18 July 1936 as an attempted right-wing military coup led by General Francisco Franco. The coup was launched with elite troops from Spanish Morocco to topple the recently elected socialist and anti-clerical Popular Front government. Franco's Nationalists failed to take Madrid, and the Republican government of President Azana remained in control of much of Spain. Both sides appealed for outside help to achieve victory. As a result, Spain became Europe's ideological battlefield. Nazi Germany and Fascist Italy intervened on the side of the Nationalists, while the Soviet Union sent aid to the Republicans. Britain and France tried to contain the war. The fighting dragged on for three terrible years, during which three-quarters of a million people perished. The civil war ended in April 1939. General Franco's dictatorship lasted until he died in 1975.

In the mid-1930s, Mussolini appeared to change course. In 1935, Italy embarked on a colonial war in Africa and a year later large-scale intervention in the **Spanish Civil War**. This opportunistic turnabout – not to mention Italy's dismal wartime performance – has led some to dismiss Fascism as an empty propaganda trick and Mussolini as the archetypal papier-mâché Mephistophelean. However, the Fascist Duce was as ruthless and determined as the Nazi Führer. Nazism and Fascism were both propelled by a distinctive revolutionary dynamic: Hitler planned to realize his race revolution through war and conquest; Mussolini also valued foreign expansion as the means to Italy's total 'fascistization'. The policies of the two regimes were shaped by similar national experiences. As recently unified states, Italy and Germany behaved like restless 'latecomers' in this era of intense Great Power rivalry and overseas imperialism. Their national aspirations had been frustrated at the Paris Peace Conference. As mass movements arising in times of social unrest, economic dislocation and political deadlock, both dictatorships claimed to be the only legitimate 'democratic' expressions of the national will.

Yet there were differences. The racism and anti-Semitism, so fundamental to Nazism, were more peripheral to Fascism (many Italians saw the Duce's race laws of 1938 as a distasteful northern import). Both regimes had been formed with the connivance of the conservative ruling elites, but Mussolini was never able to shake them off and attain the iron grip that Hitler had on the German state and its people. Italy's monarchy, the Catholic Church and the armed forces were centres of authority and power that the Duce could not ignore. Another difference lay in their ultimate goals: Hitler dreamed of total wars of racial expansion culminating in Germany's mastery of the globe; Mussolini intended to found a new Roman Empire by seizing the Mediterranean and its ocean outlets as Italy's rightful *spazio vitale*. 'Either war,' he said, 'or let's end this *commedia* of [claiming to be] a Great Power.' The obstacles to a Fascist empire were the two leading status quo Powers, Britain and France. Germany, their most formidable potential foe, was Mussolini's most important potential ally. Contacts between the Nazis and Rome stretched back to the Munich *putsch*, but Mussolini (at first anyway) and many of his advisers (long after) were wary. Undoubtedly, a resurgent Germany would create scope for a more aggressive policy, but the new Reich might also absorb Austria – one of the buffers between the two states and a focus for Italian influence in south-east Europe – and, worse, begin to demand from Italy territory taken from Austria (South Tyrol).

Italian policy reflected this uncertainty. In 1932–33, the Fascist regime proposed a new Four-Power Treaty between the Locarno Powers to arbitrate European affairs. London and Paris humoured what they saw as an Italian conceit. Apart from sidelining the League of Nations, the aim behind this *démarche* was to contain Germany for a time in a manner beneficial to Italian ambitions. Hitler, who had no interest in multilateral security systems, signed the treaty and then ignored it. On 24 July 1934, the Austrian Nazis attempted a coup and murdered the quasi-fascist chancellor, Engelbert Dollfuss. Italian troops mobilized to deter an *Anschluss*. Hitler, who denied foreknowledge of the coup, disavowed the Austrian Nazis. Italo-German relations cooled, but not for long. The two dictators were on converging ideological paths. The outbreak of the **Abyssinian War** on 3 October 1935 marked the junction point. Under the impression that he had been given a green light in April by the Western Powers for a war in Africa as a reward for Italy's condemnation of German unilateral rearmament, Mussolini was incensed by the opposition of France and Britain and the imposition of limited League of Nations economic sanctions against Italy. The Führer, who exploited the Abyssinian conflict to remilitarize the Rhineland on 7 March 1936, offered the Italians benevolent neutrality and some material support. The war ended in May 1936. Mussolini's defiance of the Western Powers and the League had impressed Hitler. In January 1936, the Duce signalled his intentions by dropping objections to Austria becoming a German satellite.

In November 1936, Mussolini announced the Rome–Berlin **Axis**. It was followed a year later by Italy's accession to the German–Japanese Anti-**Comintern** Pact. Long after the Axis was announced, British and French statesmen sought to woo Mussolini away from Hitler. The ideological bond could not be broken. Officials in Paris and London pointed to Italian support for General Franco's rebellion in Spain as the stumbling-block. The reality was that the Duce revelled in the 'dynamism' of his wars. Ironically, the Abyssinian and Spanish adventures drained Italy of its war-making potential. The Italian defence budget trebled, but the money was spent on current operations and wasteful projects such as maintaining large numbers of ill-equipped infantry instead of the in-depth preparations essential for modern warfare. In some ways, the emphasis on quantity over quality and staying power accorded well with Fascist bluster and bullying. After all, Italy was treated as a player because it possessed a big navy, a large bomber force and an army of 'eight million bayonets'. However, the Italian peninsula was vulnerable to Anglo-French naval blockade and bombardment. In a European war, Rome would have to rely on its preponderant northern ally for coal to fuel Italian war industries and for military aid. Mussolini's resolve to strike a blow against the status quo thus destined Italy to fall under the shadow of the Third Reich. This was a fate he embraced. As his son-in-law and foreign minister, Count Ciano, put it, the Axis was 'based above all upon the identity of political regimes, which determines a common destiny'.

Diplomacy and deterrence

Once the Nazi challenge gained strength, a major war became the only way by which it could be stopped. The starting date of that war would depend on the moment when the status quo Powers resisted Hitler with force. From 1933 to

Abyssinian War
On 3 October 1935, the brutal conquest of Abyssinia by Italian troops launched from neighbouring Italian Eritrea began. It arose from Mussolini's desire to exercise the martial prowess of his Fascist regime and thereby further his revolution. The war was popular inside Italy as revenge for Italy's defeat at Adowa in 1896. Emperor Haile Selassie appealed to the League of Nations, but his small kingdom was abandoned to its fate. The war ended on 5 May 1936.

Axis
A term coined originally by Mussolini in November 1936 to describe the relationship between Fascist Italy and Nazi Germany. The German–Italian Axis was reinforced by the so-called Pact of Steel signed by Rome and Berlin in May 1939. More broadly speaking, the term is often used (as in Chapter 8 of this book) to refer to the relationship between Germany, Italy and Japan. These three Powers were formally linked by the German–Japanese Anti-Comintern Pact of November 1936, which Italy signed one year later, and the Tripartite Pact of September 1940.

Comintern
The Communist or Third International founded in Moscow in 1919 as an organization to direct and support the activities of communist parties outside Russia. It was abolished in 1943 in a short-lived effort by Stalin to reassure Britain and the United States that the Soviet Union no longer sought to export Marxism-Leninism.

1938, Paris and London accommodated the Nazis. On 21 October 1933, Germany walked out of the League of Nations. In March 1935, Hitler ordered compulsory military service in Germany and announced the existence of the *Luftwaffe* (German air force). In reaction to these unilateral violations of the **Versailles Treaty**, Britain, France and Italy consulted and issued a protest in April. This deceptive display of unity between France and the Locarno guarantors was short lived. In June, Britain signed a bilateral naval agreement with Germany. In October, the Italians, who had only just signed up to military agreements which set out how they would assist France in a war against Germany, attacked Abyssinia. In March 1936, while Europe was gripped by the crisis in the Mediterranean, German troops marched into the Rhineland. In response, Britain stepped forward to propose a new round of diplomacy, France stood still and Belgium withdrew into neutrality. The emerging security framework of the 1920s was now in ruins. The sense that Europe was on the verge of a great calamity was heightened after July 1936 with the outbreak of the Spanish Civil War. Italy and Germany sent men and *matériel* to assist Franco's nationalists, while the Soviet Union supplied the same to the left-wing Republican government. As Europe's ideological fissure widened, France and Britain negotiated an international agreement on non-intervention in Spain which in practice permitted German and Italian intervention to continue.

Orthodox historians have explained this phase of retreat as the product of shortsighted and spineless leadership. Granted, French and British politicians never fully grasped the depth of Hitler's malevolence. However, hindsight combined with a half-century of scholarly inquiry into the nature of Nazism makes it difficult for us to appreciate the *uncertainty* about Germany's intentions that contemporaries had to deal with. In the cabinet rooms, foreign and defence ministries and intelligence departments of France and Britain, pessimists argued that the militaristic Germans sought to dominate Europe, for much the same reason as they did before 1914, while optimists believed that Hitler or those who purportedly had influence over him could be constructively conciliated. Pointing to the statements of the former as evidence of foresight and those of the latter as proof of inanity does injustice to the realities of statecraft. These debates – recurring again and again in the twentieth century – sprang from the inescapable dilemma of coping with what was an inherently ambiguous and menacing situation.

Uncertainty alone does not explain the initial responses of Britain and France to the expansion of German power. There were other inhibiting factors. Not least was an all-pervasive sense of revulsion at the cost of the last war. Most French and British politicians had either served in the trenches or lost someone dear. 'Never again' was not just a slogan for peace movements and pacifists; it was the moral purpose behind the foundation of the League of Nations, the Kellogg–Briand Pact and world disarmament. The identification of the status quo Powers with liberal internationalism should not be dismissed as starry-eyed idealism. Values expressed in the form of rules or norms of conduct are *potential* power. As the chief beneficiaries of post-1919 order, it was in the interest of Paris and London to outlaw force and promote institutions for the pacific settlement of disputes. As one Japanese official complained, 'The Western Powers had taught

---

Versailles Treaty
The treaty that ended the Allied state of hostilities with Germany in 1919. It included German territorial losses, disarmament, a so-called war guilt clause and a demand that reparations be paid to the victors.

see Map 7.1

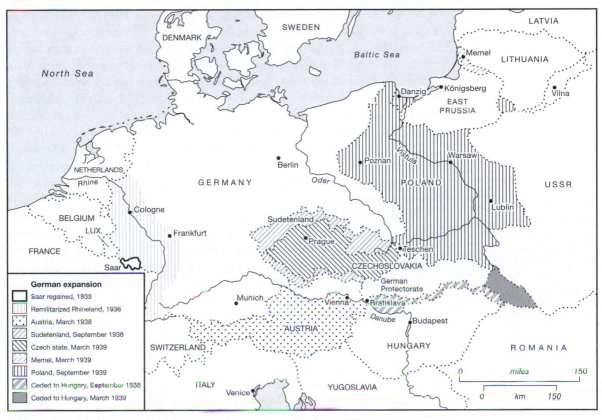

Map 7.1 German expansion, 1935–39

Source: After Lamb and Tarling (2001)

the Japanese the game of poker . . . but after acquiring most of the chips, they pronounced the game immoral and took up contract bridge.' This barb only captures the self-interested dimension of Western foreign policy. British, French and American statesmen believed that 'contract bridge' was not only good for them, but also good for the rest of the world. The problem was persuading everyone to play by the new rules. This could only be done in the first instance through diplomacy. After all, to uphold the status quo, the Western Powers could not adopt the violent methods of the revisionists without undermining the norms of the liberal state system that they had created.

Of the status quo Powers, France had the least room for manoeuvre. In *matériel* terms, Frenchmen knew that they could not equal Germany's ultimate strength. The old adversary was not only more densely populated but also more industrialized. It took a coalition of Great Powers to win in 1918. To enforce the Versailles Treaty, French soldiers had marched in 1923, but to the enormous cost of the French economy and its relations with the British and the Americans. 'A country's defence resides not only in its soldiers and its cannons,' Premier Herriot once observed, 'but also in the excellence of its legal position.' France had to have justice on its side in order to construct a coalition powerful enough to face a resurgent Germany. True, France had security treaties with Poland, Czechoslovakia, Romania and Yugoslavia. But these small states, bitterly divided among themselves, did not add up to an 'Eastern bloc'. Moreover, French influence in Eastern Europe plummeted after Germany occupied the Rhineland without a shot being fired. What about Britain and Italy, the guarantors of the Treaty of Locarno? For much of the period, the British did not see themselves as France's ally, but instead as cool-headed mediators caught between the hotheads in Paris and the bullies in Berlin. As for Italy, Pierre Laval, the French premier, concluded an accord in early 1935 with Mussolini which stipulated that the two states should consult if Germany disturbed the peace. The Duce, however, saw the deal as a go-ahead for his Abyssinian conquest. The French had no choice but to alienate Italy by siding with Britain and the League of Nations.

What about the Russians? In May 1935, France did conclude a mutual assistance treaty with the Soviet Union as well as a parallel agreement with Czechoslovakia. The negotiations for these treaties (as well as those with Italy) had begun a year before under Louis Barthou, the foreign minister of the centre-right government of 'National Union'. Some argue that Barthou's diplomacy was a transitory phase of 'realism' in French policy-making – an effort to surround Germany with powerful allies, including the Soviets. Tragically, so runs this interpretation, Barthou was assassinated in October 1934 and his *realpolitik* was abandoned in favour of a craven policy of '**appeasement**'. In fact Barthou's diplomacy did not mark such a radical break in continuity. Just like his friend Briand before him and those who followed him, Barthou hoped to build a multilateral and interlocking framework of mutual security guarantees in Eastern and Western Europe similar to those signed in 1925 at Locarno. To describe this strategy another way, Barthou was trying to persuade Germany to join in its own containment. Security talks with Russia, Poland, Czechoslovakia and Italy were designed to convince Berlin that Franco-German **détente** was the only way to alter the peace settlement. As we know, Hitler responded to this security-building effort by occupying the Rhineland and thereafter ignoring French overtures. The door on the Locarno era was slammed shut.

Domestic politics in France complicated its foreign policy. During the slump, the French witnessed a 30 per cent fall in national income and growing budget deficits, which polarized the electorate between the Right and the Left. Alignment with Fascist Italy was anathema to the Left, while a rapprochement with Soviet Russia infuriated the Right. Governments also changed frequently. Between 1933 and 1940, France was led by thirty-four separate administrations and had seven different foreign ministers. In April 1936, the election of a centre-left coalition known as the **Popular Front** exacerbated the ideological rift. Industrial unrest and social turmoil erupted. The presence of the French Communist Party in the coalition disgusted the right-wing group. Investors became jittery. The flight of capital from the Paris financial markets drove down the value of the franc. Even the unwavering commitment of the Popular Front premier, Léon Blum, a dedicated social reformer and disarmer, to a huge programme of rearmament in 1936 did not inspire national unity. Once Franco started his rebellion in Spain, the perception of imminent civil war in France (though greatly exaggerated)

appeasement
A foreign policy designed to remove the sources of conflict in international affairs through negotiation. Since the outbreak of the Second World War, the word has taken on the pejorative meaning of the spineless and fruitless pursuit of peace through concessions to aggressors. In the 1930s, most British and French officials saw appeasement as a twin-track policy designed to remove the causes of conflict with Germany and Italy, while at the same time allowing for the buildup of sufficient military and financial power to bargain with the dictators from a position of strength.

détente
A term meaning the reduction of tensions between states. It is often used to refer to the superpower diplomacy that took place between the inauguration of Richard Nixon as the American president in 1969 and the Senate's refusal to ratify SALT II in 1980.

Popular Front
The Comintern policy announced in 1935 of encouraging communist parties to form coalitions with other socialist and non-socialist parties in order to provide a common front against fascism.

became widespread. The image of a left-wing government embattled by right-wing generals was just a little too close to home. Blum's cabinet considered assisting the Spanish Republic, but feared that this might spark civil war in France as well as a general war in Europe. The Popular Front therefore championed non-intervention and worked with the British to put it into effect. After the setbacks of 1935–36, what France needed most was time to rearm and a firm embrace from the other powerful parliamentary democracy in Europe, Britain.

Unfortunately for the French, the last thing the British were prepared to do was offer security guarantees. Once again, painful memories of the First World War and a long-standing aversion to entangling alliances played an important part here. A deep hostility towards and misunderstanding of the French were equally important. In the early 1930s, many British officials believed that German recalcitrance and even the advent of Nazism were attributable to French obstinacy. Ramsay MacDonald, Britain's prime minister from 1931 to 1935, considered 'the diplomacy of France . . . an ever active influence for evil in Europe'. The ideological conflict in France that followed the election of the Popular Front only served to strengthen the deeply held conviction that it was an unreliable ally. Britain's strategic predicament also spoke in favour of isolation from Europe. Britain was a global Power. Unlike the French, the British could not focus solely on the Nazi menace. Japan threatened Britain's eastern possessions and commercial interests in China, while Italy, with its battlefleet concentrated in the Mediterranean and a large army positioned in Libya, endangered Egypt and the Suez Canal. These commitments exceeded Britain's defence resources.

The rise of the triple threat did not mean that the eyes of British strategists turned away from the German threat. A top-level committee of civilian and military officials reviewing Britain's defences in 1933–34 identified Germany as Britain's 'ultimate potential enemy'. Some influential voices advocated a retreat into isolation, but most recognized that Britain could not abandon Europe. Germany could not be allowed to crush France, occupy the Low Countries and position air and sea forces close to Britain. However, another great war to prevent Germany's domination of continental Europe would initiate another accelerated period of decline in Britain's standing as a global financial and trading nation to the benefit of the United States. Peace in Europe was therefore Britain's ultimate national interest. British diplomats accordingly drew up disarmament conventions and spoke of multilateral security accords for Eastern and Western Europe comparable to those of the French. The formula for the pacification (or appeasement) of Europe was plain: Germany would offer France a security guarantee and, in exchange, France would permit a relaxation of the Treaty of Versailles.

Britain's domestic politics reinforced this diplomatic stance. The view that the Versailles settlement had been untenable and indefensible was common among the political elite and opinion-makers. As in France, the man on the street regarded the League of Nations and disarmament as the twin pillars of foreign policy. In parliament, the Labour Party was the most vocal in support of the League, but enthusiasm for Geneva diplomacy and **collective security** cut across Right–Left boundaries. As a general election approached in the autumn of 1935, Prime Minister Stanley Baldwin, the leader of a cross-party – but in the main

collective security
The principle of maintaining peace between states by mobilizing international opinion to condemn aggression. Commonly seen as one of the chief purposes of international organizations such as the League of Nations and the United Nations.

Conservative – National Government, knew that electoral victory and parliamentary backing for his government hung on one issue: 'the question of peace and war and the future of the League of Nations'. While the initial preparations for rearmament were under way, Baldwin promised in an election speech that there would be 'no great armaments'. His first foreign secretary, Sir Samuel Hoare, discovered the perils and pitfalls of reconciling a declaratory policy of adherence to the League of Nations and collective economic sanctions with a prudent one of war avoidance. In December 1935, newspapers reported that Hoare and the French premier, Laval, were prepared to defuse the crisis in East Africa by offering Mussolini a **protectorate** over Abyssinia. Public indignation forced Hoare to resign. He was replaced by the dashing Anthony Eden, the fomer minister for League of Nations affairs, who was regarded by the British public as a League man.

However, the search for an agreement with Germany – the policy that later took on the pejorative label 'appeasement' – was not the product of Britain's material weakness or driven by public opinion. Politicians were sensible to take these factors into account, but appeasement as practised under Baldwin and his successor, Neville Chamberlain, was an interventionist policy designed to reshape Europe to suit Britain's security interests and to uphold Britain's global empire. A prime example of this sort of thinking put into practice was the conclusion of the Anglo-German naval agreement of June 1935. Hitler's offer to limit the size of his navy to 35 per cent of the size of the Royal Navy was in fact an attempt to bribe Britain into giving him a free hand in Central and Eastern Europe. While ignoring any suggestion that Britain would turn away from Europe, the British Admiralty and Foreign Office exploited Hitler's offer to advance their own strategic purposes. In terms of naval strength, the treaty would commit Germany to build a conventional battleship fleet instead of a much more dangerous one composed of small commerce raiders and cruiser submarines. In diplomatic terms, the naval accord would be integrated into the larger set of negotiations taking place between the five leading naval Powers – Britain, Japan, the United States, France and Italy – towards a new global naval armaments limitation treaty.

Hitler thus failed to procure Britain's disinterest in Europe with his naval appeasement. The British instead sought to solve Europe's troubles through the negotiation of a comprehensive settlement. Similar to French proposals, this new security system would be based on interrelated Western and Eastern treaties of mutual guarantee modelled on Locarno, combined with Germany's return to the League, as well as a general convention to restrict the use of bombing aircraft against civilians. The question was how to persuade the Germans to lock themselves into this multilateral framework. Most agreed that the answer was to redress German grievances arising from the 1919 settlement. Unfortunately, Hitler had an uncanny capacity to divine exactly the right moment to seize for himself the concession that the French and British were about to offer him in exchange for security talks. In this way, he frustrated British and French diplomacy first in March 1935, with his unilateral denunciation of the military clauses of the Versailles Treaty, and once again, a year later, with the reoccupation of the Rhineland. After March 1936, fresh efforts to extract from Hitler the basis for

protectorates
Territories administered by an imperial state without full annexation taking place, and where delegated powers typically remain in the hands of a local ruler or rulers. Examples include French Morocco and the unfederated states in Malaya.

talks went unanswered. While the Spanish Civil War appeared to begin the slide into general European war, some held out the prospect that colonial or economic concessions might induce Hitler to come to the bargaining table. However, indications that such offers might initiate progress originated not from the Führer, but from the president of the *Reichsbank*, Hjalmar Schacht. In London, the misconception that reputed moderates such as Schacht had influence over Hitler sustained the mistaken view that a general agreement with the Third Reich could be negotiated, if only the right diplomatic approach was made.

The emphasis in British and French policy on diplomacy did not exclude considerations of force. In 1936, Britain and France launched large-scale programmes of rearmament designed to compel Hitler to negotiate. As chancellor of the exchequer, Chamberlain favoured spending on the Royal Air Force over the British Army because he believed air power to be 'the most formidable deterrent to war'. Britain's planners aimed to build up by 1939 enough air and naval strength to deter Germany, but a balance had to be struck between acquiring the armaments to defeat an initial German attack and husbanding the financial strength necessary to purchase overseas supplies and to raise capital abroad for a *long* war – what was termed the 'fourth arm of defence'. The Maginot Line – a 200-mile system of fortifications along the Franco-German frontier – was France's declaration of deterrence expressed in steel, barbed wire and concrete. The French also had a large body of trained men to mobilize in case of a sudden German attack, but cuts to defence spending in the early 1930s had left some serious gaps in their air and land armaments. These gaps could not be closed until the 1936 defence programmes paid off in 1939–40. Expectations of what would happen if deterrence failed helps to explain the Western response to Germany. British and French strategists agreed that the 'next war' would be total, and would follow roughly the pattern of 1914–18. Indeed, the war was likely to begin with another German miscalculation. Hitler and his advisers might gamble that they could win a quick victory by ordering the *Luftwaffe* to deliver a devastating 'knockout blow' on London, or perhaps a **Schlieffen**-like assault on France with massed bombers and fast tanks. Once this German 'knockout blow' had been repelled, so British and French planners argued, the war would become another contest of endurance. As the First World War had shown, Germany did not have the raw materials and resources to win such a contest. Thus, while London and Paris mobilized the superior quantities of men and *matériel* available to them from their overseas empires and from the rest of the world, Allied sea and air power would cut off the Reich from seaborne supplies and pummel its industrial heartland. Once the Allies had reached a crushing level of supremacy, the final offensives would begin. In sum, the premise of British and French deterrence strategy was to *threaten* Hitler with a long war, by *convincing* him that he could not win a short one. Since most agreed that another great war would extinguish European civilization, the decision to issue threats of force could not be taken lightly.

Aversion to force thus arose from sensible strategic calculations and deep anxieties about a future apocalypse. Statesmen also saw that there was something more at stake in the arms race than relative military strength. The deterrence strategies of the status quo Powers were shaped by their national identities, values

Schlieffen Plan
The German pre-1914 plan for a pre-emptive military offensive against France, which would involve troops passing through neutral Belgium. It is named after the German army chief of staff, General Alfred von Schlieffen.

and a dedication to liberal economies and free societies. As one British minister told his colleagues, Britain could not match the arms drives of the dictators 'unless we turned ourselves into a different kind of nation'. The lure of doing so was real enough. Even the lifelong socialist Léon Blum once confessed that in 'attempting to oppose fascism's bid for power . . . one is too often tempted to follow in its footsteps'. Yet, as British and French statesmen well knew, the cost of emulating the totalitarians would have been to sacrifice everything their nations stood for.

Isolation and co-existence

For salvation from the security crisis, some Europeans looked to either the United States or Russia. Anthony Eden, Britain's foreign secretary, for instance, hoped to enlist American support to deter the aggression in Europe and the Pacific, while Pierre Cot, the French air force minister, dreamed of a formidable Franco-Soviet alliance based on air power to enforce the peace. However, most of their colleagues feared the cut-throat capitalism of the Americans and the insidious doctrine of the Russians in equal measure. From Locarno in 1925 to Munich in 1938, the pre-ferred solution for those Europeans hoping to erect a new security structure always rested on *four*-power co-operation between Britain, France, Germany and Italy.

Before 1940, there was no prospect that the United States would be willing to save Europe anyway. The slump reinforced the American desire for home-grown solutions to their problems. 'Each nation', American officials told the World Economic Conference, 'must set its own house in order.' In one of his first speeches, President Roosevelt announced that 'our greatest primary task is to put people to work'. Most of his listeners believed that the rest of the world, above all the decadent and untrustworthy Europeans, could look after themselves. This sentiment ran against Roosevelt's own inclinations. Previously, as an assistant secretary of the navy, he had served under Woodrow Wilson, and was imbued with his hero's ideals. Roosevelt was certain that the distinct American values of freedom, justice and enterprise could transform the globe, and that the Depression did not relieve Americans of their moral duty to make the world a better place. Yet Roosevelt had learned from Wilson's mistakes. 'It's a terrible thing to look over your shoulder when you are trying to lead', he reflected, 'and to find no one there.' During his first two terms, public opinion was the chief constraint on policy. Abhorrence of war was expressed through investigation and legislation. Through the Senate Inquiry into the Munitions Industry of 1934–36 (the Nye Committee), Americans tried to expose the sinister forces of militarization creeping into their economy. Through the three Neutrality Acts (1935–37) and the Johnson Act (1934), all of which restricted commerce with belligerents as well as the movement of American nationals through war zones, the United States hoped to isolate itself from any future great war. Roosevelt, who shared their hatred of war and its effects, could not ignore the isolationists. The success of the New Deal, his ambitious programme of public works, investment and reform designed to combat unemployment, depended in Congress on the votes of progressive Democrats and Republicans. As it happened, these progressives were also among the most staunchly isolationist.

Apart from the domestic constraints, officials in Washington could not turn to deterrence to make American policy felt abroad simply because of a scarcity of credible means. Granted, the United States navy, the world's second largest, exercised the minds of Japanese admirals. Yet, for force projection into Europe, the American army and air force were negligible. Before 1939, Hitler took no notice of Roosevelt's high-sounding admonitions for peace. Stormy relations with Europe's democracies also limited Washington's capacity to shape events. This was particularly true of Anglo-American relations. On the naval question, both sides buried their long-standing differences over fleet parity and cruiser strength to conclude the London Naval Treaty in March 1936. However, the chief obstacle to wider co-operation was trade. Americans saw Imperial Preference as 'economic aggression' at least as harmful to world peace and prosperity as the autarkic practices of the dictatorships. Cordell Hull, Roosevelt's secretary of state, called for an easing of the Ottawa agreements to improve Anglo-American relations. But what would London gain in exchange? Eden sought naval co-operation against Japan. Chamberlain thought that it was 'always best and safest to count on *nothing* from the Americans except words'.

In October 1937, Roosevelt delivered a speech in Chicago in which he spoke of 'the epidemic of world lawlessness' and of the need to 'quarantine' aggression. The speech provoked an isolationist backlash and subsequently he denied that he had a programme of action in mind when he called for quarantine. In November, Washington shied away from talk of economic sanctions and fleet movements at a conference convened in Brussels to mediate in the Sino-Japanese War. In December, a Japanese air attack on British and American Yangtze gunboats paved the way for *secret* Anglo-American naval talks – but nothing out in the open. There was now only one option available to the president, the so-called Welles Plan. Sumner Welles, the under-secretary of state and a close confidant of Roosevelt, first proposed in 1936 a conference to work out the world's political, armament, financial and economic problems and to establish worldwide unanimity on the 'fundamental norms' to 'govern international conduct'. In January 1938, Roosevelt suggested the Welles Plan to Chamberlain. From London's viewpoint, the idea of one big conference to discuss the world's problems was a recipe for a spectacular row that would leave Britain exposed to the wrath of the dictators. Chamberlain asked Roosevelt to wait. Roosevelt had little choice but to do so. As war over Czechoslovakia loomed large, the prime minister sought to defuse the crisis through bilateral talks with Hitler. Washington greeted the Munich Accords with misapplied moral outrage directed at London as well as relief that European war had been averted. In 1939, as the Munich settlement unravelled and war appeared imminent, Roosevelt and his top military and diplomatic officials began to turn the president's concept of 'quarantine' into an operative policy of political and military deterrence through allies and air power.

In contrast to the United States, Soviet Russia appeared eager to enter the European states system. In 1934, the Soviets joined the League of Nations and, in the following year, signed mutual security guarantees with France and Czechoslovakia. These treaties committed the Soviet Union to coming to the aid of the Czechs, if they fell victim to aggression, so long as France did so first. In 1935, communists across Western Europe were instructed to form Popular Front coalitions with democratic parties to bolster resistance to fascism. This sudden 180-degree reorientation away from vociferous hostility to the status quo to outspoken enthusiasm for collective security and the 'indivisibility of peace' was championed by Maxim Litvinov, commissar for foreign affairs since 1930, who strove tirelessly to dispel the image of Russia as a malign agent bent on world revolution.

Many historians blame the Western Powers for squandering the opportunity presented by Litvinov's exertions to forge an anti-Nazi coalition. To be sure, abhorrence of the Bolsheviks ran deep in Europe. Indeed, Hitler exploited the 'Red' bogey to mask his own revolutionary machinations. The British worked to prevent any connection between the planned eastern and western Locarno-type systems and to weaken the security guarantees negotiated between Paris, Prague and Moscow. The French high command resisted Russian invitations to begin detailed staff planning on how to enforce the 1935 guarantees. The Eastern Europeans, especially the Poles, were at least as wary of the Soviets as they were of the Nazis. In fact, Polish (and obviously German) hostility to the Soviet Union made the whole scheme for an 'eastern Locarno' unworkable. Despite Moscow's search for a way out of isolation, this arm's-length treatment of Russia by everyone else rendered the Soviet Union until 1939 in effect a *non*-Power. (No state could *act* like a Great Power, after all, so long as the Great Powers did not treat it as one.) Litvinov's dilemma was painfully exposed by the coming of the Spanish Civil War. The Soviet leadership could not afford to watch while their chief potential ally in Western Europe, France, was threatened by a fascist victory in Spain. Yet Soviet military intervention on the side of the Spanish Republic and its Popular Front government was greeted in Paris and London with great hostility, and lent substance to Hitler's claim that his fight was a European one against the forces of international communism.

Thus, the view that France and Britain 'failed' to exploit the opportunity presented by the shift in Soviet policy can only be sustained if one ignores the *interactive* nature of international politics. Ultimately, the 'failure' was the product of *mutual* hostility, divergent security interests and, to a large degree, adverse timing. When collective security appeared attractive to Moscow, Paris and London preferred to negotiate an agreement with Berlin; when Paris and London were ready to negotiate a deal with Moscow, Stalin preferred peaceful co-existence with Hitler. Finally, as we have seen, the reluctance of the Great Powers to commit to binding security alliances was *typical* of the international system of the period, and not unique to relations between the democratic Powers and the Soviet Union.

The Soviet approach to external security was shaped by Russia's history and ideology, and by internal debates over policy. In the early 1920s, the Russian economy lay devastated by war, revolution and foreign military intervention. Because the wave of workers' revolutions that Lenin had predicted would transform the world had failed to materialize, the Soviet leadership was compelled after 1919 to defend socialism with the resources of Russia alone. As the Red Army's defeat by Poland in 1920 had underscored, this could be achieved only if Russia industrialized to wage machine-age warfare. Joseph Stalin, who had out-manoeuvred his internal rivals to become sole leader of the Soviet Union in the late 1920s, recognized the need for an internal revolution before socialism could be exported abroad. In 1928, in order to build 'socialism in one country', the first Five-Year Plan of crash industrialization was launched. Industrialization, as well as the forced collectivization of agriculture, was accompanied by the merciless suppression of alleged internal class enemies and saboteurs. For orthodox Bolsheviks too, there were compelling reasons to industrialize swiftly. Soviet ideology prophesied that one day a crisis in capitalism would compel the capitalist Great Powers to unite and stamp out socialism. Hence Lenin's heirs saw it as their task to forestall the formation of an anti-Soviet coalition and to prepare for the coming struggle. 'We are fifty or a hundred years behind the advanced countries', Stalin bellowed in a 1931 speech. 'We must make good this distance in ten years. Either we do or they crush us.'

By the early 1930s, conspicuous progress had been made in equipping the Red Army with advanced weapons and readying the Soviet economy for total war. The timing appeared close indeed. The onset of the Depression, the growth of fascism and Japan's conquest of **Manchuria**, which menaced Russia's vulnerable Asian territories, all appeared to portend the long-expected capitalist onslaught. Moscow's initial response was to conclude non-aggression pacts with the Baltic States, France and Poland. Despite Hitler's brutal suppression of the German communists, the Soviets likewise hoped to co-exist peacefully with the Nazis. However, the Führer rebuffed Soviet feelers and trumpeted himself as Europe's saviour from Bolshevism. One German delegate to the World Economic Conference openly called for the dismemberment of Russia for the benefit of 'people without *Lebensraum*'. It was under these foreboding circumstances, not to mention a lack of alternatives, that the Soviets turned to collective security.

The Spanish Civil War, the alignment of Germany, Japan and Italy under the Anti-Comintern Pact and Russia's exclusion from Munich did not bode well for Soviet security through either multilateralism or bilateralism. While Litvinov spoke of collective security at Geneva, proposals for a rapprochement were offered to Berlin behind the scenes via a Soviet trade delegation. All of this was to no avail. Worse, the mass internal violence of the Great Terror and the purge of the Red Army in 1937–38, which accounted for about half of the officer corps, crippled the Red Army. In Western eyes, the terror confirmed Russia's status as an uncertain ally. The situation did not change until war appeared imminent in the summer of 1939, when suddenly Germany, France and Britain courted the Soviet Union. In May, to signal that all bids would be welcome, Stalin replaced Litvinov with the latter's most vocal internal critic, Vyacheslav M. Molotov. As the diplomacy reached a climax in August, the choice for Stalin was between a deal with Hitler, which promised to isolate Russia from the impending inter-capitalist conflict, or a triple alliance with Paris and London, which would ensure Russia's early entry into the 'second imperialist war'. Accordingly, on 23 August, Molotov and Hitler's foreign minister, Joachim von Ribbentrop, concluded a non-aggression treaty.

Manchuria

The three north-eastern provinces of China and home of the Manchu people. From 1932 to 1945, with the addition of Jehol province, it became the Japanese puppet state of Manchukuo.

Spheres of influence between the two totalitarian empires were defined and Poland was partitioned. The Nazi–Soviet embrace was consistent with Bolshevik ideology and diplomatic practice. The Soviet Union had no love for the status quo nor any faith in perpetual peace. Stalin knew that the revolution at home was not yet complete, but the opportunity to expand the socialist system into Europe was irresistible.

From Munich to European war

The twelve months before September 1939 witnessed a decisive change in European diplomacy. In 1938, British and French statesmen permitted the Reich to annex Austria and the German-speaking parts of Czechoslovakia; in 1939, London and Paris signalled their determination to stop Nazi expansion by extending security guarantees to Poland, Romania and Greece. This shift from a policy of accommodation to one of resistance placed Britain and France on a path to war. Why did British and French policy change? Why did Hitler, despite this change, press ahead with expansion?

Hitler's mounting impatience is our starting point. Before 1937, to achieve his goals, Hitler exploited opportunities as they appeared. Afterwards, Hitler accelerated the pace by initiating crises. Why? Much of the answer lies in his thirst for violence. Hitler craved war not just to satisfy his bloodlust, but also to make the law of the jungle the law of Europe. The first indication of this change in posture came at a meeting of Hitler's top officials on 5 November 1937. With a theatrical flourish that revealed how his inflated sense of destiny and mortality played on him, the Führer remarked that what he was about to say constituted his 'last will and testament'. The aim of long-range policy, he declared, was to obtain *Lebensraum* for the growth of the 'German racial core', and this could 'only' be executed with force of arms. To sustain the breakneck pace of German preparations for war and to move closer to autarky, the resources of Austria and Czechoslovakia had to be seized before 1943–45. By that stage, the military advantage that the Reich had obtained by arming early would begin to waste away as the other Powers caught up. Hitler speculated that Austria and Czechoslovakia might be taken earlier than anticipated if France was immobilized by civil war or if a war broke out between Britain, France and Italy. Although the senior army commanders present at the meeting objected to any action that might embroil the Reich prematurely in a European war, the Führer was convinced that Paris and London had already 'tacitly written off the Czechs'.

Hitler's view prevailed. In February 1938, the army generals who at the November conference had voiced anxiety about the risks of a general European war were ousted from their posts. Hitler assumed supreme command of a *Wehrmacht* which had grown from a few under-armed units to one of Europe's most operationally capable armed forces. His hold on the economy and diplomacy was also tightened. Göring, who headed the *Luftwaffe* and the Four-Year

Plan, extended his authority over the economy, while Ribbentrop, a pompous sycophant who said only what his master wanted to hear, became foreign minister. The first test for the regime, now free of conservative voices, appeared to confirm Hitler's appraisal of the European situation. On 9 March, Kurt von Schuschnigg, Austria's chancellor, took a bold step to counter German economic and political penetration into his country. He announced a plebiscite to determine whether his fellow Austrians wished to remain independent of the Reich. The tactic caught Berlin by surprise. To pre-empt an Austrian vote for sovereignty, the Nazis quickly improvised preparation for an armed intervention. A torrent of threats from Berlin persuaded Schuschnigg to cave in. On 11 March, Germany occupied Austria and Hitler proclaimed the *Anschluss*. Britain and France did not oppose him.

Attention now turned to Czechoslovakia. To keep the issue on the boil, Hitler ordered Konrad Henlein, the leader of the Nazi movement among the three million **Sudeten** Germans in Czechoslovakia, to demand minority rights that the government in Prague would find impossible to grant. War planning against Czechoslovakia (Operation Green) was stepped up to take into account the fact that German forces could now attack from Austria as well as Germany. Yet, for much of April–May 1938, Hitler was in no hurry to deal with the Czechs. Austria had to be digested first. Hitler and Ribbentrop had also learned in early May that Rome would not actively support a German attack on Prague. The timing for Operation Green was thus left open. Then, unexpectedly, on the weekend of 19–21 May, Europe was brought to the brink. Hitler's response to this 'weekend crisis' reveals much about how the stimulus of external events, his vision of *Lebensraum* and his lust for violence propelled Nazi aggression forward. The origins of the crisis remain murky. What we do know is that Czech intelligence received a *false* warning that the *Wehrmacht* was amassing to strike. Unnerved by the *Anschluss*, the Czech army prudently called up reservists and manned its frontier fortifications. Paris and London issued diplomatic warnings. Hitler was forced to deny that he planned to attack. In the world press, his denials were portrayed as a humiliating climb-down. Hitler was enraged. On 30 May, he vented his fury by revising the preamble to Operation Green to read: 'it is my unalterable decision to smash Czechoslovakia by military action in the near future'. Now bent on a short, sharp war soon after 1 October 1938, Hitler needed to invent a pretext. Henlein was ordered to intensify his internal agitation, while German newspapers began a propaganda campaign accusing the Czechs of heinous crimes against the Sudetenlanders.

The setting of the crisis of 1938 came as little surprise. After Locarno, informed observers agreed that once Germany and Russia revived, Central and Eastern Europe would become unstable. Ultimately, the fate of the 'successor' states rested on the approach Berlin and Moscow would adopt towards them. Would the intermediaries be regarded as useful buffers or prey? Nazi and Soviet ideology, the myriad revanchist claims and national hatreds that divided the region, and the limited capabilities of the small states, combined to ensure that the predatory approach would be adopted. One of the few hopes for the region was that the new nations might unite into a coherent bloc, but this was not to be. One problem was that most of the new states distrusted Hungary. Indeed, the 'Little Entente',

Sudetenland
The geographical area in Bohemia mainly inhabited by ethnic Germans. In 1919 it was placed on the Czech side of the German–Czech border and in 1938 led to an international crisis ending in the infamous Munich Agreement.

which had been formed in the 1920s between Czechoslovakia, Yugoslavia and Romania, was designed solely to deter Hungarian revanchism. Furthermore, the bitter rivalry between the Czechs and the Poles guaranteed that no one leader would emerge. Another factor that weakened the region was that the slump had led the largely agricultural and raw material-exporting economies of the Eastern European states to come under German dominance. Economic dislocation also led to right-wing dictatorships as well as the shameful persecution of Jews and other minorities. France swung between seeing its Eastern allies as assets and as liabilities. While they might help to contain Germany, they might also be the cause of the next Franco-German war. Also French influence was not always welcomed by the fiercely independent Eastern Europeans. In 1934, for instance, the Poles preferred to sign their own non-aggression treaty with Germany.

Moreover, the British never regarded Eastern Europe's frontiers as sacrosanct. To them, plunging Europe into war for the sake of a disputed border or the custody of a discontented national minority was as absurd in the 1930s as fighting a nuclear war for the sake of a united Germany or Korea appeared in the Cold War. Many sympathized with complaints that the Paris peacemakers had applied the principle of national **self-determination** unjustly against the aspirations of German nationalists. This is why the British did not attempt to reverse the *Anschluss*. What the British did not know for certain was whether Hitler was exploiting the alleged injustice of Versailles as a pretext for more far-reaching goals. The policy of appeasement rested on the mistaken belief that Hitler could be satisfied through orderly revision negotiated between Britain and Germany. For London, the danger was letting the crisis drift. An internal dispute in Czechoslovakia might trigger a Franco-German war, which would inevitably draw Britain in. The *Anschluss* only underscored the perils of allowing events to unfold without British intervention.

Chamberlain believed that Germany could be pacified, if only Hitler could be brought to the bargaining table. When he became prime minister, he had had six triumphant years as chancellor of the exchequer. Long before Baldwin stepped down in May 1937, Chamberlain, who towered in cabinet, was tipped to replace him. Neither narrow-minded nor provincial in outlook, his politics mixed a radical, reforming zeal at home with liberal imperialism abroad. He believed in the empire and in Britain's unique mission to promote peace and prosperity. He hated war, yet he did not seek 'peace at any price'; he saw spending on arms at the cost of social spending as a waste, yet he armed to deter war. 'What a frightful bill we do owe to Master Hitler,' he said, 'damn him!' And damn him he did. In no way was Chamberlain drawn to Nazism. He despised the dictators, but he knew he had to deal with the Nazi Führer if war was to be averted. The question was, how?

Convinced that the professional diplomats had blocked progress, Chamberlain's answer was to open a direct channel to Berlin. In November 1937, his friend Lord Halifax (who became foreign secretary after Eden resigned in February 1938) was sent to the Reich on an unofficial visit to explain Britain's position. Halifax told Hitler that Britain wanted a frank exchange of views on economic, colonial and territorial issues. If London and Berlin could arrive at reasonable solutions to these

self-determination
The idea that each national group has the right to establish its own national state. It is most often associated with the tenets of Wilsonian internationalism and became a key driving force in the struggle to end imperialism.

problems, then peaceful relations could be established between the European Great Powers. In reply, Hitler confessed that he too desired peace and only demanded a redress of Germany's legitimate grievances. The prime minister was delighted. The right atmosphere, he thought, had been created for bilateral talks. He wanted to say to Hitler: 'Give us satisfactory assurances that you won't use force to deal with the Austrians and Czechoslovakians, and we will give you similar assurances that we won't use force to prevent the changes you want, if you can get them by peaceful means.' Chamberlain's remark, while easy to ridicule, reveals what he was trying to achieve in 1938, and much about the wider, unfolding clash of values. Hitler craved a brutal, localized war against the Czechs to shatter the prevailing norms of European politics and thereby legitimize the use of violence; Chamberlain wanted to uphold the rule of law in international relations by facilitating peaceful revision through diplomacy and thereby to stigmatize the use of violence. For London, in the end, the process was always more important than the outcome.

Military considerations bolstered the case for a diplomatic solution. True, the arms balance was less dire than anyone at the time believed. British and French intelligence exaggerated the might of the *Wehrmacht*, especially the prospect of a knockout blow delivered by the *Luftwaffe*, while downplaying the strengths of their own forces. Planners on both sides of the Channel advised caution. The rearmament programmes of 1936 would only peak in 1939–40. By then, war could be faced with more confidence. Yet, even by that stage, the Reich could only be beaten in a protracted and ruinous war; there was no short cut to victory. 'We can do nothing to prevent the dog getting the bone, and we have no means of making him give it up', the British chiefs of staff concluded, 'except by killing him by a slow process of attrition and starvation.' Such calculations also lay behind French policy. The Czechs had a fine army, which would put up a brave fight before certain defeat, but French officials were unsure about whether France itself could withstand even a brief fight. The air force possessed only fifty modern planes. Aircraft production had slowed to a trickle. Since 1936, the franc had been devalued three times. Gold reserves dwindled and revenue declined. France faced bankruptcy. External politics did not augur well either. Poland (and Hungary) lined up with Germany to demand Czech territory, and the French were unwilling to count on the Soviets. Chamberlain and Halifax, though acutely aware that they could never forsake France, attempted to 'restrain' their French counterparts by refusing to state plainly whether they would assist France in a war against Germany. The British instead pressed French ministers to persuade their Czech allies to offer the Germans concessions. Édouard Daladier, the French defence minister and, since April 1938, premier, concluded that France could not uphold its treaty obligations to Czechoslovakia without inviting national disaster. He did not share Chamberlain's optimism that there could be lasting peace with Germany, yet one thing was certain. As General Maurice Gamelin, his top commander, advised, 'It is essential that we have Britain with us.'

During the crisis, it was Chamberlain who therefore had the initiative. He pursued the course he had laid out after Halifax's visit to Germany. In August 1938, he sent an emissary to mediate between the Sudetenlanders and Czechs. Hitler meanwhile turned up the heat with war preparations and further orders to

Henlein to become more recalcitrant. Hitler's plan for a bloodletting and Chamberlain's plan to satisfy his stated aim of uniting the German-speaking peoples peacefully collided. Twice Chamberlain flew to Germany for bilateral talks with Hitler. This was a spectacular gambit in an age unfamiliar with 'shuttle diplomacy'. On 15 September, at the first meeting, Chamberlain said 'yes' in principle to a German annexation of the Sudetenland, though Paris and Prague would also have to agree. Three days later, Daladier did agree, so long as Britain guaranteed the rump Czech state. Under pressure from London and Paris, and calculatingly mixed signals from Moscow about its intentions, the Czech president, Edvard Beneš, had little choice. On 22 September, the prime minister flew to inform Hitler that he would now get what he wanted. In reply, Hitler screamed for more, including the immediate occupation of the Sudetenland by German forces. Hitler still wanted his war by 1 October. After two difficult meetings with Daladier, Chamberlain at last told him that Britain would stand with France, and that the two governments should send a final plea for diplomacy as well as a military warning. The French army and the British navy mobilized for war. Hitler now decided to back away from a war over the timing and method of Germany's annexation of the Sudetenland. On 28 September, he took up Mussolini's proposal for a Four-Power conference, which met at Munich on the following day with the Duce, Daladier, Chamberlain and Hitler in attendance.

At Munich, the transfer of the Sudetenland was settled and the Four Powers guaranteed the frontiers of what was left of the Czech state. Munich was the sort of nineteenth-century Great Power arbitration that many considered to be the

Plate 7.1 Munich Conference, Germany, 30 September 1938. (Left to right) Prime Ministers Neville Chamberlain (UK) and Édouard Daladier (France), Nazi German Chancellor Adolf Hitler, Benito Mussolini (Italy) and Italian Foreign Minister Count Ciano gather to sign the Munich Treaty between Nazi Germany, France, Italy and the United Kingdom, authorizing Hitler to annex Czech territory. (Photo: Staff/AFP/Getty Images)

only way out of the extended crisis of the 1930s. Chamberlain thought that Munich would be the start of a general appeasement that would see Germany rejoin the League and progress towards world disarmament, and an end to autarky. It was a victory for the prime minister's shuttle diplomacy and, apparently, for the Führer. After all, he had been given what he had demanded so many times in public – the Sudetenland. Hitler was in fact enraged at having been cheated out of his Czech war. On 30 September, Chamberlain had even persuaded him to sign the notorious Anglo-German declaration, which committed Hitler to 'consultation' as the normal method of settling disputes. All Hitler ever wanted from the British was to be left alone. Now he would rid Europe of Britain.

Document 7.1

The Anglo-German declaration, 30 September 1938

We, the German Führer and Chancellor and the British Prime Minister, have had a further meeting to-day and are agreed in recognizing that the question of Anglo-German relations is of the first importance for the two countries and for Europe.

We regard the agreement signed last night and the Anglo-German Naval Agreement as symbolic of the desire of our two peoples never to go to war with one another again.

We are resolved that the method of consultation shall be the method adopted to deal with any other questions that may concern our two countries, and we are determined to continue our efforts to remove possible sources of difference and thus to contribute to assure the peace of Europe.

Adolf Hitler
Neville Chamberlain
September 30, 1938

Over the winter of 1938–39, Hitler raised the production targets for the expansion of the *Luftwaffe* and the German navy – both forces directed against the British. Ties with Tokyo and Rome were to be strengthened to paralyse the British Empire. The prerequisite to *Lebensraum* was now the subjugation of France. But the Czechs and Poles would have to be dealt with first to safeguard the eastern front. On 14–15 March 1939, under the threat of air bombardment, the Prague government was given no choice but to allow Germany to occupy what was left of the Czech state. Slovakia declared its independence under a German protectorate. Poland was a more complex problem. What Hitler wanted was extra-territorial rights in the Polish corridor, the annexation of the Free City of **Danzig** – both of which had been granted in 1919 to Poland to provide access to the sea – as well as Polish adherence to the Anti-Comintern Pact. In exchange, Hitler and Ribbentrop promised Warsaw territory in Ukraine after Germany turned eastward to deal with the Soviet Union. The implications of the German offer were clear enough: Poland was to become a vassal state of the Greater German Reich. Ribbentrop put the deal repeatedly to Josef Beck, Poland's foreign minister; each time the offer was turned down. On 3 April 1939, Hitler gave the order for war preparations against Poland to begin.

Danzig, Free City of
(Polish: Gdansk)
A historically and commercially important port city on the Baltic Sea. In 1919, the Paris peacemakers made Danzig politically independent as a 'free city' under the League of Nations in order to give the new state of Poland free access to the sea. However, the vast majority of the city's inhabitants were Germans. The return of Danzig to German sovereignty was thus a key issue for German nationalists between the wars. Hitler exploited the Danzig question as a pretext for his attack on Poland in 1939.

After Munich, the British and the French experienced a change in outlook. In London, Chamberlain and his ministers were puzzled over what was happening inside the German camp. In Paris too, politicians and officials wondered where Germany would strike next. Over the winter of 1938–39, the answers came in the form of spine-chilling intelligence, which suggested that the *Wehrmacht* was preparing a sudden attack on the Low Countries in order to seize bases for bombers. Neither the French nor the British intelligence services detected a slackening in the pace of German rearmament. Furthermore, on 9–10 November, a fierce pogrom against German Jews (*Kristallnacht*) swelled the sense of moral outrage against the Nazis that many had long tried to suppress. In both capitals, the unwinding of appeasement did not occur overnight, nor was it attributable to any single factor – yet it certainly began before Hitler occupied what was left of the Czech state. Some moved faster than others. Halifax abandoned appeasement more quickly than Chamberlain – although both men were always prepared to fight rather than see Nazi hegemony in Europe. In Paris, Daladier wished to construct a powerful Franco-British alliance, and to restore France's influence in Eastern Europe, while his foreign minister, Georges Bonnet, argued that France should adjust to a subordinate role in Europe.

The trend towards a resolute stand against Hitler was complicated by the fact that Munich had undermined French and British credibility. The solution was to offer firm commitments and guarantees. The process began in February 1939, when Chamberlain offered a public pledge to uphold French security. Conversations between British and French military staffs to draft joint war plans were scheduled. To build a barrier against the German domination of Eastern Europe, France and Britain offered security guarantees in March to Poland, Romania and Greece. Hesitantly, conversations with Moscow about an alliance also began. In May, to put military muscle behind these declarations, peacetime conscription was introduced in Britain. What was striking about this period was the way in which military perceptions altered so rapidly. British and French intelligence now highlighted German weaknesses, particularly in economic readiness for war and in trained manpower, and to underscore Anglo-French strengths as the 1936 construction programmes started to pay off. Rearmament was accelerated, so that British aircraft production would soon overtake German output. French armour, gun and aviation production now began to recover along with the French economy. 'If it comes to a duel between France and one other nation,' Daladier confidently declared, 'I would have no mortal concerns for the outcome.' British and French statesmen now knew that they could face the burdens of a protracted war with a united home front – no small thing for the fighting power of democracies. Indeed, Hitler's Prague coup had its greatest impact on the populace. No one relished war, but now there was a grim resolve to resist Hitlerism. It was not, however, public opinion, as some historians still argue, that dragged the 'peace at any price' men to war. Instead, British and French officials attempted to balance the issuing of credible threats designed to deter what they now perceived to be open-ended Nazi expansionism against the need not to throw away the chances of a German climb-down.

That such a balance should have been struck stemmed from an erroneous understanding of how Berlin worked. British and French diplomats argued that Hitler could be influenced by playing to moderates in his inner circle. In truth, Hitler was not swayed by moderates or extremists. The decisions were Hitler's alone, and the prospects in 1939 of a climb-down were nil. This was the legacy of Munich. If Hitler had gone to war even after Chamberlain had resolved the Sudeten question, then the full extent of his ambitions would have been exposed to the world, and the war could not have been localized to Central Europe. The fears of his military advisers and the downcast response of the German people to the prospect of war had also troubled his thoughts. In 1939, he was determined that he would not lose his nerve again or be drawn into diplomacy. Hitler would not permit 'at the last minute some *Schweinhund* [to] make a proposal for mediation'. His craving for violence, his growing aggravation as he tried unsuccessfully to manipulate events and the lack of brakes on his authority, all combined to produce the crucial miscalculations. In April 1939, in response to Poland's refusal to submit to his will and the granting of the Anglo-French guarantees to Warsaw, the Führer denounced the Polish–German non-aggression treaty of 1934 and the Anglo-German naval agreement of 1935. In May, to pave the way for a localized war against the Poles, Germany signed a ten-year alliance with Italy, the so-called Pact of Steel. Ribbentrop now assured Hitler that Britain and France were only bluffing; they would abandon the Poles as they had the Czechs. Hitler did not need any convincing. Dismissing signs of British and French determination and rearmament, he reached for the trump card, Soviet Russia. Actually, neither Hitler nor his commanders took the threat of Soviet arms very seriously in 1939 or earlier. The negotiations between Ribbentrop and Molotov in August were only of consequence because of the effect that a German–Russian treaty might have on Poland's guarantors. A Nazi–Soviet pact, so the Führer believed, would bring down Chamberlain's government, and provide the West with a pretext to desert the Poles. Despite the diplomatic coup, London and Paris firmed up their alliances. Count Ciano, meanwhile, said that Italy did not have the resources to join its Axis partner in a general war. Hitler pulled back, yet only briefly. The German–Polish war scheduled for 26 August was delayed until 1 September.

Conclusion

On 3 September 1939, Britain and France declared war. Hitler got his war, but it was not the localized war against the vulnerable Poles that he said he wanted. War against Britain and France came too soon for the completion of Nazi Germany's massive arms programmes. Autarky, huge war industries and a fleet fit to defeat Britain were at least five to six years away. Hitler and his commanders would now have to improvise. So too would their opponents. As British and French planners had made clear a year earlier in the Czech crisis, there was little that they could do to help the Poles. Germany would first have to be defeated in a long and grinding struggle. From the outset, in fact, the Anglo-French guarantees to Poland had a more symbolic than strategic significance. The guarantees signalled their determination to resist a Nazi bid for world mastery. To have abandoned the Poles would have meant forfeiting their rank as Great Powers, accepting the destruction of the existing system and the ushering in of a new world order based on the predatory principle of might makes right. True enough, Britain and France benefited disproportionately from the post-1919 distribution of world power, wealth and overseas territory. It was in their national interests to fight rather than watch the status quo crumble. Yet the conflict of the 1930s was always more about the essential rules and values of international politics than the distribution of material strength. The Anglo-French appeasement of Hitler's Germany until 1938 and the determination to fight Nazism in 1939 arose from the *same* set of national values and outlooks on international affairs. Once Hitler secured power in Germany, European war was only a matter of time.

Debating ideology and foreign policy in the 1930s

Many of the debates associated with the origins of the Second World War in Europe revolve around the complicated relationship between ideology and foreign policy. Obviously, it is impossible to make any sense of the diplomacy of Germany, Russia and Italy without some reference to ideology, but the real question is: to what degree were Hitler, Stalin, Mussolini and their advisers driven by the doctrines of Nazism, communism and Fascism? Was ideology really the principal driving force behind policy? Or did these statesmen often break free from their doctrines in order to play the 'perpetual' game of power politics with greater tactical freedom?

For instance, the British historian A. J. P. Taylor in his *The Origins of the Second World War* (London, 1961) sparked a bitter debate by describing Hitler as the 'supreme opportunist' in diplomacy. Hitler was a typical German statesman, Taylor argued, who sought to make the Reich dominant in Europe through the accumulation of power. As Taylor had intended, his dismissal of Hitler's beliefs as mere rhetoric designed to whip up popular sentiment at home shocked many historians. However, Taylor's challenge meant that his critics were forced to reconcile Hitler's remarkably consistent and often-stated views about race and living space with the fact that he did not have a fixed timetable for the completion of his programme.

The debate about the role of ideology is not restricted to the policies of the revisionists. Although Britain, the United States and France did not espouse monolithic, all-embracing ideologies, there is also no doubt that statesmen such as Chamberlain, Roosevelt and Daladier were in part guided by the essentials of liberal democracy as well as national values and identities. Indeed, some historians have argued that anti-Bolshevism in the West played a decisive role in blocking the formation of an anti-Hitler coalition between France, Britain and the Soviet Union. French and British statesmen were so blinded by their hatred and suspicion of the Soviet Union, according to this argument, that they failed to pursue the 'realistic' course of aligning themselves with Stalin against Hitler before it was too late.

Students should pay careful attention to the way in which arguments about ideology are framed. Normally, key personalities are categorized in one of two ways. First, there are the *ideologues*, who cannot grasp the dictates of balance-of-power politics because they cannot throw off their ideological blinkers. Second, there are the so-called *realists*, who transcend ideology and see the 'eternal' truths of power politics. So, for example, some argue that 'realists' such as Stalin and Churchill called for an alliance against Nazi Germany because they were not unduly influenced by their aversion to either capitalism or communism, while Chamberlain and Daladier could not overcome their hostility to communism and thus refused to consider an anti-German alliance with Russia. Here, the tacit assumptions are that there are 'eternal' truths about international politics and that human beings are capable of escaping their own world-views. Both of these assumptions, though widely shared by historians, are questionable.

Recommended reading

There are many very good general surveys of the 1930s, but the best two are Philip Bell's *The Origins of the Second World War in Europe*, 3rd edn (London, 2007) and Richard Overy's *The Road to War* (London, 1989). There are also some excellent essay collections: Gordon Martel (ed.), *The Origins of the Second World War Reconsidered* (London, 1992) focuses on the A. J. P. Taylor controversy, while Joseph A. Maiolo and Robert Boyce (eds), *The Origins of World War Two: The Debate Continues* (Basingstoke, 2003) deals with all the key Powers as well as major themes such as economics, intelligence and arms.

On the dual economic and political crisis, see Robert Boyce, 'World War, World Depression: Some Economic Origins of the Second World War', in Robert Boyce and Esmonde M. Robertson (eds), *Paths to War* (Basingstoke, 1989), and for a more general survey of the Depression in Europe, Patricia Clavin, *The Great Depression in Europe, 1929–39* (Basingstoke, 2000).

For students, the most useful general studies of the origins and collapse of the Weimar Republic are Eberhard Kolb, *The Weimar Republic* (London, 1988) and Detlev J. K. Peukert, *The Weimar Republic* (London, 1991). On Chancellor Brüning, see William L. Patch, *Heinrich Brüning and the Dissolution of the Weimar Republic* (Cambridge, 1998). For a fascinating and well-written book that restores much of the contingency to the advent of the Nazi regime in Germany, see Henry Ashby Turner's *Hitler's Thirty Days to Power* (London, 1996).

The best study of German foreign policy remains Gerhard L. Weinberg's *The Foreign Policy of Hitler's Germany*, vol. I: *Diplomatic Revolution in Europe, 1933–36* and vol. II: *Starting World War II, 1937–37* (Chicago, 1970 and 1980). Plenty of useful insights into the making of German foreign policy can be found in Adam Tooze's *The Wages of Destruction: The Making and Breaking of the Nazi Economy* (London, 2006). For a comparative study of Nazi Germany and Fascist Italy, and one that particularly focuses on the relationship between internal revolution and foreign expansion, see MacGregor Knox, *Common Destiny: Dictatorship, Foreign Policy and War in Fascist Italy and Nazi Germany* (Cambridge, 2000). On Italy, see also Knox's *Hitler's Italian Ally* (Cambridge, 2000).

There are several accessible and comprehensive studies of French foreign and defence policy. Anthony Adamthwaite, *Grandeur and Misery: France's Bid for Power in Europe, 1914–1940* (London, 1995) is highly critical of French states-manship and statecraft. Robert J. Young provides a concise account in his *France and the Origins of the Second World War* (New York, 1996), which sympathetically explores the ambiguities and uncertainties of French policy in the 1930s. There are two other more detailed studies of France that students can read with enor-mous profit: Martin Alexander, *The Republic in Danger: General Maurice Gamelin and the Politics of French Defence, 1933–40* (New York, 1992) and Peter Jackson, *France and the Nazi Menace: Intelligence and Policy-Making 1933–39* (Oxford, 2000).

On British appeasement policy and the origins of the war, an excellent starting point is R. A. C. Parker's *Chamberlain and Appeasement: British Policy and the Coming of the Second World War* (Basingstoke, 1993), which should be read in tandem with David Dutton's *Neville Chamberlain* (London, 2001). On deter-rence, economic appeasement and naval issues, see Gaines Post Jr, *Dilemmas of Appeasement: British Deterrence and Defence, 1934–1937* (Ithaca, NY, 1993), Callum A. MacDonald, 'Economic Appeasement and the German "Moderates" 1937–1939', *Past and Present* (1972), vol. 56, pp. 105–35, Joseph A. Maiolo, *The Royal Navy and Nazi Germany: A Study in Appeasement and the Origins of the Second World War* (Basingstoke, 1998) and Scott Newton, *Profits of Peace: The Political Economy of Anglo-German Appeasement* (Oxford, 1996).

On the policy of the Roosevelt administration, see Robert Dallek's classic, *Franklin D. Roosevelt and American Foreign Policy 1932–1945* (Oxford, 1979) and, more recently, David Reynolds, *From Munich to Pearl Harbor: Roosevelt's America and the Origins of the Second World War* (Chicago, 2001). On the troubled Anglo-American relationship, students should read David Reynolds, *The Creation of the Anglo-American Alliance 1937–1941: A Study in Competitive Co-operation* (London, 1981) and Callum MacDonald, *The United States, Britain and Appeasement 1936–1939* (London, 1981).

Scholars await a history of Soviet foreign policy in the 1930s that exploits the newly available sources and matches the detail of Weinberg's study of German policy. By far the best book so far is Jonathan Haslam's *The Soviet Union and the Struggle for Collective Security in Europe 1933–1939* (London, 1984). Geoffrey

Roberts, in *The Soviet Union and the Origins of the Second World War* (London, 1995), argues that the Soviet Union was committed to collective security. See Haslam's review of Roberts's book in 'Soviet–German Relations and the Origins of the Second World War: The Jury is Still Out', *Journal of Modern History* (1997), vol. 69, pp. 785–97. For an exploration of the influence of Bolshevik ideology and total war on Soviet policy formation, see Silvio Pons, *Stalin and the Inevitable War: Origins of the Total Security State in the USSR and the Outbreak of World War II in Europe* (London, 2002). James Harris provides the most systematic and archive-based analysis of Stalin's perceptions of the outside world in 'Encircled by Enemies: Stalin's Perceptions of the Capitalist World, 1919–1941', *The Journal of Strategic Studies* (2007), vol. 30, pp. 513–45.

The richest and most readable survey of the period from Munich to the outbreak of war is Donald Cameron Watt's *How War Came: The Immediate Origins of the Second World War, 1938–39* (London, 1989). On Eastern Europe and the war, students can now turn to Anita J. Prazmowska's *Eastern Europe and the Origins of the Second World War* (Basingstoke, 2000). Finally, there is now an excellent and wide-ranging collection of essays on Munich by Igor Lukes and Erik Goldstein (eds), *The Munich Crisis, 1938: Prelude to World War II* (London, 1999). The essays by Richard Overy on Germany, Martin Thomas on France and Igor Lukes on Czechoslovakia are of particular value.

CONTENTS

The Second World War, 1940–45

Introduction

Danzig, Free City of
(Polish: Gdansk)
A historically and commercially important port city on the Baltic Sea. In 1919, the Paris peacemakers made Danzig politically independent as a 'free city' under the League of Nations in order to give the new state of Poland free access to the sea. However, the vast majority of the city's inhabitants were Germans. The return of Danzig to German sovereignty was thus a key issue for German nationalists between the wars. Hitler exploited the Danzig question as a pretext for his attack on Poland in 1939.

see Map 8.1

Hitler's war began on 1 September 1939. At 4.45 a.m., the old German cruiser *Schleswig-Holstein* shelled a small Polish army installation at **Danzig** known as the Westerplatte. At the same time, the bulk of the German army, well over fifty divisions, including five tank formations as well as eight other lightly armoured and motorized units, began to cross the Polish frontier. The campaign was brief. The *Wehrmacht*, with a superior war-fighting doctrine that stressed aggressive movement and encirclement, exploited its numerical advantages in numbers of men, tanks and aircraft to break through the Polish defences. On 17 September the Red Army joined in by occupying eastern Poland. Warsaw fell to the German army ten days later.

Over the next twenty-one months the war expanded, combining the conflicts of Europe and Asia. The principal driving force behind this step-by-step process of escalating violence was relentless Nazi aggression. Between September 1939 and December 1941, Hitler wilfully added to the number of Great Powers arrayed against the Third Reich, but despite stunning successes on the battlefield in the early years of the conflict, he and his generals could not bring the European war to a victorious conclusion. Part of the explanation for this failure lies in the fact that Hitler's opponents resolved to fight on even after suffering the severest of military setbacks. This determination did not stem simply from a fear of

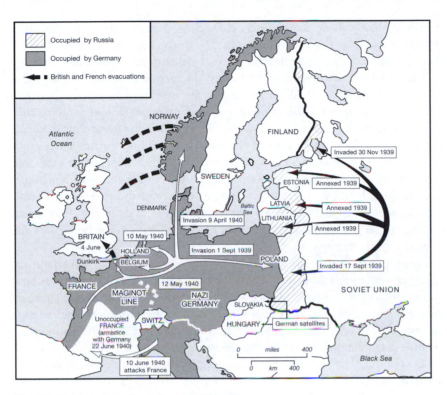

Map 8.1 German expansion in Europe, 1939–40

Source: After Nye (1993)

Germany's growing power, but more significantly from a widespread belief that Nazism, fascism and Japanese militarism stood for a new form of global barbarism that had to be stamped out before it was too late.

see Chapters 3 and 7

From European war to World War

In a speech to the Reichstag on 6 October 1939, Hitler made a vague peace overture to the Allies, Britain and France, by offering the restoration of a rump Polish state in exchange for peace. A few days later, the Allies rejected any talk of a compromise peace that legitimized Nazi conquests. However, despite their rejection of Hitler's offer, the Allies appeared to have little appetite for waging war. French troops did move forward of the Maginot Line, but only to boost Polish morale and improve France's defensive position. The Allies were equally reluctant to bomb German military and industrial targets for fear of provoking retaliatory raids against their own civilian populations. Only at sea was the war fought with intensity. The Allies disrupted German shipping and the Germans launched submarine attacks on Allied shipping. On 13 October 1939 a **U-boat** sank the

U-boat (English abbreviation of *Unterseeboot*) A German submarine.

British battleship *Royal Oak* at Scapa Flow in northern Scotland. Two months later, after a series of dramatic running battles, British cruisers forced the crew of the *Admiral Graf Spee* to scuttle their pocket battleship off Montevideo harbour.

The American newspapers aptly dubbed this period of relative lethargy the 'Phoney War'. Critics of Allied strategy at the time, and ever since, saw the 'Phoney War' as an extension of pre-war policies of '**appeasement**', arguing that Prime Minister Chamberlain and Premier Édouard Daladier never truly intended to fight the war with vigour because the 'appeasers' still held out some hope of a last-minute deal with Hitler. This critique rests on the mistaken notion that there was some short-cut to victory. However, as pre-war French and British planners foresaw, the only way to defeat Nazi Germany was first to absorb its initial attack, then to sap its strength through economic warfare, and, finally, once over-whelming strength had been accumulated by the Allies, to defeat Germany with an all-out final offensive.

Fighting a long war made strategic sense. However, there were political complications associated with it. Public opinion in France and Britain was now spoiling for a fight against 'Hitlerism', but instead, the electorates had to stomach the loss of Poland without any compensating gain. Upbeat newsreel reports about the impenetrability of the Maginot Line or the expanding size of the British army did little to quell apprehension about ultimate victory, especially as Stalin appeared to be supporting Hitler. Germany could count on Russia as a secure source of raw materials to circumvent the Allied naval blockade. Not only had the Red Army invaded Poland, but in November 1939 Russia also launched an unprovoked attack on Finland. In 1940, some in the Allied camp favoured assisting the Finns and drawing Russia into the fray. The French proposed bombing Russia's oilfields in the Caucasus to block part of the Reich's fuel supply. A foray into the Balkans to draw German divisions away from the western front was likewise proposed. The mushrooming of these perilous schemes for a quick victory reflected unease at the top, especially in Paris, about a long war. In fact, in terms of heavy armaments, the Allies were taking the lead over their foe. By May 1940, the Western forces, including those of neutral Holland and Belgium, could muster 152 divisions to oppose Germany's 135. The Allies had twice as many field guns as the Germans. France alone fielded 3,254 tanks to Germany's 2,439, including some of the world's finest. Only in the air did the Germans have a numerical edge, but even this steadily diminished as French and British aircraft production outpaced that of Germany, and contracts for modern American fighter planes were fulfilled.

On 21 March 1940 mounting political pressure in the Allied camp to do something claimed its first victim: Daladier was replaced by Paul Reynaud, his supposedly more dynamic finance minister. Ironically, Daladier had become an early enthusiast for an attack in northern Europe. Some decision-makers on both sides of the Channel looked to intervention in Scandinavia for decisive results. The key was Germany's dependence on Swedish iron ore. If ore shipments could be stopped, so experts believed, then Hitler's resource-starved war industries would soon grind to a halt. Since Sweden's ports were locked in ice most of the year, the iron ore had to be transported north by railway first to the Norwegian

appeasement
A foreign policy designed to remove the sources of conflict in international affairs through negotiation. Since the outbreak of the Second World War, the word has taken on the pejorative meaning of the spineless and fruitless pursuit of peace through concessions to aggressors. In the 1930s, most British and French officials saw appeasement as a twin-track policy designed to remove the causes of conflict with Germany and Italy, while at the same time allowing for the buildup of sufficient military and financial power to bargain with the dictators from a position of strength.

all-weather port of Narvik, and then shipped southward along the Norwegian coast to Germany. For the Western Powers, the complicating factor was that they could not openly flout Norway's neutrality. The Anglo-French Supreme War Council agreed on a plan to mine Norway's territorial waters to force German shipping out to the open seas, where the Royal Navy could intercept it. The hope was that the mining operation would force the Germans to invade Scandinavia. In turn, the German invasion would trigger the swift dispatch of an Anglo-French land force to secure Narvik, thus denying the German war economy a reliable supply of ore. The snag in this scheme was that the Führer had also become concerned about the security of Germany's prime source of iron ore and, unbeknown to Allied intelligence, had ordered his own invasion plan into motion days before the British could lay their naval mines.

On 9 April, the first day of the German attack, Denmark fell. Norway proved a much harder nut to crack. Norwegian fortress gunners sank the *Blücher* in the Oslo fjord before the German cruiser could land troops tasked to detain King Haakon VII. The Allies rushed troops across the North Sea and tried to assist the Norwegian defence, but German air power and numbers prevailed by early June. Norway cost the *Wehrmacht* more than 5,000 men, 200 aircraft and much of the surface fleet. In exchange, the Reich's northern flank was secured, and the Norwegian coast provided excellent bases for German air and sea forces to attack British shipping in the North Sea and the North Atlantic. The Norwegian debacle also accounted for the loss of more than 4,000 British servicemen. As a result, Chamberlain and his war cabinet were subjected to scorn and derision in parliament, and although the prime minister still commanded a majority in the House of Commons, he decided to resign. On 10 May, the first lord of the Admiralty, Winston Churchill, replaced him. Pugnacious, impulsive and eloquent, Chamberlain's successor benefited from a largely undeserved reputation as a pre-war advocate of coherent alternatives to appeasement. Yet, with an experience of war that spanned combat in the Boer War to ministerial rank in the First World War, Churchill's time had indeed arrived. His first weeks proved to be the most testing of his entire career.

On 10 May, the German western offensive began with air, airborne and armoured attacks into Holland, Belgium and France. Six weeks later France sued for peace. How can this triumph be explained? Scholars usually point to the German doctrine for the aggressive use of tanks in co-operation with dive-bombers and motorized infantry, what the Allies called *Blitzkrieg*. To be sure, the German army was unrivalled in operational finesse, yet France was not Poland. The German high command expected a long war in the west, and set industrial priorities for defensive weapons and entrenching equipment which reflected this expectation. The first German war plan called for a thrust into neutral Belgium and Luxembourg to outflank the Maginot Line and to lay siege to France. The plan changed from this rerun of the **Schlieffen Plan** to the now famous 'sickle cut' through the Ardennes Forest because of good intelligence and a large dose of desperation. Over the winter of 1939–40, Hitler repeatedly demanded an immediate attack in the west. His generals, convinced that an attack would fail unless they had time to accumulate greater strength, were equally certain that time

Schlieffen Plan
The German pre-1914 plan for a pre-emptive military offensive against France, which would involve troops passing through neutral Belgium. It is named after the German army chief of staff, General Alfred von Schlieffen.

was working against them, as Allied armaments and resources were growing faster than those of the Reich. Although few thought the 'sickle cut' would succeed, the gamble appealed to both Hitler and his top commanders because German intelligence officials confidently predicted that the bulk of the Allied armoured divisions would race into the Low Countries as soon as the German offensive opened. This was indeed General Maurice Gamelin's intention. The French supreme Allied commander planned to reinforce Belgium and Holland and thus block what he expected to be the German army's principal line of advance. Tragically, therefore, when the *Wehrmacht* struck on 10–11 May, the finest French and British divisions rushed headlong into a German trap.

As the French realized that metropolitan France was lost, Reynaud proposed fighting from abroad with the forces of the empire and navy, but Marshal Philippe Pétain and General Maxime Weygand, both of whom were appointed to positions of authority to stiffen French resistance, argued that the war was lost. France had to adapt to the German reshaping of Europe. For many French and Europeans, May–June 1940 did not simply herald the demise of the Third Republic; it also appeared to do the same for the values of liberty, fraternity and equality – the principles of the 1789 French Revolution. This wider meaning was not lost on Pétain and Weygand, who saw no shame in turning defeat into a witch-hunt against socialists, communists and Jews, and relished the opportunity to execute a French national revival based on order, authority and the nation in collaboration with Nazism. General Pétain, who replaced Reynaud as head of government on 17 June, signed the armistice with Hitler six days later and, on 1 July, founded a new French government, named **Vichy** after the small spa town where it was formed. Hitler set limitations on the size of the French army, imposed astronomical reparations and forced Vichy to agree to the German occupation of northern France and its coast. Hope that the Vichy regime might restore some French sovereignty through adherence to the **Nazi New Order** faded rapidly. Hitler did not want partners, least of all French ones, on his path to *Lebensraum* and World Power status.

The French defeat confronted Churchill with two problems. One was the rescue of the British Expeditionary Force, the other was whether to sue for a compromise peace. From 26 May to 3 June, under heavy *Luftwaffe* attack, the Royal Navy and a fleet of small civilian boats launched an improvised evacuation from Dunkirk. The rescue of some 338,226 British and French troops was a great success, but the British army had lost most of its heavy equipment. The question now was: could Britain fight alone? On 25 May the chiefs of staff answered yes. The Royal Navy and the Royal Air Force were strong enough to repel a German invasion, and (allegedly) there were signs that Germany's overstretched economy was weakening under the strain of war. For the next three days, the cabinet discussed the issue. Lord Halifax, the foreign secretary, argued that a balanced appraisal of the situation required an indication of what terms might be expected. Would Britain be forced to disarm? However, exploiting his position as cabinet chairman, and convinced that Britain could and should fight to either total victory or defeat, Churchill obstructed a dispassionate analysis of the pros and cons of negotiated peace, and rejected a 'parley' with Hitler as the slippery slope to

Vichy France
The regime led by Marshal Pétain that surrendered to Hitler's Germany in June 1940 and subsequently controlled France until liberation in 1944.

Nazi New Order
The German propaganda euphemism for the racial transformation and economic reordering of Europe to conform with the barbaric principles and criminal practices of German national socialism.

surrender. In Clausewitz's famous dictum, war is an extension of politics, and in wartime passion reigns over reason. In May 1940, Churchill believed that the British people were determined to fight, come what may. Most shared his belief that everything depended on American intervention. Many in the political elite, who had always despised the French alliance, were almost jubilant at the prospect of replacing France with the United States. In the meantime, Britain would have to repulse German air and sea attacks alone. On 3 July 1940, to prevent the Germans from seizing French warships, the Royal Navy attacked the French fleet anchored at its Algerian base of Mers el-Kebir.

The events of May–June 1940 had profound repercussions, especially for those states not yet engaged in the conflict. The sudden shift in the European military situation opened an opportunity for Mussolini. In April 1939 Italy had invaded Albania (a weak state long dominated by Rome) and in May had signed the Pact of Steel with Germany. However, Italy did not stand beside its northern partner in September 1939. Objections from the crown as well as strategic considerations determined the decision, for many officials argued that an early war against France and Britain would spell disaster. 'Non-belligerence' was a bitter pill for the Duce to swallow, for his policy programme and the authority of his regime were premised on military expansion and the warrior ethic. Thus when in 1940 the German battlefield victories pushed aside the *matériel* and domestic political obstacles to intervention, he decided to enter the fray. On 10 June 1940 Rome declared war on Paris and London. Ten days later the Italian army launched a poorly executed offensive into the French Alps. In his sudden bid for *spazio vitale*, Benito Mussolini spilled blood just in time to qualify for Italy's own armistice with the hapless French.

Hitler's triumph and Mussolini's intervention shattered Roosevelt's post-Munich policy. The Czech crisis had convinced the president and his advisers that they needed to contain the European dictators by supplying the Allies with arms and promoting the buildup of American air power. 'Had we had [in September 1938] 5,000 planes and the capacity to immediately produce 10,000 per year, even though I might have had to ask Congress for authority to sell or lend them to the countries of Europe,' Roosevelt said, 'Hitler would not have dared to take the stand he did.' Although more slowly than in Britain and France, American opinion also began in 1939 to shift against Nazi Germany. In this new political climate, Congress passed an amended Neutrality Act which permitted sales of American-made arms to belligerents on a 'cash and carry' basis. Since the British and French navies controlled the Atlantic, this policy favoured the Allies. While all of this was good news for London and Paris, in no way did it signal an American intention to enter the war. However, the French catastrophe, the British decision to fight alone and what appeared to be well co-ordinated **Axis** aggression in 1940–41 confronted the Americans with a stark choice: they could either convert the Americas into a fortress of isolation or take up arms and lead the anti-Axis coalition. As Roosevelt stated in late 1940, the United States would not live 'at the point of a gun'. To survive in an Axis world, he added, 'we would have to convert ourselves permanently into a militaristic power on the basis of war economy'. The first choice, which meant an end to the American way of life, was

Axis
A term coined originally by Mussolini in November 1936 to describe the relationship between Fascist Italy and Nazi Germany. The German–Italian Axis was reinforced by the so-called Pact of Steel signed by Rome and Berlin in May 1939. More broadly speaking, the term is often used (as in Chapter 8 of this book) to refer to the relationship between Germany, Italy and Japan. These three Powers were formally linked by the German–Japanese Anti-Comintern Pact of November 1936, which Italy signed one year later, and the Tripartite Pact of September 1940.

no choice at all. Therefore, in response to the escalating Axis threat, President Roosevelt authorized a gigantic American arms programme and searched for ways to keep the British fighting. In September 1940 the British agreed to lease bases in Bermuda and Newfoundland to the Americans for hemispheric security, and in exchange acquired fifty old American destroyers to escort Atlantic convoys. That same month, Japan, Italy and Germany signed the **Tripartite Pact** in an effort to deter Washington from entering the European war or interfering in Japan's southward advance, but this move quickly backfired. The United States refused to be deterred, and saw the Tripartite Pact as symbolic of the moral distinction between the two emerging coalitions: one dedicated to peace and liberty, the other to war and slavery. By March 1941, under **Lend-Lease**, the United States had saved Britain from bankruptcy and capitulation, while the US navy's Atlantic fleet began to engage in an undeclared war against German U-boats.

For Russia, May–June 1940 was a disaster. The Soviets had reckoned that the war in the west would become a prolonged deadlock, and that while the capitalists exhausted themselves, Russia would have ample time to grow stronger. Indeed, the ineffectual performance of the Red Army in the Finnish War underscored the urgent need for thorough military reform. Once France caved in, though, the Soviets faced the all-conquering *Wehrmacht* alone on the European continent. In response, Stalin turned to economic appeasement combined with unflinching territorial expansion. Convinced that Hitler would not move eastwards while Britain remained dangerous, and while Russia provided the resources Germany needed to finish Britain off, Stalin and Molotov agreed that they should display no weakness. This, after all, had been the chief lesson of Soviet relations with Japan. In 1939, when the Kwantung Army provoked fighting along the Manchurian–Mongolian frontier, Stalin, well aware from espionage that Tokyo did not desire war, ordered that the Japanese be given a bloody nose. Afterwards, relations improved.

The result was that in late 1940 and 1941 tensions with Berlin rose as Russia tightened its grip on Estonia, Latvia and Lithuania, demanded Bessarabia and Bukovina from Romania, and attempted to dominate Bulgaria. Hitler decided to attack the Soviet Union long before Molotov asserted Soviet rights, yet the latter's hard-nosed bargaining reinforced the Führer's fixation with the east. The Germans responded by wooing the Finns, signing up Hungary, Romania (a vital source of oil for the German war machine) and Slovakia to the Anti-Comintern Pact, and marshalling the bulk of the *Wehrmacht* into Eastern Europe for a knockout blow against Moscow. In reply, Stalin ordered that nothing should be done by way of military preparations that could be interpreted as provocative. The Soviet leader was convinced that 'hawks' in Berlin were trying to provoke him into some precipitous action, which would turn Hitler against him. British warnings of a German war plan were likewise dismissed as provocations designed to bring Russia into the conflict, especially after Rudolf Hess, Hitler's deputy, crash-landed a plane in Scotland in a bizarre bid to end the Anglo-German war. Although Russian intelligence and the Soviet ambassador in Berlin repeatedly warned of what was coming, the German attack on 22 June 1941 came as a surprise to Stalin.

see Chapter 3

Tripartite Pact

A mutual aid treaty signed between Germany, Japan and Italy in Berlin on 27 September 1940. The pact was intended to deter the United States from interfering in the creation of a German new order in Europe and a Japanese new order in Asia. Article 3 of the pact as well as additional secret clauses were drafted that stated that the pact did not commit the parties to go to war on each other's behalf.

Lend-Lease

With the Lend-Lease Act of March 1941, the US Congress empowered the president to lease or lend arms and supplies to any foreign government whose defence the administration considered essential to US national security. The programme, originally intended to rescue Britain, was eventually extended to more than thirty-eight states fighting the Tripartite Pact Powers.

In 1940–41, Hitler's choices had a far-reaching impact. His attack on Russia hardened American attitudes, especially towards Japan. It also initiated in Tokyo the debate that ended with Japan's decision to fight. It is worth remembering that war with Russia was not the only course open to Hitler. For instance, preparations for Operation Sea Lion, the invasion of England, began in July 1940. Air superiority over southern England, however, was a crucial prerequisite to Sea Lion. Field Marshal Göring promised that the *Luftwaffe* could achieve this, but the Royal Air Force proved a remarkably resilient foe. Even so, there were other compelling reasons for steering clear of a seaborne invasion of England. The Royal Navy had a crushing superiority in big warships. Much of the German surface fleet had been sunk or damaged in the Norwegian campaign. Many historians doubt that Hitler ever had any intention of carrying through with Operation Sea Lion and believe that the invasion preparations were only meant to intimidate the British. Moreover, even when Admiral Erich Raeder, the head of the German navy, proposed an alternative route to Britain's downfall, the Mediterranean, Hitler was not convinced. For him, southern Europe was always a minor theatre. Moreover, the capture of Gibraltar and the use of the French fleet would require co-operation with Vichy and Spain. Hitler had no desire to make General Pétain an ally, and, despite Spain's adherence to the Anti-Comintern Pact in March 1939, and General Franco's frequent declarations of wholehearted sympathy with the Axis cause, the Spanish dictator kept Spain out of the war.

Ribbentrop suggested an alliance with Russia as another way to crush Britain and counteract American interference. It was not a preposterous idea. Japan was courting Russia, and signed a neutrality pact with Moscow in April 1941. As allies, Germany, Russia and Japan would add up to an invincible Eurasian bloc. Yet Hitler made up his mind in late July 1940. From the inception of his ideological programme, Hitler looked to the creation of a vast autarkic Nazi empire and the consummation of his race revolution inside Germany through the conquest of *Lebensraum* in the east. On 31 July, he ordered the *Wehrmacht* to be ready by the spring of 1941 for Operation Barbarossa, the 'destruction' of the Soviet Union. Hitler's motives have been hotly debated. At the time, he justified his decision on strategic grounds. 'With Russia smashed,' he told his commanders, 'Britain's last hope will be shattered.' He later argued that war against Russia was a pre-emptive strike timed to knock Russia out before the Red Army became too strong. Indeed, it may be that the Soviet posture of asserting their territorial claims while supplying Hitler with the resources to wage war in the west appeared to be a long-term stratagem designed to lure him into a false sense of security while Soviet strength grew. While these explanations are plausible, the fundamental reason for Hitler's choice can be seen in the nature of his savage war in the east. Far from attacking out of fear of the Bolshevik giant, Hitler and his generals boasted that the Red Army would be crushed in a few weeks. Hitler ordered that the conduct of this campaign should be radically different from that of the west. Provision for the execution of Soviet commissars and systematic murder of Jews was made. Instead of exploiting long pent-up hatred of the Stalinist system or Ukrainian nationalism to the *Wehrmacht*'s advantage, the Germans arrived in the east as an all-conquering master race with economic and resettlement plans that pre-supposed the enslavement and death of millions.

The final step on the road to global war was Hitler's (and Mussolini's) declaration of war on the United States on 11 December 1941. This arose in part out of the parallel crisis in the Pacific that had been developing since the summer of 1940, which came to its conclusion in December 1941 when the Japanese took the decision to go to war against the United States, Britain and the Dutch East Indies. For Hitler, the outbreak of war in the Pacific provided an opportunity to take the offensive in the Atlantic. For months, the German navy had been urging Hitler to declare war on the United States so that they could unleash U-boats against vulnerable American merchant ships. The US navy, in any case, was already fighting an undeclared anti-submarine war against them. For Hitler, who had always ridiculed the war-making potential of the United States, this reason was as good as any to bring forward the final showdown.

see Chapter 3

The Axis at war

For the Axis, the way to win any one war was to start another. In 1941, this escalatory approach seemed to pay. Unable to end the war in the west, Hitler ordered Barbarossa in the east. Germany won great victories in the first six months. Russia lost a staggering 3,138,000 fighting men killed, captured or missing, as well as 20,000 tanks, 100,000 guns and 10,000 aircraft. Unable to defeat China, Japan launched the **Pacific War** with an attack on Pearl Harbor. On 7 December, Japanese carrier-based aircraft sank six American battleships, badly damaged two other battleships, wrecked 292 warplanes and inflicted 3,581 casualties. Two days later, with equal efficiency, Japanese aircraft sank the British warships *Prince of Wales* and *Repulse* and started a lightning campaign to occupy the British colony of Malaya that ended on 15 February 1942 with the capture of the naval base at Singapore.

Barbarossa and Pearl Harbor were the Axis high points. German tank crews and Japanese aviators were invincible. However, signs appeared even at this stage that the Axis advance had begun to falter. The Red Army stopped the *Wehrmacht* in front of Moscow. Admiral Isoroku Yamamoto, who had led the attack on Pearl Harbor, knew that his nation could not win a long war against the United States. 'We can run wild for six months or a year,' he said, 'but after that I have utterly no confidence.' He was right. Instead of breaking Washington's will to reverse the Japanese conquest, the Americans resolved to crush Japan. The turning point arrived in early June 1942. In the seas around the American island base of Midway, US navy aircraft carriers attained a decisive victory over the Japanese. At the battle's end, four Japanese aircraft carriers, with their magnificently trained sailors, aircraft mechanics and pilots, were lost. Midway also cost the Americans a carrier, but more of these key vessels than Japan would ever build were already on order from American shipyards. The turning point in the German–Russian war arrived

Pacific War
The phrase usually used to refer to the Allied war against Japan from 1941 to 1945.

in November 1942 when six Soviet armies broke through ill-prepared Romanian forces on the flanks of the German Sixth Army, which was besieging Stalingrad. This ruined city on the lower Volga was a compelling symbol: Hitler, who had promised the city's capture, ruled out a retreat; Stalin knew that the city bearing his name could not fall. In a few weeks, General Zhukov demonstrated that the Red Army too had mastered the art of manoeuvring massed tanks to encircle enemies. The German Sixth Army was surrounded and starved. On 31 January 1943, General Friedrich Paulus, the German commander, and 200,000 of his men surrendered.

After these two defeats – Midway and Stalingrad – the war efforts of Japan and Germany never recovered. Axis fighting power eroded while that of the Allies rapidly grew. Winning the war for the Allies was a hard slog fought at tremendous cost against often fanatical yet poorly equipped and supplied defenders. Why did the course of the war turn? One clue lies in the pre-war policies of the Axis Powers: Germany, Italy and Japan had all worked to achieve **autarky** and to build the industrial base to wage **total war**, but the target dates for the completion of their 'armaments in-depth' programmes were all well into the 1940s. Economies preparing for a long war could not be converted overnight to adjust to the sudden burst of output needed to win a short war. The Axis Powers could not therefore maximize their striking power in the early years of the conflict, when victory through knockout blows seemed possible.

Half-completed armaments factories and synthetic oil plants alone do not explain the Axis's loss of momentum. Poor organization and misguided policies also played a part. Germany, the only Axis state that could have competed economically with the United States and the Soviet Union, was the most telling case. The image of a thoroughly militarized, command economy was largely a pre-war Nazi façade. Indeed, the Reich did not make the most of its productive potential because of wartime mismanagement. Excessive layers of bureaucracy, myriad independent agencies working at cross-purposes, not to mention incompetence at the top, all combined to generate economic chaos. Output lagged and long manufacturing runs were interrupted by the military's self-defeating quest for the perfect design and an aversion to the 'American' practice of mass production. Astonishingly, up to 1943, Britain's much smaller yet more efficient economy churned out more arms in almost every category than Germany's did. The situation improved after 1942, when Hitler appointed Albert Speer, his favourite architect, as the minister for armaments. By 1944, with mass production underway and resources rationally allocated, arms manufacture had trebled. Yet, with the Allies closing on the Reich from the west and east, Speer's production miracle arrived too late.

In 1941, Japanese ministers knew that they could never equal the industrial might of their new foes. Once the gamble of a short war backfired, defeat was only a question of time. The unending war in China proved to be the largest drain on manpower and *matériel*. Though Japanese forces controlled large parts of China and South-East Asia, these resource-rich regions lacked the infrastructure and industrial development that would enable them to be systematically exploited for Japan's war effort. Moreover, Tokyo was too reliant on the seaborne supply of raw

see Chapter 7

autarky
A policy that aims at achieving national economic self-sufficiency. It is commonly associated with the economic programmes espoused by Germany, Italy and Japan in the 1930s and 1940s.

total war
A war that uses all resources at a state's disposal including the complete mobilization of both the economy and society.

see Map 8.2

Map 8.2 Japanese expansion in Asia, 1940–42

Source: After Nye (1993)

materials. Once the balance at sea turned against Tokyo, Japanese shipping suffered relentless attrition from American submarines. In 1943–44, Prime Minister Tōjō and his ministers instituted last-ditch measures to raise aircraft production at the expense of all other sectors of the economy. Output doubled, but it was too late to do anything except prolong the agony. Too few skilled pilots were available to do more than organize suicidal *kamikaze* attacks on advancing American warships, while American B-29 bombers systematically fire-bombed

Japan's large urban centres. In defence of the home islands, everyone expected that Japanese soldiers would die fighting rather than surrender. For that reason, Washington did not relish thoughts of an invasion; seizing the vital islands of Saipan, Iwo Jima and Okinawa from zealous Japanese defenders had, after all, already cost tens of thousands of American lives. In Washington, some argued that a promise to leave the emperor on his throne would promptly end the war, but no such pledge was possible as it would have contravened the Allied doctrine of demanding **unconditional surrender**. Instead, the war in the Pacific was settled with the use of atomic bombs. On 6 and 8 August, two atomic bombs destroyed the cities of Hiroshima and Nagasaki. After Hiroshima, Tokyo remained silent. After Nagasaki and the almost simultaneous entry of the Soviet Union into the war, the emperor called for peace and the Pacific War came to an end on 15 August.

Italy's military performance was briefer and far less tenacious than that of Japan. As Mussolini's officials had warned, a premature European war did spell disaster. Yet in the predatory climate of 1940–41, the expansionist zeal was irresistible. As the Duce explained, Italians 'seek to break the territorial and military chains that suffocate us in our sea'. Operationally, however, the task was well beyond Rome's reach. Italian troops who had attacked Egypt in September 1940 were three months later forced by the British to retreat back into Libya. In October, Italy's unprovoked aggression against Greece was repelled. In November 1940, British carrier-launched aircraft sank three battleships in harbour. The economy underperformed: chronic scarcities of resources and technical backwardness were reinforced by poor organization. In 1941–42, the aviation industry turned out far fewer warplanes than ordered. Instead of propelling forward the Fascist revolution, Italians resisted full mobilization. Defeat exposed how shallow the roots of the regime really were. In July–August 1943, intense Allied air attacks and landings in Sicily initiated the collapse of the Italian economy as well as Rome's defection from the Axis. Mussolini was arrested, while his military chief, Marshal Pietro Badoglio, negotiated in secret with the Allies for an armistice. Pre-emptively, Hitler ordered the *Wehrmacht* to secure northern Italy while his paratroops rescued the Duce. Meanwhile, Anglo-American armies landed in the south. Italy thus ended the war as a secondary battleground for the major combatants.

Fascist Italy's brief war underscores another reason why the Axis failed: there was no co-ordination in Axis strategy. Given the predatory norms of their shared view of world affairs, it is not surprising that each partner fought a separate war, and gave the other little notice before touching off another conflict. Hitler provoked the European war before Rome was ready. In starting his 'parallel' war, Mussolini was eager to secure gains in North Africa and the Balkans without Germany. At their meeting in October 1940, the Duce did not tell the Führer of his designs on Greece, while Hitler was silent about Russia. Days later, the German move into Romania ahead of Operation Barbarossa reinforced Mussolini's anxiety about Germany's domination of the Balkans, and confirmed his decision to attack Greece. In 1941, to prop up his Italian ally, Hitler sent forces to Libya to push the British back into Egypt and diverted divisions gathering for Barbarossa to roll into

unconditional surrender
A doctrine first articulated at Casablanca in January 1943 by President Roosevelt at the Anglo-American summit meeting. The view that there could be no negotiated peace with the Axis stemmed from the sharp moral distinction between the Grand Alliance and the Axis as expressed in documents such as the Atlantic Charter and the United National Declaration, as well as the desire on the part of the Allies not to repeat what they saw as the chief error of 1918–19 – that Germany had not been thoroughly beaten before the Versailles Treaty was imposed.

Yugoslavia and Greece. While Hitler's personal admiration for Mussolini remained unshaken, Germany's treatment of Italians as unworthy vassals became much more pronounced. After Italy's surrender, the Germans took savage revenge in the north and exploited Italian labour and wealth for their war economy. Strategic co-ordination was little better between Berlin and Tokyo. Hitler had shocked his Anti-Comintern partner by signing the Nazi–Soviet Pact in 1939. Shortly after the Japanese had signed a neutrality pact with the Soviets in April 1941, the Germans attacked Russia. Hitler's declaration of war on the United States was not an act of Axis solidarity. As Gerhard Weinberg suggests, had such unity existed, Berlin and Tokyo could have co-ordinated their wars with some success. Hitler might have sent powerful forces to break through to advance across Egypt into the Middle East, while the Japanese might have moved into the Indian Ocean and linked up with the Germans. Instead, the Japanese tried to seize Midway and later locked themselves into a long attritional battle in the Solomon Islands for Guadalcanal, while the Germans plunged deeper into Russia.

What part did values play? Were the Axis Powers, especially Germany, doomed because they stood for evil causes and fought like criminals? Perhaps there was something to Hitler's cynical formula: 'Once we have won, who is going to question our methods?' Alternatively, while values were not alone decisive, the ethical war shaped the final outcome. Certainly propagandists in Berlin, Tokyo and Rome thought it would do so, and worked to portray the struggle as a just cause, fought defensively against immoral foes who craved to wipe out their enemies. While the Axis legions were unstoppable, this case was simple to make. Once the bombs began to fall and reversals at the front could no longer be kept quiet, civilian morale flagged. The importance of morale depended on the context: in Italy, defeat undermined support for the war; in Germany and Japan, where public loyalty to national leaders ran deeper and was in part enforced by terror, both states could rely on at least the resigned consent of workers and soldiers, and often on much more. Omar Bartov argues that with the coming of the ideological war against Soviet Russia, the *Wehrmacht* became *Hitler's* army, faithful to his vision of *Lebensraum* and race war. Moreover, the army's identification with the Führer explains why so many fought tenaciously on the long road back to Berlin. Fear and greed won the Axis many temporary allies of opportunity, but dread of an Axis victory also repelled neutrals and inspired resistance movements in occupied countries. Japanese atrocities in China, Manchuria, Korea and beyond made its **pan-Asian** propaganda of 'Asia for the Asians' ring hollow. Arguably, Hitler's **Final Solution**, the murder of six million European Jews, diverted resources away from the front and denied the German economy millions of potential workers. Yet a balance sheet to measure this crime is a grim and difficult thing to draw up, and the scale of the mass murder was only fully exposed after the war. What is certain is that these revelations confirmed what many fighting on the Allied side had long known: that Hitler and his allies stood for an inhumane and barbaric world order.

pan-Asianism
The idea that Asia should free itself from Western imperialism and unite in a common effort to modernize. Espoused chiefly by Japan before 1945, but some Indian and Chinese nationalists were also attracted to the concept.

Final Solution (*Endlösung*)
The Nazi euphemism for the mass murder of European Jews.

The Grand Alliance at war

No one except Adolf Hitler could have united the United States, the Soviet Union and the British Empire for a common purpose, but even during their united struggle against Nazism, pre-war hostilities lingered. The Americans opposed British imperialism and **protectionism**. The British resented American economic dominance and anti-imperialism. Both the Americans and the British loathed Russian communism, and the Soviets remained wary of Anglo-American capitalism. Yet the 'Grand Alliance' – a term coined by Churchill – remained steadfast, and out-produced and out-gunned the aggressors. The strategic cycle of the Allied war effort followed that laid out by pre-war Anglo-French planners (albeit with the United States in France's place). The Allies initially absorbed furious Axis onslaughts, then accumulated overwhelming superiority in men and weapons while wearing down those of their enemy, and, finally, launched crushing offensives.

protectionism
The practice of regulating imports through high tariffs with the purpose of shielding domestic industries from foreign competition.

The precondition for the Allied victory over Nazi Germany was the survival of Britain, and even more so, of the Soviet Union. Had the British opted for a negotiated peace, or succumbed to an invasion, the United States would have retreated behind the walls of a 'fortress' America. Instead, faced with the *Luftwaffe*'s bombing 'blitz' of London and other cities, and the relentless menace of prowling U-boats to its merchant shipping, the British endured, and so became the heroic cause for American interventionism to rally behind. Once the United States mobilized, Britain supplied the air bases, staging areas and port facilities required for the combined bomber offensives of 1943–44 as well as the invasion of France in June 1944. Had the Soviet Union collapsed under the pressure of the *Wehrmacht*'s knockout blows in the summer of 1941, then Britain would certainly have had to sue for peace or, in the following year, yield to the full weight of the *Wehrmacht*. Few in the summer of 1941, including most British and American military and intelligence officials, gave the Red Army more than a few weeks.

Not only did Russia endure, but in the following year the Soviets began to turn the *matériel* balance. In 1943, Soviet industries produced more than twice as much steel, nearly twice as much artillery, and thousands more tanks and aircraft than the Reich. How? Part of the answer can be found in German shortcomings, specifically the *Wehrmacht*'s inability to crush the Red Army, and the failure of the German war economy to exploit its full potential. Yet the Soviet Union, and especially the Soviet war economy, suffered blows that should have initiated collapse. Barbarossa cost Stalin one-third of his rail network, 40 per cent of his electrical generating capacity and three-quarters of his steel and iron supply. From July to December 1941, however, 1,523 iron, steel and engineering plants were dismantled and relocated to the Urals–Volga–Siberian heartland, well beyond Hitler's reach. Despite this disruptive exodus, Russia out-produced Germany on a much slimmer resource base because the Soviet people sacrificed everything for military output. The rapid decline in production for civilian consumption did not result in a breakdown in popular morale. Coercive measures were enforced to keep workers working, but fear alone cannot account for a willingness of millions to toil day in, day out on meagre rations and under harsh working conditions. Perhaps this popular Soviet groundswell of resolve sprang from sources similar to those that kept the British fighting in 1940. Ultimately, it would have all been in vain had Soviet managers not displayed a remarkable capacity for planning and organization. Unlike the Germans, the Soviets dedicated resources to mass-producing a few proven designs, including the KV-1 and T-34 tanks. Abundant machines wielded by the revitalized Red Army turned the defensive battle at Stalingrad into an offensive. In July 1943, at the Battle of Kursk, where Hitler and his generals tried one last great pincer movement to blunt the Red Army advance, General Zhukov's armies ground down the Germans in the largest tank battle ever, and then counter-attacked.

Before Hitler declared war on the United States, he predicted that the Americans would take five years to organize full-scale war production. He was wrong: in 1940, the Americans built 331 tanks and 12,804 aeroplanes; in 1941, the numbers jumped to 4,052 tanks and 26,277 planes; by 1942, the figures skyrocketed to 24,997 and 47,826. Nothing explains the Allied victory over the Axis better than the magnitude of American rearmament. By 1944, Americans were cranking out 40 per cent of all the weapons produced globally, and two-thirds of the arms fielded by the anti-Axis forces. This industrial miracle was facilitated by the American political culture. The state did not need to conscript industry or labour; they volunteered. Americans embraced mass production, civilian ingenuity, healthy competition and profit. Washington issued targets, and private industry worked out clever ways to meet ever more ambitious goals. The slack in the American pre-war economy – a legacy of the slump – and North America's remoteness from the battlefronts of Europe and Asia also help to explain the gigantism of its rearmament. For instance, at an empty field called Willow Run near Detroit, the Ford Motor Company (which alone manufactured more arms than Italy) built the world's largest assembly hall in 1941 to manufacture four-engine heavy bombers, the B-25 Liberators. The 5,450-feet long assembly line covered 67 acres and orchestrated the fitting of 1,550,000 parts for each B-25 bomber. By 1944 well-fed and well-paid American workers could put together one B-25 Liberator every sixty-three minutes.

Not only did the Allies win the arms race, but they pooled resources, co-ordinated strategy and maintained a unity of purpose better than their adversaries. Lend-Lease was the principal means for the redistribution of surplus *matériel* and resources within the alliance. Precise values are difficult to calculate, but about $45–50 billion worth of food aid, military hardware, oil and industrial goods and services was sent overseas. The first and largest recipient was Britain, followed by Russia. The **Free French Forces** under General Charles de Gaulle and the Nationalist Chinese under Jiang Jieshi were also major beneficiaries. How significant was Lend-Lease? It rescued Britain from insolvency in 1941. About one-fifth of all British arms were American in origin. Moreover, the aid from the United States permitted Britain and Russia to focus their war industries on what they could do for themselves best. As Stalin said in 1942, 'Send us trucks instead of tanks.' More than 400,000 sturdy American trucks provided the Red Army with superior battlefield mobility over their increasingly horse- and wagon-reliant

Free French Forces

General Charles de Gaulle commanded an armoured division in the battle of France and then, briefly, held a junior post in Paul Reynaud's cabinet on the eve of France's defeat. In June 1940, in radio broadcasts from London, he called upon French people everywhere to join him in the struggle to free France from the Nazi occupation and, later, Marshal Pétain's Vichy regime. At first, the general's calls went largely unanswered. His abrasive, overbearing personality and his lack of diplomatic finesse ensured that his relationship with Roosevelt and Churchill was always rocky at best. By 1943, however, he had become the undisputed leader of the Free French movement, whose growing volunteer forces participated in Allied military operations in North Africa and the Middle East. In 1944, Free French Forces triumphantly participated in the liberation of France. The Allies recognized his administration as the French provisional government in October 1944, and de Gaulle, a national hero, was elected president in November 1945. He resigned shortly thereafter when the National Assembly refused to grant him American-style executive powers. He again served his country as president from 1958 to 1969.

German foe. The Americans likewise helped the Soviets to overcome serious shortages of food and machine tools. Even so, the influx of Lend-Lease was more marginal to Soviet staying power than it was to that of Britain. Large quantities of Lend-Lease goods were in fact stockpiled by Soviet officials. Nonetheless, as a sign of the commitment to Russia's war effort, few things compared with the safe arrival of a convoy carrying American cargoes, escorted by Royal Navy warships, through submarine-infested Arctic waters. Of course, we should not paint too rosy a picture, for American aid was also a source of political friction. Washington exploited Lend-Lease in order to compel London to agree to abandon imperial preference after the war, and Soviet officials always viewed any interruption to the flow of goods with a sceptical eye.

Strategy was the principal source of inter-Allied tension. For Moscow, the priority was an early 'second front' to ease the burden on the Red Army. Although America's war had begun in the Pacific, Roosevelt prioritized the war against Germany, the most dangerous foe, and his staff devoted the bulk of American strength to a campaign on the European continent. Successful landings in France, however, depended on the Red Army's continued resistance in the east. The spectre of a separate Nazi–Soviet peace never vanished. In May 1942, therefore, when Molotov questioned General George Marshall about a cross-Channel invasion of Europe during a visit to Washington, the army chief of staff, according to the president's wishes, replied that preparations were in hand for a 'second front' within the year. Few in Moscow took this promise at face value, yet it became a sore point, especially as delays mounted. Put simply, there were too many demands on scarce shipping to prepare for an early invasion. American forces, with all of their heavy kit and supplies, had to be shipped to British ports, and Britain still required large imports of food, fuel and arms to fight. The British, moreover, who had developed a healthy respect for the German army, feared that a premature invasion would fail and thus prolong the war. Time was needed to gain more experience of landing operations and to develop amphibious craft. In the meantime, Churchill and his advisers preferred a peripheral strategy of blockade, bombing and subversion against the Nazis, while the Anglo-American forces were used in North Africa and the Mediterranean against Italy. After the landing in Vichy-controlled North Africa in November 1942, and the final surrender of Italian and German troops in Tunisia in May 1943, the Americans, who never thought that decisive results could be achieved this way, found themselves drawn deeper into the Mediterranean. After Italy's defection from the Axis, the British spoke alluringly of strategic possibilities for landings in the Balkans, but the Americans refused to be diverted. The cross-Channel invasion of Europe was scheduled for 1 May 1944. This target was confirmed at the Teheran Conference in November 1943, where Churchill, Roosevelt and Stalin all met for the first time. Publicly, the Big Three affirmed their partnership in the fight against Hitler. Behind closed doors, Stalin agreed to attack Japan once Germany fell, and to mount an offensive on the eastern front to correspond with the Anglo-American landings.

Despite these bitter and persistent squabbles, therefore, the Allies fought a more co-ordinated war than the Axis. Co-operation was closest between Britain

Plate 8.1 The 'Big Three', December 1943. Left to right: Soviet Premier Joseph Stalin, US President Franklin Roosevelt and British Prime Minister Winston Churchill sit together at the Teheran Conference, Persia (now Iran), during the Second World War. (Photo: Hulton Archive/Getty Images)

and the United States. After 1941 the two governments developed an integrated organization to wage war, from the combined chiefs of staff at the top, down to an elaborate series of subsidiary committees for joint shipping, industry, technical and scientific research, and intelligence. In the first phase, the Anglo-American war emphasized naval and air power. Without command of the sea, the invasion of France was unimaginable. From 1940, when the German navy could exploit easy access to the Atlantic, U-boats organized in deadly 'wolf packs' held the upper hand, claiming a horrific toll on cargo ships and crews. Fortunately, the offensive developed slowly enough for British, Canadian and American forces to perfect U-boat counter-measures before the Germans could respond with their own countervailing innovations in submarine technology. By March 1943, when the Germans were forced to abandon the Atlantic after crippling U-boat casualties, convoys were provided with constant close air support from land-based long-range patrol aircraft or from short-range planes launched from escort carriers. Allied destroyers had also become ruthlessly proficient in locating U-boats with sonar below (or with radar above) the surface and sinking them. Information centres on both sides of the Atlantic co-ordinated the progress of convoys, aircraft and escorts, and shared excellent intelligence on U-boat locations. In addition to winning the long battle of the convoys, the Allies also devised more efficient ways to transport *more* cargo with *fewer* ships. With equal ingenuity, the Americans mass-produced thousands of replacement merchant ships. A standard design, the Liberty Ship, was built in prefabricated sections and then swiftly welded together on slipways. Try as they might, the U-boats could never sink enough shipping to starve Britain out of the war or impede the steady buildup of American ground forces assigned to the liberation of Europe.

Before the invasion of France, the British and the Americans relied entirely on air power to strike directly at German targets. In fact, only the Anglo-American air forces developed the big four-engine bombers required for mass bombing. This readiness to attempt 'strategic' bombing in part reflected pre-war anxieties about a *Luftwaffe* 'knockout' blow, and in part expressed the desire to avoid bloody land battles by fighting quick air wars. Although the German 'blitz' of London and other cities had shown that civilian morale was more resilient than anyone had anticipated, and that economies were more difficult to dislocate than air theorists had predicted, the British tried to obtain decisive results in 1940–41 with twin-engine medium aircraft. Photographic analysis of bomb damage revealed that the effort was ineffectual. However, bombing was Churchill's only reply to Stalin's sallies that the British had no stomach for the fight.

The combined Anglo-American bomber offensive was launched by Roosevelt and Churchill at Casablanca in January 1943. The appearance on British airfields of large numbers of four-engine American B-17s and British Lancasters turned the delivery of big payloads into a reality. The British, who sought to shatter German civilian morale, bombed cities at night, while the Americans, who believed that 'precision' was possible, struck industrial targets by day. Both day and night raids were costly. By the spring of 1943, the Germans had diverted 70 per cent of their fighter force and thousands of men and anti-aircraft guns to the west. In this way, the air war constituted a 'second front', but losses as high as 11 per cent per mission meant that the bomber offensive could not be sustained. The battle turned in late 1943, however, when the Allies focused their air power on the destruction of the *Luftwaffe*. British and American bomber fleets targeted the German aviation industry, while American-made fighters, equipped with disposable fuel tanks for extended range, escorted the bombers deep into the Reich. Not only did the long-range escorts offer constant protection, and thereby quickly reduced loss rates, but they also shot down attacking fighters, which began to appear in ever smaller numbers. By June 1944, therefore, when American, British and Canadian soldiers stormed the Normandy beaches, the *Luftwaffe* had been eliminated as a serious menace, while Allied aircraft pounded German troops at will. Although the fire-storms in Germany's cities did not break morale, Albert Speer observed that the Allied bombs stunted munitions production, ate up scarce labour and accelerated the collapse of the German war economy in 1944–45.

Besides strategic bombing, Britain and the United States also secured a tremendous lead in the collection, analysis and exploitation of most forms of intelligence, especially in the interception and breaking of coded Axis radio transmissions. Before the war, Germany (and later Italy) adopted an electro-mechanical encoding machine (known as the Enigma) to protect its secret diplomatic and military radio traffic from code-breakers. Most experts believed that secret messages encoded by a cipher machine were too complex to be broken.

However, thanks to the work of Polish code-breakers in the 1930s, Britain and France were able to obtain a window on to the German code. Before Warsaw fell, Polish officials turned over two Enigma machines as well as prototypes for devices known as the 'bombes', which 'solved' mechanically the settings for the Enigma machines. The British progressively developed an elaborate system for the exploitation of Enigma. The hub was a Victorian mansion north-west of London called Bletchley Park. Listening stations in Britain and abroad intercepted and retransmitted enemy signals to Bletchley Park, where teams of code-breakers and service analysts turned the secret Axis messages into useful information (code-named Ultra) for select distribution. In the first two years Ultra was of only limited value, for excellent intelligence could not make up for inadequate fighting strength. For example, although the British had forewarning via Ultra of the German plan to capture Crete in May 1941, little could be done to prevent the German paratroops from securing the island's airfields. It also took time for the British to establish secure methods to disseminate Ultra in a timely manner and to educate field commanders to integrate signals intelligence into their decision-making process.

After 1942 the secret war tilted decisively in favour of the Western Allies, when they began to collaborate. The Americans revealed Magic, the codename for the American cracking of Japanese codes, and the British unveiled Ultra. In 1943, the Allies were reading more than 4,000 German signals a day, as well as a large volume of Japanese and Italian traffic. To be sure, Ultra *alone* was not a war winner. Intelligence was a 'force multiplier'. Thanks to reliable information, the British and the Americans were able to concentrate forces where they were most needed, to seal most of their own security leaks, and to gain a day-by-day insight into the intentions and capabilities of their foes. In the Atlantic, Ultra was invaluable because listening to the constant chatter between U-boats and the German command permitted the Allies to re-route vulnerable convoys away from lurking wolf packs. Sometimes code-breaking could be decisive. The American ability to break the Japanese naval codes, for example, proved indispensable to their triumph against the odds at Midway. Usually it was the painstaking accumulation of seemingly unimpressive pieces of the enemy puzzle that supplied the edge. Insights gained in this way allowed planners to fine-tune deception campaigns to play on Axis preconceptions. Supremacy in signals intelligence likewise enabled the British to capture all of the Nazi spies sent to England and then to compel them to transmit misinformation to Berlin. Overall, the secret war reveals much about the modernity of the Western war effort. The Axis too had victories in the covert war, but the authoritarians failed to create the integrated and free-thinking institutions to exploit intelligence systematically.

Did values play a wider role in the Grand Alliance's victory? Britain, the Soviet Union and the United States were attacked and could thus call on their people to fight for the just cause of national self-defence. The war was also portrayed as an epic struggle of human progress against the nihilistic forces of slavery. Propaganda depicted the Axis dictators as carnivorous beasts bent on global domination. The Axis record afforded ample evidence: aggression in Asia and Africa, a string of broken treaties, the persecution of the Jews, the rape of Nanjing, the German terror bombing and so on. In Russia, few who experienced the Nazi occupation had any doubt about what the war meant for them. Not only was the moral high ground vital to rallying the public will at home (and, in Britain's case, within the Commonwealth and Empire), but it was also a powerful inducement to neutrals and occupied peoples to resist the aggressors. Thousands of Czechs, Poles, French, Norwegians and others fought beside or in the uniforms of the Allies to win legitimacy for their exiled governments and assure national liberation. In August 1941 Roosevelt (with Wilsonian gusto) and Churchill affirmed the principles of peace, democracy, self-determination and prosperity in the **Atlantic Charter**. In January 1942 the normative distinction was drawn sharply again with the declaration of the United Nations, which underscored the Allied aims of freedom, justice and peace in the new world order. As always in politics, the moral case was ambiguous. The Allied war effort was not free of the barbarities of modern warfare, especially city bombing, and the Alliance included some with dubious ethical credentials. Stalin, after all, had signed a wicked pact with Hitler, had occupied Poland and attacked Finland. How could the representative of this murderous regime sit in judgement on Axis officials at the war crimes trials? In the end, what counted was that the moral choices at the time were clear enough to bind the anti-Axis coalition for long enough to win.

Atlantic Charter
A document signed by Franklin Roosevelt and Winston Churchill in August 1941 which committed the United States and Britain to support democracy, self-determination and the liberalization of international trade.

The collapse of the Grand Alliance

In *Mein Kampf*, Hitler wrote, 'Germany will either be a World Power or there will be no Germany.' He tried to keep his word. As Anglo-American forces closed on the Reich from France and the Red Army marched from Eastern Europe, Hitler's soldiers fought on and on 16 December 1944, in a forlorn bid to relive the glories of June 1940, launched a surprise attack into the Ardennes to break through the American lines. While the weather grounded Allied aircraft, the German tanks made headway towards recapturing the vital port city of Antwerp. Once the skies cleared and the Americans recovered, the Germans, short of fuel and ammunition, were beaten back.

Only three things could have altered Germany's fate in 1944–45. One was a coup. On 20 July 1944 Hitler narrowly escaped a bomb planted in his head-quarters under the map table. The conservative German army officers and other high officials who had planted the bomb out of fear for Germany's future paid with their lives for this attempt on Hitler's life. The second, one Hitler had great faith in, was some secret 'wonder' weapon. New weapons, namely rockets, flying bombs, jet aircraft and advanced submarines, were already in use or nearly so with little effect. Fortunately, the Germans failed to build the one device that might have made a difference, the atomic bomb. Third, the Führer might have prolonged the war or perhaps stopped it by negotiating a separate peace with one of his foes. The Allies, however, held firm. So, the final act of Europe's long tragedy was staged in the bunker of the Reich Chancellery. As the Red Army advanced

Mein Kampf (German: *My Struggle*)
A semi-autobiographical book dictated by Adolf Hitler to his chauffeur and his personal secretary, Rudolf Hess, while he was serving a prison sentence for his part in the failed Munich beer hall *putsch* of 9 November 1923. It was published in 1925–26 in two volumes. Sales did not reach the hundreds of thousands until Hitler took power in 1933. It is a myth that the book was unread or ignored by foreign statesmen. It contained no detailed timetable for aggression; instead, *Mein Kampf* is a rambling exploration of Hitler's basic political and racial views.

towards the bombed-out suburbs of Berlin, Hitler ordered the demolition of what was left of German industry and infrastructure. On 30 April 1945 Hitler committed suicide.

It is tempting to try to pinpoint the moment when the Grand Alliance began to fall apart between Hitler's suicide and Germany's final surrender on 5 May 1945. As the purpose that had united the Allies in the first place was achieved, so runs the logic, the Alliance began to pull apart. However, the defeat of Nazi Germany is only one part of a much wider explanation of why wartime co-operation between the Big Three did not continue into peacetime. In 1944–45 a progressive breakdown in East–West relations was not a foregone conclusion. London, Washington and Moscow shared an interest in checking the re-emergence of German revanchism. Europeans of all ideological hues longed for an extended period of quiet reconstruction and resettlement. Why then did East–West relations go sour? The main part of the answer lies in the clash of values and visions of world order between the victorious Powers.

From 4 to 11 February 1945 Roosevelt, Churchill and Stalin met at Yalta in Crimea. The conference marked the high point of inter-Allied co-operation. The Big Three reiterated their demand for Nazi Germany's unconditional surrender. Stalin pledged to enter the war against Japan (the Red Army in fact attacked Japan on 8 August). With victory in sight, post-war issues took on urgency. Officials drew up plans for a Four-Power occupation of Germany (the French would occupy one zone) and the prosecution of German war criminals. Consensus was also reached on the need for a new international organization to promote **collective security** to replace the now defunct **League of Nations**. In line with the principles first set out in the Atlantic Charter, the Big Three issued a 'Declaration on Liberated Europe'. The declaration promised Europeans the right to determine their own futures through democratic institutions. Finally, they settled the long-disputed question of Poland's borders. The frontiers of the new Polish state would be drawn much further westward, at the territorial expense of Germany, and to the benefit of Soviet Russia.

Yalta could have formed the basis for a working relationship, but each of the Big Three was seeking peace and security in its own way, and officials in each capital worked to identify and remedy the likely circumstances under which new threats might emerge according to deeply entrenched doctrines. Washington, for example, was determined not to repeat the mistakes of the 1920s and 1930s. Peace would be secured through the active participation of the United States in a number of new multilateral institutions. In July 1944 the Americans thus hosted delegates from forty-four nations at **Bretton Woods** in New Hampshire in order to fashion a post-war economic order. The conference buzzed with Anglo-American ideals of liberal economics and free trade. Two institutions were established: the International Monetary Fund and the International Bank for Reconstruction and Development (or the World Bank). The mission of the first was to set up a new financial system based on fixed exchange rates to facilitate world capital flows; the second was intended to supply the capital for major reconstruction projects. Similarly, from August to October 1944, Washington played host to diplomats from thirty-nine countries for the Dumbarton Oaks

collective security
The principle of maintaining peace between states by mobilizing international opinion to condemn aggression. Commonly seen as one of the chief purposes of international organizations such as the League of Nations and the United Nations.

League of Nations
An international organization established in 1919 by the peace treaties that ended the First World War. Its purpose was to promote international peace through collective security and to organize conferences on economic and disarmament issues. It was formally dissolved in 1946.

Bretton Woods
The site of an inter-Allied conference held in 1944 to discuss the post-war international economic order. The conference led to the establishment of the IMF and the World Bank. In the post-war era the links between these two institutions, the establishment of GATT and the convertibility of the dollar into gold were known as the Bretton Woods system. After the dollar's devaluation in 1971 the world moved to a system of floating exchange rates.

Conference on the formation of the **United Nations** Organization. Just like Woodrow Wilson decades before, Roosevelt believed that the world needed a single forum for the peaceful resolution of conflicts. Yet he also recognized that the replacement for the old League had to reflect the unequal distribution of power and responsibility in international relations. Roosevelt's vision of the new UN thus included a General Assembly of all states and a select executive (the Security Council) of Great Powers, principally the United States, the USSR, China and Britain, which would act together as the world's 'four policemen'.

Roosevelt's idea of the 'four policemen' indicated his willingness to work with Moscow. As Cordell Hull, the secretary of state, said in November 1943, with the foundation of a concert of Great Powers there would no longer be the need for 'spheres of influence, for alliances, for balance of power, or for any other special arrangements through which, in the unhappy past, the nations strove to safeguard their security or to promote their interests'. These words do not, as one might think, betray a lack of political savvy and sophistication. The president and his advisers knew that Stalin was a suspicious tyrant. What they hoped was that the war had taught the Soviet leader and his officials that mutually beneficial relations with the capitalist world were possible. They were equally alert to Moscow's deep sense of insecurity. Eastern Europe, they agreed, could no longer be a hotbed for anti-communism and a launch pad for anti-communist crusades. Russia would be preponderant in the region. But how would Moscow *exercise* that power? The Americans did not object to Stalin shaping the foreign and defence policies of the Eastern European states. What the Americans rejected was the formation of an *exclusive* sphere of control. In other words, so long as the Soviets permitted the Eastern Europeans to exercise self-determination and democracy at home, and to participate in multilateral institutions and commerce abroad, then there would be little scope for future conflicts. However, if Moscow tried to impose one-party politics and closed economies within their sphere of control, then Eastern Europe would become a source of national discontent, chronic poverty and eventually general war.

The British understood too that Stalin would dominate Eastern Europe. Like the Americans, Churchill and his advisers did not object to a Soviet sphere of influence, so long as the principles in the Atlantic Charter and the Declaration on Liberated Europe were adhered to. In talks between Churchill, Stalin and their foreign ministers in October 1944, south-eastern Europe was divided between them in what came to be called the 'percentages agreement'. To protect their imperial interests in the eastern Mediterranean and Egypt, the British attained predominance in Greece, while the Soviet Union attained the dominant position in Romania and Bulgaria. Churchill also implied to Stalin that he would not oppose Soviet claims in Eastern Europe if Stalin would help him safeguard Britain's Asian empire against American pressure for rapid **decolonization.** Britain's readiness to draw spheres of influence and to shore up its declining empire with diplomacy was consistent with the view prevalent in London that Soviet Russia would behave after the war much like its tsarist predecessor. The British Empire could peacefully co-exist yet still compete with the Soviet one provided their rivalry remained circumscribed by well-defined rules. Churchill's diplomacy

United Nations (UN)
An international organization established after the Second World War to replace the League of Nations. Since its establishment in 1945, its membership has grown to 192 countries.

decolonization
The process whereby an imperial power gives up its formal authority over its colonies.

likewise indicated growing anxiety about Britain's place among the *World* Powers. The war had severely weakened Britain in relation to both the United States and the Soviet Union. No one could be sure of the continued flow of American material aid and goodwill across the Atlantic. Indeed, despite Churchill's stormy relations with General de Gaulle, who had been recognized as head of the provisional government in Paris, the British turned to France as a potential ally to help counteract Soviet influence in Western Europe. It was thus the British who persuaded Washington and Moscow that France should be responsible for a zone of occupation in Germany and that it should be given a permanent seat on the UN Security Council.

see Chapter 9

Evidence from the Soviet archives confirms that Stalin and his top advisers had no 'master plan' for Eastern Europe leading to the full communist take-over in 1947–48. Nonetheless, Soviet security policy, just like that of the United States and Britain, was the product of weighty historical and ideological factors. As American diplomats understood, the Soviets would not allow Eastern Europe once again to become the springboard for war against Russia. In November 1943, Stalin had insisted that the Soviet Union retain the territorial gains it had made under the Nazi–Soviet pact and from Finland and Romania, the absorption of the Baltic States, and the movement of Poland's frontier with Russia further westward. For Stalin and his security planners, territory equalled security. This did not necessarily mean the imposition of communist dictatorships across Eastern Europe, but where the Red Army had become the army of occupation, territory was best safeguarded through deep political and economic transformations. 'This war is not as in the past,' Stalin explained in 1945. 'Whoever occupies a territory imposes his own social systems. Everyone imposes his own system as far as his army has the power to do so. It cannot be otherwise.' To be sure, the Soviets were primarily concerned with reconstruction, recovery and freedom from aggression in this period, but their willingness to deal with the United States and Britain only reflected what they expected to be a long truce with the leading proponents of global capitalism and imperialism.

After Yalta, there were signs that the truce would not hold for long. A change of American presidents accelerated the downturn in relations. On 12 April 1945, Roosevelt died and his vice-president, Harry S. Truman, assumed the presidency. The new man in the White House had not been a member of Roosevelt's inner circle during the war and was less inclined to give Stalin the benefit of the doubt. Truman's fears that the Soviets might emerge as the next totalitarian threat to the American way of life, as well as the liberty, prosperity and security of Western Europe and Japan, also arose from a steady hardening of attitudes. The atomic bomb played an important, though alone not decisive, role in the magnification of hostilities. Before becoming president, Truman had been kept in the dark about the Manhattan Project – the codename for the American atomic programme – but Soviet intelligence had had some knowledge of the project as early as 1941. After the successful detonation of the first bomb on 16 July 1945, Truman hoped that the weapon would provide him with the lever he needed to keep the Soviets loyal to the Yalta Accords. As David Holloway has shown, Stalin and Molotov were equally determined not to be intimidated by the atomic bomb and deliberately toughened their responses to Truman's abrasive diplomacy.

Poland was the initial source of grave tension. Over Poland, Truman and Churchill saw Stalin as a contract breaker (which was a serious charge in the light of Hitler's failure to respect treaties), while Stalin and Molotov saw the West's pressure for elections in Poland as a violation of their designated sphere of control. Poland was a sensitive issue for all three states: Britain had gone to war over Poland; Polish Americans formed a powerful lobby in Washington; and twice in thirty years German troops had attacked Russia through Poland. At Yalta, Stalin agreed to form an inclusive government through free elections that would have a place for the representatives of the Polish government in exile in London. During the war, Stalin and the London Poles tried to strike an equitable bargain, but failed. Historic antagonisms ran too deep, and revelations in 1942 that the Red Army had murdered 15,000 Polish officers at Katyn Forest did not improve matters. For Moscow, the danger was that free elections would elect an anti-Soviet government in Warsaw. Since the Polish Workers Party had no base of popular support, this fear was not unfounded. Poland, as the Red Army's access route to defeated Germany, was too valuable to risk and therefore, despite concessions from Washington and London, Stalin reneged on his Yalta pledges and imposed his own subservient provisional government known as the Lublin Poles. Washington and London complained. Perhaps Stalin wanted an *exclusive* sphere of control after all? Yet, on 5 July, the two governments recognized a slightly modified cabinet of Lublin Poles as the legitimate government in Warsaw. Regardless of how much outrage British and Americans officials felt over the Polish elections, the German question still had to be settled in collaboration with the Soviet Union.

Conclusion

The Second World War left deep wounds. Fifty million perished, twenty-eight million of whom were civilians. Russia and China together accounted for thirty million killed; their principal enemies, Germany and Japan, another nine million; Poland, caught between two towering ideological foes, suffered civilian losses of about four to five million. The distinction between civilians and combatants, the rear area and the front line, had been erased in the minds of many long before the first trigger was pulled. The high proportion of civilian deaths was testimony to the boundless violence with which the war was conducted, as well as to the power of the ideologies that millions fought and willingly sacrificed their lives for. Nothing epitomized this more than Nazi Germany's systematic murder of six million Jews. To put this crime against the idea of a common humanity into context, one should recall that the Final Solution claimed *one-third* of the world's total Jewish population in 1939. In Poland alone, Hitler and his followers murdered more than two and a half million Jews, or 90 per cent of all the Jews in pre-war Poland.

The suffering did not end with the dead or those who knew and loved them. Millions staggered as refugees over the gutted remains of European civilization. Mobs meted out justice to collaborators and many more besides. Millions were forced to flee. In the wake of the conflict people were being shifted *en masse* to fit the new frontiers. 'We must expel all the Germans,' exclaimed one Polish communist, 'because countries are built on national lines and not on multinational ones.' The Germans were not alone in suffering this fate. Much of Eastern Europe witnessed the expulsion of ethnic and religious minorities. Europe's nightmare ended in a brutal peace. The old European game of Great Power competition was now over, and the continent was set to become one battlefield (albeit the most important one) in a wider Cold War world, with a divided Germany as its epicentre.

Debating why the Allies won the Second World War

At what point did the Allies win the Second World War? Was the outcome predetermined from the weight of Allied economic resources? Was victory always beyond the reach of the Axis states? In the view of many military and economic historians, the outcome of the war was no longer in any doubt after December 1941. The Japanese surprise attack on Pearl Harbor and the German declaration of war on the United States brought together a coalition of Great Powers that could not fail to win so long as they continued to fight long enough. As R. A. C. Parker put it in *The Second World War* (Oxford, 2001), 'the Allies must win if they stayed together'.

The statistics make Parker's case persuasive. Even in the year most favourable to the Axis in fighting performance and strategic advantages, the Allies still possessed a healthy margin over their foes in wealth, exploited and untapped resources, weapons and manpower. After 1942, the superiority grew at an astronomical rate. Mark Harrison, a leading historian of the economics of the Second World War, argues in *The Economics of World War II* (Cambridge, 2000) that once the initial Axis attacks petered out, the 'economic fundamentals' reasserted themselves: 'The greater Allied capacity for taking risks, absorbing the cost of mistakes, replacing losses, and accumulating overwhelming quantitative superiority now turned against the Axis. Ultimately, economics determined the outcome.'

Richard Overy, in his *Why the Allies Won* (London, 1995), rejects the large dose of determinism in explanations based on statistics alone. He locates the war's turning point much later than the end of 1941. 'On the face of things,' he writes, 'no rational man in early 1942 would have guessed at the eventual outcome of the war.' A rich account of why the Allies won, Overy asserts, must consider a whole series of *contingent* factors. The war was as much a moral, political, technical and organizational contest as it was a race to stockpile resources. Scholars must explain why Germany, Italy and Japan failed to exploit their full productive potential in 1942 and thus lost their operational and strategic momentum. If the organizational weaknesses had been overcome by the aggressors, allowing them to realize their potential, then 'the Axis by 1942 might well have proved the irresistible force'. Quantity of men and arms, moreover, tells us little about *quality*. Remarkably quickly, the Allies managed to close the qualitative gap and rally their peoples to fight the long hard battles required to destroy the Axis. Even so, the critical campaigns of 1942 were won by the Allies by slender margins.

Recommended reading

Many of the books cited in the recommended reading of Chapter 7 also cover 1940–41. On the United States, students will find Waldo Heinrichs, *Threshold of War: Franklin D. Roosevelt and American Entry into World War Two* (Oxford, 1988) indispensable. For Italy, see MacGregor Knox, *Mussolini Unleashed 1939–41* (Cambridge, 1982). For a survey of the period before the coming of global war, see John Lukacs, *The Last European War, September 1939–December 1941* (New York, 1976).

On the Phoney War, see Thomas Munch-Petersen, *The Strategy of the Phoney War: Britain, Sweden and the Iron Ore Question, 1939–1940* (Stockholm, 1981), Talbot Imlay, 'Allied Economic Intelligence and Strategy during the "Phoney War"', *Intelligence and National Security* (1998), vol. 13, pp. 107–32 and his excellent *Facing the Second World War: Strategy, Politics, and Economics in Britain and France, 1938–40* (Oxford, 2003). On France and 1940, see Martin S. Alexander, 'The Fall of France 1940', *Journal of Strategic Studies* (1990), vol. 13, pp. 10–44 and Joel Blatt, *The French Defeat of 1940: Reassessment* (Oxford, 1997). For an account of 1940 that stresses the role of intelligence, read Ernest R. May's superb *Strange Victory: Hitler's Conquest of France* (London, 2000). For the official German histories, see Bernd Stegemann *et al.* (eds), *Germany and the Second World War*, vol. II: *Germany's Initial Conquests in Europe* (Oxford, 1991) and Karl-Heinz Frieser, *The Blitzkrieg Legend: The 1940 Campaign in the West* (Annapolis, MD, 2005).

The best analytical study of the British decision to fight on in the summer of 1940 is Chapter 6 of Christopher Hill, *Cabinet Decisions on Foreign Policy* (Cambridge, 1991) and the most readable is John Lukacs, *Five Days in London: May 1940* (London, 1994). See also Philip M. Bell, *A Certain Eventuality: Britain and the Fall of France* (Farnborough, 1974) and David Reynolds, 'Churchill and Britain's Decision to Fight on in 1940', in Richard Langhorne (ed.), *Diplomacy and Intelligence during the Second World War* (Cambridge, 1985). For an essential study of the politics of Lend-Lease, consult Warren F. Kimball's *The Most Unsordid Act: Lend-Lease 1939–1941* (Baltimore, MD, 1969). For a panoramic and insightful view of the consequences of the French defeat, see David Reynolds, '1940: Fulcrum of the Twentieth Century', *International Affairs* (1990), vol. 66, pp. 325–50.

For the origins of Operation Barbarossa, a good place to start is the official German history by Horst Boog *et al.* (eds), *Germany and the Second World War*, vol. V: *The Attack on the Soviet Union* (Oxford, 1996). The finest book on Stalin's policy is Gabriel Gorodetsky, *Grand Delusion: Stalin and the German Invasion of Russia* (London, 1999). Also see Constantine Pleshakov, *Stalin's Folly: The Secret History of the German Invasion of Russia, June 1941* (London, 2005). There are also two valuable essay collections: David Dilks and John Erickson (eds), *Barbarossa: The Axis and the Allies* (Edinburgh, 1994); and Bernd Wegner, *From Peace to War: Germany, Soviet Russia, and the World, 1939–1941* (Oxford, 1997).

On the course and conduct of the war, students will be grateful to I. C. B. Dear and M. R. D. Foot for editing *The Oxford Companion to World War II* (Oxford, 1995). It offers well over a thousand pages of mini-essays on every aspect of the war, as well as plenty of maps, tables and illustrations. General surveys vary in length and detail. R. A. C. Parker, *The Second World War: A Short History* (Oxford, 2001) is the best of the short books. Gerhard L. Weinberg, *A World in Arms: A Global History of World War II* (Cambridge, 1994) is considerably longer and the best of them all. On the origins of the Holocaust, see Götz Aly, *'Final Solution': Nazi Population Policy and the Murder of European Jews* (London, 1999) and Christopher Browning, *The Path to Genocide: Essays in the Launching of the Final Solution* (Cambridge, 1992). Omar Bartov offers a fascinating and provocative analysis of the relationship between National Socialism and the German army in *Hitler's Army: Soldiers, Nazis, and the War in the Third Reich* (Oxford, 1992). On the course and conduct of the Pacific War, read Ronald H. Spector, *Eagle against the Sun: The American War with Japan* (London, 1984) and John Dower, *War without Mercy: Race and Power in the Pacific War* (New York, 1986).

This chapter relied extensively on Richard J. Overy's *tour de force*, *Why the Allies Won* (London, 1995). For an account which stresses the role of economics, see Mark Harrison's essay in *The Economics of World War II: Six Great Powers in International Comparison* (Cambridge, 2000). The essays in David Reynolds, Warren F. Kimball and A. O. Chubarian (eds), *Allies at War: The Soviet, American and British Experience, 1939–45* (London, 1994) are also valuable. On intelligence, the literature is huge and growing. Two overviews of the subject are Ralph Bennett, *Behind the Battle: Intelligence in the War with Germany* (London, 1994) and Ronald Lewin, *The American Magic: Codes, Cyphers, and the Defeat of Japan* (New York, 1982). See also John Ferris, 'Ralph Bennett and the Study of Ultra', *Intelligence and National Security* (1991), vol. 6, pp. 437–86.

On the collapse of the Grand Alliance, there is a short introduction with documents by Martin McCauley, *The Origins of the Cold War*, 2nd edn (London, 1995) and an excellent collection of essays by leading scholars, Ann Lane and

Howard Temperley (eds), *The Rise and Fall of the Grand Alliance, 1941–1945* (Basingstoke, 1995) (including an excellent chapter on the atomic bomb by David Holloway). Studies that begin with the wartime diplomacy of the Big Three include Warren F. Kimball, *The Juggler: Franklin Roosevelt as Wartime Statesman* (Princeton, NJ, 1991), Keith Sainsbury, *The Turning Point . . . the Moscow, Cairo and Teheran Conferences* (Oxford, 1985) and Vojtect Mastny, *Russia's Road to the Cold War: Diplomacy, Warfare, and the Politics of Communism, 1941–1945* (New York, 1979). More generally on the coming of the Cold War, see John L. Gaddis, *We Now Know: Rethinking Cold War History* (Oxford 1997) and Vladislav M. Zubok and Constantine Pleshakov, *Inside the Kremlin's Cold War: From Stalin to Khrushchev* (Cambridge, MA, 1996).

The 'first' Cold War in Europe, 1945 – 61

Introduction

'Who has Germany, has Europe', Lenin is reported to have said. In this he may have been correct, but in 1945 there was not much to rule in Germany. The country had been devastated by years of war, it lacked a political structure, it was under the military authority of four foreign powers, and its economy – like those in the European countries that Nazi Germany had once held under its sway – was in no condition to feed or clothe its population. This alone provides one explanation for the phenomenal rise of Soviet and American power in Europe after the Second World War: with Germany in ruins, France largely excluded from the victors' table and Britain in no condition to play a major role in continental Europe, there were, ultimately, only two major Powers capable of exercising predominant influence over the old continent. Still, it seems that the two needed each other and, even with the common enemy gone, they did not necessarily need to become bitter rivals, let alone mortal enemies.

In fact, the Soviet Union was in almost as bad a shape as its defeated German enemy. The country had suffered catastrophic human losses (estimated at twenty million deaths) and much of its economic infrastructure had been destroyed by the German invasion. Already, in order to rally the Russian population behind the war effort, Stalin had felt it necessary to abandon ideological purity in his wartime internal policies. Now in the post-war period, it appeared that unless the Soviet regime created a better standard of living, it could hardly rely on its population to regard the previous years' sacrifices as having been worthwhile. Moreover, while the Red Army was the largest standing army on the European continent, it would, sooner or later, need to be demobilized in order for the reconstruction work to begin. In addition to security guarantees, the Soviets needed money and material aid in order to rebuild their country after the war.

Ultimately, the only power that was in a position to provide significant economic assistance in the post-war years was the United States. In contrast to much of the rest of the world, including its wartime allies, the United States was in excellent shape. With the exception of Pearl Harbor, it had not suffered from bombing campaigns against its territory. In 1945 the American economy was responsible for 50 per cent of the world's industrial output. In the immediate post-war years the United States would account for one-third of total world exports. American economic power was matched by its military might: its troops were present in Asia and Europe, its navy and air force were the largest in the world, and it held a monopoly over the atomic bomb.

In short, of the two key post-war Powers, the United States clearly held the edge. Still, the Americans were at a distinct disadvantage in Europe. Ever since the American Revolution in the late eighteenth century, successive governments in Washington had proclaimed their distaste for long-term external commitments. While much of this may have been rhetoric, the Truman administration still faced a difficult task if it wished to maintain a long-term military presence in Europe, for such a departure could only be explained if a major threat to American interests and ideals existed.

The origins of the Cold War were not, though, a purely, perhaps not even primarily, a Soviet–American game. Other countries were bound to play a significant role as the battle-lines of the post-war confrontation hardened. Indeed, as one historian has forcefully argued, the United States did not become permanently engaged in Europe by imposing its will on Western Europe – the American influence was in large measure a result of West European initiatives; it was the British, for example, who pushed hard for American participation in a Western European defensive alliance. At the same time, numerous American policy-makers were eager to prevent a return to the conditions of the 1930s, when the Great Depression and the rise of right-wing totalitarian powers had prompted the onset of the Second World War. In the immediate post-war years the sorry state of the European economy and the apparent popularity of left-wing ideologies thus had an uncomfortable similarity to the events of the previous decade. That these events were coupled with the expansion of Soviet influence in Eastern Europe rapidly transformed the American image of a post-war order based on co-operative security arrangements with all the victors to one that emphasized the differences between the United States and Western Europe, on the one hand, and the Soviet Union and Eastern Europe, on the other. Within the European context this meant, primarily, two things: that the Truman administration viewed the recovery of Western Europe as a major precondition to international stability and American prosperity, and that the Soviet quest for security and recovery almost inevitably clashed with American goals.

The German question

Germany was the vital but downtrodden centre of Europe. Yet while the division of Germany (and Berlin) came to symbolize the division of Europe in decades to come, it is worth asking whether the division was inevitable. Was there room for compromise and unity as the victorious Powers grappled with the ruined enemy and defined its future role? One problem in answering such questions is the sheer ambiguity that tended to surround the agreements over Germany's future during the war. In the two major 'Big Three' conferences in 1945, the Americans, Soviets and British concurred on a number of principles and practical steps regarding the post-war status of Germany. In order to prevent the rise of a future German threat to European peace and security, the Allies agreed on a programme that comprised four elements: denazification, demilitarization, decartelization and decentralization. At the same time, they agreed that Germany and Berlin would be divided into four separate occupation zones – with the French taking the fourth piece of German territory – and that the military governor from each occupying country would have supreme authority in his zone. A separate Allied Control Commission (ACC) was set up in Berlin. In addition, it was decided that, while administratively divided, Germany was to be treated as a single economic unit.

These broad principles might have worked had there not been a number of issues that caused friction between the various occupying Powers. Perhaps the key one was the Soviet demand for $10 billion in reparations. In principle this had been agreed at Potsdam, but in 1945–46 it became increasingly clear to the Soviets that, despite the original understanding, no significant reparations deliveries were to be expected from the western zones. While this was in large part owing to the occupation costs incurred by the Western Powers, which made such reparations deliveries impracticable, the Soviets were naturally suspicious. They were further disheartened to learn in the autumn of 1946 that the British and the Americans were holding discussions regarding the fusion of their two zones; the Bizone that resulted from these talks came into being on 1 January 1947.

As the establishment of the Bizone was the first concrete step towards the eventual creation of the **Federal Republic of Germany (FRG)**, it might be assumed that the Anglo-American agreement reflected a determination to establish an independent West German state and deny the resources of the major part of Germany to the Soviet Union. However, it is important to realize that to a substantial degree this move was a result of growing American and British concern over Soviet practices in the latter's zone. For example, in the spring of 1946 the Soviets had forced a merger between the East German Communist and Social Democratic parties and handed the key administrative powers to the newly created Socialist Unity Party (SED). To many American observers this seemed a clear indication that the Soviets would only agree to a central administration for the whole of Germany if they felt they could control it.

After the fusion of the British and American zones the trend towards a formal division gradually accelerated. In 1947 the decision to include western Germany among the recipients of **Marshall Plan** aid was a clear signal of the American

Federal Republic of Germany (FRG)
The German state created in 1949 out of the former American, British and French occupation zones. Also known as West Germany. In 1990 the GDR merged into the FDR thus ending the post-war partition of Germany.

Marshall Plan
Officially known as the European Recovery Programme (ERP). Initiated by American Secretary of State George C. Marshall's 5 June 1947 speech and administered by the Economic Co-operation Administration (ECA). Under the ERP the participating countries (Austria, Belgium, Denmark, France, Great Britain, Greece, Iceland, Italy, Luxembourg, the Netherlands, Norway, Sweden, Switzerland, Turkey and West Germany) received more than $12 billion between 1948 and 1951.

Plate 9.1 Germany, 1948. A US C-47 cargo plane flies over locals amid ruins, approaching Tempelhof Airport with food and other relief supplies as part of the Berlin airlift to break the blockade of overland routes imposed by the surrounding Soviets. (Photo: Walter Sanders/Life Magazine/Time & Life Pictures/Getty Images)

intent to integrate the defeated enemy into Western Europe as much as possible. Meanwhile, the Soviets moved to clamp down even further on democratic principles in their own zone. When all three western zones instituted a currency reform in the spring of 1948, the Soviets responded by closing off all land routes to West Berlin in June 1948. The Berlin blockade did not, though, make the United States and its Allies abandon their goal of creating a separate West German state. Instead, a massive airlift of supplies to Berlin in 1948–49 allowed the western zones of the city to continue existing within East Germany. The end result was a hardening of the East–West divide and, eventually, the creation of the Federal Republic of Germany in 1949. The Soviets countered this by organizing the **German Democratic Republic (GDR)**. The two Germanies – and the two Berlins – that would symbolize the post-war international system in Europe until the late 1980s had thus been created.

German Democratic Republic (GDR)
The German state created in 1949 out of the former Soviet occupation zone. Also known as East Germany. The GDR more or less collapsed in 1989–90 and was merged into the FRG in 1990, thus ending the post-war partition of Germany.

From take-overs to conformity: the USSR and Eastern Europe

In addition to the division of Germany, the area that came to symbolize the onset of the Cold War was Eastern Europe. For many in the West, the communist take-overs in this region between 1944 and 1948 were seen as a frightening and gradually escalating sign of Stalin's true intentions. Winston Churchill, for example, had in October 1944 been willing to divide Eastern Europe into British and Soviet spheres of influence in the so-called 'percentages agreement'. About a year and a half later, however, Churchill – who was voted out of office during the Potsdam Conference – had changed his mind. In early 1946 the former prime minister declared in a speech in Fulton, Missouri, that an Iron Curtain had descended from the Baltic to the Adriatic. Calling for the Anglo-Americans to resist the expansion of Soviet-communist power, Churchill not only sounded the alarm about Soviet intentions but also expressed the public rationale for much of the Western policy that was to follow.

The fate of Eastern Europe provides important insights into the puzzle of the origins of the Cold War. In all likelihood, Soviet policies were driven by a complex set of motives in which ideology, security and concerns about the possible repetition of earlier suffering played a role. It would also be naive to assume that Western rhetoric and policy did not affect the thinking of the Soviet leadership. An additional point to stress is that the imposition of Soviet and/or communist hegemony in Eastern Europe did not take place overnight. Much depended on the specific conditions in the various East European countries, such as the strength of the local Communist Party, the position of the Red Army, the depth of anti-Russian sentiment, and the presence (or lack) of an ACC. In addition, geographical location made a difference, for while Poland, given its location in between Germany and the USSR, was central to the Soviet quest for security and had little chance of escaping Russian hegemony in the post-war years, Finland, which shared a long border with the USSR but lacked strategic significance, managed to avoid the fate of Eastern European nations.

The importance of local conditions was highlighted by the first two Eastern European communist take-overs. In Yugoslavia and Albania, the local communists established their rule in 1944–45 as patriots who had fought, often heroically, against the German invaders. In Albania, Enver Hoxha's National Liberation Movement faced little resistance when it deposed King Zog in May 1944 and established its rule firmly after the Germans left the country at the end of the year. Perhaps ironically, in the years to come, the major threat to Hoxha's rule would emanate from neighbouring Yugoslavia, where during the war Marshal Tito had manoeuvred himself and his partisans into a powerful position. After a brief coalition with the royalists, Tito's Popular Front quickly organized an election in November 1945 in which it received an astonishing (and unquestionably flawed) 96 per cent of the vote. Tito formally deposed King Peter and proclaimed the creation of the Federative People's Republic of Yugoslavia on 31 January 1946. To the increasing fury of Stalin and the growing concern of his neighbours, however,

Tito harboured dreams of creating a larger Balkan Federation, which would include the neighbouring countries to the south and east. To further such goals the newly created Yugoslavia, independently of (and contrary to) Moscow's wishes, pressed Hoxha's Albania to align with Belgrade and supported the communists in the Greek Civil War.

While Tito's independent actions would later spark the first serious internal post-war crisis of the communist movement, his path to power was in many ways an exception. In Poland, for example, the communists' route to government was far more complicated and prompted by much greater Soviet involvement. The Soviets recognized the Polish Workers Party's 'Lublin committee' as the provisional government in late 1944. As a precondition to British and American recognition, however, the Lublin government was enlarged in the spring of 1945 to include some token representatives from other parties, most significantly the Polish Peasants Party (PPS). Over the next two years the communists, headed by Wladislaw Gomulka and Boleslaw Bierut, gradually marginalized the other political parties and forced the PPS leader, Stanislaw Mikolajczyk, to choose between exile or imprisonment. In the autumn of 1947 he chose the former, thus removing the last effective opposition to the communists.

In many ways, the Polish opposition parties had poor cards to begin with, for among other things the communists were far better organized than their opponents. Moreover, the Germans had decimated the local industrial elite, thus making the post-war nationalization of the Polish economy much easier to accomplish. Territorial gains from Germany (the Oder–Niesse line) also meant that Gomulka (who was in charge of the new territories) could redistribute the properties of eight million departing Germans. The PPS could hardly match such largess and, in fact, split into two in late 1945. As later events were to show, however, Poland was a special case; indeed, some historians argue that it escaped the extreme Sovietization that befell some of its southern neighbours. This was, probably, the result of a number of interrelated factors. As the gateway to Germany, Soviet domination of Poland was considered absolutely indispensable for post-war security, and this sense was reinforced by concern over nascent Polish Russophobia. To minimize the potential for future unrest, therefore, the Soviets gave the local communist leaders comparatively more leeway than their counterparts in other Eastern European countries. As a result, the Polish communists were careful in their application of socialist ideals, allowing the Catholic Church, for example, to retain its property until 1950.

The priority accorded to securing socialist control in Poland affected Soviet policy in other countries. In Hungary, for example, Stalin felt compelled to hold back the local communists from seizing power immediately after the war. Between 1945 and 1947 the Hungarian Communist Party thus respected election results and participated in coalition governments. Meanwhile, the communist control of the Ministry of the Interior and, in particular, use of the Hungarian security police worked to marginalize political opponents one by one. In a classic example of the so-called 'salami tactics', László Rajk, the young communist minister of the interior, directed a campaign that succeeded in discrediting or removing from office several key leaders of the Smallholders Party (SHP), which, in 1945, had won 57 per cent of the popular vote. Strengthened by the presence of the Red Army, the security police became involved in selected assassinations, the sabotage of the opposition parties' offices and the closure of Catholic youth organizations. The Ministry of the Interior also blocked the SHP's plans to establish peasants' labour organizations in 1946. Yet it was only after the conclusion of the Hungarian Peace Treaty and the exit of the ACC from Hungary in 1947 that the communists moved to establish complete supremacy. Elections in April 1949 were held without opposing candidates and were followed by the adoption of a new Soviet-style constitution.

By this time Bulgaria and Romania had also become socialist republics. In Bulgaria, the local communist leaders had, in fact, constituted a respectable party prior to the Second World War and were included in a coalition government that was formed in September 1944. As in Hungary, the take-over was gradual, in part due to the presence of the ACC and the need to maintain order until a peace treaty had been signed. In September 1946 Bulgaria formally became a republic (eleven-year-old King Simeon II was sent into exile). In the following month, the Bulgarian Communist Party's leader Gheorghi Dimitrov, who had spent the war in Moscow, became head of a coalition government. From then on the communists moved quickly: in the summer and autumn of 1947 they removed major opposition figures and destroyed their organizations; in December 1947 they introduced a new constitution.

In contrast to Bulgaria, the Romanian communists had an extremely weak organization at the end of the war; by most accounts its membership was fewer than a thousand in August 1944. As a result, the Communist Party of Romania worked slowly to increase its standing, with the help of growing Soviet influence. The latter was in part a result of Soviet demands for reparations, which allowed the USSR virtual control over Romania's shipping and its oil and timber industries. However, the Soviets, who occupied Romania at the end of the war, also apparently threatened direct intervention on several occasions and by doing so empowered their Romanian allies to enact land reform that amounted to virtual nationalization in 1945–46. Meanwhile, the civil service was purged and the leaders of other parties were gaoled. The final outcome was thus clear well before King Michael abdicated in late 1947, although a complete end to Soviet occupation did not arrive until 1958.

The last European country to fall under communist rule was Czechoslovakia. Indeed, for quite some time after the return of the pre-war president Eduard Beneš in April 1945 Czechoslovakia appeared likely to remain a liberal democracy. To be sure, the Czech communists, under the leadership of Klement Gottwald, won 38 per cent of the popular vote in the May 1946 elections and occupied a number of key posts in the post-war coalition cabinet. However, the lack of any Red Army presence after December 1945 and the existence of a friendship treaty with the USSR seemed to make Czechoslovakia a special case, for the Czech communists did not resort to the strong-arm strategies or salami tactics of their Eastern European counterparts. In the second half of 1947, however, the picture began to change. Under Soviet pressure the Czech government declined to participate in the Marshall Plan, sending the Czech communists' already declining popularity into a severe downward spiral. In response, while the Red Army amassed troops on the Czech borders, Gottwald and his party staged a *coup d'état* in February 1948. Between 12 and 22 February President Beneš, probably assuming that no Western help was forthcoming, failed to take advantage of obvious popular anti-communist sentiment and effectively allowed the communists to take control of the state apparatus. Jan Masaryk, the non-communist foreign minister, was soon found dead, Beneš was forced into permanent house arrest (until his death in September 1948), and Gottwald became president. The new government quickly moved to enact socialist reforms and block any opposition.

The Prague coup of February 1948 was the last addition to what would for four decades be known as the Soviet bloc. Rumours that a similar coup was under way in Finland – which, under severe pressure, signed a 'Friendship Treaty' with the USSR in April 1948 and had previously declined the offer to join the Marshall Plan – proved false. Instead of further expansion of the bloc, the Soviet Union moved to impose conformity on Eastern Europe. In practice this meant that the Soviet bloc underwent a series of purges and show trials during which a number of national communist leaders, who were accused of Western sympathies or 'national deviation', were sent to their deaths or removed from office. Between 1948 and 1952 figures such as Rajk in Hungary, Kostov in Bulgaria and Slansky in Czechoslovakia were executed; others, including Gomulka in Poland and Patrascanu in Romania were 'merely' purged. Meanwhile, the Eastern European economies were subjugated to the Soviet economy through a series of joint Soviet–East European companies and by the imposition of Soviet-style five-year plans to promote the development of heavy industry. An organization for economic co-operation, the **COMECON**, was established in 1949 to control trade and industry further in the Soviet bloc. Following the Soviet model, Eastern Europe's agriculture was partially collectivized. Police forces, armies and internal security services were closely linked to the USSR's central command, even to the extent that East European officials' uniforms were modelled on those worn by their counterparts in the USSR. All in all, the late 1940s and early 1950s saw a clear move towards conformity behind the Iron Curtain.

The Soviet Union's increasing stranglehold on Eastern Europe can be viewed in numerous ways. It may have been a result of a grand master plan, a diabolical scheme to take over the world in steps. This, certainly, was what many Western observers argued at the time. However, Soviet policy can also be seen as part of a chronic search for security that had been prompted by the recent experience of war and destruction. In addition, Stalin may have been concerned over the implications of the Yugoslav case. In June 1948, criticizing Tito for his independent course, the **Cominform** (the Communist Information Bureau, founded in September 1947 as an umbrella organization for European communist parties) expelled Yugoslavia from its ranks. It is not clear whether this decision owed more to Stalin's own personal insecurities about a possible rival emerging within the communist world, or whether it was a response to concerns that Yugoslavia's independent actions were jeopardizing Soviet national security. Whatever the case, the Tito–Stalin split nevertheless demolished the myth of

COMECON

The Council for Mutual Economic Assistance, a Soviet-dominated economic organization founded in 1949 to co-ordinate economic strategy and trade within the communist world.

Cominform

The Communist Information Bureau, organized in 1947 and dissolved in 1956. The Cominform attempted to re-establish the links between the European communist parties that had lapsed since the dissolution of the Comintern. Dominated by the USSR, the major event in the Cominform's history was when it expelled Yugoslavia in 1948.

monolithic communism, for the Yugoslav leader's independent power base allowed him to survive all efforts to depose him and thus produced the first clear crack in the Iron Curtain. Conversely, however, it also strengthened the Soviet need to prevent any other nationalist leaders from attaining a similar independent status. Ultimately, however, the chief influence on Soviet policy was the gradual decline in co-operation with the other victorious powers, particularly the United States. In all likelihood, for example, the timing of the Soviet move from encouraging socialist take-overs to demanding subservience was linked to the developments in the West.

The United States, containment and Western Europe

There is no question that the enhanced American role in Western Europe was both a contributory source and an outcome of the tensions and divisions that characterized the origins of the Cold War in Europe. In retrospect it is easy to assume that American policy followed a straightforward logic, with its major goals being to restore and strengthen capitalism, minimize left-wing influence and prevent the Soviet Union from extending its influence beyond those areas that the Red Army controlled at the end of the war. Thus, the American response grew gradually harsher and more comprehensive, until eventually Washington permanently committed its forces to the defence of Western Europe.

That the United States would eventually engage so deeply in Western Europe was, however, by no means inevitable in 1945–46. In fact, strong domestic constituencies urged the Truman administration to disengage the United States from the old continent. For example, in the November 1946 Congressional elections the Republicans, under the influential leadership of Senator Robert Taft, defeated the Democrats for the first time in decades, and it was no secret that Taft and a large portion of the Republicans favoured a return to some form of American **isolationism** (although their more appealing message was probably the promise to cut down government expenditure by 20 per cent). President Truman, who lacked the unchallenged authority of his deceased predecessor, thus faced an uphill battle, as he became more convinced of the need forcefully to oppose the USSR.

Inexperienced in foreign affairs, Truman relied on a number of advisers who rarely agreed on the gravity of, and the correct response to, what was viewed as increasingly aggressive Soviet behaviour. To be sure, a strong anti-Soviet consensus was being formed among a number of key policy analysts who, in the spring of 1946, began to support the line advocated by George Kennan, one of the State Department's key Soviet analysts. In his so-called 'Long Telegram' of February 1946 Kennan presented an analysis of Soviet behaviour which, over the year that followed, heavily influenced the Truman administration's Cold War policies. Kennan's argument appeared straightforward: the Soviets were almost patho-

isolationism
The policy or doctrine of isolating one's country by avoiding foreign entanglements and responsibilities. Popular in the United States during the inter-war years.

logically insecure, they believed that the USSR's future security was directly dependent on minimizing their neighbours' security, and were convinced that only the destruction of American power would ultimately guarantee their survival. What Kennan thus implied was that the Soviets would not be satisfied even with the total domination of Eastern Europe but would use both overt and covert means to spread their influence to Western Europe. While Kennan would later complain he had been misunderstood and that his statements about the concurrent weaknesses of the USSR had been overlooked, he essentially restated this message in public in an anonymous July 1947 article in the influential *Foreign Affairs* magazine. In this essay he also used the term '**containment**' to describe how the United States should use its military, political and economic power to prevent further Soviet expansion.

By July 1947, though, containment was already being applied. In fact, Kennan's 'Long Telegram' was only one of many private and public statements that indicated a hardening attitude in the United States and elsewhere towards Soviet behaviour. For example, the American administration itself launched a campaign to publicize Soviet 'misbehaviour': leading Republican Senator Arthur Vandenberg made fiery speeches about Soviet aggressiveness in the Senate, while Secretary of State James F. Byrnes publicly articulated the Truman administration's tough stand against the Soviets. Moreover, outside the United States, the toughening of the American stance was also evident. This was clear as early as March 1946 when a crisis developed over the continued presence of Soviet troops in northern Iran (Azerbaijan). Faced with stern criticism from the United States and Britain, the Soviets withdrew their troops in the late spring of 1946. In a similar vein, when the Soviets made continued demands on the Turkish government for control over access routes through the Straits, the United States responded in August 1946 by sending a naval presence into the eastern Mediterranean region. The following month, the Truman administration announced that this was to remain a permanent presence. Clearly, what was of concern to the Americans was the future of the eastern Mediterranean region and the Middle East and, as with Iran, a show of strength appeared necessary to contain further Soviet encroachment into the area. Encouragingly, the Soviets appeared once again to be listening; Moscow began to back down and gradually withdrew some of the twenty-five divisions that had been deployed near the Soviet–Turkish border in 1946.

These two crises seemed to confirm one of the major principles of the policy of containment: if you are tough, the Soviets will eventually step back. Indeed, a year and a half after Germany's surrender the American administration was becoming increasingly convinced that only a firm policy of containment could stop further Soviet moves to expand their power beyond Eastern Europe. On another level, however, the events in Iran and Turkey in 1946 reflected not only Truman's growing resolve to confront the Soviets, but the obvious weakness of Britain's power and the American willingness to take over the commitments and positions previously held by the British. This trend became even clearer in early 1947, when the central focus of the emerging Cold War shifted to the ongoing civil war in Greece.

containment
The term coined by George Kennan for the American, and broadly Western, policy towards the Soviet Union (and communism in general). The overall idea was to contain the USSR (that is, keep it within its current borders) with the hope that internal division, failure or political evolution might end the perceived threat from what was considered a chronically expansionist force.

After the evacuation of German forces from Greece in late 1944, the country had experienced a brief period of civil war. However, the British forces that subsequently entered the country managed to forge a truce between the two Greek factions: the Greek communists and the royalists. In March 1946 Greece held elections, but the communists decided to boycott them, resulting in a royalist government being formed that enjoyed Britain's support. A few months later the Greek Civil War erupted and became immediately internationalized: the Greek communists received support from Yugoslavia, Albania and Bulgaria; the royalists continued to receive British assistance.

The Soviets and the Americans were not directly involved in this initial outburst of violence, but by early 1947 this began to change owing to the dire economic situation in Britain. Facing a steady drain of gold and foreign exchange reserves, and with an internal fuel and food crisis on its hands, Clement Attlee's Labour government had few resources to put into expensive foreign initiatives. Therefore in February 1947 the British informed the United States of their inability to continue aiding the Greek royalists. Simultaneously, the Greek government pleaded for American assistance. The Truman administration now sprang into action and on 12 March 1947 the president unveiled the so-called **Truman Doctrine** to Congress. This amounted to a programme to provide American assistance to the non-communist side in the ongoing Greek Civil War and further aid to neighbouring Turkey. As such, the Truman Doctrine called for the United States to step into Britain's shoes. However, while Truman's message related specifically to the requests made by the Greek government for aid in their struggle against communists, the Doctrine went a step further. In his speech to Congress, Truman made references to the global responsibility of the United States 'to support free peoples who are resisting subjugation by armed minorities or by outside pressures' and clearly stated that, if such aid was not provided, the other European countries would quickly come under threat. Congress rapidly assented. Eventually in 1949 the Greek communists were defeated.

While the Truman Doctrine was a response to a specific conflict clothed in universalistic terms, American involvement in Western Europe soon reached new heights with the announcement of the Marshall Plan. In June 1947 Secretary of State George Marshall unveiled what was to become probably the most important and popular American policy initiative in the post-war years. The European Recovery Program (ERP), as the Marshall Plan was formally known, eventually offered American financial aid to nearly all of the Western European countries. From 1948 to mid-1952, more than $13 billion was distributed to fourteen countries in the form of direct aid, loan guarantees, grants and necessities from medicine to mules. With such aid the transatlantic link between the United States and Western Europe was confirmed.

To be sure, the Marshall Plan, for all its lofty rhetoric ('against hunger and poverty'), was not an unselfish act born out of some sense of guilt and responsibility for the fate of Europe. Rather, the pumping of money into Western Europe was to counter the distressing rise of European left-wing political parties: in two key countries, France and Italy, the communists were already extremely popular. The assumption was that further economic dislocation

Truman Doctrine
The policy of American President Harry S. Truman, as advocated in his address to Congress on 12 March 1947, to provide military and economic aid to Greece and Turkey. Subsequently used to justify aid to any country perceived to be threatened by communism.

see Table 9.1

Table 9.1 Aid allocated under the European Recovery Programme

Country	Amount ($ million)
United Kingdom	3,189.8
France	2,713.6
Italy	1,508.8
West Germany	1,390.6
Netherlands	1,083.5
Greece	706.7
Austria	677.8
Belgium/Luxembourg	559.3
Denmark	273.0
Norway	255.3
Turkey	225.1
Ireland	147.5
Sweden	107.3
Iceland	29.3

could only boost their popularity and that, in turn, would strengthen the likelihood that the Soviet Union could play a role beyond the Iron Curtain. Put another way: economic recovery was considered the best antidote to leftist political tendencies. Moreover, insisting that the European recipients of the Marshall Plan use part of the aid in the United States would help stimulate the American domestic economy. The ERP was, in other words, a way of strengthening America's position as the leading Western country and a means of increasing markets for American exports.

Indeed, the announcement of the Marshall Plan put the Soviets on the defensive and effectively served to push the onus for the commencement of the Cold War onto the Kremlin's shoulders. This came about because the United States cannily offered aid to all European countries. Accordingly, in late June and early July 1947 the Soviets attended a meeting in Paris with the British and the French to discuss the particulars of the American offer. However, the Soviets, headed by Foreign Minister Molotov, soon walked out of the meeting, claiming that the whole thing was a capitalist plot, and stating that they rejected any external intrusion into the East European, let alone Soviet, national economies. In particular, the Soviets rejected the idea that East European raw materials would be shipped to boost Western recovery. The Kremlin, as previously noted, then pressed East Europeans to remain outside the ERP, thus effectively sealing the economic division of Europe.

How successful was the Marshall Plan in stimulating European recovery and meeting its political objectives? This question has yielded considerable debate, as some revisionist historians, by pointing to statistics showing that Western European recovery was well under way by 1947–48, have challenged the assumed 'boost' that the Marshall Plan provided and have claimed that the influx of dollars caused inflation and did not solve the serious balance-of-payments problem.

European Economic Community (EEC)

Established by the Treaty of Rome 1957, the EEC became effective on 1 January 1958. Its initial members were Belgium, France, Italy, Luxembourg, the Netherlands and West Germany (now Germany); it was known informally as the Common Market. The EEC's aim was the eventual economic union of its member nations, ultimately leading to political union. It changed its name to the European Union in 1992.

European Coal and Steel Community (ECSC)

Established by the Treaty of Paris (1952) and also known as the Schuman Plan, after the French foreign minister, Robert Schuman, who proposed it in 1950. The member nations of the ECSC – Belgium, France, Italy, Luxembourg, the Netherlands and West Germany – pledged to pool their coal and steel resources by providing a unified market, lifting restrictions on imports and exports, and creating a unified labour market.

North Atlantic Treaty Organization (NATO)

Established by the North Atlantic Treaty (4 April 1949) signed by Belgium, Canada, Denmark, France, Great Britain, Iceland, Italy, Luxembourg, the Netherlands, Norway, Portugal and the United States. Greece and Turkey entered the alliance in 1952 and the Federal Republic of Germany in 1955. Spain became a full member in 1982. In 1999 the Czech Republic, Hungary and Poland joined in the first post-Cold War expansion, increasing the membership to nineteen countries.

However, whether this is the case or not, it is undeniable that the ERP had a huge psychological impact on West Europe, creating greater admiration for the United States and building a sense that the reconstruction of Europe was well under way. Moreover, it forced West Europeans to co-operate seriously for the first time, brought West Germans to the same table as others and hence provided a stimulus, if not a perfect one, for the European integration process that would reshape the continent in subsequent decades.

Indeed, the Marshall Plan coincided with and encouraged a number of the economic arrangements that paved the way towards the founding of the **European Economic Community (EEC)** in 1957. On 9 May 1950 the French foreign minister, Robert Schuman, made an announcement proposing the pooling together of Western Europe's coal and steel resources. After extended negotiations, the Schuman Plan resulted in the signing of a treaty in Paris the following March that established the **European Coal and Steel Community (ECSC)**. The ECSC created a common market for coal, steel, coke, iron ore and scrap between six countries: France, the Federal Republic of Germany, Italy, Belgium, the Netherlands and Luxembourg.

The culmination of the early containment policy in Europe came approximately a year after the Marshall Plan became operational. On 4 April 1949 the United States, Canada and ten West European countries formed the **North Atlantic Treaty Organization (NATO)**. 'An alliance for peace', as the chairman of the Senate Foreign Relations Committee, Tom Connally, termed it, NATO in many ways symbolized the key role that the United States had come to play in Europe. While there had been some initial reluctance to commit the United States in this manner – a strain of latent isolationism ran deep in American politics – the pressure from Britain and a number of other European countries, as well as the need to create an institutional structure linking the United States permanently with Western Europe, eventually forced the issue. Still, in the spring of 1949 it was clear that NATO was in large part created to send yet another message to the Soviet Union, a message that conveyed US determination to object to any further expansion of Soviet influence in Europe. To a large extent NATO was at the time of its creation a political rather than a military alliance. Together with the Marshall Plan, it solidified the political and economic division of Europe by emphasizing the similarities between the participating countries' domestic systems and values. Remarkably, it would remain an important part of transatlantic co-operation even after the Cold War (see chapter 20).

NATO's success was, however, in large part linked to the numerous hiccups that slowed down European integration in the 1950s. While economic integration was remarkably successful, political integration suffered from continued national preferences and prejudices. This, in part, explains the inability of West Europeans to agree on a common defence policy; indeed, one of the early failures of European integration was the 1954 demise of the European Defence Community (EDC). In the realm of security, particularly military security, most West Europeans preferred NATO and the continued presence of the United States to an independent European defence policy. This would become evident in the mid-1960s when the departure of France – a key country in all the various integration schemes – from NATO did not encourage others to follow suit. By then, however, the nature of the Cold War confrontation had dramatically changed, for while many in the Truman administration and Western Europe viewed the Cold War initially as a political and economic contest focused on Europe, developments in late 1949 and throughout the early 1950s served both to militarize and to globalize the Cold War.

see Chapter 11

Debating the origins of the Cold War

While no one questions that the Soviets expanded their influence massively in the early post-war years, historians have debated for decades the motives behind Moscow's policies. Were the Soviets acting simply to guarantee their security in the future – that is, did East and Central Europe simply represent a first line of defence against the future rise of Germany or other Powers trying to invade the USSR? Or were the Soviets deliberately attempting to expand communism, initially to Eastern Europe, but later to Western Europe and beyond? Did Stalin have a master plan? Was he simply an opportunist, or do the take-overs in, and subsequent hegemony over, Eastern Europe provide evidence of the impact of communist ideology in Soviet foreign policy?

A closely linked debate concerns the motivations behind American involvement in Europe. Initially, most observers and a large number of historians have stressed the essentially defensive nature of American policy: that the Truman administration merely responded to the aggressive policies of the Soviet Union. In the 1960s the so-called revisionist school – led by scholars like William A. Williams – challenged this interpretation by arguing that American foreign policy was driven by a need to secure overseas markets and incorporate Western Europe firmly into an American-dominated international system. Subsequent scholarship has often taken these opposing views as the starting point of analysis, although gradually the picture of the origins of the Cold War has become increasingly complex. In particular, numerous authors have explored the role of other players (notably, the various European countries) and taken advantage of new methodological approaches to explore the cultural and social aspects of the origins of the Cold War in Europe. In general, the scholarship of the onset of the Cold War is both rich in scope and large in volume, offering no easy path for generalization.

On every front

A series of events in late 1949 and early 1950 gave the Cold War confrontation a more global and more threatening outlook. In August 1949 the Soviet Union, several years earlier than expected by Western intelligence analysts, successfully tested its first atomic bomb. The American nuclear monopoly, a key part of its national security, was thus shattered only four years after the United States had dropped the atomic bombs on Japan. In response to the Soviet tests, the United States quickly moved to develop its nuclear arsenal further, adding the thermonuclear bomb in 1952. The problem was that the Soviets followed suit only a year later. From this point on, the arms race continued to escalate, adding another frightening aspect to the Soviet–American confrontation.

But there was more. On 1 October 1949 the **People's Republic of China (PRC)** was formed, and its leader, Mao Zedong, soon travelled to Moscow to conclude a treaty with the Soviet Union. With the formation of the Sino-Soviet alliance and the prospect that an apparent 'red tide' was about to sweep across the rest of Asia, the stakes were manifestly increased. The Americans, who had already taken steps to support Japanese recovery as a counterweight against communism in East Asia, chose not to recognize the PRC; instead, they began increasing aid to both the European colonial Powers and to new non-communist governments. In short, anti-communism was increasingly influencing American policy decisions, sometimes, as later became clear in Vietnam, with disastrous results.

In fact, a full re-evaluation of American priorities was under way at the time when the Soviets and Chinese concluded their alliance. Along with ordering a rapid development of the hydrogen bomb in January 1950, Truman instructed the State and Defense departments to conduct a full review of national security policy. The end result was NSC-68 (National Security Council Paper Number 68), one of the seminal documents of the early Cold War. Concluded in April 1950, this top-secret report based its recommendations on a simplistic view of the world as divided between a monolithic communist sphere under Moscow's leadership and the 'free world' headed by the United States. It made few allowances for the differences within the communist bloc and made no references to the many non-democratic allies of the United States. Working under the assumption that the Soviet Union and its clients posed a severe military threat to the United States and the rest of the 'free world', NSC-68 called for a massive buildup of the American military. Given the global nature of the threat, moreover, the report warned that the United States and its allies would have to counter the expansion of communism anywhere in the world.

The sentiments of NSC-68 reflected the exaggerated anti-communism that was sweeping the United States in the late 1940s and early 1950s. This virulent anti-communism, which is known as **McCarthyism** after one of its leading protagonists, Senator Joseph McCarthy (WI, Republican), had its roots in earlier periods in American history; indeed, a 'red scare' had raged in the United States in the aftermath of the First World War. Already in the late 1940s sensationalized spy cases, including the trial of former high-ranking State Department official

People's Republic of China (PRC)
The official name of communist or mainland China. The PRC came into existence in 1949 under the leadership of Mao Zedong.

see Chapter 10

see Chapter 12

McCarthyism
General term for the practice in the United States of making accusations of pro-communist activity, in many instances unsupported by proof or based on slight, doubtful or irrelevant evidence. The term is derived from its most notorious practitioner, Republican Senator Joseph R. McCarthy of Wisconsin (1909–57).

Alger Hiss, had raised the level of concern over domestic communists. However, when McCarthy announced in February 1950, erroneously as it turned out, that there were hundreds of 'card-carrying' communists in the State Department, he managed to magnify what was already a widespread attack on civil liberties into a witch-hunt. In the name of democracy, hundreds of Hollywood writers and actors, government employees, professors and teachers were subsequently investigated for possible communist sympathies. While the verdicts never led to sentences equivalent to life in the gulags of the Soviet Union, many lives were ruined. Thus, the early Cold War became in the United States a period of relative conformity.

However, even with McCarthyism in full swing in the spring of 1950 the secret recommendations of NSC-68 – effectively a tripling of the American defence budget – were going to be difficult to sell to Congress. Until a 'real' military threat appeared on the horizon, doomsday scenarios could only go so far in persuading the American public that they needed to bear an additional tax burden in order to defend the 'free world' against communism. The solution, though, was not long in coming, for the Cold War rapidly entered yet another stage.

The North Korean attack on South Korea of 25 June 1950 produced outrage in the United States and around the world, galvanizing the Western alliance and leading to the first serious 'hot war' of the Cold War. With the introduction of American and other allied troops into the Korean peninsula and the later entry of the PRC into the conflict, the world seemed, indeed, close to a Third World War. While the direct impact of the events in Korea was most clearly felt in Asia, its role as the first real conflict within the wider Cold War was crucial in influencing the course of future American policy, the relations between Washington and its West European allies, and the general mood in East–West relations. In particular, the war resulted in a rapid militarization and subsequent globalization of the Cold War. In Western Europe conservative parties returned to power and defence budgets began to escalate. Prompted by fears that the USSR would attack in Europe while American troops were preoccupied in Korea, nightmare scenarios about another world war escalated, leading the West European governments to initiate plans for an independent EDC.

The United States, for its part, created the most wide-ranging alliance system in the history of the world. This included bilateral pacts with Japan (1951), the Philippines (1951), Spain (1952), South Korea (1953) and Taiwan (1954), and multilateral treaty organizations, such as in 1951 the Australian–New Zealand–United States Pact (ANZUS), and in 1954 the **South-East Asia Treaty Organization (SEATO)** which committed Thailand, Pakistan and the Philippines among other states to the defence of South-East Asia. In the Middle East, the Baghdad Pact (consisting of Britain, Turkey, Pakistan, Iran and Iraq), which was organized in 1955 without American membership, acted as the forerunner to the establishment of the American-led Central Treaty Organization (CENTO). With this proliferation of alliances and the acquisition of numerous military bases from Greenland to North Africa and Japan, the United States was, indeed, keeping a global watch on the assumed designs of the **Warsaw Pact** and the Sino-Soviet alliance.

South-East Asia Treaty Organization (SEATO)
An alliance organized in 1954 by Australia, France, Great Britain, New Zealand, Pakistan, the Philippines, Thailand and the United States. SEATO was created after the Geneva conference on Indochina to prevent further communist gains in the region. However, it proved of little use in the Vietnam War and was disbanded in 1977.

Warsaw Pact (Warsaw Treaty Organization)
An alliance set up in 1955 under a mutual defence treaty signed in Warsaw by Albania, Bulgaria, Czechoslovakia, East Germany, Hungary, Poland, Romania and the Soviet Union. The organization was the Soviet bloc's equivalent of NATO. Albania formally withdrew in 1968. The Warsaw Pact was dissolved in June 1991.

That the Cold War was becoming a 'total' war became even clearer with the strengthening of the Western economic embargo against the Soviet bloc. In 1949 the United States and its allies had already established CoCom (Co-ordinating Committee) to underpin this process. The outbreak of the Korean War gave a strong boost to the strengthening of export control legislation and agreements. In the early 1950s CoCom became a means of synchronizing the Western powers' trade policies so as to minimize the Sino-Soviet bloc's ability to strengthen its military capabilities through East–West trade. Propelled mainly by the United States, the participating countries established a series of embargoes that prohibited the export of various goods, from arms and ammunition to petroleum and other 'strategic raw materials'. It is important to note, though, that in this field differences between the United States and its allies were in evidence from the beginning: concerned over a political backlash from the USSR and/or possible domestic discontent due to the loss of trade with Eastern Europe, West European governments accepted CoCom merely as an informal set of 'gentlemen's agreements'. Although differences in Western policies would begin to undermine the US ability to keep a complete strategic embargo on the USSR and its allies, CoCom acted, particularly in the 1950s, as a fairly effective means of limiting East–West trade. Only in the 1960s, along with general criticism over American policies and the rise of European **détente**, did serious cracks in the Western embargo system begin to appear. By then, though, the general dynamics of the Cold War had dramatically shifted.

détente

A term meaning the reduction of tensions between states. It is often used to refer to the superpower diplomacy that took place between the inauguration of Richard Nixon as the American president in 1969 and the Senate's refusal to ratify SALT II in 1980.

Stability and revolts

With the death of Joseph Stalin in March 1953, the first chance to alleviate the tensions that had produced the division of Europe and contributed to the outbreak of the Korean War seemed to be at hand. In the years that followed, a power struggle in the Kremlin resulted in a period of uncertainty that undoubtedly affected the conduct of Soviet policy. The 'thaw' of the mid-1950s that followed can thus in part be attributed to the competition within the Kremlin leadership that pitted Stalin's former lieutenants – most importantly men like Georgi Malenkov, Lavrenti Beria, Nikita Khrushchev and Vyacheslav Molotov – against each other. By the time Khrushchev eventually triumphed in this competition, the Cold War had been transformed.

Indeed, the fact that Stalin's death occurred only two months after Dwight D. Eisenhower had taken over the White House added to collective hopes that an opportunity for reshaping the Cold War had arrived. Although the former supreme commander of NATO had campaigned for the White House on a tough foreign policy agenda that promised to roll back communist power, early signs that a détente was in the making were promising. At Stalin's funeral in mid-March the new Soviet leader, Georgi Malenkov, announced that there were no issues that could not be decided using peaceful means. On 16 April 1953 President

Eisenhower delivered his widely quoted 'Chance for Peace' speech, in which he stressed the opportunities for reducing East–West tensions. Yet Eisenhower also asked the Soviets to act through 'deeds' and not just 'words'. Less than a month later the ageing British prime minister, Winston Churchill, went a step further by calling for an early **Great Power** summit without preconditions.

While Churchill did not get his wish in 1953, there were several practical developments that signalled a move away from the uncompromising hostility that had characterized the early 1950s. In June 1953 the Korean armistice was concluded. In the spring of 1954 a number of key powers, including the United States, France, the USSR and the PRC, agreed to a series of agreements in Geneva that provided for the formal end of the French involvement in Indochina and, some hoped, a permanent settlement of the subcontinent's persistent wars. In 1955 the Austrian State Treaty resolved that country's uncertain status – unlike Germany, Austria was to be united and neutral. In addition, the Soviets withdrew their troops from bases in Finland (Porkkala) and Manchuria (Port Arthur). In 1955 the USSR also restored normal diplomatic relations with Tito's Yugoslavia and, in 1956, abolished the Cominform. Amid all this diplomatic activity, the British, French, Soviets and Americans held a summit in Geneva in the late summer of 1955. Although lacking in practical progress on any of the contested issues (such as Germany and possible limitations on the development of nuclear arms), the Geneva summit raised hopes that the 'spirit of Geneva' would eventually be transformed into a launching pad for substantive agreements between East and West.

Such hopes proved illusory. Not only did the nuclear arms race continue unabated, but also the future of Germany remained a sensitive and divisive issue. Already in June 1953 the Soviets had shown that, even in the aftermath of Stalin's death, they had no interest in relaxing their hold over East Germany. In that month Soviet and East German forces crushed spontaneous uprisings throughout the GDR. The German question thus remained a focal point of post-Stalin Soviet policy, and an issue the new Soviet leadership was unlikely to compromise upon. When West Germany was invited to join NATO a year later – after the long-standing effort to create the EDC had failed – the Soviets retaliated in 1955 by creating the Warsaw Pact.

Worse followed in 1956, when facing unrest in Hungary that threatened to result in that country's exit from the new alliance, the Soviets resorted to strong-arm tactics again by using the Red Army to crush Hungarian hopes for neutrality and democracy. At the time the Americans and their most important West European allies, Britain and France, were preoccupied with the **Suez crisis**. Yet it is hard to imagine that the Western response to Soviet repression in Hungary would have been much different even in the absence of the Middle East imbroglio. By protesting against Soviet activities and opening their doors to Hungarian refugees, the West effectively indicated how the division of Europe was, in their view, a *de facto* state of affairs not to be challenged through military means. While anti-Soviet propaganda and various measures of psychological warfare escalated, the costs of any direct intervention within the Soviet sphere were simply too high. If anything, the thaw that characterized the European Cold War in the years

Great Powers
Traditionally those states that were held capable of shared responsibility for the management of the international order by virtue of their military and economic influence.

see Map 9.1

Suez Crisis
The failed attempt by Britain and France in 1956 to take advantage of a war between Israel and Egypt by seizing control of the Suez Canal and bringing down the government of Gamal Abdel Nasser. It is often taken as a symbol of the collapse of European imperialism and the rise of the Third World.

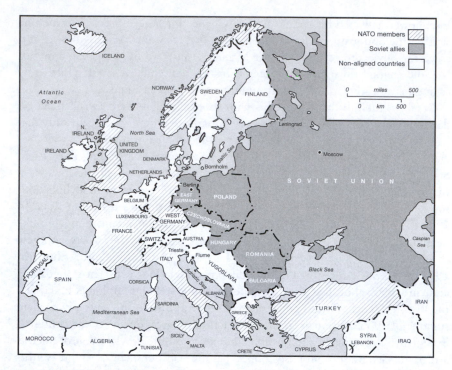

Map 9.1 The Cold War in Europe, 1955

Source: After Reynolds (1994)

de-Stalinization
The policy, pursued in most communist states and among most communist groups after 1956, of eradicating the memory or influence of Stalin and Stalinism. Initiated by the Soviet Union under the guidance of Nikita Khrushchev.

following Stalin's death thus ensured that external challenges to the legitimacy of the Soviet hold in Eastern Europe were limited to verbal condemnations. Contrary to what Eisenhower's secretary of state, John Foster Dulles, had implied during the American presidential campaign of 1952, there would be no aggressive effort to 'liberate' Eastern Europe or 'roll back' communist power.

Not that propaganda and criticism of communist repression were necessarily insignificant; in fact, the combination of **de-Stalinization** and American psychological warfare may have been partly responsible for the uprising in Hungary. One of the key causes of the revolts, however, was the Soviet effort to relax the extreme suppression that had characterized the Stalin years. The Soviet leaders who vied for a position of power in the aftermath of Stalin's death did agree upon one thing, that the personality cult and extreme repression that had characterized the pre-1953 years should not continue. Thus, once Nikita Khrushchev emerged from this power struggle as the key player, he moved to condemn Stalin's practices in his famous 'secret speech' at the Soviet Communist Party Congress in early 1956 and effectively denounced the former dictator as a criminal. Khrushchev then launched the Soviet Union upon an often unpredictable era of internal reform. In the years that followed, many of those who had suffered during Stalin's purges were released from prison camps and had their reputations restored. However, as is often the case, the promise of relaxation prompted demands for rapid transformation and, as in Hungary, an outright revolt against communism and the Soviet Union.

In fact, perhaps the most accurate way to characterize the 'thaw' is to state that it represented a period of reassessment in Soviet–American relations, stabilization of the Cold War system in Europe and the emergence of competition (rather than direct military confrontation) as the key form of waging the Cold War. Talk about **peaceful co-existence** and competition between two systems characterized the new rhetoric emanating, in particular, from the Kremlin. Nor was it just talk, for by 1957 not only was Europe divided into two 'geopolitical zones' (with a few neutral countries, Austria, Finland, Sweden and Switzerland, in the middle), but the eastern and western parts of Europe had by and large become two separate economic systems.

In Western Europe the movement, encouraged with some foreboding by the United States, towards European integration gathered steam during the 1950s with the formation of the EEC in 1957. Helped by an influx of American capital and the successful working of the **Bretton Woods** system, the EEC's economic success further highlighted the division of Europe, while its institutional arrangements marked the beginning of political integration. The development of Western European integration was undoubtedly one of the most fundamental 'side effects' of the Cold War. The various institutions, treaties and communities that knit together the basic structure of the post-Cold War European Union represented a basic shift in inter-European relations. Whereas France and Germany, for example, had previously been bitter rivals, they became, starting in the early 1950s, the two countries driving the integration process. With the signing of the Treaty of Rome in 1957, the six nations of the ECSC formed the EEC and EURATOM, which established a common market in nuclear materials (and equal access to uranium stocks). In subsequent years, the EEC states introduced further integration schemes, such as a Common Agricultural Policy, and moved towards the gradual withdrawal of all existing tariff barriers between member states. Although the process would continue throughout the rest of the twentieth century, the successful integration of Western Europe during the Cold War would succeed in uniting at least one half of the continent.

However, the EEC also exposed disagreements among West Europeans. Britain, concerned about losing the remnants of its global influence to a European body in which the French played a dominant role, preferred an arrangement limited to trade issues (that is, reduction or removal of tariffs etc.) and chose to remain outside the EEC. Instead the British, along with the Scandinavian countries, Austria and Switzerland, formed the seven-nation European Free Trade Association (EFTA) in 1960. The success of the EEC continued, though, to expose the relative decline of the British economy, so that almost immediately after the foundation of EFTA Britain applied for membership of the EEC. The debate over the future course of European integration and Britain's role in it continued through the 1960s when the French, under Charles de Gaulle's presidency, twice vetoed British membership. However, the main question was not really whether European integration should take place or whether Britain should be a member; rather, the debate focused on the nature of integration. Later this debate and the

peaceful co-existence
An expression coined originally by Trotsky to describe the condition when there are pacific relations between states with differing social systems and competition takes place in fields other than war. The idea was vital to Soviet diplomacy particularly after the death of Stalin.

see Chapter 21

Bretton Woods
The site of an inter-Allied conference held in 1944 to discuss the post-war international economic order. The conference led to the establishment of the IMF and the World Bank. In the post-war era the links between these two institutions, the establishment of GATT and the convertibility of the dollar into gold were known as the Bretton Woods system. After the dollar's devaluation in 1971 the world moved to a system of floating exchange rates.

success of Europe's economic integration would lead to a number of challenges to American leadership.

The American attitude towards European integration itself shifted during the Cold War. While the Truman and Eisenhower administrations were keen supporters of European unity – political, military and economic – and pressed the British to join the EEC early on, such unequivocal support turned in the 1960s into a profound ambivalence. In part, Americans worried over the apparent French effort to drive a wedge between a resurgent Europe and the United States. In addition, Washington was concerned about the growing economic strength of the EEC which, alongside the emergence of Japan as a major economic power, had the potential to lead to trade wars and to increase the political divergence between the United States and its European partners. Ultimately, Americans worried that an independent Europe would launch an independent détente with the Soviet bloc and that the Soviets would use every opportunity to promote divisions between the Western Powers.

see Chapter 11

In Eastern Europe the Soviet Union met the challenges to its authority in East Germany, Poland and Hungary either by strengthening its grip (as in East Germany and Hungary) or by allowing some additional autonomy in internal matters (Poland). All in all, even though violent crackdowns took place, the uniformity that had been the general characteristic of the late Stalin years – together with the terror that had been the central means of achieving it – was not nearly as evident in Eastern Europe during the Khrushchev era. The Soviet Union relied increasingly on the structural arrangements, such as the Warsaw Pact and COMECON, to keep its sphere intact. However, by doing so, the Soviets were gradually faced with an increasing amount of 'deviation' as countries such as Romania moved to emphasize their independent policies and develop ties to the West. Whatever the repressive counteractions of the USSR, Khrushchev and the 'thaw' of the mid-1950s thus managed to erode even further the myth of monolithic communism. Soon it would be shattered altogether, as the Soviet Union and China moved towards confrontation.

see Chapter 15

In the end, though, the hopes for a permanent relaxation of East–West tensions in the mid-1950s proved to be misplaced, for the thaw turned out to be but a brief interlude. By the time Khrushchev confirmed his position as the head of the Soviet Union in the summer of 1957 (when he survived an attempt to topple him), the Cold War had, in effect, become a long 'twilight struggle' that was being fought on all fronts through a mixture of confrontation and competition.

A wasting asset? Nuclear weapons

The Soviet–American rivalry over nuclear weapons was the issue that, above all others, symbolized the bipolarity of the Cold War. In the first half of the 1950s the balance stood clearly in America's favour for, although it had lost its nuclear monopoly in 1949, the United States seemed to be consistently one step ahead of its rival. Because of this edge, the Eisenhower administration relied heavily on nuclear weapons and the notion of **massive retaliation** – the idea that the United States was willing to retaliate with nuclear weapons even in response to small-scale conventional Soviet attacks – as a way of deterring possible Soviet military moves. The 'New Look' (as the overall policy was called) had the attraction of reducing the need to expand American and NATO conventional forces to match the level of their Soviet and Warsaw Pact counterparts. In 1955, for example, the United States had about 2.9 million men in arms compared with the Soviets' 5.7 million. Reliance on nuclear weapons also had another advantage: it allowed the United States to keep its military budget from mushrooming, something the Soviet Union picked up on and effectively copied in the late 1950s.

The problem was that massive retaliation could work only as long as the perception of American nuclear superiority, as well as the reality, existed. By late 1957 that was no longer the case. Between August and October of that year the Soviets stunned the world by launching their first **inter-continental ballistic missile (ICBM)** and by sending Sputnik, the first man-made satellite, into space. Given that the Americans had twice failed in 1957 to launch their Atlas ICBM, it seemed that a sudden shift in rocket technology and intelligence capabilities had taken place. As a result, the Eisenhower administration was placed under siege, as critics began to talk about a 'missile gap' in the Soviets' favour. Many cited the Gaither Report, a 1957 study that called for massive additional defence spending, as the guideline to be followed in responding to the new Soviet challenge. That American rocket scientists (headed by such former German scientists as Werner von Braun) succeeded in launching the first American satellite into space in January 1958 did little to calm increasing fears that the United States had lost, or was about to lose, its scientific edge to the USSR.

In reality, the Soviets had only scored a short-term propaganda victory, for the missile capabilities of the United States far exceeded those of the USSR. But there were two problems. First, no matter that the numerical balance favoured the United States, the sheer existence of Soviet ICBMs turned the long-standing fear that the USSR might one day be able to hit American territory with nuclear weapons into a frightening reality. Hence, threatening to strike the Soviets with nuclear weapons if they launched a conventional military attack on Western Europe became less credible; this, in turn, undermined the whole concept of massive retaliation. Second, although the Eisenhower administration knew of America's continued superiority, the means by which such intelligence was gathered made it difficult, if not impossible, to publicize it. Eisenhower had gone on record denying that the United States spied on the USSR, but in reality high-tech **U-2 spy planes** were regularly flying over Soviet airspace gathering intelligence on military installations. As it was unwilling to acknowledge this publicly, the American administration could thus not make a strong case against further missile development; the Soviets, in the meantime, made the new technological advances a centrepiece of their propaganda effort. 'Socialist science', Khrushchev would repeatedly argue, was not only equal to but had overtaken 'capitalist science'.

In such a situation it was no wonder that calls for a new American defence doctrine were heeded. John F. Kennedy, who narrowly defeated Richard Nixon in

massive retaliation
A strategy of military counter-attack prevalent in the United States during the Eisenhower administration, whereby the United States threatened to react to any type of military offensive by the Soviets or the Chinese with the use of nuclear weapons. The strategy began to lose its credibility as the Soviets developed a substantial nuclear capability in the late 1950s.

inter-continental ballistic missile (ICBM)
Any supersonic missile that has a range of at least 6,500 kilometres and follows a ballistic trajectory after launching. The Soviet–American SALT I Agreements limited the number of ICBMs that each side could have.

U-2 spy planes
An American high-altitude reconnaissance aircraft used to fly over Soviet and other hostile territories.

the 1960 presidential race, moved rapidly towards abandoning the New Look and massive retaliation. Even though his administration was later forced to 'admit' that the missile gap was, in fact, in America's favour, Kennedy adopted a more expensive defence doctrine (Flexible Response) that emphasized not only the development of nuclear weapons but additional spending on conventional and non-conventional forces.

There was, however, much more behind the shift in American military doctrines than the sudden launch of Soviet satellites and ICBMs, for the Americans were also responding to a sudden explosion of new potential trouble spots around the world. The Korean War and the decision to aid the French war effort in Indochina had been but the first expressions of the expansive view American leaders were beginning to take of their country's national interests in the Cold War. In effect, the shifting American military doctrine was part of the American decision to globalize the Cold War in response to the instability created by the rapid **decolonization** process of the 1940s and 1950s. By the late 1950s the picture was, indeed, disheartening. Between 1946 and 1960 thirty-seven former colonies became independent in Africa, Asia and the Middle East; by 1958 twenty-eight guerrilla wars were under way in these areas. Not only that, but the Soviet Union, under Khrushchev's leadership, presented itself as the champion of the 'wars of national liberation' and openly advocated socialism as a solution to economic and political problems that were endemic in the **Third World**. Nuclear weapons, it was clear, could have little practical use in the struggle over influence in these areas.

decolonization
The process whereby an imperial power gives up its formal authority over its colonies.

Third World
A collective term of French origin for those states that are part of neither the developed capitalist world nor the communist bloc. It includes the states of Latin America, Africa, the Middle East, South Asia and South-East Asia. Also referred to as 'the South' in contrast to the developed 'North'.

Culture and propaganda

The beginning of the space age coincided with an accelerated propaganda war between the United States and the Soviet Union. From the Soviet perspective, in fact, one of the chief causes of the Hungarian uprising and other unrest in Eastern Europe had been Western propaganda. Indeed, through such mediums as Radio Free Europe, the Americans had waged an active psychological warfare effort inside the Iron Curtain. The major goal had been straightforward: to encourage dissent towards communism and the tendency towards nationalism in order to incite the East European countries to move towards acts of independence similar to that of Tito's Yugoslavia.

However, the Soviet crackdown on Hungary indicated the dangers of openly challenging Moscow's supremacy. Thus, in the second half of the 1950s the cultural Cold War began to take a different form. Rather than stressing the negative, both sides now focused on the positive elements and achievements of their respective systems. While the Soviets bragged about their most recent technological achievements such as Sputnik, and 'sold' the socialist model to the newly independent countries as an antidote to imperialism, the Americans targeted Eastern Europe and the Soviet Union through a campaign of cultural infiltration. In effect, the American government sponsored the export of American mass culture to the Eastern bloc hoping that it would, however gradually, help to erode the prevailing totalitarian conformity and the stranglehold of the communist parties.

The early breakthroughs in this programme included a 1958 Soviet–American Cultural Agreement and a six-week American National Exhibition in Moscow in the summer of 1959. The exhibition is best known as the stage for the so-called 'kitchen debate' between Khrushchev and the American vice-president, Richard Nixon, in July 1959. While visiting the exhibition the two leaders sipped Pepsi-Cola and Nixon bragged about the latest products of the American consumer society. Among these were a number of kitchen gadgets that made household work much easier in the United States. While Khrushchev appeared unimpressed, the display of American consumer products clearly illustrated to the large crowds of Soviet citizens who visited the exhibition (which ran for six weeks) the material attractions of Western capitalism. In the long term, as films, exchange programmes, music, clothes and other products of the American consumer society gradually filtered into the Soviet bloc, the National Exhibition can be seen as one of the opening shots in an American effort to undermine confidence in the socialist system through peaceful means. In essence, Americans were no longer focusing on anti-Soviet diatribes but on selling the positive benefits of the 'American way of life'. While impossible to measure, such a long-term 'cultural offensive' could not have been inconsequential in gradually fostering dissent towards authoritarian conformity.

The American campaign to win 'the hearts and minds' of East Europeans was matched by efforts to persuade West Europeans that they were an integral part of the same shared system of democratic values as the United States. Indeed, the United States made a strenuous effort to 'educate' West Europeans not only about the 'evils' of communism but about the 'community of interests' and 'cultural heritage' that was at the root of the transatlantic bond. The cultural campaigns in Western Europe began with the 're-education' of West Germans and Austrians during the 1940s. However, with the launching of the Marshall Plan a genuine government-sponsored effort, supported by numerous private initiatives, sold America as the example for the Europeans to follow. By helping Hollywood to reclaim its markets in post-war Europe, by defending American notions of free trade, by flooding Europe with American consumer products, by funding various exchange programmes (such as the Fulbright scholarly exchanges), and even by Central Intelligence Agency (CIA) sponsorship of such organizations of European intellectuals as the Congress for Cultural Freedom (founded in June 1950, the same month as the Korean War broke out), the United States made a consistent effort to influence the European view of America and the debates about Europe's role in the Cold War.

One of the reasons for this effort was the fact that West European communists were not the only ones criticizing NATO and American policy. Indeed, while various communist-inspired 'peace conferences' failed to make much impact on West European public opinion in the 1950s, a persistent neutralist sentiment, strong particularly in France, remained a constant scourge of American efforts to gain unwavering European support for its policies. Indeed, the failure of the American efforts to unify political opinion in Europe played a role in enabling such independent-minded leaders as Charles de Gaulle to break ranks, if only in a limited way, with the United States in the 1960s.

In the end, much as in the Soviet bloc, American cultural programmes were relatively unsuccessful when they were geared towards explicit advocacy of specific policies. However, the spread of American popular culture and consumer products was so pervasive that it is hard to escape the conclusion that alongside the existing political, economic and military agreements, the transatlantic alliance between the United States and Western Europe was further strengthened by the relative 'Americanization' of the old continent. Even as European intellectuals at times criticized the influx of consumer products from across the Atlantic, the general public found little to fault in enhanced access to American-style fast food, clothes, music or films. While some of its policies may have invited resentment, the general lifestyle of the United States was certainly something that most West Europeans were ready to emulate. Moreover, the fact that an increasing number of East Germans were willing to risk their lives in order to benefit from such consumerism and personal freedoms created the last major European crisis of the first Cold War.

The Berlin Wall

In the late 1950s the Soviet–American relationship began to sour once again. In Europe, the focus of the confrontation was Berlin, where Americans, British and French forces retained their post-war control over the western part of the city. In November 1958 Khrushchev suddenly demanded the evacuation of the Western allies' garrisons from Berlin by the following summer, threatening that otherwise the USSR would sign a separate peace treaty with the GDR. Such unilateral action, in turn, would mean that the Western powers would either have to recognize the GDR and negotiate an access agreement with it, or accept the absorption of Berlin into East Germany. Neither alternative was appealing: the former would have created a crisis with the FRG, while the latter was likely to spark a serious confrontation, unless the Western Powers were willing to yield Berlin to the East and suffer a severe blow to their prestige.

Khrushchev's ultimatum had several objectives. First, it was a response to growing GDR demands to cut the brain drain of talented young East Germans via the open access route from East to West Berlin. Pushed by the lack of opportunity in East Germany and pulled by the prosperity in West Germany, thousands of young East Germans were by this stage taking advantage of the one remaining hole in the Iron Curtain. Indeed, not only was the GDR deprived of many of its most promising and best-educated citizens, but the constant movement from East to West was also providing welcome propaganda to Konrad Adenauer's West German government and its American supporters. Accordingly, the secondary aim of the Berlin ultimatum was to cause some rifts in the close (from the Soviet perspective disturbingly so) American–West German relationship. Finally, the Soviets hoped to create doubts within NATO at a time when the Alliance was considering whether to deploy medium-range missiles in Western Europe. Confident that the increasing Soviet nuclear capability would raise doubts about the reliability of an American deterrent, Khrushchev thus seized the opportunity both to solve an embarrassing local problem and to alter the delicate balance in Europe in the Soviet Union's favour.

Ironically, the end result of the prolonged Berlin crisis was a propaganda defeat for the Soviets and East Germans, and a reaffirmation of the status quo in Europe, for the United States and the West European Powers simply rejected Khrushchev's ultimatum. Moreover, he could not make any progress on the issue when he met with President Eisenhower at the Camp David summit in September 1959. The first Soviet leader to visit the United States, Khrushchev instead seemed to abandon the controversial issue for the time being in favour of friendly banter. The following year, however, Khrushchev's tone changed again. In May 1960 he stormed out of the Four-Power Paris Summit meeting that had been convened in order to deal with such unresolved issues as the Berlin question. The Soviet premier cited as his reason a series of American U-2 spy flights, one of which had been shot down (and the pilot, Francis Gary Powers, captured and tried) shortly prior to the summit, and demanded that Eisenhower publicly apologize for such violations of Soviet airspace. The American president, who had probably hoped to end his presidency on a hopeful note, left office early the following year with the Cold War in full flow.

In 1961, as Khrushchev came under increasing pressure both at home and abroad to live up to his tough rhetoric, the new US president, John F. Kennedy, was left to deal with the climax of the Berlin crisis. With more than 100,000 East Germans fleeing via Berlin in the first half of 1961, it was clear that the issue had to be settled. However, with both sides under pressure to remain tough, the Soviet–American summit in Vienna in June 1961 accomplished little. Hence, the war of words intensified: Khrushchev set the end of 1961 as the deadline for a solution; Kennedy shot back by reaffirming America's commitment to West Berlin and asking Congress to increase defence expenditure. As tensions mounted the Soviets and East Germans resorted to the only solution that was unlikely to provoke an open military confrontation: on 13 August 1961 East German police forces started to construct a barbed-wire fence separating East and West Berlin. They soon followed this up by erecting a concrete wall. Access between East and West Berlin was soon restricted to a number of tightly controlled checkpoints.

The building of the Berlin Wall had mixed effects. In the short term, it diffused the crisis by removing its source, for East Germans now found it virtually impossible to move to the West via Berlin. The Western Powers, including the United States, protested but they did not attempt to remove the wall, realizing that this would risk war. As a result, the Berlin question, while by no means solved, soon occupied a far less central position as a source of Cold War tension. In a sense, the Berlin Wall thus symbolized the acceptance of the status quo in Europe by both sides. To the West, Berlin was clearly not an adequate cause for going to war. To the Soviets, West Berlin's existence was acceptable as long as it no longer drained the best and the brightest from the GDR. However, Khrushchev's decision to build the wall was also indicative of the tightrope act that the Soviet premier was performing. On the one hand, he had been pressed by his East German allies to take action, but on the other hand, he was no more eager than Kennedy was to risk a nuclear exchange. In Berlin, at least, a stability of sorts – however bizarre a concrete wall dividing the former capital of the Third Reich was in the nuclear age – had set in.

In the long run, however, the more significant symbolic value of the wall was not the stability it seemed to provide, but the way in which it clarified for all to see the differences between the two political systems it separated. As Cold War propaganda wars continued, the West never stopped using to its advantage the fact that the East had had to build a wall to keep its people in. Over subsequent decades the Berlin Wall became *the* symbol of the Cold War's endurance, and the ultimate unanswerable indictment of communism.

Conclusion

When Germany surrendered on 7 May 1945 the process leading to the post-war division of Europe had already begun. Three months earlier, at Yalta, the leaders of Britain, the United States and the Soviet Union had failed to produce a workable solution for post-war Europe. In the months and years that followed, Europe, and eventually much of the rest of the world, became increasingly divided. In the process, Germany, the old enemy, was partitioned into two halves, the FRG and the GDR. On a broader scale, this was replicated by the Iron Curtain that divided communist Eastern Europe from non-communist Western Europe until the late 1980s. On both sides of the divide various measures of economic integration, military buildup and political co-operation (or domination) set in motion a process that for the next forty-five years effectively separated the European continent into two opposing blocs, each with its own military organization (NATO and the Warsaw Pact). While the Cold War in Europe never transformed itself into a hot war, it did, effectively, become a **total war** using every other means possible. For European countries, neutrality, while theoretically possible, became the privilege of the few and the small.

On a lesser scale, the division of Europe was symbolized by the quadripartite control of the victorious Powers over Berlin. Indeed, it was Berlin that remained the focal point of tension in much of the first decade and a half of the Cold War. In 1948–49 it was the scene of the Berlin blockade, and in 1961 the Soviets, worried about the corrosive political and economic impact of a large flood of East Germans to West Germany, built the Berlin Wall. But it also became a stabilizer of sorts, for after the wall was built, the 'German question', while a continued

total war
A war that uses all resources at a state's disposal including the complete mobilization of both the economy and society.

see Chapter 13

point of contention between the United States and the Soviet Union, seemed to lose some of its central character. This was hardly an accident, for by the late 1950s and early 1960s the Cold War contest in Europe appeared less likely to provoke an open East–West (or Soviet–American) confrontation than the numerous regional hot spots produced by rapid decolonization. Moreover, while new sources of tension appeared from Cuba to the Congo to Vietnam, the dangers of the nuclear age were making an open confrontation between the United States and the Soviet Union seemingly unthinkable.

The period from the surrender of Germany in 1945 to the building of the Berlin Wall in 1961 thus saw the dramatic onset and the uneasy stabilization of the Cold War in Europe. Indeed, by the early 1960s, the Cold War division of Europe was taken almost as the normal state of affairs. Thus, however abnormal it might seem to build a wall to divide the once-proud centre of Hitler's Third Reich, in reality it only confirmed the division of Europe that had emerged at rapid pace after Germany's surrender. But at the same time as that confirmation took place, the contest between the East and the West – and ultimately between the United States and the Soviet Union – was about to enter another phase, which would be dramatically highlighted by an 'eyeball-to-eyeball' confrontation in October 1962.

Recommended reading

There is no shortage of books on the issues covered in this chapter. For some of the more recent comprehensive analyses on the entire period see John L. Gaddis, *We Now Know: Rethinking Cold War History* (New York, 1997) and *The Cold War: A New History* (New York, 2006), Richard Crockatt, *The Fifty Years War* (New York, 1995), David S. Painter, *The Cold War* (New York, 1999), Melvyn Leffler, *For the Soul of Mankind: The United States, the Soviet Union, and the Cold War* (New York, 2007), Martin Walker, *The Cold War* (New York, 1994), Marc Trachtenberg, *The Constructed Peace* (Princeton, NJ, 2000), William Curti Wohlforth, *The Elusive Balance: Power and Perceptions during the Cold War* (Ithaca, NY, 1993) and David Miller, *The Cold War: A Military History* (New York, 1999).

The German question is discussed in William Glenn Gray, *Germany's Cold War* (Chapel Hill, NC, 2007), Thomas A. Schwartz, *America's Germany* (Cambridge, MA, 1991), Anne Deighton, *The Impossible Peace: Britain, the Division of Germany, and the Origins of the Cold War* (New York, 1990), Carol Eisenberg, *Drawing the Line: The American Decision to Divide Germany* (New York, 1996), Norman Naimark, *The Russians in Germany* (Cambridge, MA, 1997), Frank Ninkovich, *Germany and the United States: The Transformation of the German Question since 1945* (New York, 1995), Avi Shlaim, *The United States and the Berlin Blockade* (Berkeley, CA, 1983) and Marc Trachtenberg, *A Constructed Peace: The Making of the European Settlement* (Princeton, NJ, 1999). For the renewed crisis in Berlin, see William Burr (ed.), *The Berlin Crisis, 1958–1962* (Alexandria, VA, 1994) and Michael Beschloss, *Kennedy vs. Khrushchev: The Crisis Years, 1960–1963* (New York, 1991).

Different viewpoints on containment during the early Cold War are offered in Melvyn Leffler, *A Preponderance of Power* (Stanford, CA, 1992), Gabriel Kolko and Joyce Kolko, *The Limits of Power* (New York, 1972), Thomas Paterson, *On Every Front* (New York, 1992), John L. Gaddis, *Strategies of Containment* (New York, 1982), Thomas J. McCormick, *America's Half Century* (Baltimore, MD, 1995), Michael Hogan, *A Cross of Iron* (New York, 1998) and Arnold A. Offner, *Another Such Victory: Harry S. Truman and the Cold War* (Stanford, CA, 2002). For more specific issues, see Louise Fawcett, *Iran and the Cold War: The Azerbaijan Crisis of 1946* (New York, 1992) and John O. Iatrides and Linda Wrigley (eds), *Greece at the Crossroads: The Civil War and its Legacy* (University Park, MD, 1995). On the Marshall Plan and economic warfare, see Michael Hogan, *The Marshall Plan* (New York, 1987), Alan Milward, *The Reconstruction of Western Europe* (New York, 1984), Robert A. Pollard, *Economic Security and the Origins of the Cold War* (New York, 1985) and Michael Mastanduno, *Economic Containment: CoCom and the Politics of East–West Trade* (Ithaca, NY, 1992). For collected essays offering different perspectives on the origins of the Cold War, see David Reynolds (ed.), *The Origins of the Cold War in Europe* (New Haven, CT, 1994) and Melvyn Leffler and David S. Painter (eds), *The Origins of the Cold War* (New York, 1994).

On the role of other West European countries see David Carlton, *Churchill and the Soviet Union* (New York, 2000), John Charmley, *Churchill's Grand Alliance, The Anglo-American Special Relationship, 1940–1957* (New York, 1995), James Miller, *The United States and Italy, 1945–1950* (Chapel Hill, NC, 1986), Jussi M. Hanhimäki, *Scandinavia and the United States: An Insecure Friendship* (New York, 1997), Philip Gordon, *France, Germany and the Western Alliance* (Boulder, CO, 1995), and William I. Hitchcock, *France Restored* (Chapel Hill, NC, 1998).

NATO is covered in Michael Brenner, *NATO and Collective Security* (New York, 1998), Lawrence Kaplan, *NATO and the United States: The Enduring Alliance* (New York, 1994), Geir Lundestad (ed.), *No End to Alliance* (New York, 1998), Charles Cogan, *Forced to Choose: France, the Atlantic Alliance and NATO* (Westport, CT, 1997), Olav Riste (ed.), *Western Security: The Formative Years* (New York, 1985) and Kevin Ruane, *The Rise and Fall of the EDC: Anglo-American Relations and the Crisis of European Defence, 1950–1955* (New York, 2000).

For Soviet policy, Vladislav Zubok and Constantin Pleshakov, *Inside the Kremlin's Cold War* (Cambridge, MA, 1996) is probably the best account covering the Cold War period, while Zubok's *A Failed Empire: The Soviet Union in the Cold War from Stalin to Gorbachev* (Chapel Hill, NC, 2007) offers a comprehensive survey of the entire Soviet era. See also Vojtech Mastny, *The Cold War and Soviet Insecurity* (New York, 1996), James G. Richter, *Khrushchev's Double Bind: International Pressures and Domestic Coalition Politics* (Baltimore, MD, 1994), Donald Filtzer, *The Khrushchev Era: De-Stalinisation and the Limits of Reform in the USSR, 1953–1964* (Basingstoke, 1993) and James Goldgeier, *Leadership Style and Soviet Foreign Policy: Stalin, Khrushchev, Brezhnev, Gorbachev* (Baltimore, MD, 1994).

For Soviet policies in Eastern Europe, Zbigniew Brzezinski, *The Soviet Bloc* (Cambridge, MA, 1967) is still useful. More recent studies include Neil Fodor, *The Warsaw Treaty Organization* (New York, 1990), Bradley Gitz, *Armed Forces and Political Power in Eastern Europe* (New York, 1992), Charles Gati, *Hungary and the Soviet Bloc* (Durham, NC, 1986) and *Failed Illusions: Moscow, Washington, Budapest, and the 1956 Hungarian Revolt* (Stanford, CA, 2006), Odd Arne Westad *et al.* (eds), *The Soviet Union in Eastern Europe, 1945–1989* (New York, 1994), Karel Kaplan, *The Short March: The Communist Takeover in Czechoslovakia, 1945–1948* (New York, 1987), Kersten Krystyna, *The Establishment of Communist Rule in Poland, 1943–1948* (Berkeley, CA, 1991) and Vojtech Mastny and Malcolm Byrne (eds), *A Cardboard Castle? An Inside History of the Warsaw Pact* (Budapest, 2006). For two perspectives on American policy in Eastern Europe see Geir Lundestad, *The American Non-Policy in Eastern Europe* (New York, 1975) and Bennett Kovrig, *Of Walls and Bridges: The United States and Eastern Europe* (New York, 1991).

The various aspects of West European integration are discussed in Francis Heller and John Gillingham, *The United States and the Integration of Europe* (New York, 1996), Wolfram Kaiser, *Using Europe, Abusing the Europeans: Britain and European Integration, 1945–1963* (New York, 1996), Geir Lundestad, *'Empire' by Integration: the United States and European Integration, 1945–1997* (New York, 1998), Alan Milward, *The European Rescue of the Nation-State* (Berkeley, CA, 1992), Derek W. Urwin, *The Community of Europe: A History of European Integration* (New York, 1991), John W. Young, *Britain and European Unity, 1945–1992* (New York, 1993) and Pascaline Winand, *Eisenhower, Kennedy and the United States of Europe* (New York, 1993).

Basic works on the cultural Cold War include Volker R. Berghahn, *America and the Intellectual Cold Wars in Europe* (Princeton, NJ, 2002), Walter Hixson, *Parting the Curtain* (Basingstoke, 1997), Richard Pells, *Not Like Us* (New York, 1997), Stephen Whitfield, *The Culture of the Cold War* (Baltimore, MD, 1991), Hans J. Tuch, *Communicating with the World: US Public Diplomacy Overseas* (New York, 1990), Sig Mickelson, *The Word War: The Story of Radio Free Europe and Radio Liberty* (New York, 1983), J. D. Parks, *Culture, Conflict and Coexistence: American–Soviet Cultural Relations, 1917–1958* (Jefferson, MO, 1983), Frederick Starr, *Red and Hot: The Fate of Jazz in the Soviet Union* (New York, 1983), Reinhold Wagnleitner, *Coca-Colonization* (Chapel Hill, NC, 1994), Randolph Wieck, *Ignorance Abroad: American Educational and Cultural Foreign Policy* (Westport, CT, 1992) and Timothy Wyback, *Rock around the Bloc: A History of Rock Music in Eastern Europe and the Soviet Union* (New York, 1990).

For Soviet–American relations and the nuclear arms race in the 1950s, see Gunter Bischof and Saki Dockrill (eds), *Cold War Respite: The Geneva Summit of 1955* (Baton Rouge, LA, 2000), John Newhouse, *War and Peace in the Nuclear Age* (New York, 1988), Andreas Wenger, *Living with Peril: Eisenhower, Kennedy, and Nuclear Weapons* (Lanham, MD, 1997), David Holloway, *The Soviet Union* and the Nuclear Arms Race (New Haven, CT, 1983), David Holloway, *Stalin and the Bomb: The Soviet Union and Atomic Energy, 1939–1956* (New Haven, CT, 1994), Saki Dockrill, *Eisenhower's New Look National Security Policy* (New York, 1996), Robert Bowie and Richard Immerman, *Waging Peace* (New York, 1998), Peter J. Roman, *Eisenhower and the Missile Gap* (Ithaca, NY, 1995) and Stephen Zaloga, *Target America: The Soviet Union and the Strategic Arms Race, 1945–1964* (Novato, CA, 1993).

Asia in turmoil: nationalism, revolution and the rise of the Cold War, 1945 – 53

Introduction

When the Second World War reached its conclusion in 1945, the devastation was by no means limited to the European continent, for in Asia too destruction stretched far and wide. Moreover, just as the defeat of Germany led to a power vacuum in Europe and the start of Cold War tensions, so the capitulation of Japan on 15 August 1945 led to chaos and revolution in Asia. Over the next decade a new international order very different to that which had existed before the **Pacific War** slowly emerged from the wreckage. In South and South-East Asia indigenous nationalist movements freed themselves from the European colonial presence and a number of new independent states emerged. Meanwhile China, following the victory of the Chinese Communist Party (CCP) over the **Guomindang** (**GMD**), emerged once again as a regional **Great Power**, while Japan eschewed imperialist expansionism to concentrate on economic growth.

However, this tendency for Asian peoples to gain greater control over their own destiny was to be compromised by another development, namely the arrival of the Cold War in the region. The establishment of the **People's Republic of China** (**PRC**) in 1949 meant not only that China was now united under a strong centralized state, but that it was ruled by a communist government with close political and military ties to the Soviet Union. Fearing that such a regime posed

Pacific War
The phrase usually used to refer to the Allied war against Japan from 1941 to 1945.

Guomindang (GMD)
The Chinese Nationalist party founded in 1913 by Sun Yatsen. Under the control of Jiang Jieshi, it came to power in China in 1928 and initiated a modernization programme before leading the country into war against Japan in 1937. It lost control over mainland China in 1949 as a result of the communist victory in the civil war. From 1949 it controlled Taiwan, overseeing the island's 'economic miracle', until its electoral defeat in 2000.

Great Powers
Traditionally those states that were held capable of shared responsibility for the management of the international order by virtue of their military and economic influence.

People's Republic of China (PRC)
The official name of communist or mainland China. The PRC came into existence in 1949 under the leadership of Mao Zedong.

containment
The term coined by George Kennan for the American, and broadly Western, policy towards the Soviet Union (and communism in general). The overall idea was to contain the USSR (that is, keep it within its current borders) with the hope that internal division, failure or political evolution might end the perceived threat from what was considered a chronically expansionist force.

a danger to its economic and strategic interests in the region, the United States reacted to this apparent threat by introducing a policy of **containment** similar to that which already existed in Europe. Thus, from 1949, East and South-East Asia became the second most important battleground in the global Cold War.

The encroachment of the Cold War and its attendant reductionist logic was to have a profound effect on Asia. Indeed, in some ways the ideological conflict for control of the continent was to become even more dangerous than the parallel events in Europe. After all, Asia, unlike Europe, witnessed two 'hot wars', in Korea and Vietnam, which had the potential to develop into global conflagrations. The volatility of the Cold War in Asia came about precisely because it was an area where nationalism was on the march and where new unstable states were coming into existence. As a result, the United States and the communist bloc entered into a deadly competition for clients, established either bilateral or multilateral alliance systems, and, in order to win or guarantee loyalty, distributed large amounts of military and economic aid. Uncommitted states were pressed to align themselves, with both the East and West declaring that there could be no neutrality in the conflict between communism and democracy. So rigid was this belief that Washington even felt it necessary to support colonial Powers against the challenges posed by left-wing national liberation movements. The result, not surprisingly, was a largely polarized Asia and the development of two armed camps. However, some states refused to be coerced into line and instead sought to free themselves from the shackles of bipolarity. Rejecting the Cold War paradigm, they asserted that the priority in Asia was the final removal of colonialism, and that America's insistence on the importance of containing communism was leading it to protect European imperialism and to act as an imperialist itself.

The end of the Raj

decolonization
The process whereby an imperial power gives up its formal authority over its colonies.

Congress
Shorthand for the Indian National Congress, a nationalist party first formed in India in 1885. Congress played the most important role in bringing about Indian independence in 1947 and since then has been one of the major political parties in Indian politics.

In the aftermath of the Pacific War, the first clear sign that a new Asia was emerging from the ashes of that conflict came in 1947 with the most dramatic act of **decolonization** yet to take place – the end of British rule in India. During the inter-war period Britain had attempted to use both coercion and concession in equal measure in its efforts to remain in India. However, by the end of the Second World War this policy was no longer attractive or feasible. India was now in a state of expectation following the promises of independence that had been made during the war, and, moreover, was in danger of breaking down into inter-communal violence. This was because, while the **Congress** Party's leaders had been imprisoned, the leading voice of the Islamic community, the Muslim League, had strengthened its position to the extent that it could now effectively veto any arrangement for the transfer of power that was against its interests. In such a volatile situation it was clear that if Britain wished to reassert its control and once again drag out its withdrawal, it would have to pay a high price both financially and militarily. Britain, under the new Labour government of Clement Attlee, was in no mood to make such a commitment. After all, Britain's economic interests in India had been in decline for a number of years and the hope existed that independence would not entirely sever the connection with the subcontinent, rather that India would accept **Dominion** status and become an active member of the **Commonwealth**.

Accordingly, from 1946 Britain began actively to negotiate a transfer of power, but this did not prove to be an easy matter, for when independence was granted in August 1947 it was not to one unitary state, but to two – India and Pakistan. The partition of India occurred because Congress and the Muslim League had fundamentally incompatible ideas about how to constitute a single successor state to British rule. Put simply, the Muslim League desired a weak political centre and the devolution of power to groups of provinces, which would allow the Muslim-majority areas a good deal of autonomy, while Congress sought the construction of a strong centralized state in order to achieve its social and economic goals. With neither side willing to compromise and the country on the brink of chaos, the easiest solution was partition. The result was that the Muslim-majority areas of Baluchistan, Sind, the North-West Frontier, the western half of the Punjab and the eastern half of Bengal were amalgamated into the state of Pakistan under the premiership of the leader of the Muslim League, Muhammad Ali Jinnah. Meanwhile India gained its independence under the leadership of Jawaharlal Nehru, the head of the Congress Party. Moreover, it quickly added to its territorial area by bribing or coercing the heads of the **Princely States** to merge their states into India.

The actual partition process was a painful one, for in the Punjab and Bengal those who found themselves on the wrong side of the religious divide were forced to flee for their lives and hundreds of thousands were killed. Another terrible legacy was left in one of the largest of the Princely States, **Kashmir**, whose Hindu ruler decided to merge his kingdom into India, even though 70 per cent of the population was Muslim. Pakistan was naturally furious at this outcome, although its protests reflected the province's strategic importance as much as its demography, for it had no desire to see India control the headwaters of the Indus. However, Nehru rejected Pakistan's claim to the province, stating that the religious affiliation of the population was of no matter as India was a secular state. The outcome was a brief war in 1948 and a lingering dispute that has at regular intervals brought conflict to the subcontinent.

Despite the unintended appearance of two successor states, the independence of India was an event of great importance for Asia, for it symbolized and further stimulated the desire to rid the continent of European colonialism. Moreover, in the figure of Nehru it produced an eloquent spokesman for the interests of Asian peoples. However, in the other major area of Asia still under colonial rule, South-East Asia, the road to independence was to prove considerably more complex. Unlike India, this region saw a power vacuum develop at the end of the Pacific War, which had important implications for the return of colonial power. Furthermore, in contrast to the subcontinent, its mineral wealth made it a vital pawn in the growing ideological confrontation between the Western Powers and the Soviet Union.

Dominion
A completely self-governing colony which is freely associated with the mother country. Within the British Empire, the Dominions were Australia, Canada, the Irish Free State (1922–49), New Zealand and South Africa.

Commonwealth, The
An organization of independent self-governing states linked by their common ties to the former British Empire.

Princely States
The states in British India that remained formally under the control of local rulers rather than direct British administration. They included states such as Hyderabad and Kashmir.

Kashmir
Province in the north-west of the Indian subcontinent. Although mainly Muslim in population, the Hindu ruler in 1947 declared his allegiance to India. Pakistan reacted by seizing control of some of the province. Divided ever since by what is known as the Line of Control, Kashmir has been a perpetual sore in Indo-Pakistani relations. Terrorist campaigns by Islamic militants in the 1990s led the two countries to the brink of war on a number of occasions.

Nationalism and independence in South-East Asia

see Chapter 4

As in other areas of the world, the Second World War had a profound effect on South-East Asia. In particular, the humiliating defeats that Japan inflicted on the imperial Powers in 1941–42 dealt a severe blow to European prestige. This effect was then compounded by Japan's ambivalent record as an occupying power, which saw it offering nominal independence to the local elites in Burma, the East Indies and the Philippines, while at the same time ruling with such a harsh hand that it stimulated the rise of nationalist-based resistance movements in all the countries it subjugated. In this environment the nationalist movements, which had struggled to make much impact in the pre-war period, began to flourish.

see Map 10.1

When the war ended in 1945 the strength of indigenous nationalism meant that it was extremely difficult for colonial rule to be re-established. Even Britain, the strongest of the European Powers, did not find the task easy. Building on the precedent set in India in 1947, in January 1948 it granted independence to Ceylon (Sri Lanka) and Burma, both of which had made substantial constitutional progress in the inter-war period. In the case of Burma, it was clear that any other choice would have involved Britain in a debilitating effort to maintain order, which the decreasing economic benefits derived from controlling the colony would not warrant. Meanwhile in Malaya, which was of much greater economic importance owing to its position as one of the empire's major dollar earners through its exports of rubber and tin, Britain attempted to make its rule more efficient through constitutional reform. In 1948 it introduced a new federal governmental system that provided for strong central government control over security and finance, but also a degree of local autonomy for the Malay-dominated sultanates.

Holland and France proved to be less accommodating to the forces of nationalism than their British counterparts. Both had suffered a marked loss of prestige during the war, both in Europe and in Asia, and therefore saw the restoration of their possessions in South-East Asia as vital to their national rehabilitation. Both, however, met with strong resistance when they attempted to reassert their control. In the Dutch East Indies the Japanese had directly encouraged Indonesian nationalism by liberating leaders such as Sukarno and Hatta from Dutch custody and allowing the development of an indigenous militia. When the Japanese surrendered in August 1945 the nationalists were therefore ready to take advantage of the power vacuum to establish a Republic of Indonesia and were determined to stop the Dutch from returning. In Indochina, the opposition to the French came from the **Viet Minh**, a communist-led resistance movement against the Japanese, which in September 1945 declared the independence of Vietnam. In both areas the uncompromising attitudes displayed by both colonialists and subjects meant that a mutually acceptable political settlement was impossible, and thus wars of national liberation broke out.

These two conflicts had a significant effect on the region. Britain had hoped that, in the aftermath of the Pacific War, it could use its position as the predominant Power in the region to encourage economic integration in South-East

Viet Minh
Vietnamese, communist-led organization whose forces fought against the Japanese and the French in Indochina. Headed by Ho Chi Minh, the Viet Minh was officially in existence from 1941 to 1951.

see Chapter 12

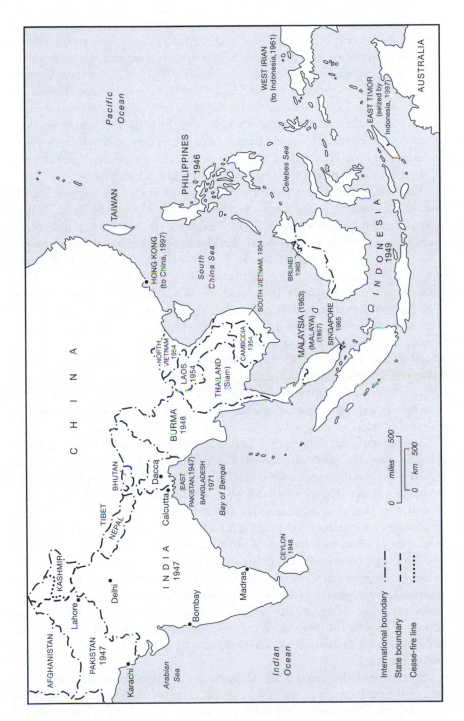

Map 10.1 Decolonization in South and South-East Asia

Source: After Brown and Louis (1999)

Asia. It believed that this would produce stability and a quick restoration of the region's favourable trade balance with the United States, which would, in turn, assist the economic recovery of the colonial Powers themselves. However, the fighting in the East Indies and Indochina frustrated this process and, as South-East Asia's economy and food distribution system remained mired in chaos, political disturbances soon spread throughout the region. The most disturbing aspect of this growing unrest was that in 1948 indigenous communists outside Indochina began to take advantage of the situation. In March communists plunged newly independent Burma into civil war, in June the Malayan Communist Party began an armed struggle against British rule, and in September the Indonesian Communist Party launched a failed coup in Java against Sukarno's government. The region thus appeared to be on the edge of political breakdown.

This was, not surprisingly, a matter of great concern for the colonial Powers, but it also became a worry for the United States. Since 1945 the Truman administration had attempted to distance itself from events in the region, merely indicating a general, if vague, desire that the European colonial Powers should allow greater self-government following the American example in the Philippines, which had been granted its independence in July 1946. However, in 1948 American thinking began to shift drastically. This was due largely to the realization that the raw materials, such as rubber and tin, that the region exported to the United States acted as one of the few ways in which key European states such as Britain and France could earn American dollars. The stability of South-East Asia therefore became linked to the main priority of the United States, the economic revival of Western Europe. Accordingly, when communist insurrections began in Burma, Malaya and Indonesia, American policy-makers assumed that these were not merely responses to local conditions but rather a co-ordinated campaign directed by Moscow designed to strike at one of the West's weakest links.

As a result of such thinking, the United States began to take a higher profile in a region that it had previously been content to see under British tutelage. Its main aim was to stem the communist tide. This involved it in what might seem to be contradictory policies, for in some areas it acted to expedite decolonization but in others it helped to perpetuate colonialism. The main focus of its effort to encourage decolonization was the Dutch East Indies. By 1948 the Dutch had still not come to terms with Indonesian nationalism, but their attempts to strangle the Republic of Indonesia had only succeeded in alienating world opinion and wasting their own scarce resources. Believing that the Dutch were involved in a fruitless and dangerous exercise, Washington's solution to this problem, safe in the knowledge that the Indonesian leaders were anti-communist, was to urge the Dutch to withdraw. In April 1949, after American threats to end economic and military aid, Holland finally conceded defeat and Indonesia moved towards full independence.

In regard to Indochina the United States took a very different tack, which was to put it firmly on the side of the imperialists rather than the forces of Asian nationalism. The situation in Indochina was not as simple as in Indonesia, for France was a vital European ally that could not be coerced in the same way as Holland. Moreover, the Viet Minh, although nominally a united front, was clearly under the control of the communists. American policy therefore tolerated the continuation of the French presence and even, albeit reluctantly, paid lip service to the latter's half-hearted gesture towards Vietnamese nationalism in the shape of the nominally autonomous Bao Dai regime.

The situation in South-East Asia in 1949 was therefore that, although much of the region had achieved independence, in one key area – Indochina – the advance of Asian nationalism had been thwarted. It was not, however, only the reverberations of the developing Cold War in Europe that had led to this outcome, for South-East Asia's destiny was also being moulded by events far closer to home. Already by the late 1940s East Asia was developing into a second front in the Cold War, a process that was completed in 1949 with the emergence of a communist regime in China.

The Chinese Civil War

In order to understand the development of the Cold War in Asia, it is first necessary to look at the respective interests of the superpowers in the region. At the end of the Second World War, both the United States and the Soviet Union sought to provide themselves with greater security in the East Asian and west Pacific regions. For Stalin, this meant a reversal of the outcome of the Russo-Japanese War, that is, the return of the southern half of Sakhalin, possession of the Kurile Islands, the re-establishment of a sphere of influence in **Manchuria** and use of naval bases in Korea. The United States, for its part, tried to ensure that there would be no more 'Pearl Harbors'. It therefore established trusteeships over what had been the Japanese **mandates** in the west Pacific, and most importantly, through its occupation of Japan, sought to transform its former enemy into a demilitarized and democratic state that would never again threaten the international order.

To a degree, the security concerns of the superpowers contained within them the seeds of strategic competition, particularly in regard to the future of Japan and Korea. In the case of the United States, one could even say that by occupying Japan it inherited the strategic concerns that had led the latter to become so sensitive about the balance of power in North-East Asia. The crucial factor, however, in determining whether the Cold War would spread to Asia was the fate of China. On the one hand, if reconciliation could be achieved between the GMD and the CCP in China, then the country could become a stabilizing influence. However, on the other hand, if the victory of one of these parties led to the Chinese tilting decisively towards one of the superpowers, it would have a significant effect on regional security.

The position in China at the end of the Pacific War was undeniably tense. At the start of the war against Japan in 1937, the GMD and the CCP had agreed to create the Second United Front, thus putting aside their mutual hostility in order to concentrate on resisting Japanese aggression. However, the two parties

Manchuria
The three north-eastern provinces of China and home of the Manchu people. From 1932 to 1945, with the addition of Jehol province, it became the Japanese puppet state of Manchukuo.

mandates
The colonial territories of Germany and the Ottoman Empire that were entrusted to Britain, France, Japan, Australia and South Africa under the supervision of a League of Nations Commission.

remained largely independent of each other, making war in parallel rather than engaging in a joint effort. Neither side was willing to move towards a true coalition for fear that the other would betray it in a repeat of the bloodshed that had accompanied the collapse of the First United Front in 1927. The Second United Front was therefore a fragile alliance that was not expected to last beyond the end of the war and, indeed, as early as 1941, clashes, such as the New Fourth Army Incident, were taking place between GMD and CCP forces.

The problem for Jiang Jieshi as the war progressed was that the CCP based at Yan'an in north China became increasingly strong, particularly if contrasted with its dilapidated state after the tribulations of the Long March. The CCP gained strength in a number of ways. In the military sphere, it adopted the principle of 'protracted war', which involved using guerrilla warfare to wear down the Japanese through attrition. This strategy proved successful and over time the CCP built itself a strong base in the rural areas of north China. Implicit in its use of guerrilla warfare was the need to work in the political sphere to foster good relations with the rural population, which it relied upon for food and intelligence. It did this by stressing its nationalist credentials and establishing relatively efficient local government. Moreover, in order to encourage the development of an anti-Japanese 'united front' of classes, it moderated the radical land reform policy it had followed in the early 1930s, so that it would not alienate rich peasants or small-scale landowners. Ideological justification of this policy was provided by Mao's 'sinified' reformulation of Marxism-Leninism, the '**New Democracy**' movement, which argued that socialism could only be achieved through the proletariat leading a broadly based alliance of classes. Military success, popular support and a coherent ideological programme led to the CCP's expansion from 40,000 members in 1937 to 1.2 million in 1945. Moreover, despite this rapid growth, party discipline was ruthlessly enforced. The CCP thus emerged as a potential challenger to the GMD's monopoly on power.

In contrast to the rise in the CCP's fortunes, the Nationalists encountered many problems during the war against Japan. The fall of Shanghai and Nanjing in 1937 meant that the GMD lost its wealthy power base in the lower Yangtze valley and, accordingly, was denied the main source of its income. In order to sustain the war effort, officials resorted to increasing the money supply, but this sparked spiralling inflation, which in turn undermined support for the government. In addition, the descent of the GMD into corruption and factionalism and the Nationalist Army's tendency to engage in forced conscription and requisition of goods without payment alienated the general population. Some of these excesses might have been excused had the Nationalists fought well against the Japanese, but Jiang's war record was far from impressive, reaching its nadir in 1944 when his armies collapsed during Japan's Ichigo offensive in south China. This lack of effective resistance led in turn to damaging speculation, fuelled by CCP propaganda, that Jiang was keeping his best forces intact for a post-war reckoning with the communists.

The GMD's reverses were, however, balanced by other factors. The strongest card that Jiang held was that the outbreak of the Pacific War strengthened his ties with the United States. After Pearl Harbor, Washington saw China as a crucial

New Democracy
The reformulation of Marxism-Leninism by Mao in the late 1930s and early 1940s in which he 'sinicized' communism and argued for the need for an alliance of classes, including both the proletariat and the peasantry, to bring about socialism.

theatre in the conflict with Japan and therefore increased its military and financial support for the Nationalists. In military terms the results of this sponsorship were distinctly advantageous, as the GMD's forces were boosted by the arrival of American advisers and, from 1944, increasing amounts of **Lend-Lease** material. In addition, American interest in China had the effect of raising the country's, and therefore by implication Jiang's, international standing. During the war Roosevelt became interested in the idea that, when peace was restored, China should become the dominant regional power in East Asia and one of the 'four policemen' of the world. In order to achieve this goal, the United States and Britain agreed in 1943 to relinquish the last of their imperial privileges in China, bar the British possession of Hong Kong. Moreover, Roosevelt supported Jiang's demand for the return of all the territories that Japan had seized since 1895, and lobbied successfully for China to become one of the five permanent members of the **UN** Security Council. In addition, Jiang was able in August 1945 to build a diplomatic bridge to the Soviet Union by signing a treaty accepting the terms laid down by the 'Big Three' at Yalta for Russian entry into the Pacific War. In essence, this meant that the Nationalists accepted Russian economic and military privileges in Manchuria, but in return they received from Stalin the promise of Soviet disinterest in Chinese internal affairs, in other words a commitment not to support the CCP.

The position therefore at the end of the war with Japan was that the GMD, although it faced a formidable CCP challenge, still remained relatively more powerful. It controlled more territory, had more party members and its army was numerically far greater than that of the communists and possessed better equipment. Moreover, Jiang, through his diplomatic manoeuvres, had managed to isolate the CCP internationally, having committed the Soviet Union to neutrality and won the outright support of the United States. The problem for Jiang, however, was how to use this advantageous position to eliminate the CCP threat. On the surface it might appear that immediate renewal of the civil war was the best option, but in late August 1945 Jiang moved instead to open negotiations with the CCP. One reason for this surprising decision was that the GMD needed a period of peace in which to regain its Yangtze stronghold and have its forces airlifted into north China by the Americans. In addition, Jiang knew that Washington desired GMD–CCP negotiations in the hope that they would lead to a democratic coalition government, and to have started a war in such circumstances would clearly have been unwise. Also, there was always the possibility that an isolated CCP might be willing to reach a political compromise, for it too was under pressure from Stalin to negotiate.

From August 1945 China thus entered into a twilight period in which negotiations, marked by grave suspicion on both sides, took place in Chongqing, while in the rest of the country the two parties vied for position. Not surprisingly, the talks soon became deadlocked. Frustrated by this lack of progress and fearing that the Soviets might take advantage of the situation, the Truman administration attempted in December 1945 to break the impasse by sending General George Marshall to mediate a general settlement. Marshall achieved an early success when he negotiated a cease-fire in January 1946, but in reality he faced an almost

Lend-Lease
With the Lend-Lease Act of March 1941, the US Congress empowered the president to lease or lend arms and supplies to any foreign government whose defence the administration considered essential to US national security. The programme, originally intended to rescue Britain, was eventually extended to more than thirty-eight states fighting the Tripartite Pact Powers.

United Nations (UN)
An international organization established after the Second World War to replace the League of Nations. Since its establishment in 1945, its membership has grown to 192 countries.

impossible task, neither side being willing to make any substantial concessions. The only hope lay in the prospect that each party feared that if it broke off the talks and renewed hostilities, it risked the prospect of losing both international and domestic support.

The fragile peace in China was undermined finally by two factors. The first was that by early 1946 the United States and the USSR were increasingly at odds. This was important because it propelled Jiang towards the conclusion that American support was guaranteed if he should go to war against the CCP. He therefore turned away from a political solution and looked for a suitable justification to renew hostilities. This then links to the second factor, which was the situation in north-east China. In the last few days of the Pacific War the Soviet Union had invaded Manchuria, thus honouring its commitment at Yalta to enter the war against Japan. After the Japanese surrender its troops remained in occupation and, despite the treaty signed with Jiang in August, allowed CCP forces to enter the region in the autumn of 1945 and take control of the rural areas. This greatly alarmed Jiang, for Manchuria was a rich prize following its industrialization under Japanese rule. Therefore when, in April 1946, the Russians withdrew from Manchuria, he ordered the airlift of GMD troops into the region in an effort to prevent the CCP from seizing complete control. With this move the cease-fire broke down and China quickly descended into civil war.

In the first year of fighting the GMD's superior numbers led to a series of victories in Manchuria and north China. This apparent success was misleading, for the CCP once again engaged in a 'protracted war' strategy, which was designed to encourage Jiang's forces to overstretch themselves and thus increase their vulnerability. By the autumn of 1947 the CCP was strong enough to go on the offensive in Manchuria, and from then on the tide of the war swung irrevocably in its favour. The victory of the CCP was also due to its broad level of political support. It gained the solid adherence of the peasantry owing to the popularity of its land requisition policy, and acquired the backing of many Chinese 'liberals' as a result of the continuation of 'New Democracy' and its reputation for discipline and incorruptibility. This contrasted with the GMD, which remained mired in factionalism and graft, and proved unable to do anything to control the increasing economic chaos. Indeed, in the midst of the civil war, the Nanjing government continued to introduce reforms designed to modernize the country and centralize power, even though such measures proved to be entirely counter-productive.

Another important miscalculation on Jiang's part was his belief that the United States would fully support his efforts to eradicate communism. In reality, Washington proved reluctant to act. Many in the Truman administration felt that Jiang had miscalculated when he had gambled on war, and believed that he should have concentrated instead on domestic reforms in order to undermine the CCP's appeal. Scepticism about Jiang and his regime became particularly noticeable after Marshall returned to Washington to take up the position of secretary of state in January 1947. Marshall had not been impressed by Jiang's regime, noting its corruption and lack of commitment to democratic values, and held that the United States should not commit itself irrevocably to the GMD's survival. Moreover, although, as Jiang had predicted, serious tensions developed between

America and Russia in 1946–47, even this did little to help his cause, for the architects of containment policy in Washington considered China to be economically weak and thus not a vital asset that must be denied to the Russians.

In 1949, after a series of catastrophic defeats, the GMD regime was forced to flee to Taiwan and the CCP proclaimed its victory by establishing the PRC on 1 October in Beijing. On taking power the CCP made it clear that the 'new China' would pursue a radically different path to its predecessor. At home it maintained

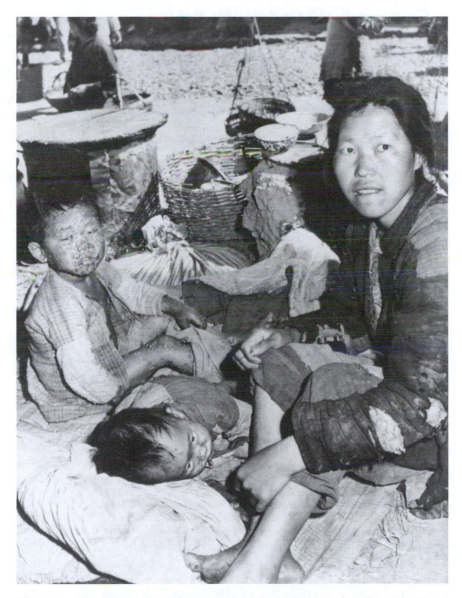

Plate 10.1 China, May 1946: a refugee family from one of China's famine areas lies on the side of the road during the civil war. Both of the children are suffering from smallpox. (Photo Bob Bryant/Keystone/Getty Images)

its 'New Democracy' approach to government, and in line with this pursued the continuation of land reform, the eradication of anti-social practices, such as corruption and prostitution, and the gradual introduction of socialist economic planning on the Stalinist model. It was, however, in the field of foreign policy that it had its greatest impact.

China, Japan and the Cold War in Asia

From the moment that it was clear that the CCP was heading for victory, the question of how the West would respond to the creation of a communist China and what direction that country would take in its relations with foreign Powers concentrated minds around the world. Some hope did exist in Western circles that the CCP might not necessarily follow Moscow's line but that it might emulate Tito and become an independent state equidistant from the two Cold War blocs.

This optimism was misplaced, for it showed a fundamental misunderstanding of the nature of the Chinese Revolution. For both nationalist and ideological reasons, the CCP had no intention of developing relations with America. It saw the United States as an imperialist-capitalist state that had armed and supported Jiang and which, in the shape of the Sino-American Commercial Treaty of 1947, had attempted to become the latest in the long line of foreign exploiters of Chinese resources. Convinced of American hostility and determined to uphold China's independence, the CCP therefore decided to strengthen its ties with its natural ideological ally, the Soviet Union. Accordingly on 30 June 1949 Mao declared that, in the context of the Cold War, China had no choice but to 'lean to one side' – that is, towards the socialist bloc. In December Mao travelled to Moscow to negotiate a Sino-Soviet treaty of alliance which, after some delay, was signed on 14 February 1950. The alliance was primarily a military agreement which committed the two sides to come to each other's aid if either was attacked by Japan 'or any other state which should unite with Japan', in other words, the United States.

The signing of this agreement, added to the fact that in January 1950 both the PRC and the USSR recognized the Viet Minh's **Democratic Republic of Vietnam (DRV)**, can be interpreted as the point at which the Cold War arrived in earnest in Asia. There was, after all, now a coherent communist bloc in the region that was determined to challenge America's interests. However, this grouping did not emerge merely in order to advance the communist cause; it was also partly defensive in character as a reaction against American activities in the region, and specifically as a response to changes in the American policy towards the occupation of Japan.

Even before the formal foundation of the PRC, the United States had begun to view East Asian affairs through a Cold War prism. One factor that had led to this development was clearly the prospect of the CCP's impending victory, but China's becoming communist was not the only factor that brought about a rapid

Democratic Republic of Vietnam (DRV)
The official name of communist Vietnam; the DRV was initially proclaimed by Ho Chi Minh in 1945. Between 1954 and 1975 it comprised only the northern part of Vietnam (North Vietnam).

Debating PRC – American relations and the 'lost chance' thesis

Of all areas in international history, study of the origins of the Cold War in East Asia has probably benefited most from the increasing availability of archival material from the former USSR and the PRC. This in turn has helped to revise some of the arguments that were put forward when only American sources were available. This is particularly evident in the case of the 'lost chance' debate about the relationship between Washington and the CCP in 1949–50. In the 1970s and 1980s some historians, such as Nancy Tucker (1983), Warren Cohen (1980) and Michael Hunt (1980), speculated about the possibility that if the United States had proved more forthcoming, it could have established working relations with the PRC and avoided the next twenty years of animosity. This 'lost chance' thesis rested largely on the discovery from American documents released in this period that in the spring of 1949 the CCP had suggested that it was willing to explore diplomatic and economic ties with America, but that no positive response had been forthcoming from Washington.

In positing this argument, the 'lost chance' historians were, however, making a large assumption, which was that the original CCP overtures were sincere rather than mere tactical gestures designed to mislead the Americans. The partial opening of the PRC's archives over the past decade has clarified the CCP's intentions and appears to demonstrate that there was little prospect of better relations. It transpires that in the spring of 1949 the CCP leadership and the Soviets were concerned about the prospect of the United States intervening in China to prevent the fall of the former treaty ports, and that the overtures had been sanctioned to thwart such an occurrence. Moreover, as noted in the main text, it seems from Chinese documents that such was the hostility felt towards the United States that there was little or no chance of any kind of diplomatic relationship with America. However, in this area some caution is still necessary, for it needs to be understood that the PRC still has strong controls over the release of documents and one cannot discount the possibility that the availability of material is influenced by contemporary political considerations.

transformation. In addition, Washington was subject to other influences, such as its concern about the fragile state of the capitalist world economy and the deterioration of its relations with the Soviet Union in Europe. This forced American decision-makers to consider what role East Asia should play both in the revival of international trade and in its policy of containment.

The most important change came in relation to the occupation of Japan. Since 1945 occupation policy in Japan had focused on democratization and demilitarization, but in 1948 the United States put aside these policies and began to stress, in what is known as the **reverse course**, the need for Japanese economic

reverse course
The change of emphasis from democratization to economic reconstruction that the United States introduced in its occupation of Japan, 1947–49.

recovery and eventually rearmament. The decision to reconstruct Japan came about as the result of a number of interlocking factors. In part, the United States moved in this direction as a result of its disillusionment with China as the latter slipped into civil war, but another significant motivation was the importance of re-establishing Japan's position within the global and Asian economies. In the inter-war period Japan had exported its consumer goods to Asian countries and in turn imported substantial quantities of raw materials. These trade patterns failed to revive after the end of the Pacific War, with the result that Japan itself and Asia as a whole remained mired in depression. This was a matter of great concern, as it constituted part of a larger picture in which the failure of countries in Europe and Asia to recover from the recent war threatened to prevent the establishment of the **Bretton Woods** international economic order. Just as Germany was considered to be the linchpin for economic recovery in Europe, so Japan was seen as vital in Asia. Indeed, in May 1947 the under-secretary of state, Dean Acheson, referred to these countries as the 'two great workshops of the world'. Thus, for economic and financial reasons, Washington considered it necessary from 1948 to provide dollar loans to help rebuild Japan.

The Americans did not, however, have only economic considerations in mind when they began the pump-priming of Japanese industry, for security motives also played a part. As in Western Europe, there was a fear that perpetual economic paralysis would prove to be a fertile breeding ground for the spread of communism. Although the situation in Japan was by no means as serious as that in France and Italy, there was real concern about the long term, particularly as the Japanese labour movement was growing at a precipitate rate. To the architects of containment the prospect of Japan turning communist was unthinkable, for it would deliver into the hands of the Soviets the productive capacity of one of the world's leading economies. The feeling in Washington was therefore that the focus on democratization must end and that attention should be concentrated instead on industrial and financial reconstruction, which would in turn lead to political stability.

The growing significance of Japan in American Cold War policy naturally also had implications for its attitude towards other areas in the region. One important effect arose from the calculation that if the Japanese economy were to recover, it needed trading partners. With China in disarray, the only way to achieve this was to encourage Japan to send its manufactured goods to South-East Asia in return for that region's raw materials. This was one other reason why from 1948 South-East Asia became of such importance to the United States. In addition, the emphasis on Japan led the United States to consider how it might strengthen its strategic position in the region and to focus on what base facilities it needed in Japan, Okinawa and the Philippines, and what role Taiwan might play should a general war break out.

However, while the Americans saw the economic rehabilitation of Japan as defensive, in that it was in part a response to the perceived threat to domestic stability posed by the Japanese Communist Party, this was not how it appeared to Russia and China. These countries had, after all, a long history of competition with Japan, and had no wish to see any renewal of Japanese aggression. To them,

Bretton Woods

The site of an inter-Allied conference held in 1944 to discuss the post-war international economic order. The conference led to the establishment of the IMF and the World Bank. In the post-war era the links between these two institutions, the establishment of GATT and the convertibility of the dollar into gold were known as the Bretton Woods system. After the dollar's devaluation in 1971 the world moved to a system of floating exchange rates.

therefore, it appeared that the United States was encouraging the rebirth of Japanese militarism and intended to use Japan as its cat's-paw for American ambitions in the region.

Conversely, in the tense environment of the Cold War the United States refused to accept that the Sino-Soviet grouping was defensive in nature. It believed instead that the CCP had betrayed Chinese nationalism by becoming a Soviet client state, and responded to the appearance of the Sino-Soviet bloc by further reassessing its strategic planning for the region and heightening its assistance to South-East Asia. In early 1950 America extended economic and military aid to Indonesia, Thailand and Burma. In addition, in the light of the Chinese and Russian recognition of the DRV, aid was given to the French in Indochina: the first fateful American commitment. Thus by mid-1950 the United States had begun to extend containment from Japan to cover South-East Asia as well. At the same time the Chinese government responded by increasing its support for the DRV, with the result that there were the makings of a proxy war in Vietnam. In the end, however, it was not Vietnam but Korea that was to lead to the eruption of a 'hot war' in Asia.

The Korean War

In August 1945 the Americans proposed to the USSR that their forces should share the responsibility for taking the Japanese surrender in the Korean peninsula. The division of their respective zones was demarcated at the 38th parallel, with the United States taking control of the south and Russia of the north. The intention was that they would then work to implement the long-term plan that had been drawn up by the Great Powers for the political future of Korea, which was that it should come under a United Nations trusteeship that would prepare the country for eventual independence.

On their arrival in Korea in the late summer of 1945 the Americans and Russians discovered that the imposition of a political solution from above was not so easy, for the Korean people were eager for immediate independence. Unfortunately, however, for the Koreans, independence was about the only matter upon which they could agree, for a vast variety of groupings emerged after the Japanese surrender, ranging across the political spectrum from far Right to far Left. This diversity of opinion was a direct consequence of Japanese colonial rule. One problem was that the period of Japanese domination had destroyed the authority and legitimacy of the traditional landowning elite in Korea which had shown a marked propensity to engage in collaboration. There was therefore no chance that a new nation could be built around the compromised monarchy or aristocracy (*yangban*). Furthermore, the Japanese authorities in Korea had been notoriously intolerant of resistance with the result that the Korean nationalist movement was atomized, its key members scattered into political exile in the United States, China and Russia. These activists drew up a number of radically different interpretations of why Korea had lost its independence in 1910 and varied prescriptions for how a strong, modern, independent state could be constructed in the future. Some, such as Syngman Rhee, leaned towards a state-driven modernization akin to that pursued by the Guomindang in China, while others, such as Kim Il-Sung, proselytized communist solutions to Korea's problems.

If the Koreans had been the masters of their own fate, it is possible that a centre-left coalition might have emerged from this confusion, but the presence of the Russians and the Americans made this an impossibility. In the Soviet zone preference was given to the formation of political groups based on the Korean Communist Party, particularly the faction controlled by Kim Il-Sung. In the American zone, authority rested with General John Hodge, who came to his post with no knowledge of Korea whatsoever. He saw his task as instilling political order, and was prepared to use the former Japanese colonial apparatus to achieve this goal. In so doing he broke with the centre-left factions, whom he saw as fomenting disorder in their desire for retribution against the collaborationist Right. Alienated from all but the right-wing factions, Hodge therefore looked to conservative former exiles such as Syngman Rhee to provide leadership.

The result of Soviet and American policy was the emergence of rival groups from the North and South, each vehemently opposed to trusteeship and to any form of unification which would favour the other. In desperation the Americans in 1947 turned the problem over to the UN. The UN solution was for nationwide elections to take place under its auspices. However, the political representatives from the North rejected this idea on the grounds that the South would interfere with any free ballot. Thus the election that took place in May 1948 was restricted to the south, and as it turned out the ballot, as the north had predicted, was far from untainted. The victor was Syngman Rhee, who in July became the first president of the **Republic of Korea (ROK)**. The response in the north was that in September the Soviets passed control into the hands of Kim Il-Sung, who became the leader of the **Democratic People's Republic of Korea (DPRK)**.

In understanding the origins of the Korean War, it is useful to refer to these two new regimes by their proper names rather than as South Korea and North Korea, for both governments saw themselves as the rightful leaders of the whole country and not just the geographical area that they currently administered. Moreover, for each, the prime goal was the destruction of the other and the assumption of leadership over the whole of Korea. In order to achieve this aim, from 1948 the DPRK supported an anti-ROK insurrection in the south by providing both weaponry and cadres. Meanwhile, the ROK attempted to provoke the DPRK into an open attack in the hope that it might win American support for an assault on the North. Thus well before the outbreak of full-scale conventional war, it is possible to see Korea as mired in civil war, a perspective that has been convincingly argued by the leading historian of the conflict, Bruce Cumings.

In 1948–49 the fighting in the Korean peninsula remained localized and inconclusive. The ROK was able to contain the insurrection against it, while the DPRK refused to be provoked into all-out war. In 1950, however, the situation

Republic of Korea (ROK)
The official name of South Korea. The ROK came into existence in 1948 under the leadership of Syngman Rhee.

Democratic People's Republic of Korea (DPRK)
The official name of North Korea. The DPRK came into existence in 1948 under the leadership of Kim Il-Sung.

changed drastically. Realizing that guerrilla warfare in the South was insufficient to topple the ROK, Kim Il-Sung appealed to Stalin in January 1950 to approve a conventional attack over the 38th parallel. Kim argued that, with the DPRK's armed forces boosted by the return of troops who had fought alongside the CCP in the Chinese Civil War, the military balance had swung clearly in Pyongyang's favour. Furthermore, he stressed that, as the ROK was only able to retain power through the use of repression, the DPRK's attack might spark a popular uprising against Rhee's government. In such circumstances, Kim predicted that victory would take a matter of days rather than weeks, and would be so sudden that the Americans would have no time to intervene.

Previously the Soviet leader had turned down such requests from Kim, but this time he provided a green light, the only proviso being that Mao should also concur. Stalin's motives are far from clear, as historians lack sufficient documentation to come to any definite conclusion. Some have speculated that he desired to divert American attention away from Europe, perhaps to pave the way for an attack on Yugoslavia. Others have seen the Soviet leader as still suspicious of Mao, and therefore keen to create a Sino-American confrontation that would draw China closer to the USSR. Another possibility is that, disturbed by American activities in Japan, Stalin desired to bring all of continental North-East Asia under communist control, thus denying Japanese militarism its traditional springboard for expansion and bringing home to Tokyo the cost of collaboration with Washington. Whatever his reason, Stalin's approval set the scene for a marked escalation of tensions within the region.

Having gained Mao's approval, on 25 June 1950 the DPRK launched its assault over the 38th parallel. In Washington news of the attack was met with horror. To Truman this act of unprovoked aggression was analogous to the tactics that had been followed by Hitler, and, drawing the lesson that **appeasement** was a morally and politically bankrupt policy, he decided that the ROK must be assisted. The Americans therefore took the ROK's case to the UN Security Council and in the absence of the Soviet delegation, which was boycotting its proceedings, a resolution was passed calling for aid to be given to Rhee's regime. Under the UN's auspices, American forces in Japan were ordered to Korea under the command of General MacArthur. In addition, in order to thwart any attack by the PRC on Taiwan, the American Seventh Fleet was ordered into the Taiwan Straits.

With American assistance the ROK forces were able to stem the DPRK offensive and by August had launched a counter-attack. The DPRK retreat became a rout when, on 15 September, MacArthur's forces initiated an amphibious landing at Inchon that threatened to cut the North's supply lines. As victory beckoned thought in Washington turned to the question of whether the UN should accept the restoration of the status quo *ante bellum*, or fulfil its mandate from 1947 and bring about the unification of Korea by advancing beyond the 38th parallel and completing the destruction of Kim's forces. The latter was a tempting proposition, as Stalin had failed to come to Kim's aid and it seemed unthinkable that the war-weary PRC would attempt to resist American might. In these circumstances Washington decided to roll back communism in Korea, and on 1 October ROK forces moved into the North.

see Map 10.2

appeasement
A foreign policy designed to remove the sources of conflict in international affairs through negotiation. Since the outbreak of the Second World War, the word has taken on the pejorative meaning of the spineless and fruitless pursuit of peace through concessions to aggressors. In the 1930s, most British and French officials saw appeasement as a twin-track policy designed to remove the causes of conflict with Germany and Italy, while at the same time allowing for the buildup of sufficient military and financial power to bargain with the dictators from a position of strength.

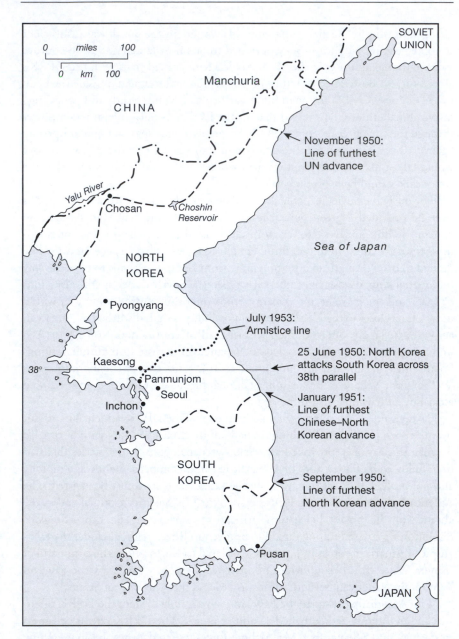

Map 10.2 The Korean War

Source: After Leffler (1992)

In retrospect, this was a foolish decision, for the crossing of the 38th parallel precipitated Chinese intervention. To Mao the American move into the DPRK, which came only three months after the US navy had started patrolling in the Taiwan Straits, was part of a broader plan to bring about a counter-revolution in China. From his perspective it appeared as though the Americans were readying themselves for a future three-front assault on China, attacking from Indochina,

Taiwan and Korea, which might be combined with counter-revolutionary agitation within China. The PRC therefore was faced with a choice: it could either wait passively for the United States to choose its moment to attack, or it could launch a pre-emptive strike to remove the Western presence from Korea before it was too late. From the first, Mao favoured the latter approach. His thinking, however, reflected more than purely strategic concerns, for he realized that to acquiesce in the destruction of the DPRK would damage the PRC's revolutionary credentials and thus undermine both its domestic and international standing. Another important factor was that Stalin was urging the PRC to intervene, although he failed to indicate clearly how much support he was willing to provide. As the Soviet Union was a guarantor of Chinese security, Mao believed that there was a need to demonstrate to Moscow that the PRC was steadfast in its allegiance to the communist cause.

Therefore in October 1950 detailed preparations were made for intervention and the People's Liberation Army (PLA) began to infiltrate its forces over the Yalu River. In late November, with American intelligence having failed to pick up warning of the impending attack, the PLA launched a massive attack on the UN/ROK forces, forcing them to retreat beyond the 38th parallel. If any event set the tone of the Cold War in Asia, it was this unexpected attack, which revealed for the first time that the PRC was a very different creature to China under the GMD. This was a regime so radical and so confident of its military prowess that it was prepared even to challenge the might of the United States. Within Washington the reaction was one of shock, even generating loose talk of the need to use atomic bombs to stem the red tide and to widen the war to attack targets in China itself.

Luckily, the fear that escalation might activate the Sino-Soviet alliance led to restraint, and the war remained limited to the Korean peninsula. The conflict continued for another two and a half years. Armistice talks began in the summer of 1951 when it was clear that neither side had the ability to win a complete victory, but they soon became bogged down in endless discussions over the fate of Chinese and North Korean prisoners. Finally the war-weariness of the Chinese and the Americans meant that the deadlock was broken, and an armistice was reached in July 1953 with the border between the DPRK and the ROK only marginally different to that of 1950.

Asia and the consequences of the Korean War

The outbreak of the Korean War had a profound effect on the development of the Cold War in Asia. The most obvious consequence was that it further exacerbated the divide between the PRC and the United States. The mixture of radical nationalism and Marxism that defined the CCP led it ceaselessly to denounce the imperialist intentions of the United States. Adding fuel to the fire was that American support for Jiang Jieshi's **Republic of China (ROC)** in Taiwan

Republic of China (ROC)
The official name for the government of China in Taiwan.

was viewed in Beijing as an unwarranted intervention in China's unfinished civil war. On the American side, its failure to appreciate the nationalist element in the Chinese Revolution led it to perceive the PRC as an unbalanced threat to the international order, which was perhaps even more dangerous, owing to its unpredictability, than the Soviet Union. Twenty years of mutual hostility were to follow.

In addition, the Korean War helped to polarize the continent into hostile alliance systems. On the communist side, the war brought the Soviet Union and the PRC closer together and encouraged the latter to expand its military assistance to the Viet Minh. In response, American fear of the Sino-Soviet bloc, particularly after the dramatic events of November/December 1950, led Washington to rationalize and expand its commitment to the region. In September 1951 the United States agreed to end the occupation of Japan, but in return forced the government in Tokyo to agree to limited rearmament and to sign a bilateral security treaty that guaranteed the United States unrestricted use of military bases on Japanese soil. Further American commitments to the region soon followed. In 1953 the United States signed a security pact with the ROK, and in 1954 military containment was extended even further with the foundation of the **South-East Asia Treaty Organization (SEATO)** and the signing of a security pact with Taiwan. In parallel to this, Washington expanded its provision of economic and military aid to its clients in the region, and, in particular, escalated its assistance to the French in Indochina (see Chapter 12).

The American determination to contain the threat posed by communism was, however, to lead to serious problems, for it prompted the United States to adopt policies that in some ways only exacerbated the tense situation in the region. One important error was that in its effort to ensure political stability, Washington tended to tie its fortunes to the conservative forces within its client states, such as the Philippines, Thailand and what, in 1954, was to become South Vietnam. So important were these conservatives that they were able to resist American pressure to introduce progressive policies, such as land reform, that might have the effect of quelling internal discontent. The unfortunate result was that, with peasant grievances largely ignored, fertile breeding grounds remained within which communism could flourish. In addition, the focus on security rather than on developing prosperity for all led to much of the financial assistance to these regimes being in the form of military rather than economic aid. Thus, despite attempts by the Japanese to argue that a large-scale aid programme was needed for the region to fuel economic growth, the states of South-East Asia continued to rely on the extraction but not the processing of raw materials.

In addition, the American concentration on the Cold War above all other issues led to difficulties. The problems arose because the United States felt that the need to contain 'Red China' was so self-evident that it found it hard to tolerate those who disagreed with its viewpoint. However, while the United States saw the PRC as nothing other than an even more belligerent extension of the Soviet Union, others saw Mao's rhetoric and actions more in terms of Chinese nationalism. This, in turn, led some non-communist Asian states to become increasingly critical of the American stance. To countries such as India, Ceylon, Burma and Indonesia,

see Chapter 15

see Chapter 14

South-East Asia Treaty Organization (SEATO)
An alliance organized in 1954 by Australia, France, Great Britain, New Zealand, Pakistan, the Philippines, Thailand and the United States. SEATO was created after the Geneva conference on Indochina to prevent further communist gains in the region. However, it proved of little use in the Vietnam War and was disbanded in 1977.

the American obsession with the threat from communism seemed to have blinded it to the real causes of instability in Asia, namely the perpetuation of colonialism and its unwelcome progeny, **neo-colonialism**. Moreover, they resented the way in which their own relationships with Washington came to be defined by the Cold War. For example, in 1951 ill feeling was generated when the American Congress attempted to link urgently needed food aid for India to Nehru's **neutralism**. Meanwhile American–Indonesian relations were hurt in 1952 by a clumsy American attempt to make economic aid conditional on Jakarta taking an overtly pro-Western attitude in the Cold War.

Another grievance was that America's narrow policy led to its being manipulated into intervening in regional disputes. The most notable example was Washington's increasingly close relations with Pakistan, which it viewed as playing an important role in the defence of the Middle East and South-East Asia. To Nehru, this reeked of naivety, for he was certain that Pakistan only sought access to American weaponry in order to strengthen its position vis-à-vis India. Concerned therefore that the emerging Cold War paradigm was a recipe for continued war and instability, leaders like Nehru and Sukarno sought to create an alternative international system, stressing neutrality from Great Power conflicts and a concentration on the fight against the perpetuation of colonialism in Asia and Africa.

neo-colonialism
The process whereby a colonial power grants juridical independence to a colony, but nevertheless maintains *de facto* political and economic control.

neutralism
The policy whereby a state publicly dissociates itself from becoming involved in Great Power conflicts. The first major advocate of the policy was Jawaharlal Nehru on behalf of post-independence India.

see Chapter 13

Conclusion

The new Asia that emerged from the ruins left by the Pacific War was therefore a continent that, despite the overthrowing of Western European and Japanese imperialism, remained susceptible to aggressive outside influences. In part, this was due to the security interests of the two superpowers, who advanced into the power vacuum left by the collapse of the Japanese Empire and came into competition over the spoils. However, it would be wrong to categorize Asia's plight as entirely the result of its being one of the areas of the world where American and Soviet interests collided, because events within the continent itself also played a key role in bringing the superpowers in. Ironically, one of the major stimuli that provoked superpower interest was the rise of indigenous nationalism, for the United States in particular found the radical Asian nationalists difficult to comprehend, often seeing them as nothing more than puppets of Moscow.

More than any other episode, it was the victory of the CCP which concentrated American and Soviet attention on the region, thus provoking the descent into a Cold War mentality. Indeed, it is important to understand that it was the CCP's own hostility towards the United States, and the fact that Washington reciprocated this animosity, which came to categorize the intensity of the Cold War in the region. This Sino-American antagonism arose from more than simple ideological differences, for the Chinese Revolution was as much a triumph for radical nationalism as it was for communism. What emerged therefore in 1949 was a strong, deeply nationalistic China that was no longer prepared to be a stage upon which the Great Powers played out their rivalries. In a sense, therefore, the troubled relationship between the PRC and the United States can be seen as the most extreme example of the problems created by the West's inability to come to terms with Asian nationalism. This can be seen in the way in which Washington reacted to the creation of the PRC, for, instead of recognizing the strength of Chinese nationalism, it classified the Beijing regime as being Moscow's stooge. Similar confusion was later to mark American policy in Vietnam, where again more emphasis was put on the communist than the nationalist side of the revolution.

The emergence of communist China had a profound effect on the United States, which perceived that this new regime necessarily posed a threat to its key interest in Asia, the security of Japan. The result was that Washington sought to contain the Chinese menace; indeed, the importance of Japan was such that, in order to defend its markets and sources of raw materials, America was prepared to extend its anti-Chinese shield ever further into Asia. In turn, its concentration upon Japan helped to deepen Cold War animosities, for the rebuilding of the Japanese economy only increased Chinese and Russian suspicion of the United States, thus cementing their military and political ties.

From 1949 therefore the Cold War began to colour international relations in Asia, but this was not a development that was generally welcomed by the newly independent states which had just freed themselves from the grip of Western and Japanese colonialism. In the tense environment of the late 1940s and early 1950s, some of these new countries, such as India and Indonesia, resented the pressure exerted on them to choose between entering either the American or the Russian camp, for they had not removed one sort of imperialism only to replace it with another. Moreover, these states were not convinced by the Cold War paradigm expounded by the superpowers, for what they saw in the Sino-American confrontation was an attempt by the United States to deny the legitimate aspirations of Asian nationalism. In this attitude lay the roots of what would become **Third World** neutralism.

Third World

A collective term of French origin for those states that are part of neither the developed capitalist world nor the communist bloc. It includes the states of Latin America, Africa, the Middle East, South Asia and South-East Asia. Also referred to as 'the South' in contrast to the developed 'North'.

Recommended reading

At present there is no international history text that covers all of the subjects raised in this chapter. Useful general studies that approach these events from an American perspective include Ronald McGlothlen, *Controlling the Waves: Dean Acheson and US Foreign Policy in Asia* (New York, 1993), Michael Schaller, *The American Occupation of Japan: The Origins of the Cold War in Asia* (New York, 1985) and Andrew Rotter, *The Path to Vietnam: The Origins of the American Commitment to Southeast Asia* (Ithaca, NY, 1987). To gauge the relative importance of East and South-East Asia to the United States in the context of the Cold War, see Melvyn Leffler, *A Preponderance of Power: National Security, the*

Truman Administration and the Cold War (Stanford, CA, 1992) and Robert McMahon, *The Limits of Empire: The United States and Southeast Asia since World War II* (New York, 1999).

For decolonization in South Asia, see M. J. Akbar, *Nehru: The Making of India* (London, 1989), Ayesha Jayal, *The Sole Spokesman: Jinnah, the Muslim League and the Demand for Pakistan* (Cambridge, 1985), R. J. Moore, *Escape from India: The Attlee Government and the Indian Problem* (Oxford, 1983), Anita Inder Singh, *The Origins of the Partition of India, 1936–1947* (Oxford, 1987) and the chapter by Judith Brown in Judith Brown and W. Roger Louis (eds), *The Oxford History of the British Empire*, vol. IV: *The Twentieth Century* (Oxford, 1999). For South-East Asia, see Nick Cullather, *Illusions of Influence: The Political Economy of United States–Philippines Relations, 1942–1960* (Stanford, CA, 1994), Robin Jeffrey (ed.), *Asia: The Winning of Independence* (London, 1981), Robert McMahon, *Colonialism and the Cold War: The United States and the Struggle for Indonesian Independence, 1945–1949* (Ithaca, NY, 1981), Tilman Remme, *Britain and Regional Co-operation in Southeast Asia, 1945–49* (London, 1994), Anthony Short, *The Communist Insurrection in Malaya, 1948–60* (London, 1975) and the chapter by A. J. Stockwell in Judith Brown and W. Roger Louis (eds), *The Oxford History of the British Empire*, vol. IV: *The Twentieth Century* (Oxford, 1999) (for readings on Indochina).

see Chapter 12

On the Chinese Civil War, the best studies of the domestic context are Suzanne Pepper, *The Civil War in China: The Political Struggle, 1945–1949* (Berkeley, CA, 1978) and Odd Arne Westad, *Decisive Encounters: The Chinese Civil War, 1946–1950* (Stanford, CA, 2003). In regard to the international aspects of the origins of the war, see Odd Arne Westad, *Cold War and Revolution: Soviet–American Rivalry and the Origins of the Chinese Civil War, 1944–1946* (New York, 1993) and Xiaoyuan Liu, *A Partnership for Disorder: China, the United States and their Policies for the Postwar Disposition of the Japanese Empire, 1941–1945* (Cambridge, 1996). For general texts on the CCP's foreign policy and its relations with Stalin, see Michael Hunt, *The Genesis of Chinese Communist Foreign Policy* (New York, 1996), Michael Sheng, *Battling Imperialism: Mao, Stalin and the United States* (Princeton, NJ, 1997) and Odd Arne Westad (ed.), *Brothers in Arms: The Rise and Fall of the Sino-Soviet Alliance, 1945–1963* (Stanford, CA, 1999). On the 'lost chance' thesis, see the symposium in *Diplomatic History* (1997), vol. 21, pp. 71–115, which contains useful essays by Chen, Garver, Sheng and Westad. Contrasting outlooks on the American domestic debate about China policy can be found in Nancy Tucker, *Patterns in the Dust: Chinese–American Relations and the Recognition Controversy, 1948–1950* (New York, 1983) and Thomas Christiansen, *Useful Adversaries: Grand Strategy, Domestic Mobilization and Sino-American Conflict, 1947–1958* (Princeton, NJ, 1996). Chinese attitudes towards America are powerfully conveyed in Chen Jian, *China's Road to the Korean War: The Making of the Sino-American Confrontation* (New York, 1994). For the 'reverse course' in the American occupation of Japan and its effects on policy towards South-East Asia, see the recommended reading in Chapter 14.

The classic exposition of the Korean War as a civil conflict is Bruce Cumings, *The Origins of the Korean War*, 2 vols (Princeton, NJ, 1981 and 1990). Other useful works that explain the complex nature of Korean nationalism and attitudes towards modernization include C. I. Eugene Kim and D. E. Mortimore (eds), *Korea's Response to Japan: The Colonial Period, 1910–1945* (Kalamazoo, 1977), Hyun Ok Park, *Two Dreams in One Bed: Empire, Social Life, and the Origins of the North Korean Revolution in Manchuria* (Durham, NC, 2005), Michael Robinson, *Korea's Twentieth Century Odyssey* (Honolulu, HI, 2007) and Andre Schimd, *Korea between Empires, 1895–1919* (New York, 2002). A different perspective that emphasizes the Sino-Soviet role in the conflict is Sergei Goncharov, John Lewis and Xue Litai, *Uncertain Partners: Stalin, Mao and the Korean War* (Stanford, CA, 1993). A good synthesis of the arguments about the conflict can be found in Peter Lowe, *The Origins of the Korean War* (London, 1996). On the course of the war, see William Stueck, *The Korean War: An International History* (Princeton, NJ, 1995), Rosemary Foot, *A Substitute for Victory: The Politics of Peacemaking at the Korean Armistice Talks* (Ithaca, NY, 1990) and Shu Guang Zhang, *Mao's Military Romanticism: China and the Korean War, 1950–1953* (Lawrence, KS, 1995).

For further reading, see the historiographical essay by Robert McMahon, 'The Cold War in Asia: Towards a New Synthesis', in Michael Hogan (ed.), *America in the World: The Historiography of American Foreign Relations since 1941* (New York, 1995) and the relevant chapters in Warren Cohen (ed.), *Pacific Passage: The Study of American–East Asian Relations on the Eve of the Twenty-First Century* (New York, 1996).

From Cold War to détente, 1962–79

Introduction

Between 1962 and 1979 the Soviet–American relationship went through a series of dramatic peaks and troughs. In October 1962 the two countries entered into a dangerous confrontation over the presence of Soviet missiles in Cuba. A decade after the Cuban Missile Crisis ended, the two superpowers signed the **Strategic Arms Limitation Treaties (SALT)** in Moscow, as well as a series of other bilateral treaties. At the highpoint of **détente** in the early 1970s it appeared that Soviet–American summitry, which commenced with President Richard Nixon's trip to Moscow in May 1972, had launched a completely new era in international relations. When the Soviet Union sent its armed forces into neighbouring Afghanistan in late 1979, however, the Carter administration in the United States undertook a series of measures that confirmed the death of Soviet–American détente. There would be no ratification of SALT II and the confrontational rhetoric that had been a mainstay of Soviet–American relations prior to the launch of détente was once again renewed. By the early 1980s the brief period of relaxation of tensions had given way to what some characterized as a new Cold War.

Explanations for the rise of détente are complex. While the Cuban Missile Crisis, for example, resulted in an apparent Soviet defeat and American victory, one of its effects was to cause an escalation in the Soviet arms buildup, which led to virtual parity between Washington and Moscow's nuclear arsenals by the late

Strategic Arms Limitation Treaties (SALT I and II)
The agreements between the United States and the Soviet Union for the control of certain nuclear weapons, the first concluded in 1972 (SALT I) and the second drafted in 1979 (SALT II) but not ratified.

détente
A term meaning the reduction of tensions between states. It is often used to refer to the superpower diplomacy that took place between the inauguration of Richard Nixon as the American president in 1969 and the Senate's refusal to ratify SALT II in 1980.

Sino-Soviet split

The process whereby China and the Soviet Union became alienated from each other in the late 1950s and early 1960s. It is often dated from 1956 and Khrushchev's speech to the twentieth congress of the CPSU, but this view has been challenged in recent years.

People's Republic of China (PRC)

The official name of communist or mainland China. The PRC came into existence in 1949 under the leadership of Mao Zedong.

Third World

A collective term of French origin for those states that are part of neither the developed capitalist world nor the communist bloc. It includes the states of Latin America, Africa, the Middle East, South Asia and South-East Asia. Also referred to as 'the South' in contrast to the developed 'North'.

Conference on Security and Co-operation in Europe (CSCE)

An agreement signed in Helsinki, Finland, in 1975, by thirty-five countries including the United States and the Soviet Union, which promoted human rights as well as co-operation in economic, social and cultural progress. It was succeeded in the 1990s by the Organization for Security and Co-operation in Europe (OSCE), which has fifty-five members, including all European nations, all former republics of the Soviet Union, the United States and Canada.

1960s. In this context, the two superpowers found it convenient – and economically sound – to agree on set ceilings for their nuclear arsenals. At the same time, centrifugal tendencies within both blocs presented new challenges to Soviet and American leadership. In particular, countries such as France and West Germany launched independent calls for détente in the 1960s, while the **Sino-Soviet split** destroyed the myth of a communist monolith and opened up new diplomatic opportunities for the United States. All of these elements came together in the early 1970s when the United States opened a relationship with the **People's Republic of China** (PRC), the Soviets and Americans launched their high-level summitry, and a number of agreements seemed to normalize the post-war status quo in Europe.

The failure of détente was, in large part, a reflection of its shortcomings in the early 1970s. In particular, one major problem was that the relaxation of Soviet–American tensions did not lead to any agreement on appropriate action in the **Third World**. Starting in the mid-1970s Moscow and Washington increasingly clashed over areas far removed from the original causes of the Cold War: the Middle East, South-East Asia and Africa. This, as well as the lack of a domestic consensus in support of détente, eventually undermined the positive gains of the Soviet–American rapprochement. Only in Europe, where détente was a far more multilateral and comprehensive construct, did the détente process last beyond the late 1970s.

It is important to underline that in any discussion of détente one needs to separate the bilateral Soviet–American détente from the multilateral East–West détente in Europe. In addition to the number of actors involved, the key difference between the two détentes lies in the nature of the areas and issues that were part of the respective processes. European détente dealt with issues limited to the specific regional context, such as the relationship between the two Germanies and the nature and level of interaction between Eastern and Western Europe. European détente thus resulted in a series of comprehensive agreements that ranged from such 'traditional' security issues as respect for the post-war borders of Europe, to increased economic and cultural links, and to such 'intangibles' as personal and human security. Much of the European agenda was codified in the 1975 Helsinki Accords, the final protocols of the lengthy all-European negotiations (the **Conference on Security and Co-operation in Europe, CSCE**) that had commenced in 1972. With thirty-five countries involved (including the United States, Canada and the Soviet Union), the August 1975 Helsinki Accords represented, at least in retrospect, the beginning of an all-European process that would last into the post-Cold War era.

Superpower détente was different. It was associated particularly with the SALT agreement and the series of summit meetings between American and Soviet leaders. While it is true that the issues discussed between the Americans and Soviets covered the entire globe, it is equally true that the agreements reached were essentially on a narrow set of bilateral issues that did not involve third parties. Yet both the USSR and the United States were engaged in various regional conflicts around the world that led almost inevitably to disagreements and, ultimately, conflicts over the perceived interests of each party in, say, Angola or Afghanistan.

Indeed, the whole process of superpower détente began with a crisis on one such Cold War periphery, a small Caribbean island off the coast of the United States – Cuba – which would ironically later also play its own important role in the decline of détente.

The Cuban Missile Crisis

Before the late 1950s Cuba was an unlikely setting for a major superpower confrontation. Ever since the Spanish–American War of the late nineteenth century this small island had effectively been a **protectorate** of the United States. This semi-colonial status, added to the extreme economic and social divisions, led to growing anti-Americanism. To many Cubans the dictatorship of the Cuban leader, Fulgencio Batista, who had been in power since the 1930s, symbolized foreign domination and inequality. Finally, after years of guerrilla warfare the revolutionary forces (the **Fidelistas**) headed by a young lawyer, Fidel Castro, entered Havana in January 1959. However, Castro knew that his success depended in large part on the willingness of the United States to tolerate his new regime. This, as well as memories of the American role in the 1954 overthrow of a leftist government in Guatemala, made the leader of the new Cuba extremely anxious about a prospective military intervention from the United States. By 1960, such concerns made Castro turn increasingly towards the USSR for support. The new Kennedy administration responded by approving the ill-fated **Bay of Pigs** invasion of April 1961.

Although Castro successfully defeated the invasion force, the Bay of Pigs experience, and growing concerns about continuing American attempts to remove him from power, made the Cuban leader receptive towards further offers of Soviet military support. The end result was one of the most dangerous crises of the Cold War era when, a year after the Bay of Pigs, Khrushchev offered to deploy Soviet nuclear missiles in Cuba. Castro accepted and by the summer of 1962 Soviet ships were delivering the necessary materials, including missiles, to their new allies. Hoping that a future public announcement about the presence of Soviet missiles stationed a mere 160 kilometres from the American heartland would be a substantial propaganda coup, the installation of these weapons was undertaken in secrecy.

However, in mid-October 1962 American **U-2 spy planes** flying over Cuba spotted the ballistic missile sites under construction. Crisis was now imminent. Although the Americans had already deployed missiles in Turkey and both Moscow and Washington had the capability of inflicting serious damage on each other with their **inter-continental ballistic missiles (ICBMs)**, the psychological impact of Soviet nuclear installations in the Caribbean – as well as the secrecy of the operation – persuaded the Kennedy administration of the need to take action. Kennedy formed a special inner cabinet of advisers, the Executive Committee of the National Security Council (ExCom), to discuss the situation. They initially

see Chapter 6

protectorates
Territories administered by an imperial state without full annexation taking place, and where delegated powers typically remain in the hands of a local ruler or rulers. Examples include French Morocco and the unfederated states in Malaya.

Fidelistas
The name used for the Cuban revolutionaries under Fidel Castro's leadership. After a long guerrilla campaign the Fidelistas eventually toppled the Batista regime on 1 January 1959.

see Chapter 16

Bay of Pigs
The site on 17 April 1961 of an unsuccessful invasion of Cuba by Cuban exiles opposed to the Castro regime. It had the support of the American government and the CIA was heavily involved in its planning. By 20 April most exiles were either killed or captured. The failed invasion was the first major foreign policy act of the Kennedy administration and provoked anti-American demonstrations in Latin America and Europe and further embittered American–Cuban relations.

U-2 spy planes
An American high-altitude reconnaissance aircraft used to fly over Soviet and other hostile territories.

inter-continental ballistic missile (ICBM)
Any supersonic missile that has a range of at least 6,500 kilometres and follows a ballistic trajectory after launching. The Soviet–American SALT I Agreements limited the number of ICBMs that each side could have.

United Nations (UN)
An international organization established after the Second World War to replace the League of Nations. Since its establishment in 1945, its membership has grown to 192 countries.

North Atlantic Treaty Organization (NATO)
Established by the North Atlantic Treaty (4 April 1949) signed by Belgium, Canada, Denmark, France, Great Britain, Iceland, Italy, Luxembourg, the Netherlands, Norway, Portugal and the United States. Greece and Turkey entered the alliance in 1952 and the Federal Republic of Germany in 1955. Spain became a full member in 1982. In 1999 the Czech Republic, Hungary and Poland joined in the first post-Cold War expansion, increasing the membership to nineteen countries.

considered several options, including a possible military invasion of Cuba and aerial attacks against the missile bases. In the end, though, the Kennedy administration chose to 'quarantine' Cuba by erecting a naval blockade to stop any further Soviet shipments reaching their destination. On 22 October, Kennedy went public in a televised address, disclosing the discovery of Soviet missiles in Cuba and announcing that a blockade was in force against all ships bound for the island. He also demanded the removal of the missiles.

For the next few days the United States and Soviet Union appeared to be moving towards a nuclear war. The Kennedy administration took its case to the UN and prepared for air strikes and a massive invasion of Cuba. The Castro government called up more than a quarter of a million Cubans ready to repel an American invasion, and the Soviet forces on the island, with their nuclear-tipped tactical missiles, were placed on full alert. In the United States, a wave of panic buying swept across the country as people tried to prepare for a possible nuclear holocaust. In the Soviet Union, some news about the crisis reached the public, causing a more limited panic. In Western Europe America's NATO allies prepared for the implications of a potential nuclear war that might easily spread to Berlin and elsewhere.

After some bargaining, under increasingly tense conditions, the crisis was finally resolved. What happened was that on 26 October Khrushchev offered to withdraw his missiles from Cuba in return for an American pledge not to invade the island. While Kennedy was considering this compromise, the Soviet leader suddenly made another demand: that the Americans must also remove their missiles from Turkey. Meanwhile, the situation was made more ominous as an American U-2 was shot down over Cuba on 27 October. On the same day, however, Robert Kennedy, the attorney general and the president's brother, struck a deal with Soviet ambassador Anatoly Dobrynin whereby Soviet missiles would be removed from Cuba in return for a subsequent, unpublicized, removal of missiles from Turkey. On Sunday, 28 October, Khrushchev announced the withdrawal of the Soviet missiles from Cuba. Under close American surveillance, Soviet ships took the missiles back home.

Debating the Cuban Missile Crisis

The Cuban Missile Crisis remains one of the most widely written-about confrontations of the Cold War. For various views on the reasons behind the Soviet decision to place the missiles in Cuba, on the decision-making during the crisis and on the impact of the crisis, readers should consult A. Fursenko and T. Naftali, 'One Hell of a Gamble' (New York, 1997), Michael Beschloss, *Kennedy versus Khrushchev: The Crisis Years* (New York, 1991) and Graham T. Allison, *Essence of Decision: Explaining the Cuban Missile Crisis* (Cambridge, 1999). For an in-depth 'insider's' view of decision-making, an indispensable source is E. R. May and P. Zelikow, *The Kennedy Tapes: Inside the White House during the Cuban Missile Crisis* (Cambridge, 1997).

Towards the world of MAD

The crisis was over, but its seriousness and potential consequences demanded, on both sides, a reassessment of the entire strategic situation. For the remainder of the 1960s two aspects of this reassessment were particularly evident. On the one hand, the United States and the Soviet Union took some tentative steps towards an easing of tensions, improving their channels of communication and working out some minimal agreements on nuclear testing. On the other hand, the arms race itself did not stop. Both sides continued their nuclear weapons programmes unabated and, in the case of the Soviet Union, massively escalated their efforts. The end result was the world of **mutually assured destruction** (MAD). Under MAD, the stability of Soviet–American relations relied, ironically, on each side possessing a large and diverse nuclear arsenal, so that even after suffering an initial nuclear strike each would retain the capability to inflict an overwhelming retaliatory attack on the other, thus meaning that neither would dare to commence hostilities.

The shock of the Cuban Missile Crisis clearly made Soviet and American leaders more aware that an accidental nuclear war was a serious possibility and required, at the minimum, improved channels of communication between the two sides. Therefore, in 1963 they set up a 'hot line', a direct communications link between the Soviet and American capitals. Several months later, the Soviet Union, United States and Britain agreed to a **Limited Test Ban Treaty** that ended atmospheric tests; future nuclear tests would be conducted underground. These limited steps were coupled, however, with a series of seemingly contradictory moves and public statements. In June 1963 in a speech at the American University in Washington, for example, Kennedy called on his countrymen to 're-examine our attitude toward the Cold War, remembering that we are not engaged in a debate, seeking to pile up debating points. We are not here distributing blame or pointing the finger of judgement.' Indeed, Kennedy added, 'We must deal with the world as it is, and not as it might have been had the history of the last eighteen years been different.' Yet, while visiting Berlin the same month, Kennedy loudly condemned Soviet policy and the wall, maintaining that 'lasting peace in Europe can never be assured as long as one German out of four is denied the elementary right of free men, and that is to make a free choice'. He then asked his listeners to 'lift your eyes beyond the dangers of today to the hopes of tomorrow, beyond the freedom merely of this city of Berlin, or your country of Germany, to the advance of freedom everywhere'.

Such statements have contributed significantly to the debate about what Kennedy might have sought to achieve had he not been killed on 22 November 1963. Would he have worked tirelessly towards improving Soviet–American relations? Would he, perhaps, have refused to dispatch American troops to Vietnam, hence avoiding another major point of contention between Moscow and Washington? Whatever the answers are to such questions, the fact of the matter remains that Kennedy's policy towards the Soviet Union after the Cuban Missile Crisis was ambivalent. He was certainly not willing to concede defeat, or risk the appearance of defeat, vis-à-vis the USSR in any field.

mutually assured destruction (MAD)
An American doctrine of reciprocal deterrence resting on the United States and Soviet Union each being able to inflict unacceptable damage on the other in retaliation for a nuclear attack.

Limited Test Ban Treaty
An agreement signed by Britain, the Soviet Union and the United States in 1963, committing nations to halt atmospheric tests of nuclear weapons: by the end of 1963, ninety-six additional nations had signed the treaty.

On the Soviet side, Nikita Khrushchev retained the reins of leadership only slightly longer than Kennedy did. In October 1964 the Soviet leader was removed from his duties by the Politburo. The new collective leadership, within which the general secretary of the Soviet Communist Party, Leonid Brezhnev, gradually took the dominant role, blamed Khrushchev for, among other things, a reckless gamble with the missiles in Cuba. More to the point, though, was the new leadership's decision to accelerate the Soviet nuclear buildup in order to reach parity with the United States. Never again would the Kremlin confront the United States from a standpoint of strategic inferiority.

By the second half of the 1960s it was evident that the continued nuclear buildup on both sides had created a grim situation. As both sides amassed nuclear weapons and increased their destructive capabilities, the prospect of a nuclear war – given its consequences – at the same time became increasingly unthinkable. Hence, many strategists were convinced that the only way of avoiding nuclear war was to rely on the deterring effects of MAD. MAD represented, in fact, a curious shift in military thinking. The Americans, for example, had previously considered superiority as the best deterrent to a Soviet nuclear attack, but they now believed that only a balance of terror – the ability of both the United States and the Soviet Union to survive a first strike and launch a massive retaliatory strike in response – could prevent a nuclear exchange.

There was an additional irony in the emerging world of MAD, for while warheads and missiles were piled up and research was undertaken into new weapons systems, nuclear arms seemed to be losing their practicality. On the one hand, the major purpose of the arms race from the 1960s onwards seemed to be to ensure that a nuclear war would not begin. On the other hand, the growing nuclear arsenals of the United States and the Soviet Union seemed to give them little additional political power, save some incalculable degree of additional 'prestige' vis-à-vis the rest of the world. Nuclear weapons could not, for example, be used in such regional conflicts as the Vietnam War. On top of all this, there was the problem of proliferation. In the 1960s France and the PRC joined the nuclear club of the United States, Britain and the Soviet Union. Other countries, such as India and Israel, hoped to acquire nuclear weapons. Thus, while the United States and the Soviet Union remained far ahead of the rest of the 'club' in terms of numbers and quality of weapons, proliferation itself undermined the presumed stability of the MAD world.

It was within the context of MAD, proliferation and the seeming waste of resources that the continued buildup represented, that the American and Soviet leaders began to warm towards the idea of some sort of agreement that would limit the expansion of their respective arsenals. In June 1967, during a meeting in Glassboro, New Jersey, between the Soviet premier, Alexei Kosygin, and President Johnson, the two sides began to exchange preliminary views about a possible treaty limiting the size of each other's strategic nuclear stockpiles. By then, however, a number of other developments in the Eastern and Western blocs were already indicating that détente was more than wishful thinking.

France, Germany and the origins of European détente

While the United States grappled with the implications of the Cuban Missile Crisis and the prospects of nuclear parity with the Soviet Union, its dominant position in the West was challenged from a number of directions. At the general level, the growing American involvement in the Vietnam War, particularly after the Johnson administration dispatched ground troops to South Vietnam, came under increasing scrutiny and criticism from America's allies. None of the NATO allies, for example, agreed to support the American war effort despite repeated pleas. Many were concerned, in fact, that the American obsession with Vietnam would seriously undermine the American commitment to maintain its ground troops in Western Europe and thus weaken NATO's collective defence capability.

see Chapter 12

This seemed a particularly pertinent concern at a time of shifting defence doctrines: whereas NATO had relied heavily on the policy of **massive retaliation** in the 1950s, the Kennedy administration shifted towards 'flexible response'. In practice, this meant that rather than threatening the Soviet Union and the Warsaw Pact with nuclear strikes should they launch military action against any part of NATO territory, the Western Alliance – prompted in part by the emergence of MAD – would now respond to such attacks 'in kind'. In other words, if the Warsaw Pact took action against Berlin or launched an invasion with ground troops against West Germany, the United States would not respond with nuclear weapons. Rather, the result would be conventional warfare. To continental Europeans such scenarios were, understandably, less than reassuring.

massive retaliation
A strategy of military counter-attack prevalent in the United States during the Eisenhower administration, whereby the United States threatened to react to any type of military offensive by the Soviets or the Chinese with the use of nuclear weapons. The strategy began to lose its credibility as the Soviets developed a substantial nuclear capability in the late 1950s.

While the Vietnam War and changing American defence doctrines undermined some of the transatlantic trust built in the years after the Second World War, the unity of the West was further complicated by the relative decline of US economic dominance. In 1945 the United States had produced roughly 50 per cent of the world's manufactured goods; by 1960 its share had declined to roughly one-third of global output. The main gains in this period had been made by Western Europe and, increasingly in the 1960s, by Japan. Both had been net beneficiaries of American post-war economic policies: the Americans had, after all, directly encouraged European integration and promoted Japanese recovery. Moreover, both Western Europe and Japan had benefited from the boom generated by the establishment of the **Bretton Woods** system, which was in turn underpinned by the strength of the American dollar. However, while this ability to generate prosperity was the cause of some satisfaction, particularly as it supplied useful propaganda for the battle of ideas with the Soviet Union, it did mean that, for the first time since 1945, the United States faced serious economic competition. Indeed, by 1971 the weight of propping up the Bretton Woods system while simultaneously fighting in Vietnam led President Nixon to end the dollar's convertibility into gold. It was within this context of emerging nuclear parity between the United States and the Soviet Union, the growing American involvement in Vietnam, the heightened European concerns about the American determination to defend Western Europe and the relative decline of

see Chapters 9 and 14

Bretton Woods
The site of an inter-Allied conference held in 1944 to discuss the post-war international economic order. The conference led to the establishment of the IMF and the World Bank. In the post-war era the links between these two institutions, the establishment of GATT and the convertibility of the dollar into gold were known as the Bretton Woods system. After the dollar's devaluation in 1971 the world moved to a system of floating exchange rates.

American economic power that the French president, Charles de Gaulle, launched his bid for West European leadership.

In power since 1958, de Gaulle's independent initiatives in the 1960s grew in large part from his desire to enhance France's position in the international arena. This, he maintained, would be possible only if France adopted a leadership role in the building of a new, more independent, Europe. This, in turn, required, as far as de Gaulle was concerned, the reduction of American influence on European diplomacy and, as he made clear with his determined opposition to its entry into the **European Economic Community** (EEC), no participation by Washington's 'Trojan horse' – Britain. Instead, he saw the partnership between France and Germany as the linchpin in realizing a new Europe, ultimately stretching from the Atlantic to the Urals. Some of the key decisions in this quest included de Gaulle's two vetoes of British membership of the EEC (1963 and 1967), the Franco-German Treaty of 1963, the development of an independent French nuclear force (the *force de frappe*), France's withdrawal from NATO's unified military structure in 1966 and de Gaulle's independent diplomacy towards the Soviet Union.

Despite de Gaulle's hectic diplomacy and grandiose rhetoric, he did not destroy the NATO alliance. Indeed, his stubborn rejection of British membership was not popular with other EEC members, his vision of a Franco-German 'axis' failed to materialize (in part because of this) and his independent diplomacy with the Soviet Union did not result in any major initiatives. What his independent initiatives managed to provoke, however, was a reassessment of Western Cold War policies in the form of the NATO Council's Harmel Report. Approved by the NATO Council in December 1967, the Harmel Report (named after the Belgian prime minister, Pierre Harmel) introduced a double-track policy for the members of the Western Alliance. On the one hand, the NATO countries agreed that the original military purpose of the pact remained valid and that they should vigilantly pursue further improvements in their collective defence capabilities. On the other hand, the Harmel Report stated, 'The second purpose of the Allies is to develop plans and methods for eliminating the present unnatural barriers between Eastern and Western Europe (which are not of our choosing) including the division of Germany.' Fostering an atmosphere of détente, either through collective or individual policies, was thus approved as a formal goal of NATO.

In the short term, the country that practised the spirit of the Harmel Report most actively was West Germany. As the Harmel Report had indicated, the reunification of Germany was an alliance goal that could be brought closer only within an atmosphere of détente. In the German context, however, this translated into a dramatic transformation of the foreign policy of the **Federal Republic of Germany** (FRG), which was made possible in part by the departure of Konrad Adenauer. As the first chancellor of West Germany and leader of the governing Christian Democrats, Adenauer had refused to entertain any contacts with the **German Democratic Republic** (GDR). Instead he had adopted the uncompromising policy of the Hallstein Doctrine, which effectively meant that the FRG would not have diplomatic relations with any country that recognized East Germany, save the USSR. Germany was one nation and one state; East Germany would eventually collapse as a result of its own internal shortcomings

---

European Economic Community (EEC)
Established by the Treaty of Rome 1957, the EEC became effective on 1 January 1958. Its initial members were Belgium, France, Italy, Luxembourg, the Netherlands and West Germany (now Germany); it was known informally as the Common Market. The EEC's aim was the eventual economic union of its member nations, ultimately leading to political union. It changed its name to the European Union in 1992.

Federal Republic of Germany (FRG)
The German state created in 1949 out of the former American, British and French occupation zones. Also known as West Germany. In 1990 the GDR merged into the FDR, thus ending the post-war partition of Germany.

German Democratic Republic (GDR)
The German state created in 1949 out of the former Soviet occupation zone. Also known as East Germany. The GDR more or less collapsed in 1989–90 and was merged into the FRG in 1990, thus ending the post-war partition of Germany.

and join the FRG. In the meantime, Adenauer anchored the FRG firmly within the EEC and NATO.

The erection of the Berlin Wall in 1961, however, raised increasing doubts about the Hallstein Doctrine and its ability to bring the reunification of Germany, the ultimate goal of Adenauer's policies, any closer. Spearheaded by the Social Democratic Party's leader Willy Brandt, the idea of *Ostpolitik* now began to gain ground among the West German electorate. Essentially, *Ostpolitik* was built on the argument that German reunification would be possible only once neighbouring states, the Soviet Union, Poland and Czechoslovakia, were satisfied that their security would not be in jeopardy if East and West Germany were joined. Moreover, the success of *Ostpolitik* relied on extensive engagement between the two Germanies (or the 'two states within one nation', as Brandt put it). In short, much like the Harmel Report, Brandt's *Ostpolitik* called for the development of détente.

The independent policies of de Gaulle's France, the adoption of the Harmel Report and the rise of Willy Brandt to power in the late 1960s (he became foreign minister in 1966 and chancellor in October 1969) signalled a growing West European interest in détente. Still, even with France's exit from NATO, there appeared little danger of serious disintegration within the West. In the early 1970s Brandt's *Ostpolitik*, for one, would be co-ordinated with the United States. Moreover, the Johnson administration showed remarkable flexibility in adapting to the European challenge by, for example, endorsing the Harmel Report. Such continued co-operation between the Western democracies presented a remarkable contrast to developments within the Soviet bloc.

Ostpolitik
The West German policy towards the Soviet Union and Eastern Europe in the 1960s and 1970s, which aimed at reducing tensions with the ultimate hope of negotiating the peaceful unification of Germany.

Trouble in the Soviet bloc

By the early 1960s the notion of a communist monolith had proved to be a myth. Already in 1948 the differences between Soviet and Yugoslav leaders had produced the Tito–Stalin split. Moreover, continued opposition to Soviet hegemony in Eastern Europe had manifested itself in unrest in East Germany in 1953 and Hungary in 1956. In each case the USSR had resorted to force and the uprisings had been suppressed. However, when the differences between the Soviet Union and the People's Republic of China began to boil over towards the end of the 1950s such measures could not be seriously considered. As their ideological differences increased, as the Chinese became more disillusioned by the nature of Soviet aid and as the doctrine of **peaceful co-existence** was rejected in Beijing as heresy, the conflict between the two communist giants eventually came out into the open. In 1960 the two countries ended their military co-operation, and by 1961 both sides were openly criticizing each other for revisionism. Meanwhile, China raced ahead to register its self-reliance through independent diplomacy and by developing its own nuclear weapon. By the end of the decade, the two countries would be in a *de facto* state of war as Soviet and Chinese troops clashed along the Ussuri River.

peaceful co-existence
An expression coined originally by Trotsky to describe the condition when there are pacific relations between states with differing social systems and competition takes place in fields other than war. The idea was vital to Soviet diplomacy particularly after the death of Stalin.

see Chapter 15

While the Sino-Soviet schism was probably the most significant development within the socialist bloc, the unity of the Soviet bloc was in question in Europe as well. Albania and, to a lesser extent, Romania moved closer to China and away from the Soviet Union; later in the 1960s Romania began to establish trade links to Western Europe. Yugoslavia continued its independent course, despite a partial rapprochement in the mid-1950s. In the meantime, the Soviets responded to the apparent trouble within their sphere by attempting to reorganize the Warsaw Pact's structure. Its effort to introduce a political consultative committee did not, though, prove a success, for decision-making could simply not be shared within the Soviet-led alliance even as a cosmetic measure. More significantly in 1966–67 the Warsaw Pact did advance similar notions of détente to those adopted by NATO in the Harmel Report in late 1967. However, its initial proposal was for a European security conference that, at this point, would exclude the United States, an idea that held little attraction for the West.

Prague Spring

A brief period of liberal reforms attempted by the government of Alexander Dubček in 1968. The period ended with the invasion by Soviet-led Warsaw Pact military forces.

The most severe challenge to Warsaw Pact unity came in 1968. A movement towards political liberation in Czechoslovakia – the so-called **Prague Spring** – ultimately resulted in a Warsaw Pact invasion of the country in August. In its aftermath Soviet policy was characterized as being based on the **Brezhnev Doctrine**, the idea that the USSR/Warsaw Pact had the right to intervene if a socialist country's internal political system was under threat. In short, the suppression of the Prague Spring was effectively a reassertion of Soviet hegemony over Eastern Europe.

Brezhnev Doctrine

The 'doctrine' expounded by Leonid Brezhnev in November 1968 affirming the right of the Soviet Union to intervene in the affairs of communist countries in order to protect communism.

The Prague invasion did not, however, kill the hopes for détente. To be sure, it did result in a momentary stall in the tentative moves towards lowering tensions that had characterized East–West relations in previous years. A prospective summit between US President Lyndon Johnson and Soviet Premier Kosygin, which had been planned for October 1968, was cancelled. However, after the victory of Richard Nixon in the American presidential election of November 1968, the new administration in Washington was ready to reassess its relationship with the Soviet Union. Moreover, the Western reaction to the Prague events – much as in the brutal crackdown on Hungary twelve years earlier – was ultimately relatively restrained. To the Soviets this seemed to indicate that the Western Powers might still be ready to pursue détente, despite the military action in Czechoslovakia. A temporary stall, in other words, did not necessarily translate into long-term hostility.

Within the socialist bloc, however, there seemed to be little prospect of détente between the two principal antagonists. To the PRC the Warsaw Pact invasion of Czechoslovakia was further proof that the Soviets were, as official Chinese rhetoric put it, 'socio-imperialists'. The Soviets, for good measure, blasted Chinese revisionism as a key obstacle to socialist unity. In the spring of 1969 it became clear that this was not merely empty rhetoric.

Triangular diplomacy and the 'two détentes'

In March 1969, when Soviet and Chinese troops clashed on several occasions along the Ussuri River, several of the conditions that resulted in the relaxation of East–West and Soviet–American tensions came together. For one, the Nixon administration, and particularly the president himself and his national security adviser, Henry Kissinger, was keen on using the Sino-Soviet hostility as a diplomatic card in the Soviet–American relationship and as a way of pressuring the North Vietnamese. To maximize such leverage, the United States pursued an opening to China and, after a long series of signals and several false starts, the Chinese finally invited Kissinger to visit Beijing in July 1971; at that time Nixon's visit was scheduled for the following February.

see Chapter 15

It seems that the 'opening to China' removed many obstacles in the way of further Soviet–American détente. In the three years that followed Kissinger's secret trip to Beijing, the two superpowers negotiated several agreements and commenced an era of Soviet–American summitry. At the Moscow Summit of 1972 the United States and the Soviet Union signed the first SALT agreement. There were, in fact, two treaties: one capping the number of offensive missile launchers (both ICBMs and **submarine-launched ballistic missiles**, or **SLBMs**), and another, which included strict limits on defensive missile systems (so-called **anti-ballistic missiles**). At the 1973 summit in the United States the two sides signed

submarine- (or sea-) launched ballistic missile (SLBM)
A ballistic missile designed for launch by a submarine (or surface ship).

Anti-Ballistic Missile (ABM) Treaty
An agreement between the United States and the USSR signed on 26 May 1972, limiting the number of ABM deployment areas, launchers and interceptors. The United States withdrew from the treaty in 2002.

Plate 11.1 Moscow, 31 May 1972. US President Richard Nixon meets General Secretary Leonid Brezhnev in Moscow after the Strategic Arms Limitation Talks (SALT). (Photo: Keystone/Hulton Archive/Getty Images)

the Prevention of Nuclear War agreement. At the November 1974 Vladivostok Summit between the new American president, Gerald Ford, and Brezhnev, the two leaders made a tentative agreement on a SALT II treaty (Nixon – having bowed out of office following the Watergate scandal in August 1974 – could only watch from the sidelines).

All in all, it was a remarkable set of deals and summits that constituted a significant break from the atmosphere of the late 1960s, when America's growing involvement in Vietnam and the Warsaw Pact's invasion of Czechoslovakia had marred the early tentative efforts at détente. The early 1970s also stood in extremely sharp contrast to the crisis years of the early 1960s. While the Soviets and the Americans had been, in October 1962, on the brink of nuclear confrontation, they signed, less than ten years later, the first strategic arms limitation agreement. From the American perspective, moreover, there were the promising prospects of the normalization of Sino-American relations in the early 1970s and the apparently permanent split in Sino-Soviet relations that had opened up. One should, though, bear in mind that the principal actors on the American side (Kissinger and Nixon) had relatively modest goals in their quest for détente. It was not aimed at ending the Cold War but rather at changing the methods and framework used in fighting it. Their major contribution was to have lived up to Nixon's promise (delivered in his inaugural address in 1969) to open 'an era of negotiations' and, with the introduction of regularized summitry in the first half of the 1970s, Soviet–American relations had, clearly, made a qualitative quantum jump.

In the meantime, the process of European détente took on a life of its own. Two key factors account for this. On the one hand, the issues involved in the European détente process were different from those discussed between Soviet and American leaders. Instead of nuclear arms, the Europeans focused on a wider range of issues from economic and cultural exchanges between East and West to the formalization of Europe's post-war borders. On the other hand, European détente was, far more than its Soviet–American sibling, a dynamic process that stretched from the mid-1960s well into the 1980s when superpower détente was already dead in its tracks.

The main treaties associated with the European détente process coincided with Soviet–American détente. The first set of agreements included the 1970 Soviet–West German and Polish–West German treaties, the September 1971 Four-Power agreement on Berlin and the December 1972 Basic Treaty between East and West Germany. All of these were, either directly or indirectly, results of the changes that had taken place in West German foreign policy during the 1960s. European détente thus appeared to signal an end to the ongoing squabbles about the division of Germany, the main point of contention in post-war Europe. In August 1975, however, European détente went far beyond the specific question of Germany. After several years of painstaking negotiations, representatives from thirty-five countries (all the European countries save Albania, as well as the United States and Canada) gathered in Helsinki to sign the Helsinki Accords, the final outcome of the CSCE. Divided into three major 'baskets', the Helsinki Accords were a remarkable series of documents that dealt with virtually all aspects related to pan-

European security issues. Basket I, for example, included provisions about the 'inviolability of borders', while Baskets II and III dealt with such issues as economic and cultural relations and human rights. In short, the CSCE extended far beyond the 'traditional' security issues of borders into economic and human security. In part because of this, it was also bound to become a very controversial document.

Indeed, even as the thirty-five countries prepared to sign the Helsinki Accords, different interpretations emerged. Most Soviet leaders assumed, and many in the West disapprovingly feared, that Basket I, which defined the 'inviolability of borders', was equal to a multilateral acknowledgement of the legitimacy of Soviet control over Eastern Europe. Defenders of the treaty, however, pointed out that the Soviet and East European acceptance of the human rights provisions in Basket III would, in turn, act as a significant boost to the various dissident and pro-democracy groups in the Soviet bloc which had traditionally been heavily suppressed. Similarly, while many West Germans feared that the combination of the 1970–72 German treaties and the CSCE's notion about inviolability of borders translated into a permanent division of Germany, others took heart from the fact that the CSCE did approve the possibility of a 'peaceful transformation of borders'.

In the long run, the CSCE's Basket III would indeed have a corrosive effect within the Soviet bloc. Already two years after the signing of the Helsinki Accords, dozens of so-called Helsinki Groups had been established with the specific purpose of monitoring human rights abuses within the Soviet bloc. The 1975 CSCE thus commenced a decade-and-a-half-long process during which individuals like the future Czech president Vaclav Havel challenged, eventually successfully, the totalitarian rule in Eastern Europe. In 1975, though, few observers seriously considered the possibility that the CSCE would yield a long-term transformation in the nature of East–West relations. Instead, most were concerned with the rapid increase in Soviet–American tension.

Détente in trouble: Watergate, Angola and the Horn of Africa

In the mid-1970s, after a promising series of summits and agreements, the hopes and promises for a permanent shift in the Soviet–American relationship began to dissipate. Soviet–American détente began to fall apart as domestic troubles plagued the second Nixon administration and as the Americans and Soviets engaged in a proxy contest for influence in the Middle East after the October War of 1973. After Nixon's ignoble exit in August 1974 the decline of détente only accelerated; the term itself became so unpopular in the United States that President Gerald Ford banned its use in his 1976 election campaign. Most disturbingly from the American point of view, the Soviets appeared suddenly to be keen on expanding their influence into Africa as they, along with Cuba, supported the winning faction in the Angolan Civil War and sent large numbers of advisers to Marxist Ethiopia. In a fascinating reversal of allegiances, the United States responded by supporting neighbouring Somalia, which had previously been a Marxist enemy of the formerly 'pro-Western' Ethiopia. Such increasingly heated proxy conflicts clearly marked the demise of American–Soviet détente.

One cannot fully comprehend the collapse of détente without briefly exploring American domestic developments. While the fall of Richard Nixon did not cause the demise of détente, it probably did accelerate the attacks on his policies. This was particularly the case with the Nixon administration's effort to move ahead with the economic side of détente. As early as 1972 the Democrat Senator Henry Jackson had picked up the anti-détente banner by insisting that any economic agreements between the United States and the Soviet Union should be tied to the Soviet Union's human rights record. As a result, plans for granting the USSR most favoured nation (MFN) status were blocked when Congress introduced an amendment that tied the MFN Bill to the relaxation of emigration measures. The Soviets, predictably, criticized such linkage as interference in their internal affairs. Various other Congressional moves in 1973 and 1974, such as legislation restricting the president's war-making capability (the War Powers Act of 1973), ending bombing in Indochina and cutting American aid to South Vietnam, further emphasized Congress's general desire to limit the executive branch's freedom of movement in foreign policy. While Nixon's resignation in August 1974 restored some of the trust between Congress and the White House, the 1975 Congressional investigations into the conduct of the CIA revealed illegalities that further undermined presidential authority.

In the 1976 presidential elections the attack on détente was twofold. On the one hand, the Republican Party's primaries were characterized by Ronald Reagan's conservative challenge. In the spring of 1976 Reagan accused the Ford administration of bargaining away America's superiority in nuclear weapons and legitimizing the Soviet Union's hegemony over Eastern Europe by participating in the CSCE. After a narrow victory over Reagan, President Ford faced similar charges from Jimmy Carter, the Democrats' presidential candidate. In Carter's campaign rhetoric, though, his main criticism of foreign policy was its lack of a moral agenda. Nixon, Kissinger and Ford had, according to Carter, adopted a *realpolitik* approach that did not represent America's democratic value system. When he won the November 1976 presidential election Carter assured the nation that he would restore moral principles and human rights as the main ideas guiding foreign policy. From Moscow's perspective, however, an emphasis on human rights was easily understood as an effort to intervene in the country's internal affairs. Carter did not, for example, win any friends within the Soviet Politburo when he called for the Soviets to allow the famous dissident Andrei Sakharov – the winner of the 1975 Nobel Peace Prize who was held in internal exile – to speak freely and publicly.

Carter's rhetoric may have been provocative but it was hardly the only reason for the demise of détente. As many critics of détente pointed out, the Soviets did their fair share to undermine détente in the mid-1970s. By intervening more boldly in areas where their national security interests appeared to have no obvious relevance, the USSR seemed to shift towards a new kind of globalism at about the same time as American domestic critics pounded the Nixon and Ford administrations for their 'immoral' and weak foreign policy. In particular, the Soviets appeared to have 'discovered' Africa as the new frontier of the Cold War. The key word, though, is 'appeared': the Soviets rarely intervened directly, choosing to prop up allies and stooges instead (such as the Cubans who went to Angola).

Soviet interventionism may have been to blame for the decline of détente, yet it is important to ask what the motivations behind it were. There are a number of possible explanations. First of all, by 1974 the Soviets had discovered that for all their talk about practising restraint and co-operating with the Soviet Union to resolve regional crises, the United States was not unwilling to seek unilateral advantages for itself if an opportunity appeared. In the 1973 Middle East War and *see Chapter 18* the peace process that followed, Secretary of State (since September 1973) Kissinger may have acted in a more even-handed manner towards the principal adversaries than his predecessors had done in the 1960s, but as Kissinger shuttled between Israel and its Arab neighbours in a successful bid for disengagement, he clearly enhanced the American role in the region. The Soviets, while acting as co-sponsors of the Geneva Peace Conference on the Middle East, were effectively excluded from the day-to-day diplomacy. This, in turn, meant that Moscow's influence in the region was severely diminished. To the Soviets, Kissinger's quest for increased influence in the Middle East was surely an indication that Washington preferred seeking unilateral advantage to co-operation.

If the United States could do this, then why should not the Soviet Union follow suit? After all, viewed through the lenses of Soviet leaders, détente had been possible because the Americans had finally been convinced that the USSR was their approximate equal. That much had, after all, been recognized in the SALT I agreements that were based on the assumption of nuclear parity. Given the CSCE process, the legitimacy of the Soviet hold in Eastern Europe was, moreover, coming to be recognized only a few years after the USSR had aroused moral outrage by the Warsaw Pact invasion of Prague. If anything, détente appeared to acknowledge Moscow's stature as the other legitimate superpower at the time when America's power was waning. And if the Soviet Union was now a superpower, it surely had the right to act in that manner; it had gained the right to be more than a mere regional Power in Eastern Europe.

An added reason for Soviet activism may have been the American inability to project its military power in the mid-1970s. In 1975 anti-interventionism in the United States received a further stimulus when the North Vietnamese launched a successful offensive against the South, resulting in the unification of Vietnam by late April. While condemning the 'treachery' of the North, President Ford was *see Chapter 12* unable to persuade Congress to approve a last-minute aid package to the South Vietnamese government. As America's longest war came to an end, a 'Vietnam syndrome' set in, restricting US willingness to risk another disastrous military engagement. In the context of the post-Vietnam fatigue and a general domestic attack on presidential war-making powers, it was inconceivable that it would, for example, use its military force to influence the outcome of the Angolan Civil War. As a number of historians have argued, the Soviets, already in a triumphant mood because of the American acknowledgement of nuclear parity, were therefore encouraged to turn even more 'confidently' to the Third World by the American withdrawal from Vietnam and the anti-interventionist domestic scene in the United States. Indeed, one way to sum up the Soviet thinking is to note that in the mid-1970s – notwithstanding the split with China – history appeared to be on the side of the Soviet Union.

Examples of Soviet interventionism in the so-called Third World included Moscow's role in the Angolan **decolonization** crisis. While no Russian troops entered Angola, the United States considered the active Cuban involvement (up to 12,000 troops by the start of 1976) and Soviet material support for the Popular Movement for the Liberation of Angola (MPLA) as signs that the communist bloc was moving into Africa. Disastrously for America's overall reputation in Africa, the Ford administration chose to encourage **apartheid** South Africa's intervention in the Angolan crisis. In part owing to the failure of this involvement and in part because of Congress's refusal in late 1975 to grant any more money for American operations in Angola, the Soviet/Cuban-backed MPLA emerged as the victor in this stage of the Angolan Civil War. By February 1976 the People's Republic of Angola was recognized by most African countries and by Portugal, the former colonial Power, but the United States vetoed Angola's membership in the UN.

While subsequent events made it clear that the new Angolan government was keen on keeping the Soviet Union at arm's length while accepting a continued Cuban presence, the United States clearly interpreted the outcome of the Angolan crisis as a net loss within the context of a Soviet–American confrontation. If the Soviets had considered American behaviour in the aftermath of the Middle East War as a breach of the 'rules of détente', the Ford administration viewed the Angolan crisis from a similar perspective. Together with the collapse of South Vietnam (and the communist take-overs of neighbouring Cambodia and Laos), the Angolan débâcle further encouraged the conservative critics of détente in the United States.

A few years later American suspicions over Soviet activity focused on the Horn of Africa, where a crisis between Ethiopia and Somalia provided a pretext for somewhat reluctant Russian intervention. By February 1978 there were about 15,000 Cuban troops in Ethiopia while the Soviets had supplied approximately $1 billion in military aid. Perhaps surprisingly, the United States did not initiate a military aid programme for Somalia. However, it did provide indirect aid via Iran, Saudi Arabia, Egypt and Pakistan, including American military equipment. Yet the Carter administration, concerned over a growing Soviet role in a region so close to the oil-rich Middle East (and in close proximity to the Red Sea naval routes), threatened the USSR with grave consequences to détente. Indeed, the United States made clear its determination to link the future of détente with Soviet action in the Horn of Africa (and other regional conflicts). While the Carter administration was deeply divided over such linkage – with Secretary of State Cyrus Vance opposing it and National Security Advisor Zbigniew Brzezinski proposing to take it further – the crisis in the Horn of Africa only further complicated the prospects for continued détente.

decolonization
The process whereby an imperial power gives up its formal authority over its colonies.

apartheid
The Afrikaans word for racial segregation. Between 1948 and 1990 'apartheid' was the ideology of the Nationalist Party in South Africa.

see Chapter 17

see Chapter 17

The death of détente: SALT II and Afghanistan

Amid the domestic backlash against détente in the United States and the increasing Soviet activity in the Third World, the two superpowers still managed to negotiate a SALT II Treaty. It was a much needed one: the SALT I Treaty had left important loopholes that allowed the further development of nuclear weapons. In particular, the SALT I agreement had excluded **multiple independently targetable re-entry vehicles (MIRVs)**, that is, the ability to place several independently targeted warheads on a single nuclear launcher (or delivery vehicle). The implication of such a device was unnerving, for without breaking the SALT I agreement on land and submarine-based nuclear delivery vehicles, each side by introducing MIRVs could vastly increase the number of its nuclear warheads. MIRVs, in short, made the escalation of the arms race possible even under the terms of SALT I. Another gaping hole in the arms control regime of the early 1970s was the lack of agreement on anything other than long-range 'strategic' nuclear weapons. This became evident when in late 1976 and early 1977 the Soviets introduced without any forewarning new medium-range nuclear missiles in Europe – the SS-20s.

Given that the 1972 treaty was of limited duration (five years), negotiations for SALT II had started already in November 1972. At the November 1974 Vladivostok summit the two sides had agreed to some tentative guidelines that were fleshed out over subsequent negotiations. The talks were complicated by a number of factors, including the American presidential elections of 1976, the

multiple independently targetable re-entry vehicle (MIRV)
A re-entry vehicle that breaks up into several nuclear warheads, each capable of reaching a different target. Not included in the SALT I agreements of 1972.

see Tables 11.1 and 11.2

Table 11.1 Détente and the Soviet–American nuclear balance: strategic launcher parity

	1969		1971		1975	
	USA	USSR	USA	USSR	USA	USSR
ICBMs	1,054	1,028	1,054	1,513	1,054	1,527
SLBMs	656	196	656	448	656	628
Bombers	560	145	505	145	422	140
Total	2,270	1,369	2,215	2,106	2,132	2,295

Table 11.2 Nuclear warheads (ICBMs and SLBMs) parity

	1971		1977		1983	
	USA	USSR	USA	USSR	USA	USSR
ICBMs	1,254	1,510	2,154	2,647	2,145	5,654
SLBMs	1,236	440	5,120	909	5,145	2,688
Total	2,490	1,950	7,274	3,556	7,290	8,342

events in Angola and the Horn of Africa, the SS-20 deployment, and the American decision to move towards full normalization with China in late 1978. Finally, after a long delay, in June 1979 the SALT II Treaty was signed at the Vienna Summit.

As an arms control agreement SALT II far exceeded the terms of its predecessor. SALT II provided for numerical equality, included restrictions on the MIRVs and committed (but did not mandate) the two sides to reduce the number of their missiles by 1982. However, negotiating and even signing an agreement did not make it binding. Indeed, as Carter returned home from Vienna, opposition to the ratification of SALT II was already vocal inside the United States. While some wanted to tie the treaty to the Soviet Union's record on human rights (citing Carter's own rhetoric on this issue), others criticized SALT II as a treaty that did not go far enough to reduce the size of each side's nuclear arsenal, hence allowing both sides to continue their nuclear buildup. In the autumn of 1979 the treaty was intensely debated on Capitol Hill. As the ratification process dragged on, events in Central Asia intervened.

see Chapter 19

While the Iranian Revolution of 1978–79 is discussed usually in terms of its being the first manifestation of a collision between political Islam and the West, the impact of this crisis on the thinking of American foreign policy-makers is also important for understanding the death of détente. The fall of the shah and the success of the deeply anti-American Islamic Revolution in 1979 came at a time when doubts about the course of American foreign policy had already been expressed following events in Angola and the Horn of Africa. In November 1979, while the SALT II ratification process dragged on, the followers of the Iranian leader, Ayatollah Khomeini, stormed the US embassy in Teheran and took sixty-six Americans hostage. Fifty-two of the captured Americans were not released until early 1981, after a long series of negotiations and an unsuccessful rescue attempt in 1980. By that year the Islamic fundamentalists had consolidated their control in Iran and a war between Iran and Iraq had sparked another of the many American shifts of allegiances in the region; throughout most of the 1970s Iraq had been considered a Soviet ally.

The significance of the Iranian Revolution to détente was twofold. On the one hand, the loss of yet another Cold War ally was an added blow to American prestige and paved the way for more aggressive leadership in Washington. Indeed, the hostage crisis contributed greatly to Ronald Reagan's victory in the 1980 presidential elections and his determination to restore American credibility, primarily through building up military strength. On the other hand, the anti-Americanism of the Iranian Revolution was another factor that transformed the oil-rich Middle East into a key strategic concern in the late 1970s. Even more than the pan-Arab movement spearheaded by Nasser in the 1950s and 1960s, the Iranian Revolution had severe implications for continued Western access to Middle East oil resources.

In this context, the December 1979 Soviet invasion of Afghanistan was easily perceived in the United States as a further menace to a beleaguered strategic nexus. In reality, the Soviets probably launched the invasion of Afghanistan not to threaten Western access to oil, but in order to prevent the rise of another fundamentalist Islamic regime on their own doorstep. In April 1978 the People's Democratic Party of Afghanistan (PDPA) had launched a successful coup against President Daoud's regime in Kabul. The PDPA, however, proved to be a deeply factional party, prone to infighting and incapable of consolidating its power within Afghanistan. This became evident in March 1979 when a four-day rebellion by a coalition of Islamist guerrillas and other anti-communist forces in the city of Herat left more than five thousand people dead (among them fifty Soviet citizens). In subsequent months the Soviets increased their presence and aid to the Afghan communists to no avail, for while opposition forces launched sporadic attacks on government strongholds, infighting within the PDPA continued. In October 1979 the deputy leader, Hafizullah Amin, killed President Nur Mohammad Taraki, the Soviet-backed Afghan communist leader, sparking an internal debate in Moscow that finally led to the decision to intervene on Christmas Day 1979.

Given the conditions inside Afghanistan, as well as the general state of international politics at the time, it is unlikely that the Soviets considered the invasion as the first step in a broad offensive to establish Soviet hegemony in Central Asia. Instead, two essentially defensive calculations lay behind what eventually amounted to a decade-long Soviet military presence. First, the Soviets were clearly concerned about the possible rise of fundamentalist Islam, which formed the major opposition to the PDPA's rule, as it presented a latent threat to Soviet control over its Central Asian republics. Second, the Soviets were aware that the United States was a major supporter of the Islamist rebels (and would for years provide major assistance to the *mujahedeen* fighting against Soviet intervention). Moreover, while the October killing of President Taraki was essentially a palace revolution, it also raised the spectre that the new leader might decide to shift Afghanistan towards the West and, possibly, to negotiate a truce with the rebels. The Soviet nightmare was that the United States would support the rise and spread of anti-Soviet fundamentalist Islam to the southern belly of the USSR. Coming on top of the Carter administration's emphasis on human rights abuses in Eastern Europe and the Soviet Union, these factors meant that what was at stake was ultimately the legitimacy of the Soviet regime.

mujahedeen (Arabic: those who struggle in the way of God) Term used for the Muslim guerrillas who fought against the Soviets in Afghanistan in 1979–89.

While the Soviets may have viewed their actions as essentially a defensive move required to safeguard the USSR's national security, the American reaction to Soviet intervention was harsh. President Carter claimed that Afghanistan represented a 'quantum jump in the nature of Soviet behaviour' and posed a serious threat to peace. He was seemingly correct, for the invasion of Afghanistan did, after all, require the largest deployment of Soviet troops outside its territory since the Second World War. Thus, Carter withdrew the SALT II Treaty from the Senate, stopped the sale of grain and high-tech items to the USSR and announced a boycott of the 1980 Olympics. In his January 1980 State of the Union address Carter made public this new confrontational approach, spelling out a link between the Soviet invasion and the oil-rich Persian Gulf area. If any outside force tried to gain control of the Gulf region, the Carter Doctrine spelled out, the United States would 'repel by any means, including military force'. While the Soviets seemed to pay little interest to Carter's rhetoric and action, the president had, rather unambiguously, declared the death of détente.

At least in the short term, Carter's efforts failed. The Soviets did not withdraw from Afghanistan and the American absence from the Moscow Olympics simply translated into more gold medals for the Soviet bloc. If anything, Carter's confrontational rhetoric and increased aid to the anti-Soviet *mujahedeen* guerrillas in Afghanistan probably confirmed to the Soviet leadership that their suspicions of American motives had been correct. At home, Carter found that his policies had won him few new friends and probably alienated a number of old ones. In the 1980 presidential election he was voted out of office. He had, however, paved the way for even more confrontational rhetoric, that of Ronald Reagan. In the early 1980s confrontation once again replaced détente in Soviet–American relations.

Conclusion

In terms of Soviet–American relations the fall of détente exposed how slender the basis for co-operation had always been. As many historians have pointed out, the Americans and the Soviets had different notions of what détente consisted of and therefore conflict was bound to replace co-operation sooner or later. Other historians, however, claim that superpower détente was never meant to achieve true co-operation in the first place. Rather, détente was an attempt, partially through covert means, to outmanoeuvre the other side and gain advantages in an ongoing Cold War. The Americans did so in the Middle East, while the Soviets responded in Angola and the Horn of Africa. In the end, the only area where meaningful agreements were possible was in the field of nuclear arms limitation. Prompted by the scare of the Cuban Missile Crisis and the emergence of virtual parity between the two sides' nuclear arsenals, both the USSR and the USA were ready to set some limits on their costly competition. Yet, even in this field, the promising start (SALT I) fell victim to other complications in the superpower relationship. Domestic political debates (particularly in the United States), persistent ideological differences, and continued geostrategic and military competition all help to explain why Soviet–American détente ultimately collapsed in the late 1970s.

In Europe, however, détente persisted to a remarkable degree even as Soviet–American relations deteriorated. To be sure, a number of NATO countries, most obviously Britain under Margaret Thatcher's Conservative leadership, joined in the critique of Soviet policy. However, the West Europeans were reluctant to lend unambiguous support to American policy in the Third World and eager to preserve the gains of East–West détente in Europe. The shift of the focus of Soviet–American confrontation from Europe to the Third World may have made the old continent less central as a Cold War arena, but for most Europeans this represented a net gain, allowing political and economic engagement between the East and the West to increase even as the Soviet–American relationship deteriorated. Indeed, the foundation for increased East–West contacts that had been built through *Ostpolitik* and the CSCE by and large survived in the years following the Red Army's incursion into Afghanistan. While still hampered by the Cold War bloc division, an all-European process continued through the 1980s with important consequences in the second half of the decade.

Soviet–American détente may have collapsed on Christmas Day 1979 when the fully fledged invasion of Afghanistan commenced, but the period that began and ended with a Soviet–American confrontation in areas adjacent to one of the superpowers witnessed a number of important shifts that played a role in the eventual transformation from the Cold War to a new era. After all, even in the field of Soviet–American relations there was no return to the hair-raising dangers that had characterized the days of the October 1962 Cuban Missile Crisis. Yet, it was neither evident nor obvious that the 1980s would end with the collapse of the international system that most had learned to take for granted over the previous decades.

Debating the rise and collapse of détente

The reasons behind the emergence of détente have created a considerable amount of debate among scholars of the Cold War. In fact, the arguments are so wide-ranging that it is hard to detect clear 'schools of thought'; the most complete account remains Raymond Garthoff's *Détente and Confrontation* (Washington, DC, 1994), which emphasizes the bilateral Soviet–American relationship and the emergence of nuclear parity in the 1960s, but also pays homage to the many other issues that impacted upon the superpower relationship. On the American side the chief among these is the Vietnam War; the links between Vietnam and détente are detailed in Keith Nelson's *The Making of Détente* (New York, 1995). In addition, a number of other historians, including Chen Jian in *Mao's China and the Cold War* (Chapel Hill, NC, 2001), have stressed the impact of the Sino-Soviet split on both Soviet and American thinking on international relations. The origins and onset of European détente and its impact on Soviet–American relations provide another interesting avenue of inquiry. And in his book *Power and Protest* (Cambridge, MA, 2003) Jeremi Suri has opened yet another provocative avenue of investigation by maintaining that the global social context of the late 1960s was a root cause of détente.

In recent years the debate about the reasons behind the USSR's invasion of Afghanistan has been reinvigorated in light of new documentary evidence from the former Soviet bloc archives. Whereas the 'official' American explanation in the late 1970s and early 1980s emphasized aggressive Soviet motivations, today's scholars, from Henry Bradsher to Odd Arne Westad, tend to stress the essentially defensive motivations of the USSR.

Recommended reading

For general works on the Cold War see Chapter 9. The most comprehensive overall account of the rise and fall of Soviet–American détente is still Raymond L. Garthoff, *Détente and Confrontation* (Washington, DC, 1994); two other, by now somewhat outdated, studies that cover most of the issues discussed in this chapter are Mike Bowker and Phil Williams, *Superpower Détente: A Reappraisal* (New York, 1988) and Robert Stevenson, *The Rise and Fall of Détente: Relaxations of Tension in US–Soviet Relations, 1953–1984* (New York, 1985).

For an account that attempts to decentre the Cold War see Odd Arne Westad, *The Global Cold War: Third World Interventions and the Making of our Times* (Cambridge, 2005); for one that ties together social and diplomatic history see Jeremi Suri, *Power and Protest: Global Revolution and the Rise of Detente* (Cambridge, MA, 2003). Westad's work is particularly good on the rationale behind the superpowers' covert and overt interventions in the Third World. Works that focus on American policy include: William Bundy, *A Tangled Web* (New York, 1998), Jussi M. Hanhimäki, *The Flawed Architect: Henry Kissinger and American Foreign Policy* (New York, 2004) and Robert S. Litwak, *Détente and the Nixon Doctrine: American Foreign Policy and the Pursuit of Stability, 1969–1976* (Cambridge, 1984); Robert Dallek's *Nixon and Kissinger* (New York, 2007) focuses heavily on these two key personalities. On Soviet policy the best works are Peter Dibb, *The Soviet Union: The Incomplete Superpower* (Cambridge, 1988), Raymond Edmonds, *Soviet Foreign Policy: The Brezhnev Years* (Ithaca, NY, 1983) and Matthew J. Ouimet, *The Rise and Fall of the Brezhnev Doctrine in Soviet Foreign Policy* (Chapel Hill, NC, 2003).

The following titles offer a non-exhaustive sample of recent writing on the Cuban Missile Crisis and related issues: Graham T. Allison, *Essence of Decision: Explaining the Cuban Missile Crisis* (Cambridge, 1999), Michael Beschloss, *Kennedy versus Khrushchev: The Crisis Years, 1960–1963* (New York, 1991), James G. Blight and David A. Welch, *On the Brink: Americans and Soviets Re-examine the Missile Crisis* (New York, 1989), Laurence Chang and Peter Kornbluh (eds), *The Cuban Missile Crisis* (New York, 1992), Anatoly Fursenko and Timothy Naftali, *'One Hell of a Gamble': The Secret History of the Cuban Missile Crisis* (New York, 1997), Ernest May and Philip Zelikow (eds), *The Kennedy Tapes: Inside the White House during the Cuban Missile Crisis* (Cambridge, 1997) and Philip Nash, *The Other Missiles of October* (Chapel Hill, NC, 1997). See also on the Kennedy period, Lawrence Freedman, *Kennedy's Wars: Berlin, Cuba, Laos and Vietnam* (Oxford, 2000).

For discussions on the various aspects of the nuclear arms race, see John D. Boutwell (ed.), *The Nuclear Confrontation in Europe* (London, 1985), McGeorge Bundy, *Danger and Survival: Choices about the Bomb in the First Fifty Years* (New York, 1988), Lawrence Freedman, *The Evolution of Nuclear Strategy* (New York, 1981), Williamson J. Murray, McGregor Knox and Alvin Bernstein (eds), *The Making of Strategy: Rulers, States and War* (Cambridge, 1994), David Holloway, *The Soviet Union and the Nuclear Arms Race* (New Haven, CT, 1983), Michael

Mandelbaum, *The Nuclear Revolution* (Cambridge, 1981), Marc Trachtenberg, *History and Strategy* (Princeton, NJ, 1991) and Andreas Wenger, *Living with Peril: Eisenhower, Kennedy, and Nuclear Weapons* (Lanham, MD, 1997).

The most comprehensive overview of the development of European détente is John van Oudenaren, *European Détente: The Soviet Union and the West since 1953* (Durham, NC, 1991). It should be complemented with such works as David Calleo, *Beyond American Hegemony* (New York, 1987), Frank Costigliola, *France and the United States* (New York, 1992), Philip Gordon, *France, Germany, and the Western Alliance* (New York, 1995), Geir Lundestad, *'Empire' by Integration: The United States and European Integration, 1945–1997* (New York, 1998), Barbara Marshall, *Willy Brandt: A Political Biography* (Cambridge, 1997), Avrill Pittman, *From Ostpolitik to Reunification* (Cambridge, 1992), Angela Stent, *From Embargo to Ostpolitik* (New York, 1981), Nicholas Wahl and Robert Paxton, *De Gaulle and the United States* (New York, 1994) and John W. Young, *Britain and European Unity, 1945–1992* (Cambridge, 1994). For a particularly comprehensive set of essays focusing on a key period see N. Piers Ludlow (ed.), *European Integration and the Cold War: Ostpolitik, Westpolitik, 1965–1973* (London, 2007).

For an analysis of Soviet policy towards Germany and Western Europe, see Michael J. Sodaro, *Moscow, Germany and the West: From Khrushchev to Gorbachev* (Ithaca, NY, 1991). Other aspects of the German question are explored competently in William Glenn Gray, *Germany's Cold War* (Chapel Hill, NC, 2007) and Mary E. Sarotte, *Dealing with the Devil: East Germany, Détente, and the Cold War* (Chapel Hill, NC, 2001). For other developments in the Soviet bloc, see Barbara Barnouin, *Chinese Foreign Policy during the Cultural Revolution* (London, 1998), Karen Dawisha, *The Kremlin and the Prague Spring* (Berkeley, CA, 1984), Charles Gati, *Hungary and the Soviet Bloc* (Durham, NC, 1986), Bennett Kovrig, *Of Walls and Bridges* (Durham, NC, 1991), John McAdams, *East Germany and Détente: Building Authority after the Wall* (Cambridge, 1985), I. Neuman and O. A. Westad, *The Soviet Union in Eastern Europe, 1945–1989* (Oslo, 1994), G. Swain and N. Swain, *Eastern Europe since 1945* (Cambridge, 1993) and Odd Arne Westad (ed.), *Brothers in Arms: The Rise and Fall of the Sino-Soviet Alliance* (Stanford, CA, 1998).

The opening to China has been of much interest to scholars in recent years. For the American president's momentous trip to Beijing see Margaret Macmillan, *Nixon and Mao* (New York, 2007). On the American side see Patrick Tyler, *A Great Wall* (New York, 1999) and James Mann, *About Face* (New York, 1998). For the Chinese perspective the best recent analysis is Chen Jian, *Mao's China and the Cold War* (Chapel Hill, NC, 2001). On the triangular diplomacy leading up to the rapprochement, emphasizing the role of the United States, see Gordon Chang, *Friends and Enemies* (Stanford, CA, 1989). For a collection of documents that highlight triangular diplomacy after the opening of China one should consult William Burr (ed.), *The Kissinger Transcripts* (New York, 1998).

A good introduction to the issues that caused the decline of Soviet–American détente is Odd Arne Westad (ed.), *The Fall of Détente: Soviet–American Relations during the Carter Years* (Oslo, 1997). For general early assessments see Harry Gelman, *The Brezhnev Politburo and the Decline of Détente* (Cambridge, 1984) and Fred Halliday, *The Making of the Second Cold War* (New York, 1986). On the Carter presidency, consult Jerel A. Rosati, *The Carter Administration's Quest for Global Community* (Columbia, SC, 1991), David Skidmore, *Reversing Course: Carter's Foreign Policy, Domestic Politics, and the Failure of Reform* (Nashville, TN, 1996), Gaddis Smith, *Morality, Reason and Power* (New Haven, CT, 1986), Robert Strong, *Working in the World* (Baton Rouge, LA, 2000) and John Dumbrell, *The Carter Presidency* (Manchester, 1995).

On the role of Africa, one should consult David E. Albright, *Africa and International Communism* (London, 1980), Andrew Bennett, *Condemned to Repetition: The Rise, Fall, and Reprise of Soviet-Russian Military Interventionism, 1973–1996* (New York, 1999), Peter Calvocoressi, *Independent Africa and the World* (London, 1985), Piero Gleijeses, *Conflicting Missions: Havana, Washington, and Africa, 1959–1976* (Chapel Hill, NC, 2001), Brian J. Hesse, *The United States, South Africa, and Africa* (Aldershot, 2001), Henry F. Jackson, *From the Congo to Soweto: US Foreign Policy towards Africa since 1960* (New York, 1984), Helen Kitchen (ed.), *Angola, Mozambique and the West* (New York, 1987) and John Seiler (ed.), *Southern Africa since the Portuguese Coup* (Boulder, CO, 1980). The best account of the rationale behind Soviet intervention in Afghanistan remains Henry S. Bradsher, *Afghan Communism and Soviet Intervention* (New York, 1999).

The Vietnam Wars, 1945–79

Introduction

The war in Vietnam is undoubtedly the best-known military conflict of the post-1945 era. This is in large part due to the extensive involvement of the United States in the war during the 1960s. Indeed, in the years following the initial dispatch of American ground troops to Vietnam in 1965, the war brought home to ordinary Americans the sacrifices which the global role of the United States demanded of them. With unexpectedly high casualty rates, the war managed to undo President Lyndon Johnson's career while dividing the nation between supporters and opponents of the conflict. Moreover, as it ultimately had the outcome successive American administrations had vowed to prevent, that is the unification of Vietnam under communist rule and the take-over of neighbouring Cambodia and Laos by communists, the Vietnam War has long since been viewed as a uniquely American tragedy.

Often overlooked in discussions about Vietnam is the obvious fact that the conflict in Indochina was much more than an 'American' war. After all, before American intervention there was a war between the Vietnamese and their French colonial masters, and after the United States withdrew in 1973, war continued to ravage Indochina for the next two decades. Thus, for the Vietnamese, the war that preoccupied them in the 1960s and 1970s was, at one level, only the latest in a series of struggles against foreign occupiers: the Americans were merely

Viet Minh
Vietnamese, communist-led organization whose forces fought against the Japanese and the French in Indochina. Headed by Ho Chi Minh, the Viet Minh was officially in existence from 1941 to 1951.

decolonization
The process whereby an imperial power gives up its formal authority over its colonies.

following in the footsteps of the Chinese, the French and the Japanese before them. The symbol of this latest Vietnamese struggle for independence, Ho Chi Minh, was to the Americans just another communist leader, but to many Vietnamese Ho and his **Viet Minh** movement represented their historic hopes for self-determination.

In the context of the Cold War, however, the interrelationship between the **decolonization** of European empires and the rise of Asian communism (most evidently seen in the success of the Chinese communist revolution in the late 1940s) almost inevitably made Indochina a subject of American interest. Such developments also invited the interest of the Soviets and the Chinese, whose aid to the Viet Minh and, after 1954, the communist North Vietnamese state played an important role in determining the final outcome of what has been called 'America's longest war'. Yet, the single most important factor determining the outcome of the war was probably the local and regional context: the North Vietnamese and their southern allies represented anti-colonialism and independence while the South Vietnamese were, not entirely incorrectly, often viewed as serving the interests of the latest 'colonizer', the United States. Ironically, the end of the 'American' phase of the Vietnam Wars did not produce an enduring peace: even after the unification of Vietnam in 1975, Indochina remained an area of continued civil and inter-state wars as genocide swept Cambodia and wars between Vietnam and Cambodia, and China and Vietnam erupted in the late 1970s. As a consequence, Indochina remains to the present day one of the poorest regions in Asia.

The origins of the conflict and the first Indochina War

Democratic Republic of Vietnam (DRV)
The official name of communist Vietnam, the DRV was initially proclaimed by Ho Chi Minh in 1945. Between 1954 and 1975 it comprised only the northern part of Vietnam (North Vietnam).

see Chapter 9

The origins of the Vietnam War lay in the Vietnamese struggle to free itself of French colonial rule. Following the defeat of the Japanese, on 2 September 1945 the Viet Minh, led by the veteran nationalist and communist Ho Chi Minh, declared Vietnam's independence from France and the formation of the **Democratic Republic of Vietnam (DRV)**. In trying to enlist the support – or at least the non-intervention – of the United States, Ho even borrowed much of the declaration from the 1776 American Declaration of Independence. However, in spite of President Franklin Roosevelt's anti-colonial statements during the Second World War, by 1946 the Americans supported France's attempts at regaining control of Indochina. Such support was in large part conditioned by the emergence of the Cold War in Europe: the United States needed France as a key West European ally throughout the late 1940s, while successive French governments stressed their need to hold on to Indochina as a key source of raw materials enabling France's economic recovery and political stability. In the late 1940s French Indochina (Vietnam, Laos and Cambodia) was thus incorporated back into the French Empire with American acquiescence. To give the French administration a 'local' flavour, the Emperor Bao Dai, who had been close to the

Japanese during the Second World War, was installed as a nominal head of state in 1949. In early 1950 the United States officially recognized this arrangement.

The Viet Minh, however, never accepted the return of the French and orchestrated a concerted war of national liberation against them. Ho Chi Minh's need for external support in this struggle also meant that the Viet Minh – which already had strong socialist leanings (Ho himself was a founding member of the Indochinese Communist Party and had spent several years in Moscow) – moved clearly towards the socialist bloc. The success of the Chinese Revolution was a crucial development: after 1949 the Viet Minh received increasing economic and military aid from the neighbouring **People's Republic of China (PRC)**. When the Sino-Soviet alliance was formed in early 1950, Moscow and Beijing both recognized the DRV as the sole legitimate government of all of Vietnam. Indeed, between 1950 and 1954 the PRC was, in effect, fighting two proxy wars close to its borders: one in Korea, the other in Vietnam. By 1954 the Viet Minh had inflicted heavy casualties on the French and was poised to take control over all of Vietnam.

This was the case despite escalating American aid to the French war effort. Between 1945 and 1954 – mostly after February 1950 – the United States provided the French with substantial material and economic support worth close to $2 billion (this was approximately 40 per cent of the total American aid to France in the first post-war decade). By 1954 the Americans were covering roughly 80 per cent of the cost of the French campaign. Equally importantly, the Eisenhower administration, which had come to power in early 1953, justified this effort by reference to the so-called 'domino theory', which postulated that if Vietnam 'fell' under communist rule, neighbouring Laos and Cambodia would be under immediate risk, and that the other countries in South-East Asia would eventually follow. The combined effect of this threat and the already significant cost of the American investment ensured that the Eisenhower administration did not accept a unified Vietnam under the DRV's rule, even after the French suffered a major military defeat at Dien Bien Phu in early May 1954.

By 1954 war-weariness was mounting in France, while the Soviet Union, the PRC and Britain were all, for various reasons, keen to see a de-escalation of the war in Indochina. The result was that in May 1954 an international conference in Geneva that had originally been convened to discuss the future of Korea directed its attention to bringing about a negotiated solution to the fighting between France and the DRV. With representatives from France, Britain, the Soviet Union, the PRC, the United States, Bao Dai's Vietnam, the DRV, Laos and Cambodia, the conference eventually settled on an agreement. The **Geneva Accords** of July 1954 introduced a cease-fire that split Vietnam into two halves, with the DRV controlling the area north of the 17th parallel, while Bao Dai's regime exerted authority over the southern half of the country. This division was only to last for a limited period until national elections were held in 1956. The Accords also provided independence to Laos and Cambodia under royal governments, and stipulated that Indochina was to be neutralized, that is, that none of its constituent parts – the two Vietnams, Laos and Cambodia – was allowed to enter into a military alliance.

People's Republic of China (PRC)
The official name of communist or mainland China. The PRC came into existence in 1949 under the leadership of Mao Zedong.

see Chapter 10

Geneva Accords (July 1954)
The international agreement that provided for the withdrawal of the French and Viet Minh to either side of the 17th parallel pending reunification elections in 1956, and for the independence of Laos and Cambodia.

The United States, however, refused to endorse the July 1954 Geneva Accords (in part because it would have implied the recognition of the PRC, which the United States still treated as a diplomatic nonentity). Instead, the United States started supporting the construction of an independent non-communist regime in South Vietnam. Washington backed the new South Vietnamese prime minister, Ngo Dinh Diem, who quickly moved to undermine Bao Dai. In 1955 Diem refused a North Vietnamese call for talks about the prospective national elections the following year. Instead, he held his own referendum on turning the South into the **Republic of Vietnam (RVN)** with himself as president, and won an astonishing – and clearly fraudulent – 98.2 per cent of the vote (including 600,000 votes from the Saigon electoral district, which only had 450,000 eligible voters). The Eisenhower administration not only supported Diem with financial aid and a growing cohort of military advisers but also established the **South-East Asia Treaty Organization (SEATO)** in September 1954. The major purpose of SEATO – whose membership included the United States, France, Britain, Australia, New Zealand, Thailand, Pakistan and the Philippines – was to 'contain' the PRC and its efforts to support communist revolutionaries in Indochina. In short, by the mid-1950s, the United States had extended the **containment** doctrine to South-East Asia. The inevitable result was that in subsequent years the division of Vietnam – as well as the future of Laos and Cambodia – became the linchpin of the globalized Cold War where the East–West confrontation and decolonization, as well as regional nationalism and communism, fuelled a long and deadly conflict.

Divided Vietnam and American nation-building

In the period between the 1954 Geneva Conference and the 1963 coup against Ngo Dinh Diem, the conflict in Vietnam gradually intensified. Already in 1956, as Diem refused to accept nationwide elections that would almost certainly have given the edge to Ho Chi Minh, the DRV in the North and Diem's regime in the South were poised to begin an all-out war. Yet, both the North and the South faced internal difficulties in the late 1950s. While Diem moved against real and suspected Viet Minh supporters in the South, the DRV launched a disastrous effort to move towards collectivization in the North. Both Diem and Ho Chi Minh had to crush internal opposition movements, although the southerners faced a far wider array of 'enemies' (in addition to Viet Minh supporters, there were several organized military groups that refused to accept Diem's rule). Despite continued Soviet and Chinese aid to Hanoi, the DRV found it much easier to present itself as the standard-bearer of Vietnamese nationalism than Diem, a French-speaking former colonial administrator, who came from the minority Catholic population. Diem made his position worse by his blatant nepotism, for by appointing a number of his family members to prominent positions of power he further antagonized a number of potential allies in the South, including senior officers in the new Army of the Republic of Vietnam (ARVN). Furthermore,

Republic of Vietnam (RVN)
The official name of South Vietnam until re-unification in 1975.

South-East Asia Treaty Organization (SEATO)
An alliance organized in 1954 by Australia, France, Great Britain, New Zealand, Pakistan, the Philippines, Thailand and the United States. SEATO was created after the Geneva conference on Indochina to prevent further communist gains in the region. However, it proved of little use in the Vietnam War and was disbanded in 1977.

containment
The term coined by George Kennan for the American, and broadly Western, policy towards the Soviet Union (and communism in general). The overall idea was to contain the USSR (that is, keep it within its current borders) with the hope that internal division, failure or political evolution might end the perceived threat from what was considered a chronically expansionist force.

Diem, while ready to accept annual American aid of approximately $300 million, was supremely reluctant to listen to Washington's advice about the need for political and economic reforms.

By the late 1950s Diem's policies were clearly working to the advantage of the DRV and their southern supporters. In 1959 the northerners, having managed to solidify their own internal situation, began sending aid to southern rebels. In December 1960 a number of anti-Diem organizations joined forces to form the **National Liberation Front (NLF)**, a communist-dominated political group that became the major southern force fighting against the Saigon regime and for the unification of Vietnam. Using guerrilla tactics and taking advantage of growing rural discontent, the NLF quickly grew into a major force throughout South Vietnam.

In 1960–61, however, the major trouble spot in Indochina appeared to be Laos rather than Vietnam. Granted independence in Geneva in 1954, the Laotians had tried to isolate themselves from the effects of the Cold War. In 1957 the nationalist leader Souvanna Phouma chose **neutralism** and formed a coalition government with the local communists, the Pathet Lao. However, in 1958 a CIA-backed coup replaced Souvanna and the Pathet Lao with a pro-American regime that soon received help from American military advisers. In 1960, Souvanna managed to return to power and turned towards the Soviet Union and North Vietnam for help. After only four months, however, he was forced to flee amid an escalating civil war. Finally, when it was clear that not even American aid could help their clients in Laos to crush the Soviet-supported Pathet Lao, another Geneva Conference, focusing on the Laotian conflict, commenced in May 1961. In June 1962 the conferees finally agreed to a compromise solution of sorts: Laos was banned from entering military alliances or having foreign troops on its soil, while it would be ruled by a coalition government headed by Souvanna Phouma (and including four Pathet Lao cabinet members, as opposed to two in 1957). However, despite this agreement on the neutralization of Laos, the civil war soon resumed, but this time with covert outside intervention. Over the next few years the Americans moved to supply Souvanna with military aid via CIA channels, while North Vietnam and the USSR armed the Pathet Lao. Moreover, by 1964 American bombing raids regularly hit the Pathet Lao, while the North Vietnamese expanded their use of Laotian (as well as Cambodian) territory as a supply route and operational base for the escalating war in South Vietnam.

As the negotiations leading to the neutralization of Laos progressed, the Diem regime in South Vietnam was losing its ability to control the country. Initially the United States tried to control the situation by increasing its aid package and sending an increasing number of military advisers, including special forces trained in guerrilla warfare and counter-insurgency methods, to help the ARVN. However, the record was far from encouraging: in October 1961 the American military estimated that the Diem government had lost its ability to control 80–90 per cent of South Vietnam's rural areas. To stop further deterioration of the situation, the Kennedy administration ultimately raised the number of American 'advisers' in Vietnam to 16,700 in the autumn of 1963 (there had been about 900 such 'advisers' at the time Kennedy took office). By then, though, civil unrest had

National Liberation Front (NLF)
Established in 1960 as an umbrella organization for those opposing the rule of President Ngo Dinh Diem in South Vietnam. Supported by North Vietnam, the NLF played an important role in the Vietnam War throughout the 1960s.

neutralism
The policy whereby a state publicly dissociates itself from becoming involved in Great Power conflicts. The first major advocate of the policy was Jawaharlal Nehru on behalf of post-independence India.

spread into the major cities, where students and Buddhists launched major protests throughout 1963 (the most famous of which was the self-immolation of a Buddhist monk, Thich Quang-Duc, in Saigon in June 1963).

The Kennedy administration's response to the deteriorating situation in South Vietnam was to support, or at least not discourage, a military coup against Diem and his entrenched family oligarchy. On 1 November 1963 Diem was arrested and killed, along with his brother, Nhu. This dramatic move did not, however, do anything to stem the haemorrhaging of power from the RVN regime. The problem was that no effective replacement could be found for Diem; instead he was succeeded by what amounted to a series of military juntas that lacked both political legitimacy and administrative competence. Moreover, recognizing the RVN's weakness, now that Diem had been removed, Hanoi in December 1963 decided to increase its support for the NLF. This in turn allowed the latter to begin to engage in larger unit actions against the ARVN, with the result that the situation on the ground grew steadily worse for the Saigon regime.

As if this were not enough, from 1963 to 1965 the United States also faced a deteriorating situation in the South-East Asian region at large. During this period, the fighting was renewed in Laos and there were fears that a serious communist insurgency might also begin in Thailand. Furthermore, these years witnessed a Chinese diplomatic offensive to win over radical anti-imperialist governments in the **Third World**. In South-East Asia, this led to Beijing developing increasingly close relations not just with Hanoi, but also with elements within the governments of Indonesia, Cambodia and Burma. Of these, the relationship that caused the greatest concern for Washington was that with Indonesia, where a delicate balance of power existed between President Sukarno, the army and the Indonesian Communist Party, the PKI, which was the largest communist party outside the socialist bloc. The United States was thus faced with a situation where any demonstration of weakness in Vietnam might lead to a general loss of confidence in its ability to live up to its alliance commitments. This might in turn lead to unwelcome consequences, such as Thailand seeking security in neutrality and a weakening of the army's resistance to the PKI in Indonesia. Policy towards Vietnam could not be decided in a vacuum.

For the Johnson administration, which took over after Kennedy was assassinated on 22 November 1963, the choices in regard to Vietnam were far from appealing. Abandonment of Vietnam and its almost certain unification under the DRV's rule was unthinkable, both for the regional reasons laid out above, but also because of the immense damage that would have been caused worldwide to American prestige. This left two choices: either the United States could launch an all-out assault on North Vietnam, thus risking a Chinese entry into the conflict, or it could follow a policy of limited war, using ground troops in South Vietnam and air power over the DRV, to contain and eventually reverse the communist offensive. The first of these alternatives held little appeal, for there was no wish to fight another Korean War. Policy-makers therefore concentrated on the second option, hoping that an American military presence in South Vietnam would help to stabilize that country, while simultaneously a limited bombing campaign against the North would force Hanoi to the peace table.

Third World
A collective term of French origin for those states that are part of neither the developed capitalist world nor the communist bloc. It includes the states of Latin America, Africa, the Middle East, South Asia and South-East Asia. Also referred to as 'the South' in contrast to the developed 'North'.

see Chapter 15

The Americanization of the Vietnam War

Two incidents in the Gulf of Tonkin in August 1964 provided the pretext for the eventual introduction of American ground troops into Vietnam. According to the official record at the time, which was highly contested afterwards, on 2 and 4 August two American destroyers came under fire from North Vietnamese patrol boats. Three days after the second incident, Congress passed the **Gulf of Tonkin Resolution**, authorizing the president to use all necessary measures to counter and prevent any further such military attacks, thus effectively giving Johnson a blank cheque to pursue a war in Vietnam.

Johnson used this authority in August to launch a short, sharp attack on the DRV's naval facilities, but with the presidential election coming up in November he was wary of escalating the war any further, at least in the short term. However, after his re-election to office, and with both the military and political situation in South Vietnam deteriorating rapidly, he used his new powers in February 1965 to order the beginning of a limited bombing campaign against the DRV and the dispatch of American marines to defend the air base at Da Nang in South Vietnam. Even this escalation, however, was not enough to stem the communist flood, for by the late spring both the NLF and for the first time regular army units from the DRV escalated the ground war in the South, believing that Saigon's collapse might be imminent. Faced with the urgent need to stabilize the situation in the South, Johnson was therefore quickly forced to raise the level of American troops markedly and in July 1965 agreed to a deployment of 200,000 men. However, in order not to alarm the American people unduly or risk Congress diverting funds away from his radical domestic agenda, Johnson refused to put the United States on a war footing. Thus, the reserves were not called up and taxation was not increased.

As with most wars, the idea was that this significant commitment of American forces would achieve a quick and comprehensive victory, but this was not to be the case, for the war soon developed into a quagmire. By 1968 Johnson had committed more than 500,000 American troops to the war in South Vietnam and engaged in a massive bombing campaign against targets throughout Vietnam, as well as neighbouring Laos and Cambodia (the United States is said to have dropped three times more bombs on Vietnam between 1965 and 1973 than were dropped by all combatants during the entire Second World War). The United States also tried to bolster South Vietnam through further injections of economic aid. Overall, while not expanding the ground war to North Vietnam, because of concerns that the Chinese might enter the fray and create a situation similar to the Korean War, the United States pursued the war with few limitations after 1965.

The impact of the Americanization of the war was gruesome. Lacking clear front lines, the war quickly developed into a series of 'search-and-destroy' missions as the American forces and the ARVN combed the countryside for suspected rebels. In the process tens of thousands of civilians died, while countless others were forced to flee their villages. The use of napalm, Agent Orange and other

see Map 12.1

Gulf of Tonkin Resolution
A resolution passed by the US Congress in August 1964 following alleged DRV attacks on American ships in the Gulf of Tonkin, which authorized the president to employ all necessary measures to repel attacks against American forces and all steps necessary for the defence of American allies in South-East Asia. Presidents Johnson and Richard M. Nixon used it to justify military action in South-East Asia. The measure was repealed by Congress in 1970.

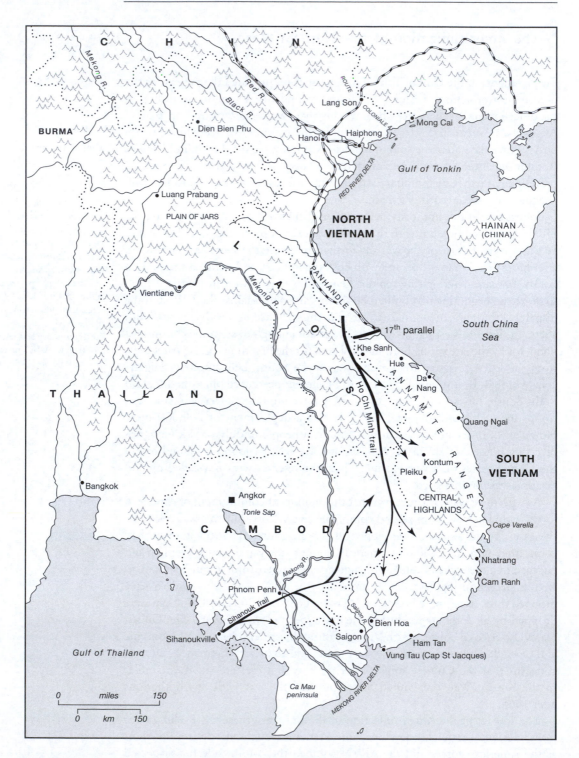

Map 12.1 The Vietnam War in the 1960s

Source: Sheehan (1990)

chemicals as a way of denying the opponents a hiding place in the jungle or access to food crops resulted in extensive defoliation (and caused damage to both combatants and civilians alike). By 1967 the number of refugees, many placed in overcrowded relocation (or pacification) camps, grew to roughly four million, or 25 per cent of the South Vietnamese population. While the South Vietnamese regimes, headed by Generals Nguyen Cao Ky and Nguyen Van Thieu, were able to retain a fairly consistent grip on power after 1965, the American policy hardly created favourable conditions for sustainable civil government. In fact, the deadly consequences of the American intervention were in large part responsible for the ability of the North Vietnamese and the NLF to garner continued support from the South Vietnamese population. Throughout the 1960s the NLF – who had been dubbed the Viet Cong (Vietnamese communists) by Diem – also sustained its struggle through an increasing flow of supplies and men via the so-called **Ho Chi Minh trail** that ran from North Vietnam via Cambodia and Laos to South Vietnam. US efforts to destroy the Ho Chi Minh trail by bombing raids were surprisingly unsuccessful: between 1965 and 1967 the influx of troops from North to South grew from 35,000 to 90,000. The bombing raids and the continued presence of foreign troops in Laos and Cambodia did, however, manage to destabilize the fragile neutrality of these two countries.

To be sure, the United States was not the only external player shaping the events in Indochina. Throughout the period of American escalation Hanoi received increasing amounts of support from both Moscow and Beijing. As a result of the **Sino-Soviet split**, in fact, the North Vietnamese were able to play their two benefactors against each other and receive consistent support from both: while Soviet aid was mainly in the form of heavy military machinery (including, later on, aircraft), the Chinese provided foodstuffs, rifles and other 'lighter' forms of aid. Both the Soviets and the Chinese also sent advisers to North Vietnam, albeit never in similar numbers to those dispatched by the Americans to the South. Indeed, while there is no question that the Vietnam War was to some extent a proxy war for the three major external players, the DRV was clearly more successful than the RVN in retaining its independence from its allies during the war, which, in turn, enabled it to portray itself as the embodiment of Vietnamese nationalism and paint the Saigon regime as a mere American stooge.

The Americanization of the Vietnam War between 1965 and 1968 had other important consequences, both for the region and for the Cold War generally. Within the region, while the lack of a clear victory meant that disquiet about the future continued to surface, the American display of resolve reassured the Thai government and arguably emboldened the army in Indonesia when it turned on the PKI in the autumn of 1965. Most important for the long term, however, was that the Johnson administration decided from 1965 to encourage the economic development of South-East Asia in an effort to contain any further spread of communism. While the war limited the resources that Washington could make available, valuable aid was supplied to countries such as Thailand, where it was used to improve infrastructure and local government. In addition, the United States in 1966 sponsored the creation of the Asian Development Bank and encouraged Japan to invest in the region. By concentrating American attention

Ho Chi Minh trail
A network of jungle paths from North Vietnam through Laos and Cambodia into South Vietnam. Used as a military route by North Vietnam to send supplies and troops to the south.

see Chapter 15

Sino-Soviet split
The process whereby China and the Soviet Union became alienated from each other in the late 1950s and early 1960s. It is often dated from 1956 and Khrushchev's speech to the twentieth congress of the CPSU, but this view has been challenged in recent years.

on the region, the war therefore acted as a springboard for the future prosperity of South-East Asia, although it brought precious little benefit for the countries of Indochina itself.

In the wider world, America's war in Vietnam led to much dissent. Washington's **NATO** allies, for example, refused to support the war effort in South-East Asia; even the British government, traditionally the closest to Washington, distanced itself from American policy. Others, most obviously (and ironically, given its past involvement) the French government of Charles de Gaulle, were openly critical. The sheer cost of the war also contributed to growing American government deficits and weakened its relative position vis-à-vis its major economic competitors. At home in the United States the massive military spending on the war cut into Johnson's ambitious social and economic programmes, collectively known as the Great Society. Thus, despite his efforts in 1965 to play down the conflict in order to defend his domestic priorities, in the end his desire to wage a successful 'war on poverty' at home was sacrificed to what he once referred to as 'that bitch of a war on the other side of the world'. More broadly, the American inability to subdue a seemingly far inferior opponent hurt its credibility, while its support for an obviously undemocratic regime in the South eroded America's claim of moral superiority over its Cold War adversaries.

The war also created an unprecedented, and extremely vocal, protest movement that challenged not only the Johnson administration's conduct of the war but, ultimately, the very premises of American Cold War policies. By late 1967, with close to 30,000 Americans dead, the anti-war movement, which had started on college campuses, was gathering strength throughout the United States, and a number of prominent politicians, such as the Democratic Senator Eugene McCarthy, were calling for a gradual American withdrawal. Moreover, Robert McNamara, the secretary of defence, resigned in the autumn of 1967 largely because of his disenchantment with the Vietnam policies that he had personally overseen. Still, at the end of 1967, as internal and external pressure was mounting for an American withdrawal, the Johnson administration claimed that 'victory' in Vietnam was just around the corner.

By exposing the inflated nature of such claims the National Liberation Front's (NLF) **Tet Offensive** in early 1968, although a military defeat for the NLF, turned out to be a major turning point in the American phase of the Vietnam War. On 30 January 1968, the NLF initiated a series of attacks throughout South Vietnam; within days, thirty-six out of forty-four provincial capitals and five of the six major cities were under fire. Most spectacularly, the NLF attacked the American embassy in Saigon and briefly occupied parts of this symbol of US presence in Vietnam. In Hue, the old imperial capital of Vietnam located just south of the 17th parallel, the NLF, supported by large numbers of North Vietnamese troops, was even more successful. After capturing the city on 31 January, it held back an American–ARVN counter-offensive for three weeks.

The NLF had launched the Tet Offensive with two political aims in mind. Its optimum ambition was to cause the complete collapse of the Saigon regime. This it failed to do, and indeed in some ways it was the NLF itself that emerged the weaker party, for it suffered heavy casualties (approximately 40,000 Viet Cong

North Atlantic Treaty Organization (NATO)

Established by the North Atlantic Treaty (4 April 1949) signed by Belgium, Canada, Denmark, France, Great Britain, Iceland, Italy, Luxembourg, the Netherlands, Norway, Portugal and the United States. Greece and Turkey entered the alliance in 1952 and the Federal Republic of Germany in 1955. Spain became a full member in 1982. In 1999 the Czech Republic, Hungary and Poland joined in the first post-Cold War expansion, increasing the membership to nineteen countries.

Tet Offensive

The attack launched by the NLF in South Vietnam in late January and early February 1968, named after the country's most important holiday, the lunar new year. Although the offensive was not a military success for the NLF, it was a political and psychological victory as it dramatically contradicted optimistic claims by the American government that the war had already been won.

Plate 12.1 Tet Offensive, January 1968. A youthful hard-core Viet Cong squats down under the watchful eye of a Nationalist guard with rifle drawn, shortly before his interrogation following capture in attacks on the capital city of Saigon during the Tet Offensive in the Vietnam War. (Photo: Time Life Pictures/USTA/National Archives/Getty Images)

guerrillas were killed in the fighting, compared with 1,100 Americans and 2,300 ARVN regulars) and saw its organization in large parts of South Vietnam virtually destroyed. However, this setback was balanced by the successful achievement of the offensive's secondary aim, which was to reveal to the American government and people that the war was far from over. To critical politicians and most of the general public in the United States the offensive demonstrated exactly what the NLF set out to achieve: namely, it proved the hollow nature of the Johnson administration's policy and widened the already existing credibility gap between the White House and the American people. In one fell swoop Johnson's claims that the situation was under control and that victory was in sight were refuted; instead Tet suggested that further bloodletting would be necessary. When news leaked to the press that General William Westmoreland, the American commander in Vietnam, had requested more troops, the Johnson administration lost even more of its fragile credibility. Furthermore, the American establishment itself became jittery when it appeared that uncertainty over the war was causing a flood of gold to leave the country.

By late March President Johnson became convinced that further escalation could not be sanctioned. In a dramatic television appearance he declined to seek re-election and announced a halt to the bombing and his intention to seek a peaceful resolution of the war. A number of openly anti-war candidates, most prominently Senator Robert F. Kennedy, entered the 1968 presidential race. In mid-May peace talks began in Paris after the United States had scaled down its bombing campaigns against the North. Yet, by the time Americans selected the former vice-president, Richard Nixon, as Johnson's successor in November 1968 the war was far from over. In fact, American troop levels in Vietnam peaked at 543,000 in the spring of 1969.

Strategic Arms Limitation Treaties (SALT I and II)
The agreements between the United States and the Soviet Union for the control of certain nuclear weapons, the first concluded in 1972 (SALT I) and the second drafted in 1979 (SALT II) but not ratified.

see Chapter 11

'Peace' and unification

Nixon's first term from 1969 to 1973, which saw such remarkable foreign policy feats as the 'opening to China' and the signing of the **SALT** I agreement between the United States and the USSR, was constantly overshadowed by his attempts to find an 'honourable' end to the Vietnam War. Unwilling to concede defeat and still aiming to prevent the unification of Vietnam under communist rule, Nixon tried to force the DRV into signing a truce that would have made permanent the temporary division initially agreed upon at Geneva in 1954. Thus, instead of moving to disengage the United States, the Nixon administration initially escalated the war by ordering sustained bombings against the NLF's supply routes (the Ho Chi Minh trail). As a result, Cambodia, which had tried to preserve a neutral position under Prince Norodim Sihanouk's leadership, was drawn into the war. In May 1970, following a *coup d'état* against Sihanouk, the Nixon administration dispatched American troops against NLF–North Vietnamese supply bases in Cambodia, thus widening the war further. In February 1971, the

ARVN, supported by American air power, launched a series of raids into Laos. In the end, such efforts to disrupt the Ho Chi Minh trail were unsuccessful, but they did manage to destabilize the already fragile situation in Vietnam's two neighbours.

Meanwhile, the Nixon administration had commenced a programme dubbed 'Vietnamization'. The basic idea was simple: the United States would gradually transfer the actual burden of the ground war to the ARVN by withdrawing its troops and simultaneously expanding its military aid. At one level, Vietnamization was a success, for the number of American troops did decline to approximately 140,000 by the end of 1971 with a concomitant decrease in casualty rates. Vietnamization thus partially removed one of the focal points of the domestic critique of the Vietnam War. At the same time, however, the ARVN did not emerge as a credible fighting machine that was capable of holding back, let alone defeating, its opponents. The ARVN's invasion of Laos in 1971 ended in a humiliating retreat, while the Saigon government had to rely on massive American air power to prevent an imminent collapse following the North Vietnamese Spring Offensive in 1972.

By 1972 it was clear that the Americans had to agree to a negotiated settlement. In fact, two sets of peace talks had been under way for years for, in addition to the official discussions that had commenced in 1968, Nixon's national security adviser, Henry Kissinger, had embarked on a series of secret discussions with North Vietnamese representatives in the autumn of 1969. Both sets of talks were held in Paris but yielded few results until the second half of 1972. By that point, the continued stalemate on the ground, massive American bombing campaigns (including the so-called Christmas Bombings of December 1972), diplomatic pressure from China and the Soviet Union (on both the United States and North Vietnam), and the Nixon administration's willingness to allow approximately 200,000 North Vietnamese regulars to remain in the South combined to produce the **Paris Peace Accords** of January 1973. In this agreement the DRV promised not to support subversion in the South and the United States pledged to withdraw all remaining American troops from Vietnam. Kissinger and his major negotiation partner, Le Duc Tho, were awarded the Nobel Peace Prize later in the year.

But the war was not truly over. The continued presence of North Vietnamese troops in the South created an untenable solution and in late 1973 the war flared up again. In this new war the Saigon government was at a decisive disadvantage. Although Nixon had made a personal promise to continue supporting South Vietnam with air power and military aid, Congress passed a series of resolutions that diminished the presidential war-making capabilities. The War Powers Act of June 1973 put strict limits on the length of time that the president could keep American troops abroad without Congressional approval, and in August Congress passed a bill that put an end to further military activity in Cambodia. Nor could Nixon, facing an all-out assault on his authority as the Watergate scandal unfolded, prevent the cuts in military aid to South Vietnam that Congress insisted upon. At the time of Nixon's resignation in August 1974, the North Vietnamese, who could count on continued Soviet (and, to a lesser extent, Chinese) aid, were already planning the final offensive against the South. Hanoi was undoubtedly

Vietnamization
President Nixon's policy of gradually withdrawing US ground troops from Vietnam while simultaneously building up the strength of the South Vietnamese armed forces. The policy was implemented starting in 1969 when there were more than half a million US troops in Vietnam; the programme of withdrawals was effectively completed in the autumn of 1972.

Paris Peace Accords
Signed on 27 January 1973, the Paris Agreements provided for a cease-fire in Vietnam, the withdrawal of remaining American troops and the return of American prisoners of war.

further encouraged in November 1974 when Congress cut in half the Ford administration's proposed military aid budget for South Vietnam in 1975: from $1.5 billion to $700 million.

The end of the 'post-American' Vietnam War was relatively quick. Beginning in early 1975 the North Vietnamese troops gradually advanced to take over a series of South Vietnam's provincial capitals. Finally in late April the NLF and North Vietnamese troops entered Saigon, while Americans desperately airlifted their embassy staff and selected South Vietnamese officials to safety (Nguyen Van Thieu himself would live most of the rest of his life in the United States; he died in 2001 in Boston). Vietnam was finally unified and Saigon was renamed Ho Chi Minh City (Ho Chi Minh himself had died in September 1969).

The war had been costly to all participants. The Americans lost 58,000 lives during their 'longest war'. Since 1950 the United States had spent approximately $155 billion in South-East Asia; an additional $200 billion would be paid in subsequent decades to those Americans (approximately two million) who had returned home alive. The war had also fuelled inflation at home and become the focal point of civil unrest in the United States. However, such figures paled in comparison to the suffering of the Vietnamese. Perhaps as many as half a million South Vietnamese civilians were killed during the last decade of the war, hundreds of thousands suffered injuries, and more than 5 million (out of a population of 16–17 million) became refugees. The combined NLF and North Vietnamese military losses ran up to half a million; the number of North Vietnamese civilian casualties is still unknown. Such losses, when combined with the incalculable material and psychological damage caused to all of Indochina in the three decades after the Second World War, clearly justify the Vietnam War's place as one of the worst human-made catastrophes in post-1945 international history. Worse still, the crucible had not yet ended.

Debating America's Vietnam War

Much of the historiographical debate on the Vietnam War has focused on the reasons behind American involvement in the conflict and the specific strategies and policies that led to the eventual withdrawal and communist victory. In short: why did the United States get involved in this conflict and why did Americans stay engaged for as long as they did?

One popular explanation stresses the role of bureaucratic inertia, the misreading of historical lessons and the lack of expertise on Indochina among American policy-makers. This viewpoint is exemplified, for example, in George Kahin's *Intervention* (New York, 1986). Others, most prominently the historian Gabriel Kolko in *Anatomy of a War* (New York, 1985), have stressed economic explanations. According to Kolko, the United States intervened in Vietnam because it was trying to uphold its economic dominance over the Third World.

Another major controversy has to do with the American failure to 'win' in Vietnam. Two opposing viewpoints dominate the literature. On the one hand, many have argued that the United States could have won had it followed a different military strategy. In particular, such authors as Harry G. Summers, Jr. in *On Strategy: The Vietnam War in Context* (New York, 1981) argued that the United States should simply have isolated and then invaded North Vietnam. Others, including the author of the most widely read survey of American involvement in Vietnam, George Herring, maintain that the strength of Vietnamese nationalism, the destructive American conduct of the war and the false premises of the containment doctrine lay at the heart of America's failure.

Indochina in turmoil after 1975

In 1975 there were, in fact, a series of communist victories in Indochina. At the same time as Hanoi's forces clinched victory in their war, the **Khmer Rouge** and the Pathet Lao took over in Cambodia and Laos respectively. To some observers this meant that the domino theory rang true after all, for with the Americans out of the way, communism was on the march. To other observers, however, it was clear that while the new ruling elites were composed of communists, the respective loyalties and interests – internal, regional and international – of the Cambodians, the Laotians and the Vietnamese did not mean that a monolithic communist force had suddenly subdued a large part of South-East Asia. National leadership in each country was influenced by nationalist sentiments as much as by communist ideology, and they were wary of external influences. Indeed, by the late 1970s self-inflicted war and genocide rather than peaceful reconstruction were the order of the day throughout much of Indochina.

In Vietnam itself, the forced reunification of the country was followed by efforts to unify the nation under the leadership of the Communist Party. However, Hanoi's leadership faced many obstacles. In addition to the massive human suffering described above, the country lacked the resources for a successful reconstruction programme. While there had been some hope that American aid would be offered in the immediate aftermath of the 1973 Paris Agreements, the continued war and unification had frozen the Vietnamese–American relationship. In the North, the Sino-Vietnamese relationship, which had begun its decline in the late 1960s, was growing worse by the day. As a result, for external aid the DRV depended largely on the Soviet Union. Indeed, one irony of the unification was that it made Hanoi more, rather than less, dependent on Moscow.

Even without the newly exaggerated dependency on the USSR, Vietnam was bound to suffer. One reason was the sheer number of South Vietnamese who,

Khmer Rouge
The Western name for the communist movement, led by Pol Pot, which came to power in Cambodia in 1975. The new government carried out a radical political programme that led to 1.5 million deaths. In 1979 it was overthrown by Vietnam, but continued to fight a guerrilla war campaign into the 1990s.

rather than remain in the unified country, chose to leave after 1975. Estimates of the numbers of the so-called boat people run as high as 1.4 million, including 50,000 who were killed during their flight. Almost a million Vietnamese have found new homes elsewhere in the world, predominantly in the United States (the home of roughly 700,000 Vietnamese immigrants since 1975). Those who stayed in Vietnam often suffered immeasurably in labour and 're-education' camps set up by the DRV. Economically, Vietnam was effectively condemned to poverty after 1975, a fate made no easier following the collapse of its major external supporter, the Soviet Union, in 1991. While the Hanoi leadership in the 1990s launched economic reforms similar to those in China, political power was kept in the hands of the Communist Party in a manner also similar to events in China.

see Chapter 15

However, while the Chinese experienced massive, if uneven, economic growth during the 1990s, Vietnam remained poor. The average per capita income was approximately $700–800 at the end of the twentieth century.

In Cambodia, the situation after 1975 was far worse. Under the leadership of Pol Pot, the Maoist-influenced Khmer Rouge initiated virtual genocide after it took over the country in that year. Declaring that 1975 was 'Year Zero' of the new Cambodia, the Khmer Rouge launched a homicidal effort to cleanse the country of any remaining 'bourgeois' elements and create a pastoral communist utopia. Much of the urban population was forcefully transferred to rural areas. Libraries, schools and temples were destroyed. Between 1975 and 1978 an estimated two million Cambodians were killed, with countless others fleeing the country. To guard its independence from the more populous and better-armed Vietnam, Pol Pot's regime established close ties with China, a country eager to prevent Soviet-backed Vietnamese hegemony in Indochina. However, at the same time the Khmer Rouge provoked Vietnam by initiating a series of border incidents and persecuting ethnic Vietnamese within Cambodia.

Finally in December 1978, Vietnam's patience snapped and it launched an invasion of Cambodia, which drove Pol Pot out of power and established a puppet government to replace the Khmer Rouge. China followed up by invading Vietnam in February 1979. In a brief inconclusive war 35,000 people died. Meanwhile, Pol Pot gathered his troops and fought a prolonged guerrilla warfare campaign against the new regime of the People's Republic of Kampuchea. Vietnamese troops, approximately 140,000 of them, remained in the impoverished country until 1989. Only in the late 1990s was the Khmer Rouge finally defeated and Pol Pot captured, although the latter committed suicide before he could be put on trial for genocide. The end result of this lengthy civil war was that Cambodia remains a country even worse off economically than Vietnam.

Laos may have escaped the genocide of neighbouring Cambodia but it too came under the domination of the DRV. Landlocked and bordering on Vietnam, Cambodia and China, the Laotian economy was severely weakened by the continued turmoil in the region. The Pathet Lao refused to hold elections in the country until 1989; the country remains among the poorest in the world (indeed, its per capita income was even lower than that of Cambodia and Vietnam in 2000).

In short, the 'dominoes' that fell in 1975 were not much better off a quarter-century after the last American soldiers had left Saigon. Political dogmatism, the politics of revenge and the continued interest of external powers in the region – it should be noted that the United States, in effect, approved of China's attack on Vietnam in 1979 – continued to wreak havoc in Cambodia, Laos and Vietnam throughout the remainder of the Cold War. While this, in turn, proved that American fears of the continued spread of communism had been exaggerated, the United States (as well as the French, the Soviets, the Chinese and others) still shares some responsibility for the casualties and massive economic dislocation that have continued to plague Indochina to the present day.

Conclusion

The fate of Indochina after 1945 stands as a horrific example of the way in which developments in international politics and a tense regional setting can coincide to create a serious and protracted conflict. In the early post-war years issues of imperial prestige were pre-eminent in determining the French resolve to restore its rule in Indochina. Without external support, however, the French Empire could hardly have been even temporarily reincarnated after the Second World War. In fact, the demands of the Cold War created a convoluted situation: the return of an imperial Power (France) was supported by a country that presented itself as the champion of national self-determination (the United States). By 1954 the colonial Power was defeated but the Cold War had been transformed and as a result the United States ended up supporting, and trying to sustain, the southern half of Vietnam as an anti-communist bastion. In the end, such efforts proved not only costly but counter-productive, for ironically the United States lost much of its international prestige in its misguided effort to preserve its credibility as an ally; the Chinese and the Soviets became more deeply involved in Indochina than they probably would have been without the American involvement; and the Vietnam War shook the American people's trust in their own government's foreign policies.

The post-1975 genocides, the continued political instability and Indochina's general economic dislocation thus owe much to the way in which its fate was determined within the context of the Cold War. While such local actors as Ho Chi Minh, Ngo Dinh Diem, Pol Pot and others were in large part responsible for the sad fates of their populations, the support that such actors received from the outside – from France, the United States, the Soviet Union and the PRC, in particular – inexorably shaped the fates of the millions who inhabited Cambodia, Laos and Vietnam. Perhaps most tragically, at the end of the twentieth century the state of Indochina remains bleak. Whereas a number of Asian countries – from Japan and China to the fast-growing 'tigers' of the 1980s – have become part of the global economy and have seen in many cases spectacular economic growth, the former French colonies remain poor economically and unstable politically. The bitter irony here is, of course, that the relative prosperity of Indochina's neighbours, under the aegis of the **Association of South-East Asian Nations**

Association of South-East Asian Nations (ASEAN) Organization founded in 1967 by Indonesia, Malaysia, the Philippines, Singapore and Thailand to provide a forum for regional economic co-operation. From 1979, and the Third Indochina War, it took on more of a political and security role. Membership increased with the accession of Brunei in 1984, Vietnam in 1995, Burma in 1997 and Cambodia in 1999.

(ASEAN), was built on the back of the wars that ravaged that region. Whether the countries of Indochina can escape from poverty and share the fruits of ASEAN's success in the new century remains to be seen.

Finally, it is important to note that the cost of American intervention had a profound impact on US willingness to send its ground troops into far-away military conflicts – at least until the end of the Cold War. In this sense, the so-called 'Vietnam syndrome' played a restraining role on American admini-strations from 1975 until 2001; no occupant of the White House was willing to suffer the political fate that befell Johnson in the late 1960s. While the nation hardly retreated into becoming a fortress America after 1975, the sending of hundreds of thousands of troops overseas became inconceivable. This changed after the end of the Cold War, starting with the 1991 Gulf War, and continuing with the 2001 global war on terror, military intervention in Afghanistan, and the 2003 invasion of Iraq. While casualties in the first Gulf War were low, the opposite holds true for the second Gulf War. And it is in this context that the spectre of Vietnam has once again come to haunt US politics.

see Chapter 22

Recommended reading

The Vietnam War is probably the most heavily studied military conflict of the post-1945 era. The focus of most books has, however, been almost exclusively on the American side, but three works that do address the broader context of the war are Stanley Karnow, *Vietnam: A History* (New York, 1983), Peter Lowe (ed.), *The Vietnam War* (London, 1998) and Ralph B. Smith, *An International History of the Vietnam War*, 3 vols (New York, 1984–90).

Some of the key works on Vietnamese history include Joseph Buttinger, *Vietnam: The Unforgettable Tragedy* (New York, 1977), William J. Duiker, *Sacred War: Nationalism and Revolution in a Divided Vietnam* (New York, 1995), Thomas L. Hodgkin, *Vietnam: The Revolutionary Path* (New York, 1981) and Timothy J. Lomperis, *From People's War to People's Rule: Insurgency, Intervention, and the Lessons of Vietnam* (Chapel Hill, NC, 1996). For Cambodia, see Ben Kiernan, *How Pol Pot Came to Power: A History of Communism in Kampuchea, 1930–1975* (London, 1985), Ben Kiernan, *The Pol Pot Regime: Race, Power, and Genocide in Cambodia under the Khmer Rouge, 1975–79* (London, 1992), Stephen J. Morris, *Why Vietnam Invaded Cambodia: Political Culture and the Causes of War* (Stanford, CA, 1999) and David P. Chandler, *The Tragedy of Cambodian History: Politics, War and Revolution since 1945* (New Haven, CT, 1991). On Laos, see Timothy Castle, *At War in the Shadow of Vietnam: United States Military Aid to the Royal Lao Government, 1955–75* (New York, 1993) and Martin Stuart-Fox, *A History of Laos* (Cambridge, 1997). For biographies of two of the most important leaders in Indochina, see William Duiker, *Ho Chi Minh* (New York, 2000) and David P. Chandler, *Brother Number One: A Political Biography of Pol Pot* (Boulder, CO, 1992).

The best overviews of American involvement in Indochina include William J. Duiker, *US Containment Policy and the Conflict in Indochina* (Stanford, CA, 1994), George C. Herring, *America's Longest War* (New York, 1996), Gary R. Hess, *Vietnam and the United States: Origins and Legacy of War* (Boston, 1990), Alan J. Levine, *The United States and the Struggle for Southeast Asia, 1945–1975* (Westport, CT, 1995), James S. Olson and Randy Roberts, *Where the Domino Fell: America and Vietnam, 1945–1990* (New York, 1996), Robert Schulzinger, *A Time for War* (New York, 1997), William S. Turley, *The Second Indochina War: A Short Political and Military History, 1954–1975* (Boulder, CO, 1986) and Marilyn B. Young, *The Vietnam Wars* (New York, 1990). For a challenging revisionist account, see Gabriel Kolko, *Anatomy of a War: Vietnam, the United States, and the Modern Historical Experience* (New York, 1985).

For studies that cover particularly important points of decision-making, see David L. Anderson (ed.), *Shadow on the White House: Presidents and the Vietnam War, 1945–1975* (Lawrence, KS, 1993) and John P. Burke, Fred I. Greenstein *et al.*, *How Presidents Test Reality: Decisions on Vietnam, 1954 and 1965* (New York, 1989). An influential argument regarding the origins and end of American involvement can be found in Leslie H. Gelb and Richard K. Betts, *The Irony of Vietnam: The System Worked* (Washington, DC, 1979). For the cleavage between American military leaders and political decision-makers, see the award-winning Robert Buzzanco, *Masters of War: Military Dissent and Politics in the Vietnam Era* (Cambridge, 1996).

There are hundreds of more specialized studies on the various aspects and periods of the Vietnam War. On the French Indochina War, see Anthony Short, *The Origins of the Vietnam War* (London, 1989), Jacques Dalloz, *The War in Indochina, 1945–54* (New York, 1990), Peter M. Dunn, *The First Vietnam War* (London, 1985), Lloyd C. Gardner, *Approaching Vietnam: From the Second World War through Dienbienphu* (New York, 1988), Gary R. Hess, *The United States' Emergence as a Southeast Asian Power, 1940–1950* (New York, 1987), Andrew J. Rotter, *The Path to Vietnam* (Ithaca, NY, 1983) and Martin Shipway, *The Road to War: France and Vietnam, 1944–1947* (Oxford, 1996). On the battle of Dien Bien Phu and its significance, see Howard R. Simpson, *Dien Bien Phu: The Epic Battle America Forgot* (McLean, VA, 1994).

On America's early involvement in Vietnam during the Eisenhower and Kennedy presidencies, consult David L. Anderson, *Trapped by Success: The Eisenhower Administration and Vietnam, 1953–1961* (New York, 1991), James R. Arnold, *The First Domino: Eisenhower, the Military, and America's Intervention in Vietnam* (New York, 1991), Melanie Billings-Yun, *Decision against War* (New York, 1988), Ellen J. Hammer, *A Death in November: America in Vietnam, 1963* (New York, 1987), John M. Newman, *JFK and Vietnam: Deception, Intrigue, and the Struggle for Power* (New York, 1992) and William J. Rust, *Kennedy in Vietnam* (New York, 1985). On the internal Vietnamese situation, see Carlyle Thayer, *War by Other Means: National Liberation and Revolution in Viet-Nam, 1954–60* (Cambridge, MA, 1989).

The period of the massive escalation and subsequent de-escalation of direct American engagement in Vietnam has produced a number of recent works. A few of the key studies include Larry Berman's trilogy, *Planning a Tragedy: The Americanization of the War in Vietnam; Lyndon Johnson's War*; and *No Honor, No Peace* (New York, 1982, 1989, 2001), Larry Cable, *Unholy Grail: The US and the Wars in Vietnam, 1965–8* (New York, 1991), Lloyd C. Gardner, *Pay Any Price: Lyndon Johnson and the Wars for Vietnam* (Chicago, 1995), George C. Herring, *LBJ and Vietnam: A Different Kind of War* (Austin, TX, 1994), Michael H. Hunt, *Lyndon Johnson's War: America's Cold War Crusade in Vietnam, 1945–1965* (New York, 1996), Jeffrey Kimball, *Nixon's Vietnam War* (Lawrence, KS, 1999), Frederick Logevall, *Choosing War* (Berkeley, CA, 1999), Edwin E. Moïse, *Tonkin Gulf and the Escalation of the Vietnam War* (Chapel Hill, NC, 1996) and Andrew Preston, *The War Council: McGeorge Bundy, the NSC, and Vietnam* (Cambridge, MA, 2006). For the collapse of South Vietnam and the communist take-overs throughout Indochina, see Arnold Isaacs, *Without Honor: Defeat in Vietnam and Cambodia* (Baltimore, MD, 1983), William Shawcross, *Sideshow: Kissinger, Nixon and the Destruction of Cambodia* (New York, 1987), Olivier Todd, *Cruel April: The Fall of Saigon* (New York, 1990), Ralph S. Watts, *Saigon: The Final Days* (Boise, ID, 1990) and Jussi Hanhimäki, *The Flawed Architect: Henry Kissinger and American Foreign Policy* (New York, 2004).

For China's role in Indochina, see Cheng Guan Ang, *Vietnamese Communists' Relations with China and the Second Indochina Conflict, 1957–1962* (Jefferson, NC, 1997), Barbara Barnouin and Yu Changgen, *Chinese Foreign Policy during the Cultural Revolution* (London, 1998), William J. Duiker, *China and Vietnam: The Roots of Conflict* (Berkeley, CA, 1986), Anne Gilks, *The Breakdown of the Sino-Vietnamese Alliance, 1970–1979* (Berkeley, CA, 1992), Steven J. Hood, *Dragons Entangled: Indochina and the China–Vietnam War* (Armonk, NY, 1992) and Qiang Zhai, *China and the Vietnam Wars* (Chapel Hill, NC, 2000). On the Soviet role the only full-length account remains Iliya Gaiduk, *The Soviet Union and the Vietnam War* (Chicago, 1996), but see also R. A. Longmire, *Soviet Relations with South-East Asia: An Historical Survey* (London, 1989) and Ramesh Thakur and Carlyle Thayer, *Soviet Relations with India and Vietnam* (New York, 1992).

A few more specialized works worth mentioning are Robert Brigham, *Guerrilla Diplomacy* (New York, 1999), John Hellmann, *American Myth and the Legacy of Vietnam* (New York, 1986), John C. Rowe and Rick Berg, *The Vietnam War and American Culture* (New York, 1991) and Neil Sheehan, *After the War was Over: Hanoi and Saigon* (New York, 1992).

For analyses of Indochina in the last quarter of the twentieth century the reader should turn, in addition to several works cited above, to Robert S. Ross, *The Indochina Tangle* (New York, 1988), Borje Ljunggren, *The Challenge of Reform in Indochina* (Cambridge, MA, 1993), Stephen J. Morris, *Why Vietnam Invaded Cambodia* (Stanford, CA, 1999), Marie A. Martin, *Cambodia: A Shattered Society* (Berkeley, CA, 1994), Robert Schulzinger, *A Time for Peace: The Legacy of the Vietnam War* (New York, 2006), Kenneth J. Campbell, *A Tale of Two Quagmires: Iraq, Vietnam, and the Hard Lessons of War* (New York, 2007), and Jon Roper and Saki Dockrill, *Over Thirty Years: The United States and the Legacy of the Vietnam War* (London, 2007).

Neutralism, development and the rise of the Third World, 1945–2007

Introduction

While the Cold War was in progress it was common for people to assume that it was the dominant paradigm that shaped the international system, and that no state, large or small, could fail to be drawn into the bipolar competition between the United States and the Soviet Union. However, during the years of this monumental conflict some states did attempt to distance themselves from its effects by declaring their neutrality and remaining aloof from both of the Cold War alliance systems. For some states in Europe, such as Switzerland and Sweden, the decision to be neutral was a matter of tradition based on an internationally recognized concept of neutrality that had existed since the sixteenth century. However, for other states, particularly the newly independent nations of Asia and Africa, the desire to remain free of entanglement in the competition between the superpowers represented far more than this. Their rejection of the global Cold War rested not only on their conviction that involvement in this conflict represented an unnecessary threat to their national security, but also on the belief that it directed attention away from the issues that they found most important. Reflecting their own experiences, their priorities were expediting Western **decolonization** and tackling the causes of economic underdevelopment.

decolonization
The process whereby an imperial power gives up its formal authority over its colonies.

Non-Aligned Movement
The organization founded in 1961 by a number of neutral states which called for a lowering of Cold War tensions and for greater attention to be paid to underdevelopment and to the eradication of imperialism.

Third World
A collective term of French origin for those states that are part of neither the developed capitalist world nor the communist bloc. It includes the states of Latin America, Africa, the Middle East, South Asia and South-East Asia. Also referred to as 'the South' in contrast to the developed 'North'.

Warsaw Pact (Warsaw Treaty Organization)
An alliance set up in 1955 under a mutual defence treaty signed in Warsaw by Albania, Bulgaria, Czechoslovakia, East Germany, Hungary, Poland, Romania and the Soviet Union. The organization was the Soviet bloc's equivalent of NATO. Albania formally withdrew in 1968. The Warsaw Pact was dissolved in June 1991.

North Atlantic Treaty Organization (NATO)
Established by the North Atlantic Treaty (4 April 1949) signed by Belgium, Canada, Denmark, France, Great Britain, Iceland, Italy, Luxembourg, the Netherlands, Norway, Portugal and the United States. Greece and Turkey entered the alliance in 1952 and the Federal Republic of Germany in 1955. Spain became a full member in 1982. In 1999 the Czech Republic, Hungary and Poland joined in the first post-Cold War expansion, increasing the membership to nineteen countries.

The desire to further their own agenda meant that the activist states in Asia and Africa, such as India, Egypt and Algeria, did not pursue neutrality in isolation, but attempted to form groupings, such as the **Non-Aligned Movement**, that would allow them to speak with a stronger collective voice. Thus from the 1950s onwards a number of conferences and summits took place that called for the world's attention to be redirected towards the plight of what came to be known as the '**Third World**'. Specifically, this meant a demand for greater concentration on the economic and social problems caused by underdevelopment. However, whether this attempt to construct a new paradigm could succeed in supplanting the Cold War or whether the competition between the superpowers would define the Third World's future was to be a matter of much struggle and debate.

Neutrality in Cold War Europe

While neutrality is often associated in the post-1945 period with the Third World, it is important to realize that the roots of the concept lay in Europe and the European states system. Indeed, one of the most overlooked issues in studies of the Cold War in Europe is the role of the neutral countries. In part this is an understandable omission; after all the countries that did not join the **Warsaw Pact** or **NATO** were small states of only marginal significance to the broader ideological, political, military and economic aspects of the East–West confrontation. Yet to some degree in the 1940s, but even more so in the 1950s, neutrality and the idea of '**neutralism**' helped to influence the direction of the Cold War in Europe.

When discussing European neutrality, it is important to bear several facts in mind. First, one must differentiate between the traditional policy of neutrality, as practised by such countries as Switzerland and Sweden, from the emergence of Cold War neutrality and **non-alignment** in Austria, Finland and Yugoslavia. Neither Swiss nor Swedish neutrality was an outcome of the Cold War: in the former case neutrality dates back to the sixteenth century; for Sweden, the policy emerged in the aftermath of the Napoleonic Wars of the early nineteenth century. Moreover, while neither state joined a Cold War alliance, it was no secret that ideologically and economically both Sweden and Switzerland belonged to the 'West'. In contrast, the neutrality and non-alignment of Austria, Finland and Yugoslavia were products of the Cold War. Austria's neutrality was, in effect, a compromise solution imposed from the outside as a way of ending that country's occupation ten years after the end of the Second World War. Much like neighbouring Switzerland, however, Austria clearly gravitated to the West after 1955.

The cases of Finland and Yugoslavia provide an interesting contrast. In Finland, post-war political leaders (such as presidents Juho K. Paasikivi and Urho K. Kekkonen) considered a cordial relationship with their powerful neighbour, the USSR, to be a precondition for maintaining internal democracy. Thus, Finland made important security and foreign policy concessions to the Soviet Union (most notably by signing a Security Pact in 1948) but managed, through a series of political and diplomatic manoeuvres, to avoid membership in the Warsaw Pact and retain its political traditions and pro-Western sentiment largely intact. Moreover, while its exports to and imports from the USSR represented 25–35 per cent of its foreign trade throughout the Cold War, Finland also associated itself with various Western economic organizations such as EFTA in the early 1960s, and over time managed to distance itself from the USSR.

If Finland was a Western state practising 'Soviet-friendly' neutrality during the Cold War, Yugoslavia was the first socialist state to break with Moscow's leadership and establish independent links with the West. Following the Tito–Stalin break of 1948 Yugoslavia received military assistance from the United States, which saw it as a potential agent for breaking the Soviet Union's monolithic control over Eastern Europe. Such hopes proved, in the end, illusory, for Tito had no desire to leave one camp to enter another. Indeed, Yugoslavia from the mid-1950s used its neutrality to develop links with like-minded countries in the Third World, and in the 1960s became a leading member of the Non-Aligned Movement.

While the policies of these five states probably had a limited impact on the unfolding of the Cold War in Europe, it is important to note that the relative success of the neutral states had broader implications. Perhaps most importantly, their sheer existence made neutrality a potentially credible policy choice for other countries both inside and outside Europe and a corresponding headache for the leading protagonists in the Cold War. In Western Europe, neutralist sentiments were particularly strong in such countries as France and helped President de Gaulle's efforts to adopt a more independent course in the 1960s. Moreover, in the 1970s one worrying, albeit much exaggerated, spectre for American policy-makers was that West Germany's *Ostpolitik* was leading that NATO country down the dangerous path towards neutralism. More broadly, there was even talk of West Europeans adopting a similar posture towards the USSR to that of Finland; the popular, if much misused, term 'Finlandization' became a way to refer to such potential dangers to NATO unity in the latter part of the Cold War. In contrast, the Soviets worked diligently to avoid the cancer of neutralism in their sphere. In 1956, for example, the Soviets, despite having touted the 'neutralization' and unification of Austria as a possible model for ending the division of Germany, reacted violently to Hungary's attempt to leave the Warsaw Pact and adopt a neutral posture.

In the end, however, neutrality remained the privilege (or burden) of a few selected countries in Cold War Europe, and even the independent initiatives of de Gaulle's France or Willy Brandt's West Germany did little to shake the division of the continent. Yet neutrality and the existence of strong neutralist sentiments served as expressions of a continued reluctance on the part of large segments of European opinion to be mere pawns in the Soviet–American confrontation. Similar sentiments, if in dramatically different contexts, were shared by a large group of countries throughout the developing world that wished to remain non-aligned in the Cold War.

neutralism
The policy whereby a state publicly disassociates itself from becoming involved in Great Power conflicts. The first major advocate of the policy was Jawaharlal Nehru on behalf of post-independence India.

see Chapter 9

non-alignment
A state policy of avoiding involvement in 'Great Power conflicts', most notably the Cold War. It was first espoused by India on its becoming independent in 1947.

Ostpolitik
The West German policy towards the Soviet Union and Eastern Europe in the 1960s and 1970s, which aimed at reducing tensions with the ultimate hope of negotiating the peaceful unification of Germany.

see Chapter 9

India and the path to Bandung

The emergence of neutralism outside Europe followed a very different trajectory to that which existed in Europe. Strictly speaking, the tendency among states in Asia and Africa was not to be neutral but to be non-aligned. Non-alignment meant that states did not necessarily have to be rigidly neutral (they could, for example, be members of alliances in order to preserve their national security), but that they should avoid involvement in **Great Power** conflicts. The fundamental starting point of what became 'Third World' non-alignment was that the states that espoused this position had only recently shaken off the shackles of colonialism. They were therefore deeply protective of their newly won independence and believed that involvement in Great Power politics and alignments would necessarily compromise their sovereignty and freedom of action. Moreover, they felt that the Cold War was an unwanted distraction from concentration on what they saw as the key moral issue affecting international politics, namely the eradication of imperialism.

The first state that clearly set out the tenets of non-alignment was India under the leadership of Jawaharlal Nehru. Even before independence was granted in 1947, Nehru made it clear in a number of speeches that India would 'follow an independent policy, keeping away from the power politics of groups aligned one against another'. Moreover, from the first, he argued that the other newly independent states in South and South-East Asia should live by this creed, so that these regions would never again become fields for Great Power competition. In order to further this line, in April 1947 Nehru organized an Asian Relations Conference in New Delhi, and followed this in January 1949 by convening a second conference specifically to protest against the recent Dutch attack on the Indonesian Republic. That non-alignment rather than Asian solidarity was Nehru's chief concern is demonstrated by his attitude towards another meeting held at this time. In May 1950, concerned about the establishment of the **People's Republic of China (PRC)**, Elpidio Quirino, the president of the Philippines, organized a conference of Asian states at Baguio to call for defence collaboration against the communist bloc. Nehru, however, rejected any arrangement that would align the region with the American side in the Cold War, and thus Quirino's initiative came to nothing.

The independent policy followed by Nehru and his dismissal of the Cold War as the key paradigm in international affairs naturally led to problems with the two superpowers, for neither cherished the idea that their ideological conflict was not the supreme moral and political struggle of the day, which was the implicit subtext of Indian rhetoric. The Soviet Union saw Nehru's position as bourgeois posturing, and dismissed India as being in reality within the Western camp. Relations were also not helped by the Communist Party of India's agitation against the government in New Delhi and the latter's attempt to suppress this dissent. The relationship between India and the United States was more complex, for both parties found it difficult to understand each other. Perceiving Nehru as a morally driven figure, American officials could not understand why he failed to appreciate

Great Powers
Traditionally those states that were held capable of shared responsibility for the management of the international order by virtue of their military and economic influence.

see Chapter 10

People's Republic of China (PRC)
The official name of communist or mainland China. The PRC came into existence in 1949 under the leadership of Mao Zedong.

Defining the Third World

Identifying the terminology to use when one groups together the states of Asia, Africa and Latin America is a difficult problem. The common shorthand has been to refer to these areas as the 'Third World', but this is a loaded expression that requires explanation as its meaning has changed over time. The term was coined in the early 1950s by the French demographer Alfred Sauvy who used it to describe the poor Afro-Asian countries and peoples who belonged to neither the Western capitalist bloc, the 'First World', nor the communist bloc, the 'Second World', and which he saw, in an allusion to *ancien régime* France, as being equivalent to a disenfranchised global 'third estate'. Sauvy argued that, in time, it would, like the 'third estate', demand that its voice be heard. With the attempt to move towards Afro-Asian solidarity in the mid-1950s, it appeared that this prediction had come true. However, with the emergence of a common economic agenda on the part of Asia, Africa and Latin America in the 1960s, the term came to refer not just to the neutralist states but to all countries struggling with the issues of dependency and underdevelopment, and its meaning began to broaden to include all of the post-colonial nations, no matter what their political stance. If anything, it is this economically derived definition that has lasted longest. However, even in this field its vague inclusiveness has proved problematical, for the states that made up the 'Third World' have had widely differing economic trajectories. For example, from the 1970s a number of countries in East and South-East Asia, such as Taiwan, the **Republic of Korea** and Singapore, saw rapid economic growth, while at the same time some of the states in Africa, such as Burkina Faso and the Central African Republic, experienced negative growth. To put all of these states under the same label naturally seemed incongruous, and there was some talk of applying the term 'Fourth World' to the very poorest states. The expression has also become less useful since the end of the Cold War for the very good reason that much of the so-called 'Second World' became extinct. Moreover, those communist states that remained, such as the PRC and Vietnam, were the very ones that had already identified themselves with 'Third World' concerns. To a degree this problem has been addressed by the wider usage of a practice that had appeared in the 1970s, namely to refer to the 'Third World' as the 'South', in contradistinction to the advanced economies of the 'North', but like 'Third World', this construction does little justice to the diversity of Asia, Africa and Latin America. The expression 'Third World' has therefore continued to be more widely used, for, although ill-defined and often abused, it nevertheless serves a useful purpose.

Republic of Korea (ROK)
The official name of South Korea. The ROK came into existence in 1948 under the leadership of Syngman Rhee.

Kashmir
Province in the north-west of
the Indian subcontinent.
Although mainly Muslim in
population, the Hindu ruler in
1947 declared his allegiance to
India. Pakistan reacted by
seizing control of some of the
province. Divided ever since
by what is known as the Line
of Control, Kashmir has been
a perpetual sore in Indo-
Pakistani relations. Terrorist
campaigns by Islamic militants
in the 1990s led the two
countries to the brink of war
on a number of occasions.

United Nations (UN)
An international organization
established after the Second
World War to replace the
League of Nations. Since its
establishment in 1945, its
membership has grown to 192
countries.

peaceful co-existence
An expression coined
originally by Trotsky to
describe the condition when
there are pacific relations
between states with differing
social systems and competition
takes place in fields other than
war. The idea was vital to
Soviet diplomacy particularly
after the death of Stalin.

see Chapter 12

the moral core of the Cold War. Moreover, they believed that India's bellicosity
over the issue of **Kashmir** contradicted Nehru's claim of high-mindedness.
Meanwhile, Indians were disturbed that the Truman administration's single-
minded concentration on the Cold War was leading it to compromise on what
had been one of the central tenets of American political beliefs, namely its resolute
abhorrence of colonialism. Reinforcing this, as Andrew Rotter has recently argued,
was a pervasive sense of mutual cultural incomprehension brought about by
different religious and social values. Thus, Americans tended to patronize the
Indians as being hopelessly idealistic and childish, while the Indians characterized
the Americans as arrogant, racist capitalists.

Relations between the United States and India worsened as the Cold War in
Asia heightened. During the Korean War, India agreed to the initial **United
Nations (UN)** effort to support the Republic of Korea, but voted against the
resolution declaring the PRC an aggressor state and called for the Beijing regime
to be allowed to take up China's seat in the Security Council. Furthermore, in
September 1951 India refused to sign the San Francisco peace treaty ending the
state of hostilities with Japan on the grounds that the United States had forced
the former to sign a security treaty committing it to America's side in the Cold
War. Neither stance endeared India to the United States government, which saw
it as an increasingly unreliable presence on the world stage.

American criticism did not, however, deter Nehru from following his path
of preaching non-alignment, working to achieve an Asia free of Great Power
influence and attempting to integrate the PRC into the Asian international
political system. Indeed, following the end of the Korean War, India became
more active than ever. In April 1954, in a move symbolic of Nehru's aims, India
and China signed a border treaty which stated that relations between the two
states would be regulated by reference to the 'five principles of **peaceful co-
existence**'. These principles included mutual respect for sovereignty and territorial
integrity, non-aggression, non-interference in the internal affairs of the other
country, equality and mutual benefit, and peaceful co-existence. Then, in line
with Chinese policy, Nehru emerged during the period of the Geneva Conference
as a significant and vociferous supporter of the idea of the neutralization of
Indochina as the best way to bring stability to that troubled region.

The prospect of Great Power intervention in Indochina in 1954, and of the
United States and Britain attempting to form a Cold War alliance in Asia, led
Nehru and the like-minded leaders of Ceylon, Burma and Indonesia to seek to
generate a sense of non-aligned solidarity in Asia. In April 1954 they, along with
representatives from Pakistan, met in Colombo in Ceylon (Sri Lanka) to decide
how to further this interest. The result was a decision to convene a conference of
African and Asian states at Bandung in Indonesia with the aim of promoting
goodwill and providing a forum within which issues of common interest, such as
opposition to colonialism, could be investigated. This was, however, not to be a
conference of non-aligned countries, for it was decided that states that had ties
with the superpowers could attend. In part, this came about for pragmatic reasons,
for India wished to invite the PRC, while Pakistan was on the verge of signing a
mutual defence pact with the United States. In addition, however, there was a

genuine desire on the part of the convenors to foster a sense of solidarity and mission between the newly independent states.

Accordingly, the **Bandung Afro-Asian Conference** opened in April 1955 with representatives from twenty-nine states. Most of these came from Asia, for this meeting took place prior to the collapse of the European empires in Africa; the latter was only represented by delegations from Egypt, Libya, Sudan, Ethiopia, Liberia, and two states that were at least on their way to independence, Ghana and Algeria. Of the Asian countries, most were not committed to either side in the Cold War, but there were representatives from front-line states, such as the PRC, Japan, the Philippines, Thailand and Turkey. It is also worth noting that, despite the claims about being inclusive, a number of countries were excluded as their presence would have been divisive; thus there were no representatives from Israel, South Africa and Taiwan, or from either of the Korean regimes.

Measured by the resolutions passed at the conference, Bandung did not have the substantial impact that many had anticipated and, indeed, that the West had feared. Restricted by the presence of the Philippines and Pakistan, criticism of the Cold War was fairly muted, and even the expected denunciation of colonialism was not as violent as expected. However, some issues that would later become central to the Non-Aligned Movement's agenda were raised, such as the need for the prohibition of weapons of mass destruction and, in the economic sphere, for commodity prices to be fixed. Moreover, those present voted to endorse the general application of the 'five principles of peaceful co-existence'. Thus, even though the presence of Cold War participants compromised some of the conference's intended results, the meeting should be judged a qualified success.

One sign that the development of an Afro-Asian group had raised the profile of the newly independent states, and particularly those that practised non-alignment, was that from 1954 onwards the superpowers became more forth-coming in terms of aid and assistance. The transformation was most apparent on the part of the Soviet Union, which, in the period following Stalin's death in 1953, turned its back on the 'two camps' paradigm that had been used since 1948 and adopted a more flexible policy towards the non-aligned states. While the Soviet Union could not outbid the West in the amount of aid it could provide, it attempted to win favour by offering assistance without ostensibly demanding anything in return. This contrasted with the United States, which generated the impression that its aid was always tied in some way to the recipient's backing for Washington in the Cold War. Soviet money thus flowed to states such as India and Indonesia to fund the building of steel mills and other industrial complexes. Moreover, in the case of Egypt's Aswan High Dam, the Soviet Union achieved a considerable propaganda coup when, following the American and British withdrawal of funds in the summer of 1956, it stepped into the breach.

The Soviet interest in the non-aligned countries led in turn to a change in the American viewpoint. On taking office, the Eisenhower administration, and particularly the secretary of state, John Foster Dulles, had shown little tolerance of non-alignment. Indeed, in one notorious speech Dulles had denounced neutralism as a morally bankrupt concept. However, as the Soviets began to display interest in independent Asia and Africa, and it became clear that states

Bandung Afro-Asian Conference
The conference of Asian and African states held in Bandung in Indonesia in 1955. Commonly seen as the first move towards the establishment of a Third World lobby in international politics.

such as India were serious in their adherence to non-alignment, the United States was forced to become more forthcoming. For example, in 1958 the United States responded to an economic crisis in India by providing two tranches of aid: first, a series of unilateral loans worth $225 million, and then a contribution to a multilateral aid package under the auspices of the World Bank. American largess increased even further under the Kennedy administration, as the new president was convinced that the United States had to do more to win the sympathy of the non-aligned countries.

The birth of the Non-Aligned Movement

In the wake of Bandung, the question for Nehru and the other non-aligned leaders was whether they should continue with their focus on Afro-Asian solidarity or seek some other more effective and coherent forum for expressing their concerns. After much deliberation, the decision was made to move towards the latter by the formation of a loose conglomeration of non-aligned states. The drift towards a more overt non-aligned stance came about for a number of reasons. One of the most important was the emergence of Gamal Abdel Nasser of Egypt and Josip Tito of Yugoslavia as enthusiastic supporters of the principle of non-alignment. While they recognized that the struggle against colonialism was important, both stressed the even greater need, based on both moral and pragmatic grounds, for the non-committed states to do their utmost to try to ease the ideological confrontation between the two superpowers. This was, of course, of particular importance for Yugoslavia, owing to its exposed position in East Europe, especially after the Soviet invasion of Hungary in 1956. This emphasis on non-alignment towards the Cold War as the overriding priority clearly argued against any continuation of the attempt to follow the Afro-Asian path, for any forum based on the latter necessarily included states that were allied to the superpowers.

In addition, the cause of Afro-Asian solidarity was undermined, somewhat ironically, by the surge in the late 1950s in the number of states eligible to attend such a forum. The problem here was that, although a large number of states in Africa received their independence in this period, they were deeply divided between the Casablanca Group of radical governments inspired by **pan-African** ambitions, which included Egypt and Ghana, and the more conservative, pro-Western states, such as Nigeria, Ethiopia and the former French colonies which constituted the Monrovia Group. The obvious implication of this schism was that the entry of the Monrovia Group into any Afro-Asian forum would seriously compromise any attempt to take a critical stance towards the Cold War. However, it was clear that the Casablanca Group would be sympathetic towards any grouping based on a common adherence to non-alignment.

Another important stimulus to the emergence of the Non-Aligned Movement was that the rhetoric used by Nasser and Tito about the urgent need to dampen down Cold War tensions appeared to be confirmed by the trend in world affairs.

pan-Africanism
The belief that Africans wherever they live share common cultural and spiritual values. Pan-Africanism was an important influence on the rise of nationalist movements in Africa in the first half of the twentieth century, but after decolonization its impact waned as the new states were reluctant to compromise their independence.

see Chapter 17

After all, the late 1950s witnessed a resurgence of the Cold War in the shape of the crises over Berlin and Taiwan, and in 1960, following a brief period of **détente**, the Four-Power Summit at Paris was cancelled abruptly amid American–Russian recriminations. In addition, the fact that these years witnessed a peak in the decolonization process and the rise of national liberation movements posed a number of challenges to international stability. On the one hand, there was the problem that, while the colonial Powers were beginning to divest themselves of their possessions in Sub-Saharan Africa, in some areas they were still bent on frustrating nationalist movements and holding on to their imperial privileges, as, for instance, in the French war to maintain control of Algeria. On the other hand, there was the danger that decolonization would leave behind a power vacuum which the superpowers would seek to fill, thus bringing their Cold War baggage into regions that had previously escaped their grip. To an extent this had already taken place in the Middle East, where the collapse in British and French prestige following the Suez Crisis of 1956 had allowed the United States to develop its presence in the region, leading to its intervention in Lebanon in 1958. The non-aligned states therefore felt duty-bound to express their concerns in a louder and more coherent voice than ever before, in an effort to mobilize world opinion against the perpetuation of imperialism and make clear that the newly independent states had the right to live free from foreign intervention.

The result was that in 1961 the leading non-aligned states decided, following a preparatory meeting in Cairo, to hold a non-aligned summit in Belgrade. This conference, which met in September 1961, was attended by twenty-five states; most of the delegations were from Asia and Africa, Yugoslavia and Cyprus were the only representatives from Europe, and Cuba alone came from Latin America. Because of the absence of superpower clients, the Belgrade Summit was a far more radical affair than Bandung. Its main significance lay in two areas: first, that the states present agreed that they should form a pressure group that would focus attention on political problems, such as lowering Cold War tensions and opposing colonialism and **apartheid**, and, second, that they should lobby on economic development issues. In the short term both of these interests were to have an impact on international relations, but in the long term it was the economic rather than the political agenda that was to have the most influence on international politics. This might seem surprising since the non-aligned states had concentrated until this point on political issues first and foremost, but in fact there was a good reason for this, namely that it was far easier for them to cohere around their economic objectives than to achieve a political consensus. Indeed, in the years following the Belgrade summit it was by no means clear that the Non-Aligned Movement would be able to survive, for divisions over its political direction and other distractions threatened to bring about its rapid extinction.

One problem that emerged was that, for a number of reasons, India's role as the 'leader' of the non-aligned came into question in the early 1960s. In part, this arose from Nehru's ambivalence about the non-aligned summit, for he was concerned that, by forming their own distinct group, the non-aligned were merely becoming yet another bloc in international politics. In addition, a number of the newly independent states questioned India's leadership role, because they felt that

détente
A term meaning the reduction of tensions between states. It is often used to refer to the superpower diplomacy that took place between the inauguration of Richard Nixon as the American president in 1969 and the Senate's refusal to ratify SALT II in 1980.

apartheid
The Afrikaans word for racial segregation. Between 1948 and 1990 'apartheid' was the ideology of the Nationalist Party in South Africa

it was not assertive enough in regard to colonial issues. Indeed, the Indian seizure of the Portuguese colony of Goa in 1961 can be seen as an attempt by Nehru to dampen down such criticism. The most damaging development, however, was the disastrous Sino-Indian border war of October–November 1962. This conflict compromised India's international standing for, after suffering a rapid series of reverses, a deeply shaken Nehru accepted an offer of large-scale military aid from the United States and Britain. Nehru never really recovered from these humiliating experiences, and died in May 1964 a disappointed man.

While India's star waned, a major challenge to the definition of non-alignment propagated by Nehru, Nasser and Tito came from the Indonesian president, Ahmed Sukarno, who believed that the non-aligned should take on a still more radical position. Sukarno's argument was that the primary duty of the non-aligned states was to oppose imperialism, both in its familiar guise and in its meta-morphosis into **neo-colonialism**. His interest arose largely from Indonesia's own experience. From 1950 Indonesia had engaged in a long campaign to force the Dutch to cede control over West Irian, and finally it achieved this goal in 1961. This was followed in 1963 by the start of its campaign to destabilize the new federation of Malaysia, which it saw as a neo-colonial construct designed to maintain British influence in South-East Asia. Sukarno's rhetoric was not without appeal, particularly for the radical independent states in Africa, such as Ghana, which were deeply disturbed at recent events such as the **Congo Crisis**.

In addition, however, there was another aspect to Sukarno's position, which was that he challenged the existence of the newly established Non-Aligned Movement by reviving the cause of Afro-Asian solidarity. To a substantial degree Sukarno was put up to this by his Great Power patron, the PRC, which wished to increase its influence in the Third World. The PRC could clearly not do this in the context of a non-aligned grouping, but it had every right to attend an Afro-Asian forum. Moreover, the PRC was moved to action by its disdain for the revisionist regime in Yugoslavia and its increasingly tense relations with India.

In October 1964, partly in an effort to head off Sukarno's challenge, a second non-aligned summit was held in Cairo. This time it was attended by forty-seven governments, most of the new participants coming from the more conservative African states that had not been invited in 1961. Owing to the new mood of détente in superpower relations following the high drama of the Cuban Missile Crisis, there was less concentration in this summit on East–West relations and more criticism aimed at intervention by the Great Powers in the Third World. This was not enough to assuage Sukarno, who was already putting into operation his plans for a second Afro-Asian conference. At a preparatory meeting in Jakarta in 1964 Ahmed Ben Bella, the president of Algeria, offered to host the conference in Algiers in 1965. However, matters did not proceed smoothly, for, in an effort to sabotage the conference, the Soviet Union got its client states to argue that it too should be invited on the grounds that it was, after all, an Asian power. Moreover, in June 1965 a coup in Algiers overthrew the government of Ben Bella and this was followed in October by the political disturbances in Indonesia that marked the start of Sukarno's fall from power. With its plans in disarray, the PRC had no choice but to call for the conference to be postponed, and with this the

neo-colonialism
The process whereby a colonial power grants juridical independence to a colony, but nevertheless maintains *de facto* political and economic control.

see Chapter 17

see Chapter 15

Congo Crisis
The civil war that took place in the Congo (the former Belgian Congo) from 1960 to 1963. The crisis was caused largely by the attempt of the copper-rich province of Katanga to secede from Congo. The secession was defeated eventually by a UN force, but in the process there were scares that the dilatory UN response would lead the Congolese government to turn to the Soviet Union for support.

dream of Afro-Asian solidarity finally came to an end, while non-alignment was left licking its wounds.

Development and the Group of 77

While the ability of the Non-Aligned Movement to make a significant impact on the politics of the Cold War world was blunted by its internecine disputes, in the economic field its legacy was more important, for here it acted as a catalyst to the opening of a dialogue between the West and the Third World over development issues. By the start of the 1960s there was considerable interest in economic development not just among the non-aligned states, but also on the part of other developing countries, no matter what attitude they had towards the Cold War. For example, America's allies, such as Pakistan and the Philippines, were as interested in this area as India and Egypt. The common link between these states was that their economies were still substantially influenced by their colonial heritage; that is, their chief sources of income were derived from the production of commodities for export to the rich, capitalist countries of Western Europe and North America. This was a fragile foundation on which to build a country, for the prices paid for commodities on the world market could fluctuate wildly, thus making economic planning on the basis of a predictable flow of revenue extremely difficult. Moreover, the development agenda also appealed to the states of Latin America: even though most of them had long been independent, they still suffered from the same unfavourable terms of trade as those states that had only just received their freedom. Indeed, work in the 1950s by a number of Latin American economists, such as Raul Prebisch, had shown that the continent's terms of trade were getting worse rather than better.

Rejecting the Cold War paradigm that relegated issues such as development to the periphery of international relations, the Non-Aligned Movement played an important part in turning the vague discontent of the amorphous Third World into more constructive channels. In 1960, even before the Belgrade summit, some of the key non-aligned states had attempted to place development on the international agenda by making use of the fact that the wave of decolonization sweeping Africa meant that the developing states now constituted a majority in the UN General Assembly (UNGA). In two symbolic moves in December 1960 they mobilized this newly acquired voting power to pass UNGA Resolution 1514, which called for the independence of all states under colonial rule, and Resolution 1522, which called for the 1960s to be a 'development decade'. In July 1962 the Non-Aligned Movement sponsored an economic conference in Cairo, attended by thirty-six states, including some from Latin America. At this and subsequent gatherings the economic objectives of the developing countries coalesced around two issues: first, that the price of commodity exports should be fixed, and, second, that the Western Powers and the **Bretton Woods** international financial institutions, such as the IMF and the World Bank, should provide financial aid on more

Bretton Woods
The site of an inter-Allied conference held in 1944 to discuss the post-war international economic order. The conference led to the establishment of the IMF and the World Bank. In the post-war era the links between these two institutions, the establishment of GATT and the convertibility of the dollar into gold were known as the Bretton Woods system. After the dollar's devaluation in 1971 the world moved to a system of floating exchange rates.

import substitution
The process whereby a state attempts to achieve economic growth by raising protective tariffs to keep out imports and replacing them with indigenously produced goods.

see Chapter 17

'modernization' theory
The idea that rapid economic development is achieved by a state going through a 'take-off' stage in which an entrepreneurial class and high investment in economic growth play a crucial part. The theory is closely associated with the Massachusetts Institute of Technology (MIT) economist Walt Rostow, who served in both the Kennedy and Johnson administrations.

see Chapter 16

Alliance for Progress
The American assistance programme for Latin America begun in 1961, which called for an annual increase of 2.5 per cent in per capita income, the establishment of democratic governments, more equitable income distribution, land reform, and economic and social planning. Latin American countries (excluding Cuba) pledged $80 billion over ten years, while the United States pledged $20 billion. After a decade of mixed results, the Alliance was disbanded in 1973.

favourable terms, free of Cold War considerations. More generous provision of aid would, it was hoped, assist with the development of **import substitution** industries, which would in turn reduce the dependence of the newly independent states on commodity production and trade with the West.

Another factor that allowed for greater progress to be made in the economic field was that by the start of the 1960s the Western Powers were beginning to show considerable interest in this area. One reason for this was that the European colonial Powers had, even prior to independence, been concerned to encourage economic development, and had indeed invested considerable sums of money in their African colonies. Their initial interest naturally had been to develop the colonial economies as useful adjuncts to that of the metropole, but over time they came to see that a certain degree of largess could help to maintain economic links even after independence. The United States, in turn, had its own perspective on the development question. Influenced by the development in the late 1950s of **'modernization' theory**, the Kennedy administration believed that, through the judicious use of financial and technical aid, and advice on how to construct a modern capitalist economy, the United States could assist developing countries to achieve economic 'take-off'. Conversely, failure to assist, it was held, might mean that the process of modernization would be drawn out needlessly and that the resultant economic and social tensions might provide a breeding ground for the dissemination of communism. This was particularly pressing, for it was believed that the Third World was undergoing a population explosion that would only exacerbate its discontents. There was therefore a need to act quickly before conditions deteriorated even further, with the attendant danger that this might lead to a rise in anti-American sentiment. It was in this spirit that Kennedy in 1961 initiated the **Alliance for Progress** in Latin America. Thus, while the developing states saw the development agenda as separate from the Cold War, this was not how it was interpreted in the West.

Influenced by such ideas, and afraid that refusal to discuss the developing world's concerns would constitute a propaganda reverse, the Western states proved receptive to the need for talks. In 1964, following a declaration issued under the authority of seventy-five developing states calling for the UN to take action, a conference took place in Geneva where the West agreed, although somewhat reluctantly, to the formation of the United Nations Conference on Trade and Development (UNCTAD). The developing states, which had by this point organized themselves outside the Non-Aligned Movement's auspices into the **Group of 77 (G-77)**, tried over the coming years to use UNCTAD as a forum to press for fairer terms of trade and for greater access to development aid. However, while UNCTAD was able to make some progress by loosening the IMF's lending rules and bringing about a slight lowering of the West's protective tariffs, overall the results were disappointing, for there were strict limits on how far the Western states were willing to compromise.

The failure to achieve all of their goals naturally led to increasing anger on the part of the developing states, which began to believe that nothing less than a major transformation of the international economic order would address their concerns. The disenchantment of what was now becoming an increasingly self-conscious

Third World was stimulated further by the intellectual environment surrounding development issues. As early as the 1950s a Harvard economist, Paul Baran, had argued that underdevelopment was largely the result of the dominant presence of foreign firms in the economies of the developing countries. These companies, he argued, contributed little to economic growth because they exported their profits back to their home country, leaving little capital for local investment. These ideas were developed further in the late 1960s and early 1970s in a series of studies on Latin America by André Gunder Frank, who argued that the operation of the capitalist world economy meant that the Third World had to be kept in a permanent state of underdevelopment. These conclusions reinforced the impression that only fundamental change could assist the G-77 countries.

Clearly, however, the advanced capitalist states were not likely of their own volition to accept such a transformation; rather, it rested with the Third World to force them to meet its demands. In the early 1970s it appeared that the moment had come, for the United States, after its débâcle in Vietnam, was perceived to be weaker economically and politically, and thus susceptible to pressure. This realization helped to contribute in 1970 to a revival of the Non-Aligned Movement, which, after a period of inactivity in the late 1960s, held its third summit at Lusaka in Zambia. Using its moral weight and increasing organizational coherence, the Non-Aligned Movement now concentrated on pushing the Third World's economic interests, although it continued also with more political concerns such as calling for the ostracism of South Africa and Israel. However, it did not prove to be the most important organization in the economic field, for that prize went to another body – the **Organization of Petroleum Exporting Countries (OPEC)**.

OPEC had been founded in 1960 as a group designed to further the interests of the oil-producing states of the Third World in the struggle against the rapaciousness of the Western-owned oil companies. At first it had made little impact, but by the early 1970s it began to acquire more power. This development arose for two reasons: first, the developed economies were becoming increasingly reliant on oil produced by OPEC members, and, second, OPEC had begun, following an example set by Libya, to force the oil companies to allow its members to set the price of oil. Initially OPEC used its new influence tentatively and purely for economic gain, but in the autumn of 1973 its position changed dramatically. The issue that sparked this transformation was a political one, and one, indeed, that was dear to the Non-Aligned Movement, that is, opposition to Western support for Israel in the October 1973 war in the Middle East. Outraged by a massive American airlift of arms to Israel, OPEC announced a fourfold increase in oil prices. The commodity producers were finally having their revenge.

Although their own members also suffered from having to pay more for oil, the G-77 countries and the Non-Aligned Movement expressed their approval of OPEC's action. Furthermore, emboldened by this challenge to the West, in April 1974 the Non-Aligned Movement, led by President Houari Boumédienne of Algeria, used the occasion of a special session of the UN General Assembly on the energy crisis to press for the establishment of a **New International Economic Order (NIEO)**. The NIEO proposals once again reiterated the G-77's stance on

Group of 77 (G-77)
An organization, originally of seventy-seven nations, that has lobbied at the United Nations for the need to equalize the terms of trade between the developed and developing worlds and to ease access to international aid from institutions such as the World Bank and the IMF.

Organization of Petroleum Exporting Countries (OPEC)
The organization founded in 1960 to represent the interests of the leading oil-producing states in the Third World.

New International Economic Order (NIEO)
The proposal put forward by the Non-Aligned Movement and adopted by the UN in 1974 for major changes to be made to the international trading and financial order.

fixed prices for commodities, but added demands for sweeping changes in the operating methods of the World Bank and the IMF, including greater voting rights for Third World countries. Using their majority in the General Assembly, the non-aligned nations were able to pass a resolution supporting the NIEO. This was a dramatic moment, for it appeared that the Third World, in the face of Western weakness, was now setting the international agenda and that the development paradigm was now centre stage. However, turning these aspirations into reality proved to be a difficult undertaking and, in retrospect, the demand for the NIEO can be seen as the zenith of the Third World's ability to influence international relations and to act as a cohesive bloc.

The fragmentation of the Third World

There are a number of reasons why the Third World states were not able to achieve the goals that they proclaimed for themselves in the mid-1970s. The fundamental difficulty was that, although the concentration on development issues had sealed the construction of a sense of Third World identity, the mere fact that a North–South dialogue had begun did not guarantee that the developing states would receive any substantial benefits. Thus, while the Third World had helped to bring about a new paradigmatic shift that rejected the universality of the East–West divide, the tangible gains from this realignment of international politics were strictly limited.

Clearly one major problem the Third World faced was that the advanced capitalist states, despite the energy crisis, showed little enthusiasm for the idea of introducing significant modifications of the international trading regime. Thus, while the issues connected to the NIEO proposals dominated the UN's debates about development, very little progress was achieved. Indeed, a major summit at Cancún in Mexico in 1981 proved to be an almost total failure. In fact, it might be said that the only dramatic effect of the Third World's attempt to speak with a firmer voice was to force the Western states to pull together more than ever before. Notably, in November 1975 a meeting of the major capitalist states was convened in Rambouillet in France to discuss economic issues in the wake of the energy crisis. This meeting set in train the idea of an annual summit of the seven leading capitalist economies, the United States, Japan, West Germany, Britain, France, Canada and Italy, referred to as the **Group of 7 (G-7)**. While initially intended to broker agreement on issues such as currency stabilization, over time the creation of the G-7 forum allowed the major states of the 'North' to present a united front in the face of the Third World's demands. Moreover, the West started to respond to Third World domination of international organizations by simply withdrawing from them. The most noted case came in 1985 when the United States pulled out of the United Nations Educational, Scientific and Cultural Organization (UNESCO), after which Washington also began to withhold its payments to the UN itself, arguing that too much money was being wasted.

Group of 7 (G-7)
The Group of 7 was the organization of the seven most advanced capitalist economies – the United States, Japan, Canada, Germany, France, Italy and Britain – founded in 1976. The G-7 held and continues to hold annual summit meetings where the leaders of these countries discuss economic and political issues.

Underpinning the West's refusal to accept the Third World's remedies for economic underdevelopment was the fact that, once again, there was a fundamental shift in the way in which development issues were approached intellectually. By the late 1970s the rise of neo-liberal economic thinking in the West led to the view that the underdeveloped states had approached development in the wrong way. Instead of establishing inefficient state-run import substitution industries, it was argued, they should have concentrated on areas in which they possessed a comparative advantage. Moreover, the rapid growth of the newly industrializing countries in Asia confirmed the World Bank in its belief that the developmental programmes that had been followed in Latin America and Africa had been fundamentally flawed, and thus reinforced its determination to change the nature of its aid provision. The result was that as the 1980s began the World Bank introduced what it termed 'structural adjustment programmes', the aim of which was to encourage governments to privatize state assets, to introduce austerity measures and to devalue their currencies. Aid on the terms proposed by the NIEO was thus not on the West's agenda.

Given that the West was able to make a largely united response to the NIEO proposals, it was tragic that from the late 1970s the conglomeration of nations that made up the Third World lacked effective leadership and grew increasingly divided. In the political realm, while the Non-Aligned Movement was far better organized in the 1970s and by the end of that decade had an extensive membership of just under one hundred states, its record in achieving its goals was not impressive. For example, while détente between the superpowers did emerge in the 1970s, it could not be said that this was in any way a reaction to lobbying by the non-aligned. Indeed, at the Algiers non-aligned summit in 1973 a number of resolutions were passed that criticized détente on the grounds that the superpowers were merely dividing the world between themselves, and that the Third World had not received any benefits from this process. Moreover, the ability of the Non-Aligned Movement to lobby the West was compromised by a number of factors. One was the increasingly prominent role played by Cuba, which, particularly after its interventions in Angola and Ethiopia, was hardly seen as neutral. In 1979 the non-aligned summit was held in Havana, and, although a Cuban resolution declaring the Soviet Union to be 'a natural ally' of the Third World was rejected, this naturally raised Western suspicions about the movement as a whole. In addition, the Non-Aligned Movement's use of the Third World majority in the UN General Assembly to pass a resolution in 1975 declaring Zionism to be racist hardly endeared it to Israel's friends in the West.

Another problem was that, just as in the early 1960s, the cohesiveness of the movement was strained by differences and rivalries between its members. This included splits over such issues as the Angolan Civil War and the Soviet invasion of Afghanistan. These problems might have been overcome had a new generation of leaders displaying the vision of the three founding fathers, Nehru, Nasser and Tito, emerged and been able to mobilize the movement. However, this did not happen, and in fact some of the states which had previously acted as leaders tended to retreat into the background. For example, India under Indira Gandhi largely concerned itself with the security of South Asia. In 1971 it went to war with

structural adjustment programme
The idea propagated by the World Bank from the end of the 1970s which linked the provision of development aid to Third World states to the latter committing themselves to balanced budgets, austerity programmes and the sale of nationalized industries and property.

Pakistan in order to ensure the successful secession of Bangladesh, and in the same year signed a treaty of friendship with the Soviet Union. In 1974 it proceeded to explode its first nuclear device. Because of its new sense of regional responsibility, India tended to take a more moderate line on Third World issues and did not provide the leadership that Nehru had once given. Among the other leading states, Egypt, following its peace treaty with Israel in 1979, found its moral authority within the Non-Aligned Movement severely undermined, while Algeria's and Yugoslavia's voices became more subdued after the deaths of Boumédienne and Tito in 1978 and 1980 respectively. Thus, while the Non-Aligned Movement continued to meet, its last summit to date being at Durban in South Africa in 1998, it failed to make much impact on either political or economic issues.

While the West strengthened its position and the Third World once again lost its cohesion, in the most appalling irony of all the failure to redefine the workings of the global economy through the introduction of the NIEO was to have a catastrophic effect on many of the developing countries in the 1980s. The chief reasons for this were increasing indebtedness and the collapse of commodity prices. Indeed, if any one factor symbolized the inability of the G-77 to change the nature of the international economy it was the debt crisis that racked Latin America and Africa from the late 1970s onwards. This crisis was directly linked to the first 'oil shock', for after 1973 many Third World states were forced to raise loans in order to cover purchases of oil, while simultaneously pursuing development programmes. Loans were reasonably easy to arrange as Western banks were awash with the petrodollars that had flowed into the OPEC countries, and interest rates were fairly low. The Third World states therefore took on considerable debts; indeed between 1970 and 1982 long-term debt in Latin America increased from $27.6 billion to $238.5 billion.

This level of indebtedness would clearly have led to problems no matter what happened in the global economy, but in fact events in the world exacerbated the difficulties to a very significant degree. The catalyst for the worsening of the debt crisis was the revolution in Iran in 1979, which led to the second 'oil shock', when prices rose by 160 per cent as a result of the shortages caused by the tailing off of Iranian production and the general sense of fear about the future security of the Persian Gulf. The second 'oil shock' led to inflation and recession for the Western advanced capitalist economies, and thus to large increases in interest rates, which were, in turn, passed on to the Third World debtors, vastly increasing their debt-servicing commitments. For example, by 1982 African debt from all sources stood at $51.3 billion and the annual debt-servicing accounted for $5.46 billion or 12.6 per cent of the value of Africa's exports of goods and services. The difficulties in meeting such high debt repayments were increased by the fact that the recession in the West in the early 1980s and the rise of oil production from non-OPEC sources led to a dramatic fall in commodity prices. By 1990 the real price index for commodities demonstrated a drop of 35 per cent in their value compared with 1980; for Africa this meant that in the 1980s it had lost one-sixth of the income that it might have expected. Naturally, the plummeting value of the commodities that constituted the main exports of the Third World countries made the task of meeting debt commitments extremely difficult. In 1982 Mexico was forced to negotiate a rescue package to avoid defaulting on its payments, while Peru also came close to defaulting in 1985.

Thus by the end of the 1980s, when the Cold War paradigm finally came to its unexpectedly rapid end, although the organizations established by the Third World states had managed to raise interest in development issues, they had achieved little in terms of substantive results. The years following the end of the Cold War were to be no better. With the Soviet Union now vanquished it was no longer possible for countries in the Third World to use the influence of the communist bloc to balance pressure from the United States and its allies or vice versa. They were therefore more amenable to pressure than ever before. Moreover, the triumph of free market capitalism over communism meant that the West was now in a strong position to push its own prescriptions for development on the Third World. The 1990s therefore saw the World Bank and the IMF put increasing emphasis on 'good governance' and democracy as conditions for aid, allied with pressure on states to engage in the further liberalization of markets.

The result was that the Third World was pitched into the era of **globalization**, in which the sovereignty and independence for which they had fought in the middle years of the century stood in danger of being eroded by the forces of international finance. Despite the potential threat, there was initially little resistance to this new paradigm, which reached its peak in 1995 with the establishment of the World Trade Organization. Indeed, instead of attempting to create a Third World united front in order to resist globalization being imposed upon them, the tendency was for regional groupings, such as **Mercosur** in South

globalization

The cultural, social and economic changes caused by the growth of international trade, the rapid transfer of investment capital and the development of high-speed global communications.

Mercosur

Or the Southern Cone Common Market. A Latin American trade organization established in 1991 to increase economic co-operation in the eastern part of South America. Full members include Argentina, Brazil, Paraguay and Uruguay. Bolivia and Chile are associate members. Mercosur's goals include the gradual elimination of tariffs between member states and harmonization of external duties.

Plate 13.1 Dohar, Qatar, Group of 77, 15 June 2005. The second summit of the South, an alliance of 132 developing countries which gathered 50 heads of state or government officials from the Group of 77 and China, opened with the issues of South–South co-operation, South–North relations and the huge debt crisis of poor nations. (Photo: Rabih Moghrabi/AFP/Getty Images)

America or the **Association of South-East Asian Nations (ASEAN)**, to engage in negotiations with the United States and the **European Union** to try to gain the best trading conditions possible through collective bargaining. This did not mean, however, that the idea of globalization was universally welcomed for, as the world moved from the 1990s into the twenty-first century, resistance began to manifest itself in a variety of forms, such as the rise of political Islam and the emergence of a new generation of radical socialist leaders such as Hugo Chavez of Venezuela. However, whether such disparate voices could ever provide the Third World with power and unity was a moot point.

Conclusion

The practical significance of neutrality, neutralism and non-alignment as forces in international politics in the Cold War period and after is not easy to measure. In Europe 'neutrality' remained the privilege of a few small Western-oriented countries that played only a minimal role in the diplomatic, military, economic and political evolution of the Cold War. Moreover, while neutralism had some resonance within a number of NATO countries (most obviously France and West Germany), it never really posed a serious threat to these countries' alignment in the East–West confrontation. When looking outside Europe, the picture is more mixed. On the face of it, one might argue that the Non-Aligned Movement had little influence, for its activities did not lead to any abatement of the Cold War, and many states in the Third World remained allied to one side or the other until the superpower competition came to its conclusion. However, if one looks more broadly at the activities of the non-aligned, it is possible to say that its impact was not negligible. One key consequence was that from the seed of the Bandung Conference there developed a growing sense of a shared consciousness between those states that constituted the Third World. The rise of Third World consciousness, as exemplified by the Non-Aligned Movement, was significant in that it forced the superpowers to compete for the favour of the new states, which resulted in increased levels of economic and military aid. In addition, the United States and the Soviet Union found themselves having to couch policies in language that met Third World sensibilities.

In addition, non-alignment had an impact because in its rejection of the centrality of the Cold War paradigm it posed a positive alternative, namely the development paradigm. While it is difficult to contend that the attempts by the Non-Aligned Movement to redress the terms of trade between the 'North' and the 'South' had much substantial effect, the simple fact that these issues were raised had ramifications for the way in which international politics operated. Thus, even if the non-aligned states did not achieve major breakthroughs in their attempts to press the advanced industrialized countries to make concessions over trade and aid, they did place a number of their favoured issues firmly on the international agenda. Thus, by the time the Cold War ended, the Third World had acquired a voice in world affairs that could not be entirely ignored and had

see Chapter 21

see Chapter 19

Association of South-East Asian Nations (ASEAN)
Organization founded in 1967 by Indonesia, Malaysia, the Philippines, Singapore and Thailand to provide a forum for regional economic co-operation. From 1979, and the Third Indochina War, it took on more of a political and security role. Membership increased with the accession of Brunei in 1984, Vietnam in 1995, Burma in 1997 and Cambodia in 1999.

European Union (EU)
A political and economic community of nations formed in 1992 in Maastricht by the signing of the Treaty on European Union (TEU). In addition to the agreements of the European Community, the EU incorporated two inter-governmental – or supra-national – 'pillars' that tie the member states of the EU together: one dealing with common foreign and security policy, and the other with legal affairs. The number of member states of the EU has expanded from twelve in 1992 to twenty-seven in 2007.

created normative changes that meant that development was a central issue in international politics.

Recommended reading

There are relatively few historical studies of non-alignment and its influence on international politics, although much more has been written from an international relations and political science perspective. Useful introductions include Peter Willetts, *The Non-Aligned Movement: The Origins of a Third World Alliance* (London, 1978), Robert Mortimer, *The Third World Coalition in International Politics* (Boulder, CO, 1984), Rikhi Jaipul, *Non-Alignment: Origins, Growth and Potential for World Peace* (New Delhi, 1987) and Marc Williams, *Third World Cooperation: The Group of 77 in UNCTAD* (London, 1990). An interesting account of the rise and fall of Third World identity is Robert Malley, *The Call from Algeria: Third Worldism, Revolution and the Turn to Islam* (Berkeley, CA, 1996). For the 1990s and globalization, see Louise Fawcett and Yezid Sayigh (eds), *The Third World beyond the Cold War* (Oxford, 1999).

On European neutrality, see Jürg Martin Gabriel, *American Conception of Neutrality after 1941* (New York, 1989), Harto Hakovirta, *East–West Conflict and European Neutrality* (Oxford, 1988), Efraim Karsh, *Neutrality and Small States* (London, 1988), Joseph Krüzel and Michael H. Haltzel, *Between the Blocs: Problems and Prospects for Europe's Neutral and Nonaligned Countries* (New York, 1989), Alan T. Leonhard (ed.), *Neutrality: Changing Concepts and Practices* (Lanham, MD, 1988), Hanspeter Neuhold and Hans Thalberg (eds), *The European Neutrals in International Affairs* (Boulder, CO, 1984), Jukka Nevakivi (ed.), *Neutrality in History* (Helsinki, 1993) and Victor Papacosma and Mark Rubin (eds), *Europe's Neutral and Nonaligned States: Between Nato and the Warsaw Pact* (Wilmington, DE, 1988). On Austria and Finland, see Gunter Bischof, *Austria in the First Cold War, 1945–1955: The Leverage of the Weak* (London, 1999) and Jussi Hanhimäki, *Containing Coexistence* (Kent, OH, 1997).

For American attitudes towards the Third World in general, see Scott Bills, *Empire and Cold War: The Roots of US–Third World Antagonism, 1945–47* (Basingstoke, 1990), H. W. Brands, *The Specter of Neutralism: The United States and the Emergence of the Third World, 1947–1960* (New York, 1989), Gabriel Kolko, *Confronting the Third World: United States Foreign Policy, 1945–1980* (New York, 1988), Zachary Karabell, *Architects of Intervention: The United States, the Third World, and the Cold War, 1946–1962* (Baton Rouge, LA, 1999), Peter Rodman, *More Precious than Peace: The Cold War and the Struggle for the Third World* (New York, 1994) and Kathryn Slater and Andrew L. Johns (eds), *The Eisenhower Administration, the Third World and the Globalization of the Third World* (Lanham, MD, 2006). For the influence of 'modernization' theory on the Kennedy administration, see Michael E. Latham, *Modernization as Ideology: American Social Science and 'Nation Building' in the Kennedy Era* (Chapel Hill, NC,

2002) and for the population issue, see Matthew Connelly, 'To Inherit the Earth: Imagining World Population from the Yellow Peril to the Population Bomb', *Journal of Global History* (2006), vol.1, pp. 299–319. For Soviet policy, see Margot Light (ed.), *Troubled Friendships: Moscow's Third World Ventures* (London, 1993), Galia Golan, *The Soviet Union and National Liberation Movements in the Third World* (London, 1988) and Andrjez Korbonski and Francis Fukuyama (eds), *The Soviet Union and the Third World: The Last Three Decades* (Ithaca, NY, 1987). For a general overview of the linkages between superpower confrontation and the Third World, see Odd Arne Westad, *The Global Cold War: Third World Interventions and the Making of our Times* (Cambridge, 2005).

On Indian relations with the Great Powers, see Robert C. Horn, *Soviet–Indian Relations: Issues and Influence* (New York, 1982), Dennis Merrill, *Bread and the Ballot: The United States and India's Economic Development, 1947–1963* (Chapel Hill, NC, 1990), Anita Inder Singh, *The Limits of British Influence: South Asia and the Anglo-American Relationship, 1947–56* (London, 1993), Robert McMahon, *Cold War on the Periphery: The United States, India and Pakistan* (New York, 1994) and Andrew Rotter, *Comrades at Odds: The United States and India, 1947–1964* (Ithaca, NY, 2000). For readings on China and the Third World see Chapter 14.

The best book on the history of the economic relationship between the North and the South is David Fieldhouse, *The West and the Third World* (Oxford, 1999), but see also Stephen Krasner, *Structural Conflict: The Third World against Global Liberalism* (Berkeley, CA, 1985). For explanations of dependency and under-development theory, see Ian Roxborough, *Theories of Underdevelopment* (Basingstoke, 1979), Vicky Randall and Robin Theobald, *Political Change and Underdevelopment: A Critical Introduction to Third World Politics* (Basingstoke, 1998), Thomas C. Patterson, *Change and Development in the Twentieth Century* (Oxford, 1999) and R. Kingsbury, J. Remenyi, J. McKay and J. Hunt, *Key Issues in Development* (Basingstoke, 2004). A useful introductory overview of the world economy since 1980 is Robert Solomon, *The Transformation of the World Economy* (Basingstoke, 1999).

The 'developmental states': Japan, South Korea and Taiwan, 1945 – 2007

Introduction

An important feature of the post-war era was the incredible economic growth achieved by the non-communist states of East Asia, and in particular the record of Japan, which by the 1970s had become the second largest capitalist economy in the world after the United States. For a region that lay in ruins in 1945 as the result of Japan's doomed challenge to the West, this was a remarkable change in fortunes. Moreover, this success is especially noteworthy when it is contrasted with the far less impressive growth rates in Latin America and Africa, and begs the question whether the methods used by the East Asian states could be exported to other developing countries.

To understand why the capitalist states in East Asia have been able to achieve this 'economic miracle', as it is sometimes called, it is necessary not only to concentrate on economic factors, but also to examine the political environment within the region. In particular, it is important to analyse the impact that both the legacy of the **Pacific War** and the course of the Cold War had on developments in East Asia. For example, all too often the history of post-war Japan is written as though the country existed in its own universe, in which it selfishly concentrated

Pacific War
The phrase usually used to refer to the Allied war against Japan from 1941 to 1945.

on economic growth while other countries engaged in the serious business of resisting communism. In fact, its relationship with the Cold War was far more extensive and significant than this image would imply in terms of both Japan's international relations and its domestic politics. This becomes even clearer if Japan is seen in its regional context, for in East Asia, as the histories of South Korea and Taiwan attest, the Cold War was a permanent and inescapable fact of life. Indeed, it can be argued that the 'economic miracle' in East Asia would not have happened outside the Cold War environment, and that this alone suggests that the model of development that worked in the region is too historically specific to be exported to the outside world.

The American occupation of Japan

On 2 September 1945 Japan signed the official document of surrender ending the Pacific War in a ceremony led by General Douglas MacArthur, the Supreme Commander Allied Powers (SCAP, an acronym also given to the occupying bureaucracy under his control). For the next seven years the United States occupied Japan, and initiated a massive campaign of reform designed to remove all vestiges of militarism and feudalism so that the defeated Power could never again threaten the international order. Notably, in contrast to the situation in Germany, it decided to keep a Japanese government in being, as well as allowing the emperor to stay on his throne. The rationale behind this was that if the Japanese themselves implemented the American reforms this would help to legitimize the 'new' Japan, making it difficult for the elite to turn the clock back once the occupation was over.

The American occupation of Japan can be divided into two distinct eras. From 1945 to 1947 SCAP concentrated on establishing democracy and pluralism. In pursuit of these goals it encouraged the growth of the labour movement, enfranchised women and engaged in an extensive agricultural reform policy to eradicate land tenancy, which was seen as having contributed to the rise of ultra-nationalism in the 1930s. In addition, many of those associated with militarism were either put on trial or purged from public life. This affected former army and navy personnel and some right-wing politicians, but in a spirit of conservative pragmatism was not applied to the royal family or to the bureaucrats and industrialists needed to run the country. Most important of all, in 1947 a new constitution was promulgated. This vested all political authority in the prime minister and the Diet, stated that the emperor was merely to be a 'symbol' of the state, and, in **Article 9**, declared that Japan renounced the right to go to war and, accordingly, to possess armed forces.

By 1948 this 'liberal' phase of the occupation had run its course, for in that year, in what is referred to as the '**reverse course**', the United States began to change tack and stress instead the need for economic recovery and eventually rearmament. This transformation in occupation policy was caused by a number

Article 9
Article in the Japanese Constitution of 1947 barring the country from going to war and possessing armed forces. Later interpreted to mean that Japan still had the right to self-defence and could maintain armed forces designed with that purpose in mind.

reverse course
The change of emphasis from democratization to economic reconstruction that the United States introduced in its occupation of Japan, 1947–49.

of concerns, such as the need to re-establish Japan as a key player in the world economy, and the fear that continued economic dislocation would encourage the growth of communism. In order to create a stronger economy, SCAP introduced in 1949 a policy of financial austerity, designed to curb government expenditure, reduce inflation and encourage the growth of the export sector by giving it preferential access to raw materials and foreign currency earnings. Significantly for the future it also pegged the yen at the competitive exchange rate of ¥360 to $1. Assisting SCAP in its new policy was the government of Shigeru Yoshida, which came to office in October 1948. Yoshida was a former diplomat of marked anti-communist views. Like many of the Japanese conservative elite, he felt that the 'liberal' period in the occupation had gone too far, and he welcomed the 'reverse course' with its emphasis on building for prosperity and reining in the Japanese Left. In addition, Yoshida was keen to co-operate because he believed that the rapid re-establishment of economic and social stability would help lead to the end of the occupation.

see Chapter 10

By 1951 Washington decided that the time had come to bring the occupation to a conclusion. Accordingly, in September a peace treaty was signed at an international conference in San Francisco, which stated that Japan would regain its full sovereignty in April 1952. The treaty was a deliberately lenient document. It formally ended Japanese control over its empire and stated that it should pay reparations to the states that it had occupied in South-East Asia. One of the few punitive measures was that Japan did not regain control over the Ryukyu Islands, which were to remain indefinitely under American control. The settlement did not, however, end Japan's state of war with all countries, for the Soviet Union and India refused to sign the treaty and neither Chinese regime had been invited to attend the conference.

At the same time as this rather bland document was signed into international law, another treaty was also being concluded – a security pact between Japan and the United States. This controversial treaty has been at the centre of Japanese foreign and security policy ever since, and is therefore worth studying in some detail. During the first part of the 'reverse course' security had not been an important issue; indeed, in the late 1940s most American policy-makers were content to see Japan as a neutral, demilitarized state in line with the constitution. However, by 1951 the Korean War meant that this was no longer deemed to be a feasible option. Instead, American policy-makers believed that if Japan was again to become a sovereign state it must rearm and join the Western alliance system. It might be thought that the Japanese conservative elite would have greeted this complete reversal in American policy with great satisfaction, for the ban on possessing armed forces was a humiliating reminder of Japan's defeat and its new lowly status. However, while Yoshida was desperate to win back Japan's independence, he was in fact loath to rearm. He feared that military expenditure would direct scarce economic resources away from domestic growth, and felt that both politically and socially it was too early to contemplate the revival of those elements that had plunged Japan into the disastrous Pacific War. He therefore sought in his talks with the Americans in 1951 to place Japan under America's protection, but to avoid having to reconstruct its armed forces.

American commentators in the 1980s frequently argued that Yoshida successfully achieved his goal, for the Security Treaty did not commit Japan to full-scale rearmament. This, it has been contended, laid the foundations for what is referred to as the 'free ride', in which Japan, liberated from the burden of paying for its own defence, was able to concentrate on generating economic growth under an American security umbrella. However, the reality of the situation was that Yoshida's refusal to contemplate full rearmament cost Japan dearly in the short term. Unable to rely on the Japanese to protect themselves, the United States decided to use the Security Treaty to turn its bases in Japan into a bastion for the defence of East Asia, even if this compromised Japanese sovereignty. Accordingly, under the conditions of the treaty, Washington won the right to use bases in Japan for regional defence without having to consult the Japanese government. In addition, in a separate administrative agreement signed in February 1952, American forces in Japan were given virtually extra-territorial rights. Moreover, in the wake of the San Francisco conference, Washington acted to limit Japan's diplomatic freedom of movement by making it clear that Congress would not ratify the peace treaty unless Japan opened relations with Jiang Jieshi's government on Taiwan rather than with the **People's Republic of China** (PRC). This was a bitter blow for Japan, which traditionally had close commercial ties with mainland China, but under American pressure it had no choice but to comply.

Thus, as the occupation came to an end, Japan was already heavily influenced by the Cold War between the United States and the Soviet Union. Its economic revival was being sponsored by Washington in order to assist with the stabilization of Asia and to forestall the growth of communism in Japan, while strategically and politically it was locked into the Western alliance system as a distinctly unequal partner. The question for Japan as it regained its independence was whether it was content to remain in this subordinate position and take advantage of America's interest in its stability and growth, or whether it should seek to improve its position and gain greater flexibility and equality of status.

People's Republic of China (PRC)
The official name of communist or mainland China. The PRC came into existence in 1949 under the leadership of Mao Zedong.

The '1955 system' and the revision of the Security Treaty

In 1952 a number of views existed about Japan's future. On the Left all shades of opinion were opposed to the security ties with America, but while the communists favoured alignment with the Soviet Union, moderate socialists felt that Japan should occupy a more neutralist and pacifist position that would remain true to the spirit of the constitution. Among the conservative parties there was also division. On one side, Yoshida and his supporters felt that Japan should adhere to the status quo, thus concentrating on economic growth while maintaining a low security posture. On the other, recently de-purged right-wing politicians, such as Yukio Hatoyama and Nobusuke Kishi, believed that Yoshida had given too much away in the Security Treaty and that Japan should seek to rearm and establish a more equal relationship with the United States. Yoshida's government was thus under attack from both the Right and the Left. Furthermore, the United States itself was by no means reconciled to Japan's low security posture. In 1953 the Eisenhower administration pressed Japan to transform its existing paramilitary force, which had been established in 1950 to maintain internal order, into a proper army. It was difficult for Yoshida to refuse this request, for Japan still relied on American economic aid. During the Korean War the Japanese economy had begun to recover, due largely to the American need for trucks, clothing, bedding and other goods for its armed forces. Indeed, the Japanese motor company Toyota was saved from imminent bankruptcy by American military procurements. However, once the conflict in Korea ended in 1953 there was widespread concern that if American military procurements were curtailed, the economy would tip back into recession. Therefore, under pressure from the Right, and fearing that refusal would jeopardize American procurements, Yoshida agreed in May 1954 to set up the Self-Defence Force (SDF), an army, navy and air force in all but name, with a ceiling of 150,000 men. This, however, was to be Yoshida's last major act, for in December of that year he was forced out of office and replaced by a new government led by his rival, Hatoyama.

Yoshida's fall from power seemed to presage a resolution to the question of where Japan was heading, for it suggested that those who favoured remilitarization had won the debate on the Right. This assumption appeared to be confirmed when, in the wake of Yoshida's dismissal, a radical realignment of political forces took place that was to set the structural framework for Japanese politics over the next forty years. In November 1955 the socialists, who had split into moderates and radicals earlier in the decade, managed to put their differences behind them and merged to re-establish the Japanese Socialist Party (JSP). The vision of a newly united democratic left wing in Japanese politics was deeply alarming to the politicians on the Right and to the business community and resulted in the conservative parties merging into one organization, the Liberal Democratic Party (LDP). This was a dramatic shift, for at a stroke it internalized the Cold War within Japanese politics by formalizing a strict Right–Left polarization. Moreover, by bringing the various conservative groupings under one umbrella, this new '1955 system' overcame the instability of the previous years and set the road for LDP dominance over Japanese politics.

To many observers the modern era in Japan can be traced back to this rearranging of the political jigsaw, for the LDP was to rule from this point uninterruptedly until 1993, with the JSP as the main opposition party. However, while the structure of Japanese politics was established in 1955, the policy agenda remained in a state of flux, with Hatoyama and Kishi pushing for a rearmed and politically assertive Japan while Yoshida and his followers continued to argue for a low security profile and concentration on economic development.

When the LDP formed, its first task was to support Hatoyama's government. Hatoyama was a veteran party politician and former cabinet member from the pre-war era, who felt aggrieved at Japan's new lowly status in world affairs. He was determined to follow a more independent line in foreign policy than Yoshida, and this was manifested in his desire to negotiate a peace treaty with the Soviet Union and to expand Japanese trade at an unofficial level with the PRC. His

Federal Republic of Germany (FRG)
The German state created in 1949 out of the former American, British and French occupation zones. Also known as West Germany. In 1990 the GDR merged into the FDR, thus ending the post-war partition of Germany.

see Chapter 9

United Nations (UN)
An international organization established after the Second World War to replace the League of Nations. Since its establishment in 1945, its membership has grown to 192 countries.

North Atlantic Treaty Organization (NATO)
Established by the North Atlantic Treaty (4 April 1949) signed by Belgium, Canada, Denmark, France, Great Britain, Iceland, Italy, Luxembourg, the Netherlands, Norway, Portugal and the United States. Greece and Turkey entered the alliance in 1952 and the Federal Republic of Germany in 1955. Spain became a full member in 1982. In 1999 the Czech Republic, Hungary and Poland joined in the first post-Cold War expansion, increasing the membership to nineteen countries.

U-2 spy plane
An American high-altitude reconnaissance aircraft used to fly over Soviet and other hostile territories.

diplomatic efforts were not, however, wholly successful. Talks with Moscow in 1955–56 foundered over the issue of the future of the southernmost four islands in the Kurile island chain in the north-west Pacific. Hatoyama demanded that these islands, which were under Soviet occupation, should be returned to Japanese control, but for strategic and prestige reasons Russia was only willing to agree to pass back two of the four. Unwilling to make an agreement on these terms and, moreover, under considerable American pressure not to do so, Hatoyama decided to follow the formula that Adenauer had adopted for **FRG**–Soviet relations, that is, to agree to mutual diplomatic recognition without a formal peace treaty. This had the limited advantage that the Soviet Union was willing to waive its veto over Japanese entry into the **United Nations** (**UN**), which finally took place in 1956. Meanwhile, there was some expansion of trade with the PRC, but there were strict limits owing to the American-led sanctions regime against China.

Hatoyama resigned at the end of 1956 and after a short interregnum Nobusuke Kishi emerged as the new LDP leader and prime minister. Kishi was an even more controversial figure than Hatoyama, for he had acted as the minister of munitions in General Tōjō's wartime cabinet and in 1946 had been arraigned as a Class A war criminal, although the case against him never came to trial. Like Hatoyama before him, Kishi yearned to strengthen Japan, but in contrast to his predecessor he intended to do this by first putting the alliance with the United States on a more equal basis before turning to regional matters and the issue of further rearmament. He therefore made his priority the revision of the Security Treaty. Talks about this began in 1958 and a revised treaty was finally signed in Washington in January 1960. Under its terms the United States had to consult the Japanese government before using its forces to counter a threat to Japan or to the region, and the administrative agreement was brought into line with those that regulated the conduct of American troops in **NATO** countries.

Once the treaty was signed, it had to be ratified by the legislatures in both countries. This process led to the biggest political crisis in post-war Japanese history. In order to understand why this issue became so controversial it is necessary to look at it from a number of angles. One important factor was that since 1954 the pacifist movement in Japan had made great strides as the country slowly came to terms with the scale of devastation at Hiroshima and Nagasaki. During the occupation the Americans had suppressed the evidence that the atomic bombs had long-term implications for public health, but from 1952 this material entered the public domain. Moreover, Japan's sense of being a victim of the atomic age was exacerbated further by the *Lucky Dragon* incident in 1954, when the crew of a Japanese trawler was irradiated during an American nuclear test. Pacifism was also stimulated by the Cold War and particularly the bitter Sino-American hostility, which in 1958 threatened to escalate into war in the second offshore islands crisis. If this were not enough, in the spring of 1960, just before the Diet began to deliberate on the Security Treaty, East–West relations were disturbed by the shooting down of an American **U-2 spy plane** above the Soviet Union, which led to the cancellation of a four-power summit in Paris. Security issues were thus increasingly controversial.

Pacifism, however, was not the only stimulus to dissent. Equally significant was that the Left increasingly perceived Kishi to be a dangerous throwback to Japan's militaristic past because of the reactionary nature of his domestic programme. In particular, his government's abortive attempt in 1958 to widen police powers of arrest suggested that it had authoritarian tendencies similar to those that had existed in the 1930s. Added to this was Kishi's arrogant hostility towards the need for political consensus, which was viewed by left-wing intellectuals as showing a basic lack of sympathy for democracy. This image of Kishi made it easy to believe that he had a more sinister agenda than just gaining equality with the United States, and that he intended to use revision of the Security Treaty as a stepping stone to abrogating Article 9 and perhaps committing Japan to a multilateral defence pact in Asia. Moreover, adding extra tension to an already combustible situation was the fact that the Security Treaty debate coincided with a deep crisis in labour relations, the fractious Miike coal-mine dispute, which further polarized Japanese politics.

With a large measure of support for its stance, the JSP therefore tried to obstruct the ratification of the treaty when it arrived in the Lower House in May 1960. Kishi reacted in typically intolerant style by forcing through a quick vote in a manner that did nothing to enhance his democratic credentials. The JSP and its allies then took the battle on to the streets, and a series of large-scale demonstrations took place in which one female participant was killed. These protests did not deter the Upper House from ratification on 20 June which finally made the treaty law, but they did lead to the cancellation of the first American presidential visit to Japan as it was deemed that Eisenhower's security could not be ensured. Taking the blame for this humiliation, and having lost the support of his party and the business community, who were aghast at the social instability unleashed by treaty revision, Kishi announced on 24 June his decision to stand down as prime minister.

Kishi was quickly replaced by a new LDP prime minister, Hayato Ikeda. Ikeda was a protégé of Yoshida, and his government saw Japan take a new very different political course. Recognizing that Kishi had brought Japan to the brink of a political abyss through his obsession with the security issue and his undemocratic tendencies, Ikeda played down national defence, created a new atmosphere of consensus by rebuilding dialogue with the JSP, and introduced a policy agenda whose central theme was that by the end of the 1960s Japan should have doubled its national income. Ikeda's 'income-doubling' concept was a vital turning point in Japanese history, for in accepting the country's discomfort with its expansionist past, and therefore eschewing defence and instead emphasizing economic growth, he set the policy parameters for Japanese politics for the next three decades. It can thus be argued that while 1955 was significant, in that the developments of that year established the structure of Japanese politics, 1960 was in the end more important because the policy decisions of that year created modern Japan.

High-speed growth and its discontents

Ikeda's decision to concentrate on economic growth had a solid foundation, for the Japanese economy had begun to expand markedly from the mid-1950s onwards. In particular, this period had witnessed an increase in the productivity of heavy industry with a substantial rise in steel production and Japan becoming the world's largest shipbuilder. In addition, under the protection of tariffs on foreign goods, Japan was able to make progress in **import substitution** by, for example, building up its automobile and electronic industries. Ikeda worked to stimulate growth by further stressing the importance of exports, thus leading to a huge increase in Japan's trade with both the developed and the developing nations. As a result, his ambitions for Japan were met beyond anyone's wildest expectations, for in the 1960s the economy grew at an average rate of 10.4 per cent per annum, overtaking those of France, Britain and West Germany.

Japan was able to achieve such rapid growth for a number of reasons. One of the most important was the way in which the government acted to create an economic environment that stimulated growth. A vital element in this strategy was the **Ministry of International Trade and Industry (MITI)**, which utilized methods that had previously been adopted during wartime to direct national resources to stimulate growth in certain sectors of the economy, such as steel production and shipbuilding. For example, MITI used its control over the distribution of imported raw materials and foreign currency earnings to favour those sectors of industry that were seen as vital to future economic growth, and used tariffs and other mechanisms to protect Japanese companies. It also worked to diffuse good practices, such as quality control and the lifetime employment system, and encouraged companies to disseminate technology and patents. Moreover, it worked closely with the Ministry of Finance and the Bank of Japan

import substitution
The process whereby a state attempts to achieve economic growth by raising protective tariffs to keep out imports and replacing them with indigenously produced goods.

see Table 14.1

Ministry of International Trade and Industry (MITI)
The Japanese government ministry most closely associated with directing Japan's economic growth.

Table 14.1 Japanese economic growth, 1955–65

Year	Growth rate (as % change over previous year)
1955	8.8
1956	7.3
1957	7.4
1958	5.6
1959	8.9
1960	13.4
1961	14.4
1962	7.0
1963	10.4
1964	13.2
1965	5.1

Source: Johnson (1982, p. 237)

to ensure that public and private capital was made widely available to the key industrial sectors.

In retrospect, the political scientist Chalmers Johnson has characterized Japan as constituting a '**developmental state**'. What he means by this is that, in contrast to the American model of capitalism, where the government acts largely to ensure fair competition, and to the communist model, in which the state both plans and controls industrial growth, in Japan the state played a direct role in planning the development of a capitalist economy. As Johnson argues, perhaps the best way to conceptualize this is to say that Japan maintained the tools of a wartime economy during a period of peace.

However, as well as these domestic factors, Japan was assisted by the fact that the international environment favoured growth. For many of the industrialized nations the period between the Korean War and the first oil shock of 1973 was one of steady progress because of the stability provided by the American-dominated **Bretton Woods** financial and trading system, with its fixed exchange rates and steady reduction of protective tariffs. The expansion of international trade in this period was naturally advantageous to a state that had orientated itself towards exports. In addition, it is important to note that the stability of the capitalist economies at this time was underpinned by the low cost of the major new energy source for industry – oil. Japan was particularly well placed to take advantage of the shift towards oil for much of its industrial plant was new, replacing factories that had been destroyed during the war. In addition, Japan, as the world's most cost-effective shipbuilder, was able to benefit from the ever-growing demand for ocean-going oil tankers.

Another vital factor in Japan's rapid growth was that, primarily for Cold War reasons, the United States was prepared to go to great lengths to nurture and sponsor its development within the Bretton Woods system. During the 1950s Washington continued to adhere to the view that Japanese economic growth was the one sure way to undermine the appeal of the Left within Japanese politics. Added to the belief that a strong Japanese economy would have a beneficial effect on Asia, this meant that it was very much in American interests to ensure that the Japanese economy remained healthy. In order to assist Japan economically the United States provided help in a number of areas. For example, it maintained its procurements for the American military throughout the decade, and eased Japan's path into the world economy by sponsoring its entry into the **General Agreement on Tariffs and Trade (GATT)** organization in 1955. Moreover, Washington tolerated Japan's use of protectionist restrictions, such as high tariff barriers and limits on foreign direct investment, to defend its growing heavy industry sector. In addition, noting that Japan was denied access to the Chinese market and that South-East Asia was not sufficient to soak up Japan's exports, the Eisenhower administration in 1955 allowed Japanese goods, such as textiles, access to the American domestic market. The United States therefore acquiesced in the protectionist policies pursued by MITI and helped to provide an international trading environment for Japanese exports. This policy continued in the 1960s. Disturbed by the storm over the revision of the Security Treaty, the Kennedy administration lowered American trade barriers, as it believed that this would

developmental state
A term coined by the political scientist Chalmers Johnson to refer to a state which plays a direct strategic role in planning the development of a capitalist economy. First used in relation to Japan, but subsequently utilized more broadly to refer to South Korea, Taiwan and the developing countries in South-East Asia.

Bretton Woods
The site of an inter-Allied conference held in 1944 to discuss the post-war international economic order. The conference led to the establishment of the IMF and the World Bank. In the post-war era the links between these two institutions, the establishment of GATT and the convertibility of the dollar into gold were known as the Bretton Woods system. After the dollar's devaluation in 1971 the world moved to a system of floating exchange rates.

General Agreement on Tariffs and Trade (GATT)
An international agreement arising out of the Bretton Woods conference covering tariff levels and codes of conduct for international trade. The progressive lowering of tariffs took place in a succession of negotiating rounds. In 1995 it passed its work on to the World Trade Organization.

Debating Japan's 'economic miracle'

The most volatile debate in regard to modern Japanese history has been that over the methods Japan used to achieve its remarkable economic growth after 1945. In the 1950s and early 1960s American political scientists and historians, such as Edwin Reischauer, suggested that the Japanese recovery was a testament to the enlightened guidance provided by the United States. Japan was accordingly presented as an example of how the modernization theories of economists such as W. W. Rostow could work in practice. This in turn led to a backlash in Japan, in which Japanese economists proclaimed the indigenous, cultural roots of its success. This debate is described in a fascinating article by Laura Hein, 'Free-Floating Anxieties on the Pacific: Japan and the West Revisited', *Diplomatic History* (1996), vol. 20, pp. 411 – 37.

The nature of the analysis changed dramatically in 1982 with the appearance of Chalmers Johnson's highly influential book, *MITI and the Japanese Miracle* (Stanford, CA, 1982) in which he argued that the Japanese state, in the form of MITI, had been the key element in guiding the economy towards rapid growth. Japan, he argued, was a 'developmental state' that operated in a fundamentally different way to the American capitalist system. This thesis not only sparked off a new historical discourse, but also substantially influenced the contemporary debate in the United States about how it should deal with Japan and its ever-increasing trade surplus, and inspired a number of commentators to engage in 'Japan-bashing' books and articles. Gradually, a number of Johnson's contentions have been challenged. Writers such as Daniel Okimoto (1989) have demonstrated that MITI's record of 'administrative guidance' was far from flawless, while others, such as Kent Calder (1993) and Mark Mason (1992), have put more emphasis on the role of the large industrial companies. Furthermore, as the economic history of the Cold War becomes subject to greater scrutiny, the manner in which the United States encouraged Japanese growth is once again being studied, most notably in Aaron's Forsberg's book *America and the Japanese Miracle* (Chapel Hill, NC, 2000). The idea that there is a monocausal explanation for Japan's success is thus not sustainable.

Moreover, the nature and intensity of the debate have changed over time. In the 1980s the Japanese model appeared as a threat to the United States and as a possible panacea to the development conundrum, and therefore became one of the central research areas in the field of political economy. However, Japan's poor economic performance in the 1990s has undermined the relevance of the debate, making it increasingly of academic rather than political interest. Indeed, those working in this field now have to account for the relative failure of the Japanese system in the 1990s.

assist in the stabilization of Japanese politics. As a result, Japanese automobiles and motorcycles began to enter the American market for the first time and in 1965 the United States suffered its first trade deficit with Japan.

In addition, Japan continued to benefit commercially from the Cold War tensions in the region. As Sino-American tensions escalated in the mid-1960s and the situation in South Vietnam began to worsen, the United States was keen to use Japan's growing economic power to stabilize the region. In 1965 the United States brokered the opening of diplomatic relations between Japan and South Korea which previously had proved impossible owing to the lingering animosity between the two countries. This move, which in part was designed by Washington as a means of strengthening the Korean economy and reducing its reliance on the United States, opened a major new market for Japanese goods and investment. In addition, as the Vietnam War reached its peak, Washington encouraged Japan to expand its trade links with South-East Asia. Accordingly, in 1966 Japan extended credits to Thailand and Malaysia, helped with the restructuring of Indonesia's debt burden and became one of the largest contributors to the newly established Asian Development Bank. These economic measures helped to stimulate the regional economy, thus benefiting Japanese exports. Japan also gained directly from the Vietnam War, for the fact that the United States was engaged in a major war in East Asia meant that once again the procurement tap flowed freely, with hundreds of millions of dollars being earned every year.

see Chapter 12

Japan's economic success was thus achieved through the happy combination of a variety of domestic and international factors. However, such marked progress brought with it its own problems, particularly when it appeared to Washington that Japan was profiting from the Cold War but doing very little to contribute to the struggle against communism. This problem first arose during the Vietnam War. The Japanese government of Eisaku Sato, who replaced Ikeda in 1965, took an ambivalent attitude towards the war. On the one hand, Sato recognized that participation in the war would reopen the wounds that had appeared during the 1960 Security Treaty crisis, and that a low-key approach was therefore preferable. On the other, he acknowledged that the United States was, after all, the guarantor of Japanese security, and that he had therefore to prove Japan's loyalty to its ally. Moreover, by the mid-1960s a new issue had arisen that required Japan to woo the United States – its desire to see the rapid retrocession of Okinawa. Sato therefore followed a cautious line in which he expressed his public support for the American cause in Vietnam while at the same time not committing Japan in any substantial way to assist the war effort.

This policy succeeded in keeping the peace within Japan, but it did not impress Washington and helped to create a backlash that was to have pro- found consequences. The difficulties began for Sato with the appearance in Washington in January 1969 of the new Republican administration of Richard Nixon. Almost from the outset Nixon created problems for Japan by redefining American policy towards East Asia. His aim, as set out in the Nixon Doctrine of July 1969, was to reduce American commitments to the region by forcing allies such as Japan to take greater responsibility for their own defence. At first this new initiative seemed to have its desired effect. In November 1969 Sato held a summit conference with Nixon in Washington in which the former declared that Japan saw the security of South Korea and Taiwan as essential to its own. In return Nixon agreed that Okinawa would return to Japanese sovereignty in 1972, but that the United States would retain its military bases.

This promising start was, however, derailed by another issue – trade. At the summit Sato committed Japan to introduce new voluntary limits on its textile exports to the American market, but on his return to Tokyo he quickly reneged on his promise. Feeling betrayed, President Nixon decided to engage in a demonstration of power in the two 'Nixon shocks' of 1971. The first 'shock' came in July when he announced his intention to visit the PRC in the following year. In a calculated insult, Sato was only given one hour's notice of this major reorientation of American foreign policy. This shift in American thinking towards China suited Japan's purposes, for it brought the prospect of its finally being able to open trade links with the PRC, but the manner in which the announcement was made was disquieting. The following month saw a further surprise when, on 15 August, the anniversary of Japan's surrender, Nixon declared that the dollar would devalue and that a 10 per cent surcharge would be placed on imports entering the United States. In one fell swoop this action brought down the Bretton Woods order that had helped to nurture Japan's rise to prosperity and returned the international economy to a period of instability.

These two shocks made it clear that the United States was no longer prepared to ease Japan's path, and that the latter could not expect prosperity without responsibility. The era in which Japan, as a result of its vital position in the Cold War, could afford to 'hide under America's skirt' was thus drawing to an end. While the strategic alliance with the United States was not under threat, it was clear that Japan could and should do more to contribute to the stability of the international order by using its now enviable economic power.

Japan as an economic superpower

Group of 7 (G-7)
The Group of 7 was the organization of the seven most advanced capitalist economies – the United States, Japan, Canada, Germany, France, Italy and Britain – founded in 1976. The G-7 held and continues to hold annual summit meetings where the leaders of these countries discuss economic and political issues.

The years from 1972 to 1989 saw Japan become a major player in international politics in consequence of its economic power. Moreover, as a model of how to achieve prosperity, it provided inspiration to the newly industrializing states in Asia. During this period Japan became one of the key powers in the **Group of 7 (G-7)** and emerged as the largest provider of foreign aid to the Third World. However, its success came with a price, for the trade friction with the United States worsened, and it was faced with continuing calls from Washington for it to take a much greater share in the Cold War and the policing of the international system.

The LDP's immediate reaction to the 'Nixon shocks' and the growth of domestic discontent was to recognize the need for the country to change direction once again. Facing both external setbacks and domestic opposition, in 1972 Sato resigned and was replaced by a figure more attuned to the times, Kakuei Tanaka.

In foreign affairs Tanaka sought to take a more independent line than Sato. In 1972 he opened diplomatic relations with the PRC and sought to emulate Nixon's achievements by encouraging **détente** in the troubled Japanese–Soviet relationship. A further spur to this spirit of independence came in 1973 with **OPEC**'s decision during the October War to raise oil prices. This sudden move revealed Japan's alarming reliance on the Middle East for its energy requirements and led to a drive to improve relations with the oil producers, which included adopting a pro-Arab stance on Middle Eastern issues.

This marked the start of a new policy of 'omni-directional diplomacy' in which Japan sought to move beyond the Cold War paradigm and to secure its economic standing by widening its diplomatic links and encouraging international stability. One key aspect in this campaign was its effort to increase its provision of overseas development aid (ODA) to developing countries, and particularly those on which Japan relied for its raw material imports. The most important recipients of Japanese ODA were the member states of the **Association of South-East Asian Nations (ASEAN)**, which provided a key market for Japanese goods, supplied vital raw materials, including oil, and stood astride the communications route with the Middle East. ASEAN was keen to reciprocate Japan's interest and during the premiership of Takeo Fukuda from 1976 to 1978 the first Japan–ASEAN forum met to discuss economic ties and Fukuda became the first foreign visitor to an ASEAN summit. The late 1970s also saw an improvement in relations with the PRC. In 1978 a peace treaty was finally signed between the two countries and Japan became a major investor in Deng Xiaoping's modernization campaign.

While Japan was able to create better ties with the **Third World** and to cement its economic security, its relations with the United States entered a difficult period. In the economic field, the basic problem was that, compared with its competitors, Japan was too successful. The Japanese economy weathered the difficulties engendered by the oil-price hikes of 1973 and 1979 better than its rivals, and the result was that its trade surpluses with the United States and the **European Community (EC)** began in the early 1980s to spiral out of control. This process was assisted by the fact that the first Reagan administration allowed the dollar to increase in value, thus making Japanese goods more competitive than ever in the American market. In 1985 the United States decided that the dollar should be devalued, and a mechanism to ensure this was arranged by the major economic powers in the **Plaza Accord**. Unfortunately, such was Japanese productivity by this stage that even this move made little difference to its inroads into the American economy, particularly as companies such as Toyota and Nissan ran subsidiary producers in the United States. By the late 1980s therefore there was increasing pressure from Congress on the American executive to take tougher action against Japanese exports and foreign direct investment.

In the field of security too, Japan's relations with the United States remained strained. From the late 1970s Japan deepened its security relationship with the United States in response to the Soviet Union's increasing capacity to project its maritime power into the Pacific. In 1978 the 'Guidelines for Japan–US Defence Co-operation' were adopted which spelt out the division of labour should there

détente
A term meaning the reduction of tensions between states. It is often used to refer to the superpower diplomacy that took place between the inauguration of Richard Nixon as the American president in 1969 and the Senate's refusal to ratify SALT II in 1980.

Organization of Petroleum Exporting Countries (OPEC)
The organization founded in 1960 to represent the interests of the leading oil-producing states in the Third World.

see Chapter 21

see Chapter 15

Association of South-East Asian Nations (ASEAN)
Organization founded in 1967 by Indonesia, Malaysia, the Philippines, Singapore and Thailand to provide a forum for regional economic co-operation. From 1979, and the Third Indochina War, it took on more of a political and security role. Membership increased with the accession of Brunei in 1984, Vietnam in 1995, Burma in 1997 and Cambodia in 1999.

Third World
A collective term of French origin for those states that are part of neither the developed capitalist world nor the communist bloc. It includes the states of Latin America, Africa, the Middle East, South Asia and South-East Asia. Also referred to as 'the South' in

contrast to the developed 'North'.

European Community (EC)
Formed in 1967 with the fusion of the European Economic Community (EEC, founded in 1957), the European Atomic Energy Community (EURATOM, also founded in 1957), and the European Coal and Steel Community (ECSC, founded in 1952). The EC contained many of the functions of the European Union (EU, founded in 1992). Unlike the later EU, the EC consisted primarily of economic agreements between member states.

Plaza Accord
The agreement reached by the G-5 (G-7 minus Canada and Italy) finance ministers at the Plaza Hotel in New York in 1985 to raise the value of the yen and the Deutschmark and to lower that of the dollar. The accord helped to lead to the Japanese 'bubble economy' of the late 1980s.

Plate 14.1 Tokyo, Japan, 1998. Neon lights in the Ginza area, Tokyo's most famous shopping and entertainment district. (Photo: Brad Rickerby/Getty Images)

be an armed attack on Japan. This was followed in 1983 by a Japanese commitment to undertake maritime patrols up to 1,000 kilometres into the Pacific Ocean. The prime minister by this time, Yasuhiro Nakasone, shared the anti-communist attitude of Ronald Reagan, and was keen to meet American demands for increased Japanese defence spending and greater co-operation in the development of defence technology, including the 'Star Wars' project. However, Nakasone had to tread carefully to avoid reawakening Japan's antipathy to security issues, and his effort to raise Japanese defence spending above 1 per cent of gross national product (GNP) yielded only temporary success. As a result, the United States maintained its doubts about whether Japan was pulling its weight.

It was at this point in the 1980s that the Americans accused Japan of having taken a 'free ride' on the back of the American security commitment in East Asia. As a result, a number of commentators in both Japan and the United States began to urge that now was the time for the country to revise the constitution, to rearm and become a 'normal state'. In other words that Japan should now put its guilt about the Pacific War to one side and translate its economic might into political power and play a full role within international politics. This, however, was not to prove easy, for the pacifism engendered by the disasters of 1945 was still strong in Japan, as were memories of the 1960 crisis over revision of the Security Treaty. Knowing that the Japanese public was suspicious of this new direction, the political elite was duly cautious, and thus, although there was much rhetoric about constitutional revision and rearmament, little progress was made.

The troubled nineties

Japan's failure to reform in the 1980s was to a large degree a result of the continuing effect of the '1955 system', which, as Gerald Curtis has argued, meant that the Cold War had become internalized within Japanese politics. Put simply, the LDP could not risk abrupt change which might alienate voters and allow the JSP into power, for the latter was influenced by Marxism and was far from being a social democratic party along the lines of those that existed in Western Europe. However, this major obstacle to reform was removed between 1989 and 1991 with the collapse of the Soviet Union, which at one fell swoop made the stark Right–Left polarization of politics an anachronism. It was therefore possible for the radical conservatives who sought to make Japan a 'normal state' to contemplate breaking the LDP's monopoly on power. Further destabilizing the situation was the fact that the Gulf War of 1990–91 painfully revealed the limitations of Japan's reliance on economic power. Although Japan provided the money that bankrolled the campaign, it won little thanks from the United States for this essentially passive role and its efforts to persuade the Diet to allow it to contribute forces ended in a humiliating retreat. The case for Japan to reassess its role in world affairs was thus becoming painfully urgent.

Faced with this situation, various dissident elements within the LDP, of whom the most important was Ichiro Ozawa, decided to gamble on a realignment of the forces within Japanese politics by allying with the JSP. The result was that in June 1993 Ozawa and his supporters helped to bring down the LDP government of Kiichi Miyazawa. In the subsequent election in July the LDP failed to retain its majority and was replaced in government by a coalition of the opposition parties led by Morihiro Hosokawa, but with Ozawa as its *éminence grise*. The dramatic end to the LDP's monopoly on power suggested that Japan was on the verge of major changes to its domestic and international political agendas and that it would perhaps emerge from the reform process stronger and more assertive than before. However, the events of 1993 turned out to be but the beginning of a long drawn-out transformation of Japanese politics rather than a short, sharp revolution. Over the next seven years Japan went through a further six prime ministers and even the return of the LDP to power in 1994 failed to bring about a restoration of political stability.

One of the main reasons for this instability was that this period of political turmoil coincided with a previously seemingly unthinkable phenomenon, namely a prolonged economic slump. Japan's economic downturn had its roots in the exuberance of the 1980s. In 1985 the Ministry of Finance, fearing that the Plaza Accord might lead to a recession, had decided to ease controls over the money supply in order to allow firms to raise cheap loans that could be invested in increasing productivity. The problem was that this increase in liquidity went too far and sparked off a wave of speculative investments in property and share values. The result was the 'bubble economy' of the late 1980s, during which the value of the shares traded on the Japanese stock exchange between October 1987 and December 1989 increased by 120 per cent. This upward trend could not be sustained for ever and in 1990 the 'bubble' burst, leaving Japanese banks and companies with a heavy debt burden. At first it was assumed that this was merely a temporary downturn as the continuing vitality of the export-orientated companies led to an underestimation of the increasing weakness of the financial sector and the hope that Japan would move back towards growth without having to undertake any substantial reforms. Unfortunately in 1997 this hope was dashed when an increase in the consumption tax led to an abrupt fall in consumer spending and Japan sank into a stubborn recession, which even the traditional means of stimulating demand, increased public works, failed to cure.

Exacerbating Japan's problems was the fact that its moment of greatest economic weakness in 1997 coincided with a severe downturn in the wider Asian economy. The 1980s and early 1990s had seen investment capital pour into South-East Asia in order to bankroll that region's rapid industrialization and urban development, which, as in Taiwan and South Korea, took their inspiration from the Japanese model. However, in mid-1997 the severe current account deficit and lack of effective supervisory institutions in Thailand led to speculation against the Thai baht, forcing a 50 per cent devaluation, and the haemorrhaging of foreign capital out of the country. In what was seen as a textbook example of the perils of economic globalization, the speculators then turned on other Asian economies, wreaking havoc, particularly in Indonesia where the rupiah lost 60 per cent of its value.

For many Western observers Japan's continuing stagnation, allied to the Asian financial crisis, demonstrated that the 'developmental state' did not after all represent the way of the future. Indeed, by the end of the 1990s some speculated as to whether the only solution was some sort of neo-liberal revolution of the type introduced in the 1980s by Reagan and Thatcher. The problem though, as ever, was whether there was anyone within Japanese politics who was both bold and powerful enough to contemplate an assault on the social and political consensus. In 2000 the LDP finally found a leader with the will to act – Junichirō Koizumi. From 2000 to 2006 Koizumi's government introduced measures that sought to revitalize the Japanese economy by cutting bad debt and by allowing inefficient businesses to go under, even at the cost of unemployment running above 5 per cent. Some success was achieved, but the results struggled to live up to the rhetoric. Moreover, once Koizumi stepped down from power, political instability and doubts about Japan's future direction quickly re-emerged.

Japan's neighbours: South Korea and Taiwan

At the same time as Japan dealt with its political and economic woes, it also found its attempts to take a more assertive role in the world became unstuck. This was not rooted solely in continued uneasiness about its own history and domestic suspicion of 'normal state' rhetoric, but was also a response to its troubled relationship with the other countries in East Asia, both communist and non-communist. At first glance this might seem strange, for in a number of ways the post-war historical trajectory of South Korea and Taiwan, the other two leading non-communist states in East Asia, was similar to that of Japan, and their trade links have been extensive. One might therefore have expected Tokyo to provide a measure of regional leadership. But this was not to be.

The greatest degree of similarity between these three states lay in the economic field. The rise of South Korea and Taiwan as economic powers in their own right began in the 1960s, when these countries shifted from a concentration on import substitution to a focus on the production of manufactured goods for export. The success of this formula can be seen in the fact that between 1960 and 1990 both countries achieved growth rates of more than 8 per cent per annum and by the early 1990s produced jointly 8 per cent of the world's manufactured goods. Obviously, one similarity with Japan was the emphasis on exports, but in addition one can note that in all three countries the state invested heavily in selected sectors of industry and, through highly trained bureaucrats, played an important role in directing the growth of the economy. Moreover, in all three countries the emphasis on economic growth as the main priority of the state, instead of social issues and welfare provision, appears to have met with general consensus. Thus South Korea and Taiwan can also be defined as following the 'developmental state' model.

The roots of these similarities can be found in a number of common historical and political factors. The first is that, to a degree, the three states share the same bureaucratic tradition. After all, both Korea and Taiwan had been Japanese colonies until 1945 and therefore some of their civil servants had been exposed to Japan's wartime efforts to mobilize the economy. A second important factor was that Japan's defeat in 1945 created the conditions in which it was possible, as in Japan itself, for sweeping land reform programmes to be undertaken in South Korea and Taiwan, thus removing the landlord class as an obstacle to state activity. Third, for South Korea and Taiwan, perhaps even more so than for Japan, economic development was inspired by an atmosphere of crisis, in the knowledge that poverty would only heighten both the internal and external threat from Cold War enemies.

Adding an extra layer of common experience was the fact that all three states displayed a remarkable degree of political continuity, even though they possessed very different governmental systems. In Japan, although a democratic parliamentary system existed throughout the period, the LDP's hold on power meant that the country was in reality under one-party rule, albeit one in tune with the electorate. As a result Japan did not suffer the abrupt changes of policy that sometimes marred growth in the economies of Western Europe where parties from the Right and the democratic Left tended to alternate in government.

In the case of South Korea and Taiwan continuity was largely the result of repression rather than consensus. The fact that these states existed on the frontier of the Cold War divide meant that they needed strong autocratic leadership and could not afford to indulge in the luxury and uncertainties of democracy. The result in South Korea was that it suffered repressive rule under Syngman Rhee from 1948 to 1960 and then, after a brief and unstable brush with democracy in 1960–61, was governed by a military regime led first by Park Chung Hee

Guomindang (GMD)
The Chinese Nationalist party founded in 1913 by Sun Yatsen. Under the control of Jiang Jieshi, it came to power in China in 1928 and initiated a modernization programme before leading the country into war against Japan in 1937. It lost control over mainland China in 1949 as a result of the communist victory in the civil war. From 1949 it controlled Taiwan, overseeing the island's 'economic miracle', until its electoral defeat in 2000.

Republic of China (ROC)
The official name for the government of China in Taiwan.

Republic of Korea (ROK)
The official name of South Korea. The ROK came into existence in 1948 under the leadership of Syngman Rhee.

(1961–79) and then by Chun Doo Kwan (1980–87). Meanwhile, in Taiwan the **Guomindang (GMD)** completely controlled the state, with Jiang Jieshi remaining president until his death in 1975 and then being succeeded by his son, Jiang Jingguo, who died in 1988. Thus in each country, power was exercised by a powerful elite, which owing to its longevity was able to put into practice a coherent long-term programme designed to achieve and perpetuate rapid economic growth. In the end this economic growth, allied in the last years of the Cold War with a general global trend that emphasized democratization and human rights, led in both countries to the rise of a middle class that was determined to install representative government. The result was that by the late 1980s South Korea and Taiwan were on their way to becoming liberal democracies.

Finally, there are important parallels in the way in which the United States interacted with all three states. For the United States, Taiwan and South Korea were vital buffers to the expansion of the communist bloc towards Japan, but in consequence of their partitioned status they were also important as showcases to demonstrate that capitalism was superior to communism. Accordingly, as in the case of Japan, Washington was willing to provide these countries with extensive economic and military aid and to give them preferential access in the 1960s to the American market. The degree of American interest can be seen in the fact that between 1946 and 1978 South Korea received $6 billion in economic aid, which was only a little less than the total amount given to the whole of Africa over the same period. In addition, the United States played a vital role in facilitating the development of economic ties between Japan and the two front-line states. In 1952 it forced Tokyo to open ties with the **Republic of China (ROC)** and in 1965 played a key role in facilitating the normalization of relations between Japan and the **Republic of Korea (ROK)**. This was important because these interventions created the conditions whereby Japan became one of the key sources for capital investment in its neighbours.

The degree of shared experience and Japan's positive role in the industrialization of its neighbours did not, however, mean that Tokyo's relations with Seoul and Taipei were close and uncontroversial, for, just as memories of the Pacific War shaped Japan's desire to take a low security posture, so the experiences of South Korea and Taiwan as territories subsumed within the Japanese Empire influenced their attitudes towards their former colonial masters. In addition, as they represented partitioned nations, it was important for South Korea and Taiwan to emphasize their nationalist credentials. The danger was that otherwise a too compromising line might provide the PRC and North Korea with an opportunity to produce damaging propaganda. This fear was confirmed in 1965 when the normalization of Japan–ROK relations led to large-scale protests in Seoul and other cities, and denunciations from Pyongyang.

This lingering distrust has not dissipated over time. If anything, with politicians such as Nakasone, Ozawa and Koizumi talking of the need for Japan to become a 'normal state' and to take greater pride in its history and achievements, the suspicion has grown. Thus, when this discourse in Japan translated itself into events such as, in 1982 and 2005, the revision of Japanese school textbooks to play down its aggressive past, and the visits in 1985 and from 2000 to 2006 by

Nakasone and Koizumi respectively to honour the war dead at the Yasukuni shrine, the reaction among Japan's Asian neighbours was one of outrage. Both the PRC and South Korea were particularly vociferous in their criticisms of Japan, as they felt that the latter, far from being racked by guilt, had never atoned for its past crimes with either an apology or full reparations. This view was reinforced as revelations emerged that wartime Japan had experimented with biological weapons and conscripted women from its imperial possessions, in particular Korea, to service the sexual needs of the military.

Moreover, the strategic position in the region did not require Taiwan and South Korea to bury their grievances against Japan, for they were able to rely on America for security against their most direct enemies – the PRC and North Korea. Indeed, for all three states – Japan, South Korea and Taiwan – their closest bilateral relationship has always been the one with Washington. Tellingly, the only times that South Korea and Japan have moved closer together in the political field have coincided with periods when the American security commitment to the region was in doubt, namely in the aftermath of the Nixon Doctrine and President Carter's abortive move to withdraw American troops from the Korean peninsula in 1977–78.

The damage that these strained relations with its neighbours could cause to Japanese interests was made abundantly clear in 2005. One of the key aspects of Japan's quest to become a 'normal state' was its bid to acquire a permanent seat on the United Nations Security Council. By directly linking itself to other aspirants who sought this prestigious goal, such as Germany, India and Brazil, and increasing its aid to the Third World, the Japanese government appeared to be manoeuvring towards a successful outcome, particularly as it was clear that it had the support of the United States. Japan's optimism was, however, short lived, for in 2005 renewed controversy over its apparent lack of remorse for its conduct during the Second World War gave both the PRC and South Korea ample excuse to frustrate its aspirations. Indeed, that year saw Sino-Japanese relations deteriorate to their worst point since the reopening of diplomatic relations in 1972. Japan's tense relationship with its neighbours thus clearly continued to act as an important restraint on its efforts to turn its economic power into political might. By the mid-2000s Japan was therefore caught between two stools – it wished to transform itself into a 'normal state' in the future, but still found it difficult to escape its past.

Conclusion

The history of non-communist East Asia can therefore be seen as the result of the influence of both the Pacific War and the Cold War. Within Japan the dire outcome of the Pacific War inculcated a desire among the populace never to repeat the follies of that conflict. This led to an ingrained distrust of militarism and an emphasis on the need to respect consensus. Thus, although both Japanese conservative politicians and the United States sought to ensure that Japan played a full role as an ally in the Cold War, domestic opposition meant that this did not come about. Japan's significance within the Cold War was not, however, limited to a security role, for it was also a key element in the economic strength of the Western alliance. As such, the United States keenly sponsored its growth within the Bretton Woods system, and this, allied to the ingenuity of Japanese businessmen and bureaucrats, sparked Japan's phenomenal economic growth. Japan thus developed during the Cold War period into an anomalous entity – a purely economic superpower.

At the same time, South Korea and Taiwan were themselves transformed into economic powerhouses. Here too historical and political factors played a key role. Anchored in one of the 'hottest' regions in the Cold War, these two states had to strengthen themselves to cope with the external threat, and thus invested heavily in economic growth. In this their success was shaped both by their experience as colonies within the Japanese Empire and by the immense support provided by their superpower sponsor, the United States, which tolerated their **protectionism** and provided them with access to the vast American consumer market.

The rise of East Asia as the fastest-growing regional economy in the world was therefore crucially influenced by historically specific factors, and the success of the 'developmental state' model needs to be seen in this light. This in turn suggests that the idea that the East Asian model of development can readily be adopted by other developing states is surely mistaken, for it is not easy to replicate the conditions that existed within the region. Moreover, the fact that in the 1990s both Japan and South Korea experienced a marked economic downturn also suggests that the 'economic miracle' had been closely linked to the certainties of the Cold War years and that without this prop, the future success of the 'developmental state' was considerably less certain.

protectionism
The practice of regulating imports through high tariffs with the purpose of shielding domestic industries from foreign competition.

Recommended reading

There are a number of general introductions to the history and politics of Japan since 1945. Probably the best of these is J. A. A. Stockwin, *Governing Japan: Divided Politics in a Major Economy* (Oxford, 1999), but see also W. G. Beasley, *The Rise of Modern Japan* (London, 1990), Dennis Smith, *Japan since 1945: The Rise of an Economic Superpower* (Basingstoke, 1995) and Chushichi Tsuzuki, *The Pursuit of Power in Modern Japan 1825–1995* (Oxford, 2000). An important study that links security issues with domestic politics is John Welfield, *An Empire in Eclipse: Japan in the Postwar American Alliance System* (Atlantic Highlands, NJ, 1988). A good edited collection dealing with various aspects of modern Japan is Andrew Gordon (ed.), *Postwar Japan as History* (Berkeley, CA, 1993). The best introductions to Korea since 1945 are Bruce Cumings, *Korea's Place in the Sun: A Modern History* (New York, 1997), Adrian Buzo, *The Making of Modern Korea* (London, 2002) and Michael Robinson, *Korea's Twentieth Century Odyssey*

(Honolulu, HI, 2007). On Taiwan, see Murray Rubinstein, *Taiwan: A New History* (New York, 1999) and John Copper, *Taiwan: Nation-State or Province?* (Boulder, CO, 1999).

On the occupation of Japan and the effect of the American reform policies, see Michael Schaller, *The American Occupation of Japan: The Origins of the Cold War in Asia* (New York, 1985) and John Dower, *Embracing Defeat: Japan after World War II* (New York, 1999). Japanese politics in the period immediately after the end of the occupation are dealt with in Tetsuya Kataoka's interesting study, *The Price of Constitution: The Origin of Japan's Postwar Politics* (New York, 1991) and the classic analysis of the 1960 crisis, George Packard, *Protest in Tokyo* (Princeton, NJ, 1966). The Vietnam era is the subject of Thomas Havens, *Fire across the Sea: The Vietnam War and Japan, 1965–1975* (Princeton, NJ, 1987). Modern Japanese politics are covered by B. Richardson, *Japanese Democracy* (New Haven, CT, 1997), Gerald Curtis, *The Logic of Japanese Politics: Leaders, Institutions, and the Limits of Change* (New York, 1999) and Glenn Hook and Gavan MacCormack, *Japan's Contested Constitution: Documents and Analysis* (London, 2001).

A number of studies deal with American–Japanese relations during the Cold War, the most notable being Roger Buckley, *US–Japan Alliance Diplomacy, 1945–90* (New York, 1992) and Michael Schaller, *Altered States: The United States and Japan since the Occupation* (New York, 1997). Okinawa as an issue in American–Japanese relations is covered in Nick Sarantakes, *Keystone: The American Occupation of Okinawa and US–Japanese Relations* (College Station, TX, 2000). Other aspects of Japan's foreign relations are covered well in Sadako Ogata, *Normalization with China: A Comparative Study of US and Japanese Processes* (Berkeley, CA, 1988), Victor Cha, *Alignment despite Antagonism: The US–Korea–Japan Security Triangle* (Stanford, CA, 1999), Michael Green, *Reluctant Realism: Japanese Foreign Policy in an Era of Uncertain Power* (Basingstoke, 2001) and Glenn Hook, Hugo Dobson, Julie Gilson and Christopher Hughes, *Japan's International Relations: Politics, Economics and Security* (London, 2001). Japan's attitude towards the security question is covered in Michael Green, *Arming Japan: Defense Production, Alliance Politics and the Postwar Search for Autonomy* (New York, 1995) and Peter Katzenstein, *Cultural Norms and National Security: Police and Military in Postwar Japan* (Ithaca, NY, 1996).

The best place to start in the debate about the reasons for Japan's phenomenal economic growth is with Chalmers Johnson, *MITI and the Japanese Miracle: The Growth of Industrial Policy, 1925–1975* (Stanford, CA, 1982). Refutations of his 'developmental state' thesis can be seen in Daniel Okimoto, *Between MITI and the Market: Japanese Industrial Policy for High Technology* (Stanford, CA, 1989) and Kent Calder, *Strategic Capitalism: Private Business and Public Purpose in Japan* (Princeton, NJ, 1993). An important study of the American sponsorship of the Japanese economy is Aaron Forsberg, *America and the Japanese Miracle: The Cold War Context of Japan's Postwar Economic Revival, 1950–1960* (Chapel Hill, NC, 2000). A useful survey of the developmental state thesis is Meredith Woo-Cumings (ed.), *The Developmental State* (Ithaca, NY, 1999), but see also Robert Wade, *Governing the Market: Economic Theory and the Role of Government in East*

Asian Industrialization (Princeton, NJ, 1990) and Stephen Haggard, *Pathways from the Periphery: The Politics of Growth in the Newly Industrializing Countries* (Ithaca, NY, 1990).

For South Korean and Taiwanese economic growth, see Thomas Gold, *State and Society in the Taiwan Miracle* (Armonk, NY, 1986), Alice Amsden, *Asia's Next Giant: South Korea and Late Industrialization* (New York, 1989), Hyung-A Kim, *Korea's Development under Park Chung Hee: Rapid Industrialization, 1961–1979* (London, 2003) and Jung-en Woo, *Race to the Swift: State and Finance in Korean Industrialization* (New York, 1991). For political developments see D. Oberdorfer, *The Two Koreas: A Contemporary History* (Reading, 1998), Whan Kihl Young, *Transforming Korean Politics: Democracy, Reform and Culture* (Armonk, NY, 2005) and R. L. Edmonds and S. Goldstein (eds), *Taiwan in the Twentieth Century: A Retrospective View* (New York, 2001).

For advice on further reading, see Warren Cohen (ed.), *The Study of American–East Asian Relations on the Eve of the Twenty-First Century* (New York, 1996).

The People's Republic of China and North Korea: ideology and nationalism, 1949–2007

Introduction

As the twentieth century came to its close, China, which in 1900 had been one of the extra-European empires that had been brought to its knees by the might of the West, was emerging as a nascent superpower. By the 1990s it appeared as though the **PRC** was engaged in an inexorable cycle of growth that had the potential in the long term to transform it into the second largest economy in the world. This economic power in turn led to the prospect that the world's most populous country, possessing 1.2 billion people, might pose a substantial potential threat to American hegemony and the Western-dominated international system.

The ability of China to play an important part in international politics is not, however, a new development, for during the period of the Cold War the PRC took on a number of roles that influenced the course of the confrontation between the Soviet Union and the United States. Under the leadership of Mao Zedong, the People's Republic of China was in its early years a key ally of the Soviet Union. Over time it developed into the world's leading revolutionary state, threatening

People's Republic of China (PRC)
The official name of communist or mainland China. The PRC came into existence in 1949 under the leadership of Mao Zedong.

not just the interests of the Western liberal democracies and their clients but also Moscow's claim to primacy within the socialist bloc. As China was significantly weaker than either of the two superpowers, this was a dangerous position to adopt for too long and finally, after deciding that Russia posed a greater danger than the United States, it leaned towards the latter, helping to create the conditions that brought about **détente** in the 1970s.

To understand the positions the PRC adopted and the motives behind its dramatic shifts in policy, it is important to look at a number of themes in Chinese policy-making and how they influenced the development of its diplomacy. Key factors here are the interplay between domestic events and foreign policy, the legacy of China's 'one hundred years of national humiliation' as a semi-colonized country and, perhaps most significant in Mao's period, the role of ideology in the survival and furthering of the revolution.

The rise and decline of the Sino-Soviet alliance

When the Chinese Communist Party (CCP) took power in 1949 it inherited a country that had been ravaged by more than a decade of war. It therefore faced an immense task in its intention to transform China into a modern socialist state that would raise the people's standard of living and be treated as an equal by all within the international community. Moreover, it had to begin the construction of socialism in the knowledge that both domestic and foreign opponents still existed, for the **Guomindang (GMD)** had not been annihilated but had retreated to Taiwan, and the world's leading capitalist power, the United States, was vociferously hostile to the idea of a communist China. In these conditions the CCP was naturally drawn towards an alignment with the Soviet Union which, as the unchallenged centre of the communist world, could obviously assist in the building of socialism and act as a guarantor of China's national security.

The Sino-Soviet alliance was signed in February 1950 and first bore fruit later that year when China was able to risk intervening in the Korean War without provoking an American attack on its own soil. The alliance worked reasonably well during the Korean conflict, for the Soviet Union assisted China with the provision of air support and supplied a great deal of military *matériel*. However, the fly in the ointment was that Stalin demanded payment for the Soviet supplies. This naturally irritated the Chinese, who were after all fighting on behalf of world communism and who needed all the resources they could muster to fuel domestic economic growth.

Some scholars have been tempted to date the **Sino-Soviet split** from these early tensions, but that is a dangerous *post-facto* reading of events. In reality these initial problems were overcome, in part because two linked events in 1953 promised a brighter future. The first of these was that March witnessed the death of Stalin, which was important because, while Stalin was alive, Mao had sometimes resented his bullying attitude and self-interested policies, but had not had the temerity to

---

détente

A term meaning the reduction of tensions between states. It is often used to refer to the superpower diplomacy that took place between the inauguration of Richard Nixon as the American president in 1969 and the Senate's refusal to ratify SALT II in 1980.

Guomindang (GMD)

The Chinese Nationalist party founded in 1913 by Sun Yatsen. Under the control of Jiang Jieshi, it came to power in China in 1928 and initiated a modernization programme before leading the country into war against Japan in 1937. It lost control over mainland China in 1949 as a result of the communist victory in the civil war. From 1949 it controlled Taiwan, overseeing the island's 'economic miracle', until its electoral defeat in 2000.

see Chapter 10

Sino-Soviet split

The process whereby China and the Soviet Union became alienated from each other in the late 1950s and early 1960s. It is often dated from 1956 and Khrushchev's speech to the twentieth congress of the CPSU, but this view has been challenged in recent years.

disobey Lenin's heir. Stalin's removal from the scene therefore allowed a more equal relationship between Russia and China to be constructed. In addition, his passing was significant because the new Soviet leadership, based around Georgi Malenkov and Nikita Khrushchev, was keen to introduce a thaw in the Cold War. Obviously one way of achieving this was to bring the Korean War to a speedy conclusion, which was a policy that also appealed to the PRC's leaders. Accordingly, in July 1953 the second key event of the year took place, namely the end of the conflict in Korea. With Stalin and the Korean War removed from the scene, the Sino-Soviet relationship was able to turn towards a more promising area of co-operation.

Now that the PRC was at peace, its main priority was to construct a socialist economy by adopting the Soviet five-year plan model of industrialization and moving towards state ownership of all property. To help it achieve these goals, the Soviet Union sent thousands of advisers and technicians to China to provide assistance across a broad range of state activities. Soviet aid also arrived in other forms, such as up-to-date weaponry, including jet fighters such as the MiG-15, and credits that allowed China to acquire the latest Russian industrial technology. In addition, by 1955 the Soviets started to assist with the development of a Chinese nuclear capability. Meanwhile, on the world stage the Soviet Union and China co-operated effectively at the Geneva Conference in 1954, with both benefiting from the neutralization of Indochina.

In retrospect the years between 1953 and 1957 can be seen as the highpoint of the alliance, but even so, this period did contain the germs of later problems. Most notably difficulties were created when, in February 1956, Khrushchev made his wide-ranging and controversial '**de-Stalinization**' speech, in which he sharply criticized the cruelties and failings of Stalin, called for a move towards **peaceful co-existence** with the West, and announced that there was more than one path to the goal of constructing a socialist society. The conventional view among scholars used to be that this new Soviet agenda was anathema to Mao and that accordingly the speech marked the start of the Sino-Soviet split. In fact the situation was more complex. It certainly does appear that Mao was not amused about the lack of forewarning, and that he felt that the attack on Stalin was tactically injudicious. However, in a number of ways the speech was important not because of the anger that it stirred but for the opportunities it provided for Mao, and ironically it was these aspects that paved the way for the split.

One positive aspect of the speech was that, by attacking Stalin, Khrushchev allowed the Chinese leadership to follow suit and to engage in criticism of the late Russian leader's '**Great Power** chauvinism' towards China. The implication of such a line was obvious: the Soviet Union should treat the PRC as an equal. Even more significant was Khrushchev's acknowledgement that other socialist states did not have to adhere rigidly to the Soviet model. This was important because by 1956 Mao was beginning to doubt whether economic development based on centrally planned heavy industrialization was suited to a country like China, which still possessed a relatively small industrial sector. Mao believed instead that the PRC could build socialism by concentrating on a massive increase in agricultural production, allied with the development of infrastructure projects and localized

see Chapter 12

de-Stalinization
The policy, pursued in most communist states and among most communist groups after 1956, of eradicating the memory or influence of Stalin and Stalinism. Initiated by the Soviet Union under the guidance of Nikita Khrushchev.

peaceful co-existence
An expression coined originally by Trotsky to describe the condition when there are pacific relations between states with differing social systems and competition takes place in fields other than war. The idea was vital to Soviet diplomacy particularly after the death of Stalin.

Great Powers
Traditionally those states that were held capable of shared responsibility for the management of the international order by virtue of their military and economic influence.

Great Leap Forward
The movement initiated by the CCP in 1958 to achieve rapid modernization in China through the construction of communes and the utilization of the masses for large-scale infrastructure projects.

industrialization, such as the building of 'backyard furnaces'. Essential to this rapid economic transformation of China, labelled the '**Great Leap Forward**', was the idea of devolving power from the centre to rural communes containing thousands of households.

Document 15.1

Mao's conversation with the Soviet ambassador, Pavel Yudin, 31 March 1956

He [Mao] noted that Stalin, without a doubt, is a great Marxist. However, in his great work in the course of a long period of time he made a number of great and serious mistakes, the primary ones of which were listed in Khrushchev's speech. . . . Mao . . . noted that Stalin's mistakes accumulated gradually, from small ones growing to huge ones. . . . The spirit of criticism and self-criticism and the atmosphere which was created after the [twentieth CPSU] congress will help us, he said, to express our thoughts more freely on a range of issues. It is good that the CPSU has posed all these issues.

Source: Westad (ed.) (1999, document ix, pp. 341–42)

The Great Leap Forward was launched formally with many fanfares in 1958. In order to stir the Chinese people into action, a fervent domestic propaganda campaign was begun. Simultaneously, the state unleashed a new confrontational phase in Chinese diplomacy, with the intention of creating a pervading atmosphere of crisis that would reinforce the people's revolutionary ardour. This was, however, only partly due to domestic factors, for in addition the desire to confront Western interests was influenced by Mao's reading of current international affairs. By 1958 Mao was beginning to express doubts about Soviet policy towards the West, which appeared to centre upon its desire to establish peaceful co-existence, thus guaranteeing the security of its empire in Eastern Europe. Mao believed that, as a result of recent events in Asia and Africa and the technological advances symbolized by the launch of Sputnik, the communist bloc was now in a superior position to the West and did not need to pursue such a cautious line. He therefore argued that socialism should be more radical in its denunciations of imperialism and in the provision of support for revolutionary national liberation movements and newly independent states in the **Third World**. In addition, Mao still hungered for equality in the PRC's relationship with the USSR, and felt that China needed to assert itself by following a more independent line in foreign and security policy.

All of these goals came together in August 1958 when Mao initiated a propaganda campaign calling for the liberation of Taiwan and ordered the bombardment of Jinmen (Quemoy), an island off the coast of Fujian province which was still occupied by the GMD. The issue of Taiwan's control of various offshore islands had already sparked a crisis once before in 1954–55, which had led the United States to sign a mutual defence pact with Jiang's regime. This second 'Taiwan Straits' crisis therefore immediately turned into a dangerous confronta-

Third World
A collective term of French origin for those states that are part of neither the developed capitalist world nor the communist bloc. It includes the states of Latin America, Africa, the Middle East, South Asia and South-East Asia. Also referred to as 'the South' in contrast to the developed 'North'.

tion between the PRC and the United States. This suited Mao's purpose, for it created the necessary sense of crisis, demonstrated the socialist will to tackle imperialism and constituted a daring declaration of independence from Moscow.

The Soviet Union responded with dismay to Mao's brinkmanship, for, with its attention focused on Europe, it saw little value in heightened Cold War tensions in East Asia. However, as criticism of Mao might be counter-productive, it felt it necessary to give limited support to the PRC in the hope that this would allow some Soviet control over events. In September 1958 therefore Khrushchev warned the United States not to use nuclear weapons against the PRC. Mao, however, with the desire for independence as one of his key motives, was loath to co-ordinate China's activities with those of the Soviet Union, and continued to follow his own line.

Having achieved his initial purpose, Mao allowed the tensions with the United States to dissipate, but the crisis left a legacy of unease in Sino-Soviet relations. The Soviet leadership was greatly concerned by the belligerency and unpredictability of Chinese policy, and sought to restrict the PRC's ability to undermine international stability. In 1959 the Soviet Union therefore abruptly reneged on a promise to provide the PRC with a prototype atomic bomb and took a studiously neutral position when a border dispute developed between China and India, which Moscow had been courting with military and economic aid. For Mao, this behaviour confirmed his belief that the Soviets were temperamentally incapable of respecting China's independence and were sliding towards a 'revisionist' foreign policy. However, arguably the greatest provocation was that it appeared to Mao that the Soviet Union was intervening in Chinese domestic politics.

The occasion for this intervention came when the CCP leadership gathered at Lushan in the summer of 1959 to discuss the future of the 'Great Leap Forward'. China's bid to achieve socialism had begun promisingly, but by the spring of 1959 it was clear that too many people were being diverted into infrastructure projects and rural industrialization and that greater control needed to be exerted over agricultural production. Mao himself was aware of these difficulties and therefore convened the Lushan conference to assess the situation. However, the conference did not go according to plan, for during its proceedings the minister of defence, Peng Dehuai, wrote to Mao criticizing the 'Great Leap'. Mao interpreted this as an act of *lèse-majesté* and accused Peng, who had just visited Moscow, of having been put up to it by Khrushchev, who saw the 'Great Leap' as a challenge to Russia's ideological predominance. The result was that Peng was purged, further poison entered into the Sino-Soviet relationship and the 'Great Leap' continued for a further disastrous year. Moreover, adding insult to injury, in July 1960 the Soviet Union suddenly called home all its advisers, just when they were needed to rebuild China's stricken economy.

While clear ideological and geostrategic divisions had opened up by the start of the 1960s, the Sino-Soviet split was at this stage not irrevocable. Indeed, military co-operation continued and the polemical battle that erupted briefly in 1960 subsided in the following year. In part this arose from China's weakness after the failure of the Great Leap, which through arrogance, incompetence and indifference had led to more than twenty million deaths from starvation. In addition, the Great Leap's demise had the effect of forcing its main protagonist, Mao, to retreat from the political front line. This allowed the more moderate Liu Shaoqi and Deng Xiaoping to set to work to repair the damage at home, but also had the effect of reducing Sino-Soviet animosity.

However, the uneasy truce that developed in 1961 proved to be only temporary, for Mao had no intention of allowing his eclipse to become permanent. Indeed, he saw his re-emergence in 1962 as essential to the revolution, because in his view, if the PRC once again returned to a close relationship with Moscow,

Debating the Sino – Soviet split

The history of the foreign relations of the PRC is another field in which our knowledge has been vastly increased by growing access to primary source material. This has been most valuable and enlightening in respect to the history of the Sino-Soviet split. Ever since the split first became apparent to the West in the 1960s, there has been an effort to understand how and why it took place. The problem initially, however, was that in the absence of archival sources the only documents available were the polemics issued by each side, decrying the other for past and present mistakes and provocations. Based largely on these polemics, the orthodox view, epitomized by writers such as John Gittings (1968) and Donald Zagoria (1962), was that the split began with Khrushchev's secret speech of February 1956 and that it was caused largely by his adoption of the policy of 'peaceful co-existence' with the West. Building on this foundation, the common assumption came to be that the split represented a classical example of divergent security concerns leading to the end of an alliance. However, not all scholars accepted this realist approach, for some, such as Stuart Schram (1989), continued to emphasize the importance of ideology as an influence on the PRC's foreign policy.

The newly available documents on the formulation of Chinese and Soviet foreign policy during the period of the alliance have opened up the study of this area enormously. A number of works, including most notably the essays in Odd Arne Westad (ed.), *Brothers in Arms: The Rise and Fall of the Sino-Soviet Alliance, 1945 – 1963* (Stanford, CA, 1998) and Chen Jian, *Mao's China and the Cold War* (Chapel Hill, NC, 2001), have attempted to draw conclusions from this material. The consensus that has emerged has been that the split came later than previously assumed and that 1958 was the crucial turning point. Moreover, in line with Schram's reading of events, great emphasis has been put on the significance of ideological divisions in causing Sino-Soviet alienation. The documents have thus led us to a far more nuanced interpretation of the reasons for the split, which also adds considerably to our understanding of the Cold War in the 1950s and 1960s.

it risked being itself infected by the revisionism that he saw as endemic in Khrushchev's Russia. By the early 1960s Mao was convinced that the Soviet Union was turning into a bureaucratically controlled form of state capitalism and a status quo power. The ignominious withdrawal of Soviet missiles from Cuba in November 1962 and its agreement in the following year to sign the **Limited Test Ban Treaty** with the United States and Britain only confirmed him in his contempt. The result of Mao's re-emergence was therefore that in 1963–64 the PRC unleashed an unrestrained polemical assault against its erstwhile ally, culminating in diatribes such as 'On Khrushchev's Phoney Communism', and with this the split finally became irreversible.

In retrospect, the Sino-Soviet split can be seen as arising out of a number of issues that divided these two communist powers, such as ideological differences over the future evolution of socialism and their diverging national security interests as the nature of the Western threat changed. It is also important, however, to see that at the centre of the dispute lay the heightened sense of nationalism in communist China and the idea that it had not thrown off the shackles of Western imperialism just to be dominated by the Soviet Union. As such, China was never a compliant client within the Soviet Empire, and this fact lay at the core of its divisive relationship with Moscow.

Revolutionary China and the Third World

At the same time as the Sino-Soviet alliance collapsed, the PRC once again moved towards a more assertive and revolutionary foreign policy directed at winning over adherents in Asia and Africa. Ever since the creation of the PRC Mao had recognized that China, which was itself a relatively underdeveloped Asian country, could play a leadership role in the Third World and encourage the states of Asia and Africa in their struggle against imperialism. Its first bid to assume such an influential position came in April 1955 when it attended the **Bandung Conference** of Asian and African states. At this stage it posed as a respectable state to the extent that it developed a close relationship with neutralist India and renounced its claim to authority over the **overseas Chinese** population in South-East Asia. However, from the time of the Great Leap and the border clashes with India over Tibet in 1959, the PRC moved towards a more divisive policy towards the Third World. This more confrontational stance was marked by denunciations of the new concept of **non-alignment** espoused by Nehru and Tito, and support for the more overtly anti-imperialist line taken by President Sukarno of Indonesia.

From 1963 anti-imperialism and support for the newly independent revolutionary states and national liberation movements became the centrepiece of Chinese diplomacy. Leaders such as Zhou Enlai and Peng Zhen engaged in extensive tours of Asia and Africa, attempting among other things to win support for a second Asian–African conference to be held at Algiers that would steal the

Limited Test Ban Treaty
An agreement signed by Britain, the Soviet Union and the United States in 1963, committing nations to halt atmospheric tests of nuclear weapons; by the end of 1963, ninety-six additional nations had signed the treaty.

see Chapter 11

Bandung Afro-Asian Conference
The conference of Asian and African states held in Bandung in Indonesia in 1955. Commonly seen as the first move towards the establishment of a Third World lobby in international politics.

overseas Chinese
The descendants of the Chinese who immigrated to South-East Asia in the nineteenth and early twentieth centuries. They have tended to act as a merchant class and as such have stirred up a good deal of resentment among the indigenous people who envy their wealth and doubt their loyalty to their adopted countries.

non-alignment
A state policy of avoiding involvement in 'Great Power conflicts', most notably the Cold War. It was first espoused by India on its becoming independent in 1947.

see Chapter 13

Non-Aligned Movement
The organization founded in 1961 by a number of neutral states which called for a lowering of Cold War tensions and for greater attention to be paid to underdevelopment and to the eradication of imperialism.

see Chapter 12

Democratic Republic of Vietnam (DRV)
The official name of communist Vietnam; the DRV was initially proclaimed by Ho Chi Minh in 1945. Between 1954 and 1975 it comprised only the northern part of Vietnam (North Vietnam).

Gang of Four
The radical group centred upon Mao's wife, Jiang Qing, that helped to initiate and perpetuate the Cultural Revolution. They were purged in 1976 following Mao's death, put on trial for treason and later executed.

limelight from the **Non-Aligned Movement**. In addition a Beijing–Jakarta axis was developed with Indonesia and its communist party, the PKI, and close relations were established with Pakistan on the basis of mutual hostility towards India. Most significant of all was that the PRC became the key foreign supporter of the campaign by the **Democratic Republic of Vietnam (DRV)** to unify Vietnam under communist rule. Thus, freed from what it considered to be the shackles of its alliance with the Soviet Union, the PRC became a crusader for revolution and threatened to export its ideology to the Third World, to the detriment of both Washington and Moscow. In this sense the revolutionary diplomacy espoused by the PRC provided an essential backdrop to the escalation of the American commitment to the Vietnam War, for Chinese ambitions suggested that the domino theory could become a reality.

The PRC's ability to provide an effective challenge to the international order was, however, compromised by two factors. The first was that the PRC had very little of substance to offer its potential clients apart from rhetoric. China could, after all, not provide much in the way of economic assistance or advanced military hardware. Even in Vietnam the PRC found itself outbid technologically once American air attacks began on the DRV, for Hanoi quickly turned to the Soviet Union in the recognition that only the latter could provide the air defence equipment that was urgently needed. Moreover, the PRC's ability to create its own bloc was limited by the fact that it could not come to the aid of its clients if they were challenged by internal or external enemies for it lacked the capability to project its power. For example, the PRC may have exploded its first atomic bomb in October 1964 but it lacked an adequate delivery system. Its relative weakness was illustrated all too graphically by its inability to influence the outcome of the Indo-Pakistan War of September 1965, and its powerlessness when, in October, the Indonesian army turned on the PKI and began to marginalize Sukarno. China's bark was therefore considerably worse than its bite, and this made it a poor and increasingly unappealing patron.

The second factor which led to the curtailment of the diplomatic offensive was that by 1965–66 Mao's attention had turned to domestic issues, for by this time he had become convinced that the cancer of revisionism had infected his own party. One of his main concerns was that the post-Leap retrenchment policies pursued by Liu and Deng, which included a return to peasants cultivating their private plots, had gone too far and were tantamount to pursuing the 'capitalist road' to socialism. He also contended that the CCP cadres were turning into a new ruling class, and that this transformation promised a continuation of class inequality rather than the egalitarian society that the revolution had been intended to achieve. The obvious solution to this threat to his life's work was to mobilize the people to make revolution against the party. At first Mao struggled to turn his ideas into practice, for he had lost influence in the early 1960s. However, by 1965 he was able to form a coalition that supported his new line. His supporters included the People's Liberation Army (PLA) under the control of the minister of defence, Lin Biao, and the ultra-left group centred on what retrospectively has been referred to as the **Gang of Four**, of which his wife, Jiang Qing, was the key member. In addition, Mao was able to rely on the tacit support of Premier

Zhou Enlai, who was under attack from the Liu/Deng camp for the PRC's failures in foreign policy.

The **Cultural Revolution** began in earnest in the summer of 1966 when Mao encouraged students to criticize the running of universities and in particular their elitist admissions and examination policies. These students quickly formed themselves into the **Red Guards**, the foot soldiers of Mao's campaign, and steadily expanded their range of targets to attack former landlords and capitalists and then finally party officials themselves. At the same time ultra-left workers' groups emerged which took the struggle into the factories. The Cultural Revolution swept away the 'capitalist roaders', Deng being forced into internal exile while Liu died in custody in 1969, but its effects did not end there, for once Mao unleashed the revolutionary spirit it proved very difficult to control. Within months the Red Guards and workers' groups split into factions that fought between and among themselves. In 1967 cities such as Guangzhou and Wuhan were thrown into chaos and the whole country teetered on the brink of anarchy.

The effect on the PRC's foreign relations was that the country began to cut itself off from the outside world. Ambassadors were called back to Beijing for re-education and diplomatic relations were left in suspension. The only manifestations of China's foreign policy agenda were the pronouncements of support for like-minded communist parties, such as those in Burma, Cambodia and Albania, and the vitriolic polemics unleashed against both capitalism and the 'phoney communism' of the Soviet Union. Its retreat from the active revolutionary diplomacy of the mid-1960s suggests that, during the most intense revolutionary period in its history, China was more of a danger to itself than it was to the outside world. Indeed, it may be that China's retreat into the Cultural Revolution to a degree eased American security concerns in South-East Asia, and by doing so made the de-escalation of the Vietnam War possible.

However, not all of China's foes took comfort from its latest change of direction. To the Soviet Union, China's revolutionary folly showed it to be a dangerous and distinctly unstable neighbour. Following the ousting of Khrushchev by Aleksei Kosygin and Leonid Brezhnev in October 1964, the new Soviet leadership, after its initial conciliatory overtures had been rejected, decided to take a tough line against the PRC, and began strengthening massively its forces on the border and targeting nuclear weapons against its former ally. The Cultural Revolution only exacerbated this tendency. The sharp growth of Soviet hostility had in turn two major effects on the PRC. The first was that it contributed to Mao's decision to abandon the Red Guard stage of the Cultural Revolution. In particular, Mao was concerned when in August 1968 the Soviet Union used the Red Army to crush the '**Prague Spring**' in Czechoslovakia and issued the **Brezhnev Doctrine**, which claimed that the USSR had the right to intervene in other countries in order to put down deviations from Soviet-style communism. This clearly could be construed as a threat to the PRC, and seems to have influenced the decision to use the PLA to bring the Red Guards under control. The second effect was that, in the light of a number of serious clashes on the Sino-Soviet border, Mao began to realize that China's international isolation was endangering its security, and that it might be necessary to deter Russia from attacking by developing relations with

Cultural Revolution
The movement initiated by Mao in 1966 to rid the CCP of 'revisionists' whom he accused of seeking to introduce the type of state capitalism that existed in the Soviet Union. The Cultural Revolution was at its height between 1966 and 1969, but did not end officially until Mao's death in 1976.

Red Guards
The students and workers who acted as the foot soldiers of the Chinese Cultural Revolution, 1966–69.

Prague Spring
A brief period of liberal reforms attempted by the government of Alexander Dubček in 1968. The period ended with the invasion by Soviet-led Warsaw Pact military forces.

Brezhnev Doctrine
The 'doctrine' expounded by Leonid Brezhnev in November 1968 affirming the right of the Soviet Union to intervene in the affairs of communist countries in order to protect communism.

see Chapter 11

the United States. Thus, in another irony, by causing a worsening of Sino-Soviet relations, the Cultural Revolution encouraged Mao to tone down the struggle against Western imperialism.

The opening to America and the death of Mao

Mao's desire to build a relationship with the United States was reciprocated by the new administration in Washington, led by President Richard Nixon, which took office in January 1969. Even before announcing his nomination Nixon had affirmed that the United States could not go on pretending that a state which ruled more than a quarter of humankind did not exist, and that China could not be left in isolated hostility indefinitely. Once in office Nixon was also influenced by two other considerations, first, that better relations with China would reduce tensions in Asia and thus allow the United States to retreat from Vietnam, and second, that he could use the prospect of a Sino-American alignment to put diplomatic pressure on the Soviet Union, thus paving the way for détente.

The normalization was a long-drawn-out affair, in part because events in Indochina, such as the American incursion into Cambodia in the spring of 1970, led to delays in the negotiations between the two sides. In addition, Mao faced some internal resistance to his new diplomatic revolution, most notably from Lin Biao, his over-ambitious political heir. Lin, however, steadily lost influence in 1970 and in 1971 died in mysterious circumstances, possibly after launching an abortive coup. The breakthrough in the talks came in July 1971 when Nixon's national security adviser, Henry Kissinger, travelled in secret to Beijing for talks with Zhou Enlai. This was followed in February 1972 by Nixon's visit to China and his meetings with both Zhou and Mao.

The Sino-American opening was a complicated process, because neither Nixon nor Mao had any intention of moving towards any kind of alliance or doing anything that would sacrifice diplomatic independence. For both leaders the normalization process was a limited but eminently practical expedient. Both sides therefore recognized that there was no need to try to settle all of their differences and that, in fact, any attempt to do so could wreck the whole exercise. As a result they agreed to disagree over a large range of issues, most notably the fractious issue of Taiwan. The PRC's position was that Taiwan was nothing more than a renegade province of China. The United States, however, still recognized the **Republic of China (ROC)** in Taiwan as the legitimate government of the whole country. There were clearly no grounds for complete settlement of this issue, but it was possible for the United States to declare that it saw Taiwan as an integral part of China and therefore would not support its independence, while the PRC promised to pursue peaceful liberation, thus allowing the Americans an opportunity to reduce their forces on the island. The problem of Taiwan had one other effect which is often forgotten, namely that, despite Nixon's visit, the United States did not at this time open full diplomatic relations with the PRC.

Republic of China (ROC)
The official name for the government of China in Taiwan.

Plate 15.1 Mao and Nixon, February 1972. Chinese communist leader Chairman Mao Zedong shakes hands with American President Richard Nixon in Beijing during his visit to China. (Photo: Keystone/Getty Images)

The normalization process brought the PRC out of its international isolation in other ways as well. In 1971 the **United Nations (UN)** voted in favour of the PRC taking over the Chinese permanent seat on the Security Council. Then in 1972 the new Japanese prime minister, Kakuei Tanaka, followed Nixon's example and visited China. However, unlike the Americans, the Japanese were so entranced by the prospect of trading with the PRC that they were willing to break off relations with Taiwan and recognize the Beijing regime instead. Over the following years this practice became an international trend, leading to Taiwan's international isolation at least at the level of formal diplomatic ties.

There were, however, limits to how far China's position could change. Both in the United States and in the PRC obstacles meant that it was difficult to build on the foundations laid down in 1971–72. From 1973 the Nixon administration became mired in the Watergate affair, which naturally forestalled any further initiatives. Moreover, the weakening of the executive branch temporarily strengthened the hand of Taiwan's supporters in Congress. In the PRC further progress was hindered by the declining health of both Mao and Zhou and the attacks made on the latter by the Gang of Four. Zhou sought during this period to repair some of the damage caused by the Cultural Revolution and Deng briefly re-emerged to help with this process. However, early in 1976 Zhou died and shortly afterwards Deng was again purged. Then on 9 September Mao himself passed away.

Mao's death clearly marked the end of an era in Chinese history. Ever since the foundation of the PRC he had dominated its political life by creating and then

United Nations (UN)
An international organization established after the Second World War to replace the League of Nations. Since its establishment in 1945, its membership has grown to 192 countries.

see Chapter 14

destroying the alliance with the Soviet Union, initiating the Great Leap, turning the people against the party in the Cultural Revolution, and finally in his twilight years making the opening to Washington. This undoubtedly constituted dynamic leadership but had anything been gained? Under Mao standards of education and health and the position of women in society had improved, but steady economic development had all too often been sacrificed to ideological principle. Moreover, his frequent changes of policy had come at a high human cost with many lives lost and shattered as a result of his arrogance and his predilection for unleashing violence in the cause of class struggle. In addition, his imaginative rhetoric and feel for brinkmanship might have brought China to international prominence, but the country was by no means a superpower, for it remained economically, technologically and militarily backward. Thus Mao may have been a great revolutionary but once in power he failed his people.

Deng and the 'Four Modernizations'

Mao's death left China at a crossroads, for it was by no means clear what would follow him. On one side there was the possibility that his removal from the scene might lead to a new phase in the Cultural Revolution with the Gang of Four taking power. On the other side of the political spectrum was the prospect that the more moderate policies which Liu and Deng had espoused in the early 1960s might now be revived. Mao tried to ensure that neither would be the case by making the relatively inexperienced party loyalist Hua Guofeng his political heir. At first Hua lived up to the expectations placed in him by turning on the Gang of Four almost as soon as Mao was dead. However, marginalizing Deng was not such an easy matter. Deng had many important supporters within the CCP and, moreover, stood as the figure who could deliver the one thing which most Chinese wanted – the end of the Cultural Revolution. With these attributes on his side Deng did not take long to sideline Hua, and in 1978 he emerged as the PRC's new paramount leader.

Deng's taking on of the mantle of leadership coincided with dramatic events in foreign affairs as Indochina once again slid into war, this time between pro-Soviet Vietnam and pro-Chinese Cambodia. Alarmed by what it perceived as Vietnam's attempt to achieve hegemony in Indochina, which threatened to increase Soviet encirclement of China, the PRC negotiated a peace treaty with Japan ending the state of hostilities left over from the Sino-Japanese War, and co-operated with the **Association of South-East Asian Nations (ASEAN)** to support the **Khmer Rouge** and its allies. Most significantly, the United States, which was itself concerned about Soviet power in Indochina, finally decided to open diplomatic relations with the PRC and cut off its formal ties with Taiwan.

In some ways this was a fortunate harvest for Deng, for it strengthened not only the PRC's international position but also his own domestic standing. More was to follow. Over the next few years Cold War tensions deepened even further,

Association of South-East Asian Nations (ASEAN)
Organization founded in 1967 by Indonesia, Malaysia, the Philippines, Singapore and Thailand to provide a forum for regional economic co-operation. From 1979, and the Third Indochina War, it took on more of a political and security role. Membership increased with the accession of Brunei in 1984, Vietnam in 1995, Burma in 1997 and Cambodia in 1999.

see Chapter 12

Khmer Rouge
The Western name for the communist movement, led by Pol Pot, which came to power in Cambodia in 1975. The new government carried out a radical political programme that led to 1.5 million deaths. In 1979 it was overthrown by Vietnam, but continued to fight a guerrilla war campaign into the 1990s.

with the Soviet intervention in Afghanistan in December 1979 and the suppression of the Solidarity Movement in Poland. This benefited China because it meant that the Reagan administration in Washington, which had threatened to take a more positive view of Taiwan, was in fact forced through circumstance to deepen the American relationship with Beijing by, for example, sharing intelligence on Soviet activities in Central Asia.

The heightened tensions along China's borders did, however, reveal one major problem. In the winter of 1979 the PRC launched a limited incursion into the north of Vietnam in order to intimidate the government in Hanoi. The invasion, however, was not a success, for the PLA fought poorly and clearly suffered from inadequate material and organization. Here in microcosm was the main dilemma that China faced, that its efforts to exert influence in Asia were compromised by its technological and economic inferiority.

The desire to overcome China's relative backwardness was to prove to be the main hallmark of Deng's rule over the next twenty years. His policy, which was first announced in 1978, was to push the PRC to engage in the 'Four Modernizations' – of agriculture, industry, science and national defence. The first major changes came in agriculture, with a marked shift away from collectivization to cultivation based on private family plots, resulting in a substantial increase in productivity. For the long term, however, the most significant move was that state controls over industry were loosened, with private industrialists allowed to operate in a capitalist manner. In order to create rapid growth China also looked to outside assistance. This meant not only purchasing Western goods and technology, but also encouraging foreign companies to invest in China. In 1980 four 'Special Economic Zones' (SEZs) were created, of which the most important was Shenzhen which bordered on Hong Kong. Foreign investors were allowed to establish factories in the SEZs and use cheap Chinese labour to produce goods for export.

The PRC's pursuit of economic growth naturally affected the shape of its foreign policy: trade and investment, for example, became the cornerstone of its relationship with Japan. It also influenced the PRC's stance towards a number of territorial issues left over from the days of imperialism and civil war. One of these was the issue of the future of Hong Kong. The island itself and the peninsula at Kowloon were British in perpetuity, but the New Territories had been acquired by Britain as a ninety-nine-year lease in 1898. As the colony was not viable without the New Territories this naturally raised the question of what would happen in 1997. Owing to the need to eradicate China's past humiliation at the hands of the imperialists, Deng was determined that Hong Kong should be returned, but at the same time he recognized its value as a hub of capitalist trade and investment. To demand its complete integration into socialist China risked capital flowing out of Hong Kong, and therefore Deng negotiated the return of the colony under the auspices of a 'one country, two systems' model, in which the territory would retain substantial autonomy. The agreement was sealed by the signing of a Joint Declaration in 1984. By accepting this compromise Chinese policy was also serving another function, namely trying to assure Taiwan that if it returned to the fold it too could prosper under the 'one country, two systems'

scenario. Reunification did not in fact make any progress, but the more conciliatory stance taken by Beijing did encourage the development of closer trade
links between the PRC and Taiwan during the 1980s.

In the late 1970s and into the 1980s the PRC was therefore able to strengthen
itself by throwing off the last vestiges of its years of international isolation and
achieving high rates of economic growth. To a substantial degree it appeared that
the country had turned its back on Mao and his legacy, even if in public due
respect was shown to his memory. Some commentators even questioned whether
the PRC could still be defined as a Marxist-Leninist state. Such assessments were,
however, dangerously naive, for the CCP still reigned supreme and, moreover, still
could not rid itself of Mao's ghost.

Tiananmen and after: causes and consequences

By the end of the 1980s some leaders of the CCP were beginning to express
concern about the rapidity of economic change, which threatened to unleash
damaging forces within society, such as demands for democracy and a loosening
of party control. Their assessment of the situation was correct, for discontent was
clearly emerging from 1987 onwards. One of the reasons for this was the inherent
danger in the type of economic development sponsored by Deng, namely that
the CCP had no experience in such a field. As a result, serious problems arose,
including a steep increase in inflation. Reinforcing popular dissatisfaction was the
fact that, while ordinary families found their purchasing power declining, some
CCP cadres began to enrich themselves by indulging in corruption.

As in the Cultural Revolution it was students who most publicly voiced these
complaints. In April 1989 the death of a leading CCP moderate, Hu Yaobang,
and a visit to Beijing by the Soviet president, Mikhail Gorbachev, inspired
students' calls for greater democracy in China and a purging of the corrupt from
the CCP. The centre of the protests was the student occupation of **Tiananmen
Square** in Beijing, but demonstrations also took place in another twenty or so
cities, and increasingly involved workers and other non-student groups. At first
the party hesitated about how to react to this wave of dissent, but once it became
clear that the movement would not dissipate of its own accord, a military
clampdown was ordered. On 3 June units of the PLA entered the square and
dispersed the demonstrators with some loss of life. In the aftermath mass arrests
took place. The heavy-handed response of the CCP leadership to this challenge
to its authority was in part simply a clear rejection of the students' democratic
agenda, but in addition it has to be acknowledged that fear played a part. After
all, many of the leadership, including Deng himself, had fallen victim to the
previous wave of student unrest – the Red Guards movement.

The violent suppression of the Tiananmen Square protests naturally had an
unfortunate effect on China's international image. Even before this the growth in
the West of interest in human rights had led to some criticisms of Chinese
behaviour, particularly in regard to Tibet, where it was seen as propagating a brutal

Tiananmen Square
The main square in Beijing
where Mao declared the
foundation of the PRC in
October 1949 and where
students protested against
communist rule in the spring
of 1989. The student
movement was crushed on 3
June 1989 by units of the
PLA.

policy of assimilation that was intended to destroy Tibetan society and culture. After Tiananmen this criticism of the PRC's human rights record became a tide of disapproval which Western governments found difficult to ignore. In addition, China's position in the world was further damaged by a development beyond its control, namely the end of the Soviet–American Cold War and the collapse of the Soviet Union and its empire. The removal of Soviet communism from the international system left the PRC as the major surviving Marxist-Leninist state. This was not a desirable position to be in, particularly following Tiananmen, because it allowed Western critics to portray the PRC as a potential future hegemonic threat and to argue that a policy of **containment** should be adopted similar to that which had existed during the Cold War. China's discomfort was particularly evident in relation to the future of Hong Kong, where the long road towards the hand-over in 1997 became increasingly fraught owing to fears that the Chinese intended to extinguish human rights in the colony. China's belligerent rejection of criticism only heightened the impression that it intended to rule with an iron hand, but fortunately in the end the hand-over took place with little controversy and in the years that followed the legal framework that protected freedom of speech remained in place.

The Clinton administration, while sharing some of these concerns, did not agree with the idea that the best solution was containment and argued instead that the best way to manage China was by promoting engagement rather than confrontation, on the grounds that the granting of respectability was likely to do more in the long term for human rights than constant pin-pricking. Thus, Clinton chose to promote the PRC's entry into the World Trade Organization and to encourage American investment in China's booming economy. However, despite Washington's adoption of this liberal line, Sino-American relations retained an air of tension. One of the main reasons was the issue of Taiwan. Repulsed by the PRC's behaviour in 1989, the island began to flirt with the idea of independence as a separate sovereign entity. The PRC reacted with fury every time Taiwan inched towards this status and in 1996 a new Taiwan Straits crisis briefly erupted following the visit by the Taiwanese president, Lee Teng-hui, to the United States. In response, in 1997 the Japanese and American governments agreed to expand the remit of the Security Guidelines that lay at the heart of their alliance and Japan reaffirmed its strategic interest in Taiwan and South Korea. In 1999 Sino-American relations were further strained when the Chinese embassy in Belgrade was bombed by NATO aircraft in the Kosovo conflict.

With the arrival of the highly ideological administration of George W. Bush in 2001 there was some expectation that a tougher American line towards the PRC would ensue and this impression was soon strengthened when two American pilots were temporarily seized for allegedly infringing Chinese airspace. However, the start of America's 'war on terror' led to a limited Sino-American rapprochement for both were concerned about the threat posed by militant political Islam and, in particular, were keen to ensure the survival of President Pervez Musharraf's government in Pakistan.

A permanent closer understanding, however, still proved difficult simply because China's economic, and thus also political and military, power continued

containment
The term coined by George Kennan for the American, and broadly Western, policy towards the Soviet Union (and communism in general). The overall idea was to contain the USSR (that is, keep it within its current borders) with the hope that internal division, failure or political evolution might end the perceived threat from what was considered a chronically expansionist force.

to grow at such a rapid rate. China attempted to blunt the trepidation caused by this resurgence of power by describing itself as being engaged in a 'peaceful rise' that would not dislocate or threaten international society. Many in the West hoped that this would be the case, but some aspects of Chinese policy did not inspire confidence. One particular area of concern for the West was that China's insatiable appetite for raw materials to power its economic growth led it to cultivate good relations with states that Western opinion saw as morally dubious. This was especially the case in regard to Sudan, where the PRC proved to be an implacable opponent of American efforts to enforce a solution of the Darfur crisis by introducing tough UN sanctions against the government in Khartoum. Meanwhile in Asia, China's neighbours sought insurance policies in a variety of ways. For example, Vietnam joined ASEAN in 1995 in order to boost its security, while other ASEAN members embarked on a marked increase in military spending. For its part, in 2007 Japan pushed the idea of strategic co-operation with fellow democracies in Asia and the Pacific in the shape of a Quadrilateral Initiative with the United States, Australia and India.

North Korea: the last Stalinist state

Democratic People's Republic of Korea (DPRK)
The official name of North Korea. The DPRK came into existence in 1948 under the leadership of Kim Il-Sung.

see Chapter 10

China was not, however, the only or even the most serious threat to regional security in the 1990s, for that honour went to the last surviving (as of 2007) Stalinist state, North Korea, or to give it its proper name, the **Democratic People's Republic of Korea (DPRK)**. The menace posed by the DPRK has often been ascribed in the Western media to the supposedly irrational and peculiar personality of the country's leader since 1994, Kim Jong-Il, but, as with all such situations, the instability caused by North Korea has to be put into a broader context. In the case of the DPRK this means coming to terms with a state whose attitude towards international politics and domestic development has been largely shaped by its disastrously obsessive pursuit of national reconciliation.

As noted in Chapter 10, the DPRK came into existence in 1948 as the result of both superpower and Korean disagreements about how to unify the peninsula under one administration. As its launching of a full-scale war in 1950 shows, from the very first it saw itself as the legitimate government of the whole of the Korean peninsula and was determined to oust what it saw as the puppet regime in Seoul. It is, of course, hardly peculiar that this should have been such an important goal, but what is surprising is the tenacity with which the government in Pyongyang was to pursue this aim over the following half-century. To a great extent this was down to the drive, vision and beliefs of one man – Kim Il-Sung.

When the Soviet Union backed Kim Il-Sung for the leadership of North Korea from 1946 onwards, it elevated from relative obscurity a man with a good revolutionary pedigree who it appeared would be loyal to Soviet interests. Kim's background was that he had fought in Manchuria in the 1930s as the Korean-born leader of an anti-Japanese communist guerrilla group. He had the advantage of not being a Russian-born Korean, of not being strongly linked to the CCP and having not had a dubious collaborationist past under Japanese colonial rule. If the Soviets thought, however, that he would be a malleable figure who could provide uncontroversial leadership, they were soon to be faced with uncomfortable reality, for Kim was his own man whose outlook on the world was primarily shaped by his harsh, isolated experience as a guerrilla fighter. For Kim, the priority above all else was Korean unification under communist rule, to such an extent that the DPRK became a means to that end. Thus for his regime, economic growth was largely seen as having the primary purpose of creating a strong military that was ready to take advantage of any sign of weakness in the **Republic of Korea (ROK)**. Moreover, his rule was shaped by profound suspicion of those, both inside and outside North Korea, who had not been through similar adversity. He was therefore intolerant of domestic opposition and determined to pursue an independent line in terms of relations with the Soviet Union and the PRC.

Initially Kim's policies in government were not out of keeping with developments elsewhere in the socialist bloc. Influenced by his wartime years in the Soviet Union, his ideas for building a socialist society drew heavily on the Stalinist model, including the collectivization of agriculture and the construction of an extensive personality cult. By the mid-1950s, however, it became clear that Kim was seeking to pursue a more independent line. He began to introduce a more **autarkic** economic policy and in December 1955 referred for the first time to the idea of 'juche' (self-reliance) as the ideological underpinning of the state. Simultaneously, he worked assiduously to undermine those factions within the Korean Workers Party (KWP) that leaned towards Beijing and Moscow and finally achieved success at a party congress in March 1958, which saw his main rivals expelled from the party. This was, of course, a dangerous line to follow during the years of Khrushchev's push for de-Stalinization, but Kim was saved by the fact that Sino-Soviet differences had begun to emerge and that his radical policies appeared to complement those of Mao in China. For example, the Ch'ollima Movement in the DPRK which called on all citizens to engage in voluntary work and for the development of local factories clearly echoed some of the major tenets of the Great Leap Forward.

With his domestic political situation strengthened and with the Sino-Soviet split allowing him greater autonomy, Kim was well placed from the late 1950s to accelerate the policies that he believed would ready the state for reunification. In 1962 an Equal Emphasis policy was introduced, which stressed the need for high economic growth to go hand in hand with high levels of arms production. This was followed in 1964 by the announcement of the 'three fronts' policy, which called for the building up of military power, support for the Left in the ROK, and confronting the United States in order to persuade it to withdraw from the Korean peninsula. In pursuit of the 'first front', military spending was vastly expanded. In 1964 it took up 6 per cent of total state expenditure, but by 1967 this had grown to 30 per cent. This excessive focus on the militarization of the DPRK led to some discontent in the KWP, but in October 1966 a fresh purge was introduced which silenced the opposition and filled the top ranks of the party with Kim loyalists who had fought alongside him in the 1930s.

Republic of Korea (ROK)
The official name of South Korea. The ROK came into existence in 1948 under the leadership of Syngman Rhee.

autarky
A policy that aims at achieving national economic self-sufficiency. It is commonly associated with the economic programmes espoused by Germany, Italy and Japan in the 1930s and 1940s.

Unfortunately Kim's excessive emphasis on the development of an autarkic, militaristic state based on the tenets of 'juche' had a disastrous effect on the country. In the 1950s the DPRK, having inherited a fairly advanced industrial infrastructure from the period of Japanese colonial rule and having used state control to expand production, had an economy that rivalled that of the ROK. By the 1970s, with Park Chung-hee's regime beginning its export-orientated economic growth, the DPRK's obsession with military spending meant that it fell far behind.

In the 1980s there was an attempt to change, when relations improved with the Soviet Union and a deal was struck that allowed the DPRK access to cheap oil and gas. This, however, proved to be a double-edged sword, for when the Soviet Union collapsed in 1991, the DPRK found that the new Russia was no longer prepared to settle for anything less than the market price for its fuel. The end of the Cold War had, however, another potentially harmful ramification, for, with the PRC increasingly turning towards capitalism and seeking trade relations with South Korea, it appeared that the DPRK was becoming increasingly diplomatically isolated and thus open to a security threat from Seoul and Washington. There were two potential answers to the DPRK's twin dilemma of its need for security and its lack of fuel: it could either negotiate a new relationship with its neighbours, which would give it a security guarantee and access to oil, or it could kill two birds with one stone by developing an indigenous nuclear energy programme. The latter option, though, had the extra advantage that it could also be used to blackmail North Korea's neighbours into agreeing to the former.

In 1993 the increasingly isolated regime in Pyongyang acted to reassert itself by withdrawing from the **Nuclear Non-Proliferation Treaty (NPT)**, thus raising the fear that it intended to acquire nuclear weapons. The United States reacted with great alarm and in 1994 there was talk of a pre-emptive strike against North Korea's nuclear facilities. The crisis was only averted in June when former President Jimmy Carter flew to Pyongyang for talks with Kim Il-Sung. This meeting laid down the basis for an agreement whereby North Korea would continue to respect the NPT in return for American, South Korean and Japanese assistance with oil supplies and developing light-water nuclear reactors. This agreement, which was signed in October 1994, led to an uneasy peace returning to the peninsula. Almost at the same time another development occurred which confirmed the image of the DPRK as a mysterious, contradictory regime, for in July 1994 a dynastic succession took place when Kim Il-Sung died and was succeeded as leader by his son Kim Jong-Il. The dynastic nature of the regime appeared perverse to the West, but in reality it was once again an expression of the elder Kim's extraordinary obsession with reunification on his terms. He had decided as early as the 1970s that if his ideas were to continue to shape the DPRK's future, this could only be done by someone of his own blood.

By the end of the 1990s there was some hope that a period of détente was emerging. In part this was due to the DPRK's clear economic plight and its failure to deal with the dire effects of a number of natural disasters that left it unable to feed its own population. In June 2000 the newly elected South Korean President Kim Dae-jung inaugurated his 'sunshine policy' by flying to Pyongyang for a

Nuclear Non-Proliferation Treaty (NPT)

Proposed by the USSR and the United States in 1968, and subsequently approved by the UNGA, the treaty prohibits the proliferation of nuclear weaponry to 'new' countries. It has been ratified by more than 180 nations but has not prevented some states from either openly or secretly acquiring a nuclear weapons capability.

summit meeting with Kim Jong-Il. This temporary thaw in relations did not, however, develop much momentum. In the face of the clear hostility of the George W. Bush administration, which in January 2002 declared the DPRK to be part of the 'axis of evil', Kim pushed ahead with the policy of developing a nuclear capacity. At the end of 2002 it expelled the last two remaining UN inspectors in the country and then in January 2003 once again announced its intention to leave the NPT. A few months later, as American forces were invading Iraq, the North Koreans restarted their nuclear programme in earnest, arguing that this was necessary for self-defence and in October 2005 duly declared that it had become a nuclear power. It then used this capability to negotiate for itself a deal with the United States, the ROK and Japan that guaranteed its security and access to energy resources. In essence, as a result of the fact that even its conventional forces could bring down a rain of death on Seoul, the DPRK had finally managed to blackmail the West into allowing it to survive.

see Chapter 22

Conclusion

Since its creation in 1949 the PRC has therefore played an important role in the international arena. Within the Cold War it began as an ally of the Soviet Union but ended as a state that was willing to co-operate, although not ally itself, with the United States. It played a key role in the escalation of the Korean and Vietnam wars but also helped to create the conditions that led to the limited détente of the 1970s. It preached Maoist revolution to the Third World in the 1960s, but in the 1980s moved towards a redefinition of Marxism-Leninism that allowed for the creation of a partly capitalist economy. Thus, as the historian Chen Jian has noted, China consistently helped to shape the course of the Cold War and no understanding of that conflict can be complete without an acknowledgement and understanding of its influence.

However, as the above demonstrates, assessing China's role means coming to terms with a series of paradoxes, for its external policy has often been marked by dramatic shifts in direction. To a degree these paradoxes can be explained in terms of its permanent security concerns, for within the context of the Cold War it sought to defend its own interests by maintaining a balance of power between the two superpowers. It is important though to put more flesh on this vague realist assumption in order to come to any true understanding of China's course. In essence two linked factors have shaped the PRC's foreign policy. The first, which applied throughout the period under examination, was its desire to maintain and assert its independence. After casting off its hundred-year-long virtual subjugation by the imperial Powers, China was determined that it would not be subject to further attempts to erode its sovereignty, either by the United States or by the Soviet Union, and that it would fully unite the country, bringing Hong Kong, Macao and Taiwan home to the motherland. The need to assert China's independence has therefore had a considerable influence on policy, and in particular on the way in which the PRC has represented itself to the outside world. The second factor, which applied most of all to the Maoist years but re-emerged with a vengeance in the Tiananmen Square massacre, was the influence of ideology on the PRC and the importance of defending the revolution. Ideology complemented and, indeed, strengthened Chinese nationalism to the extent that China was even prepared to be an international pariah if that was the price to be paid for ideological purity. The result was a foreign policy that veered between a desire for international acceptance and a tendency to sink into sullen isolation.

Beyond these factors, however, is one more driving force, which is simply that China is an immense country with huge resources at its disposal. Just as its weakness in the nineteenth century led to international disorder as the imperial Powers competed for its considerable spoils, so its recovery from that low point has led to instability. The slow road towards Chinese resurgence began before the communists took power – indeed it was one of the main contributory factors to the outbreak of the **Pacific War** – but since 1949 it has gathered speed, and reached new peaks in the 1990s. Thus, even if China did not bring its troubled historical and ideological legacy to the formulation of its foreign policy, one of the key challenges for the twenty-first century would still be how the world will manage China's almost inevitable move towards superpower status.

However, while the PRC has undergone a great process of change and the question of how smoothly the world can adapt to its growing power is now one of the key debates in international politics, a very different discourse exists in relation to its neighbour, North Korea. Here the issue is not so much how to cope with a rising power, but what to do about an unreconstructed Stalinist state that refuses to die. Most commentators would predict that in the long term the DPRK is doomed to failure and Korea will be reunified, but how that will come about and whether it can be achieved peacefully is a matter for conjecture.

Pacific War
The phrase usually used to refer to the Allied war against Japan from 1941 to 1945.

Recommended reading

The best places to start in understanding the history of the PRC are volumes XIV and XV of the *Cambridge History of China* (Cambridge, 1987 and 1990) and the later chapters of both Jonathan Spence's magisterial *The Search for Modern China* (New York, 1999) and Jack Gray's *Rebellions and Revolutions: China from the 1880s to the 1990s* (Oxford, 1990). A number of overviews of Chinese communist foreign policy exist, including John Garver, *Foreign Relations of the People's Republic of China* (Englewood Cliffs, NJ, 1993) and Thomas Robinson and David Shambaugh (eds), *Chinese Foreign Policy: Theory and Practice* (Oxford, 1994). A useful review of American attitudes towards China is Rosemary Foot, *The Practice of Power: US Relations with China since 1949* (Oxford, 1997).

For Mao's China, see Roderick MacFarquhar's three-volume series, *The Origins of the Cultural Revolution* (New York, 1974–97), Stuart Schram, *The Thought of*

Mao Zedong (Cambridge, 1989), Michael Schoenhals, *China's Cultural Revolution, 1960–1969: Not a Dinner Party* (London, 1996), Frederick Teiwes, *China's Road to Disaster: Mao, Central Politicians, and Provincial Leaders in the Unfolding of the Great Leap Forward, 1955–1959* (Armonk, NY, 1999) and Joseph W. Esherick *et al.* (eds), *The Chinese Cultural Revolution as History* (Stanford, CA, 2006). For Mao's foreign policy, see Chen Jian's provocative study, *Mao's China and the Cold War* (Chapel Hill, NC, 2001). The Sino-Soviet alliance has been much misunderstood, but Odd Arne Westad (ed.), *Brothers in Arms: The Rise and Fall of the Sino-Soviet Alliance, 1945–1963* (Stanford, CA, 1998) provides a useful corrective. On Sino-American relations until the rapprochement, see Harry Harding and Yuan Ming (eds), *Sino-American Relations 1945–1955: A Joint Assessment of a Critical Decade* (Wilmington, DE, 1989), Gordon Chang, *Friends and Enemies: The United States, China and the Soviet Union* (Stanford, CA, 1990), Shu Guang Zhang, *Deterrence and Strategic Culture: Chinese–American Confrontations, 1949–1958* (Ithaca, NY, 1992), Robert Ross and Jiang Changbin (eds), *Re-examining the Cold War: US–China Diplomacy, 1954–1973* (Cambridge, MA, 2001) and Simei Qing, *From Allies to Enemies: Visions of Modernity, Identity, and US–China Diplomacy, 1945–1960* (Cambridge, MA, 2006).

For China's relations with the Third World, Gerald Segal, *The Great Power Triangle* (Basingstoke, 1982), Ronald Keith, *The Diplomacy of Zhou Enlai* (New York, 1989) and Andrew Wedeman, *The East Wind Subsides: Chinese Foreign Policy and the Origins of the Cultural Revolution* (Washington, DC, 1987) contain useful information. For the Cultural Revolution period and the Sino-American rapprochement, see John Garver, *China's Decision for Rapprochement with the United States, 1968–1972* (Boulder, CO, 1982) and Barbara Barnouin and Yu Changgen, *Chinese Foreign Policy during the Cultural Revolution* (London, 1998). On the Vietnam War, see Cheng Guan Ang, *Vietnamese Communists' Relations with China and the Second Indochina Conflict, 1957–1962* (Jefferson, VA, 1997), Zhai Qiang, *China and the Vietnam Wars, 1950–1975* (Chapel Hill, NC, 2000) and Priscilla Roberts (ed.), *Behind the Bamboo Curtain: China, Vietnam, and the Cold War* (Stanford, CA, 2006).

China in the post-Cultural Revolution period is covered by Richard Baum, *Burying Mao; Chinese Politics in the Age of Deng Xiaoping* (Princeton, NJ, 1994), Kenneth Lieberthal, *Governing China: From Revolution to Reform* (New York, 1995), D. Shambaugh (ed.), *Deng Xiaoping: Portrait of a Chinese Statesman* (Oxford, 1995), Colin Mackerras, Pradeep Taneja and Graham Young, *China since 1978* (London, 1998) and Maurice Meisner, *Mao's China and After: A History of the People's Republic* (New York, 1999). Works that deal with post-Cultural Revolution Sino-American diplomacy are Harry Harding, *A Fragile Relationship: The United States and China since 1972* (Washington, DC, 1992), Robert Ross, *Negotiating Cooperation: US–China Relations, 1969–1989* (New York, 1995), James Mann, *About Face: A History of America's Curious Relationship with China: From Nixon to Clinton* (New York, 1998), Patrick Tyler, *A Great Wall: Six Presidents and China* (New York, 1999) and Ezra Vogel, Yuan Ming and Akihiko Tanaka (eds), *The Golden Age of the US–China–Japan Triangle, 1972–1989* (Cambridge, MA, 2002). A good survey of China and its role in the contemporary international system is Andrew Nathan and Robert Ross, *The Great Wall and the Empty Fortress: China's Search for Security* (New York, 1997).

For the evolution of North Korea under Kim Il-Sung, see Adrian Buzo, *The Guerilla Dynasty: Politics and Leadership in the DPRK 1945–1994* (London, 1999), Charles K. Armstrong, *The North Korean Revolution, 1945–1950* (Ithaca, NY, 2003) A. N. Lankov, *From Stalin to Kim Il Sung: The Formation of North Korea, 1945–1960* (London, 2001), and Balázs Szalontai, *Khrushchev versus Kim Il-sung: Soviet–DPRK Relations and the Roots of North Korean Despotism, 1953–1964* (Stanford, CA, 2005). The international crisis created by North Korea's nuclear ambitions is covered by Leon Sigal, *Disarming Strangers: Nuclear Diplomacy with North Korea* (Princeton, NJ, 1997), Victor D. Cha and David C. Kang, *Nuclear North Korea: A Debate on Engagement Strategies* (New York, 2005), Selig S. Harrison, *Korean Endgame: A Strategy for Reunification and US Disengagement* (Princeton, NJ, 2003), Michael O'Hanlon and Mike M. Mochizuki, *Crisis on the Korean Peninsula* (New York, 2003), Gavan McCormack, *Target North Korea: Pushing North Korea to the Brink of Nuclear Catastrophe* (Washington, DC, 2004), and Ted Galen Carpenter and Doug Bandow, *The Korean Conundrum: America's Troubled Relations with North and South Korea* (London, 2004).

The United States and Latin America, 1945 – 2007

Introduction

Given the domination of the United States over continental affairs and the Soviet Union's inability to project its power beyond its immediate neighbours, Central and South America remained in the 1940s rather distant from the issues that lay at the heart of the East–West division. By the early 1980s, however, President Ronald Reagan was quoting the **Truman Doctrine** as he exhorted Congress to back his crusade against communism in Central America. Thus, while direct Soviet involvement outside the island of Cuba remained limited, Latin America gradually claimed a place as one of the hottest battlegrounds of the Cold War.

This development owed much to Latin American dissatisfaction with the reality and implications of American domination. American economic and political dominance of the Western Hemisphere had been well established in the first half of the twentieth century and was justified under the principles of the **Monroe Doctrine**. Whether through direct intervention, as had been the case until the early 1930s, or via local dictators (such as the Somozas in Nicaragua, Batista in Cuba or Trujillo in the Dominican Republic), the United States effectively controlled its Central American neighbours to its own economic and political advantage. The South American countries were exempt from the presence of American troops, but their economies depended heavily on the United States. The Second World War, by removing any serious challengers to

Truman Doctrine
The policy of American president Harry S. Truman, as advocated in his address to Congress on 12 March 1947, to provide military and economic aid to Greece and Turkey. Subsequently used to justify aid to any country perceived to be threatened by communism.

Monroe Doctrine
The doctrine declared by President James Monroe in 1823 in which he announced that the United States would not tolerate intervention by the European Powers in the affairs of the Western Hemisphere.

Washington's hegemony (such as Britain, Germany or Japan) from Latin American markets, only heightened American influence.

However, in the aftermath of the Second World War, the United States discovered that it could no longer take for granted this troubled continent where economic and social dislocation was widely spread and where American dominance ('Yankee imperialism') was often identified as the chief reason for the pervasive inequality. If in Washington military dictators were generally considered the only force that could ensure stability south of the Rio Grande, the post-war years saw these same dictators become targets of popular revolts fuelled by persistent economic inequality, anti-Americanism, nationalism and socialism. Thus, even as direct Soviet involvement in Latin America remained negligible, calls for removing the 'yoke of American imperialism' created a problem of massive proportions for American policy-makers. Their responses – whether covert or overt, economic or military – helped sustain the reality of American dominance throughout much of Latin America in the decades following the Second World War.

Hemispheric unity, internal dislocation

In 1945, given that few Latin Americans had participated directly in the Second World War, there were no massive victory parades in Santiago, Caracas or Mexico City. Still, the Latin Americans had high expectations. After all, they had played an important role in the Allied war effort as suppliers of raw materials and foodstuffs and, with minor exceptions, all had formally joined the Allied cause (even Argentina declared war on Germany in 1945). At the same time, the war confirmed the US dominance over the Western Hemisphere. Trade with any other part of the world was now virtually impossible for the Latin Americans, for the war had either destroyed (Germany, Japan, Italy) or severely weakened (Britain) the power of those countries that could have presented any semblance of a challenge to American supremacy in the region. By 1945 the Monroe Doctrine had triumphed as never before.

Nor did the obvious clash between America's regional interests in Latin America (and the Monroe Doctrine) and the internationalism embedded in the founding of the **United Nations (UN)** change much in inter-American relations. In February 1945 a pan-American conference in Chapultepec, Mexico, had foreshadowed the formation of a post-war military alliance in the Western Hemisphere. Later in the year, the United States pressed for the inclusion of Articles 51–54 in the UN Charter, giving regional bodies the right to deal with crises without 'external intervention'. In the 1947 **Rio Treaty** the American republics concluded a collective defence pact that created a regional institution – dominated by the United States – which could be used to legitimize American intervention. In effect, from 1945 to 1947 the United States managed to forge a marriage of sorts between its oldest foreign policy principle (the Monroe

United Nations (UN)
An international organization established after the Second World War to replace the League of Nations. Since its establishment in 1945, its membership has grown to 192 countries.

Rio Treaty (Inter-American Treaty of Reciprocal Assistance)
Signed on 2 September 1947, and originally ratified by all twenty-one American republics. Under the treaty, an armed attack or threat of aggression against a signatory nation, whether by a member nation or some other power, will be considered an attack against all.

Doctrine) and its new internationalist emphasis. The **Organization of American States (OAS)** – a regional body established to settle inter-American disputes – was launched in 1948 and formally established in 1951.

However, beneath the surface of this formalized treaty structure lay a growing Latin American nationalism that, given the US dominance of the region, translated into an escalation of anti-Americanism. Continued high levels of poverty, illiteracy and inadequate health care further intensified such sentiments, as did a population explosion not deterred by high infant mortality rates. The structure of dependency and the dominance in the commercial sphere of American-based multinational companies seemed to many to bear responsibility for the stark levels of inequality. Moreover, Washington's support for right-wing dictatorships, which often ruled with the support of American-trained and armed militias, further fed the antipathy that Central and South Americans felt towards the colossus of the north.

The dependency and inequality in the inter-American relationship can be illustrated with a few simple statistics. In 1950 the gross domestic product of all of Latin America was roughly one-seventh of that of the United States ($41 billion and $287 billion respectively) while the population size was roughly the same (155 million in Latin America and 152 million in the United States). In the same year Latin America accounted for 28 per cent of the total of American exports and 35 per cent of US imports. These figures were particularly stark when limited to the Caribbean basin. The American share of Cuban, Guatemalan and Nicaraguan exports, for example, was between 70 and 80 per cent of these countries' total exports. In short, the economically weak 'South' was clearly dependent on the prosperous 'North'.

There is little doubt that the emergence of the Cold War was a contributory factor to the continuation of American domination over Latin America. However, during the early post-war years the recovery of Europe quite understandably dominated American thinking, while the civil war in China and the apparent threat of communism in East Asia forced Washington to concentrate on the need to resuscitate Japan's economy. In such a context there were only limited resources available for aid to South or Central America where the spectre of communism could, or so it seemed, be kept in check by relying on the political stability provided by strong military dictators. In short, there seemed little need, from the perspective of national security, for a **Marshall Plan** for Latin America. Even though most American observers acknowledged the difficulties that such an approach might produce in the long run, they appeared confident that the best, not to say the least expensive, way of containing communism in the Western Hemisphere was to rely on those locals who saw their interests best served by continued dependency upon the United States.

The situation facing the United States in 1950 was summarized neatly by one of the key architects of the policy of **containment**, George Kennan, who maintained that the United States needed to take the threat of communism seriously and not be too squeamish about the methods used in fighting it. As indicated in Kennan's memorandum, which reflected the general US attitude towards Latin American political systems, the Cold War was starting to dominate

Organization of American States (OAS)
An organization formed in 1948 for the purpose of co-ordinated action in economic, political and military matters. Its members include all countries in the Western Hemisphere.

see Map 16.1

see Chapter 13

Marshall Plan
Officially known as the European Recovery Programme (ERP). Initiated by American Secretary of State George C. Marshall's 5 June 1947 speech and administered by the Economic Co-operation Administration (ECA). Under the ERP the participating countries (Austria, Belgium, Denmark, France, Great Britain, Greece, Iceland, Italy, Luxembourg, the Netherlands, Norway, Sweden, Switzerland, Turkey and West Germany) received more than $12 billion between 1948 and 1951.

containment
The term coined by George Kennan for the American, and broadly Western, policy towards the Soviet Union (and communism in general). The

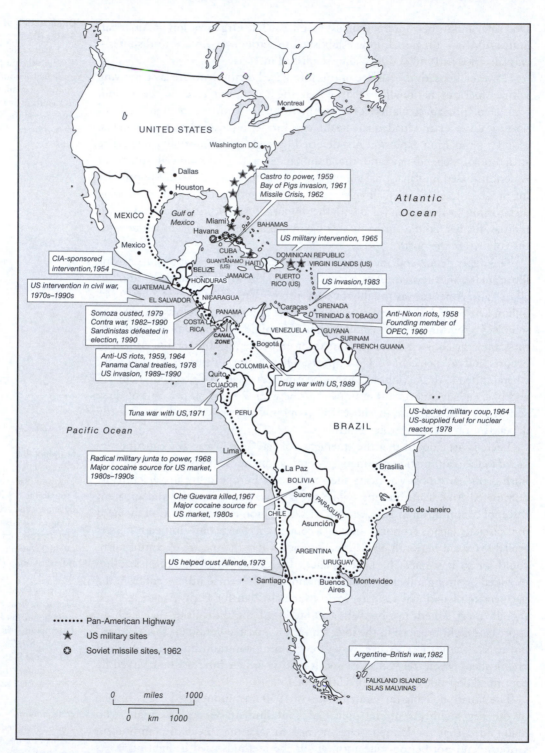

Map 16.1 The United States and Latin America since 1945

Source: After Paterson *et al.* (1999)

American thinking about Latin American problems. Kennan further reflected the traditions of the Monroe Doctrine: the need (and assumed right) to defend American interests in the Western Hemisphere against an 'alien' force: communism. Illustrating this argument, he referred to one particular country where this alien force appeared to be making some headway – Guatemala.

overall idea was to contain the USSR (that is, keep it within its current borders) with the hope that internal division, failure or political evolution might end the perceived threat from what was considered a chronically expansionist force.

Document 16.1

George Kennan on the United States and Latin America, March 1950

We cannot be too dogmatic about the methods by which local Communists can be dealt with . . . where the concepts and traditions of popular government are too weak to absorb successfully the intensity of the Communist attack, then we must concede that harsh governmental measures of repression may be the only answer; that these measures may have to proceed from regimes whose origins and methods would not stand the test of American concepts of democratic procedure; and that such regimes and such methods may be preferable alternatives, and indeed the only alternatives, to further Communist successes.

Source: George Kennan to State Department, March 1950, in Foreign Relations of the United States, 1950

Guatemala

Between 1931 and 1944 Jorge Ubico had ruled the small Central American nation of Guatemala with an iron hand. A typical Latin American dictator, Ubico had nurtured his relationship with the United States and the largest single landowner in Guatemala, the United Fruit Company (UFCO). Ubico suppressed efforts to organize the Guatemalan labour force, repressed any political dissent and showed little interest in the large native Indian population. In July 1944 Ubico was forced to resign and, following a brief interval when General Federico Ponce ruled with the help of the local military, Guatemala held presidential elections. The winner of the December 1944 elections was Juan José Arévalo, a professor of literature and philosophy. During his six-year rule Arévalo championed political, social and economic reform, provoking General Ponce to brand him a communist. Beset with other priorities and concerned about the negative impact that any overt intervention might have at a time when Washington was building hemispheric unity, the United States did not respond positively to Ponce's requests for support. The combination of Arévalo's reform efforts and Ponce's warnings of 'Moscow's growing influence' in Guatemala did, however, encourage the type of thinking embodied in George Kennan's summary of the need to contain communism in Latin America.

While Arévalo was able to complete his six-year term, Jacobo Arbenz Guzmán, a reform-minded military officer who took over the presidency in 1951, was not as fortunate. On taking office Arbenz began an ambitious reform programme of progressive taxation, new social welfare programmes and increased wages for labour. In 1952 he ensured the enmity of UFCO when he expropriated approximately 400,000 acres of non-cultivated UFCO land. Consequently UFCO launched a massive lobbying effort inside the United States, portraying Arbenz as a communist and Guatemala as a breeding ground for the spread of Soviet influence in the Western Hemisphere. Although lacking any real evidence that Arbenz was a communist, the Eisenhower administration concluded in 1953 that events in Guatemala were too ominous to be left alone. Accordingly Eisenhower approved a CIA plan to overthrow the Arbenz regime with American-trained Guatemalan exiles. In 1953–54 training camps were set up in Nicaragua and Honduras, headed by Castillo Armas. In addition, the United States initiated a resolution in the OAS that declared the communist domination of any state in the Western Hemisphere a threat to the security of all member states. The resolution was passed in early 1954 by seventeen votes to one (with Guatemala as the lone objector). By now the United States had also cut off all assistance to Guatemala.

Events advanced rapidly. Arbenz, convinced that a campaign to topple his government was under way, turned to the Soviet bloc in a desperate search for arms. In May 1954 a Swedish ship carrying Czech-made weapons arrived in Guatemala. The following month Castillo Armas and his small contingent attacked from Honduras while American planes bombed Guatemala City. After Arbenz had fled, Guatemala, ruled by Armas until his assassination in 1957, returned to 'normalcy'. UFCO lands were returned, left-wing critics imprisoned and the Guatemalan rulers remained loyal supporters of the United States, to the extent that in the early 1960s Guatemala would be a training ground for another CIA force of Latin American exiles: the Cubans preparing to overthrow Fidel Castro's regime.

However, while the CIA, and its legendary director Allen Dulles, were widely congratulated within the Eisenhower administration (and by UFCO) for its successful operation, the overthrow of Arbenz did little to blunt the growing criticism of the United States throughout Latin America. To many Latin American intellectuals, students and others, the not-so-hidden hand of the Eisenhower administration in Guatemala only confirmed that the real source of the region's economic and social problems lay in the north. As the links between the CIA, Armas and UFCO entered the folklore of a growing group of radicals throughout Latin America, nationalism and anti-Americanism easily blended with various left-wing groups demanding social and economic reform. 'Yankee go home' thus became a widespread slogan.

It was Vice-President Richard Nixon's unenviable fate to experience the growth of anti-Americanism at first hand. In April to May 1958 Nixon toured South America on a goodwill visit. In Uruguay and Peru he encountered a mix of supporters and protesters, but in Caracas, the capital of Venezuela, he felt the full force of regional anti-Americanism. Earlier in the year the United States had provided asylum for the country's recently deposed dictator, Marcos Perez Jimenez, as well as for Jimenez's much hated chief of police. Venezuelan crowds therefore took out their frustrations on Nixon, whose motorcade was surrounded by hostile crowds. The vice-president narrowly escaped before actual shooting broke out and eventually returned to the United States unharmed, but the incident brought home to Washington the unpopularity of its policies and persuaded the Eisenhower administration that the threat of communism in Latin America was growing.

In response, the United States therefore started to increase its aid programmes south of the border, abandoning Eisenhower's previous 'trade not aid' approach to economic development. In a characteristic move, however, the US administration emphasized military over economic aid and stressed the need to bring home to Latin American opinion the dangers of communism. The new approach did little to answer the general demands that lay at the heart of Latin American nationalism, namely an end to American interference in their internal affairs and increased control over raw materials.

In 1959 the United States supported the establishment of the **Inter-American Development Bank** and pledged $500 million for projects that would be managed by the new body. However, the same year saw further problems emerge. In Panama there were widespread riots and demonstrations against continued American ownership of the Canal Zone. Even more dramatically, in Cuba the American-supported dictator Fulgencio Batista, who had ruled the country for almost three decades, was overthrown by a movement headed by a man who would end up leading the small Caribbean nation for an even longer period of time.

Inter-American Development Bank
Organized in 1959 to foster the economic development of the Western Hemisphere. It is mainly funded by the United States.

The Cuban Revolution

In the late 1950s few expected Fidel Castro's revolution in Cuba to survive into the twenty-first century. The island's location alone, 150 kilometres or 90 miles south of Florida, made it a special case for American foreign policy. As Theodore Roosevelt had made clear in the early twentieth century, the United States would never willingly allow Cuba to be dominated by a hostile (or in fact any other) foreign Power. Moreover, the 1954 overthrow of the Arbenz government in Guatemala had been a reminder of the American determination to maintain its grip on countries immediately south of its border.

Castro was eager to avoid the fate of Arbenz, but he was equally aware that his domestic popularity was heavily based on the anti-Americanism of the '**Fidelista**' revolution. Moreover, a truly independent Cuba could hardly emerge if he did not take active measures to minimize the stranglehold that American financiers and corporations had on the country's economic and political life. Initially therefore Castro followed a cautious line, implementing only partial nationalization of foreign interests while at the same time making overtures to Washington. However, when the Eisenhower administration ignored these overtures, Castro began to gravitate towards Moscow, where the Soviet leader, Nikita Khrushchev, eager to build upon his self-proclaimed image as a promoter of wars of national liberation, offered Cuba economic assistance. Castro responded by deciding to

Fidelistas
The name used for the Cuban revolutionaries under Fidel Castro's leadership. After a long guerrilla campaign the Fidelistas eventually toppled the Batista regime on 1 January 1959.

purchase oil from the USSR. Furthermore, when American companies refused to refine this oil, he retaliated by nationalizing their refineries and then proceeded to take similar action against other American interests.

The combination of Soviet support, nationalization of American business interests and domestic pressure to remove the 'cancer' of communism so near to the shores of Florida prompted both the Eisenhower and Kennedy administrations to initiate – ultimately unsuccessful – actions to remove Castro's regime. As early as November 1959 the Eisenhower administration had effectively decided that Castro had to be overthrown. In March 1960 Eisenhower signed an executive order authorizing the CIA to train Cuban exiles; meanwhile, Washington instituted a complete trade embargo against Cuba.

In April 1961 the growing Cuban–American antipathy climaxed in the **Bay of Pigs** invasion. Following the model that had proved to be such a success in Guatemala seven years earlier, the operation was based on the idea that the CIA would train a force of Cuban exiles to invade their homeland and overthrow Castro's regime. This plan was put together during the last months of the Eisenhower administration and was inherited by the new president, John F. Kennedy, who, having used tough language about Cuba during the presidential campaign, felt that he had to agree to the invasion plan. Accordingly, on 16 April 1961 the CIA-trained force of 1,500 guerrillas landed at the Bay of Pigs, 125 miles (200 kilometres) south of Havana. However, faced with international criticism for allowing American planes to engage in bombing attacks to assist the invaders, Kennedy on the second day of the operation cancelled any further air support with the result that the small Cuban air force quickly destroyed the ships that were carrying vital ammunition supplies for the invaders. Stranded without adequate supplies, and unable to garner any significant indigenous support, the invaders were either captured or killed by 19 April.

Although Castro successfully defeated the invasion force, the Bay of Pigs was a clear reminder of the strength of the new American government's antipathy towards Cuba. Indeed, the failure of the invasion did not keep the Kennedy administration from considering other ways in which to overthrow Castro. The CIA, which lost much of its credibility in the eyes of Kennedy as a result of the Bay of Pigs fiasco, tried to assassinate the Cuban leader (Operation Mongoose). In the meantime Castro looked towards the USSR for further support. In return, Nikita Khrushchev offered to deploy Soviet nuclear missiles in Cuba, setting the stage for the October 1962 Missile Crisis.

Although it is discussed in more detail above, it is necessary to stress here that, from the Cuban perspective, the crisis yielded both positive and negative results. On the positive side, in return for the Soviet withdrawal of missiles, the Kennedy administration pledged not to try and overthrow the Castro regime by force. Castro could therefore breathe a sigh of relief. However, the negative side-effects of the crisis were manifold. In particular, the United States continued to pressurize Cuba economically and politically, resulting in the island's virtual isolation from the rest of the Western Hemisphere. This became increasingly clear as the United States put into practice an ambitious economic aid programme for Latin America.

Bay of Pigs
The site on 17 April 1961 of an unsuccessful invasion of Cuba by Cuban exiles opposed to the Castro regime. It had the support of the American government and the CIA was heavily involved in its planning. By 20 April most exiles were either killed or captured. The failed invasion was the first major foreign policy act of the Kennedy administration and provoked anti-American demonstrations in Latin America and Europe and further embittered American–Cuban relations.

see Chapter 11

The Alliance for Progress

The failed Bay of Pigs invasion represented one method of fighting the spectre of communism in Latin America. Yet the Kennedy administration recognized more clearly than its predecessor that military intervention, even when successful, could yield only short-term solutions to the structural problems that had led to the growth of anti-Americanism and nationalism in Central and South America. The Soviet Union's successful courting of Castro was, moreover, an indication that the various revolutionary movements had the potential to turn America's 'backyard' into a Cold War battleground. To avert any repetition of Cuba, therefore, the Kennedy administration seized the moment in the spring of 1961, even as the Bay of Pigs invasion went ahead, to launch an ambitious aid programme aimed at boosting Latin American development.

As noted above, the need to increase economic aid to Latin America had been acknowledged during the later stages of the Eisenhower administration. However, bodies such as the Inter-American Development Bank paled in comparison with the Kennedy administration's **Alliance for Progress**. Soliciting an enthusiastic response from south of the border, the new president announced in March 1961 an ambitious aid programme that was quickly compared to the Marshall Plan. In the speech which set out the programme Kennedy engaged in typical rhetorical excess, making references both to 'this very moment of maximum opportunity', as well as to 'the alien forces that once again seek to impose the despotisms of the Old World on the people of the New'. In short, Kennedy expressed the boundless opportunities that modernization held for the people of Latin America as well as the dangers of the 'despotism' of Soviet-style communism. Much as in post-war Europe, the major problem, Kennedy repeatedly stressed, was poverty. To counter the negative political consequences of continued social and economic inequality in Latin America Kennedy thus called for 'a vast co-operative effort, unparalleled in magnitude and nobility of purpose, to satisfy the basic needs of the American People for homes, work and land, health and schools'. Kennedy's words were reminiscent of George Marshall's 1947 call for a campaign in Europe against 'hunger, poverty, and chaos'.

Formally launched in August 1961 at Punta del Este in Uruguay, with all Latin American countries except Cuba in attendance, the Alliance for Progress pledged $20 billion of American money for development over the subsequent decade. The recipient countries were to match the American aid effort with equal amounts of funding. Through trade, aid and co-operation the Alliance would attack the massive economic inequalities, poor living conditions, inadequate health care and high levels of illiteracy that plagued Latin American countries. While the United States did not intend to force full-scale democracy upon the countries south of its borders, aid was to be dependent on political change. The assumption was that with the creation of a substantial Latin American middle class, the need for military dictatorships as a protective shield against communism would dwindle, and ultimately the entire Western Hemisphere would be transformed into a bastion of modernized liberal democracy.

Alliance for Progress
The American assistance programme for Latin America begun in 1961, which called for an annual increase of 2.5 per cent in per capita income, the establishment of democratic governments, more equitable income distribution, land reform, and economic and social planning. Latin American countries (excluding Cuba) pledged $80 billion over ten years, while the United States pledged $20 billion. After a decade of mixed results, the Alliance was disbanded in 1973.

The Kennedy administration moved to initiate the Alliance for Progress in large part as a result of the Cuban revolution and the emerging links between the Soviet Union and Castro's regime. One important provocation was that in early 1961 the Soviet leader, Nikita Khrushchev, made a public pronouncement in which he pledged support for wars of national liberation and cited Soviet economic assistance to Cuba as a case in point. This, and the danger that Cuba might seek to export its revolution, undoubtedly added to the sense of urgency. Indeed, another way of interpreting the aims of the Alliance is to say that it sought to prevent any more Cubas, because the new programme would remove the sort of social and economic circumstances that had led to the Cuban revolution.

For all its promise, however, the Alliance for Progress did not dramatically transform the relationship between the United States and its neighbours to the south. While the announcement of the Alliance for Progress, as well as Kennedy himself, was extremely popular in Latin America, the practical application of the ambitious programme proved immensely difficult. On the one hand there were simply too many vested interests at stake. On the other was the fact that the Alliance for Progress could only offer a long-term solution to the structural problems that impeded growth in Latin America. This was unfortunate, for the fact that it did not lead to an immediate 'cure' meant that American policy-makers in the 1960s increasingly looked to 'proven' methods of direct and covert intervention to counter any challenges to stability.

Another problem that emerged was that, despite all the hopes engendered by **'modernization' theory**, the authorities in many recipient countries – as well as American governmental bureaucracies and private firms with significant investments in Latin America – were generally opposed to any form of social engineering. Over the preceding decades political and economic power in most of Latin America had been controlled by relatively small oligarchies. These groups naturally had little interest in abandoning their hold on power or engaging in serious land reform or social welfare efforts. Therefore by the mid-1960s, in order to accommodate these local interests and to avoid enraging the nationalists any further, the United States abandoned the initial requirement that aid was to be tied to political reform. As a result corruption became a constant problem. Latin American elites pocketed portions of the aid money, refused to engage in significant land reform and opposed any far-reaching plans for progressive taxation. In retrospect, it seems that political change was required before the Alliance could have any chance of achieving its goals. However, American officials had no interest in working against the traditional friendly elites, while Congress specifically banned the use of American funds for land redistribution to the poor. Coupled with the lack of an effective 'master plan' or a coherent overall organizational structure, this inevitably made the Alliance for Progress a half-hearted effort.

American businesses were equally keen on safeguarding the stability provided by local rulers. It was not, for example, in the interest of UFCO to support policies that would raise wages and improve the social standing of cheap labour in countries like Guatemala; it made little sense voluntarily to raise one's operating costs. American investors also encouraged local landowners to use Alliance funds

'modernization' theory
The idea that rapid economic development is achieved by a state going through a 'take-off' stage in which an entrepreneurial class and high investment in economic growth play a crucial part. The theory is closely associated with the Massachusetts Institute of Technology (MIT) economist Walt Rostow, who served in both the Kennedy and Johnson administrations.

to develop export crops (such as coffee) rather than staple foods (such as beans). While local elites and American investors made large profits from such exports, inadequate food supplies in Latin America remained a constant problem.

Moreover, there was the additional problem that the Alliance's efforts to initiate change took place during a population explosion. While infant death rates declined in part as a result of improvements in medical care, of greater significance was the fact that the Roman Catholic Church, the dominant religion in Latin America, continued to resist any plans for birth control. Thus, whatever economic expansion and improvements in living conditions may have trickled down to the poorest parts of Latin America were of little substantial consequence to regions with an average annual population growth exceeding 2.5 per cent per year. This was the rate of increase even though the Alliance for Progress failed to meet its ambitious goal of halving infant deaths by the end of the 1960s. In 1968, for example, the death rate for children under one year of age remained 75 per 1,000 in Peru, 86 in Chile and a regional 'high' of 94 in Guatemala. In the case of Guatemala the rate had actually increased (but the population still grew).

The Alliance also fell short of achieving its aim of an annual GDP growth rate of 5.5 per cent by the mid-1960s. Only Nicaragua, where the continued stranglehold of the Somoza family and their allies allowed little of the new wealth to trickle down to the majority of the population, could boast such a rate by 1965. Other countries' GDP growth rates in the first half of the 1960s varied from Colombia's 1.6 per cent to El Salvador's 3.7 per cent. Moreover, the benefits of such admittedly positive but relatively modest growth tended to translate into more money for those who already had it: of every $100 of new income generated in the 1960s only $2 trickled down to the poorest one-fifth of the population.

The inflated promises and meagre results of the Alliance for Progress did little to reduce the attraction of revolutionary ideas. In the 1950s and 1960s almost thirty separate revolutionary groups and guerrilla organizations emerged to challenge the existing political power structures. A few of them, such as Nicaragua's Sandinistas, were eventually successful in seizing power, but most guerrilla groups, including the Rebel Armed Forces in Guatemala and the Armed Forces of National Liberation in Venezuela, remained a somewhat marginalized but constant threat to their country's internal stability. Perhaps most worryingly from the American point of view, several Cuban revolutionaries did try to export their movement to the rest of the Western Hemisphere. In a spectacular, if ultimately doomed, effort the Argentine-born Ernesto 'Che' Guevara, Castro's most famous lieutenant, organized the so-called *foco* group in the Bolivian highlands in the mid-1960s.

Despite the idealistic rhetoric of the Alliance for Progress, the United States and most Latin American governments responded with force to the proliferation of revolutionary movements. Washington provided increasing amounts of military aid while many Latin Americans actively repressed any discontent and hunted down the guerrillas (Guevara, who was unable to gain the mass support he had hoped for, was killed in October 1967). Moreover, the Johnson administration, concerned over the leftward shift in the area's largest country, supported a 1964 military coup in Brazil; indeed, the United States was even ready to send troops

Plate 16.1 Ernesto Guevara, 17 December 1964. Profile portrait of Argentine-born Cuban Marxist revolutionary Ernesto 'Che' Guevara, wearing a beret and smoking a cigar in an airport, probably New York City. (Photo: Bob Parent/Hulton Archive/Getty Images)

there if that proved necessary. For Brazil, the result was two decades of military rule; only in 1985 did the country again experience democratic elections.

Nor did the United States shy away from direct intervention in the 1960s. In 1965 20,000 American marines landed in the Dominican Republic in the largest American intervention in the Caribbean since the 1920s. The return of such 'gunboat diplomacy' had been in the making for several years. Following the assassination of the American-supported military dictator, Rafael Trujillo, in May 1961 the Kennedy administration, fresh from the Bay of Pigs fiasco and fearing 'another Cuba' on its watch, had dispatched a naval force to the Dominican capital, Santo Domingo. In addition to this gesture, the United States had boosted the Council of State that ruled the Dominican Republic through extensive economic aid and assistance to the local security forces and by training the Dominican army in counter-insurgency methods. After presidential elections in late 1962 the journalist-politician Juan Bosch had ruled the country between January and September 1963, at which point he succumbed to a military coup and took refuge in Puerto Rico. Even this had not brought about stability, for General Donald Reid Cabral's presidency came to an abrupt end on 24 April 1965 when a coalition of Bosch supporters and young officers set up a rival government. The Dominican Republic – and more specifically its military forces – was now divided between the Constitutionalists (those who called for the return of Bosch) and the Loyalists (who worked to restore a military junta).

The Johnson administration was in a dilemma. It did not wish to take a clear stand in favour of either side but also had no desire to see the Dominican Republic descend into a long civil war that might bring into power a left-wing politician or even encourage Cuban (or worse yet Soviet) intervention. The administration thus settled on a 'third way': it would restore stability, install a provisional junta and hold elections (in which it would ensure that an undesirable candidate, such as Bosch, would not be able to triumph). Thus, in the same year as the United States began dispatching ground troops to Vietnam, marines returned to the Dominican Republic after a four-decade hiatus. Despite the lofty promises of the Alliance for Progress, interventionism thus re-emerged as an official American policy option in the mid-1960s. 'Gunboat diplomacy', many charged, had been revived.

see Chapter 6

Revolutionaries and reformers from Chile to Nicaragua

Neither the Alliance for Progress nor the return to gunboat diplomacy could, however, dampen the growth of anti-Americanism or the spread of revolutionary ideas. Throughout much of Latin America the United States was still perceived as the chief obstacle to true independence, either because the Americans supported the ruling elites and effectively sanctioned their repressive policies or simply because change did not come rapidly enough to answer the demands of a growing population. However, as the United States found itself increasingly trapped in the quagmire in Vietnam, the likelihood of another Dominican Republic-type invasion became unlikely. Thus, by the 1970s, while Latin American demands for social and economic change continued, the American ability to intervene overtly was dampened by the need to avoid being bogged down in another guerrilla war.

The reluctance to use American troops was clear in the case of Chile where Salvador Allende, the leader of the Unidad Popular movement that was supported by both communists and socialists, was elected as president in 1970. The election itself was extremely tight. In the popular vote Allende, who ran unsuccessfully for the presidency six years earlier, won a narrow plurality of the votes – 36.6 per cent in contrast to the right-wing National Party's Jorge Alessandro's 34.9 per cent and the centrist Christian Democrats' Radomiro Tomic's 27.8 per cent – but did not have the majority needed to make him president automatically. The decision was thus transferred to the Chilean National Congress, which, in previous cases of this kind, had always favoured the candidate that had won the most votes. True to this established civic tradition, in late October 1970 the Congress confirmed Allende as the president of Chile.

The Nixon administration was duly outraged. Between the September popular vote and Allende's confirmation as president, the so-called Forty Committee (headed by National Security Advisor Henry Kissinger with representatives from the CIA, State and Defense Departments) had tried to prevent an Allende presidency through a series of schemes that involved bribes and various clandestine manoeuvres. However, neither 'Track I' (a plan to prevent Allende's confirmation) nor 'Track II' (the encouragement of an outright military coup) prevented the inauguration of the democratically elected left-wing president. Therefore the Nixon administration adopted a longer-term strategy to bring down Allende and install a 'friendly' government in Chile. Finally, after three years of economic pressure, during which American economic aid ceased and generous support was provided to Allende's opponents, the Chilean military assumed command of the country in September 1973. Headed by General Augusto Pinochet, the junta launched a brutal crackdown to rid Chile of 'the cancer of Marxism'. At least 3,000 Chileans and a number of foreign nationals were killed or disappeared, scores of others were detained and tortured, socialist and communist party headquarters were raided, labour unions were dissolved, and universities were placed under close government surveillance.

It is worth pondering why a democratically elected government in the furthest corner of Latin America should have made the Nixon administration so anxious. After all, although Chile hosted two American intelligence stations that monitored the movements of the Soviet Pacific fleet, the country had limited strategic significance; as Kissinger is known to have quipped, Chile was 'a dagger pointed at the heart of Antarctica'. However, American economic interests in Chile were substantial: American companies had approximately $1 billion worth of investment there in 1970, and fears of nationalization did prompt conglomerates such as International Telephone and Telegraph (ITT) to offer the CIA $1 million to prevent an Allende presidency. Yet, it is unlikely that either the strategic or the economic considerations weighed heavily in the American administration's determination to bring Allende down. What seems to have concerned Nixon, Kissinger and others was the prospect that a democratically elected socialist government would prove itself a viable political alternative in the Western Hemisphere. For while Castro's Cuba had clear links to the USSR and could be isolated within the Western Hemisphere, Allende's Chile, if allowed to survive, could prove that socialism could flourish in the Western Hemisphere without external support. In other words, if a 'Cuban model' held little attraction throughout the Western Hemisphere, a 'Chilean model' had the potential of answering many of the problems left unresolved by the Alliance for Progress. Given its potentially broad appeal, it was not enough to 'contain' Chilean socialism; it needed to be 'rolled back'.

As in the case of Guatemala in the 1950s, however, the overthrow of Allende did little to solve the structural flaws in inter-American relations. The Chilean president – who either committed suicide on 11 September 1973 (as the new military junta announced) or was killed – became another martyr for those political forces within Latin America that considered the pervasive presence of the United States to be the major source of their economic and social ills. There was a certain historical irony in all this. For the reality was that while the absolute figures (or dollar amounts) for American investment in and trade with Latin American countries grew throughout the Cold War, the region's relative economic importance to the United States was clearly in decline. For example, in 1950 Latin America had received roughly 37 per cent of all American direct investment abroad, but by 1970 this figure had declined to 18 per cent and by 1990 was about 10 per cent. Similarly, in 1950 American exports to Latin America had amounted to 28 per cent of the total, but by the mid-1970s the figure was down to 15 per cent (where it would remain through the 1980s).

In the 1970s and 1980s the decreasing economic significance of Latin America to the United States did not have any discernible positive consequences for the continent. Lacking any other obvious external outlets, the continent's economic growth rates in fact declined in the late 1970s and became negative in the early 1980s. Argentina, for one, 'boasted' a –8.4 per cent GDP growth rate in 1981. Moreover, the region's external debt rapidly escalated. Between 1975 and 1985 Brazil's external debt more than quadrupled, from $25 billion to $106 billion (in 1988 dollars). Nor, as the Chilean example indicates, did the declining economic significance of Latin America to the United States translate into a more relaxed political attitude in Washington. Thus, the call to rise against 'Yankee imperialism' remained as potent a political force in the 1970s as it had been in the 1950s. Given the fate of such socialist reformers as Allende, moreover, it was no wonder that guerrilla movements, rather than democratic socialism, became the focal point of anti-American resentment.

see Chapter 13

While numerous guerrilla movements challenged governmental authority in South America, including the Nineteenth April Movement in Colombia and the Shining Path in Peru, the ones that caught Washington's attention were based in Central America. In El Salvador several groups joined forces in the late 1970s to form the Farabundo Marti National Liberation Front (FMLN), which challenged the ruling civilian–military junta throughout the 1980s. More than 80,000 lives were lost in the protracted conflict. In Guatemala various guerrilla groups continued a similar struggle. However, it was the 1979 victory of the Sandinistas in Nicaragua that truly provoked the United States and led to a protracted, albeit mostly secret, war.

The July 1979 victory of the Sandinista National Liberation Front, headed by Daniel Ortega, brought down one of the longest-standing dictatorships in Latin America. The Somoza family had ruled the country since the 1930s with consistent backing from the United States. By the 1970s, however, the ruling family had lost the support of the local oligarchy as well as that of the general population. The Americans, however, continued to support the Somozas almost to the bitter end. Even the Carter administration refused to talk with the

Sandinistas until they were poised to seize power. Such a stand, which was presumably based on a need to preserve stability, did little to win points for the United States throughout Central America, for the Somozas had few rivals when it came down to abusing human rights.

As was the case with Castro's Cuba, the Sandinistas were able to take power because of fortuitous local and external circumstances. Also, following the Fidelistas' example, the Sandinistas did not initially show much interest in joining the Soviet bloc. Instead, they opted, ultimately in vain, to pursue **non-alignment** in their foreign policy while proclaiming social justice and a mixed economy as their major internal goals. Between 1979 and 1982 Nicaragua looked for and received aid from a number of different sources: other Latin American countries provided more than 30 per cent, while the Soviet bloc's aid package and its share of Nicaragua's foreign trade remained at roughly 20 per cent (in the same period Mexico gave twice as much aid as the Soviet Union). Based on such figures, it is fairly clear that in the early 1980s Nicaragua was hardly 'another Cuba'. The Sandinistas were instead merely looking for a way to avoid renewed dependency upon the United States by diversifying their external ties.

That, though, was apparently enough to alarm the Reagan administration in the United States. Bent on reinstating America's influence, the administration that came to power in early 1981 moved, at least rhetorically, towards a policy of global containment. The danger of 'communist infiltration' was, according to Reagan and his foreign policy team, particularly pervasive in America's backyard, where the so-called 'Moscow–Havana axis' was busily promoting the creation of 'Cuba-model states'. Reagan's secretary of state, Alexander Haig, put it in simple, gangster-like terms: the Soviets, he maintained in March 1981, had a 'hit list' of Central American states with Nicaragua and El Salvador at the top.

The perception that Moscow had targeted Central America for revolution led the Reagan administration to pursue a policy not of containment but of eradication. In El Salvador, while the Reagan administration may not have created the civil war conditions, it certainly provided strong support for the right-wing opposition to the left-wing FMLN rebels, including assistance to the infamous death squads. Moreover, in time-honoured fashion, in 1984 the CIA distributed funds to ensure that the Christian Democratic Party leader, José Napoleón Duarte (who was a graduate of Notre Dame University in Indiana), was elected in the presidential election. On taking office, Duarte entered into talks with the FMLN, but these soon collapsed and the civil war erupted anew, continuing through to the late 1980s. The 1989 election of Alfredo Cristiani, leader of the right-wing ARENA party, to the presidency did nothing immediately to restore peace in El Salvador, but in 1991 his government, with help from the United Nations, renewed negotiations with the FMLN. In early 1992, a peace treaty with the rebels was signed, ending the bloody twelve-year conflict. The FMLN demobilized and participated in the 1994 elections, although the ARENA party continued to hold the presidency through the 1990s. Yet, while terrorism and violence, by both Left and Right, greatly decreased, El Salvador's land redistribution programme, which was one of the government's concessions in the 1992 peace accord, was

non-alignment
A state policy of avoiding involvement in 'Great Power conflicts', most notably the Cold War. It was first espoused by India on its becoming independent in 1947.

implemented slowly and the country's economy continued to pay the price of decades of turmoil.

While trying to tilt the Salvadoran civil war in the 'right' direction, the Reagan administration also worked hard to overthrow the Sandinistas in Nicaragua. All foreign aid was cut off in 1981 and in 1985 the administration imposed an economic embargo. Nicaraguans responded by inviting Cuban medical specialists and teachers, as well as military advisers. A 1982 Congressional resolution forbade the Reagan administration to try to overthrow the Sandinistas, but the CIA attempted to get round it by providing extensive funding to the Contras, an anti-Sandinista force based in Honduras and Costa Rica. By the mid-1980s the Contras were conducting extensive raids into Nicaragua, sabotaging the infrastructure, destroying crops and spreading terror. The American link to the Contras soon became apparent, but although the World Court condemned CIA involvement in activities that included the mining of three Nicaraguan harbours and Congress suspended all aid in 1984, the Reagan administration continued to channel money to the rebels via private organizations. In 1985–86, in a most spectacular and bizarre case that almost led to impeachment hearings against Reagan, Lieutenant-Colonel Oliver North, an officer on the staff of the National Security Council, funnelled profits from a secret arms deal with Iran to the Contras.

Against this background, it was no wonder that in the 1980s the Sandinistas looked increasingly towards Cuba and the Soviet Union for help. However, the results were hardly comforting, for, once clear links were established between Managua, Havana and Moscow, Reagan was able to get $100 million from the Congress to fund 'humanitarian' aid to the Contras. Meanwhile a number of Latin American countries launched peace initiatives that were effectively snubbed by the United States. In 1987, for example, the Costa Rican president, Oscar Arias Sanchez, offered a plan providing for a cease-fire and national reconciliation.

Relative peace returned to Nicaragua only after the Reagan administration left office and the collapse of the Soviet bloc indicated how inflated the fears of a communist conspiracy to seize Central America had been. Building on the foundations of the Arias Plan, a meeting of five Central American presidents in February 1989 produced the so-called 'Tesoro Beach Accord', which called for free elections and the disbanding of the Contras. In February of the following year, after the Sandinistas agreed to allow opposition groups to operate and the Bush administration began to distance itself from the Contras, an extensively monitored election resulted in two surprises. First, the National Opposition Union headed by Violeta Barrios de Chamorro, whose husband had been killed in 1978 by the Somoza forces, soundly defeated the Sandinista leader Daniel Ortega. Second, Ortega, who had served as president for the previous five years, accepted the result. Thus, after a prolonged civil war that had claimed at least 30,000 lives, fighting finally ceased in Nicaragua.

A similar series of events transpired in Guatemala, which had been plagued by intermittent civil war between the government and leftist opposition groups since the 1954 overthrow of the Arbenz government. In 1986 a civilian government headed by Marco Vinicio Cerezo Arévalo took office, which in 1991 was succeeded by one led by Jorge Serrano Elías. Ironically, a peace agreement was only signed in 1996, after the Guatemalan military had deposed Serrano and allowed the inauguration of de Leon Carpio, the former attorney general for human rights, in 1993. Thus ended the longest civil war in Latin American history, which had left approximately 200,000 Guatemalans dead over three-and-a-half decades. Echoing general hopes for a more peaceful future, in 1997 UNESCO awarded the new Guatemalan president, Álvaro Arzú Irigoyen, and the guerrilla movement leader, Ricardo Ramirez, the Houphouët-Boigny Peace Prize. In short, as the Cold War ended, a number of Central American countries moved towards the difficult, but far less violent, phase of national reconciliation.

Into the new millennium: an age of uncertainty

According to conventional wisdom in the 1980s, the United States was, in part by default, losing some of its dominance in the Western Hemisphere. The revolutions in Central America, the growing independence of the Latin American economies and the reluctance of the United States to intervene abroad in the post-Vietnam era were seemingly bringing to an end the era of the Monroe Doctrine. Statistics seemed to confirm this: American trade (including arms shipments to) and direct investment in the Western Hemisphere had, in fact, been in constant decline since the 1950s. Moreover, the Americans had been forced to accept the survival of a communist regime in Cuba and even the Reagan administration was reluctant to intervene openly in places other than the small island of Grenada. By the end of the Cold War, it appeared therefore that Latin America was destined for a new era of independence and, perhaps, prosperity that would, in the long run, result in ever-diminishing American influence (let alone hegemony) in the southern half of the Western Hemisphere.

Yet, throughout the 1990s, it was clear that the economic dependency of Latin America on the United States remained strong. In part this was due to the traditional disparity in wealth. In the 1990s the gross domestic product of the United States was still seven times as high as that of all of Latin America; meanwhile, the Latin American population, which had been roughly equal to that of the US in 1950, was 75 per cent higher in the 1990s (436 million compared with 250 million). In short, in contrast to the United States, Latin America remained relatively poor and overpopulated, which was one reason for the large-scale illegal migration towards the north. Moreover, while American trade with the region as a whole may have been in relative decline in the 1970s and 1980s, the United States was still the largest single trading partner of all Latin American countries in 1990. Even as Japan and the **European Union** made some relative gains in the 1990s (Japan becoming Chile's most important customer), investment by the United States remained twice as high as that of its two major competitors combined. Yet, perhaps most significantly, the United States retained

European Union (EU)
A political and economic community of nations formed in 1992 in Maastricht by the signing of the Treaty on European Union (TEU). In addition to the agreements of the European Community, the EU incorporated two inter-governmental – or supra-national – 'pillars' that tie the member states of the EU together: one dealing with common foreign and security policy, and the other with legal affairs. The number of member states of the EU has expanded from twelve in 1992 to twenty-seven in 2007.

its preponderant political influence in the Western Hemisphere throughout the first post-Cold War decade.

In fact, the post-Cold War era in the Western Hemisphere began with an American military intervention. On 20 December 1989 13,000 American troops joined a group of similar size that permanently guarded American rights in the Panama Canal area to capture Manuel Noriega, the notorious leader of the Panamanian Defence Forces who had earlier in the month had himself declared the chief of government. In early 1988 Noriega, a former intelligence chief and ally of the Reagan administration, had been convicted for money-laundering and drug-trafficking by a US federal court in Florida, but instead of accepting an offer of immunity if he left Panama, Noriega had struck a defiant note. Finally, the Bush administration, identifying the Panamanian leader as a symbol of the illegal drug trade, launched 'Operation Just Cause' without consulting the member states of the OAS. Noriega was captured and eventually tried and convicted in Miami. Amid wide protests throughout Latin America (as well as much of the rest of the world), the American public generally cheered the intervention as a victory in the so-called 'war on drugs'. Perhaps underlying this was a certain satisfaction that the United States had been able to wield its power so effectively and unilaterally. However, Noriega's removal did little to address the real problem, for the drug trade from Latin America to the United States flourished throughout the 1990s.

In 1994 American marines were, once again, poised for intervention in the Caribbean, this time in Haiti. On this occasion the cause had little to do with drugs. Instead, the supposedly non-interventionist Clinton administration launched 'Operation Uphold Democracy' as the result of a mounting refugee crisis in Haiti caused by the actions of a succession of repressive regimes. Throughout the 1980s the Reagan and Bush administrations had repatriated Haitians attempting to flee the brutal regime of Jean-Claude 'Baby Doc' Duvalier; only 28 of the almost 23,000 Haitian 'boat people' were given asylum in the United States. Duvalier was ousted in 1986 and Jean-Bertrand Aristide, a populist priest, won a democratic election in 1990. In September 1991, Aristide himself was ousted in a military coup that was roundly condemned by the OAS and the United States alike. This time, as the flow of refugees escalated, the American coastguard gave temporary safe haven to thousands of Haitians at the Guantanamo Bay military base in Cuba. By the time Clinton, who had called for a more active policy against the military regime in Haiti, took office in early 1993 the prospect that up to 200,000 Haitians would take to the seas was creating a difficult humanitarian and political crisis. Reinforcing the pressure on the new administration was the awareness that public opinion in the United States was clearly concerned about a rapid increase in the number of immigrants of Caribbean descent.

As various mediation efforts to curb this flow of refugees failed, the United States stepped up military pressure and in September 1994 the president openly called for the government of General Raoul Cedras to resign. Eventually, the military rulers agreed to step aside and accept the return of Aristide, who was by no means uniformly supported within the Clinton administration, in exchange for an amnesty. American troops duly arrived in Haiti to restore order and were in turn replaced in 1995 by a Canadian-led UN peacekeeping force, while the

Haitian military itself was gradually demobilized. However, the country has remained politically unstable and economically chaotic up to the present day.

The operations in Panama and Haiti were clear expressions of continued American hegemony in the Caribbean region. Yet in both cases the justification for intervention was remarkably different from those of the Cold War years. Both the Bush and Clinton administrations used the rhetoric of **Wilsonian internationalism** and referred to the need to uphold democracy, but in truth the post-Cold War policy was closely linked to American domestic considerations. In Panama, the Bush administration rationalized intervention as part of its war against drugs; in Haiti, the obvious concern was the prospect of 200,000 poor, mostly uneducated and non-white refugees arriving on US shores. To be sure, the operations were mostly successful in meeting their goals: Noriega was captured and imprisoned, the flow of refugees from Haiti stalled, and both Panama and Haiti were unquestionably 'more democratic' after US intervention. Yet, another lesson of the intervention was also obvious: even in the post-modern age the United States was a regional hegemon capable of intimidation and military action against smaller countries in its neighbourhood.

The changes that took place in the first post-Cold War decade in the Western Hemisphere hardly amounted to a revolution. In the political and economic spheres the United States retained, and in some ways strengthened, its dominant position vis-à-vis its neighbours, while in the military field American troops did engage in small-scale military interventions, although the justifications were rather different from those of the Cold War years. The predominance of the United States and the trend towards globalization led, however, only to partial economic integration and no serious efforts were made to pool political sovereignty.

In the new millennium, though, the North–South relationship started to look rather different. Anti-American attitudes, which had been always prevalent in the region, hardened, with more than half of Latin Americans polled in 2007 proclaiming a negative view of the United States. This reflected in part the global trend towards criticism of the United States that increased after the American-led invasion of Iraq in 2003. In a more regional context, though, the antipathy towards the colossus to the north was a legacy of the historically unequal relationship that continued to bedevil Washington's dealings with its southern neighbours. At times, as in the case of the United States' continued attempts to isolate Cuba or the Bush administration's open campaign in favour of right-wing candidates in Nicaragua's 2007 presidential election, there was a distinctive Cold War flavour to US policies.

In many ways these policies appeared to be counter-productive. In Nicaragua the return of Manuel Ortega, the leader of the Sandinista revolution of the 1970s, to the presidency in 2007 through free elections was clearly a blow to the Bush administration. Cuba, where the ailing Fidel Castro passed the reins of leadership to his brother Raoul in 2006, remained defiant. Such defiance was in part made possible by the generous economic support of the most flamboyant of the twenty-first-century anti-Americans, Hugo Chavez of Venezuela. As president of his oil-rich country since 1999, Chavez spearheaded a 'Bolivarian' revolution, which was designed to free Venezuela from American influence by using the abundant oil

Wilsonian internationalism
Woodrow Wilson's notion, outlined in his so-called fourteen points, of trying to create a new world society, which would be governed by the self-determination of peoples, be free from secret diplomacy and wars, and have an association of nations to maintain international justice.

see Chapter 21

revenue at his disposal, and to create a regional network of like-minded countries. His public stand against the United States included a much-publicized visit to Iraq in 2000 as part of a tour of OPEC nations and the severing of decades-old military ties with the United States. On a broader level, Chavez became one of the world's most open critics of liberal capitalism and a fierce proponent of alternative routes for economic development. A number of other new Latin American leaders either openly sympathized with him, such as Bolivia's Evo Morales, or at least silently applauded his policy of distancing South America from the United States, such as Argentina's Nestor Kirchener.

see Chapter 13

Whether Chavez represents the future, in other words a conflict-ridden North–South relationship in the Western Hemisphere, remains to be seen. What is clear from the vantage point of 2008, however, is that the United States is no longer as dominant a presence in Latin America as it was in the last decades of the twentieth century. Economically, owing in large part to globalization, the increase in trade within the region and the diversification of its external trade relations, Latin America is less dependent on the United States now than at any time since the Second World War. Politically, it has left behind the dark era of dictatorships (often promoted by the United States) and has, in most cases, consolidated democratic governance. Equally importantly, since 11 September 2001, the United States has not regarded Latin American countries as presenting more than a 'potential' threat to its security interests. Although there is no denying the United States' preponderant influence in the region, the Western Hemisphere can no longer be regarded as merely Washington's 'backyard'.

Debating the impact of the Cold War in the Western Hemisphere

One of the basic questions worth asking about the US – Latin American relationship during the Cold War is: how did the structure of interaction in the Western Hemisphere differ from that in Eastern Europe? For accounts that discuss the level of symmetry in the two cases, see Gaddis Smith's *The Last Years of the Monroe Doctrine* (New York, 1993) or Walter LaFeber's *Inevitable Revolutions* (New York, 1983).

Although the various American covert and overt interventions have created much controversy, a more complex debate has to do with the goals and results of the Alliance for Progress initiative. While the early interpretations tended to stress the 'good intentions' behind the Alliance, later scholarship has tended to stress the lack of firm direction and the way in which it veered between at times 'conservative' and at times more 'progressive' aspects of the Alliance's intentions. The latest works exploring the Alliance for Progress in detail are Stephen Rabe, *The Most Dangerous Area in the World* (Chapel Hill, NC, 1999) and Michael Latham, *Modernization as Ideology* (Chapel Hill, NC, 2000). The causes of Latin American resentment towards the United States, an issue that the Alliance for Progress tried to address, are also discussed in these two books.

For a fuller understanding of the United States' policy towards Latin America, it is also important to explore the prevalent 'Northern' attitude towards the 'South'. As Lars Schoultz, among others, has argued, the 'belief in Latin American inferiority is the essential core of the United States policy toward Latin America' (*Beneath the United States*, Cambridge, MA, 1998, p. xv). How far American policy towards Latin America can be explained within such a 'cultural' paradigm is, of course, open to debate. A more 'realist' version can be found in Cole Blasier, *Hovering Giant: US Responses to Revolutionary Change in Latin America* (Pittsburgh, PA, 1986).

Conclusion

From the 1950s to the 1980s Latin America's place in the Cold War vacillated between being seemingly peripheral to being crucially central. And yet one of the ironies of Cold War history is that this continent, which was so far removed from the initial causes of the East–West confrontation, not only became one of its 'hottest' battlegrounds in the early 1980s, but still hosts one of the few surviving communist regimes in the world.

In meeting what it perceived as the communist challenge in Latin America, the United States responded essentially in one of two ways. At one extreme it launched a series of interventions aimed at toppling undesirable governments. With two exceptions, the 1965 landing of marines in the Dominican Republic by the Johnson administration and the Reagan administration's intervention on the small island of Grenada in 1982, these were covert operations. In 1954 the CIA helped train and provide logistical support for the overthrow of the leftist government of Arbenz in Guatemala; in 1961 it attempted but failed miserably in a similar effort in Cuba; between 1970 and 1973 it worked hard to destabilize the socialist government of Salvador Allende in Chile; and in the 1980s the Reagan administration provided support for right-wing guerrillas in Central America.

While such interventions were often counter-productive or produced only short-term successes, American administrations also tried to use economic aid and the building of hemispheric institutional structures to counter the appeal of left-wing causes and anti-American sentiments. Perhaps most notably, in the early 1960s the Kennedy administration launched the Alliance for Progress, an ambitious programme using a combination of American economic aid and matching Latin American efforts that was designed to combat the economic and social problems in the target countries. While hailed initially as a major undertaking, the Alliance for Progress soon ran into difficulties and, in the eyes of its critics, served only to perpetuate the hold on power of Latin American military governments and oligarchies. Furthermore, US administrations were not loath to combine more traditional strong-arm tactics with the lofty promises of economic and social transformation.

Of all the countries in Latin America, it was Cuba that caused the greatest problem for US administrations. Under Fidel Castro, Cuba symbolized many of the failures of previous American policies and posed a constant, if at times exaggerated, challenge to its influence in the region. From the US perspective Cuba provided a base for Soviet operations in the Western Hemisphere, served as a 'model' for other revolutionaries, and acted as an active exporter of revolutionary ideas to countries as distant as Nicaragua and Chile. Indeed, one of the notable 'successes' of US covert action in Latin America in the 1960s was the assassination of Ernesto 'Che' Guevara. There is no question that the Soviet Union took a special interest in seeing the Cuban Revolution, and Fidel Castro, succeed. Yet the Soviet–Cuban relationship was never one of complete dependency, something that in part explains the survival of Castro's regime beyond the Cold War. Since the early 1990s, though, Cuba's economic troubles have multiplied and the country has increasingly been forced to rely on such 'capitalist' industries as tourism in order to obtain the hard currency necessary to purchase foreign imports.

As the Guatemalan, Cuban, Chilean and Nicaraguan cases in particular indicate, Latin American peoples were hardly content with being passive subjects of American foreign policy. In various ways, both violently and peacefully, political movements in a number of South and Central American countries tried to find ways of reducing their economic dependency on the United States. Their problem was that in the context of the Cold War, the only country that could provide a significant external balance to the American dominance was the Soviet Union. As the Cuban and Nicaraguan cases indicated, the United States reacted violently as soon as even the slightest indication of Latin American links to the USSR was evident. Unable to form an effective regional co-operative body that could challenge American hegemony, most countries were thus left with the alternative of trying to adjust their policies in a way that could at least minimize Washington's influence. It would, however, take the end of the Cold War before such policies yielded significant success.

Recommended reading

The best recent overview of US–Latin American relations that pays due attention to developments and policies throughout the Western Hemisphere is Peter H. Smith, *Talons of the Eagle: Dynamics of US–Latin American Relations* (New York,

2000). Some of the other recent overviews of US policy towards Latin America during the Cold War include John H. Coatsworth, *Central America and the United States: The Clients and the Colossus* (New York, 1994), R. H. Holden and E. Zolov, *Latin America and the United States* (New York, 2000), John J. Johnson, *A Hemisphere Apart: The Foundations of United States Policy toward Latin America* (Baltimore, MD, 1990), Walter LaFeber, *Inevitable Revolutions: The United States in Central America* (New York, 1983), Lester D. Langley, *The United States and the Caribbean in the Twentieth Century* (Athens, GA, 1982), Lars Schoultz, *Beneath the United States: A History of US Policy toward Latin America* (Cambridge, MA, 1998) and Gaddis Smith, *The Last Years of the Monroe Doctrine* (New York, 1993). For a somewhat outdated account of the Soviet role, see Cole Blasier, *The Giant's Rival: The USSR and Latin America* (Pittsburgh, PA, 1988).

The Latin American perspective is assessed in such works as Pope Atkins, *Latin America in the International Political System* (Boulder, CO, 1989), Paul Drake (ed.), *Money Doctors, Foreign Debts, and Economic Reforms in Latin America from the 1890s to the Present* (Wilmington, DE, 1994), Victor Bulmer-Thomas, *The Economic History of Latin America since Independence* (Cambridge, MA, 1994), Jennie Lincoln and Elizabeth Ferris, *Latin American Foreign Policies: Global and Regional Dimensions* (Boulder, CO, 1981) and Thomas Skidmore and Peter Smith, *Modern Latin America* (New York, 1996).

On Guatemala, see Piero Gleijeses, *Shattered Hope: The Guatemalan Revolution and the United States, 1944–1954* (Princeton, NJ, 1991) and Richard Immerman, *The CIA in Guatemala* (Austin, TX, 1982). For a broader assessment of US–Latin American relations in the 1950s, see Stephen G. Rabe, *Eisenhower and Latin America: The Foreign Policy of Anticommunism* (Chapel Hill, NC, 1988).

On the Cuban Revolution and its impact, see Jules R. Benjamin, *The United States and the Origins of the Cuban Revolution: An Empire of Liberty in an Age of National Liberation* (Princeton, NJ, 1990) and Thomas Paterson, *Contesting Castro: The United States and the Triumph of the Cuban Revolution* (New York, 1994). On the Bay of Pigs, see Thomas Higgins, *The Perfect Failure* (New York, 1987). An overall account of Castro's Cuban foreign policy is Jorge Dominguez, *Making the World Safe for Revolution: Cuba's Foreign Policy* (Cambridge, MA, 1989). A good study assessing the impact of the Cuban Revolution on the rest of Latin America is Thomas Wright, *Latin America in the Era of the Cuban Revolution* (Westport, CT, 2001). An older account, with a more 'realist' perspective, is Cole Blasier, *The Hovering Giant: US Responses to Revolutionary Change in Latin America* (Pittsburgh, PA, 1986).

Some early accounts of the Alliance for Progress include Jerome Lewinson and Juan de Onis, *The Alliance that Lost its Way: A Critical Report on the Alliance for Progress* (Chicago, 1970) and William D. Rogers, *The Twilight Struggle: The Alliance for Progress and the Politics of Development in Latin America* (New York, 1967). A more recent version with numerous insights is Ronald Scheman (ed.), *The Alliance for Progress: A Retrospective* (New York, 1988). For a study that puts the Alliance in the broader context of 'modernization theory', see Michael E. Latham, *Modernization as Ideology* (Chapel Hill, NC, 2000). For general assessments of Kennedy's policy towards the region, see Edward Martin, *Kennedy and Latin America* (Lanham, MD, 1994) and Stephen Rabe, *The Most Dangerous Area in the World* (Chapel Hill, NC, 1999).

American interventions from the 1960s to the present have produced numerous studies. The 1965 Dominican intervention is treated in Abraham Lowenthal, *The Dominican Intervention* (Cambridge, MA, 1972) and Piero Gleijeses, *The Dominican Crises: The 1965 Constitutionalist Revolt and American Intervention* (Baltimore, MD, 1978). Events in Chile are covered in Nathaniel Davis, *The Last Two Years of Salvador Allende* (Ithaca, NY, 1985), Jonathan Haslam, *The Nixon Administration and the Death of Allende's Chile: A Case of Assisted Suicide* (London, 2005) and Paul Sigmund, *The United States and Democracy in Chile* (Baltimore, MD, 1993). For post-Allende Chile, see Pamela Constable and Arturo Valenzuela, *A Nation of Enemies: Chile under Pinochet* (Baltimore, MD, 1991) and Peter Kornbluh (ed.), *The Pinochet File* (New York, 2005).

The last decade of the Cold War is covered in Thomas Carothers, *In the Name of Democracy: US Policy toward Latin America in the Reagan Years* (Berkeley, CA, 1991), Roy Gutman, *Banana Diplomacy* (New York, 1987), Anthony Lake, *Somoza Falling* (Boston, CO, 1989), Thomas Walker, *Revolution and Counter-revolution in Nicaragua* (Boulder, CO, 1990), Thomas Walker (ed.), *Reagan vs. the Sandinistas* (Boulder, 1987) and William Leogrande, *Our Own Backyard* (Chapel Hill, NC, 1998).

For the post-Cold War era see Thomas E. Skidmore and Peter H. Smith, *Modern Latin America* (New York, 2002), R. H. Holden and E. Zolov, *Latin America and the United States* (New York, 2000) and Greg Grandin, *Empire's Workshop: Latin America, the United States and the Rise of the New Imperialism* (New York, 2006). On the impact of Hugo Chavez, see Richard Gott, *Hugo Chavez and the Bolivarian Revolution* (New York, 2005) and Nikolas Kozloff, *Hugo Chavez: Oil, Politics, and the Challenge to the US* (London, 2006).

CONTENTS

apartheid
The Afrikaans word for racial segregation. Between 1948 and 1990 'apartheid' was the ideology of the Nationalist Party in South Africa

Third World
A collective term of French origin for those states that are part of neither the developed capitalist world nor the communist bloc. It includes the states of Latin America, Africa, the Middle East, South Asia and South-East Asia. Also referred to as 'the South' in contrast to the developed 'North'.

Africa: decolonization and independence, 1945 – 2007

Introduction

In most accounts of the history of the twentieth century it is fair to say that references to Africa are often few and far between. Arguably this is because the prevailing image in the West of the continent is that it is one locked in an endless cycle of corruption, poverty and political violence, which brings misery to Africans but has little impact on international politics as a whole. However, it is wrong to see Africa in this simplistic way, for the history of the continent involves some of the key themes of the second half of the twentieth century, such as the end of European imperialism, the debate about underdevelopment and the degree to which the Cold War paradigm dominated international politics. Indeed, few areas of the world have changed so drastically in a political sense since 1945. When the Second World War came to an end, Africa remained very largely under the control of European imperial Powers and with no prospect of independence being offered in the immediate future. Yet within the space of twenty years most of the continent had thrown off the shackles of direct colonial rule, and by 1994 the last vestiges of white minority rule had disappeared completely with the collapse of **apartheid**. In addition, Africa is important because it is seen so often in the West as a prime example of how **Third World** poverty perpetuates itself. This naturally raises the question of why this should be so. Has Africa simply been singularly unfortunate in its rulers since independence? Or are its problems the result of the global Cold

War and the machinations of international capitalism? Or is it that the factors that have led to endemic corruption and instability are inextricably linked to its colonial past?

The end of empire

Apart from the campaigns in East and North Africa, Africa largely escaped the fighting that ravaged the world between 1939 and 1945. The continent was not, however, by any means isolated from the war, for the Allied need to mobilize colonial resources to defeat the Tripartite Powers led to a number of significant developments. The most obvious was that the loss of the raw materials of South-East Asia in 1941–42 necessitated the rapid expansion of production of resources such as rubber and tin in the African colonies. In addition, the war was important because it saw an even more extensive mobilization of the population than had occurred in 1914–18, some 374,000 Africans being recruited into the British armed forces alone. Those who served overseas were often changed by the experience, returning home more politically conscious than before and keen to achieve European standards of living.

Recognizing that the continent was changing, some of the colonial Powers, most notably Britain and France, saw the necessity during and immediately after the war for a degree of constitutional reform that, by increasing local representation, would legitimize the drive towards economic development. In 1944 the French held a conference at Brazzaville in Equatorial Africa, at which it was agreed to end forced labour, to expand African involvement in local politics and to establish a constituent assembly in Paris that would draw up a constitution for a new French Union. Meanwhile in West Africa, Britain decided in 1946 to establish an African majority in the legislative councils of Nigeria and the Gold Coast (Ghana) and to extend the powers of these bodies.

It would, however, be a mistake to see these reforms as part of a programme that was intended to lead to independence in the near future. The French at Brazzaville made it clear that independence was not on their agenda, while in 1943 the British colonial secretary, Oliver Stanley, ruled out a transfer of power in Africa for generations to come. Instead these political reforms were designed to perpetuate imperial control, for the colonies, both during and after the war, were seen as vital for the future prosperity and security of the metropole. Indeed, once the Second World War came to an end, the European colonial Powers diverted more resources than ever to develop their African possessions. In 1945 the Labour government in Britain passed the second Colonial Development and Welfare Act, which provided £120 million for its colonies in Africa, the Caribbean and South-East Asia, while in 1947 the French established the *Fonds d'Investissement et de Développement Economique et Social des Territoires d'Outre-Mer* (FIDES). Between 1943 and 1957 FIDES invested $542 million in French West Africa alone, far outstripping the British effort to develop its colonies. This push for development came about because it was believed in Britain and France that an expansion of raw material production would increase the ability of their empires to earn dollars, thus assisting the post-war recovery of their metropolitan economies. In addition, it was hoped that greater mobilization of African resources would help to maintain Britain and France as world Powers able to operate independently of the United States and the Soviet Union.

The hope that Africa would contribute to a return to prosperity and power turned out to be a chimera, not least because the very act of encouraging development led, as in the case of India before, to increasing political, economic and social unrest. Indeed, the drive for development proved to be one of the main causes of the rapid shift towards **decolonization** in Africa in the 1950s, for the social and economic discontent that it generated meant that those who preached the cause of liberation from colonial rule began to find a ready audience for their rhetoric.

decolonization

The process whereby an imperial power gives up its formal authority over its colonies.

see Map 17.1

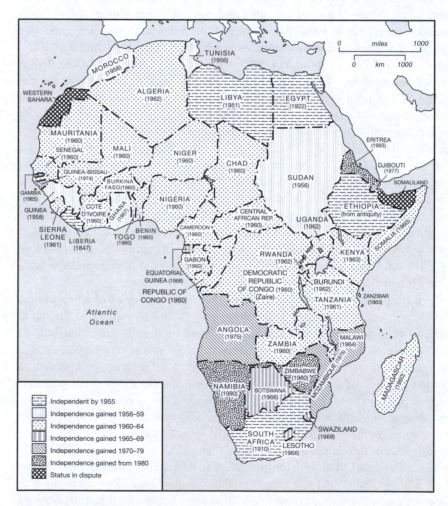

Map 17.1 Decolonization in Africa

Source: After Brown and Louis (1999)

This first became evident in February 1948 when riots broke out in Accra in the Gold Coast. The roots of this urban unrest lay in a number of factors arising out of the push for development, such as high inflation and discontent about employment prospects, particularly among recently demobilized soldiers, and the virtual monopoly that British companies exercised over imports. The initial British reaction was to use the mailed fist and to arrest the leaders of the newly established nationalist party, the United Gold Coast Convention (UGCC), including an organizer who had recently returned from university studies in the United States and Britain, Kwame Nkrumah. However, after investigating the causes of the rioting, the British government decided that only further constitutional reform could bring about a return to stability. Accordingly, in 1949 the British introduced a new parliamentary system of government, believing that this would quieten discontent. This hope proved to be misplaced, for in 1951 Nkrumah's new political party, the Convention People's Party, which took a far more radical stance on self-government than the UGCC, won the first legislative elections. Aware that the choice lay between a rapid move towards self-government within the **Commonwealth** or prolonged political instability, Britain chose the former, setting the Gold Coast towards its path to independence as Ghana in 1957.

The case of the Gold Coast is instructive, for it provides a classic example of the way in which many transfers of power in Africa were not planned but were forced upon the colonial authorities in a series of *ad hoc* retreats and compromises. In many colonies the imperial Powers had clear ideas about what they wanted to achieve, but found that circumstances forced them to make compromises acceptable to African opinion. For example, Britain desired to establish a multi-racial political system both in Kenya and in the Central African Federation (an entity that brought together Nyasaland [Malawi] with Northern and Southern Rhodesia [Zambia and Zimbabwe]), but was eventually forced to abandon these plans in the early 1960s and agree to independence under African majority rule. France, meanwhile, declared in 1958 its intention to turn its empire into a French Community which would allow the Equatorial and West African colonies to become states that controlled their own domestic affairs but co-operated with Paris over foreign affairs, security issues and overall economic policy. This bold initiative was, however, fatally undermined when Guinea voted against joining the Community and soon after Senegal and French Sudan (Mali) opted for full independence, leading to a general exodus which France had little choice but to accept. The Belgian Congo too was affected by this pattern of events. In January 1959, following riots in Leopoldville (Kinshasa), Belgium announced its intention to transfer power in four years' time, but the mounting pressures in the colony forced it to truncate this to a period of eighteen months, granting independence in June 1960.

Reinforcing this trend was the fact that where the colonial Powers did attempt to resist nationalism through the use of force, the results were often disastrous. The most obvious example of this was the French effort to defeat the challenge posed by the *Front de Libération National* (FLN) in Algeria between 1954 and 1962. The fact that Algeria contained a large number of European settlers and that it was constitutionally part of France meant that, as far as the government in

Commonwealth, The
An organization of independent self-governing states linked by their common ties to the former British Empire.

Paris was concerned, its status was not negotiable. It therefore reacted to the FLN's war of national liberation with a savage campaign of repression. However, while France was able to stem the tide militarily, the political costs of the conflict proved very damaging and gradually sapped its spirit of defiance. A key element in this was that the FLN was very effective in presenting its cause to international opinion as symbolic of the Third World's struggle against colonialism. Accordingly, France's effort to force the Algerians into submission generated much international criticism, for it was made to appear as though it was attempting to hold back an irresistible moral force. French efforts to win back its esteem and to isolate the FLN, such as its decision in 1956 to grant independence to Morocco and Tunisia, proved to be in vain, for in the end there was no alternative to full Algerian independence. Eventually, realizing the damage that had been caused to French prestige and unity, in 1962 President de Gaulle consented in the Évian agreement to a transfer of power.

In the light of its agony in Algeria, it is not surprising that France largely avoided resisting African nationalism elsewhere. Indeed, Algeria generally heightened European sensitivities to the costs of 'holding on', for no state wished to find itself in the same morass. For example, the hard-line policy that the Conservative government of Harold Macmillan followed over Kenya and the Central African Federation was dealt a fatal blow in 1959 when there was public outcry over the revelation that the police in both colonies had acted with unnecessary brutality. In addition, Algeria was important because the FLN's ties with the leading Third World states and its occasional flirtations with the communist bloc confirmed to both the colonial Powers and the United States that it was better to make concessions over self-government in the short term than to risk radical or pro-Soviet national liberation movements taking power in the long term. The other side of the coin was that, for their part, nationalist governments and movements in the Third World played on the fears of the colonial Powers and their American patron by lauding the FLN, seeking ties with the Afro-Asian movement and hinting at the possibility of finding a sympathetic voice in Moscow or Beijing. They were therefore able to manipulate the Cold War for their own benefit.

Apart from the costs of resistance, one other factor played a key role in African decolonization, namely that as the capitalist world economy flourished under the umbrella of the **Bretton Woods** system, the imperial Powers found themselves less reliant on trade with their colonial possessions. Not surprisingly, this sapped their will to spend precious resources on areas that were now a drain on rather than a benefit to the metropolitan economy. Moreover, there remained the broad hope that the granting of independence in good time would involve a political transfer of power but not necessarily a change in economic ties, and that the large European trading concerns, such as Britain's United Africa Company, would therefore continue to flourish.

The result of the above pressures was that by 1966, when Botswana became independent, the majority of the territories that made up Africa had become sovereign states, the only significant exceptions being those colonies controlled by Portugal, the anomaly of Southern Rhodesia and South-West Africa (Namibia),

Bretton Woods
The site of an inter-Allied conference held in 1944 to discuss the post-war international economic order. The conference led to the establishment of the IMF and the World Bank. In the post-war era the links between these two institutions, the establishment of GATT and the convertibility of the dollar into gold were known as the Bretton Woods system. After the dollar's devaluation in 1971 the world moved to a system of floating exchange rates.

which remained under the rule of South Africa. However, while this was a victory for the cause of **self-determination**, it came at a price, for now the new states faced the difficult task of plotting both their individual and collective fortunes. This involved a vast array of issues, including not just economic development and constitutional reform, but also whether there should be a move towards regional federations and perhaps eventually a united government of Africa.

The rise and fall of pan-Africanism

One of the most important strands in the nationalist movements that developed in Africa from the early twentieth century onwards was the influence of pan-Africanist thought. **Pan-Africanism**, which stresses the cultural and spiritual unity of people of African descent, had its roots not in Africa itself but in the African diaspora, its leading lights being such figures as the American academic and writer W. E. B. Dubois and the Jamaican activist Marcus Garvey. However, in the 1930s and 1940s a number of African students from the British colonies, such as Nkrumah, Jomo Kenyatta from Kenya and Julius Nyerere from Tanganyika (Tanzania), became interested in pan-African thinking, and used its tenets in their respective struggles for liberation. Meanwhile, in the French Empire, figures such as the Senegalese poet Léopold Senghor developed their own *négritude* movement, which also stressed the cultural affinity of African peoples.

When the process of independence began in the mid-1950s, one important question was that of what influence pan-Africanism would have on the new Africa. As its fundamental belief was that all African peoples shared common social and cultural ties, the logic of pan-Africanism suggested that the continent should cast aside the artificial state boundaries established by the Europeans and move towards a federal form of government. This was certainly the view of Nkrumah who, as the leader of the first major Sub-Saharan state to achieve independence, was in a strong position to further this agenda. In April 1958 he convened a conference of the independent African states in Accra, and in December followed it with an All-African People's Conference which included delegates from countries still under colonial subjugation. In these gatherings he preached the cause of African unification, and added weight to his words by deeds, such as agreeing in November 1958 to form a loose union between Ghana and Guinea, to which Mali was added in 1961.

Nkrumah's ideas proved, however, to be extremely divisive. On one side, Ghana's stance won support from its fellow radical states in the Casablanca Group, such as Guinea, Mali, Morocco and the United Arab Republic. On the other, Nkrumah was opposed by the more numerous Monrovia Group – the traditionally independent states of Ethiopia and Liberia, as well as Nigeria, Sierra Leone and the majority of the former French colonies. Their opposition to Nkrumah's ideas rested on two factors. The first and most obvious was that the leaders who made up the Monrovia Group saw little benefit to themselves in merging their

self-determination
The idea that each national group has the right to establish its own national state. It is most often associated with the tenets of Wilsonian internationalism and became a key driving force in the struggle to end imperialism.

pan-Africanism
The belief that Africans wherever they live share common cultural and spiritual values. Pan-Africanism was an important influence on the rise of nationalist movements in Africa in the first half of the twentieth century, but after decolonization its impact waned as the new states were reluctant to compromise their independence.

states into a larger political entity. Indeed, Nkrumah's vision only exacerbated disputes that had already appeared at a regional level. One of the reasons why the French Community had collapsed between 1958 and 1960 was the fact that tensions had grown up over the question of whether French West Africa should continue as a federation or become a series of sovereign independent states. In the end, the latter solution had been chosen, largely as a result of the vehement opposition to federalism of one of the most influential figures in Francophone Africa, Félix Houphouët-Boigny of the Ivory Coast. Having won the battle once, Houphouët-Boigny had no intention of losing the second round of this struggle against Nkrumah and became his bitter enemy.

The second reason for opposition to Nkrumah was that the policies which he pursued as Ghana's leader provoked resentment among his neighbours. The defining issue here was his stance towards the major international issue affecting Africa in the early 1960s, the **Congo Crisis**. This began in July 1960 when, shortly after the granting of independence, Belgian troops unleashed a unilateral military intervention to suppress a mutiny by the Congolese army, while almost simultaneously the copper-rich southern province of Katanga announced its secession. In order to defend itself against this double-pronged attack, the Congo government of Patrice Lumumba appealed to the **United Nations** (**UN**) for assistance. This was granted and the Belgians were persuaded to withdraw, but the UN then proved reluctant to assist with the defeat of Katanga. Exasperated by this attitude, Lumumba made overtures to the Soviet Union for support, but in doing so he signed his own death warrant, for in January 1961, as the Congo slid into full-scale civil war, he was assassinated by a coalition of both domestic and international conservative forces. The Congo Crisis then dragged on for a further two years until the Katangan secession was ended.

The significance of the Congo Crisis for African international politics was not so much that it brought the Cold War into the continent, for in 1960 the Soviet Union clearly lacked the capability to intervene effectively, but that it further radicalized those regimes that were appalled by the West's connivance in the ousting of Lumumba. Chief among these was Nkrumah, who had strongly backed Lumumba on the basis that they shared a common pan-African, socialist vision. Following Lumumba's assassination, Nkrumah's rhetoric became increasingly radical and confrontational, while reports circulated that Ghana was creating links with disaffected groups in other countries in order to promote the over-throw of their 'bourgeois governments'. For example, in January 1963 Ghana was implicated in the assassination of President Olympio of Togo. This naturally did little to widen the appeal of Nkrumah's pan-African vision, and even those, such as Nyerere, who sympathized with his agenda, advised him to adopt a more gradualist approach.

The final defeat for Nkrumah's pan-African schemes came in May 1963 with the holding of a conference of the independent African states in Addis Ababa, which agreed that rather than moving towards continental federation, the African states should become members of an **Organization of African Unity** (**OAU**). While the name paid due respect to the ideals of pan-Africanism, the reality was that the OAU's main function was to uphold the status quo. Indeed, in 1964 the

Congo Crisis
The civil war that took place in the Congo (the former Belgian Congo) from 1960 to 1963. The crisis was caused largely by the attempt of the copper-rich province of Katanga to secede from Congo. The secession was defeated eventually by a UN force, but in the process there were scares that the dilatory UN response would lead the Congolese government to turn to the Soviet Union for support.

United Nations (UN)
An international organization established after the Second World War to replace the League of Nations. Since its establishment in 1945, its membership has grown to 192 countries.

Organization of African Unity (OAU)
The organization of African states founded in Addis Ababa in 1963. It has upheld the territorial status quo in Africa and acted in the 1960s and 1970s as an important forum for attacks on colonialism. At the July 2002 Durban Summit the OAU was formally disbanded and became the African Union (AU).

OAU passed a resolution pledging member states 'to respect the frontiers existing on their achievement of national liberation'. From this point on the pan-African dream faded, a process that was accelerated by Nkrumah's losing power in a coup in 1966.

Imperialism and 'white rule' in southern Africa

While the OAU supported the territorial status quo in Africa, it naturally took a more radical line in regard to the perpetuation of imperialism on the continent and the existence of white minority governments. Accordingly, it offered its support to the national liberation movements in these countries. By the early 1960s the areas concerned were mainly in southern Africa, consisting of two Portuguese colonies, Angola and Mozambique, South Africa and its satellite, South-West Africa, and Rhodesia. The only important exception was Portuguese Guinea (Guinea-Bissau) in West Africa.

The strongest and most significant of these states was South Africa. The Union of South Africa had become an independent state within the British Empire in 1910. Its political life was, ironically, dominated by the very people whom Britain had defeated in the Boer War, the **Afrikaners**. Imbued with racist ideas of white supremacy and the desire to concentrate South Africa's mineral wealth in white hands, the Afrikaners had long supported the idea of racial segregation and of using the black population as nothing more than a cheap migrant labour force in the mines and factories. For example, in 1913 the Native Land Act forbade the purchase or lease of land by Africans outside certain reserved areas, while in 1923 municipalities were given the right to segregate Africans from Europeans. In 1948, in the wake of the wartime expansion of black labour in urban areas, a rise in worker militancy and black political agitation for equal rights, a more radical government took power under the leadership of D. F. Malan. The National Party, which Malan headed, won the 1948 elections on a programme of introducing apartheid (the separate development of the races). The idea behind apartheid was to safeguard white control of the country by vastly increasing the degree of segregation in South Africa. This was accomplished in the following years by banning mixed marriages and sexual relationships, introducing separate residential districts and amenities, controlling the movements of all blacks, Indians and coloureds, and giving limited autonomy to black rural homelands, dubbed 'Bantustans'.

At first, apartheid won the support of only a minority of the white population, mainly Afrikaners, but over time it widened its appeal. One reason for this was that apartheid all too predictably provoked resistance by the black population, which under the leadership of the African National Congress (ANC) became increasingly militant. In 1961, following the killing of sixty-seven black demonstrators at Sharpeville near Johannesburg, the ANC adopted a policy of armed struggle, which led to a number of acts of sabotage. The government reacted by

Afrikaners
The white population in South Africa who are of Dutch descent, also known as Boers.

introducing a security clampdown, and by 1964 a number of senior ANC figures, including Nelson Mandela, the head of the movement's armed wing, had been imprisoned. The rise in political violence, along with the fact that much of Africa was either already, or in the process of coming, under black majority rule, created a sense that the state was under siege. Accordingly, those of British descent now came to accept apartheid as the only guarantee of their security and continued social privilege. In addition, apartheid won support because it delivered sustained economic prosperity for the whole of the white population. During the 1960s the South African economy grew at 5 per cent per annum as it rapidly developed **import substitution** industries. Assisting this process was a rich flow of capital investment from Britain and the United States, which was in itself a sign of confidence in South Africa's future. Thus by the 1960s apartheid was no longer the policy of a militant Afrikaner minority, but had the support of a broad white coalition.

North of South Africa was another state – Rhodesia – that had much to lose from any shift towards black majority rule; indeed it unilaterally declared its independence from Britain in 1965 over exactly this issue. Faced with pressure from London to introduce a more equitable electoral system before independence could be granted, the government of Ian Smith decided that the only way to preserve white privilege was by going it alone. This was a risky policy, but the Smith regime survived, in part because the Labour government in Britain was loath to implement a military intervention against people of British descent, but also because the international sanctions introduced by the United Nations in 1966 were undermined by the support it received from South Africa and Portugal.

The last element in the white redoubt in southern Africa was the Portuguese Empire. That Portugal was able to survive as a colonial Power in Africa longer than Britain, France and Belgium might seem surprising. This, however, was based on the fact that, unlike the other imperial Powers, Portugal was an autocracy which, under the leadership of António de Oliveira Salazar, had developed an **autarkic** economy that was largely based on trade with its colonies. The Salazar regime thus relied on continued control over its African possessions and was willing to pay the necessary blood-price to hold on to them.

That the states still under white domination were neighbours was clearly a vital element in their ability to resist the 'wind of change' sweeping across the continent, but, in addition, they were bolstered by the fact that they could take advantage of their value to the West. Portugal was a member of **NATO** and, moreover, controlled the Azores in the mid-Atlantic, where the United States maintained extremely valuable air and naval bases. Salazar was therefore able to blunt American criticism by threatening to withdraw access to these facilities. South Africa was not a member of any Cold War alliance, but its virulent anti-communism, its gold, diamond and uranium deposits, and its strategic position as the power that dominated the Cape route from Europe to Asia, meant that it too was in a good position to manipulate Western governments. Rhodesia was in a much weaker position, but even it was able to find some room for manoeuvre as a result of its position as one of the world's largest producers of chrome. Apart from the very practical ways in which these states used their assets to their own

import substitution
The process whereby a state attempts to achieve economic growth by raising protective tariffs to keep out imports and replacing them with indigenously produced goods.

autarky
A policy that aims at achieving national economic self-sufficiency. It is commonly associated with the economic programmes espoused by Germany, Italy and Japan in the 1930s and 1940s.

North Atlantic Treaty Organization (NATO)
Established by the North Atlantic Treaty (4 April 1949) signed by Belgium, Canada, Denmark, France, Great Britain, Iceland, Italy, Luxembourg, the Netherlands, Norway, Portugal and the United States. Greece and Turkey entered the alliance in 1952 and the Federal Republic of Germany in 1955. Spain became a full member in 1982. In 1999 the Czech Republic, Hungary and Poland joined in the first post-Cold War expansion, increasing the membership to nineteen countries.

advantage, it has to be said that there also existed in the West some residual sympathy for these regimes, particularly among Republicans in the United States and the Conservative Party in Britain.

Convinced that there was no need to compromise with the forces of African nationalism and with the tacit support of the West protecting them from world opinion, the white governments in southern Africa resisted all calls for change. The result, not surprisingly, was that resistance manifested itself in the shape of armed struggle. This was very different from what had transpired in other regions of the continent, where, apart from Algeria and Kenya, the decolonization process had been remarkably peaceful. The need to resort to violence in the confrontation with imperialism in southern Africa was to have very important consequences, because the national liberation movements that emerged sought international sponsors for their wars of resistance. Unable to broker support from the West, some of them naturally inclined towards the Soviet bloc, thus helping to bring the Cold War into Africa.

The Cold War in Africa

In the wake of the transfer of power some of the new African states, including Ghana, Guinea, Mali, Congo (Brazzaville) and Tanzania, had adopted an overtly left-wing stance. Although this had caused some concern among the Western states, the international impact of the phenomenon was in the end fairly limited. One reason for this was that the new African leaders, having won independence, were determined not to replace one imperial master with another, and were therefore wary of becoming too close to Moscow. Underlining this point is the case of Guinea, whose leader, Sékou Touré, accepted Soviet technical aid in 1960, but then ordered the withdrawal of Soviet diplomatic personnel in 1961 after learning that they were in contact with his domestic opponents. Another important factor was that, although leaders such as Nkrumah and Nyerere were keen to introduce socialist-style planning for economic development, they were far from being orthodox Marxist-Leninists. Their ideas reflected instead what was loosely described as 'African socialism', which held little appeal to the ideologues in the Kremlin. Doubting the revolutionary potential of Africa and seeing it as a low global priority, the Soviet Union therefore diverted few of its resources to the continent, concentrating its efforts instead on winning over India and the radical Arab states. The main exception was the close relationship that developed between the Soviet Union and Somalia, which was prized for its naval facilities at Berbera. At the same time the United States saw Africa as being of little significance within the Cold War and felt that the former colonial Powers should take the primary responsibility for the continent's security.

The extension to southern Africa of the struggle against imperialism began to change this picture and force the superpowers to pay greater attention to Africa. This tendency began in the early 1960s, when national liberation struggles started in the Portuguese colonies with the appearance of the Liberation Front of Mozambique (FRELIMO) as the main party in Mozambique and of the National Front of Liberation of Angola (FNLA), the Popular Movement for the Liberation of Angola (MPLA) and the National Union for the Total Independence of Angola (UNITA) as contending voices of nationalism in Angola. From relatively early on both FRELIMO and the MPLA relied for much of their support on the communist bloc, and this pattern was mirrored in the case of South Africa, where the exiled ANC developed links with the Soviet Union, and in Rhodesia, where Joshua Nkomo's Zimbabwe African People's Union (ZAPU) followed the ANC's example, while Robert Mugabe's Zimbabwe African National Union (ZANU) was closer to the **People's Republic of China** (PRC). Naturally the association of these parties with communist regimes alienated them from the political mainstream in the West, who saw them as nothing more than Soviet puppets. In reality, however, communist support did not initially bring these parties significant advantages, for the degree of military and political assistance provided by the Soviet Union, the PRC and Cuba was too insubstantial to make any serious impact.

This situation changed drastically in April 1974 when Salazar's successor, Marcello Caetano, was overthrown by a military coup. One of the major factors behind his ousting was that elements in the Portuguese army were determined to withdraw from the debilitating colonial wars in Africa. Consequently the new regime in Lisbon rapidly negotiated transfers of power in Guinea-Bissau, Mozambique and Angola. This in turn provoked a chain of events that led to increasing superpower intervention in Africa and the erosion of white rule in the south of the continent.

The most important of these events was the civil war that erupted in Angola. Under the January 1975 Alvor Agreement Angola was due to become independent in November of that year, while in the interim elections were to be held to determine the character of the new government. The problem was that the three leading political parties were unwilling to work together. Their mutual contempt in part reflected ideological differences, but was also shaped by tribal and ethnic animosities and by a simple hunger for power. The result of this inability to co-operate was that each party sought to strengthen its position by appealing to outside forces, the FNLA to Zaire and the United States, UNITA to South Africa and the United States, and the MPLA to Cuba and the Soviet Union.

Once the Angolan parties had generated foreign interest in their civil war, the fighting in the country quickly escalated. The first major foreign intervention came in October 1975 when South African forces invaded in order to prevent an MPLA victory. The danger that South Africa might assist the recently formed FNLA–UNITA coalition to seize Luanda led in turn to Cuba sending its own troops to support the MPLA. The United States interpreted the arrival of Cuban forces, which numbered 12,000 by early 1976, as a Soviet attempt to establish Angola as a client state, but it was not able to respond in kind as Congress refused to supply the appropriate funds. The result was that the Cuban troops, well equipped with Soviet weaponry, were able to assist the MPLA to defeat the South African and the FNLA–UNITA forces. Angola thus emerged on independence as

People's Republic of China (PRC)

The official name of communist or mainland China. The PRC came into existence in 1949 under the leadership of Mao Zedong.

a state with strong links to the communist bloc. Moreover, it threatened the wider security of southern Africa by offering support to SWAPO, the leading force fighting for the liberation of Namibia.

At the same time the regional balance of power was also being transformed by the appearance of a FRELIMO government in Mozambique, for this meant that Rhodesia was now bordered on three sides by hostile states. In particular ZANU, which was able to operate from Mozambique with the open support of FRELIMO, greatly benefited from this new environment. The subsequent escalation of the guerrilla war within Rhodesia and the possible encroachment of Cold War tensions transformed the situation in that country, and made the Smith government more susceptible to pressure from Britain and the United States for a political settlement that would deliver majority rule. Smith tried at first to avoid having to deal with the ZANU/ZAPU Patriotic Front by seeking an internal solution, by which in 1979 a moderate black political figure, Bishop Abel Muzorewa, formed a government. However, this solution, which retained many white privileges, was not acceptable to the Patriotic Front or to world opinion. Faced with a worsening security position, Rhodesia was finally forced at the Lancaster House talks in London in 1979 to agree to majority rule and in April 1980, after elections won by Robert Mugabe's ZANU, Zimbabwe came into being.

The spread of the Cold War was not limited to the southern part of the continent, for it also affected East Africa. In 1974 a coup in Ethiopia dethroned Emperor Haile Selassie. The new republic was controlled by a military council, the Dergue. This body espoused vaguely socialist ideas, but it came to rely increasingly on Marxist advisers as it introduced policies designed to modernize what was still a largely feudal country. This transformation was completed in 1977 with the emergence of Mengistu Haile Mariam as the key political figure. Ethiopia's shift to the left alienated the country's former patron, the United States, but attracted the interest of the Soviet Union, which believed that at last a truly Marxist-Leninist regime was emerging in Africa. Accordingly in 1977, when Somalia launched a war against Ethiopia to seize the province of Ogaden, whose population was ethnically Somali, the Soviet Union cut its ties with the Siad Barre regime in Mogadishu and began shipping large quantities of arms to Mengistu's government instead. In addition, in a repeat of events in Angola, some 10,000 Cuban troops arrived to assist in warding off the Somali challenge. Ethiopia thus became another Soviet client state. This in turn created the impression that communism was on the march in the continent, and raised the danger that the application of Marxist-Leninist ideas might be perceived within the continent as the best way for African states to achieve rapid economic development.

While the events of the middle to late 1970s suggested that Africa could be on the verge of being divided along Cold War lines, in the end the impact was less substantial. In part, this was because the Marxist regimes in Africa faced such severe domestic problems that it was impossible for them to export their beliefs to their neighbours. In the case of Ethiopia, the radical land reform policy launched by the Mengistu government and its refusal to make any concessions to the secessionist movements in Eritrea and Tigre helped to spark a debilitating civil war, while Angola was beset by the continued resistance offered by UNITA, which was able to draw on support from the United States and South Africa. Another important constraint on the spread of communism was the fact that the West could still massively outbid the Soviet bloc in the provision of economic aid. The relative weakness of the Soviet position in Africa was graphically illustrated in 1980, when Mozambique's application to join **COMECON** was rejected on the grounds that it would prove too great a strain on that organization's resources. Desperate to find trading partners, Mozambique was forced to turn instead to the **EEC**, and negotiated its entry into the Lomé Convention agreement that regulated trade between the Community and African, Caribbean and Pacific countries.

COMECON

The Council for Mutual Economic Assistance, a Soviet-dominated economic organization founded in 1949 to co-ordinate economic strategy and trade within the communist world.

European Economic Community (EEC)

Established by the Treaty of Rome 1957, the EEC became effective on 1 January 1958. Its initial members were Belgium, France, Italy, Luxembourg, the Netherlands and West Germany (now Germany); it was known informally as the Common Market. The EEC's aim was the eventual economic union of its member nations, ultimately leading to political union. It changed its name to the European Union in 1992.

The end of apartheid in South Africa

The collapse of the Portuguese Empire not only heightened Africa's profile within the Cold War, but also had profound implications for the future of the apartheid regime in South Africa, which became more isolated than ever. With the buffer between it and Black Africa now removed, the South African government felt that its country was under siege by hostile forces linked to the Soviet Union. South African self-confidence was thus replaced by a restless sense of insecurity, which led it to introduce greater repression at home and to try to browbeat its neighbours into denying sanctuary to the ANC. Thus, South Africa steadily isolated itself even further from the international community, while turning its domestic politics into a powder keg.

In retrospect it can be said that the end of apartheid began in June 1976, when an uprising erupted in the black township of Soweto, outside Johannesburg, which was rapidly followed by protests, strikes and riots across the country. The primary causes of this upsurge in unrest were domestic factors, such as the rise of the Black Consciousness movement, the deteriorating economic conditions after the oil price hike of 1973 and anger at the attempt to introduce the compulsory learning of Afrikaans in black schools. It was therefore a largely spontaneous, indigenous phenomenon that had few direct links with the Soviet-backed ANC. However, the government in Pretoria saw these events through a Cold War prism, and thus believed that, rather than a sudden explosion of fury, it was the premeditated work of ANC agitators encouraged by news of the MPLA victory in Angola. Accordingly, the initial conclusion drawn from the Soweto uprising was that South Africa needed to toughen both its external and internal security policies. It was within this context that in 1977 the Black Consciousness leader Steve Biko was murdered while in police custody. South Africa's claim that its new campaign of repression was justified by the threat from communism did not, however, win much sympathy abroad, and in October 1977 the UN General Assembly introduced a mandatory embargo on arms sales with which even the United States and Britain complied.

Plate 17.1 Cape Town, South Africa, October 1976. After clashes in Soweto in June 1976, new incidents erupted between demonstrators and police in Cape Town. In that month the UN Security Council condemned the South African government for the repression of black protests in Soweto that resulted in hundreds of deaths and thousands of injured. (Photo: AFP/Getty Images)

Faced with international condemnation and a deteriorating security situation, the government of P. W. Botha, which took office in 1978, introduced limited reform of the apartheid system, removing some of its more objectionable, ideologically derived features in an attempt to appease its domestic and foreign critics. Thus labour laws were relaxed and the law banning mixed marriages was repealed. In addition, in the late 1970s and early 1980s a number of the Bantustan homelands were given nominal independence and in 1983 a new constitution was introduced which gave limited rights to coloureds and Indians. However, these steps were not enough to pacify black opinion or critics within the international community. From the mid-1980s the pressure on the Botha government escalated both at home and overseas. In 1985 a new wave of political mass action began, including outbreaks of violence, which soon forced the government to introduce a formal state of emergency over much of the country. Reflecting broad international distaste with the South African government, the US Congress in 1986 passed the Comprehensive Anti-Apartheid Act, overriding President Reagan's veto. The Act introduced sanctions against a wide range of South African goods and banned the export of oil products. Botha's government had no answer to its mounting problems, a point that was underlined when the prime minister's much touted 'Rubicon' speech of August 1985 emphatically rejected the idea of 'one man, one vote'.

The effect of the National Party's paralysis in the face of this worsening situation was that the white coalition which had sustained apartheid since its heyday in the 1950s and 1960s began to break up. In particular, faced with the fact that apartheid could no longer deliver economic prosperity or social order, the business community signalled its dissatisfaction by holding private talks with the ANC leadership. This change in attitude was reflected in the elections that took place in September 1989, shortly after Botha had passed the reins of power to F. W. de Klerk. In this election, for the first time since 1958, the National Party won less than half of the total votes cast, losing support both to liberals and to right-wing Afrikaner parties whose supporters felt that too much had already been conceded. Influenced by this disarray in white ranks and the unceasing violence in the black townships, de Klerk staggered his country and the world on 2 February 1990 by announcing the end of apartheid and the lifting of the ban on the ANC. Ten days later Mandela was freed from custody and South Africa began the tortuous road to its first democratic elections in 1994, which culminated in a sweeping ANC victory.

These dramatic changes in South Africa were rooted in domestic factors, which boiled down to the fear that apartheid was unsustainable and that if it collapsed involuntarily, it could lead to economic chaos and political violence on an unprecedented scale. However, the Cold War also had some influence on events, for it was arguably the Soviet Union's withdrawal from the Third World in the Gorbachev period that made the ANC acceptable as a potential government of South Africa. This was important for two constituencies that played a crucial role in the collapse of apartheid, namely the business community within South Africa and the countries, such as the United States, that tightened the sanctions noose from 1986 onwards. Thus, the de-escalation of the Cold War was important, because it created a new situation in which a shift towards black majority rule was not as terrifying a prospect for the white community and for America and its allies as it had once been.

The African state and the legacy of empire

While southern Africa moved towards decolonization and the end of white minority rule, the history of much of the rest of the continent from the early 1960s onwards was defined by the tasks of stimulating economic development and creating new nation-states from the colonial legacy that they had inherited from the Europeans. However, these proved not to be easy undertakings, and the euphoria generated by the granting of independence soon dissipated as the new states became mired in an apparently unending cycle of corruption and factionalism at best, and at worst descent into coups and civil wars.

To a considerable degree the problems that the new states faced were the result of the legacy of colonial rule, which created a number of obstacles to the establishment of effective government. One important factor that hindered development and the practice of good governance was the shortage of qualified professionals capable of providing key services. For example, on independence in 1961 Tanzania had two trained engineers and nine doctors for a population of nine million people, of whom 85 per cent were illiterate. The situation was similar in the Congo, which in 1960 contained only sixteen university graduates. While these shortcomings could be overcome by expanding university education and sending young men and women to study abroad, this solution took time to produce results, causing frustration among a population who had come to expect that independence meant the rapid extension of social provision.

More significant still was the very nature of the struggle for independence, which arguably had come too early for the good of the successor states. The independence movements that developed in Africa in the 1940s and 1950s tended to consist mainly of the educated classes from the urban population and the leaders of organized labour movements. Once it was clear that the drive for independence could not be suppressed, the colonial Powers came to collaborate with the nationalist elites in the belief that figures such as Nkrumah and Houphouët-Boigny could deliver a peaceful transition of power. In many ways these leaders appeared to offer a better prospect for the future than the traditionally minded tribal chiefs who had been dominant in the years of indirect rule, for men such as Nkrumah had been educated in the West and were seen as aspiring to create modern states based on constitutional government, the rule of law and a rational approach to economic planning.

The problem with this approach was that it was unduly optimistic. The newly independent states had no tradition of pluralist political institutions upon which to draw and were therefore all grossly ill prepared to act as parliamentary democracies. Indeed, the reality of the situation was that the political figures who took power on independence did not rely on well-organized political parties based on the Western model with roots in class identification. Rather they looked to support from regional, tribal and familial groups linked to them by ties of patronage that had developed under colonial rule. Patron–client relations had been vital in the colonial era, because in this period the best way to get access to jobs and other privileges and to avoid tasks such as forced labour was to find a patron using one's tribal or family ties. However, there was naturally a cost involved for the client in this relationship, for the patron expected to be rewarded for his services with political support.

On independence, with the resources of the state now open to them, the irresistible temptation for the new leaders was to cement their rule by building on the patronage system. Thus, the members of their political parties and other supporters were rewarded with access to appointments in state-run organizations and to state funds and contracts as a means of ensuring their loyalty. This drift towards a position where 'clientelism' became the political norm was reinforced by the fact that the new leaders inherited the autocratic state apparatus that had underpinned colonial rule. This provided them with an all-too-effective means of silencing their opponents, meaning that effective peaceful opposition to the government became virtually impossible. The result was a steady drift towards the establishment of one-party states in which the civil service and party more or less merged and in which the state itself became the supreme patron. Accordingly, corruption became a normal part of political and bureaucratic activity; it was the price that had to be paid for loyalty. In some cases, such as Zaire (as the Congo was renamed in the early 1970s) under Mobutu Sese Seko, the looting of the state's resources became so huge that the regimes were described as 'kleptocracies'.

The rapid move away from parliamentary democracy towards a one-party state did not, however, mean that governments became all-powerful, for other obstacles inherited from the colonial era acted to frustrate their ambitions. One of the most important was that a key feature of the colonial period in Africa had been the propensity, particularly in British colonies, towards '**indirect rule**' as a form of governance. Indirect rule had been attractive because, by finding collaborators among tribal chiefs and allowing them to raise taxes and administer customary law, the colonial Powers did not have to direct scarce resources towards developing an administrative network to cover the sparsely populated rural peripheries of their territories. What proved convenient for the colonial Powers was less so for their successors, for the consequence of indirect rule was that the leaders of the newly independent states discovered that they had only tentative control over much of their respective countries, as the state apparatus tended to be underdeveloped in rural areas.

This had a number of dangerous ramifications. One of the most important was that the tribal chiefs who had benefited from indirect rule were loath to give up their privileges and, being able to draw on the tendency towards tribalism that had been cultivated in the colonial period, often set themselves up as alternative centres of power to the government. The position of such tribal groupings was a challenge for many African states. In some countries, such as Tanzania and Guinea, where a large number of tribes existed without any one predominating, the one-party state was able to take rapid action on independence to break tribal power, seeing this as a prerequisite for the creation of national unity. However, where large and powerful tribes existed, they could lead to perpetual instability.

One example of this phenomenon is Uganda, where before transferring power the British decided in the face of pressure from the kingdom of Buganda to establish a federal constitution that would allow the latter considerable autonomy. However, this arrangement proved to be a serious obstacle to nation-building and political stability. Accordingly, in 1967 President Milton Obote declared the existing situation to be unsustainable and introduced a new centralized constitution that gave the presidency sweeping powers. The result was a wave of Bagandan agitation, which culminated in 1971 with the tribal elders supporting the successful coup against Obote launched by Idi Amin. Amin then promptly followed his predecessor's centralizing policies, recognizing that this was the only way to maintain power. Uganda only escaped from this cycle of violence in 1986 when, following Amin's fall and Obote's disastrous second term, Bagandan peasants led by Yoweri Museveni launched their own rebellion against both their own elite and Obote's state. Meanwhile in Nigeria, the existence of three powerful tribal groupings, the Hausa, the Yoruba and the Ibo, rapidly led to problems that culminated in 1967 with the secession of the Ibo-dominated south-east of the country, which named itself Biafra. The Biafran War lasted for three bloody years until eventually the rebellion was broken.

Another important problem that was in part inherited from the colonial era was the urban–rural divide which appeared in many of the newly independent

indirect rule
The system whereby a colonial power delegates limited powers to indigenous institutions.

see Chapter 4

African states. The key difficulty here was that the European colonial states had tended to raise revenue through taxing trade rather than land. Accordingly, when the Europeans sought to encourage economic development in their colonies from the 1940s they had concentrated on the expansion of agricultural exports as a way of generating wealth. In particular, they had developed the use of marketing boards, which bought goods cheaply from farmers and then sold them on the world market for a considerable profit, which could be invested in development. This model had great appeal to the largely urban elites that took office on the transfer of power, for they saw the profits from cash crops as a way of creating capital for investment in import substitution industries.

This proved to be a dangerous path to follow for, as both Ghana and Senegal discovered in the 1960s with their exports of cocoa and groundnuts respectively, one could not rely on a single cash crop to generate sufficient revenue to fund import substitution. In addition, the concentration of taxation on cash crops for export led to few funds being allocated to diversifying agricultural production for the domestic market and to general neglect of rural areas. The result was that governments lacked any political or economic incentive to develop such regions, and therefore areas of low population density saw little state activity. This reached its apogee in Zaire under Mobutu, where the state was reduced to the capital, Kinshasa, and the mineral-rich region of Katanga, whose population relied ironically on food imports rather than on domestically produced crops. It is thus not surprising that, in the 1990s, the country disintegrated into civil war.

Debating the African state

One of the key issues for historians of Africa when dealing with the period since the transfer of power is why so many African states have found it difficult to achieve political stability and sustained economic development. One school of thought that was particularly prevalent in conservative circles in the West in the 1970s was that the fault lay with the political elites in African states, who abused power and squandered development aid in order to enrich themselves and the cliques that had gathered around them. Accordingly, it was argued that the answer to Africa's problems was to reduce the state sector in the economy and let future development be shaped by market forces. While accepting that the exercise of power has been seriously flawed, other observers have noted that this tendency was not an arbitrary development, but rather one rooted in the legacy of colonial rule and the continuation of neo-colonialism. For example, David Fieldhouse has argued, in his *Black Africa 1945–80: Economic Decolonization and Arrested Development* (London, 1986), that one of the key errors committed by the new leaders was to continue the colonial policy of regulating the export of cash crops through marketing boards.

Other writers have gone even further in their analysis of the colonial state and the way in which it shaped the policies and politics of the new states. Crawford Young, in *The African Colonial State in Comparative Perspective* (New Haven, CT, 1994), has outlined the importance of the autocratic nature of the colonial state, arguing that this has played a crucial role in encouraging the centrality of the bureaucracy and intolerance of opposition. Conversely, Mahmood Mamdani, in *Citizen and Subject: Contemporary Africa and the Legacy of Late Colonialism* (Princeton, NJ, 1996), has argued that the legacy of colonialism was a weak rather than a strong state. Mamdani has pointed to the problems caused by indirect rule, which has helped to exacerbate the tendency towards tribalism in Africa and thus widened the urban–rural divide. Jeffrey Herbst, in *States and Power in Africa: Comparative Lessons in Authority and Control* (Princeton, NJ, 2000), has taken this idea even further, noting that state formation in Africa has been blighted by the problems caused by the difficulty of extending control over countries with relatively low population densities. This, in turn, has meant that the attempt to construct states in line with the traditional European model has been enormously problematical.

structural adjustment programme
The idea propagated by the World Bank from the end of the 1970s which linked the provision of development aid to Third World states to the latter committing themselves to balanced budgets, austerity programmes and the sale of nationalized industries and property.

neo-colonialism
The process whereby a colonial power grants juridical independence to a colony, but nevertheless maintains *de facto* political and economic control.

see Chapter 13

Another unfortunate colonial legacy was that the state boundaries did not respect religious divisions. For example, a swath of countries bordering on the Sahara inherited states that contained both Muslims and Christians, and the different attitudes of these religions towards social and political questions only helped to exacerbate tribal and ethnic confrontations. This was one of the issues that caused problems in Nigeria, where the Hausa are followers of Islam. However, the difficulties were even greater in Sudan, where the religious divide led to a cycle of violence that has plagued the country ever since independence.

Other factors blighted the quest for stability and development. One important point to remember is that the promises made on independence were always unrealistic, for African states faced serious natural obstacles to any increase in agricultural production. These included poor soil quality and the inability to use draught animals because of the tsetse fly. Most serious of all, however, was the unreliability of the climate. In the 1970s the countries bordering on the Sahara saw food production hit by a series of drought years that set back some of the progress that had been made in the 1960s. African states were also, of course, prey to the problems that afflicted developing countries more broadly, including fluctuations in the world economy and the frequent changes in thinking among economists about development issues. For example, African states suffered badly from the debt crisis and the collapse of commodity prices in the 1980s, and were poorly placed to benefit from the **structural adjustment programmes** urged on them by the World Bank. They were also in many cases trapped in **neo-colonial** relationships with their former imperial masters, this particularly being the case for the former French colonies. This had some advantages in terms of ensured access to markets, but also perpetuated a relationship of dependency.

Even those states that possessed great mineral wealth did not necessarily do well. For example, oil-rich Nigeria, which saw its overseas earnings soar in the 1970s as a consequence of the **OPEC** oil price hike, did not use its new prosperity to fund a breakthrough in development. Instead, much of Nigeria's oil wealth was dissipated on the financing of imports for the urban population. Moreover, imagining that oil prices would remain high, in the late 1970s the government sought vast loans from Western banks in order to finance its plans for import substitution. This proved, however, to be a costly error of judgement, for when oil prices fell in the early 1980s, Nigeria found itself weighed down by its debt burden. However, it is worth noting that some resource-rich states did prosper: for example, Botswana with its vast diamond deposits has been able to ensure political stability and a rising standard of living. That these states have prospered while others with rich reserves of raw materials have not implies that the colonial inheritance cannot be used as a blanket excuse for Africa's current state, and that the quality of African leadership needs also to be studied. In addition, the fact that those African states with a long tradition of independence, such as Liberia and Ethiopia, have also suffered from severe political and economic problems suggests that the colonial legacy cannot explain everything.

Organization of Petroleum Exporting Countries (OPEC)
The organization founded in 1960 to represent the interests of the leading oil-producing states in the Third World.

Poverty, resources and the troubled road to democracy

The sense of increasing pessimism that had replaced the immediate post-independence euphoria did, however, begin to lift in the late 1980s and early 1990s. The victory of liberal democracy over socialist autocracy in the Cold War quickly emboldened opposition groups in Africa into demanding a shift away from the one-party state towards a more pluralistic political system. For example, in 1990 the first freely contested local elections were held in Algeria and in 1992 democracy returned to Ghana after a prolonged absence. Meanwhile, the end of the Cold War also helped to bring about the termination of the civil wars that had racked Angola and Mozambique since independence and sealed the fate of Mengistu's regime in Ethiopia. Above all, however, the new spirit of optimism in the continent was symbolized by South Africa's unexpectedly smooth transformation into a fully democratic state and by the statesmanship displayed by Nelson Mandela.

However, in a number of countries the shift towards democracy proved to be a false dawn. All too often the new leaders turned out to be just as corrupt as those who had been voted out of office. Another problem was that some opposition parties proved to be unacceptable to the established elite. For example, in Algeria in January 1992 the army stepped in to re-establish martial law in an effort to prevent the *Front Islamique du Salut* from winning the country's first free national election. This in turn sparked a savage civil war that lasted for the rest of the decade.

The most tragic case, and the one with the greatest consequences for those bordering upon it, was that of Rwanda. Ever since 1959, shortly before independence from Belgium in 1962, politics in Rwanda had been dominated by the Hutu majority, with the Tutsi elite who had traditionally controlled the country being forced into either submission or exile. In the late 1980s economic problems caused by a rapidly increasing population, land pressure, declining commodity prices and anger at government corruption led to calls for the authoritarian Hutu government of President Juvenal Habyarimana to agree to multi-party elections. The apparent weakness of the Habyarimana regime, in turn, led the Rwandese Patriotic Front (RPF), a group of Tutsi exiles in Uganda, to launch an abortive invasion of the country in October 1990. While this invasion did not succeed, it did spur on the democracy movement, consisting of both Hutus and Tutsis, to increase its pressure on Habyarimana. Consequently, in 1992 Habyarimana was forced to form a coalition government and then in 1993 to sign the Aruya peace agreement with the RPF, which would allow the latter to become part of a transitional administration that would steer the country towards free elections.

At this point radicals within the Hutu elite decided to take violent action in order to ward off the threat of democracy and overcome the economic crisis by seizing Tutsi land and property. Utilizing the government propaganda machine and their own client networks, they inculcated among poor and unemployed Hutus a fervent hatred of the Tutsis, drawing on the memory of what was perceived as the latter's gratuitous repression prior to the breaking of their hold on power in 1959. The trigger for genocide came in April 1994, when following the assassination of Habyarimana, the Hutu extremists proceeded to carry out genocide against the Tutsi population and against Hutu moderates who supported the trend towards democracy. Over the next two months some 800,000 Tutsis, about 11 per cent of the total population of the country, were slaughtered.

The potential for genocidal violence in Rwanda was clear to anyone willing to observe the situation, but both before and during the events of the spring of 1994 the international community showed little interest or willingness to act. Indeed, such was the level of international inaction that the genocide in Rwanda soon spread to infect much of southern central Africa. To a substantial degree this occurred because the action taken by the Hutu extremists provoked the RPF into launching a new and this time successful invasion of Rwanda. Fearing Tutsi retribution, more than two million Hutu refugees fled into Tanzania, Burundi and Zaire, bringing disaster to the latter two countries. In Zaire the ensuing crisis was particularly serious, for the influx of refugees led to increasingly serious outbursts of inter-communal violence, particularly against Tutsis living in the eastern province of Kivu. Citing concern for this community, but also motivated by an interest in gaining access to Zaire's abundant raw materials, the Rwandan and Ugandan governments intervened by providing assistance to anti-Mobutu rebels led by Laurent Kabila.

The ensuing civil war brought about Mobutu's fall from power in 1997, but the nightmare was not yet over, for, soon after he gained power in Kinshasa, Kabila broke with his Rwandan and Ugandan backers. As a result the newly renamed Democratic Republic of Congo (DRC) became immersed in a prolonged and bitter conflict, in which rebels in the east of the country received armed support from Rwanda and Uganda, while Kabila himself turned to Angola, Zimbabwe and Namibia for military assistance. This escalation of the fighting into an international war once again arose largely out of the desire of the DRC's neighbours to gain access to its vast mineral wealth, which included coltan, a mineral vital in the production of mobile phones. The result was the bloodiest African conflict of the post-colonial period in which it is reckoned that more than three million people died. Eventually in January 2001 Laurent Kabila was assassinated. He was succeeded by his son, Joseph, who quickly acted to start talks with his father's political enemies. The result in July 2002 was a negotiated settlement that brought a measure of peace to the country, although violence continued to erupt periodically, particularly in the areas bordering on Uganda and Rwanda.

Competition for control over mineral wealth also led to conflict elsewhere in Africa. The worst case came in Sierra Leone. From 1991 rebels against the government in Freetown started to receive support from the warlord Charles Taylor, whose fiefdom in neighbouring Liberia bordered on the diamond-rich eastern provinces of Sierra Leone. This sparked a nine-year war that brought misery to both Liberia and Sierra Leone. At first, the international community distanced itself from this chaos, leaving the restoration of order to the neighbouring states in the region in the form of the Economic Community of West African States Monitoring Group (ECOMOG). ECOMOG, which in reality was a vehicle for Nigerian claims to be the regional hegemon, proved, however, to be incapable of bringing peace and found its forces dragged into the morass. In the end the hopeless anarchy in Sierra Leone and the inability of ECOMOG to restore order led in 2000 to a British intervention followed by the arrival of a large UN peace-keeping force, and soon after the rebels were defeated. Following on from this reverse of his fortunes, Taylor, who had prospered enormously from the diamond trade, was forced in 2003 to stand down as president of Liberia and peace finally returned to the two war-torn countries.

While some countries in Africa leaned towards becoming failed states, in other areas notable progress was achieved. For example, Botswana continued to act as a beacon of democracy, while Mozambique and Tanzania made rapid economic progress, achieving annual growth rates of 8 per cent and 5 per cent respectively. However, even in these areas of relative stability, problems still existed. The most serious was the rapid spread of AIDS/HIV. According to UN calculations, by 2000 there were 24.5 million people infected with the virus in Sub-Saharan Africa, with the rate of infection being particularly serious in the southern half of the continent. For example, in Botswana, 35 per cent of the population were believed to be infected. Another serious issue was that many of the African states still suffered from the high level of indebtedness inherited from the 1970s. This debt burden was hard to shake off, for the continuing fluctuations in commodity prices and the refusal of the West to accept free trade in agricultural production restricted the ability of African states to earn sufficient revenue from exports. What Africa needed therefore was for the West to agree both to a coherent programme of debt relief and to the reduction of subsidies to agriculture, particularly in the United States, Japan and the **European Union (EU)**.

European Union (EU)
A political and economic community of nations formed in 1992 in Maastricht by the signing of the Treaty on European Union (TEU). In addition to the agreements of the European Community, the EU incorporated two inter-governmental – or supra-national – 'pillars' that tie the member states of the EU together: one dealing with common foreign and security policy, and the other with legal affairs. The number of member states of the EU has expanded from twelve in 1992 to twenty-seven in 2007.

However, in order to persuade the West that Africa was worth supporting, it was necessary for the continent's leading political figures to demonstrate that they were willing to act responsibly in the cause of development, thus banishing the image of corruption and ineptitude. An important move in this direction was made in 2001 with the launching of the New Partnership for African Development (NEPAD), which was the brainchild of the South African president, Thabo Mbeki. The fifteen governments that signed the NEPAD agreement committed themselves to the pursuit of good governance, democracy and sound economic management and in return sought better terms of trade with the West allied to debt relief. To a degree, NEPAD met with a positive response in the West, but the rhetoric and promises made by leaders such as the US president, George W. Bush, and the UK prime minister, Tony Blair, at events such as the G-8 summit at Gleneagles in 2005 were frequently not matched by actions. In part, this was because Africa remained a low political priority but it also reflected the ingrained belief that many governments in Africa were simply not deserving of support. In particular, Mbeki himself was tarnished in Western eyes by his blindness to the causes of the AIDS epidemic in South Africa and by his unwillingness to criticize the increasingly harsh and inept government of Robert Mugabe in Zimbabwe.

Africa therefore continues to be plagued by the colonial legacy and its poor terms of trade with the West. While some success has been achieved in terms of the spread of democracy and higher economic growth, and while the continent has largely benefited from the emergence of South Africa as a significant voice within the international community, old and new problems ensure that progress remains fitful. Moreover, all too often Western governments and institutions either ignore or misunderstand Africa's problems.

Conclusion

In the second half of the twentieth century, Africa was shaped to a considerable degree by events and trends in international politics. Above all else, the most important was decolonization, in which, of course, Africans themselves played a vital role. However, the winning of independence was a long-drawn-out struggle, and as anti-colonialism failed to make headway into southern Africa in the 1960s it increasingly dragged the Cold War into the continent as well, as some of the national liberation movements in Angola, Mozambique, Zimbabwe and South Africa turned to Moscow and Beijing for support. During the 1970s and 1980s the Cold War shaped the struggle against both imperialism and white minority rule, in some cases hastening victory and in other areas, such as South Africa, acting to delay the end-game.

In the long run though, the effects of the Cold War were not as significant for the future of the continent as those of the colonial inheritance. It was the latter, above all, in the form of the inadequate preparations for transferring power, the consequences of indirect rule and the colonial approaches towards taxation and development, that shaped the problems which African leaders faced and unfortunately in many cases influenced the way in which they responded to these challenges. Moreover, at the international level it was the state boundaries that the imperial Powers had left behind which lay at the basis of the African states system, the short-lived attempt by Nkrumah and others to shake off this legacy failing miserably. Africa therefore may have freed itself from direct colonial rule, but it has still not shaken off the effects of what in most cases had only been a half-century of European domination.

Recommended reading

There are a number of good surveys of African history; these include Peter Calvocoressi, *Independent Africa and the World* (London, 1985), John Iliffe, *Africans: The History of a Continent* (Cambridge, 1995), J. D. Fage, *A History of Africa* (London, 1995), Bill Freund, *The Making of Contemporary Africa* (Basingstoke, 1998), Frederick Cooper, *Africa since the 1940s: The Past of the Present* (Cambridge, 2002) and Martin Meredith, *The State of Africa: A History of Fifty Years of Independence* (London, 2005). An interesting and controversial overview of the legacy of colonialism is Basil Davidson, *The Black Man's Burden: Africa and the Curse of the Nation-State* (Oxford, 1992).

The struggle for independence has been the focus of many studies. Two useful overviews are Robert Holland, *European Decolonization 1918–1981: An Introductory Survey* (Basingstoke, 1985) and John Hargreaves, *Decolonization in Africa* (London, 1996). Important essays on many aspects of the decolonization process and its legacy can be found in Prosser Gifford and W. Roger Louis (eds), *The Transfer of Power in Africa: Decolonization 1940–1960* (New Haven, CT, 1982) and Prosser Gifford and W. Roger Louis, *Decolonization and African Independence: The Transfers of Power 1960–1980* (New Haven, CT, 1988). The transfer of power in the British colonies is also covered in the essays by Falola and Roberts, Lonsdale and Marks in Judith Brown and W. Roger Louis (eds), *The Oxford History of the British Empire*, vol. IV: *The Twentieth Century* (Oxford, 1999), while good summaries of developments in the French Empire are provided in Raymond F. Betts, *France and Decolonization, 1900–1960* (Basingstoke, 1991) and Tony Chafer, *The End of the Empire in French West Africa* (Oxford, 2002). On the Algerian revolution, see Martin Thomas, *The French North African Crisis: Colonial Breakdown and Anglo-French Relations, 1945–62* (Basingstoke, 2000), Irwin Wall, *France, the United States and the Algerian War* (Berkeley, CA, 2001) and Matthew Connelly, *A Diplomatic Revolution: Algeria's Fight for Independence and the Origins of the Post-Cold War Era* (New York, 2002). On the Congo Crisis, see Madeleine Kalb, *The Congo Cables: The Cold War in Africa from Eisenhower to Kennedy* (New York, 1982), D. N. Gibbs, *The Political Economy of Third World Intervention: Money, Mines and US Policy in the Congo* (Chicago, IL, 1992) and Ludo de Witte, *The Assassination of Lumumba* (London, 2001).

For the debate on the problems facing African states in the post-colonial period, see Carl Rosberg and R. H. Jackson, *Personal Rule in Black Africa: Prince, Autocrat, Prophet, Tyrant* (Berkeley, CA, 1982), David Fieldhouse, *Black Africa 1945–80: Economic Decolonization and Arrested Development* (London, 1986), Jean-François Bayart, *The State in Africa: The Politics of the Belly* (London, 1993), Crawford Young, *The African Colonial State in Comparative Perspective* (New Haven, CT, 1994), Christopher Clapham, *Africa in the International System: The Politics of State Survival* (Cambridge, 1996), Mahmood Mamdani, *Citizen and Subject: Contemporary Africa and the Legacy of Late Colonialism* (Princeton, NJ, 1996), Jeffrey Herbst, *States and Power in Africa: Comparative Lessons in Authority and Control* (Princeton, NJ, 2000) and John Harbeson and Donald Rothchild (eds), *Africa in World Politics: The African State in Flux* (Boulder, CO, 2000).

The Cold War in Africa can be studied in R. E. Albright (ed.), *Africa and International Communism* (Basingstoke, 1980), Thomas J. Noer, *Cold War and Black Liberation: The United States and White Rule in Africa, 1948–1968* (New York, 1985), Chris Coker, *NATO, the Warsaw Pact and Africa* (Basingstoke, 1985), Herbert Ekwe-Ekwe, *Conflict and Intervention in Africa: Nigeria, Angola, Zaire* (Basingstoke, 1990), P. J. Schraeder, *United States Foreign Policy towards Africa: Incrementalism, Crisis and Change* (Cambridge, 1994) and Odd Arne Westad, *The Global Cold War: Third World Interventions and the Making of our Times* (Cambridge, 2005). The Angolan crisis is dealt with very ably in Fernando Andresen Guimaraes, *The Origins of the Angolan Civil War: Foreign Intervention and Domestic Political Conflict* (Basingstoke, 1988) and Piero Gleijeses, *Conflicting Missions: Havana, Washington and Africa, 1959–1976* (Chapel Hill, NC, 2002). On the Cold War in the Horn of Africa, see Christopher Clapham, *Transformation and Continuity in Revolutionary Ethiopia* (Cambridge, 1988), Robert Patman, *The Soviet Union in the Horn of Africa* (Cambridge, 1990) and Andargachew Tiruneh, *The Ethiopian Revolution 1974–1987: A Transformation from an Aristocratic to a Totalitarian Autocracy* (Cambridge, 1993).

For South Africa and the apartheid system, useful overviews are provided in James Barber, *South Africa in the Twentieth Century* (Oxford, 1999), Nigel Worden, *The Making of Modern South Africa* (Oxford, 2000) and Rodney Davenport and Christopher Saunders, *South Africa: A Modern History* (Basingstoke, 2000). For more detailed studies, see Deborah Posel, *The Making of Apartheid 1948–61: Conflict and Compromise* (Oxford, 1991), Robert Price, *The Apartheid State in Crisis: Political Transformation in South Africa, 1975–1990* (London, 1991) and Allister Sparks, *Tomorrow is Another Country: The Inside Story of South Africa's Negotiated Revolution* (London, 1995). For accounts of the Rwandan genocide and its consequences, see Gérard Prunier, *The Rwanda Crisis, 1959–1994: The History of a Genocide* (London, 1995), Arthur Jay Klinghofer, *The International Dimension of Genocide in Rwanda* (Basingstoke, 1998), Christopher Taylor, *Sacrifice as Terror: The Rwandan Genocide of 1994* (Oxford, 1999), Mahmood Mamdani, *When Victims Became Killers: Colonialism, Nativism and the Genocide in Rwanda* (Princeton, NJ, 2001) and Johan Pottier, *Re-Imagining Rwanda: Conflict, Survival and Disinformation in the Late Twentieth Century* (Cambridge, 2002).

The Arab – Israeli conflict, 1949 – 2007

Introduction

The first Arab–Israeli war ended in 1949 with a series of armistice agreements between Israel and its Arab neighbours. It did not, however, resolve the issues at the heart of the conflict. In fact, it added further problems. Moreover, the inconclusive outcome set in motion dynamics which would lead to further wars such as Israel's search for recognition and security which propelled it to adopt an aggressive defence policy grounded in retaliation, pre-emption and expansion of its strategic depth. The Palestinians, too, saw violence as the only option. Dispossessed and betrayed by Israel, the Arab states and the international community, they embarked upon the road of armed struggle, guerrilla warfare and terrorism in their quest for statehood. And last but not least, the repeated defeats, territorial losses and humiliation experienced by the Arab states triggered instability and crises of legitimacy in the Arab world as well as a determined struggle for political equality, strategic parity and an honourable solution to the conflict. While the four Arab–Israeli wars discussed in this chapter – the 1956 Suez–Sinai campaign, the 1967 June War, the 1973 October War and the 1982 Lebanon War – each have different triggers, the broad parameters are the same and are thus key to understanding the overall dynamics of the conflict as well as the peace process.

see Chapter 20

The 1956 Suez–Sinai campaign

Israel's victory in the 1948 war bought the country almost ten years in which to focus on the difficult process of nation- and state-building. During this period, Israel's *Mapai* (Labour) Party under Prime Minister and Defence Minister David Ben Gurion strengthened its grip on Israeli domestic politics to such an extent that it virtually controlled the political scene, despite the existence of small right-wing, religious and Marxist parties. The main task of the politicians was the absorption of more Jewish immigrants, attaining economic self-sufficiency, and finding allies who could provide Israel with arms and the technology necessary to build up both a viable civilian and defence industry. During this early period France became Israel's main foreign supporter, despite the 1950 Tripartite Agreement in which the United States, Britain and France agreed not to arm either side in the Arab–Israeli conflict.

The defeated Arab states also turned inwards to focus on nation- and state-building, as they too had either just achieved independence shortly before the 1948 war or were struggling to achieve it in the period thereafter. The defeat had also delegitimized many of the Arab governments and left them open to radical challenges. Syria, for example, suffered three military coups in 1949 alone and became the most unstable of Israel's neighbours during the 1950s. Jordan's King Abdullah was assassinated in 1951 and was replaced first by Talal and then in 1953 by Hussein while Lebanon's President Camille Chamoun was unsuccessfully challenged in a coup in 1952. The most important changes, however, took place in Egypt. On 23 July 1952, Egypt's King Farouk was overthrown and sent into exile by the Free Officers whose aim was to replace what they saw as a reactionary monarchy with a progressive republic based on a strong army, social equality, an end to colonialism, rapid economic development and free universal education. Far-reaching socio-economic reforms were instituted by the new president and prime minister, Mohammed Naguib, and his deputy, Gamal Abdel Nasser. In October 1954, Nasser replaced Naguib. His charisma and his policies of **non-alignment**, Arab unity and Arab socialism not only made him the darling of the people, but also propelled Egypt into a position of leadership in the Middle East and among the recently decolonized states. This attracted Israel's interest, as well as that of the superpowers, the United States and the USSR.

Israel initially welcomed the changes in Egypt, believing that the revolution presented a window of opportunity in the search for peace. Back-channel negotiations were opened through Paris by the then Israeli foreign minister, Moshe Sharett, who believed that only negotiations would produce a lasting peace. His assumption of the premiership in 1953 upon Ben Gurion's retirement raised hopes for a breakthrough with Egypt. His efforts, however, were foiled by his pre-decessor, who continued to exert influence over policy-making as he believed Sharett to be weak and misguided with respect to the Arabs, who, according to Ben Gurion, only understood one language – force.

The cautiously constructed and nurtured Egyptian–Israeli secret negotiations unravelled in a succession of events starting with the 1954 Lavon affair. In July

non-alignment
A state policy of avoiding involvement in 'Great Power conflicts', most notably the Cold War. It was first espoused by India on its becoming independent in 1947.

see Chapter 13

1954, a group of Israeli agents, in collaboration with Egyptian Jews, attacked British and American property in Egypt in order to create discord between that country and the West. This plan, which had been contrived behind Sharett's back, was the work of the defence minister, Pinhas Lavon, who shared Ben Gurion's fear that Nasser would successfully negotiate a withdrawal of British troops from the Suez Canal zone, effectively removing the buffer between Egypt and Israel, and that Egypt would become eligible for American military aid. The sabotage operation failed when the saboteurs were caught, virtually scuppering the secret negotiations. It also provided the opportunity for Ben Gurion to manoeuvre himself back into the premiership.

The Lavon affair, the end of the back-channel talks and the continuous backdrop since 1948 of border tensions between Egypt and Israel, most of which were triggered by Palestinian refugees crossing into Israel to harvest their fields, reunite with family or carry out attacks against Israeli property or persons, persuaded both Egyptian and Israeli leaders that a second military round was imminent. On 28 February 1955, Israel launched the so-called Gaza raid against Egypt in retaliation for the killing of a cyclist near Rehovot allegedly by an Egyptian intelligence-gathering squad. Israeli forces killed thirty-eight Egyptian soldiers in line with Ben Gurion's new policy of hard-hitting military retaliation. For Nasser the Gaza raid was the final straw. He responded to this 'deliberate, brutal and unprovoked' Israeli attack by turning to the Soviet bloc for arms. In September 1955, he concluded the Czech arms deal. This, in turn, set in motion Israeli plans for a ground operation against Egypt.

While Egyptian–Israeli tensions were increasing almost daily and war appeared to be just a matter of time, Egypt's relations with France, Britain and the USA were also deteriorating rapidly. The main issue of contention for the French government was Nasser's support for the Algerian nationalist movement. French policy-makers believed that only by removing Nasser would they be able to hold on to Algeria. Britain, too, believed that Nasser was turning the Arabs against the West and was thus threatening Britain's position in the Middle East and particularly its regional oil production. The United States, which initially had high hopes for Nasser, also began to entertain doubts as a result of Nasser's flirtation with the Soviet bloc. The Czech arms deal, as far as Washington was concerned, was a clear sign that Egypt was rapidly sliding into the communist camp. In a desperate attempt to halt such developments, the United States decided to cancel its funding of the Aswan Dam, the symbol of Nasser's modernization programme. Nasser, in turn, felt compelled to nationalize the Suez Canal on 26 July 1956 in order to obtain the necessary money to finance the dam. While the nationalization of the Suez Canal provided the *casus belli* for Britain and France, it was Nasser's closure of the Straits of Tiran in September that was the determining factor for Israel. However, all three had far broader motives and plans than these respective *casus belli* suggest. For Britain and France the loss of the Suez Canal was tantamount to the loss of empire and thus they felt that action had to be taken to protect their presence and influence in the region. Britain's stance, moreover, was driven by Prime Minister Anthony Eden's personal antipathy towards Nasser and his determination not to repeat the mistakes of appeasement in the 1930s. Finally,

Israel's plans were a mixture of the need to display its strength through retaliation and Prime Minister Ben Gurion's grander scheme to use war to change the geostrategic make-up of the Middle East in Israel's favour. In fact, with respect to the latter, Ben Gurion envisioned the attack on Egypt being followed by a second phase, intervention in Lebanon, replacing in one stroke the hostile regimes of Israel's southern and northern neighbours with friendly ones.

In late July, France started to consider military co-operation with Israel against Egypt. Britain proved more reluctant to collaborate with Ben Gurion's govern-ment as Anglo-Israeli relations had never been good. This was exacerbated by the fact that Britain had a defence arrangement with Jordan at a time when Israeli–Jordanian border tensions were high. Thus it was only on 16 October, at a meet-ing in Paris, that Britain agreed to Israel's participation in the Suez War.

On 29 October 1956, as planned, Israeli troops crossed into the Sinai; by 30 October, they had reached the Suez Canal. Britain and France issued an ultimatum for both sides to withdraw, but as predicted, Nasser rejected it, thereby 'provoking' the British and French bombing of Egyptian airfields and economic targets on 31 October in order to protect international shipping. Two days later British and French paratroopers invaded, only to be forced to halt their military operation as a result of American pressure. Thus, neither Israel nor Britain nor France achieved its war aims but all were, instead, condemned for their aggres-sion in the UN and had economic sanctions imposed upon them. Nevertheless, it was only Britain and France who emerged as losers in this war, while Israel had proved its military strength and consequently emerged as a regional superpower.

The American intervention, which had the effect of saving Nasser, was moti-vated by a combination of domestic and international considerations. On the domestic side, the Suez War coincided with Eisenhower's re-election campaign in which he was stressing his commitment to peace and prosperity. With votes to be cast on 6 November, Eisenhower had little choice but to condemn the Israeli–British–French operation. Moreover, he resented what he saw as Israel's deliberate attempt to exercise pressure on the administration through the Jewish vote. On an international level, the United States felt betrayed by its allies, Britain and France, which had started a conflict that had the potential to trigger a superpower confrontation in the Middle East and one that threatened American oil supplies and its relations with the Arab states. Finally, American condemnation of the Soviet Union's invasion of Hungary made it impossible for it not to condemn the invasion of Egypt. Indeed, Eisenhower was furious that the Suez War had diverted international attention from Soviet actions in Europe.

American hopes that a superpower confrontation in the Middle East had been avoided thanks to its intervention, however, proved premature. The British and French decline in the Middle East which followed the Suez disaster left a power vacuum that was soon filled by the United States and the USSR. Superpower involvement had thus only been postponed. American intervention had also only postponed another full-scale Arab–Israeli confrontation, as the key issues of security, recognition and refugees remained unresolved. Indeed, Nasser's ascen-dancy to the position of the leader of the Arab world on the grounds that he had expelled the imperialist powers, Israel's demonstration of its military might by

United Nations (UN)
An international organization established after the Second World War to replace the League of Nations. Since its establishment in 1945, its membership has grown to 192 countries.

occupying the Sinai in only one day and the Cold War framework ensured that a third round would be only a matter of time.

The 1967 June War

The origins of the Six-Day War lay, on the one hand, in the long-term issues of Israel's quest for security and recognition, and the Arab states' belief that they could defeat Israel and liberate Palestine if sufficiently armed. On the other hand, a series of events from 1966 onwards paved the short-term road to war. On 23 February 1966 a group of militant **Ba'thists** rose to power in Syria. Their hostile anti-Israeli rhetoric exacerbated the already bad Israel–Syrian border relations to such an extent that in August Syria and Israel engaged in a fierce clash in the area of the Sea of Galilee. In November, in a search for allies, Syria signed a mutual defence pact with Egypt. Israel now appeared to be caught between allied hostile states to the north and south, as well as fighting an ongoing low-intensity conflict against Palestinian guerrillas operating from Jordan. Consequently, Israeli decision-makers adopted a more hard-line security response. On 13 November Israel launched its most extensive ground operation since the Sinai campaign, raiding the Jordanian villages of as-Samu, Jimba and Khirbet Karkay. Fifteen Arab legion soldiers and three Jordanian civilians were killed and another fifty-four wounded in this operation. A clinic, a school and 140 houses were also destroyed. Thus it is not surprising that by the end of the year the region, once again, seemed to be on the brink of war.

The first half of 1967 saw no decline in hostilities. On 7 April Israeli aircraft shot down seven Syrian MiGs in an air battle over Damascus. On 13 May a Soviet intelligence report falsely claimed that Israeli troops were massing along the Syrian border. Neither Israeli nor UN claims to the contrary were able to defuse the situation. On 14 May Egyptian troops moved into the Sinai in order to reassure Syria as well as to deter Israel. Nasser's request for a partial withdrawal of the United Nations Emergency Force (UNEF) which had been stationed in the Sinai since 1956 was met by the UN insisting that he choose between 'no withdrawal or complete withdrawal'. Not about to lose face, Nasser opted for the latter, effectively removing the buffer between Israel and Egypt. On 22 May Nasser closed the Straits of Tiran in another attempt to counter Arab criticism that his actions did not live up to his rhetoric. As in 1956, Israeli decision-makers saw the closure of the straits as a *casus belli*, especially in the context of Egyptian troop movements and general Arab mobilization. On 30 May, Jordan, in order to avoid isolation, joined the Egyptian–Syrian defence pact. By June 80,000 Egyptian troops and 900 tanks, 300 Syrian tanks, 300 Jordanian tanks, and some 250,000 Israeli troops, 1,093 tanks and 203 planes were ready for war. The Arabs demanded the liberation of Palestine and the Israeli population demanded immediate government action. Moreover, Israeli probing of American thinking about a pre-emptive strike produced an amber light. In this context, it was no surprise that last-minute

Ba'th (Arabic: Renaissance) The name given to the pan-Arab socialist party founded by Michel Aflaq and Salah Bitar in 1947. Its first congress was held in Damascus. It subsequently spread to Lebanon, Jordan and Iraq and eventually resulted in the establishment of two rival Ba'thist regimes, one in Syria since 1963 and one in Iraq 1968–2003.

Israeli–Egyptian negotiations in Washington on 3 June had little chance of succeeding. On 4 June Israel's prime minister, Levi Eshkol, formed a National Unity government and handed the defence portfolio to Moshe Dayan who tipped the balance in the cabinet in favour of a decision to launch a pre-emptive strike.

It was this succession of events that has allowed some historians to claim that the 1967 June War was an accident – the result of brinkmanship gone over the brink. Others have asserted that it was, in fact, Israel's quest for hegemony and territory that was the driving force. Israeli historians, conversely, have tended to blame Nasser, who by closing the Straits of Tiran left Israel with no alternative. The most interesting explanation, however, is that the war was the result of American–Soviet manipulation and that the Soviet intelligence report had been fabricated in order to entangle the United States in another arena of conflict while its forces were already under pressure in Vietnam.

see Chapter 12

On 5 June 1967 Israel's air force attacked the Egyptian, Syrian and Jordanian airfields simultaneously, destroying 304, 53 and 28 planes respectively, mostly on the ground. Having gained complete air superiority, the Israel Defence Forces (IDF) crossed into the Sinai and into the West Bank. The ground war lasted until 10 June. As a result of the lack of co-ordination between the Arab states and the Syrian failure to engage the IDF until the end of the war, Israel was able to defeat first Egypt, then Jordan and then Syria one after the other rather than having to fight a proper three-front war. Israel's swift victory left it in control of the Sinai, the West Bank, the Golan Heights and, importantly, East Jerusalem, increasing Israeli territory threefold, uniting its capital and returning to Israel the Jewish holy places lost in 1948. Israel had now gained strategic depth, which it saw as vital to its security, and had territory that it believed could be exchanged in return for full peace and recognition.

see Map 18.1

Peace, however, remained elusive. The 1967 defeat had not only discredited the Arab leaders and notions of Arab unity, and caused another large wave of Palestinian refugees, but also resulted in a superpower stalemate with respect to attempts at resolution. Above all, it had further widened the gap between Israel and the Arab states. While the subsequent UN Resolution 242 laid the foundation for future negotiations by stressing the need for recognition, inadmissibility of acquiring territory by war, freedom from acts of force, peace and a just solution of the Palestinian refugee problem, Israel's strength and territorial expansion did not encourage concessions and Arab weakness made it impossible to negotiate from a position of equality.

The 1973 October War

pan-Arabism
Movement for Arab unity as manifested in the Fertile Crescent and Greater Syria schemes as well as attempted unification of Egypt, Syria and Libya.

The defeat of the Arab states in 1967 set in motion some far-reaching changes in the Arab world. The war had shown the failure of Arab unity and as a result strengthened local nationalisms over **pan-Arabism**. Political disillusionment, moreover, was coupled with widespread economic problems following the war,

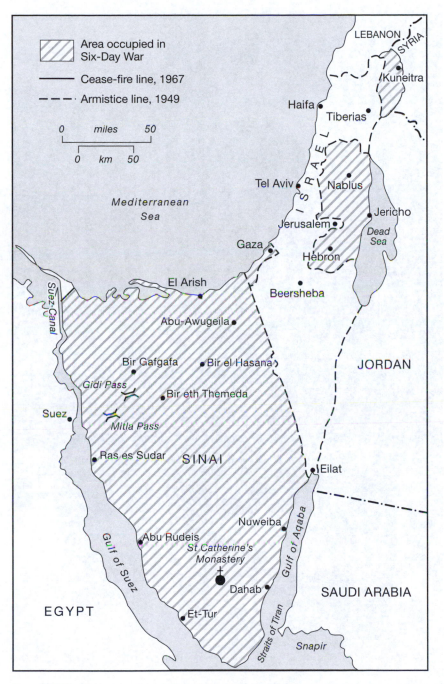

Map 18.1 The Six-Day War

Source: After Schulze (1999)

Plate 18.1 Israeli Defence Minister Moshe Dayan, centre, flanked by army chief of staff, Yitzhak Rabin, right, and General Uzi Narkiss, enter the Old City of Jerusalem through the Lions Gate after its capture from Jordanian forces in the June 1967 Middle East War. (Photo: Israeli GPO/Newsmakers/Getty Images)

providing the seeds for ideological reorientation, resulting, on the one hand, in the emergence of political Islam and, on the other, in economic and political liberalization, in other words, a transition to capitalism and limited democracy.

see Chapter 19

The response of the Arab states in the context of the ongoing conflict with a now dramatically stronger Israel can loosely be divided into three categories. The first path was that of negotiation to end the conflict and to achieve political and economic parity. This was the option adopted by Egypt under Anwar Sadat, who took over the presidency in 1970 following Nasser's fatal heart attack. The second was further militarization, seeking strategic parity and ultimately a military solution. This path was chosen by Syria, which in 1970 came under the leadership of Hafez al-Asad. The third option was to pursue neither open confrontation nor official negotiations, but *de facto* to withdraw from the conflict while still paying lip-service to the liberation of Palestine. As internally weak states, Jordan and Lebanon fell into this category, out of necessity rather than choice.

Ironically, Sadat's search for peace and willingness to negotiate with Israel led to the next Arab–Israeli war in October 1973. Shortly after Sadat succeeded Nasser in September 1970 he made contact with American officials to test the waters for both realigning Egypt with the West and negotiating with Israel. The driving force behind Sadat's decision to change the direction of Egyptian foreign policy was his desire to distance himself as far as possible from his predecessor, Nasser, on the one hand, and to improve the country's failing economy, on the other. Sadat believed that peace with Israel would allow him to regain the Sinai. It would also result in the reduction of Egypt's defence burden, create the stability required to attract foreign investment and hopefully pave the way for American economic aid. Consequently, Sadat in 1971 offered to open the Suez Canal, to declare a cease-fire and to negotiate a peace agreement on the basis of UN Resolution 242. His proposal, however, was rejected by Israel which believed that its new boundaries were vital for its national security. As a result of this rejection, Sadat started planning another war in order to persuade Israel to make peace on terms acceptable to the Arabs and in order to garner the attention of the United States which was preoccupied with **détente**. An attack on Israel, it was hoped, would also break the defeatist attitude of the population, boost Egypt's regional standing and allow Sadat to emerge from Nasser's shadow.

see Chapter 11

détente
A term meaning the reduction of tensions between states. It is often used to refer to the superpower diplomacy that took place between the inauguration of Richard Nixon as the American president in 1969 and the Senate's refusal to ratify SALT II in 1980.

In order for the manoeuvre to have the desired effect, Egypt could not attack Israel alone. Once the decision to go to war had been taken on 30 November 1972, Sadat initiated a series of private meetings with Syrian President Asad. On 31 January 1973, Syria and Egypt's armed forces were placed under joint command. Detailed planning began in March, followed by intricate deception manoeuvres aimed at lulling Israel into complacency, and culminating in the Egyptian–Syrian surprise attack on 6 October 1973.

The October War went down in history as one of Israel's greatest intelligence failures. It revealed how Israel had underestimated Arab frustration over its occupation of the Golan Heights, Sinai, West Bank and the Gaza Strip. Israel had perceived the Arabs as weak and not ready for another war. Intelligence analysts had also failed to take into consideration the possibility of limited war, while political and military decision-makers had grown complacent, convinced of their own invincibility. As a result, Egyptian forces were able to cross the Suez Canal and Syrian forces invaded the Golan Heights. In the first few days Israel was close to defeat and the tide only started to change during the second week of the war when Israel had recouped and moved towards a counter-offensive, aided by a massive American airlift which replenished its firepower. Despite the fact that Israel was able to drive back the Arab forces and the cease-fire agreed on 22 October reaffirmed the 1967 boundaries, Arab and particularly Egyptian confidence had grown dramatically while Israel's had been severely shaken. Sadat had captured Israeli and American attention, had restored Egyptian pride and was now able to negotiate as an equal. Israel realized that territory was no substitute for peace. Israel's new weakness and Egypt's new strength closed the power gap sufficiently to bring both sides to the negotiating table. The disengagement talks that began in 1973 eventually resulted in the first Arab–Israeli peace treaty in 1979 on the basis of land for peace. Egypt not only recovered the Sinai, but also used the process to move from the Soviet camp into the American camp, as well as laying the foundation for economic and political liberalization. This peace, however, came at a high price. Egypt was immediately expelled from the Arab League and, in 1981, Sadat was assassinated by militant Islamists.

While Egyptian–Israeli relations improved, Israeli–Syrian relations escalated into an arms race. Asad had no intention of following Sadat into negotiations as his decision to go to war in 1973 had been motivated by his wish to regain the Golan Heights, to legitimize himself domestically, to strengthen his regional position in the bid for Arab leadership and finally to prove to the USSR that he was a worthy ally. Negotiations were not part of the equation. In fact, Syria, unaware of Sadat's plans for limited war, had pursued a military strategy of all-out confrontation, followed by a disengagement agreement at the end of the fighting which served the purpose of rearming and regrouping for the next round.

The 1982 Lebanon War

Palestine Liberation Organization (PLO)
Founded by Nasser in 1964, it comprises the Palestine National Council as its supreme body, the Palestine Executive Committee for everyday affairs, and the Palestine Liberation Army. Initially chaired by Ahmad Shuqairy and after the 1967 war by Yasser Arafat. In 1989, the PLO Central Council nominated Arafat as Palestinian president with the PLO assuming the role of government in exile until the 1993 Oslo Accords.

The next round came in 1982 and the dynamic giving rise to Israel's invasion of Lebanon, officially named Operation Peace for Galilee, was the increasing Israeli–Syrian struggle for hegemony in the Levant. Israel's decision to launch a 'war of choice' was prompted by five developments. First, in 1975 Lebanon erupted into civil war. This created a security vacuum which was exploited by the **Palestine Liberation Organization (PLO)** in order to attack targets in northern Israel from southern Lebanon. Second, in 1976 Syria intervened in Lebanon in order to contain the sectarian conflict and prevent it from spilling across the border. The Syrian presence raised fears in Israel that Syria now had the possibility of a two-front war. Third, in 1977, for the first time in Israeli history, the Labour Party lost the elections. It was replaced by a right-wing Likud government under Prime Minister Menachem Begin who advocated a 'hawkish' policy with respect to the PLO and who increasingly saw it as Israel's moral obligation to help Lebanon's beleaguered Maronite Christian minority in their struggle against the Muslims. Fourth, in 1978 Begin's views were confirmed when Palestinian guerrillas hijacked a bus travelling from Haifa to Tel Aviv which resulted in thirty-eight Israeli dead and seventy-eight wounded. In response, Israel launched 'Operation Litani', a limited invasion of southern Lebanon with the aim of destroying the PLO infrastructure. Israel also embarked upon a process of transforming loose contacts with Maronite Christians into a full alliance, establishing the South Lebanese Army (SLA) as a proxy along Israel's border and entering into close relations with the Beirut-based Lebanese Forces headed by Bashir Gemayel. Fifth and finally, in 1981, with the election of the second Likud government, Begin's 'dovish' foreign and defence ministers, Moshe Dayan and Ezer Weizman, were replaced by 'hawkish' Yitzhak Shamir and Ariel Sharon. This was important because Sharon in particular saw a war with Syria and the PLO not only as inevitable, but also as a means of bringing about much broader geostrategic changes in the Middle East.

Israeli plans for the invasion of Lebanon were triggered by a two-week war of attrition between Palestinian guerrillas, who were firing rockets at northern Israel, and the IDF and SLA who were shelling Palestinian positions. An estimated 5,000 Israeli civilians fled the area, putting pressure on the Israeli government to act. This two-week war was followed by an American-mediated cease-fire in June 1981, which not only deprived the IDF of the opportunity to take punitive action, but also elevated the PLO's international standing. It was at this point that the decision to launch another ground operation was taken. All that was needed was an act of 'clear provocation' to which Israel could respond. This was provided by the assassination attempt on 3 June 1982 on the Israeli ambassador in London, Shlomo Argov.

Plans which had already been co-ordinated between Sharon and Gemayel in January 1982 were put into motion on 6 June under the name of Operation Peace for Galilee. While the operation was 'sold' to the Israeli cabinet and the public as a limited operation similar to Operation Litani, its actual aims were much broader: first, expelling the Palestinian presence from Lebanon; second, creating a new political order in Lebanon by establishing a Maronite government under Gemayel; third, the expulsion of Syrian troops; and fourth, the destruction of Palestinian nationalism in the West Bank and Gaza Strip.

Sharon's 'grand strategy', however, started to disintegrate quickly when Gemayel's Lebanese forces failed to link up with the advancing Israeli army and then refused to carry out their side of the bargain, namely to 'clear out' the PLO from Muslim West Beirut so that Israel would not be seen as occupying an Arab capital. As a result Israel laid siege to the city on 1 July. The siege ended on 22 August with the evacuation of Palestinian guerrillas and the relocation of the PLO headquarters to Tunis. In the meantime, Gemayel was busy campaigning and indeed won the presidential elections on 23 August. His success, however, was short lived. On 14 September he was killed in the bombing of his party's head-quarters.

The death of Gemayel was also the death-knell for Sharon's Lebanon plans. No other Maronite leader combined the ability to govern Lebanon with a political orientation acceptable to Israel. Israel had lost its key ally and the 'grand strategy' turned into a heated debate on how to extract Israeli troops from the ongoing civil war in Lebanon. American efforts at mediation eventually produced a Lebanese–Israeli agreement on 17 May 1983. However, this agreement fell far short of Israel's security needs and Lebanon's political requirements. The treaty terminated the war without installing peace; it was no more than a glorified armistice which Lebanon, under pressure from Syria, decided to abrogate on 5 March 1984. Without any tangible gains, Israel withdrew its troops to southern Lebanon where they remained until May 2000 to secure Israel's northern border.

The Palestinian armed struggle from the 1948 *naqba* to the 1987 *intifada*

What is interesting about the Arab–Israeli wars post-1948 is the comparative absence of the Palestinians. The establishment of the state of Israel and the declaration of war by the neighbouring Arab states had clearly transformed the conflict from a Zionist–Palestinian struggle into an inter-state Israeli–Arab one. While this change in dynamic put the Palestinians at a disadvantage in real power terms, which was further reinforced by their dispersion and dispossession, it did not make them any less important to either the conflict or its resolution. In fact, it is crucial to look at the evolution of Palestinian resistance during this period in order to understand the underlying dynamic of the Arab–Israeli wars, as well as the process of emancipation from over-reliance upon Arab leaders, which ultimately propelled the Palestinians back into the centre of the conflict.

The first decade after the loss of Palestine was characterized by high hopes that the Arab states would liberate it and that the refugees would soon return to the houses they had left behind. Yet as time went by, it became increasingly clear that Arab leaders such as Nasser, while verbally committed to the Palestinian cause, were doing little to engage Israel militarily. Moreover, with the exception of Jordan, they also had placed Palestinians living in refugee camps under severe restrictions, fearing that they would be a politically and economically destabilizing element. It was in this context that the Palestinian national liberation movement was born.

The first stirrings of revolution occurred in the overcrowded camps of the Egyptian-administered Gaza Strip and among Palestinian students and migrant workers in Kuwait. It was in the latter that in 1957 *Fatah* was formed and Palestinian resistance, which already existed in the form of guerrilla or *fedayeen* raids from Gaza and the West Bank, was organized by Yasser Arafat, Khalil Wazir and Salah Khalaf, who advocated a strategy of armed struggle. The increase in *fedayeen* activity met with a harsh Israeli response against the Arab host states which, in turn, were faced with the dilemma of how to support the Palestine cause without becoming the target of Israeli reprisals. Thus, in an attempt to control the *fedayeen*, Nasser established the PLO as an umbrella organization in January 1964 at an Arab summit meeting in Cairo.

Fatah
Palestinian guerrilla organization founded in 1957 in Kuwait by, among others, Yasser Arafat. It became the core of the PLO.

fedayeen (Arabic: guerrillas; suicide squads)
Originally associated with the Ismaili 'Assassins' in medieval history. After 1948 the term was used to describe Palestinian guerrilla groups.

Nasser's success in temporarily harnessing Palestinian revolutionary activity only increased the already existing regional rivalry between Egypt, Iraq and Syria, to which the PLO quickly became hostage until the 1967 war. It was not until after the Arab defeat and Israel's territorial expansion, which took control of further Palestinian territory with a population of 665,000 Palestinians and turned another 350,000–400,000 Palestinians into refugees, that the PLO embarked upon a path of emancipation. This was reflected at both the political and military level. With respect to the first, Palestinian nationalism lost some of its pan-Arab flavour. It also started to shift its aims from the total destruction of Israel towards the notion of a secular democratic state of Palestine in which Muslims, Jews and Christians could co-exist peacefully. Militarily, there was a return to guerrilla warfare from within the newly occupied territories and from Jordan.

The Palestinian struggle entered a new phase in 1970–71 when it was dealt a severe blow with the expulsion of the PLO from Jordan. Jordan had provided the *fedayeen* with access to the longest Israeli border as well as a considerable degree of autonomy, popular support and governmental goodwill. However, this relationship was ruptured in 1970, after the PLO began to establish a 'state within a state' on the East Bank and engaged in a spate of plane hijackings to Jordanian airfields, which led Jordan to become a regular target of Israeli retaliation and international condemnation. The last straw came when the more left-wing Popular Front for the Liberation of Palestine (PFLP) attempted to assassinate King Hussein. As a result of these actions, on 17 September 1970, in what came to be known as **Black September** or the Jordanian civil war, the Jordanian army moved against Palestinian positions. When the fighting ended ten days later, the Palestinians had suffered an estimated 1,500 dead and Palestinian–Arab relations had soured, leaving a bitter aftertaste of betrayal. Over the next year the PLO was ousted from Jordan and moved to Lebanon.

The expulsion and subsequent move to Lebanon triggered two new strategic developments. The first was the decision to take the armed struggle to the West in order to place the Palestinian question back on to the international political agenda. This highly controversial, and some would argue counter-productive, campaign included the attack on the Israeli athletic team at the 1972 Munich Olympics. The second was the unification of all PLO factions under one command in Lebanon, accompanied by institution-building and the acquisition of medium and heavy arms. Once again the PLO was establishing a 'state within a state', but this time it was building up a semi-regular army as well.

As Palestinian attacks on Israel increased and Israeli reprisals pounded Lebanon in an attempt to get the Lebanese army to react like the Jordanian one, Lebanon's multi-religious society collapsed into civil war in April 1975. For the PLO this meant greater freedom of movement for operations against Israel. For Lebanon's neighbours Israel and Syria, it provided the opportunity to intervene with the aim of attaining hegemony over the Levant and resolving regional problems at Lebanon's expense. Accordingly, Syria intervened in 1976 and Israel in March 1978 and again in June 1982.

Israel's 1982 invasion is of particular interest with respect to the Palestinian national movement, for one of the aims was the removal of the Palestinians from

Black September

The confrontation between the Jordanian army and Palestinian guerrillas in Jordan in September 1970, as a result of which the PLO was expelled from Jordan and relocated its headquarters to Beirut, Lebanon.

Lebanon and the destruction of the emerging Palestinian nationalism in the Israeli-occupied territories, the West Bank and Gaza Strip. While the operation succeeded in forcing the evacuation of the PLO, it failed to quell nationalist sentiments. In fact, the massacres of the Palestinian and **Shi'a** refugees in the Sabra and Shatilla camps in September 1982, following the assassination of Gemayel, served to fuel Palestinian steadfastness and, in the long run, contributed to the anger which triggered the *intifada* uprising in December 1987. Moreover, the banishment of the PLO to the far-away shores of Tunisia strengthened the diplomatic option over the military one, raising the PLO's international standing and with it the pressure upon Israel finally to address the Palestinian question. Thus, while Israel may have achieved a short-term victory over the Palestinians in Lebanon in 1982, it ultimately lost the Lebanon War and its quest to exclude the Palestinians from the settlement of the Arab–Israeli conflict. With the *intifada* the Palestinians were back on the international agenda, not as terrorists but as women and children who were intent on shaking off the occupation by throwing stones.

This almost four-year-long popular uprising in the West Bank and Gaza Strip centred on civil disobedience in the form of strikes, demonstrations, the boycott of Israeli products and non-payment of taxes. While it did not achieve the liberation of the occupied territories, it restored the green line (the armistice frontiers in 1949), erased the belief held by many that the Palestinians did not really mind Israeli rule, questioned the notion that the territories constituted a buffer zone, and raised questions about whether the continued occupation was compatible with the Jewish state's commitment to democracy. Also the images of Israel's response to the *intifada*, the so-called 'iron-fist' policy which resulted in well-trained and fully armed soldiers beating unarmed children, shifted international opinion. Israel was no longer 'David', as in 1948, but had become 'Goliath'. Israel realized that it could not fully control the West Bank and Gaza Strip and that occupation came at a price. The international community realized that maintaining the status quo, which had been the preferred option throughout the Cold War, was no longer the best option. This, along with the 1990–91 Gulf War, paved the way for the Middle East peace conference and, for the first time, a Palestinian presence at the negotiating table.

The peace process, its collapse and attempts to revive it

The environment which allowed for the construction of a workable and sustainable Middle East peace process began to emerge in the late 1980s as the result of a combination of international, regional and domestic factors. At the international level, the collapse of the Soviet Union removed the Cold War framework which had been an obstacle to conflict resolution. At the regional level, the 1990 Iraqi invasion of Kuwait, which was supported by the PLO, revealed to the majority of Middle Eastern players, as well as the remaining superpower, the

---

Shi'a Islam

Muslim sect which emerged out of the struggle over the succession following the death of the Prophet Muhammad. Derived from Shi'a Ali (the Party of Ali) or those who supported the Prophet's son-in-law Ali's accession to the Caliphate. An estimated 15 per cent of Muslims are Shi'a. They are concentrated in the areas of Iran, Iraq and southern Lebanon, with smaller communities scattered throughout the Muslim world.

intifada (Arabic: shaking off) Name given to the Palestinian uprising against Israeli occupation which began on 9 December 1987 and lasted until the signing of the 1993 Oslo Accords between the PLO and Israel.

see Chapter 20

United States, that regional stability could only be achieved if the Arab–Israeli conflict was resolved, as this would undermine the legitimacy of either Arab nationalists or Islamists who advocated expansion, revolution or war in the name of the liberation of Palestine. Finally, at the domestic or Israeli–Palestinian level, the *intifada* made Israeli occupation increasingly costly and difficult at a time when an expected one million Jews from the former Soviet Union needed to be absorbed. It also raised uncomfortable questions about the nature of the Israeli state, democracy and human rights. All these factors together made it possible for the United States, together with Russia and the European Union, to provide a framework for talks. In addition, the **Great Powers** also provided numerous sticks and carrots to get Arabs and Israelis to the negotiating table: carrots, such as desperately needed loan guarantees for Israel, and sticks, such as reminders to the PLO that it had backed Saddam Hussein in the Gulf War and therefore was not in a position to make demands.

The Madrid Conference which opened on 30 October 1991 officially initiated a peace process which divided the negotiations into bilateral and multilateral tracks. The bilateral tracks aimed at achieving separate peace treaties between Israel and its Arab neighbours Syria, Lebanon, Jordan and the Palestinians. The multilateral track was designed to resolve broader regional problems such as water, the environment, arms control, refugees and economic development. Although the framework was put in place, the negotiations themselves quickly became hostage to domestic politics as well as popular fear and mistrust. Indeed, it was not until the 1992 Israeli elections and the replacement of Yitzhak Shamir's centre-right Likud government with Yitzhak Rabin's centre-left Labour government that real negotiations rather than posturing started to take place.

The key to peace with the Arabs was an Israeli–Palestinian agreement as none of the Arab states was otherwise willing to sign any treaty with Israel. Cautious Israeli–Palestinian talks were initiated in early 1993 in Oslo out of the limelight of the media and the official negotiations, which by that point had been moved to Washington. The first contacts took place between Israeli academics such as Ron Pundak and Yair Hirschfeld and Palestinian representatives. As progress was made, Israeli academics were upgraded to civil servants and lawyers, ultimately including Foreign Minister Shimon Peres. The product of the negotiations was the Declaration of Principles (DOP), more commonly known as the Oslo Accords, signed on 13 September 1993 on the White House lawn by Rabin and Arafat.

While falling short of establishing a Palestinian state, the DOP provided for mutual recognition and outlined arrangements for Palestinian interim self-government, election of a Palestinian Legislative Council, Israeli redeployment and final status negotiations. Under the Rabin administration Israeli–Palestinian negotiations proceeded with a series of smaller arrangements and agreements, most notably the 1994 Cairo Agreement which included provisions for Israeli military withdrawal, the transfer of authority to the Palestinian Authority (PA) and Palestinian police force, and the 1995 Israeli–Palestinian Interim Agreement which aimed at broadening Palestinian autonomy, but also addressed security, elections, economic relations and the release of prisoners.

Great Powers
Traditionally those states that were held capable of shared responsibility for the management of the international order by virtue of their military and economic influence.

The DOP also opened the way for negotiations with the Arab states. Jordan was the first to follow suit with a full peace treaty in October 1994. With few contentious issues to resolve, the absence of major conflict since 1967 and a history of secret amicable relations, this treaty was easily concluded. Negotiations with Lebanon and Syria were, in comparison, more problematic. The most difficult issue here was Syria's insistence on a full return of the Golan Heights and a peace treaty based on mutuality, equality and reciprocity in all areas including security.

Rabin's assassination on 5 November 1995 and the 1996 election of the Likud leader Benjamin Netanyahu as prime minister put an end to further progress in Israeli–Palestinian relations and to Israeli–Syrian negotiations, as well as severely disrupting normalization with Jordan. While Netanyahu under American pressure concluded two more agreements with the Palestinians – the 1997 Hebron Agreement and the 1998 Wye Accords – the former was at best only partially implemented, and the latter not at all. In the meantime the Palestinians in their own 1996 elections endorsed Arafat's leadership of the PA. However, as relations with Israel deteriorated, Arafat and the PA were increasingly challenged by the rejectionist left-wing Popular Front for the Liberation of Palestine (PFLP) and the Democratic Front for the Liberation of Palestine (DFLP) as well as the Islamist **Hamas**. Their charges of a political sell-out were further exacerbated by the increasing corruption within the PA; both resulted in considerable disillusionment for the Palestinians with their own leadership and the peace process as a whole.

The election of Labour leader Ehud Barak in May 1999 set in motion the collapse of the peace process when efforts to restore the negotiations with the Palestinians and Syria ultimately failed. Barak chose to start with Syria but his reluctance to commit himself to a full withdrawal to the 4 June 1967 line, despite acknowledging the fact that Rabin had made such a commitment, left the Syrians feeling that Israel had backtracked and was therefore lacking seriousness and good-will. Barak then moved towards final status negotiations with the Palestinians, making what Israel considered 'an unprecedented offer'. For the Palestinians, however, the offer did not go far enough as it failed to meet Palestinian needs on the status of Jerusalem, the future of Israeli settlements, Palestinian refugees and viable Palestinian statehood. While the Israeli offer, which had in fact been an American bridging proposal, failed to meet Palestinian expectations and while the Camp David Summit itself was marred by Barak's lack of interpersonal skills, it was ultimately Arafat who made the decision to walk out of the talks. This decision-making error was only surpassed by the Palestinian decision to launch another uprising – the second *intifada*.

The so-called al-Aqsa *intifada* erupted on 29 September 2000 and was triggered by the visit of Likud leader Ariel Sharon to the Temple Mount/Haram ash-Sharif on the previous day. Sharon's visit aimed at shoring up Israel's claim to a united Jerusalem as well as undermining Barak. The widespread violence that followed was the result of anger at Sharon's presence but also of long-term pent-up Palestinian frustration with a peace process perceived as supporting Israeli hegemonic ambitions, of discontent with the lack of change in the everyday life of the average Palestinian, of dissatisfaction with their own leadership, and of rage

Hamas
The acronym for *Harakat al-Muqawama al-Islamiyya* (Islamic Resistance Movement). Emerged during the first *intifada* in 1987 in the Gaza Strip.

see Map 18.2

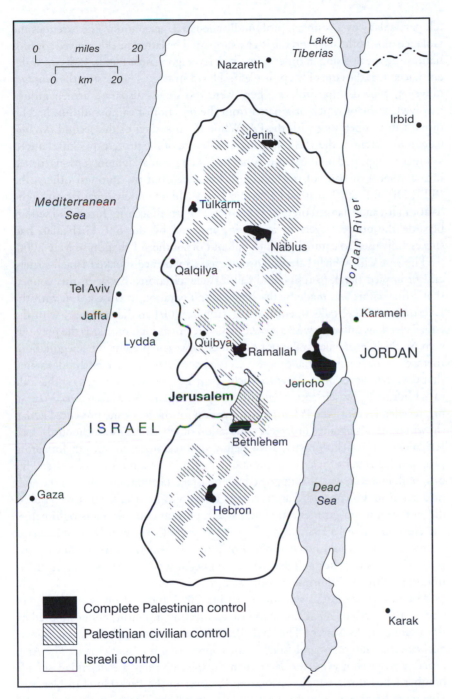

Map 18.2 The West Bank in 2000

Source: After Bregman (2003)

felt particularly by a younger, profoundly alienated, generation. The extent of the violence took both Israel and the PA by surprise. The latter quickly moved towards harnessing the uprising in order to use it as leverage against Barak. Indeed, Arafat embraced it as the core of his post-Camp David strategy. Harnessing the *intifada*, however, proved impossible as there were too many disparate armed groups involved, many of which originated from the rejectionist camp and thus had no interest in co-operating with the PA. While the first days of the second *intifada* were reminiscent of the 1987 uprising, the nature of the protest quickly changed as firearms appeared on the street. What had been popular demonstrations turned into a volatile mixture of riots and attacks carried out by, amongst others, the PFLP, DFLP, Fatah Tanzim, Hamas and Islamic Jihad loosely organized into the 'Nationalist and Islamic Forces of Palestine'. The Israeli security forces and settlers became the prime targets in a strategy inspired by the one **Hizb'allah** had successfully used to compel Israel to pull out of southern Lebanon in May 2000.

The ease with which Palestinians reverted to violence shocked Israeli society and prompted Barak to resign and call for new elections. It was in this context that a final effort was made by the Barak administration to close a deal with the Palestinians. These talks opened on 21 January 2001 in Taba, Egypt, with the Israeli elections only two weeks away. They were not as high profile as the previous summit. Neither Barak, Arafat nor the Americans were present. The negotiations themselves made substantial progress on the issues. After a week both sides stated that they 'had never been closer to reaching an agreement'. The gaps on the scale of withdrawal, the settlements and security arrangements were reduced. In an unprecedented move the Palestinian delegation for the first time presented a map showing their acceptance of Israel's annexation of Jewish neighbourhoods in East Jerusalem. An Israeli minister, Yossi Beilin, in a reciprocal move, put forward a proposal for Israel to take in a quota of refugees over a number of years. This proposal, however, was not supported by the Israeli negotiating team. In the end, no agreement was concluded as the timing was simply not right. The Israeli public did not want its government to make such important commitments right before the elections. The Palestinian representatives feared that even if commitments were made they would not be upheld by a new Israeli government. And in any case, what was on offer at Taba, while significantly closer, still fell short of the minimum that the Palestinians could accept.

The next peace initiative came in spring 2002 and was proposed by Saudi Crown Prince Abdullah at the Arab League meeting in Beirut, being adopted by the League on 28 March. The Arab Peace Plan called for a full normalization between the Arab states and Israel in the context of a final settlement. The Arab peace message, however, was lost when on the same day a Palestinian suicide bomber killed thirty people celebrating Passover in the Park Hotel in Netanya. Five more bombings followed over the next five days. The Arab Peace Plan did not stand a chance. There have been a number of attempts to revive the plan since 2002, the most recent in spring 2007. None has so far been successful.

In July 2002 the 'Quartet' of the US, EU, UN and Russia picked up the tattered pieces of the Arab Peace Plan and put together the so-called 'Roadmap for Peace'. However, it was not until the appointment of Mahmoud Abbas as

Hizb'allah (Arabic: Party of God)
Lebanese Shi'a Islamist group which emerged in reaction to the 1982 Israeli invasion of Lebanon. Its primary aim until the Israeli withdrawal in May 2000 was the liberation of southern Lebanon.

Palestinian prime minister in April 2003 that the 'Roadmap' was officially initiated so that neither the US nor Israel had to deal with Arafat. The 'Roadmap' was a performance-based plan in three phases, which ultimately envisaged a safe and secure Israel co-existing with a viable, sovereign and democratic Palestine. The first phase focused on ending the violence on both sides, followed by a normalization of Palestinian life, the building and rebuilding of Palestinian institutions and civil society, and the dismantling of settlements begun since March 2001. The second phase saw democratic Palestinian elections, a new democratic Palestinian constitution, comprehensive security performance, and the creation of a Palestinian state with provisional borders and sovereignty as a way station to a permanent status settlement. The third phase would produce a permanent status agreement and result in the end of the Israeli–Palestinian conflict. This would come in the context of an international conference and would be based on UN Security Council Resolutions 242, 338 and 1397, including a just and fair solution to the Palestinian refugee situation, the status of Jerusalem and full normalization. The 'Roadmap' was endorsed by both Israeli and Palestinian leaders as a way forward but it has so far not been implemented. Moreover, with the election of Hamas it has been questioned whether the Palestinians are still committed. Nevertheless it remained the 'only game in town' as far as the international community was concerned.

In the absence of a political solution, violence on the ground only intensified. Hamas's Qassem rockets and its suicide bombings proved so effective that they were copied not just by other Islamists but also by secular Palestinian groups. With violence ruling the day, the earlier revival of the revolutionary structures was further reinforced and the opportunity arose for the re-emergence of the 'insiders', the local leadership of 1987–92. The rejectionists were also strengthened and Hamas, in particular, started to mount a credible challenge to Fatah. This led to battlefield competition between Hamas's Izz al-Din al-Qassem Brigades and Fatah's Al-Aqsa Martyr Brigades, increasing the militancy of all Palestinian armed groups. Israel, now under Prime Minister Ariel Sharon, opted for a strategy of unilateral disengagement. Underlying this strategy was Sharon's belief that Arafat was not a partner, that the Oslo process was finished and that there would not be an immediate resumption of negotiations. Sharon's separation strategy comprised four key elements. First, to isolate Arafat and the PA politically in order to force the former to resign and the latter to reform. Second, to target the PA structures militarily in order to weaken Arafat's power base and to punish it for participating in the violence against Israel. Third, to 'decapitate' Hamas and Islamic Jihad by arresting or killing their leaders as well as destroying their command structures and support bases in order to reduce their military capacity and threat against Israel. And fourth, to separate Israeli and Palestinian territory physically in order to make Israel's border more defensible. This territorial separation started with the building of a fence along the West Bank and was followed by disengagement from Gaza and the northern West Bank in August 2005.

As Israeli strategy was implemented Palestinian popular opinion started to shift away from supporting an ineffective, internationally isolated PA towards supporting Hamas, which was seen as doing something about the occupation and which had not agreed to unacceptable compromises with Israel. This became clear with the death of Arafat in November 2004. The US and Israel hoped that his successor, Mahmoud Abbas (Abu Mazen), who was elected president of the PA on 9 January 2005, would be able to bring the violence under control, reform the PA and resume negotiations. However, despite the fact that Abbas received agreement from Hamas in March 2005 that they would honour a 'period of calm', he was perceived as weak by Israel and the US as well as by the Palestinian population. Only a year later, on 25 January 2006, Hamas won the legislative elections, taking 74 out of 132 seats. The Hamas victory was not necessarily the result of popular desire for an Islamic state, but a reflection of how disillusioned the people were with Fatah.

The election of Hamas was a challenge for Israeli Prime Minister Ehud Olmert who had succeeded Sharon after the latter had suffered a stroke and fell into a coma on 4 January 2006. It was also a challenge for Fatah which refused to accept the Hamas victory, resulting in conflict that erupted between Hamas and Fatah cadres as well as their supporters. And finally it was a challenge for the international community which reacted by freezing development funds and economic aid. Not surprisingly this had an overall detrimental impact on the already ailing Palestinian economy. Israel, backed by the US, announced that there would be no resumption of talks under these circumstances as they did not negotiate with terrorists. Abbas, who vacillated between trying to bring Hamas in from the cold and marginalizing it completely, found himself, in turn, marginalized by the Hamas prime minister, Ismail Haniyyeh, as violence on the ground turned internecine. By spring 2007 the Palestinians were embroiled in a civil war, with the result that Abbas dismissed the Hamas government.

The collapse of the Hamas-led coalition government also gave impetus to the renewal of negotiations. On 27 November 2007, after a seven-year period without talks, President Mahmoud Abbas met with Prime Minister Olmert in Annapolis under the auspices of the US and the Quartet in order to talk about the resumption of negotiations with the aim of concluding a final status agreement by the end of 2008.

The 2006 Lebanon War

When Israel pulled out of southern Lebanon in 2000 Hizb'allah and indeed Lebanon and the Arab world as a whole saw it as a victory. Israeli fears that Hizb'allah would pursue the retreating troops across the border and then proceed to target Israel did not materialize. Instead the Israeli–Hizb'allah battleground shifted to the area known as the Sheba'a farms. While Israel maintained that it had fully withdrawn from Lebanon, as the Sheba'a farms according to UN maps were part of Syria, Hizb'allah argued that it was Lebanese land as the farmers were Lebanese and thus Israel's withdrawal remained incomplete. Hizb'allah's attitude was largely determined by its domestic position. It needed a continuing area of conflict with Israel in order to resist pressure to disarm and dissolve its military wing. And Syria supported Hizb'allah in its interpretation of landownership as Syria too needed an area from where pressure could be exerted on Israel. Hizb'allah also saw continuing military action against Israel as an act of solidarity with the Palestinians following the outbreak of the second *intifada*. However, until 2006 the Hizb'allah–Israeli battle was sporadic, remained confined to this area and had 'rules'. Hizb'allah knew how Israel would respond to a strike against its forces and vice versa. This changed in July 2006.

On 12 July 2006 Hizb'allah launched an ambush on an Israeli patrol, in which two Israeli soldiers were captured and three others killed. In the IDF rescue mission another five Israeli soldiers were killed and one Merkava tank was destroyed. Hizb'allah was ecstatic as its operation had exceeded expectations. The attack was aimed at opening a second front to take the pressure off Hamas, which was at that point on the receiving end of a fully fledged Israeli offensive. Hizb'allah also saw the ambush as an opportunity to demonstrate its own offensive capacity and to boost popular admiration, which had been fading since May 2000. Its leaders also believed that Israel's new prime minister, Ehud Olmert, was weak, inexperienced and too preoccupied with Hamas to strike back. Hizb'allah's assessment could not have been more wrong. Israeli leaders since late 2005 were almost itching for a fight with Hizb'allah. They were tired of the constant taunting over Sheba'a and they perceived Hizb'allah's position as having been weakened during 2005 as a result of the pro-Western and pro-democracy 'Cedar Revolution' following the car bomb assassination of Lebanese Prime Minister Rafiq al-Hariri on 14 February, Syria's implication in the Hariri assassination and its forced withdrawal from Lebanon in April, and the victory of the anti-Syrian camp led by Hariri's son Saad al-Din in May. There were also fears that Hizb'allah was developing a first-strike capability. Moreover, Israel was angry, having monitored correspondence between Hizb'allah and Hamas in which the former had urged the latter not to compromise over the return of an Israeli soldier captured in Gaza in June 2006. And last, but certainly not least, there seems to have been American encouragement for a more extensive Israeli operation against Hizb'allah, which suited the US 'war on terror'. Indeed, in early summer Israeli and US officials met in Washington and made plans for a crushing attack on Hizb'allah.

A day after Hizb'allah's ambush, Israel's retaliatory offensive began. By 14 July Lebanon was blockaded from the sea, Beirut airport was hit and shut down, and Hizb'allah's main offices in the capital were bombed. Israeli strategy relied on air power and artillery bombardment from northern Israel into Lebanon. Its stated goal as articulated by Olmert was the return of the two Israeli soldiers, a complete cease-fire and the deployment of the Lebanese army all the way to the border with Israel. However, what emerged quickly was that its primary objective was to destroy Hizb'allah's military capacity by destroying its rocket arsenal, cutting its supply lines, targeting its leaders and removing its support base. In the first few days Israel had moral superiority as it was the victim of an unprovoked attack. Even Arab states such as Saudi Arabia, Egypt, Jordan and the United Arab Emirates publicly criticized Hizb'allah's action. However, sympathy for Israel disappeared quickly as it became clear that cutting off Hizb'allah from its supply lines and support base meant targeting the civilian population in southern Lebanon and effectively emptying the area.

Hizb'allah responded by firing rockets into Israel at a rate of around 150 per day. If Israel had thought that Hizb'allah had been weakened during the previous year and would be easily subdued, it was mistaken. Not only was Hizb'allah able to maintain its firing capacity, it had also acquired longer-range capabilities. It was no longer just Israeli towns and villages along the border that were coming under attack but large coastal cities such as Haifa. Moreover, rather than undermining Hizb'allah's support base, Israel's attacks on southern Lebanon bolstered it. This was the result of Israeli bombings such as that of Qana on 30 July in which twenty-eight civilians were killed, as well as Hizb'allah's immediate pledges to compensate anyone losing their home with between $10,000 and $12,000. There was no doubt that the Shi'a population rallied around Hizb'allah during this war. The reaction of the rest of the Lebanese population was mixed, with Christian voices denouncing Hizb'allah and calling for its disarmament as years of post-civil war reconstruction fell victim to Israeli bombs.

In mid-August the UN finally managed to broker a cease-fire. The July War, as it is referred to in Lebanon, or the Second Lebanon War, as it is called in Israel, lasted thirty-four days. During this time 500,000 residents of northern Israel and 900,000 residents of southern Lebanon were displaced. Israel counted 43 and Lebanon 1,109 civilian deaths. Military casualties comprised 118 Israeli soldiers, 28 Lebanese soldiers and 200 Hizb'allah fighters. Material losses amounted to $500 million in Israel and $4 billion in Lebanon. Hizb'allah's 'victory' was celebrated across the Arab world and among Islamists. However, Hizb'allah admitted it was a hollow victory and that had it known what Israel's response would be, it would never have kidnapped the soldiers. For Israel it left the bitter taste of defeat, not because it had truly been defeated, but because it seemed that Israel had learned nothing from the 1982 Lebanon War.

Debating the Cold War in the Middle East

The 1956 Suez Crisis is generally credited with the introduction of the Cold War into the Middle East. The power vacuum left by the defeated former colonial Powers, Britain and France, was quickly filled by the United States and the USSR. Scholars have since debated the impact of the Cold War on the Middle East, looking at the relationship between local states and external Powers. The question at the centre of the debate with respect to the Arab – Israeli conflict is a simple one: to what extent did Israel, the Palestinians and the Arab states fight to a globalist superpower agenda and to what extent did regional leaders manipulate the superpowers for their own domestic and regional gains? In trying to answer this question, two broad schools of thought have emerged, the globalist or systemic school and the regionalist school. According to the globalist or systemic school, external forces played a decisive role. Some analysts, in fact, have gone as far as suggesting that local powers had no real will of their own, no freedom of action, no control over their own destiny. They were mere pawns in the superpower game.

Those who argue that the impact of the Cold War was the decisive dynamic in the Middle East and the Arab–Israeli conflict point to the post-Suez split in the Arab world between Western-supported reactionary states, which in the Arab–Israeli sphere included Lebanon and Jordan, and Soviet-supported revolutionary states such as Nasser's Egypt, Ba'thist Syria, and many of the Palestinian guerrilla groups which had started to organize since 1957. Israel eventually joined the Western camp, despite the continued reservations by Britain and the United States that relations with Israel would jeopardize their relations with the Arab oil states. As a result Israel received its first American arms shipment in 1962 from the Kennedy administration, but it was not until after the 1967 Six-Day War that the American–Israeli special relationship developed.

Superpower manipulation of local players is evident in the issuing of the false intelligence report by the Soviets in May 1967, which put the region on the road to war. The Israeli–Syrian arms race in the 1970s and 1980s is also seen as a clear manifestation of the Cold War by proxy. Furthermore, the last phase of the 1973 war has been described as the most serious superpower confrontation in the Middle East. When the Egyptian Third Army was trapped by Israeli forces, Russia rallied to the aid of its Egyptian ally, threatening to take action in the Middle East if the United States did not curb Israel. Washington responded to the Russian threat by issuing a nuclear alert, Defcon III. Last but not least, it has been argued that the Cold War made the resolution of the Arab–Israeli conflict impossible, for the superpower rivalry led to both sides using their vetoes in the UN Security Council to maintain the status quo of 'no all out war and no peace'. Thus it was only in 1991, with Russia and the United States pulling in the same direction, that a comprehensive Middle East peace conference could be convened.

According to the regionalist school of thought, local powers have not just been acted upon. Regionalists have assigned greater weight and more leverage to local forces. Some analysts have gone as far as to suggest that the external–local power relationship is, in fact, inverse and that more often than not local powers successfully manipulated the superpowers for their own ends and that the superpowers struggled with the complexities of the regional dynamics.

Those who argue that the impact of the Cold War was less significant point to the fact that the causes of the Arab–Israeli conflict as a whole, as well as each of the wars, were regional in nature, both pre-dating the Cold War and outliving it. They also point to the fact that while the United States and USSR were supplying their local allies with arms, they had no control over how or when these arms were used and repeatedly proved incapable of restraining their allies and stopping the descent into war. In 1967, the United States and the USSR each urged Israel and Egypt respectively not to appear to be the aggressor. Yet Israel launched a pre-emptive strike. Israel's decision was based on domestic economic and security considerations, such as the population's pressure for decisive action, the fact that it could not remain mobilized for an indefinite period of time, and that it did not have the strategic depth to absorb an attack and consequently needed to fight any war in enemy territory.

An example which clearly points to a case of the 'tail wagging the dog' is Egypt's expulsion of the Soviet advisers in 1972 and its subsequent realignment with the United States. This decision was not grounded in ideological conversion but in Egypt's desire to improve its economy and regain the Sinai. Courting the United States was a pragmatic choice as only the latter could put pressure on Israel and provide large amounts of economic aid. With respect to the Middle East peace process, regionalists argue that while the end of the Cold War made the international environment more conducive to negotiations, these would not have produced results if it had not been for the changes in attitude of Israel, the Palestinians and the Arab states, changes that were the direct product of years of confrontation and the realization of the limits of the use of force.

Conclusion

The Arab–Israeli conflict, like so many others in the twentieth century, emerged as one of competing nationalisms laying claim to the same territory. The Zionist–Palestinian nature of the conflict changed with the establishment of the state of Israel and its subsequent invasion by Egypt, Jordan, Syria, Lebanon and Iraq. The 1948 war turned the Palestinians from a nation that had been allocated a state in half of Palestine into a refugee problem. The Arab–Israeli conflict was now being fought on an inter-state level, complicated by inter-Arab rivalries, Cold War politics and the emergence of both Muslim and Jewish religious fundamentalism. Thus, it was not until the outbreak of the *intifada* in 1987 and the end of the Cold War that the Palestinian–Israeli dynamic re-emerged, making it clear that the Palestinians could not be bypassed or marginalized in the search for *see Chapter 20* regional peace and stability. The 1991 Madrid peace process set in motion the process of negotiation over Palestinian statehood, recognition of Israel, secure boundaries, regional peace and normalization. Yet while considerable progress in resolving the Arab–Israeli conflict had been made by the end of the century, the circle of peace remained to be completed.

Recommended reading

Of the books covering the whole period of the Arab–Israeli conflict, four in particular stand out in terms of scope and scholarship: Mark Tessler, *A History of the Israeli–Palestinian Conflict* (Bloomington, IN, 1994), Yezid Sayigh, *Armed Struggle and the Search for State: The Palestinian National Movement, 1949–1993* (Oxford, 1997), Benny Morris, *Righteous Victims: A History of the Zionist–Arab Conflict* (New York, 1999) and Avi Shlaim, *The Iron Wall: Israel and the Arab World* (London, 2000). Avi Shlaim, *War and Peace in the Middle East: A Concise History* (London, 1995) offers a general introduction to the international politics of the region and Kirsten E. Schulze, *The Arab–Israeli Conflict* (London, 1999) provides an overview of the wars and the peace process. There are also three detailed military histories of the conflict: Trevor N. Dupuy, *Elusive Victory: The Arab–Israeli Wars, 1947–1974* (New York, 1978), Chaim Herzog, *The Arab–Israeli Wars* (New York, 1982) and Anthony H. Cordesman, *Arab–Israeli Military Forces in an Era of Asymmetric War* (Westport, CT, 2006). And finally, addressing historiography there is Jonathan B. Isacoff's *Writing the Arab–Israeli Conflict: Pragmatism and Historical Enquiry* (Lanham, MD, 2006).

Books on the Suez Crisis include Mordechai Bar-On, *The Gates of Gaza: Israel's Road to Suez and Back, 1955–1957* (New York, 1994), Benny Morris, *Israel's Border Wars, 1949–1956* (Oxford, 1993), Mohammed Heikal's *Cutting the Lion's Tail: Suez through Egyptian Eyes* (London, 1986), Keith Kyle, *Suez* (New York, 1991) and S. I. Troen and M. Shemesh (eds), *The Suez–Sinai Crisis 1956: Retrospective and Reappraisal* (London, 1990). The most useful collection of documents on this period is Anthony Gorst and Lewis Johnman, *The Suez Crisis* (London, 1997).

The role of the superpowers is discussed by Fawaz Gerges, *The Superpowers and the Middle East: Regional and International Politics, 1955–1967* (Boulder, CO, 1994), Galia Golan, *Moscow and the Middle East: New Thinking on Regional Conflict* (New York, 1992), Mohammed Heikal, *The Sphinx and the Commissar: The Rise and Fall of Soviet Influence in the Middle East* (New York, 1978) and Yezid Sayigh and Avi Shlaim (eds), *The Cold War and the Middle East* (Oxford, 1997).

As the declassification of documents is still under way, large-scale historiographical debates on the post-1967 period have yet to emerge. Nevertheless, there are some good books on the Six-Day War. An in-depth, thoroughly researched, day-by-day account is provided by Michael Oren, *Six Days of War: June 1967 and the Making of the Modern Middle East* (New York, 2002). The Arab perspective is advanced by Ibrahim Abu Lughod, *The Arab–Israeli Confrontation of June 1967: An Arab Perspective* (Evanston, IL, 1987) and Elias Sam'o, *The June 1967 Arab–Israeli War: Miscalculation or Conspiracy?* (Wilmette, IL, 1971). Good retrospective re-evaluations are Richard Parker (ed.), *The Six Day War: A Retrospective* (Gainesville, FL, 1996) and J. Roth, *The Impact of the Six Day War: A Twenty Year Assessment* (Basingstoke, 1988).

Books that deal with the 1973 war include Michael Brecher, *Decisions in Crisis: Israel 1967 and 1973* (Berkeley, CA, 1980) and Ray Maghroori, *The Yom Kippur*

War (Washington, DC, 1981). Important Egyptian contributions to the literature have come from journalist Mohammed Heikal, *The Road to Ramadan* (London, 1975) and Field Marshal Mohamed El-Gamasy, *The October War* (Cairo, 1993). They stand alongside Israeli accounts such as Chaim Herzog, *The War of Atonement: The Inside Story of the Yom Kippur War* (London, 2003). A reconsideration of the 1973 war was undertaken by P. R. Kumaraswamy (ed.), *Revisiting the Yom Kippur War* (Portland, OR, 2000) and Richard B. Parker (ed), *The October War: A Retrospective* (Gainesville, FL, 2001).

Compared with the 1973 war, Israel's 1982 invasion of Lebanon generated a much larger body of literature. Good analyses of the war can be found in George Ball, *Error and Betrayal in Lebanon: An Analysis of Israel's Invasion of Lebanon and the Implications for US–Israeli Relations* (Washington, DC, 1984), Yair Evron, *War and Intervention in Lebanon* (London, 1987), Itamar Rabinovich, *The War for Lebanon, 1970–1985* (New York, 1985), Richard Gabriel, *Operation Peace for Galilee: The Israel–PLO War in Lebanon* (New York, 1984), Zeev Schiff and Ehud Ya'ari, *Israel's Lebanon War* (London, 1984) and Kirsten E. Schulze, *Israel's Covert Diplomacy in Lebanon* (Basingstoke, 1998).

In order to understand post-1982 developments with respect to Israel's presence in Lebanon it is crucial to study Hizb'allah. The most authoritative books on Hizb'allah are Hala Jaber, *Hezbollah: Born with a Vengeance* (New York, 1997), Amal Saad-Ghorayeb, *Hizbullah: Politics and Religion* (London, 2001), Ahmed Nizar Hamzeh, *In the Path of Hizbullah* (New York, 2004), Naim Qassem, *Hizbullah: The Story from Within* (London, 2005) and Augustus Richard Norton, *Hezbollah: A Short History* (Princeton, NJ, 2007).

As the literature on the individual wars often only addresses the Palestinians in passing, it is important to broaden this particular aspect through further reading. In addition to Yezid Sayigh's above-mentioned excellent book, useful books on the PLO include John W. Amos, *Palestinian Resistance: Organisation of a National Movement* (New York, 1980), Helena Cobban, *The Palestine Liberation Organisation: People, Power, and Policies* (Cambridge, 1984), Alain Gresh, *The PLO: The Struggle Within: Towards an Independent Palestinian State* (London, 1985), Shaul Mishal, *The PLO under Arafat: Between Gun and Olive Branch* (New Haven, CT, 1986), Barry Rubin, *Revolution until Victory?: The Politics and History of the PLO* (Cambridge, 1994), Alan Hart, *Arafat: A Political Biography* (London, 1994), Samih K. Farsoun and Naseer H. Aruri, *Palestine and the Palestinians: A Social and Political History* (Boulder, CO, 2006) and Rashid Khalidi, *Iron Cage: The Story of the Palestinian Struggle for Statehood* (Boston, MA, 2006).

The *intifada* has engendered its own body of literature, which has been more journalistic and anecdotal than scholarly in nature. The most readable and analytic accounts of the uprising are Don Peretz, *Intifada: The Palestinian Uprising* (Boulder, CO, 1990), Zeev Schiff and Ehud Ya'ari, *Intifada: The Palestinian Uprising – Israel's Third Front* (London, 1989) and Zachary Lockman and Joel Beinin, *The Palestinian Uprising against Israeli Occupation* (London, 1989). For greater understanding of Hamas, an organization born out of the *intifada*, see Shaul Mishal and Avraham Sela, *The Palestinian Hamas: Vision, Violence and Coexistence* (New York, 2000), Khaled Khroub, *Hamas: Political Thought and*

Practise (Washington, DC, 2000), Andrea Nüsse, *Muslim Palestine: The Ideology of Hamas* (London, 2002) and Jeroen Gunning, *Hamas in Politics: Democracy, Religion, Violence* (London, 2007). This last book is particularly interesting as it challenges the image of Hamas as inflexible and dogmatic.

The first step on the road to peace between Israel and the Arabs came with the 1978 Camp David Accords. Good analyses of the issues and negotiations can be found in Yaacov Bar Siman Tov, *Israel and the Peace Process, 1977–1982: In Search of Legitimacy for Peace* (Albany, NY, 1994), Shibley Telhami, *Power and Leadership in International Bargaining: The Path to the Camp David Accords* (New York, 1990) and William Quandt, *Camp David: Peace Making and Politics* (Washington, DC, 1986), as well as in the first-hand accounts of Moshe Dayan, *Breakthrough: A Personal Account of the Egypt–Israel Peace Negotiations* (New York, 1981) and Ibrahim Kamel, *The Camp David Accords: A Testimony* (London, 1986).

Books on the Madrid peace process have been written by many participants such as Hanan Ashrawi, *This Side of Peace: A Personal Account* (New York, 1995), Shimon Peres, *Battling for Peace: A Memoir* (London, 1995), Mohamed Heikal, *Secret Channels: The Inside Story of Arab–Israeli Peace Negotiations* (London, 1996), Uri Savir, *The Process: 1,100 Days that Changed the Middle East* (New York, 1998), Itamar Rabinovich, *The Brink of Peace: The Israeli–Syrian Negotiations* (Princeton, NJ, 1998). Academic analyses are provided by Ziva Flamhaft, *Israel on the Road to Peace: Accepting the Unacceptable* (Boulder, CO, 1996), Rashid al-Madfai, *Jordan, the United States and the Middle East Peace Process, 1974–1991* (Cambridge, 1993), Moshe Maoz, *Syria and Israel: From War to Peacemaking* (Oxford, 1995), Joel Peters, *Pathways to Peace: The Multilateral Arab–Israeli Peace Talks* (London, 1996), Edward Said, *Peace and its Discontents: Gaza-Jericho, 1993–1995* (London, 1995), Yehuda Lukacs, *Israel, Jordan and the Peace Process* (New York, 1997), George Giacaman and Dag Jorund Lonning (eds), *After Oslo: New Realities, Old Problems* (London, 1998), Adnan Abu Odeh, *Jordanians, Palestinians and the Hashemite Kingdom in the Middle East Peace Process* (Washington, 1999) and Dona J. Stewart, *Good Neighbourly Relations: Jordan, Israel and the 1994–2004 Peace Process* (London, 2007).

And last but not least, books are starting to appear on the collapse of the Oslo process and the second *intifada*. Interesting analyses are provided by Edward Said, *The End of the Peace Process: Oslo and After* (London, 2000), Tim Youngs, *The Middle East Crisis: Camp David, the 'Al-Aqsa Intifada' and the Prospects for the Peace Process* (London, 2001), J. W. Wright, Jr, *Structural Flaws in the Middle East Peace Process: Historical Contexts* (New York, 2002), Wendy Pearlman, *Occupied Voices: Stories of Everyday Life from the Second Intifada* (New York, 2003), Oded Balaban, *Interpreting Conflict: Israeli–Palestinian Negotiations at Camp David II and Beyond* (New York, 2005), Tanya Reinhart, *Road Map to Nowhere: Israel/Palestine since 2003* (London, 2006) and Yoram Meital, *Peace in Tatters: Israel, Palestine and the Middle East* (Boulder, CO, 2006). Fascinating personal insights are provided by Bill Clinton, *My Life* (New York, 2004), Dennis Ross, *Missing Peace: The Inside Story of the Fight for Middle East Peace* (New York, 2005) and Gilead Sher, *Israeli–Palestinian Negotiations 1999–2004: Within Reach* (New York, 2006).

shari'a
Islamic law which covers all
aspects of life, not just
religious practices.

see Chapter 18

Arab nationalism
The belief that all Arabic-
speakers form a nation that
should be independent and
united.

The rise of political Islam, 1928–2000

Introduction

Political Islam or Islamism is a political ideology which seeks the establishment of an Islamic state based on Islamic law or *shari'a*. It differs from Islam as a religion or Islamic society and culture. It is an ideology embraced by choice and through conscious decision. Moreover, contrary to the impression given by many Islamist movements in the twentieth century, namely that it embodies the return to the time of the Prophet Muhammad, the notion of an Islamic state is actually a recent one and, to a large degree, can be seen as the Muslim response to the notion of the Western nation-state. Moreover, the emergence of distinct movements seeking the establishment of such an Islamic state is a twentieth-century phenomenon. It began with the establishment of the Muslim Brotherhood in Egypt in 1928 and has proliferated particularly since the Arab defeat in the 1967 June War with Israel, which marked the decline of secular **Arab nationalism**.

This chapter looks at the conditions that paved the way for the rise of political Islam and the forces driving the quest for an Islamic state. It will outline the historical circumstances that led to the Islamic resurgence, particularly in the second half of the twentieth century, as well as the Muslim political debate. Drawing upon the case studies of the Islamic revolution in Iran and Islamic resistance in the Middle East, Central and South-East Asia, it will analyse the emergence of Islamist movements, their aims, their strategies, their philosophical underpinnings and the specific conditions that have shaped them. Finally, it will discuss the shifts in political Islam triggered by the end of the Cold War, American hegemony and **globalization**.

The rise of political Islam

Islam provides a blueprint for social and religious interaction – the relations between individuals and those between the individual and God. Yet there is very little in the original Islamic sources, such as the Quran, about what form or structures states should take or what type of governance is preferable. What Islamists therefore are positing as the foundation for an Islamic state is the implementation of the body of jurisprudence formulated by the early jurists, a body of work that was prescriptive at the time of writing and is being taken as descriptive today.

The modern concept of the Islamic state was developed by Muhammad Rashid Rida (1865–1935) in response to the dissolution of the **Caliphate**, the increasing influence of the Western colonial Powers on Muslim societies and the emerging Zionist movement. Two key factors need to be considered when looking at the notion of the Islamic state. The first is a historical one which situates the emergence of the Islamic state in the context of European physical and, more importantly, cultural encroachment. Rida's own circumstances were influenced by the British occupation of Egypt in 1882 and the need for Egyptians to formulate a response, in either nationalist or religious terms, not just to the occupation but also to the European ideas that were penetrating Egyptian society. An Islamic state encompasses both. The second factor is a conceptual one. The Western concept of the state, which developed from the Renaissance, the Enlightenment and the growth of capitalism, emphasizes individualism, liberty and law. It sees the state as the guarantor of individual freedoms. In comparison, the Islamic concept of the state cannot be divorced from the group (*jama'a*), justice (*'adala*) and leadership (*qiyada* or *imama*). The state thus becomes the guarantor of communal justice. Consequently it is not surprising that the driving force in Iran's Islamic revolution was the desire for socio-economic and political justice and that Islamist movements ever since have framed their political, military and social agendas in terms of justice, ranging from the eradication of corruption to liberating Palestine.

The emerging political expressions of Islam in the late nineteenth and early twentieth centuries became known as Islamic modernism. It saw Islam as a blueprint for all aspects of life and as flexible and thus able to adapt itself. The label 'modernists' derives from the fact that this school of thought, which is based on the works of Jamal al-Din al-Afghani (1839–97), Muhammad Abdu (1849–1905) and Rida, emerged from the encounter with the West, and more specifically Western technological superiority and consequent Western colonial occupation of Muslim lands. This encounter raised the question of compatibility between Islam and modernity and how Muslims should respond to the West. They opted

globalization
The cultural, social and economic changes caused by the growth of international trade, the rapid transfer of investment capital and the development of high-speed global communications.

Caliphate
The office of the successor to the Prophet Muhammad in his political and social functions. The Caliphate was abolished by the Turkish president Mustafa Kemal Atatürk, in 1924 after the dismemberment of the Ottoman Empire and the establishment of the Turkish Republic.

see Chapter 4

for internal reform – hence sometimes they are also referred to as Islamic reformists – designed to purify the Muslim community from all the elements that had weakened it and to embrace elements of modernity and technology in order to strengthen it.

From the beginning, modernist Islam was in competition with emerging secular nationalist ideologies and, in the first half of the twentieth century, nationalism was clearly the stronger force in the Muslim world. Indeed, it was the failure of secular nationalist ideologies to deliver what they promised that allowed political Islam to emerge as a viable alternative. In the Arab world this process was triggered by the defeat of Egypt, Jordan and Syria in the 1967 June War with Israel. Until then the Arabs believed that by uniting against Israel under the banner of Arab nationalism they would be able to liberate Palestine. The 1967 June War drove home very clearly that **pan-Arabism** was an ideal which was not borne out by reality. Israel not only won the war but increased its own territory almost four-fold, swallowing the 'rest of Palestine'. Criticism from Islamic ranks focused on the moral bankruptcy of pan-Arabism and the assertion that secularism itself and Arab nationalisms were mere imitations of alien ideologies. They advocated a return to indigenous values and claimed that the reason the Arabs had lost the war against Israel was because they had strayed from the righteous path of Islam. Islam would provide for justice and the liberation of Palestine.

The bankruptcy of secular nationalism also applied to the domestic situation. Many of the newly independent Middle Eastern states such as Egypt, Syria, Algeria or Iraq had opted for a policy of Arab socialism, promising equality and prosperity to their populations. By the 1970s these socialist command economies, like their Eastern European counterparts, started to fail, living standards declined and in some cases food shortages brought people into the street in 'bread riots'. The situation was further exacerbated in the 1980s and 1990s by the decline in oil wealth, the dramatic population increase and a soaring rate of unemployment. The inability of the state to deliver economically provided an opening for Islamists to push Islam as an alternative model of developmentalism based on the Islamic principles of equality and justice. Islamists also started to fill the gap in social, health and welfare institutions, particularly for the urban poor.

Since the 1970s, Muslim South-East Asia has also undergone a process of Islamic renewal as characterized by a dramatic rise in the building of new mosques, the proliferation of religious schools and educational programmes, an expansion of the market for Islamic publications, and the growth of Muslim cultural but also distinctly political organizations. This Islamic resurgence took some inspiration from developments in the Middle East, most notably the 1979 Iranian Revolution. It also clearly shared in the disenchantment with secular nationalism and the search for an alternative response to modernity. At the same time, however, Islamic renewal in South-East Asia was highly region- and even state-specific, driven above all by the economic marginality of the Muslims in the corporatist states of Malaysia and Indonesia. Islam, since the 1965 expulsion of Singapore by Malaysia, became a means by which to redefine Malay identity and with it the New Economic Policy which favoured Muslim Malays over non-Muslim Chinese. Unlike in Malaysia, Islam did not become part of the discourse

see Chapter 4

pan-Arabism
Movement for Arab unity as manifested in the Fertile Crescent and Greater Syria schemes as well as attempted unification of Egypt, Syria and Libya.

of the state in Indonesia. Islamization instead occurred at a popular level where it served as a way of challenging traditional hierarchies, but it did not arise as a challenge to the state until the fall of President Suharto in 1998. Yet, as in Malaysia, Islamism was driven by economic factors – the 1997 Asian financial crisis, widespread corruption, the failure of the state's development policies, and the descent of the majority of Indonesians into unemployment and poverty.

Islamist movements: aims, strategies and political philosophies

The majority of twentieth-century Islamist movements share a number of grievances. Among their aversions are bankrupt Western-derived ideologies, corruption, authoritarianism, urbanization, rapid industrialization, Westerniza-tion, the unqualified American support for Israel, double standards in Western policy, social dislocation, the decline in public morality and the uncertainties created by globalization. Yet their emergence has been context specific. As a result, the aims and strategies of different organizations vary and their strategies, in particular, are more often than not a reflection of the limitations of the state rather than free choice. Broadly speaking, these movements can be located along a continuum from political Islamists at one extreme to militant Islamists at the other. Political Islamists rely predominantly on political, social and educational means to achieve their aim of an Islamic state. They work from within the given state system and political structure to Islamize society and reform the state. They seek to achieve their aims in three important ways. First, they function as political parties, each with its own distinct political platform, and, like other political parties, field candidates and stand for elections. Second, Islamist movements also function as pressure groups, which lobby political parties, politicians and institutions to adopt more Islamic practices, to include Islamic law as a source in the state's legal system, and ultimately to adopt their model of an Islamic state. Third, they function as an alternative social welfare network by establishing community assistance projects including clinics, schools, day care centres, publishing houses and Islamic banks.

The key difference between militant Islamists and political Islamists is that the militants do not believe in working within the existing system, which in their eyes is corrupt, ungodly and beyond redemption. They oppose the political strategy on the grounds that working from within effectively legitimizes failed regimes and are thus anti-systemic in nature. They not only see the use of force to overthrow such illegal governments as acceptable, but advocate it as just and holy – as *jihad.*

Historically, *jihad* was central to the expansion of the Arab Caliphate, especially during the Umayyad period. Yet contrary to much thinking in the West, physical warfare is only a minor part of the concept of *jihad* while at its core is 'striving in the way of God', which is effectively an internal struggle for every Muslim to be a better person. What is interesting is how militant Islamists have appropriated this religious concept of *jihad* and have reinterpreted it to suit their own strategies.

jihad
Struggle in the way of God. A fundamental tenet of Islam consisting of the Greater *jihad* which is above all a personal struggle to be a better Muslim and the Lesser *jihad* which is physical fighting.

see Map 19.1

salafi

Pertaining to the good
ancestral example and
tradition of the Prophet
Muhammad, his companions
and the first four Caliphs.

If one way of categorizing Islamist movements is by strategy, another way is in
philosophical terms. This can be done by dividing them broadly into revolutionary Islamists and reformist Islamists or by looking at them more in terms of
schools of thought. Revolutionary Islamists seek to Islamize society through state
power in a top-down fashion, while reformist Islamists see Islamization as the
result of social and political, bottom-up activities. With respect to specific schools
of thought, three warrant closer inspection: *salafis* or neo-*salafis*, fundamentalists
or neo-fundamentalists, and *khawarij* or seceders.

Salafi Islam is exclusive in terms of beliefs and doctrine. *Salafis* believe that
Islam after the time of the Prophet Muhammad and the four righteous caliphs
was corrupted. Consequently their movement strives to return to this purer
period, and this puts them directly at odds with Islamic mysticism and pluralism.
Their scripturalist and traditionalist orientation gave rise to the eighteenth- and
nineteenth-century puritanical desert movements such as the Wahhabiya of
Arabia, the Sanussiya of the Sahara and the Mahdiyya of present-day Sudan.
Salafis are strict Sunnis opposed to any forms of popular Islam such as saint
worship. Probably the most influential thinker for *salafism* is Ibn Taimiya
(d. 1328) who emphasized the supremacy of *shari'a* over the unity of the community. He focused on ideological unity in order to compensate for the reality of
political and social divisions. This interpretation is in juxtaposition to mainstream
Sunni juristic theory in which unity of the community takes precedence above
all, including pious and just government.

In the latter part of the twentieth century there has been a revival of *salafi*
Islam, what some have labelled neo-*salafism*, including a branching out into new
geographic areas. In addition to the Middle East, *salafi* movements are active in
Central and South-East Asia. This spread of *salafism* can be directly linked to Saudi
educational activities in Muslim countries, but also to the increasing insecurity
in the face of globalization which makes a return to the moral clarities of the time
of the Prophet Muhammad appealing.

Islamic fundamentalists share with the *salafis* the desire to return to the early
sources of Islam. However, unlike the *salafis*, they do not focus on jurisprudence,
but see Islam holistically as *din* (religion), *dunya* (way of life) and *dawla* (state).
In the latter part of the twentieth century a number of more radical or militant
splinter groups developed. These have become known as neo-fundamentalists.
The latter are eclectic in their reading of Islamic sources and generally are action-
oriented. Examples of neo-fundamentalists include Takfir wa al-Hijra, the group
which was initially blamed for the assassination of Egyptian President Anwar
Sadat in 1981.

The final category to be discussed here is that of *khawarij* or seceders. The
original *khawarij* movement emerged when a group of soldiers seceded from the
army of Ali because they disagreed with the issue of arbitration or consultation in
the context of Ali's accession to the Caliphate. The philosophical basis of these
seceders was that any decision, whether religious or political, had to be God's
decision and that commission of a grave sin was grounds for excommunication.
The *khawarij* thus became the first religio-political opposition movement against
the state. The emergence of the nation-state in the twentieth century has given

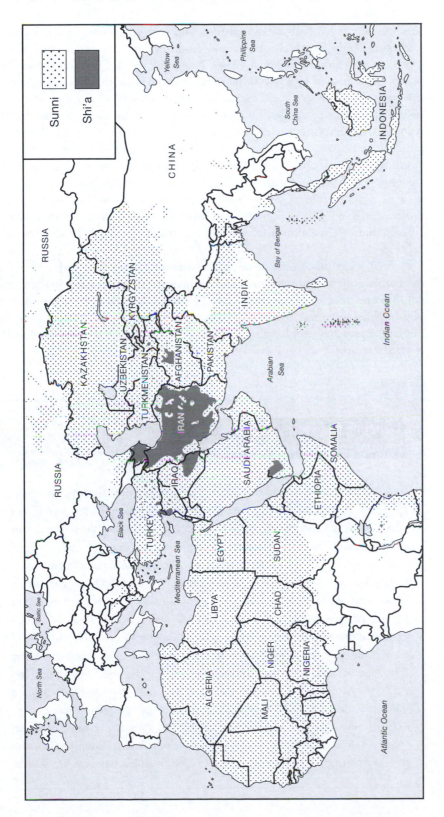

Map 19.1 The Muslim world

new momentum to anti-state opposition and with it a revival of the *khawarij* tradition. The first such challenge came from the Egyptian intellectual Sayyed Qutb to the regime of Gamal Abdel Nasser in the 1950s and 1960s. The philosophy espoused by Qutb was absolutist in the sense that in his world-view the choice was between 'God's absolute rule' or *al-hakimiyya l'illah* and 'total pagan ignorance' or *jahiliyya*. This was also reflected in his views on who did not belong to the community, which ranged from the exclusion of non-Muslims from political participation to the *takfir* (excommunication) of Nasser himself by labelling him an unbeliever. This, in turn, allowed Qutb's followers, who as Sunnis were not permitted to rise against a Muslim ruler no matter how unjust, to take up arms against Nasser. Qutb was ultimately imprisoned for his 'rebellion' and executed in 1966. His notion of *takfir*, however, was taken up by a number of Islamist movements, not all of which are, strictly speaking, in the *khawarij* category.

A final point that needs to be made when looking at the various ways of categorizing Islamist movements is that the majority of movements do not clearly fall into one category or another. Many embrace select elements from different philosophies and most have adopted strategies which combine political and militant approaches, emphasizing one over the other merely as a way of adjusting to state responses.

Debating the state strategies and responses to the Islamist challenge

State responses to the Islamist challenge can broadly be divided into two categories: co-optation and suppression. Co-optation means engagement by the government with the Islamists and their inclusion either through permitting them to stand for elections and to take up seats in the government or through partially adopting their discourse and agenda. The government of Jordan has pursued a strategy of co-optation since the mid-1980s, allowing the Muslim Brothers to organize, stand for elections and participate in the governance of the state as long as they do not resort to violence. Malaysia under Prime Minister Mahathir Mohamed has pursued a slightly different path. It has allowed for an official Islamic opposition in the form of the Partai Islam seMalaysia (PAS), while at the same time trying to undermine this opposition by adopting a more Islamic discourse for the state. The co-optation strategy is, of course, easier when the state faces political rather than militant Islamists but it has also been relatively successfully used to moderate militants. For example, **Hizb'allah**'s aims have been moderated through its participation in Lebanon's electoral politics. Co-optation, however, has proved difficult with die-hard anti-systemic Islamists who are not interested in participation. Here states have often

Hizb'allah (Arabic: Party of God)
Lebanese Shi'a Islamist group which emerged in reaction to the 1982 Israeli invasion of Lebanon. Its primary aim until the Israeli withdrawal in May 2000 was the liberation of southern Lebanon.

opted for suppression. Suppression has also been the preferred choice of states which fear opening up their political system to any form of opposition, irrespective of whether or not it is Islamic, and of states whose overall domestic and foreign policy has been built upon coercion. For instance, in the late 1970s and early 1980s Syria's **Ba'thist** regime was challenged by the Muslim Brothers. The challenge was met by force and Syria descended into a spiral of violence until the Syrian army unleashed its full force on the Islamists in 1982 in their stronghold of Hama. The Islamists were brutally crushed, resulting in up to 20,000 dead. A more recent example is that of Algeria which had embarked upon a path of cautious political liberalization with its first democratic elections in 1991. When it was clear that the Islamic Salvation Front would capture more popular votes than the government party, the elections were cancelled half-way through and the army moved against the Islamists, resulting in a brutal civil war which lasted for much of the 1990s.

Yet, just as Islamists do not necessarily fall into clear-cut categories, some states also shift back and forth between responses. For instance, Egypt has shifted between a policy of suppression under President Gamal Abdel Nasser, to 'encouraging' Islamists under President Anwar Sadat, and to both co-opting moderates and marginalizing extremists under President Hosni Mubarak. If the success of the state's response to the Islamist challenge is measured purely by whether a particular government or regime has been able to stay in power, both strategies appear to have worked. However, that would be oversimplifying the issues at hand. The majority of Islamists are playing a long game and believe that not only God but also time is ultimately on their side. Thus the state faces a dilemma in that neither suppression nor co-optation has proved effective in truly eliminating the challenge. The security approach of suppression has ignored the socio-economic dimensions and, in some cases, has even increased the popularity of Islamists by making them into martyrs. Co-optation has often been interpreted by the Islamists as weakness and has encouraged them to push harder. Similarly, the state's adoption of a more Islamic discourse has been seen as a partial victory.

Ba'th (Arabic: Renaissance) The name given to the pan-Arab socialist party founded by Michel Aflaq and Salah Bitar in 1947. Its first congress was held in Damascus. It subsequently spread to Lebanon, Jordan and Iraq and eventually resulted in the establishment of two rival Ba'thist regimes, one in Syria since 1963 and one in Iraq 1968–2003.

The 1979 Islamic revolution in Iran

On 11 February 1979, the Iranian monarchy was overthrown and the Islamic Republic of Iran was proclaimed. Iran thus became the first modern state to adopt an Islamic ideology and proved an inspiration to Islamist movements across the Middle East, Central and South-East Asia. While American policy-makers were caught by surprise at the rapid descent of Iran into revolution, close analysis of the key events preceding the fall of Shah Muhammad Reza Pahlavi shows that popular discontent had been festering below the surface for quite some time.

The causes of the Iranian Revolution can be divided into long-term and short-term factors. Key among the former are the modernizing reforms of the first Pahlavi Shah, Reza Khan, in the 1930s and 1940s, the 1953 coup, and the second set of reforms promoted by his son, Muhammad Reza, known as the 1963 White Revolution. The latter included the rapid industrialization and Westernization of Iran in the 1970s and the fact that the authoritarian and increasingly suppressive nature of the Shah's regime provided no avenues for voicing discontent.

Reza Khan's programme of reforms and modernization aimed at making Iran self-sufficient. Inspired by Turkey's founding father, Mustafa Kemal Atatürk, he started by reorganizing the military, equipping it with modern weapons and improving its training. He then proceeded to curtail the power and the wealth of the clergy (the *ulama*), replaced *shari'a* with a Westernized judicial system and religious with secular schools, and imposed a ban on the wearing of the veil. The final set of reforms concerned Iran's economy. Reza Khan adopted an étatist policy, set up a comprehensive system of monopolies and pushed for rapid industrialization at a time when more than 75 per cent of the population was rural.

During the Second World War Reza Khan was succeeded by his son Muhammad Reza. Muhammad Reza followed in his father's reformist footsteps, but his hold on power was less secure. In addition to the disgruntled *ulama* and bazaar merchants who had been the main victims of the first reforms, communists and nationalists started to challenge the monarch in the 1940s and 1950s. Muhammad Reza outlawed the Communist Party in 1949 following an abortive attempt on his life, but the nationalists proved far more difficult to deal with. They were led by the prime minister, Muhammad Mussadiq, who had gained popularity by nationalizing the Anglo-Iranian Oil Company in 1951. Worried about the direction Iranian politics was taking, both Britain and the United States colluded with the shah to engineer the dismissal of Mussadiq. Not surprisingly, Mussadiq refused to accept his enforced resignation, upon which the shah panicked and fled the country. The fact that he was ultimately only restored to power in 1953 by the British and Americans meant that he lost legitimacy in the eyes of the people. Over the coming years this resulted in his heavy reliance upon repression domestically and upon assistance from his closest foreign ally, the United States. Both only served to alienate the population further.

It was in this context that the shah launched in 1963 a second set of comprehensive reforms known as the White Revolution which included land reform, the nationalization of forests, village education, voting rights for women, and further industrialization and modernization. This effort to modernize Iran was underscored by the vast oil revenue of the 1970s. It was further accompanied by an intensification of the shah's drive towards Westernization as well as his aim of transforming Iran into one of the five largest conventional military Powers at the time. From 1975 onwards the Shah's fortunes started to change when the GNP fell and the budget deficit rose dramatically. Iran had overreached itself through military purchases of more than $6 billion by 1977. Industrialization had been accompanied by rural–urban migration with the result that the population of the capital, Teheran, swelled from one million to five million. By 1978 almost half the Iranian population was urban and most of them were poor. The education

ulama
Clerics or Islamic scholars who are learned in theology and the *shari'a*.

programme had pushed students into schools and universities but the number of graduates could not be absorbed into the economy. At the same time, the ruling elite continued to flaunt its wealth, the gap between rich and poor widened, social discontent and any form of criticism were heavily suppressed, and, rather than listening to the voices of the people, the shah was seen as listening only to the United States.

Opposition to the shah, the ruling elite and the foreign community which was associated with them came from a variety of quarters: the middle class who had become impoverished, the *ulama* who resented the secularization, Westernization and consequent moral decline of society, the intellectuals who were suffocating in the oppressive environment, the bazaar merchants who had been pushed out of the market by the monopolies, students who had been assured good job opportunities after graduation but faced unemployment, and the increasing number of poor who had been promised everything and received nothing. In the absence of avenues to express the growing discontent, for the media were under heavy censorship, public meetings were controlled by the security services and all political parties with the exception of the regime's Rastakhiz Party had been dissolved, the mosque and Islam became the central means for mobilization.

The fact that **Shi'a Islam** had been born out of opposition shortly after the death of the Prophet Muhammad and had since been the voice of the disinherited minority lent itself well to express the popular grievances against the shah and stoke the fire of revolution. The charisma and leadership of the Ayatollah Ruhollah Khomeini, a cleric and philosophy teacher who had been forced into exile, first in Iraq and then in Paris, brought together the different strands of opposition. It ultimately placed Khomeini in a position to transform the revolution from what began as a coalition to overthrow the shah into an Islamic revolution aimed at the establishment of an Islamic republic in Iran.

The new government was based on the concept of *velayet e-faqih*, meaning the rule of the jurist. Khomeini's notion of an Islamic republic was twofold. On the one hand, it stressed Islamic government as the rule of divine law over the people where the sovereignty lies not with the people but with God. On the other, it called for a republic based on democratic structures. Thus an Islamic republic, according to Khomeini, was a democratic state in its real meaning as it was based on a religion which was grounded in equality and justice.

The Shi'a discourse on government, however, was far from monolithic and evolved around the ideas of not only Khomeini, who is sometimes described as a fundamentalist Islamic republican, but also Ali Shariati, who died before the revolution, as well as Mehdi Barzagan and Abolhassan Banisadr, who were in the liberal Islamic republican camp. For instance, Shariati saw Shi'a Islam as a religion of protest, struggle and revolution, not of surrender and dogmatism. The main point of contention with respect to his fellow Islamists was that Shariati rejected both democracy, which he did not believe the people were ready for, and theocracy. Instead, he advocated an Islamic state led by a vanguard of progressive intelligentsia, not clergy. Barzagan, who became the first prime minister of the provisional government but was forced to resign nine months later when students

Shi'a Islam
Muslim sect which emerged out of the struggle over the succession following the death of the Prophet Muhammad. Derived from Shi'a Ali (the Party of Ali) or those who supported the Prophet's son-in-law Ali's accession to the Caliphate. An estimated 15 per cent of Muslims are Shi'a. They are concentrated in the areas of Iran, Iraq and southern Lebanon, with smaller communities scattered throughout the Muslim world.

occupied the American embassy, advocated a democratic and humanist Islam based on the system of governance through *shura* (consultation) in the days of the Prophet. Finally, Banisadr, despite the fact that he was a member of the revolutionary leadership, was critical of the whole notion of Islamic government from the outset. It was this position that ultimately led to his forced resignation in 1981. His ideas, however, remained within the public domain, especially those which sought to diminish the centrality of violence in the struggle for freedom and those on Islamic economics. With respect to the latter he maintained that any scarcity of resources was a social rather than natural phenomenon as God had created enough of everything.

The internal Iranian debate was to a large degree overshadowed by Khomeini's charisma, but was also cut short by the Iran–Iraq War which broke out a year into the revolution in September 1980. The end of the war in 1988 and the death of Khomeini in 1989 ushered in a post-revolutionary 'second republic' in which internal debate re-emerged. The struggle between 'hawks' and 'doves', extremists and moderates, conservatives and liberals, or totalitarians and democrats within the Islamic camp led to a gradual opening up of Iran towards the outside world. It resulted in a change in foreign policy from emphasizing the 'export of the revolution', which had led Iran to support a number of Islamic resistance movements in the Middle East in the 1980s, to mainstream government-to-government relations. This change coincided with the emergence of the newly independent Muslim states in Central Asia from the 1990s. Economic pragmatism, which was Iran's way out of isolation, also allowed for political moderation. At the same time, however, Iran remained wary of the forces it saw as furthering Western cultural imperialism, and the fear of losing the younger generation in any liberalization process shifted the tide back in favour of the revolutionaries. This was exemplified by the election of the former mayor of Teheran, Mahmoud Ahmadinejad, as Iran's new president in August 2005. He reversed Iran's pragmatism and moderation, instead pursuing confrontational foreign and more isolationist domestic policies.

Fundamentalist Islam: Afghanistan and the Taliban

There is no doubt that the establishment of an Islamic republic in Iran served as an inspiration to other Islamist movements. However, the revolutionary circumstances and the fact that Shi'ism was the dominant Islamic discourse were specific to Iran. Islamist movements were neither able to emulate them nor did the majority have the desire to do so. Instead, each searched for its own specific way and each set its own boundaries for compromise. As a result some found accommodation within secular states such as Jordan, Lebanon or Egypt; others agreed to formulas whereby parts of otherwise secular states would come under *shari'a* law, such as the northern states in Nigeria, Mindanao in the Philippines or Aceh in Indonesia. Yet others succeeded in establishing Islamic states through conflict and civil war, for example Sudan and Afghanistan. These, however, differed significantly from the Iranian model.

In order to illustrate just how different the interpretation and implementation of *shari'a* law can be and how each Islamic state has been shaped by specific historic and cultural circumstances, it is useful to look at Afghanistan under the **Taliban**. After the 1989 withdrawal of Soviet forces, which was claimed as a victory by the Afghan resistance or the *mujahedeen*, Afghanistan turned in upon itself and in 1992, following the fall of the communist regime in Kabul, disintegrated into a full-blown civil war along tribal, as well as Islamist, lines. In 1994, a new political force emerged from the turmoil, the Taliban, which has been described as the ultimate product of person-centred, tribal Pashtun political culture. At the core of this new movement were Afghan men who since the Soviet invasion had found refuge in neighbouring Pakistan where many of them studied in Islamic seminaries or *madrasas*. Some also received military training from Pakistan's Inter-Services Intelligence (ISI) which built them up in an effort to control Afghanistan. To the ISI the Taliban not only represented the largest ethnic group, the Pashtun, but also seemed to be one of the more moderate groups. The latter changed around 1995 when in an internal struggle extreme Islamists ousted the traditionalists. Moreover, Pakistan saw the Taliban as a natural support base for radical Muslim groups in Kashmir, and Afghanistan as providing strategic depth in Pakistan's conflict with India. The other key supporter of the Taliban was Saudi Arabia which saw them as an ally in spreading puritanical Islam, as well as a Central Asian foothold in their hegemonic struggle with Shi'a Iran.

When the Taliban rose to power in 1994, they were initially welcomed by the people as a new leadership that was more honest but above all could deliver stability. In 1996 the Taliban took Kabul and by 1998 their position in power had been consolidated to such an extent that they went on the offensive against the Tajik Northern Alliance, leaving them in control of two-thirds of the country. However, by the time they collapsed under the pressure of the post-11 September 2001 US-led bombing campaign, the popular mood had shifted. While the Taliban had brought some of the sought-after stability, their initial appeal as more moral leaders was undermined by their involvement in the drug trade and their harsh treatment of the civilian population.

Under the leadership of Mullah Mohammed Omar, who had proclaimed himself Caliph, the Taliban advocated a strict, ultra-conservative form of **Sunni Islam** and an Islamist ideology that was anti-modern, anti-Shi'a, anti-Western, anti-women and anti-democratic. This was also reflected in their interpretation of *jihad* as the physical struggle against heretics ranging from 'Western crusaders' to fellow Muslims whose interpretation of Islam differed. The 'heretics' most immediately affected were the Shi'a who were persecuted and the non-Muslim minorities, the Hindus, Sikhs and Jews, who until 1992 had played a significant role in the country's economy.

The Taliban saw themselves as the bearers of true Islamic justice, including the enforcement of the harshest principles of *shari'a* such as the amputation of limbs for thieves, the stoning to death of adulterers, the total segregation of women and the public execution of murderers by the victim's relatives. This latter practice,

Taliban (Arabic: students)
Term used to refer to the fundamentalist Muslim militia of Pashtun Afghans and Pakistanis that overthrew the Afghan ethnic coalition government of Ahmad Shah Masood in 1998.

mujahedeen (Arabic: those who struggle in the way of God)
Term used for the Muslim guerrillas who fought against the Soviets in Afghanistan in 1979–89.

Sunni Islam
The main body of Muslims, who follow the path (*sunna*) of the Prophet Mohammed and the Quran and the *hadith*.

however, was repeatedly condemned by non-Afghan Sunni clerics as being merely the enforcement of the Pashtun tribal code of behaviour cloaked in Islamic language. The Taliban also rejected the concept of doubt except as sin and considered debate as a form of heresy.

The literal interpretation of the Quran, *hadith* and *shari'a* placed the Taliban firmly in the fundamentalist category. This was further reflected in the destruction of all forms of art depicting the human form, ranging from photography to paintings and, most infamously, the dynamiting of two 1,800-year-old giant Buddha statues in Bamyian in February 2001. Fundamentalism also lay at the heart of their banning all forms of entertainment including sports and games; football stadiums were instead transformed into public execution grounds.

The model of Islamic state in Afghanistan under the Taliban could not be more different from that prevailing in Iran. While Iran enforced Muslim dress and standards of morality, Iranian women continued to carry out their professions, to vote and stand in elections, to drive cars and to own property. Women in Afghanistan under the Taliban were given no such rights. Veiled from head to toe, they had to give up their jobs, were deprived of all education beyond primary school, and were confined to their homes in the belief that their mere presence in public provoked immorality. Similarly, while Iran and the Taliban were equally suspicious of Western values and culture, Iran embraced modern technology to spread its revolution and to raise the living standards of the population, while the Taliban rejected modernity altogether, resulting in a ban on television, cinemas and music, as well as the decline of the country into starvation. These differences reveal the extent to which each interpretation of what constitutes an Islamic state is the product of a very specific environment and historical circumstances. It can be interpreted as compatible with democracy or as its total antithesis. It can embrace progress or stand in complete opposition to it.

hadith
The traditions collected by witnesses to the Prophet Muhammad's life at Medina. An estimated 7,000 were handed down through oral traditions, collected, edited and recorded by Bukhari (d. 807) and Muslim (d. 875).

Islamic resistance: Hizb'allah, Hamas and Laskar Jihad

Hamas
The acronym for *Harakat al-Muqawama al-Islamiyya* (Islamic Resistance Movement). Emerged during the first *intifada* in 1987 in the Gaza Strip.

Unlike their co-religionists in Iran and Afghanistan, the majority of Islamists have not been able to establish a state. They have neither functioned within a revolutionary context nor adopted extreme doctrinal positions. Instead a large number of Islamist movements have emerged within the context of conflict. They fall into the militant category in the sense that they use force but their armed struggle is not necessarily directed against a particular regime which they see as illegitimate. Rather, they have taken on the role of the defender of a particular community. The conflict which has probably given rise to the largest number of Islamist movements is the Arab–Israeli conflict. While all Islamist organizations born from this conflict share the desire to deal a decisive blow against Israel and while they all tend to be anti-American in the sense that they oppose Washington's unconditional support for Israel, they differ in terms of ideology, tactics and strategy, as well as the specific aims they hold with respect to their own Arab societies. This can best be illustrated by looking at **Hamas** and Hizb'allah.

The Islamic Resistance Movement or *Harakat al-Muqawama al-Islamiya* (Hamas) is a Palestinian Islamist organization which emerged in the early months of the first Palestinian *intifada* in 1987–91. Its origins are rooted in the Gaza branch of the Muslim Brotherhood, which operated under the name of the Islamic Association, *al-Mujamma' al-Islami* and focused on religious and social activities. Until 1987, Israel, in an attempt to divide and rule the Palestinians under its occupation, encouraged the Islamic Association's work in the field of education, health care, social welfare and charity. However, the outbreak of the *intifada* and Israel's iron-fist response transformed the Islamic Association into a politico-military organization, Hamas. *Jihad* was defined no longer in terms of internal struggle but as physical warfare, and the focus shifted from the welfare of family and community to establishing an Islamic state.

The doctrine of Hamas is one of Islamic nationalism, meaning that it functions within the context of defined nation-state boundaries, those of Palestine. It does not have transnational aims such as creating an Islamic state in the Fertile Crescent or all of the Middle East but instead seeks the liberation of Palestine and its transformation into an Islamic state. Unlike the **PLO**'s definition of Palestine, which is based on historical claims and thus allows a two-state compromise in which Israel and Palestine can co-exist, Hamas's definition of Palestine is based on Islamic *waqf* (endowment). In simple terms, this means that as the land is endowed by God, humans have no right to give it away, effectively ruling out compromise. The strategy adopted to achieve this aim involves armed struggle, including suicide bombings, to secure its territorial ambitions, and socio-political activity to secure Islamization. Hamas thus poses a twofold challenge: first, to Israel as a result of its commitment to liberate all of Palestine through *jihad*, which effectively means replacing the Jewish state with an Islamic Palestine, and second, to the secular PLO leadership which it ultimately hopes to supersede.

This dual aim has placed Hamas in the dilemma of balancing maximalist military and ideological aims against the accommodationist imperatives of internal Palestinian political considerations. The result has been a dynamic in which Hamas has, at times, co-operated with the PLO against Israel, such as during the first and second *intifada*, the latter of which erupted in September 2000. At other times, however, such as during the Israeli–Palestinian peace process, Hamas has worked against the PLO, coming out in opposition to Oslo and subsequent agreements. Moreover, during both periods of co-operation and non-cooperation, Hamas has never stopped competing for the hearts and minds of the Palestinian people, as it ultimately believes that the PLO is not capable of liberating Palestine.

Another product of the Arab–Israeli conflict is Hizb'allah, which shares with Hamas the desire to liberate Palestine and to introduce Islamization. However, as a Lebanese Islamist organization, Hizb'allah's liberation struggle has been primarily aimed at liberating southern Lebanon from Israeli occupation, coupled with a desire to liberate Jerusalem and return it to Islamic rule. Similarly, the target of Islamization is Lebanon, although it is clear that Hizb'allah started out with a broader revolutionary agenda which has moderated into an Islamic nationalist and reformist one.

intifada (Arabic: shaking off) Name given to the Palestinian uprising against Israeli occupation which began on 9 December 1987 and lasted until the signing of the 1993 Oslo Accords between the PLO and Israel.

Palestine Liberation Organization (PLO) Founded by Nasser in 1964, it comprises the Palestine National Council as its supreme body, the Palestine Executive Committee for everyday affairs, and the Palestine Liberation Army. Initially chaired by Ahmad Shuqairy and after the 1967 war by Yasser Arafat. In 1989, the PLO Central Council nominated Arafat as Palestinian president with the PLO assuming the role of government in exile until the 1993 Oslo Accords.

Hizb'allah (the Party of God) emerged in 1982 in reaction to the Israeli invasion of Lebanon. Unlike Hamas which is Sunni, Hizb'allah is one of the few Shi'a Islamist movements. The Shi'a link, as well as the fact that Iranian revolutionary guards had a hand in its establishment as part of the policy of 'exporting the revolution', influenced Hizb'allah's early ideology in no uncertain terms. Hizb'allah's doctrine was Islamic revolutionary in the Iranian mode. It was universalist rather than nationalist. It transcended the virtually non-existent borders of the equally non-existent state of Lebanon which had been racked by civil war since 1975, invaded and occupied by Syrian troops since 1976, turned into an operational base and state-within-a-state by the Palestinian resistance movement, invaded by Israel in 1978 and again invaded and occupied by Israeli forces in 1982. Like Iran, Hizb'allah also drew heavily upon the Shi'a discourse of dispossession and martyrdom. Ultimately, it sought to contribute to a greater Islamic revolution which would engulf, first, the Middle East, and then the rest of the Islamic world.

Hizb'allah's aims have clearly moderated since its establishment. It is no longer universalist but Islamic nationalist. It is no longer revolutionary but reformist. Two key factors have contributed to this transformation. The first was the end of the Lebanese Civil War with the 1989 Tai'f Accord which allowed the state to re-establish itself. Hizb'allah had the choice between adjusting to this new national reality or placing itself fundamentally at odds with the Lebanese regime and its Syrian guarantors. Adjustment was the more attractive option as Hizb'allah was curtailed neither in its socio-political activities nor in its continued military confrontation with Israel. In fact, Hizb'allah benefited greatly as it now competed for elections and had representatives in the government. It could bring policy more in line with Islamic values and also had access to resources for its community projects, which included a wide range of social, health, welfare and educational institutions. The second key factor, which not only allowed for this moderation but encouraged it, was the transition of Iran into a post-revolutionary phase with the death of Khomeini. 'Export of the revolution' was no longer the top priority of the Iranian foreign policy agenda and Hizb'allah thus did not have to fear disrupting a well-functioning relationship which was still crucial to its other main goal, liberating southern Lebanon from Israeli occupation.

While Hizb'allah's domestic strategy 'went political', its strategy in the Arab–Israeli conflict remained militant, relying heavily on guerrilla warfare. It aimed at pushing Israeli troops out of Lebanon by making the occupation too costly to maintain financially and in human terms. As part of this strategy Hizb'allah targeted not only Israeli soldiers but also all symbols of occupation. It attacked Israel's ally, the South Lebanese Army, as well as putting pressure upon Israeli villages across the border by shelling them with short- and medium-range rockets such as katyushas. It also attacked Israeli and American interests abroad, as manifested in the 1992 and 1994 bombings in Argentina and the 1996 Khybar Towers bombing. While Hizb'allah in military organizational terms is not that different from Hamas, as both are cellular in structure, it has made full use of its links with Iran and Syria which have enabled it to acquire standard military equipment, placing it more on a par with Israel and thereby reducing the need for suicide bombings. Not surprisingly, Hizb'allah attributed the Israeli withdrawal from southern Lebanon in May 2000 to the effectiveness of its strategy.

Hizb'allah, despite its rhetoric of liberating Jerusalem, concentrated its military efforts on the liberation of southern Lebanon from Israeli occupation. When Israeli troops withdrew, Hizb'allah did not pursue the retreating forces across the border. It also did not launch concerted attacks on Israeli settlements in northern Galilee. Instead, Hizb'allah focused on the one piece of disputed territory – the Sheba'a farms. Thus it is also clear that, with respect to the Arab–Israeli conflict, Lebanon has clearly served as the definitive context for Hizb'allah's military actions.

The Arab–Israeli conflict is, of course, not the only conflict to produce Islamic resistance. Another interesting case study is Indonesia, the world's largest Muslim country, which was racked by conflicts in the wake of the fall of Suharto's authoritarian New Order in May 1998. One of these conflicts on the spice island of Ambon led to the emergence of Laskar Jihad (Holy War Troops). Laskar Jihad was officially formed in January 2000 in response to the Indonesian government's failure to act to suppress the violent social conflict which had erupted between Muslims and Christians in Ambon in January 1999. (It was officially dissolved in October 2002, a week before the Bali bombing.) Its aims, like those of Hamas and Hizb'allah, were, on the one hand, conflict related and, on the other, Islamization.

Like Hamas and eventually Hizb'allah, Laskar Jihad falls into the Islamic nationalist category. Not only did it recognize state boundaries and function within them but it also assigned itself the role of protector of the unity and integrity of the Republic of Indonesia. This role was directly linked to its interpretation of the conflict in Ambon, which it saw as a separatist conflict instigated by Christians who sought to expel local Muslims and to turn the southern Maluku islands into an independent Christian republic. Defending the Muslim community and preventing separatism were pursued through armed *jihad*. Laskar Jihad was effectively a paramilitary organization, emulating the structure of the Indonesian army. It was arranged into battalions, companies, platoons and squads supported by special forces, intelligence and logistics. Its strategy was determined by the internal nature of the conflict and the fact that small arms, home-made explosives and traditional weapons, such as long knives, spears and poisoned arrows, characterized much of the fighting. It took on the form of 'communal cleansing' typical of other internal civil war or ethnic conflict situations.

Laskar Jihad's aims, however, encompassed more than Ambon. Territorially its paramilitary presence was extended to other conflict areas, especially those faced with a real or perceived separatist challenge such as Poso, Papua and Aceh. Ideologically, it was not just protecting Muslims and Indonesia's unity and integrity but also Islamizing society and the state. Laskar Jihad relied on a social rather than political strategy. It refrained from setting up a political party as it saw politics in Indonesia as inherently corrupt and immoral and believed that its own values would be tainted by association. Instead it offered educational, social welfare and health services through which it promoted its *salafi* interpretation of Islam. It is in this area of doctrine and philosophy that the Arab influence, in this case Saudi and Yemeni, was most obvious, revealing that, while the emergence of

Plate 19.1 Surabaya, Indonesia, May 2000. Indonesian police display the Holy Quran found among the belongings of a member of the militant Muslim Laskar Jihad group (which vowed to launch a *jihad* (holy war) against Christians in the Indonesian Spice Islands) before his departure from the Surabaya seaport, East Java, 10 May 2000. Several hundred Muslim militants left for Ambon in the strife-torn Maluku. (Photo: Yudhi Pardi/AFP/Getty Images)

Islamist movements is case specific and while the majority function within given state boundaries and are Islamic nationalist in nature, there are transnational ideological influences.

Transnational Islamism, international *jihadism*, global Islamism and the al-Qaeda phenomenon

Islam's concept of community is determined by faith rather than territory. Similarly, the political power required to protect and govern the relations of the community of believers, the *umma*, has no territorial definition. Thus the Islamist concept of the state is a universal one which arguably stands at odds with the existing state system and even the existing world order. While all Islamist movements support this ideal in purely abstract philosophical terms, most very clearly recognize the existing nation-state boundaries and have worked within them. Some, however, have gone beyond pure Islamic nationalism, leading to three trends developing in the twentieth century: transnational Islam, international *jihadism* and global Islamism.

Transnational Islamist movements are not a recent phenomenon. In fact, the oldest Islamist organization, the Muslim Brotherhood or Ikhwan al-Muslimim, falls into this category. Established in 1928 by Hassan al-Banna in Egypt, it now has branches in seventy countries spanning the Middle East and Central and South-East Asia as well as Europe and the United States. All branches share a *salafi* philosophy and the aim of establishing an Islamic state, but each has also very clearly adjusted to given nation-state contexts. For instance, in Egypt and Jordan the Muslim Brothers have members in parliament who lobby for the incorporation of Islamic values into politics and the legal system, while in Europe and the USA they focus on education, family and community.

A different type of transnational Islam is represented by organizations such as Hizbut Tahrir and **Jemaah Islamiyya** (JI) which also have branches internationally, but these have often been more closely linked and are actively pursuing 'unification' projects. For instance, JI in the South-East Asian states of Malaysia, Indonesia, Singapore and the Philippines has been working not only for Islamization of these individual states but also towards unifying them into a greater Islamic state – Negara Islam Nusantara. Similarly, in Central Asia, Hizbut Tahrir is seeking to unify the Ferghana valley states of Uzbekistan, Tajikistan and Kyrgyzstan in a 'revival' of the Caliphate of Ferghana.

Yet another form of transnational Islam has come in the shape of foreign policy, particularly that of Saudi Arabia and Iran. Iran's explicit aim to 'export the revolution' triggered a Saudi–Iranian hegemonic struggle. While Iran focused on Shi'a minorities and supporting revolutionary movements in Arab states, Saudi Arabia went down the educational route, funding and establishing a vast network of Islamic schools and foundations through which it proselytized *salafi* Islam. Saudi Arabia's wealth and the support of America, which equated Saudi victory with Iranian defeat, ensured that the 'export of education' became probably the most successful – and arguably the most destructive – element of the Wahhabi kingdom's foreign policy. While few have paid much attention to it, its long-term effects have become increasingly visible in the extent to which local Islamic practices, particularly in non-Arab Muslim societies, have been infused not only with *salafism* but also with Arabization. Indonesia is a case in point.

The second trend, international *jihadism*, was triggered by the 1979 Soviet invasion of Afghanistan. It evolved from two separate but interlinked dynamics, one internal and one external. The internal Muslim dynamic was solidarity within the Muslim world with the Afghan *mujahedeen*. For the first time this solidarity transcended political statements and financial contributions, for individual Muslims from the Middle East and South-East Asia and even Muslims living in the West volunteered to join the armed struggle. The external dynamic came in the form of concerted efforts by the United States and Saudi Arabia to recruit Muslim volunteers, particularly from North Africa, to aid in the war with the Soviets. Saudi-backed CIA training camps in Egypt, and later in Afghanistan itself, served as a means to achieve a victory over Soviet imperialism.

The war in Afghanistan provided a generation of young Muslims with a sense of purpose and military skills, thus giving new meaning to *jihad*. The 1989 Soviet withdrawal was nothing less than an Islamic triumph over a superpower. It restored Islam's place in history and the *mujahedeen*'s self-esteem; it confirmed their belief that armed struggle was superior to any political strategy, and when the volunteers returned to their countries of origin these were the lessons they

Jemaah Islamiyya (JI) (Arabic: Islamic Community) Southeast Asian Islamist Organization established by Indonesians Abdullah Sunkar and Abu Bakar Ba'ashir in 1995. JI seeks to establish a Southeast Asian Islamic state encompassing Indonesia, Malaysia, Singapore, Brunei, southern Thailand and the southern Philippines through militant means.

see Chapter 22

carried with them. The Afghan experience served to radicalize Islamist movements. For example, graduates from the Afghan War used their newly acquired skills in a ruthless campaign against Copts and foreign tourists in Egypt between 1992 and 1997. They also contributed to the splits and militarization of the Islamist movement in Algeria after 1991. Moreover, volunteers from all parts of the Muslim world joined Islamic struggles in other countries such as Bosnia, Chechnya, Somalia, Sudan, Indonesia and Palestine.

The third trend, global Islamism, emerged in the context of increasing globalization, financial interdependency and new technologies which have made the world a smaller place. The consequent 'proximity' resulted in closer international co-operation and free flow of information, on the one hand, but it also increased the North–South divide, emphasized the prosperity gap between the small number of industrialized nations and the rest of the world, as well as casting questions of socio-economic justice, humanity and dignity in a new light. The challenge of how to manage the rapid pace of change and how to respond to these uncertainties gave rise to popular reactions grounded in the search for meaning and identity. In the non-Muslim world this resulted in a resurgence of a 'back to basics' type of nationalism and xenophobia. In the Muslim world it strengthened the search for Islamic authenticity and community. The availability of the Internet also allowed for the emergence of new 'imagined' Islamist communities, bypassing the nation-state boundaries, the establishment *ulama* and traditional Muslim education, and uniting the ideologically like-minded. *Salafi* movements, in particular, have taken advantage of the technology to form global networks.

Al-Qaeda is in many ways a product of these combined developments. It was established in the context of the end of the Afghan War and the dispersion of the international *jihadists*. Osama Bin Laden, who had fought with the *mujahedeen* and whose money aided the Islamic welfare institutions set up to channel American and Saudi funds into Afghan operations, returned home to Saudi Arabia. There he set up al-Qaeda which drew upon international *jihadism*, but initially functioned within the Islamic nationalist paradigm. It sought internal reform, criticizing the Saudi royal family's policies and corruption, but also offered to protect the Muslim holy sites and the Saudi state's boundaries when Iraq invaded Kuwait in August 1990. The Saudi regime's inability to deal with any kind of criticism resulted in the rejection of Bin Laden's offer, followed by house arrest and his escape to Sudan in 1991. Throughout all this he watched the buildup of American forces in Saudi Arabia, seeing them as 'infidel forces' invited on to 'holy soil' by a ruling family who no longer deserved to be seen as believers. This labelling of the Saudi regime as *kafir* puts Bin Laden clearly in the *khawarij* category.

In 1994, in an effort to clip Bin Laden's wings, Saudi Arabia revoked his citizenship and stripped him of some of his financial assets. However, Bin Laden and al-Qaeda were neither contained nor controlled but had shifted outside state boundaries and transformed themselves into a global network with shifting territorial bases, cells in a large number of Muslim countries and a globalized support community which ranged from the technophobe fundamentalist Taliban at one extreme to the new 'imagined' Islamist Internet communities at the other.

al-Qaeda (Arabic: Base) Islamist umbrella organization established by Osama Bin Laden drawing upon the network of international *jihadists* established during the Afghan War to support the *mujahedeen*. Founded as early as 1988, al-Qaeda emerged into the public eye in 1990.

The expulsion from Saudi Arabia was clearly a turning point in the evolution of al-Qaeda's doctrine from an Islamic nationalist challenge to Wahhabi legitimacy in Saudi Arabia to a global Islamist challenge to the one remaining superpower which, according to Bin Laden, sought the destruction of Islam. In this context he initially demanded the expulsion of 'infidel forces' from Saudi soil. He then added to his list of grievances the UN sanctions on Iraq, which he saw as American-inspired, and Washington's support for Israel, both policies which resulted in the killing of Muslims. For Bin Laden, American policies in the Middle East were no less than a declaration of war on God and the Prophet Muhammad.

Al-Qaeda's strategy clearly falls into the militant category as demonstrated by the 1992 attempt to kill American soldiers in Somalia, the 1993 attempt to blow up the World Trade Center, the 1995 Riyadh car bombing, the 1995 assassination attempt on Egyptian President Hosni Mubarak, the 1998 bombings of the US embassies in Kenya and Tanzania, the 2000 attack on the USS *Cole* in Yemen, and the destruction of the World Trade Center on 11 September 2001. Al-Qaeda is believed to have 3,000–5,000 members, organized in cell structures which are thought to be active in Afghanistan, Pakistan, Saudi Arabia, Yemen, Sudan, Uzbekistan, Egypt, Syria, Lebanon, Jordan, Palestine, Algeria, Libya, Eritrea, Somalia, Bosnia, Chechnya, Indonesia, the Philippines, Malaysia, Germany, Britain and the United States. It is also feared that it may be able to draw upon an even larger support network of veterans of the Afghan War, international *jihadists*, and other Islamists who trained in Afghanistan under the Taliban, together numbering 50,000–70,000.

The exact relationship between Islamist groups and al-Qaeda, however, remains unclear. While many American policy-makers tend to see close links, scholars of political Islam maintain that Bin Laden's links with other groups have been overstated. They have found it more useful to see al-Qaeda as a franchise or an idea inspiring other Islamists. While it may have provided individual militants with training and finance, the fact remains that, unlike Bin Laden, the vast majority of Islamist groups continue to function in a very specific local context with very specific aims, under a leadership for whom engagement and compromise are possible. Al-Qaeda is a fundamentally different phenomenon and thus poses a new challenge to states and to the international community as a whole. *see Chapter 22* This is further complicated by its populist appeal which is truly global in nature, tapping into feelings shared by the majority of Muslims worldwide, namely that as nations and people they have been treated without fairness, equality, justice, honour or dignity.

Conclusion

Islamism as a distinct political ideology is a twentieth-century phenomenon. While Islam addresses all aspects of relations between individuals and relations between the individual and God, including politics, it does not prescribe a particular form of government. Islamism, Islamist movements and the quest for an Islamic state as a political alternative are rooted in the abolition of the Caliphate with the collapse of the Ottoman Empire, the encounter of the Muslim world with modernity, the traumas of Western colonialism, the failure of secular nationalism, pervasive corruption and authoritarianism, the inability of developmentalist policies to bridge the prosperity gap with the West, the failure to liberate Palestine, the perception that US foreign policy has promoted injustice, and the uncertainty resulting from globalization. The appeal of the Islamist alternative lies in its focus on social justice and the belief that the introduction of religion and morality will eradicate corruption, nepotism, prostitution, discrimination and poverty. In many states, Islamism has also become the only viable form of protest as opposition movements or political parties are banned and clamped down upon, leaving the mosque as the only space from which to articulate grievances. At the same time, each Islamist movement is the product of its own specific environment, differing in aims, strategies and guiding philosophy, and thus needs to be considered in its own right. The vast majority of Islamist movements fall into the Islamic nationalist category, meaning they function within the given boundaries of a particular state or a particular regional conflict. The 1979–89 war in Afghanistan, Cold War rivalry and, in particular, American policy contributed to the emergence of international *jihadism* which has flourished in the context of globalization. Ultimately it laid the foundation for the emergence of global Islamism as represented by al-Qaeda. The emergence of al-Qaeda, in turn, has posed new challenges for policy-makers by functioning outside the nation-state context and by questioning prevailing assumptions such as the idea that Islamism is bred by poverty. Finally, it has thrown down the gauntlet to both advocates of political engagement and advocates of military solutions.

Recommended reading

There has been a proliferation of books on Islam, Islamism and Islamist movements since the events of 11 September 2001. However, many of the books published shortly after this date have been of a journalistic nature or hastily put together. In order to get a firm grounding in the subject, it is useful to look at the historical and philosophical underpinnings of political Islam. W. Montgomery Watt's classic *Islamic Political Thought* (Edinburgh, 1968) and Antony Black, *The History of Islamic Political Thought: From the Prophet to the Present* (Edinburgh, 2001) are a good starting point as well as the very readable books by Karen Armstrong, *Islam: A Short History* (London, 2000) and *Muhammad: Biography of the Prophet* (London, 2001). For a more contemporary focus, John Esposito (ed.), *Political Islam: Revolution, Radicalism or Reform?* (Boulder, CO, 1997), Nazih Ayubi, *Political Islam: Religion and Politics in the Arab World* (London, 1991), Olivier Roy, *The Failure of Political Islam* (London, 1994), Ahmad Moussalli,

Moderate and Radical Islamic Fundamentalists: The Quest for Modernity, Legitimacy, and the Islamic State (Gainesville, FL, 1999), Gilles Kepel, *Jihad: The Trail of Political Islam* (London, 2002), Barry Rubin, *Revolutionaries and Reformers: Contemporary Islamist Movements in the Middle East* (Albany, NY, 2003) and Barry Rubin, *Political Islam: Critical Concepts in Islamic Studies* (London, 2003).

For those interested in the Islamic revolution in Iran, see Misagh Parsa, *Social Origins of the Iranian Revolution* (New Brunswick, NJ, 1998), Mansoor Moaddel, *Class, Politics, and Ideology in the Iranian Revolution* (New York, 1992), Masoud Kamali, *Revolutionary Iran: Civil Society and State in the Modernization Process* (Brookfield, IL, 1998) and Saskia Gieling, *Religion and War in Revolutionary Iran* (London, 1999). This reading should be complemented by Ali Ansari, *A History of Modern Iran since 1921* (New York, 2002) and Anoushiravan Ehteshami, *After Khomeini: The Iranian Second Republic* (London, 1995). For a look at broader implications, John Esposito (ed.), *The Iranian Revolution: Its Global Impact* (Miami, FL, 1990) is insightful. For those interested in the Afghan model of Islamic state, three books stand out: William Maley (ed.), *Fundamentalism Reborn? Afghanistan and the Taliban* (London, 1998), Peter Marsden, *The Taliban: War, Religion and the New Order in Afghanistan* (London, 1998) and Ahmed Rashid, *Taliban: The Story of the Afghan Warlords* (London, 2000). Another model of Islamic state not specifically discussed in this chapter but key for those interested in Islam in Africa is that of Sudan which is discussed in depth by Donald Petterson, *Inside Sudan: Political Islam, Conflict, and Catastrophe* (Boulder, CO, 1999).

Islamism in Egypt is of particular interest for current events as it produced both Sayyed Qutb, whose ideas of *jahiliyya* and perpetual revolution still inspire Islamists, and Ayman Zawaheri, arguably the most important man in al-Qaeda. Richard P. Mitchell's seminal work *The Society of the Muslim Brothers* (London, 1969) is an excellent point from which to start the study of Egyptian Islamists. It is only surpassed by Gilles Kepel's *The Roots of Radical Islam* (London, 2005). More specific works on Qutb are Adnan Musallem, *From Secularism to Jihad: Sayyid Qutb and the Foundations of Radical Islamism* (Westport, CT, 2005) and Sayed Khatab, *The Power of Sovereignty: The Political and Ideological Philosophy of Sayyid Qutb* (London, 2006).

A number of good books have been written about Islamic resistance movements. The most authoritative on Hizb'allah are Hala Jaber, *Hezbollah: Born with a Vengeance* (New York, 1997), Amal Saad-Ghorayeb, *Hizbullah: Politics and Religion* (London, 2001), Ahmed Nizar Hamzeh, *In the Path of Hizbullah* (New York, 2004), Naim Qassem, *Hizbullah: The Story from Within* (London, 2005) and Augustus Richard Norton, *Hezbollah: A Short History* (Princeton, NJ, 2007). For further reading on Hamas, see Shaul Mishal and Avraham Sela, *The Palestinian Hamas: Vision, Violence and Coexistence* (New York, 2000), Khaled Khroub, *Hamas: Political Thought and Practise* (Washington, 2000), Andrea Nüsse, *Muslim Palestine: The Ideology of Hamas* (London, 2002) and Jeroen Gunning, *Hamas in Politics: Democracy, Religion, Violence* (London, 2008).

For a general discussion on Islam in South-East Asia, covering Malaysia, Indonesia and the Philippines, see Ahmad Ibrahim, *Readings on Islam in Southeast Asia* (Singapore, 1985) and Robert W. Hefner and Patricia Horvatich, *Islam in an*

Era of Nation States: Politics and Religious Renewal in Muslim Southeast Asia (Honolulu, 1997). Hussin Mutalib's *Islam and Ethnicity in Malay Politics* (Singapore, 1990), Robert W. Hefner, *Civil Islam: Muslims and Democratisation in Indonesia* (Princeton, NJ, 2000) and Bahtiar Effendy, *Islam and the State: The Transformation of Islamic Political Ideas and Practise in Indonesia* (Singapore, 2001) provide more detailed analyses of Malay and Indonesian Islam. Militant Islam in South-East Asia is discussed by Paul J. Smith (ed.), *Terrorism and Violence in Southeast Asia: Transnational Challenges to States and Regional Security* (Armonk, NY, 2005). A closer look at Islamist separatists in the southern Philippines and southern Thailand is provided by T. J. S. George, *Revolt in Mindanao: The Rise of Islam in Philippine Politics* (Kuala Lumpur, 1980), W. K. Che Man, *Muslim Separatism: The Moros of Southern Philippines and the Malays of Southern Thailand* (Singapore, 1990), Thomas M. McKenna, *Muslim Rulers and Rebels: Everyday Politics and Armed Separatism in the Southern Philippines* (Berkeley, CA, 1998), Eric Gutierrez, *Rebels, Warlords and Ulama: A Reader on Muslim Separatism and the War in the Southern Philippines* (Quezon City, 2000) and Joseph Liow, *Muslim Resistance in Southern Thailand and Southern Philippines: Religion, Ideology, and Politics* (Washington, DC, 2006). Books on militant Islam in Indonesia, especially JI, include Kumar Ramakrishna and See Seng Tan, *After Bali: The Threat of Terrorism in Southeast Asia* (Singapore, 2003), Greg Barton, *Jemaah Islamiyah* (Singapore, 2005), Zachary Abuza, *Militant Islam in Southeast Asia: Crucible of Terror* (New York, 2006) and Ken Conboy, *Second Front: Inside Asia's Most Dangerous Terrorist Network* (Jakarta, 2006).

Relations between Islam and the West have become the subject of heated debate ever since Samuel Huntington's *The Clash of Civilisations and the Remaking of the World Order* (London, 1996), which is worth reading to obtain at least one side of the argument. Less polemical assessments of the same topic can be found in John Esposito, *The Islamic Threat: Myth or Reality?* (New York, 1999) and Fawaz Gerges, *America and Political Islam: Clash of Cultures or Clash of Interests?* (Cambridge, 1999).

On the subject of international *jihadism*, globalized Islam and al-Qaeda, numerous books have been appearing since 11 September 2001. Olivier Roy's *Globalised Islam: Fundamentalism, De-territorialisation and the Search for a New Ummah* (London, 2000) looks at the subject from a broad perspective while most other books focus on al-Qaeda. The latter are often sensationalized, overly focused on profiling or based on non-attributable, often incorrect, intelligence sources. Nevertheless many are worth reading, even if just to gain a feeling for the challenges of researching such a subject as well as obtaining a firm grasp on the debate among scholars, such as Rohan Gunaratna, *Inside Al Qaeda: Global Network of Terror* (London, 2002), Paul Williams, *Al Qaeda: Brotherhood of Terror* (Parsippany, NJ, 2002), Jason Burke, *Al-Qaeda: Chasing Shadows of Terror* (London, 2003), Muntasir Zayatt, *The Road to Al-Qaeda: The Story of Bin Laden's Righthand Man* (London, 2004) and Mohammad Mahmoud Ould Mohamedou, *Understanding Al-Qaeda: The Transformation of War* (London, 2007).

Finally, for those interested in primary sources, a range of short writings can be found in Mansoor Moaddel and Kamran Talattof (eds), *Contemporary Debates in Islam: An Anthology of Modernist and Fundamentalist Thought* (New York, 1999). The writings and speeches of those who have inspired revolution include Sayyid Qutb, *Milestones* (Indianapolis, 1990), Imam Ruhollah Khomeini, *Islam and Revolution: Writings and Declarations of Imam Khomeini* (Berkeley, CA, 1980) and Bruce Lawrence (ed.), *Messages to the World: The Statements of Osama Bin Laden* (London, 2005), while those who have inspired reform include Mahathir Mohamad, *The Challenge* (Subang Jaya, 1986) and Abdullah Ahmad Badawi, *Islam Hadhari: A Model Approach for Development and Progress* (Petaling Jaya, 2006).

The end of the Cold War and the 'new world order', 1980–2000

Third World
A collective term of French origin for those states that are part of neither the developed capitalist world nor the communist bloc. It includes the states of Latin America, Africa, the Middle East, South Asia and South-East Asia. Also referred to as 'the South' in contrast to the developed 'North'.

Warsaw Pact (Warsaw Treaty Organization)
An alliance set up in 1955 under a mutual defence treaty signed in Warsaw by Albania, Bulgaria, Czechoslovakia, East Germany, Hungary, Poland, Romania and the Soviet Union. The organization was the Soviet bloc's equivalent of NATO. Albania formally withdrew in 1968. The Warsaw Pact was dissolved in June 1991.

Introduction

Although there is disagreement among historians as to when the Cold War began to fade as an international system, most recent surveys point to the decade between 1975 and 1985 as the beginning of the end. In order to grasp that argument, one needs to look beyond the superpower conflict itself and see what broader developments made the Cold War less important within international politics. Among the most important changes were those in the economic field; for example, the increase in international trade, the rise of the 'Tiger' economies in Asia and the decline in commodity prices all enriched the capitalist countries while impeding those of the communist bloc and their allies in the **Third World**. In addition, technological change, such as the rapid evolution of communications and computers, almost all of which were developed in the West, had an important effect.

As the 1980s began, however, the political effects of the economic and technological changes were difficult to predict and, if anything, the challenges to the West were seen as large, if not larger, than those facing the **Warsaw Pact** countries. In terms of productivity and economic management, many Americans saw Japan as rapidly surpassing the United States and feared the long-term economic consequences of a less dominant American role in the global economy.

The election of a right-wing Republican, Ronald Reagan, as president in 1980 reflected therefore not only the international challenges facing the United States, the breakdown of **détente**, the Soviet invasion of Afghanistan and the Iranian Revolution, but also a general perception that America's position in the world was in decline and that a stronger American response was needed. Reagan, with his willingness to intervene against revolutionary regimes and the massive buildup of American military power, clearly represented that mind-set.

However, as the 1980s unfolded, the new challenges that both superpowers faced made it clear that fundamental changes were taking place in international relations. By the late 1980s the Soviet bloc economies were in crisis and the new policies introduced by the Soviet leader Mikhail Gorbachev after he took over the leadership in 1985 signalled the beginning of the end for the Communist Party's repressive control. As so-called *perestroika* (restructuring) in the Soviet Union began to stall by the late 1980s, increasing numbers of Soviet citizens lost faith in Gorbachev's ability to renew the system from within. Although the challenges to the West were of a less essential nature, the drive towards economic neo-liberalism associated with Thatcher and Reagan and the massive American trade and budget deficits still made many people ask questions about the stability of the Cold War international system. Finally in 1989, with the collapse of the East European communist parties' grip on power, the Cold War system began its rapid demise. By the end of 1991 the Soviet Union itself had collapsed, while Germany, one of the key sources of East–West tensions in Europe, was reunified. With these changes it was evident that the Cold War, which for many had defined the general nature of international politics for four decades, was no more. The question that emerged was simple. What now? There is no straightforward way of describing the post-Cold War international system. At one level, the world experienced an imbalance of power never seen before: throughout the 1990s the United States was, as many observers have pointed out, the *only* superpower capable of flexing its economic, military and political muscles around the globe. Yet, despite such apparent American omnipotence, the world was increasingly unpredictable, heterogeneous and, ultimately, dangerous. Amid unprecedented peace and prosperity there was continued, often exacerbated, poverty and conflict. While democracy and capitalism appeared to have history on their side, genocide and terrorism also thrived in the 1990s. If anything, the end of the Cold War had only removed one, and by the 1980s an increasingly irrelevant, aspect that had governed the international system since the end of the Second World War.

The superpowers and the Third World

In the early 1980s the Soviet leadership appeared hopeful that global trends favoured, and would continue to favour, communism. The sense inside the Kremlin – in retrospect based on unrealistic assumptions – was that 'the world was going our way'; that the United States and capitalism had entered an era of

détente
A term meaning the reduction of tensions between states. It is often used to refer to the superpower diplomacy that took place between the inauguration of Richard Nixon as the American president in 1969 and the Senate's refusal to ratify SALT II in 1980.

perestroika (Russian: restructuring)
The term attached to the attempts (1985–91) by Mikhail Gorbachev to transform the command economy of the Soviet Union into a decentralized market-oriented economy. Industrial managers and local government and party officials were granted greater autonomy, and open elections were introduced in an attempt to democratize the Communist Party organization.

stagnation and decline. Such apparent victories of communism as the unification of Vietnam (1975), the success of the Soviet-supported MPLA in Angola and the emergence of Ethiopia as Moscow's most important client state in Africa seemingly confirmed that in the international arena the Soviet-led socialist camp was riding the wave of history.

In contrast, a sense of economic and political malaise marked the 1980 presidential elections in the United States. The Republican candidate, Ronald Reagan, received just over half of the popular vote and ousted the incumbent Democratic president, Jimmy Carter (owing to the presence of a strong third-party candidate, John Anderson, Carter received approximately 41 per cent of the vote). Upon taking office in early 1981 Reagan offered to reinvigorate America's foreign policy by confronting the communist menace globally, from Afghanistan to Central America. Yet neither Reagan nor his advisers envisioned the drama that would begin to unfold after his re-election in 1984. Initially, Reagan's election simply confirmed the increase in Soviet–American tensions that had, in the late 1970s, caused the demise of détente.

A key element in the cooling of Soviet–American relations was the war in Afghanistan. However, its significance went beyond the damage that it inflicted on détente, for in the 1980s, it was this war above all other factors that forced the Soviet Union towards reform of its internal system; indeed, a number of writers have compared the USSR's efforts to bolster a friendly communist regime in Kabul to the American engagement in Vietnam in the 1960s and 1970s. Like Vietnam for the Americans, the war in Afghanistan – although Soviet casualties and troop numbers in Afghanistan were more limited than those of the United States in Vietnam – quickly turned into an endless guerrilla campaign in which the Red Army and its local allies battled various local groups. Approximately 14,000 Soviet soldiers were killed in Afghanistan between 1979 and 1989, as opposed to close to 60,000 US soldiers in Vietnam. At the peak of the Vietnam War the United States had 540,000 troops in Vietnam; Soviet troop strength in Afghanistan – a country five times the size of Vietnam – never exceeded 104,000. Just as the Soviets had supported the North Vietnamese, the Americans provided assistance to the *mujahedeen* in Afghanistan; the *mujahedeen*'s extreme Islamic views were no obstacle in this regard, for the Reagan administration saw them as 'freedom fighters' fighting against a godless communist menace. For the ailing Soviet leaders who succeeded Leonid Brezhnev, Yuri Andropov (1982–84) and Konstantin Chernenko (1984–85), the mounting costs of the war in Afghanistan, as well as the policy of helping various other Third World revolutionaries, threatened to bankrupt the Soviet state.

There was a historical irony in all of this. The Soviets had consistently preached anti-imperialism as part of their ideological hostility towards capitalism, and had accordingly presented themselves as the champions of the struggle against colonialism. However, just as their campaign finally appeared to be yielding success, the Soviets, perhaps because they increasingly appeared to be 'just' another **Great Power**, found that the recipients of their aid were reluctant to do anything to compromise their sovereignty and independence. In other words, they saw the Soviet Union as merely yet another foreign master. Nor did the Angolans,

mujahedeen (Arabic: those who struggle in the way of God)
Term used for the Muslim guerrillas who fought against the Soviets in Afghanistan in 1979–89.

Great Powers
Traditionally those states that were held capable of shared responsibility for the management of the international order by virtue of their military and economic influence.

Ethiopians, Vietnamese or Afghans see the East–West confrontation as the eternal leitmotif of their respective histories. The collapse of the Cold War as an international system was thus to a large extent a result of the Third World's rejection of the need to see every issue from the increasingly arcane context of the clash between capitalism and socialism.

The disintegration of the Soviet bloc

The cost of the external military engagements and the growing opposition to Soviet hegemony were exacerbated by the deepening crisis of socialism as an economic system. The inability of centrally controlled socialist economies to deliver rising living standards and the failure to adopt the new technological innovations produced in the West exacerbated the need for fundamental change. Meanwhile, pressure for the relaxation of the stringent controls over the press was building up in a number of East European countries and several internal dissident movements began to challenge the local communists' monopoly on political power. By the mid-1980s, therefore, the communist bloc in Europe – the core of the Soviet-dominated part of the international system – was facing a deep economic and political crisis.

The Soviets also had to accept further unwelcome developments even closer to home. In 1980 workers in Poland led by Lech Walesa formed the **Solidarity Movement** and engaged in a series of strikes which undermined the authority of the country's communist leaders. Accordingly, Moscow was faced with the decision of whether or not to intervene to save the Polish regime. Coming on the heels of the unsuccessful intervention in Afghanistan, both the political and military leaders in the Soviet Union hesitated, preferring that the Polish communists themselves handled the situation, even if that meant a military take-over. The Solidarity Movement meanwhile had more than a year to organize and prepare for the showdown with the communists. When martial law was finally introduced and Solidarity outlawed in December 1981, the Polish Communist Party also lost whatever legitimacy it had. The military crackdown was roundly condemned in Western Europe, including by the powerful Italian Communist Party, which made the Polish crisis the final step in its break with Soviet and East European communism.

Mikhail Gorbachev, who was elected general secretary of the Soviet Communist Party in 1985, understood that major initiatives would have to be taken to improve the position both at home and abroad, but had no blueprint to implement. Instead, Gorbachev attempted to reduce tension with the United States and Western Europe in order to buy time for a reorganization of the Soviet economy. These initiatives led to a series of agreements in which the nuclear arms race was curbed, even beyond the limitations envisaged during détente. Believing Soviet communism to be in retreat internationally and under threat at home, Ronald Reagan had no hesitation in reducing the danger of nuclear war since it

Solidarity Movement
Polish independent trade union federation formed in September 1980, which, under Lech Walesa's leadership, soon posed a threat to Poland's communist government. In December 1981, the Polish government banned it and imprisoned most of its leaders. However, it persisted as an underground organization and played a major role in the negotiations that, in 1989, led to the end of communist rule in Poland.

appeared that history, after all, was on the side of the United States. The April 1986 nuclear accident at Chernobyl and growing resistance within his own party forced Gorbachev to adopt, in 1987, more radical policies in his search for *perestroika* – including some form of freedom of speech (*glasnost* – openness). Towards the end of the decade, both the Soviet Union and the Cold War seemed to be undergoing rapid change.

The final push came from Eastern Europe. Tired of economic deprivation and political oppression, a number of dissident leaders were encouraged by Gorbachev's rhetoric to become more vocal. His repeated assurances persuaded many reformist leaders that the Soviet Union under Gorbachev would not act, as the Soviets had done before, to defeat their political demands. The changes started in Poland, where already in 1988 General Jaruzelski's government realized that some kind of settlement with the banned Solidarity Movement was a precondition for much-needed Western loans and economic progress. In 1989 Jaruzelski held talks with Lech Walesa (the so-called round-table negotiations) which led to *partially* free elections being held in June that year. Although it was only allowed to contest a minority of seats in the *Sejm* (parliament), Solidarity received an overwhelming majority of the votes cast. In August 1989 Jaruzelski appointed Tadeusz Mazowiecki as the first non-communist prime minister in Eastern Europe since the 1940s.

Gorbachev's acceptance of a non-communist government in Poland opened the floodgates for political change in Eastern Europe. Just as conflict over Poland

glasnost (Russian: openness) Initiated in 1985 by Gorbachev, *glasnost* refers to the public policy within the Soviet Union of openly and frankly discussing economic and political realities.

Plate 20.1 Geneva, Switzerland, November 1985. US President Ronald Reagan talks to Soviet President Mikhail Gorbachev during a two-day summit between the superpowers in Geneva. (Photo: AFP/Getty Images)

had signalled the beginning of the Cold War system in Europe, the resolution of that issue signalled its end. In the summer of 1989, round-table negotiations similar to those in Poland produced a new government in Hungary which, having been promised a half-billion-dollar West German loan, in September decided to open its borders with the West. Soon thousands of East Germans flocked to Hungary in the hope of emigrating to West Germany. By late September, the East German regime was coming under pressure from protesters who demanded reforms similar to those in Poland and Hungary. On 18 October Erich Honecker was forced to resign, and the Politburo began work on new liberal laws and instructions, especially for travel to the West. As the draft laws became known on 9 November, East Berliners began assembling at the Berlin Wall, demanding to be allowed to cross, and demoralized **GDR** border guards opened the barriers. That weekend somewhere between two and three million East Germans visited West Berlin, and the wall, the paramount symbol of the Cold War, became a thing of the past.

In Czechoslovakia the Communist Party leaders, fearful of having to face the consequences of their actions in 1968, at first tried using force to stop the demonstrators. After street battles in Prague on 17 November, the opposition responded by calling strikes and boycotts, and the journalists took over control of most of the mass media, supporting the protesters. By the end of the month, the party leaders had resigned and in December the veteran dissident writer Vaclav Havel was elected president and Alexander Dubček, the leader overturned by the Soviets in 1968, was made chairman of the Federal Assembly. Only in Romania, which for a long time had been only half-connected to the Soviet bloc, were the changes accompanied by widespread violence. On 21 December the communist dictator Nicolae Ceauşescu made a televised address to a hand-picked crowd in Bucharest, but was interrupted by protesters. Over the week that followed, armed protesters, gradually joined by the army, fought Ceauşescu loyalists in the streets. Ceauşescu and his wife were captured and executed on Christmas Day, 1989.

While the events in Eastern Europe were unfolding, Gorbachev insisted on absolute Soviet non-intervention (the so-called 'Frank Sinatra Doctrine'). As he explained to his Politburo, the Soviet Union could not afford to intervene, for the financial costs and potential damage to the relationship with the West would be too high. But most importantly, Gorbachev believed that it would not be *right* to intervene, for he felt that just like the Soviets, the East Europeans should decide their own futures. He attempted to use his willingness to allow change as a bargaining chip in his relationship with the new administration of George Bush, but the latter proved cautious and was unwilling to give much in return, economically or politically. Steadily, though, the relationship between the two countries did improve, especially in terms of arms control, to the point that by 1990 both sides spoke of a partnership rather than a 'Cold War'.

The American hesitancy in providing tangible support for Gorbachev's reforms made the Soviet relationship with Western Europe, and especially with West Germany, even more essential to Moscow. At the same time Helmut Kohl's government in Bonn had more to gain than any other Western country from a close relationship with Gorbachev, not least as reunification would boost the

German Democratic Republic (GDR)
The German state created in 1949 out of the former Soviet occupation zone. Also known as East Germany. The GDR more or less collapsed in 1989–90 and was merged into the FRG in 1990, thus ending the post-war partition of Germany.

Federal Republic of Germany (FRG)

The German state created in 1949 out of the former American, British and French occupation zones. Also known as West Germany. In 1990 the GDR merged into the FDR, thus ending the post-war partition of Germany.

North Atlantic Treaty Organization (NATO)

Established by the North Atlantic Treaty (4 April 1949) signed by Belgium, Canada, Denmark, France, Great Britain, Iceland, Italy, Luxembourg, the Netherlands, Norway, Portugal and the United States. Greece and Turkey entered the alliance in 1952 and the Federal Republic of Germany in 1955. Spain became a full member in 1982. In 1999 the Czech Republic, Hungary and Poland joined in the first post-Cold War expansion, increasing the membership to nineteen countries.

see Map 20.1

Christian Democrats' domestic standing and seal Kohl's place in history. As the East German regime withered from within after the fall of the Berlin Wall, Kohl sought Soviet support for rapid reunification and was willing to offer significant economic aid in return. In 1990, Gorbachev agreed to the **FRG** absorbing East Germany, and approved the idea that the new reunified Germany should remain in **NATO**. Gorbachev's decision effectively sidelined those West European leaders, including the French president, François Mitterrand, and the British prime minister, Margaret Thatcher, who feared the consequences of a quick German reunification.

However, German loans were not enough to stop the Soviet slide towards economic chaos and political instability. Encouraged by the events in Eastern Europe, the Baltic States, which had been forcibly incorporated into the Soviet Union in 1940, began a campaign for independence. A similar movement flourished in Stalin's home state of Georgia, and violent conflicts broke out between the Soviet republics of Armenia and Azerbaijan over the control of the Nagorno-Karabakh area. As Gorbachev in early 1991 began to slow down his drive towards liberalization, Boris Yeltsin, who had been elected president of Russia, by far the biggest of the constituent republics, began to challenge his authority. In August 1991 conservatives within the Soviet Communist Party attempted to grab power in order to turn the clock back, but their coup against Gorbachev was defeated by their own indecisiveness, the army's unwillingness to follow their orders and Yeltsin's defence of the sovereignty of his Russian republic. The failed coup effectively brought about the end of the Soviet Union. The Baltic States broke away immediately, and one after another all the Soviet republics declared their independence, including Russia. Gorbachev remained in the Kremlin as the president of a union that had ceased to exist, until he resigned on Christmas Day, 1991. After seventy-three years of uneasy existence, the Soviet Union was no more.

Debating the end of the Cold War

The sudden end of the Cold War has produced a substantial amount of scholarly debate. Among the central questions are why and how did the post-1945 era come to such a rapid conclusion in the late 1980s, who won the Cold War, and was the 'victory' worth its price? In general, the disagreements relate to the fact that different answers are given to one specific question: did internal or external factors play the key role in bringing down the Soviet Union and its empire?

Those stressing the external factors as central to the demise of the USSR essentially argue that the massive military expansion of the United States during the Reagan years and the president's vocal anti-communism prompted the Soviet leadership to respond in kind. However, given the dire state of the Soviet economy, its military buildup forced it to attempt to introduce internal reforms but these only revealed

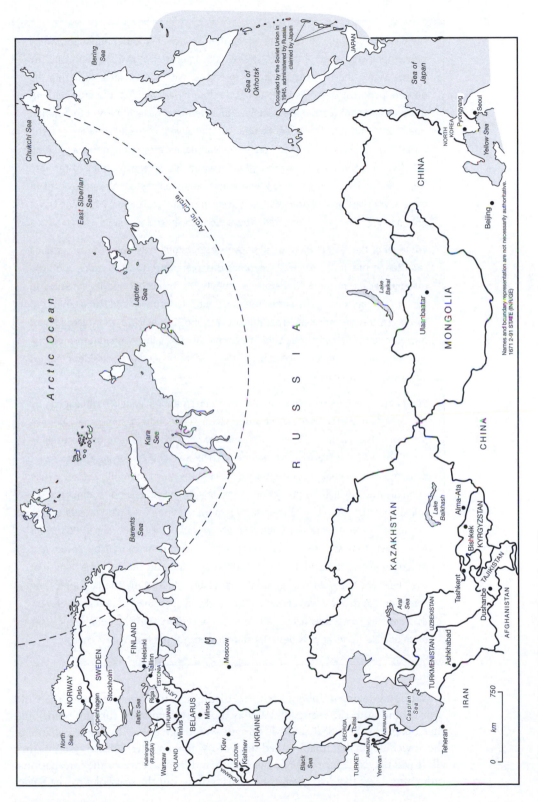

Map 20.1 States of the former Soviet Union after 1991

Source: After Lindeman et al. (1993)

the bankruptcy of the Soviet state, which then collapsed. Another argument, which also emphasizes external factors, stresses the importance of the attempt by the United States and the West generally to engage with the Soviet bloc during the détente period. It contends that, alongside the military buildup, the growing links between East and West Europeans helped to undermine the legitimacy of totalitarian rule. In addition, it has been argued that with the advent of the information age, the Soviet bloc was economically and technologically lagging further and further behind the West and this forced it to change its isolationist policies in order to tap into 'capitalist' markets and know-how. For various arguments, students should consult the essays in Odd Arne Westad (ed.), *Reviewing the Cold War* (London, 2000) and David Kotz and Fred Weir, *Revolution from Above* (London, 1997).

While all of the factors mentioned above were undoubtedly important in eroding totalitarian rule in the Soviet bloc, other observers have focused more upon the internal decline of the Soviet state. By the 1980s, the USSR and its satellites in Eastern Europe, it is argued, lacked internal political legitimacy and had been forced to accept the existence of a permanent and growing black market. Decades of mismanagement could not be cured by Gorbachev's well-intentioned reforms alone but required a complete overhaul of the system, a fact that dissident groups advocated increasingly vocally.

What about the demise of the Cold War as an international system? While it can be partly explained as a result of one side's victory over another, some analysts have pointed to the relative decline of both superpowers. Indeed, one of the best-selling titles of the late 1980s was Paul Kennedy's *The Rise and Fall of the Great Powers* (London, 1988), a book that essentially predicted the fall of the United States! While Kennedy was wrong in his prediction in this regard, the general point about the so-called 'imperial overreach' of the two superpowers during the Cold War still carries resonance. In a more recent book, *The Global Cold War* (Cambridge, 2005), Odd Arne Westad stresses the importance of the resentment caused by Soviet and American interventions in the Third World as an important cause for the demise of the USSR and the Cold War international system. Indeed, by the late 1980s, he contends that the Cold War division of the world had become increasingly irrelevant as a defining characteristic of the international system. Understanding the causes of its demise, however, provides important lessons for the twenty-first century.

While a growing number of scholars distinguish between the end of the Cold War (pointing to the events of 1989 as the most significant turning point) and the collapse of the USSR, most historians would agree that it was the collapse of the Soviet Union that finally ended the Cold War as an international system. After all, it was the existence of the Soviet Union and its challenge to the international order after 1945 that had given rise to this system. But the story of why the Soviet

Union collapsed is in itself intimately linked to many of the other events that shook the international system in the early 1990s. None of these was more closely watched than the events in the Persian Gulf.

The First Gulf War

The 1990–91 Gulf War was the first conflict of the post-Cold War environment. It was also the first challenge to the evolving unipolar world in which the United States, as the remaining superpower, set the international agenda of war and peace. The war began with the Iraqi invasion of Kuwait on 2 August 1990 and was officially based on Iraq's territorial claim to Kuwait as a district which had been administered from Basra during the Ottoman Empire. The incentives for Iraq to go to war, however, went far deeper than the fact that it did not recognize the independence of its neighbour. Broadly speaking, the causes for the invasion of Kuwait can be found in the legacy of the 1980–88 Iran–Iraq War, Saddam Hussein's need for domestic legitimacy and stability, and Iraq's quest for regional hegemony. A not inconsequential factor was Kuwait's vulnerability and the belief that Iraqi moves, while not condoned, would ultimately be tolerated.

Eight years of war with Iran had left the Iraqi regime in a difficult position. The war had depleted the country's resources and had plunged it into considerable debt, much of it owed to Kuwait and Saudi Arabia. In addition to debts totalling $80 billion and the war-related destruction, Iraq had incurred an economic loss from lower oil revenues and higher military expenditure of $208 billion. Iraq's dire economic conditions meant that it had difficulties repaying its debts, the servicing of which amounted to $8 billion a year alone. It also was not able to deliver on popular post-war expectations such as reconstruction and better living standards, turning the cease-fire, which had been hailed as a great victory, into a farce.

Moreover, economic stagnation in the year following the end of the war with Iran made it difficult to demobilize the 1.5 million soldiers, many of whom lacked education and employment skills. Indeed, with respect to the army Saddam Hussein found himself faced with nothing but unpalatable options. Demobilization would result in large-scale unemployment, which, in turn, could result in social unrest. The potential for unrest was further exacerbated by the fact that the majority of soldiers due to be released were **Shi'a** and therefore constituted a potential threat to the regime owing to their sectarian affiliation. The option of maintaining a large standing army was only marginally better as it further drained the state's coffers and, without a war to occupy the officers, Saddam Hussein feared they might turn against him in a military coup. Indeed, in 1989, believing that exactly such plans were about to be carried out, Saddam Hussein arrested and executed scores of army and air force officers. In short, he was faced with a choice between a threat from the lower ranks, which ran the risk of turning into a communal Shi'a revolt against a **Sunni** minority government, or a threat from the

Shi'a Islam
Muslim sect which emerged out of the struggle over the succession following the death of the Prophet Muhammad. Derived from Shi'a Ali (the Party of Ali) or those who supported the Prophet's son-in-law Ali's accession to the Caliphate. An estimated 15 per cent of Muslims are Shi'a. They are concentrated in the areas of Iran, Iraq and southern Lebanon, with smaller communities scattered throughout the Muslim world.

Sunni Islam
The main body of Muslims, who follow the path (*sunna*) of the Prophet Mohammed and the Quran and the *hadith*.

higher ranks, who during the war had built up their own power bases, and saw the opportunity to remove a civilian president.

The invasion of Kuwait promised a cure to both the economic and military legacy of the Iran–Iraq War. Kuwait's oil wealth would enable the Iraqi regime to reconstruct the state and to pay its non-Arab creditors. It would keep the army busy and far away from the capital. The claims of victory over Iran would be replaced with a real victory over Kuwait. The invasion was also seen as a way to project Iraqi hegemony not just over Kuwait but also over the Gulf as a whole. This would allow Iraq to dictate oil prices and quotas to serve its own interests, as it would control 21 per cent of **OPEC**'s total production. And, ultimately, the extension of military and economic power would enable Iraq to claim the mantle of **pan-Arab** leadership as the region's most powerful country, especially as it was the only country which had never even signed so much as an armistice with Israel and the only Arab state left to embrace the PLO wholeheartedly.

The invasion itself was made easier by two underlying beliefs: first, that Kuwait had provoked this attack through its unreasonable behaviour, and, second, that both Arab and Western states would not intervene. With respect to the first, in May 1988 Iraq had approached Kuwait with the aim of leasing (or annexing) the two strategically important islands at the entrance of the Shatt al-Arab river, Iraq's sole access to the Gulf. Kuwait refused. In February 1989 Iraq tried to extort territorial concessions from Kuwait as a reward for fighting the war against Iran on behalf of the Arab world, but to no avail. Iraq believed not only that it was being cheated of rightful compensation – after all, more than 200,000 Iraqis had been killed, 400,000 wounded and 70,000 taken prisoner – but also that it was being cheated of oil revenues. According to Iraq, Kuwait had stolen $2.4 billion from the Iraqi Rumaila oilfield. By invading Kuwait, Iraq was only taking what Saddam Hussein believed to be rightfully his.

With respect to the second, Saddam Hussein interpreted a meeting he had with the American ambassador, April Glaspie, on 25 July 1990 as signalling that the United States would not intervene should Iraq invade Kuwait, as Washington did not wish to get involved in inter-Arab disputes. Taking into consideration prior invasions and occupations by other Middle Eastern players and the lack of any Western or Arab reaction, Saddam calculated there would ultimately be acquiescence as long as the oil flow was not disrupted. After all, no action had been taken to dislodge Israeli forces from the West Bank, Gaza and Golan since 1967 or to dislodge Syrian troops from Lebanon since 1976. Thus Saddam Hussein discounted the likelihood of military action against his forces, the possibility of an Arab front emerging against Iraq, and arguably even the implementation of economic sanctions by the **United Nations** (**UN**).

The extent of Iraq's miscalculation and its misreading of the positions not only of the United States and Britain but also of its former allies in Moscow and its Arab brothers became clear on 16 January 1991. After months of UN Security Council resolutions, diplomatic moves, the freezing of Iraq's and Kuwait's assets, and the imposition of sanctions aimed at compelling Iraq to withdraw voluntarily, an American-led multinational coalition launched Operation Desert Storm to liberate Kuwait militarily. While the coalition relentlessly bombed Iraqi targets in

Organization of Petroleum Exporting Countries (OPEC)
The organization founded in 1960 to represent the interests of the leading oil-producing states in the Third World.

pan-Arabism
Movement for Arab unity as manifested in the Fertile Crescent and Greater Syria schemes as well as attempted unification of Egypt, Syria and Libya.

United Nations (UN)
An international organization established after the Second World War to replace the League of Nations. Since its establishment in 1945, its membership has grown to 192 countries.

Kuwait, Saddam attempted to split the coalition by creating a linkage with the Israeli–Palestinian conflict and by firing Scud missiles at Israel in an attempt to provoke the latter's entry into the conflict. American assurances and the speedy delivery of Patriot missiles kept Israel from retaliating. Nevertheless, a linkage had been created, as became evident in the efforts to push for a comprehensive Middle East peace process to resolve the Arab–Israeli conflict only a couple of months later.

On 27 February 1991, forty-three days after launching Desert Storm, a cease-fire was declared. By that point an estimated 120,000 sorties had been flown by coalition air forces and some 84,000 tons of ordnance had been dropped, including 7,400 tons of 'smart' bombs. Iraq's adventure in Kuwait had been stopped by the use of overwhelming air power and this became a strategy emulated in attempts to resolve other post-Cold War conflicts such as Kosovo in 1999. However, while Iraqi forces had been pushed out of Kuwait and had even been pursued across the border by coalition ground forces, the Iraqi regime emerged relatively unscathed. Fears of body bags and the spectre of Vietnam weighed heavily in the American decision not to commit itself to a prolonged ground operation. This was further underlined by the belief that toppling Saddam Hussein would result in the territorial disintegration of Iraq with the possibility of a Shi'a fundamentalist state appearing in the south of the country. Moreover, the coalition did not have a mandate to move against the Iraqi regime and the Arab coalition partners, France and Russia would not have supported such action.

The restoration of Kuwait to the Sabah royal family was read as a victory for the West and as a defeat for Saddam Hussein in his bid for hegemony – an interpretation which in the long term proved illusory. In particular, the demon-stration of American power in support of **collective security** led to the idea that the Cold War had now been replaced by a fresh paradigm – the New World Order – in which Washington would impose its values, for good or for ill, on the rest of the world. As such, the disparity between the victorious United States and the now almost irrelevant former Soviet Union could not have been starker.

collective security
The principle of maintaining peace between states by mobilizing international opinion to condemn aggression. Commonly seen as one of the chief purposes of international organizations such as the League of Nations and the United Nations.

The unipolar moment: America at the apex

The domination of the United States over the international order in the 1990s constituted, according to many observers, a 'unipolar moment'. In contrast to the decades of the Cold War when America was involved in a fearsome rivalry with the Soviet Union (and to some extent the **PRC**), the United States during the last years of the twentieth century had no serious rival within the international system. Its military and political might was second to none and, although the 1992 presidential election was overshadowed by a looming economic crisis, the 1990s saw America as the unchallenged global economic superpower. In particular, by the mid-1990s entrepreneurs based in the United States dominated the 'new global economy' and its most obvious by-product, the Internet. Indeed, one of

People's Republic of China (PRC)
The official name of communist or mainland China. The PRC came into existence in 1949 under the leadership of Mao Zedong.

Dow Jones Industrial Average (DJIA)
The statistical tool used to measure the performance of the New York Stock Exchange.

globalization
The cultural, social and economic changes caused by the growth of international trade, the rapid transfer of investment capital and the development of high-speed global communications.

General Agreement on Tariffs and Trade (GATT)
An international agreement arising out of the Bretton Woods conference covering tariff levels and codes of conduct for international trade. The progressive lowering of tariffs took place in a succession of negotiating rounds. In 1995 it passed its work on to the World Trade Organization.

the Clinton administration's most significant initiatives may well have been the deregulation of the World Wide Web, which quickly became a virtual marketplace in its own right. In the late 1990s, the American stock market began a rapid rise and the **Dow Jones Industrial Average (DJIA)** passed what many considered the 'magic' 10,000 mark. In part as a result of the Clinton administration's welfare reforms but even more because of the economic boom of the late 1990s, unemployment figures in the United States plunged to their lowest levels since the 1960s. By the late 1990s, as the biggest problem in the United States (aside from President Clinton's private conduct) appeared to be what to do with a mushrooming federal budget surplus, few observers doubted that the twenty-first century would only enhance its power and prestige.

Fittingly, the United States projected its economic power into the wider world, driving forward the process of **globalization**. In regard to international trade, Washington played a key role in sponsoring the metamorphosis of the **General Agreement on Tariffs and Trade (GATT)** in 1995 into a permanent institution, the World Trade Organization (WTO), that would work for the progressive lowering of tariffs. In addition, it laboured to persuade the newly industrializing countries, such as those in South-East Asia, to liberalize their economies and open themselves up to international investment. Behind this transformation of the global economy was the sense that the American victory in the Cold War had proved the superiority of its neo-liberal capitalist model of economic development. Indeed, so dominant did the mixture of neo-liberalism and democracy appear to be that some enthusiasts proclaimed an end to the twentieth century's perpetual competition between different social systems: the world had come to the 'end of history'. Such hubris was soon to look foolish.

By contrast, the new Russia of the 1990s was a nation hampered by a series of economic and political crises. Boris Yeltsin, the first president of the new independent Russian Federation, faced a plethora of insurmountable challenges. In the economic sphere, Russia tried to move towards Western practices: prices were deregulated, a number of state enterprises were privatized and the Russian Federation tried to boost foreign trade. However, the results were hardly encouraging. In 1992 inflation in Russia reached a staggering 2,500 per cent while the gross national product declined almost 40 per cent in the first half of the decade. Most disturbingly, those who prospered most from the wave of deregulation had close links to organized crime or, in a number of cases, were former Communist Party officials turned private entrepreneurs. Russia's stability was further weakened by a rising tide of separatism. In 1994 the Russian army was sent into the small republic of Chechnya in the Caucasus in order to bring the breakaway state back to the fold (Chechnya had declared its independence in October 1991). Notwithstanding the external criticism of the supposedly democratic Russia's actions, the war continued through the 1990s in various forms and raised the prospect of 'another Afghanistan'.

The chaotic state of the Russian economy was reflected in the country's chronic political instability. Given the lack of a democratic tradition, a constitution dating to the Soviet era and a parliament elected in 1990, the power struggle between the president and an aggressive legislature culminated in October

1993 when Yeltsin finally managed to disband the Congress of People's Deputies. The December 1993 parliamentary elections, however, resulted in a virtual parliamentary deadlock, as right-wing nationalists and other populist parties gained large numbers of seats in the legislature (Vladimir Zhirinovsky's far-right party won the most votes of any single party). Two years later, the parliamentary elections resulted in an even more surprising outcome when the supposedly defunct communists edged Zhirinovsky and his supporters from the top spot. Equally worrying to outside observers was Boris Yeltsin's deteriorating health. Moreover, although he won the 1996 presidential election (which was marred by extensive corruption) and remained the dominant politician in the country, Yeltsin's declining physical condition exacerbated the continuing political and economic uncertainty in Russia. Finally, on New Year's Eve 1999, Yeltsin resigned and Vladimir Putin, a former KGB (Soviet intelligence service) officer, became acting president of Russia. After his formal election in the following year, Putin promised a crackdown on organized crime and managed to restore some stability to the still turbulent Russian Federation.

The obvious internal weakness and instability of the new Russian Federation undoubtedly enhanced the relative position of the United States as the sole remaining superpower. Yet the persistent lack of central authority and the economic weakness of Russia created numerous challenges and potential security threats. Concerns about the fate of its large nuclear arsenal, its possession of other weapons of mass destruction (such as chemical and biological weapons) and the necessity to incorporate the post-communist state into the growing global economy were but some of the most obvious challenges facing not only Russia but also the United States and the wider Western community.

In the 1990s there were numerous attempts to minimize the risk of nuclear war and the possibility that the former Soviet Union's vast nuclear arsenals might fall into the 'wrong' hands. The United States and Russia continued to negotiate bilateral nuclear arms reduction treaties. In July 1991 they signed the **Strategic Arms Reduction Talks (START)** agreement in which the two countries pledged to halve the number of nuclear warheads (to about 6,000) by 1998. When the Soviet Union ceased to exist only five months later, START was supplemented by the Lisbon Agreement of March 1992 in which three of the successor states, Belarus, Ukraine and Kazakhstan, agreed to eliminate nuclear weapons from their respective territories. Early in 1993 the START II agreement further reduced the number of American and Russian nuclear weapons to approximately 3,000–3,500 on each side. A potentially important moment in limiting the proliferation of nuclear weapons was reached in 1995 when the 1968 **Nuclear Non-Proliferation Treaty (NPT)** was made permanent and the United States, Russia and the United Kingdom committed themselves to a moratorium on nuclear testing. Yet such treaties did not produce foolproof methods of preventing the proliferation of nuclear weapons, as was made clear when India and Pakistan conducted a series of well-publicized (and retaliatory) nuclear tests in 1998.

Indeed, by the end of the millennium it was evident that, while the danger and prospect of nuclear war might have changed, it had hardly disappeared. To be sure, the prospect of an American–Russian nuclear exchange was more remote

Strategic Arms Reduction Talks (START)
Begun in 1982, after the failed ratification of the SALT II Agreement, the START negotiations between the United States and the USSR led first to the 1987 Intermediate Nuclear Forces (INF) treaty to eliminate intermediate-range nuclear forces. In 1991 START I committed both sides to additional reductions in American and Soviet nuclear arsenals as well as on-site inspections. This was followed in 1993 by START II which called for a reduction in nuclear warheads by two-thirds by 2003. START also provided a framework for the nuclear disarmament of Ukraine, Belarus and Kazakhstan.

Nuclear Non-Proliferation Treaty (NPT)
Proposed by the USSR and the United States in 1968, and subsequently approved by the UNGA, the treaty prohibits the proliferation of nuclear weaponry to 'new' countries. It has been ratified by more than 180 nations but has not prevented some states from either openly or secretly acquiring a nuclear weapons capability.

than it had ever been, but what concerned the established nuclear powers was the spectre that some of the so-called 'rogue states', or even a terrorist organization, might acquire a nuclear weapons capability. Accordingly, the United States continued with the experiments it had begun in the 1980s to develop a national **missile defence programme** that would make it immune to attack. This, however, was a controversial field of activity, for it threatened to disturb the existing nuclear balance and risked provoking a new arms race.

While successive American administrations agonized over the transfer of nuclear weapons technology from the former Soviet Union to 'rogue states' and terrorist organizations, the West in general worried about the prospects for the new Russia, and the consequences of its political and economic instability. The general question was seemingly straightforward: how to incorporate Russia into a new security and economic system dominated by countries that had, by and large, been its adversaries for the past seven decades. In the security area the first major initiative was the so-called Partnership for Peace (PfP), which was established in January 1994 to provide some degree of defence co-operation between NATO and Russia. In the long run, however, the PfP failed to become a major agent of security in Europe, owing to problems over NATO expansion and the proliferation of other multilateral security organizations, such as the Organization for Security and Co-operation in Europe (OSCE) and the Western European Union (WEU), vying for a central role.

In the economic and political field, the major effort to anchor Russia into its new Western orientation was its inclusion in the **G-7** organization of leading industrial powers, which thus became the G-8 (or G-7 + 1). This probably meant more on the psychological than the economic level, for in reality Russia's economy was far smaller than that of any of the original G-7 members. Indeed, many argued that according respectability to Russia, in effect, compromised Western democracies, making them partners with what remained a 'semi-democratic' country willing to use armed force against rebellious minorities (such as the Chechens). In its post-Soviet life span, Russia also practised highly questionable and even dangerous policies in the eyes of many observers (the sale of nuclear technology to Iran being one example). Yet, given the sheer size of Russia, its still considerable military capability, and its geopolitical significance and economic potential, there appeared to be few alternatives available for Western democracies than continued 'peaceful engagement' with the (semi-democratic and semi-capitalist) successor state of their Cold War nemesis. In the early twenty-first century, with a rapid boom in energy prices boosting Russia's economic standing, it would gradually start once again to become a force to be reckoned with.

The 'new world order' and ethnic conflict

The United States was thus able to manage some of the problems that emerged in the Cold War's aftermath and clearly now dwarfed its former Russian rival in

missile defence programme
Or missile defence initiative, or national missile defence. A futuristic plan to provide the United States (and possibly other countries) with a missile shield against potential attacks.

Group of 7 (G-7)
The Group of 7 was the organization of the seven most advanced capitalist economies – the United States, Japan, Canada, Germany, France, Italy and Britain – founded in 1976. The G-7 held and continues to hold annual summit meetings where the leaders of these countries discuss economic and political issues.

terms of its military and economic power. The idea, however, that arose in the wake of the First Gulf War, that the United States might be able to use its paramount position in world politics to bring about a 'new world order', was soon to be tested. In some areas there were signs that with the Cold War over and the United States willing to exert its power, formerly intractable issues were now capable of solution. The most celebrated of these initiatives was the Clinton administration's eventually abortive effort to bring an end to the Israeli–Palestinian dispute. In addition, however, its ability to act as an 'honest broker' was important in the settlement of the Northern Ireland conflict.

see Chapter 18

The conflict in Northern Ireland, which erupted in 1969 on the back of the emergence of a Catholic civil rights movement, had little if anything to do with the Cold War, but the end of the East–West confrontation created a conducive environment for its resolution. Britain and the Republic of Ireland were able to focus fully on developments in Northern Ireland and the sole superpower status allowed the Clinton administration to become actively involved in the negotiations. The official beginning of the peace process came in the form of the August 1994 republican and October 1994 loyalist cease-fires, which were then followed by the 1995 Framework Documents and the 1996 elections to the negotiations. The negotiations were divided into three strands: internal Northern Irish relations, North–South relations with the Republic of Ireland and East–West relations between Britain and Ireland. Crucial to the resolution of the conflict was the establishment of a unionist/loyalist (Protestant)–nationalist/republican (Catholic) power-sharing government, regional autonomy or devolution, the decommissioning of paramilitary weapons, police reform, and the Irish Republic relinquishing its territorial claims. This was embodied in the 1998 Belfast Agreement, which was endorsed overwhelmingly by referendum in both Northern Ireland and the Republic. From 1998 the main challenge was to ensure the full implementation of the agreement, in particular the disarmament of the paramilitaries which were reluctant to relinquish weapons that they felt might still be needed to protect their communities and that provided them with status and influence within Northern Ireland. It was only after 11 September 2001 and under tremendous American pressure that the first act of decommissioning by the **Irish Republican Army (IRA)** finally took place.

However, while it was possible for the United States to use its power positively to try to end those conflicts in which it had a particular interest and where both combatants saw potential benefits from appealing to American opinion and largess, the limit of its influence soon became evident. The first sign of this came as early as 1992–93, when the United States intervened in Somalia following public concern about the collapse of governmental authority after the fall of the Siad Barre regime. At first, this humanitarian intervention, which seemed to tally neatly with the optimistic sentiments that existed in the wake of the UN's successful campaign against Saddam Hussein, went well. However, slowly but surely the American forces began to be sucked into the Somalian civil war, and, with the death of eighteen US Rangers at the hands of the forces of General Aideed in October 1993, public opinion in the United States soon did an abrupt about-turn. Thus, President Clinton's first major policy act was to withdraw from

Irish Republican Army (IRA)
Militant Irish nationalist organization formed in 1919 as the military wing of Sinn Fein. The IRA's original aim was to establish an Irish Socialist Republic in all of Ireland. In 1969 the IRA split into the Official and Provisional IRA. The Provisionals or Provos carried out a militant campaign in Northern Ireland in order to expel the British. In 1994 the IRA called a ceasefire and Sinn Fein entered into negotiations that resulted in the 1998 Belfast Agreement which provided for power-sharing in Northern Ireland.

see Chapter 17

see Map 20.2

Somalia. Farce was quickly followed by profound tragedy, for, influenced by its inability to project American power into the Horn of Africa, in 1994 the United States did nothing to prevent the genocide in Rwanda.

If this was not enough, the ability of the United States to shape the world was also called into question in Europe, where a new crisis threatened to bring wide-scale war to the Balkans. In retrospect, the disintegration of Yugoslavia should have come as no surprise. Already in the 1970s there was a trend towards growing autonomy for the six republics and two autonomous provinces that comprised Yugoslavia after the Second World War. Following the death of Tito in 1980, the economic problems and ethnic divisions continued to deepen and finally in the early 1990s Yugoslavia violently splintered along ethnic lines. After a failed attempt by Serbia, headed by the former communist leader Slobodan Milošević, to impose its authority on the rest of the country, Slovenia and Croatia declared their independence from Yugoslavia on 25 June 1991. The federal army responded with a brief, abortive intervention in Slovenia and a more serious effort to support the Serb minority in Croatia. However, once the genie of independence was out of the bottle, its influence soon spread. In September 1991 Macedonia declared its independence, and in October the citizens of Bosnia-Herzegovina voted for independence. Pressure from the international community helped initially to contain the crisis. In early 1992 a cease-fire was negotiated in Croatia, to be

Map 20.2 The former Yugoslavia

Source: After Lindeman *et al.* (1993)

supervised by a 14,000-strong UN peacekeeping force. At the same time the EC recognized Croatia and Slovenia as independent states, and this was followed in April by the EC and American recognition of Bosnia's sovereignty. Thus, although Serbia and Montenegro declared a new Yugoslavian federation under Milošević's leadership, the UN and the EC refused to accept that this regime was the legal descendant of former Yugoslavia, arguing that the federal state's rights and obligations had now been devolved to the new republics.

But, despite the rapid collapse of the old Yugoslavia, the Balkan wars were far from over, for very quickly Bosnia-Herzegovina fell into a long and bloody ethnic war. Almost as soon as Bosnian independence was declared, the Bosnian Serbs, about 30 per cent of the population, seized most of Bosnia's territory and proclaimed the Serbian Republic of Bosnia and Herzegovina. The Bosnian Croats, in turn, seized about half the remainder of the land and proclaimed the Croatian Community of Herceg-Bosna, leaving the poorly armed Muslims, who comprised more than 40 per cent of the population, to hold the rest (15–20 per cent) of the republic's territory. In a subsequent campaign of 'ethnic cleansing' carried out mostly by the Bosnian Serbs, thousands of Muslims were killed, and many more fled the country or were placed in Serb detention camps. In response, in May 1992 the UN imposed economic sanctions on Serbia and Montenegro and called for an immediate cease-fire in Bosnia. However, this attempt to end the conflict had little effect for there was no will at this point in the major Western European states or in the United States to use coercive power. As a result, a UN Protection Force (UNPROFOR) entered Bosnia but was inhibited from making any active moves to contain the conflict.

The Clinton administration's reluctance to intervene directly in the conflicts of former Yugoslavia until it was manifestly too late to contain the brutality of ethnic cleansing was in part related to the assumption that the conflict lay within Europe's realm of responsibilities. However, Washington was perhaps even more influenced by the impact of the débâcle in Somalia, which coincided with the debate over possible intervention in Bosnia. American public opinion was clearly against placing its troops in harm's way again, unless the administration could present a strong case to show that intervention in the former Yugoslavia was clearly in the national interest. This the administration was unable, or unwilling, to do until shocking pictures of Bosnian prisoners in concentration camps and evidence of mass killings by Serb troops began to appear regularly in the news in 1994. Even then, however, instead of military intervention, the United States opted for the 'safer' route of tightening economic sanctions. This policy, though, became unsustainable after July 1995 when Serbian forces entered the supposed UNPROFOR 'safe area' around Srebrenica and brutally massacred 7,000 Bosnian Muslims. When this event was revealed to an appalled outside world, Washington finally began to adopt a more belligerent attitude towards the Serbs. Eventually in late 1995, with the threat of American coercion in the air, the Serbs were forced to participate in talks in Dayton, Ohio, which led to a peace accord between Bosnia, Croatia and Serbia (Yugoslavia).

Even then, however, peace was not permanent. In 1997, with Milošević newly re-elected as the president of the new Yugoslav federation, another conflict began in the province of Kosovo, where the ethnic Albanian Kosovo Liberation Army launched a guerrilla warfare campaign against Serbian rule. In consequence of the mounting repression of the ethnic Albanians, the breakdown of negotiations between separatists and the Serbs, and fear that a new campaign of Serbian 'ethnic cleansing' was imminent, in March 1999 NATO, in its first-ever military action, began bombing strategic targets throughout Yugoslavia. In the ensuing conflict thousands of ethnic Albanians were forcibly deported from Kosovo by Yugoslav troops. At last in June, with NATO now finally talking of full-scale military intervention, Milošević agreed to withdraw from Kosovo, and NATO peacekeepers entered the region. Meanwhile, Montenegro sought increased autonomy within the federation and began making moves towards that goal. The turbulence in the Balkans was hardly over when in September 2000 Slobodan Milošević unexpectedly lost the presidential elections in Yugoslavia. Initially he refused to accept the victory of Vojislav Kostunica, but a series of public demonstrations and external pressure forced him to step down, and by the end of the year the United States and the European Union had begun to lift their economic sanctions against Yugoslavia. In 2001 Milošević was arrested and indicted as a war criminal by the International Court in The Hague. His trial began in February 2002 and lasted until his death from illness in March 2006.

By the beginning of the new century the wars in the Balkans had thus come to an end and a process of reconstruction and reconciliation had begun. Yet, in an ethnically divided region plagued by memories of ethnic cleansing and the knowledge that countless war criminals were still at large, the task of building a civil society remained daunting.

Conclusion

The 1990s thus proved a bewilderingly complex decade. By its conclusion neither the promise of globalization nor that of the 'new world order' had been fulfilled. Indeed, the apparent success of free market capitalism and the eclipse of state-controlled socialism did not lead, either at the global or the regional level, to the elimination of economic hardship or to the reduction of political instability. Moreover, the interdependence of the globalized world meant that the impact of hardship and regional instability became more difficult to contain than ever before. For those in the West, who ironically had come to see the Cold War as the years of a 'long peace', in which conflict had been kept at bay by the terrible logic of MAD, the 1990s were a dangerous, uncertain time. As the Cold War receded, old nationalist conflicts such as those in the Balkans re-emerged and new ideological challenges that had in part been nourished by the confrontation between the superpowers in Afghanistan and Iran came into sharp focus. Thus while at the dawn of the new millennium the Cold War may have been relegated into history, its legacy lived on, influencing the world of the twenty-first century. In short, even as talk about the new American global empire proliferated, the world continued to be plagued by conflict and change. The major difference compared with the situation a century earlier was that as the pace of change accelerated it led to a transformation in the nature and scope, if not necessarily the causes, of conflict. As nuclear weapons proliferated and new terrorist threats emerged the world was no safer than before.

Recommended reading

The best, if exhaustive, overview of Soviet–American relations at the end of the Cold War is Raymond Garthoff, *The Great Transition: American–Soviet Relations and the End of the Cold War* (Washington, DC, 1994). For various perspectives on the end of the Cold War readers should consult Beth Fischer, *The Reagan Reversal: Foreign Policy and the End of the Cold War* (Columbia, MO, 1997), Archie Brown, *The Gorbachev Factor* (Oxford, 1996), Michael H. Bernhard, *The Origins of Democratization in Poland: Workers, Intellectuals, and Oppositional Politics, 1976–1980* (New York, 1993), Timothy Garton Ash, *The Magic Lantern: The Revolution of 1989 Witnessed in Warsaw, Budapest, Berlin and Prague* (New York, 1990), Charles S. Maier, *Dissolution: The Crisis of Communism and the End of East Germany* (Princeton, NJ, 1997), Jack F. Matlock, *Autopsy on an Empire: The American Ambassador's Account of the Collapse of the Soviet Union* (New York, 1995), Gale Stokes, *The Walls Came Tumbling Down* (New York, 1997), Jacques Lévesque, *The Enigma of 1989: The USSR and the Liberation of Eastern Europe* (Berkeley, CA, 1997) and Odd Arne Westad, *The Global Cold War: Third World Interventions and the Making of our Times* (Cambridge, 2005).

For an analysis of the Soviet disengagement from Afghanistan and its impact on the collapse of the USSR (as well as a useful comparison of Vietnam and Afghanistan), see Sarah E. Mendelson, *Changing Course: Ideas, Politics, and the Soviet Withdrawal from Afghanistan* (Princeton, NJ, 1998). For an analysis stressing the role of the Communist Party elite in the process leading to the dissolution of the USSR, see David Kotz and Fred Weir, *Revolution from Above: The Demise of the Soviet System* (London, 1997). See also Michael McGwire, *Perestroika and Soviet National Security* (Washington, DC, 1991) and Robert English, *Russia and the Idea of the West* (New York, 2000).

A large number of books have been written on the 1990–91 Gulf War. A comprehensive analysis of the decision-making processes of both Iraq and the United States can be found in Amatzia Baram and Barry Rubin (eds), *Iraq's Road to War* (New York, 1993). Two books situating the Gulf War in the broader context of the new world order are Tareq Ismael, *The Gulf War and the New World Order: International Relations in the Middle East* (Gainesville, FL, 1994) and Lawrence Freedman, *The Gulf War 1990–1991: Diplomacy and War in the New World Order* (London, 1993). The Arab perspective is well articulated by Mohammad Heikal, *Illusion of Triumph: An Arab View of the Gulf War* (London, 1992).

For general accounts of globalization and international relations in the 1990s, see William Greider, *One World, Ready or Not: The Manic Logic of Global Capitalism* (New York, 1997), Hans-Henrik Holm, *Whose World Order? Uneven Globalization and the End of the Cold War* (Boulder, CO, 1995) and Ian Clark, *The Post-Cold War Order: The Spoils of Peace* (New York, 2002). For works on the relations between the United States and the new Russia, see David Remnick, *Resurrection: The Struggle for a New Russia* (New York, 1998), James Scott, *After the End: Making US Foreign Policy in the Post-Cold War World* (Durham, NC, 1998) and M. Bowker and C. Ross, *Russia after the Cold War* (New York, 2000). Various assessments of the US role in the world can also be found in Robert J. Lieber, *Eagle Adrift* (New York, 1997), Robert W. Tucker and David C. Hendrickson, *The Imperial Temptation* (New York, 1992), Peter Gowan, *Global Gamble* (New York, 1999), Michael Cox, *US Foreign Policy after the Cold War* (London, 1996), Michael Cox *et al.* (eds), *US Democracy Promotion* (New York, 2000) and William G. Hyland, *Clinton's World* (Westport, CT, 1999). For an account of post-Cold War American defence planning and policy, see Michael Klare, *Rogue States and Nuclear Outlaws* (New York, 1999).

For reading on the Northern Ireland peace process, see Eamonn Mallie and David McKittrick, *The Fight for Peace: The Secret Story behind the Irish Peace Process* (London, 1996), George Mitchell, *Making Peace: The Inside Story of the Making of the Good Friday Agreement* (London, 1999) and Thomas Hennessy, *The Northern Ireland Peace Process: Ending the Troubles* (Dublin, 2000). For a comparative perspective on Northern Ireland and other ethnic, sectarian or communal conflicts see John McGarry, *Northern Ireland and the Divided World: Post-Agreement Northern Ireland in Comparative Perspective* (Oxford, 2001).

On the Balkan crisis, see Misha Glenny, *The Fall of Yugoslavia* (New York, 1992), Slobodan Drakulic, *The Balkan Express* (New York, 1993), Thomas Ali, *Masters of the Universe? NATO's Balkan Crusade* (New York, 2000), A. Wachtel, *Making a Nation, Breaking a Nation* (Stanford, CA, 1998) and Brendan Simms, *Unfinest Hour: Britain and the Destruction of Bosnia* (London, 2001).

CHAPTER TWENTY-ONE

The rise of a new Europe: the history of European integration, 1945–2007

Introduction

While it is easy to draw a picture of the twentieth century as steeped in blood and conflict, it is important also to see that this period witnessed many different efforts by both states and individuals to overcome national rivalries and to encourage co-operation between countries and peoples. The initial hope in the wake of the First World War was that future peace and prosperity could be guaranteed through the establishment of a universal international organization, the **League of Nations**. This, however, proved to be a false dawn, for this body was compromised from its very inception by the absence of the United States and then proved unequal to the task of co-ordinating 'collective security' in the 1930s. After the defeat of the Tripartite Powers at the end of the Second World War, hope revived again with the formation of the **United Nations** (UN) and its attendant bodies. But here too, disillusion soon set in as a result of the fact that the Cold War helped to paralyse the organization and because of the way in which the permanent members of the Security Council used and abused their powers of veto to uphold their national interests.

However, while internationalist dreams of a move towards enlightened world governance were dashed on these rocks, a new path began to emerge in the post-1945 era – the emergence of continental or regional supra-governmental

League of Nations
An international organization established in 1919 by the peace treaties that ended the First World War. Its purpose was to promote international peace through collective security and to organize conferences on economic and disarmament issues. It was formally dissolved in 1946.

collective security
The principle of maintaining peace between states by mobilizing international opinion to condemn aggression. Commonly seen as one of the chief purposes of international organizations such as the League of Nations and the United Nations.

United Nations (UN)
An international organization established after the Second World War to replace the League of Nations. Since its establishment in 1945, its membership has grown to 192 countries.

European Economic Community (EEC)
Established by the Treaty of Rome 1957, the EEC became effective on 1 January 1958. Its initial members were Belgium, France, Italy, Luxembourg, the Netherlands and West Germany (now Germany); it was known informally as the Common Market. The EEC's aim was the eventual economic union of its member nations, ultimately leading to political union. It changed its name to the European Union in 1992.

European Community (EC)
Formed in 1967 with the fusion of the European Economic Community (EEC, founded in 1957), the European Atomic Energy Community (EURATOM, also founded in 1957), and the European Coal and Steel Community (ECSC, founded in 1952). The EC contained many of the functions of the European Union (EU, founded in 1992). Unlike the later EU, the EC consisted primarily of economic agreements between member states.

organizations that aimed at the development of economic, social and even political integration. The most successful of these experiments in the pooling of sovereignty took place in Europe with the birth of the **European Economy Community (EEC)** in 1958 and its evolution into, first, the **European Community (EC)** and, finally, the **European Union (EU)**. The fact that the EEC was able through economic integration to transform war-torn Western Europe into a zone of peace and prosperity not surprisingly inspired statesmen in other parts of the globe to try to follow suit. They were to do so with mixed results. Some regional organizations, such as the **Association of South-East Asian Nations (ASEAN)**, echoed the achievements of the EEC by also bringing economic and political cohesion to previously troubled regions. Others though, such as the largely abortive calls for integration in East Asia, have been less effective. In these cases, however, the reasons for failure, such as the fear of the consequences of pooling sovereignty and the lack of strong political incentives underpinning the integration process, are still important to study, for ironically they help to highlight the causes of success in Europe and South-East Asia.

The idea of Europe

The idea of a united Europe was not an invention of the post-1945 era. Indeed, most of the great conquerors of Europe's long and bloody history – from the Romans to Charles V and from Napoleon to Hitler – justified their quest in part as a way of bringing stability and order through unity. This idea of a Europe dominated by one hegemonic nation has thus been a constant feature in the annals of European history, but it has little in common with the twenty-first-century understanding of economic and political integration.

The idea of integration based on principles of democratic governance and common markets was new to the post-1945 era. Its impressive appeal was based on a number of factors. The most obvious was that in regard to national security, the West Europeans who championed integration viewed their countries as too weak to stand up against the real or imagined Soviet military threat. At the same time most Western European politicians were not content with a simple abdication of power to American dominance and leadership. The answer therefore was to attempt to create strength through unity, even though this necessarily meant bringing together previously quarrelsome neighbours, such as Germany and France. There was, though, some element of historical continuity in this, for, after all, in previous times Europeans had been more willing to cooperate when they perceived a common external threat. For some parts of Europe, the Soviets were the reincarnation of the Persians, Muslims, Mongols or Turks; they were 'barbarians' at the gates of Europe.

The modern idea of Europe is not, though, based simply on the need to confront an external enemy or on the profitability of common markets, but also looks to the belief that there is a specific European identity. Since the 1940s, when the Italian historian Federico Chabod wrote the first book on the idea of Europe, the argument that 'Europeans' share a common set of values that are rooted in ancient Greece and reached their maturity in the Enlightenment has gained wide acceptance. The notion of a common European identity is, however, controversial because many consider Christianity to be the cornerstone of the continent's value system. Increased immigration from non-Christian parts of the world, as well as the debate over the potential accession of Turkey, a Muslim nation, into the EU, has naturally raised fundamental questions about this interpretation. What is clear, however, is that underpinning the experiment that led to the EEC and EU was a fundamental commitment to liberal democracy and the rule of law.

From the Second World War to the Treaty of Rome

In the aftermath of the Second World War it was, however, issues of high politics rather than reflections on identity that led West European leaders to consider the necessity of integration, for the problems that faced them were immediate and pressing. The first fact that they had to face was that the experience of the two world wars had shown clearly the catastrophic impact that national ambition and nationalist rivalries could have in the age of modern technology. Put simply, Europe had to take another, more peaceful course or risk destroying itself entirely. The second key factor was that the years of war brought about a relative decline in Europe's influence. Europe's overseas empires were toppling. The colonized peoples in the European empires were demanding greater independence and France, Holland and Britain did not, in the long run, have the will or resources to resist. As the prospect of **decolonization** threatened to translate into a dramatic reduction in the individual European countries' global power and influence, the temptation was to remedy this decline through a pooling of national resources through integration. Moreover, once this process began it had the effect of accelerating decolonization, for the European Powers could only find common cause if they abandoned their imperial rivalries, which included dropping the preferential trade that had existed with their colonies. However, more disturbing than the prospect of imperial decline was that even within their own continent the individual European Powers were now relatively weak compared with the two superpowers, the Soviet Union and the United States. Pooling resources, both economic and military, appeared the only sensible way of redressing this new weakness. In short, integration was the only way in which the nations of Western Europe could avoid becoming mere pawns in the emerging Cold War international system.

Of course, there were plenty of obstacles to the process of integration, for not every European nation had the same interest. Although the former British prime minister Winston Churchill expressed his support for a 'United States of Europe' in 1946, Britain rejected anything that went beyond establishing a free trade area. The initial steps therefore were tentative. The first significant move came in 1949

European Union (EU)
A political and economic community of nations formed in 1992 in Maastricht by the signing of the Treaty on European Union (TEU). In addition to the agreements of the European Community, the EU incorporated two inter-governmental – or supra-national – 'pillars' that tie the member states of the EU together: one dealing with common foreign and security policy, and the other with legal affairs. The number of member states of the EU has expanded from twelve in 1992 to twenty-seven in 2007.

Association of South-East Asian Nations (ASEAN)
Organization founded in 1967 by Indonesia, Malaysia, the Philippines, Singapore and Thailand to provide a forum for regional economic co-operation. From 1979, and the Third Indochina War, it took on more of a political and security role. Membership increased with the accession of Brunei in 1984, Vietnam in 1995, Burma in 1997 and Cambodia in 1999.

decolonization
The process whereby an imperial power gives up its formal authority over its colonies.

Marshall Plan

Officially known as the European Recovery Programme (ERP). Initiated by American Secretary of State George C. Marshall's 5 June 1947 speech and administered by the Economic Co-operation Administration (ECA). Under the ERP the participating countries (Austria, Belgium, Denmark, France, Great Britain, Greece, Iceland, Italy, Luxembourg, the Netherlands, Norway, Sweden, Switzerland, Turkey and West Germany) received more than $12 billion between 1948 and 1951.

see Chapter 9

European Coal and Steel Community (ECSC)

Established by the Treaty of Paris (1952) and also known as the Schuman Plan, after the French foreign minister, Robert Schuman, who proposed it in 1950. The member nations of the ECSC – Belgium, France, Italy, Luxembourg, the Netherlands and West Germany – pledged to pool their coal and steel resources by providing a unified market, lifting restrictions on imports and exports, and creating a unified labour market.

Federal Republic of Germany (FRG)

The German state created in 1949 out of the former American, British and French occupation zones. Also known as West Germany. In 1990 the GDR merged into the FDR, thus ending the post-war partition of Germany.

with the founding of the Council of Europe, which was a pan-European body set up to protect democratic principles and sponsor the integration of legal norms. With its seat in Strasbourg, the Council remains the oldest body that specifically promotes Europe-wide standards and integration. In six decades its membership has risen from ten to forty-seven countries. The European Convention of Human Rights (1950) and the European Court of Human Rights (founded in the same year) remain its most significant achievements.

From early on, though, it was clear that the two key continental Powers, France and Germany, preferred a much 'deeper' form of co-operation that looked beyond the espousal of values to real economic and political integration. For both countries integration was a means of enhancing prosperity and security and thus aiding the massive task of reconstruction. Above all, however, they were faced with the knowledge that their national rivalry, which had contributed so significantly to the calamity of the world wars, could not be allowed to continue and that it could only be tempered through mutually advantageous co-operation. They were not the only ones to realize this, however, for one of the great ironies of European integration was that in the immediate post-war period it received a strong push from the United States. An integral part of the **Marshall Plan** was that it was intended to provide a stimulus for the breaking down of tariff barriers within Europe. In 1947–48, participating countries were required to design a joint plan for recovery, which forced them to work together in the Organization of European Economic Co-operation. In April 1948 the inclusion of West Germany in the plan further clarified the American position, indicating that they viewed the economic integration of the former enemy states as a key to Europe's future peace and prosperity.

The United States thus helped to stimulate integration, but it was the Europeans who were behind the first major step. The creation of the **European Coal and Steel Community (ECSC)** in 1951 represented the first milestone. Coal and steel production was not only essential for the reconstruction of countries in Europe, but they were also the economic sectors that had been most important for the production of munitions in the two world wars. Accordingly, even after the foundation of the **Federal Republic of Germany (FRG)** in 1949, France initially maintained its occupation of the main German steel production area, the Saarland region, in order to deny Germany any chance of rearming. However, in 1950 the French foreign minister, Robert Schuman, proposed the creation of a supra-national institution that would oversee coal and steel production, thus neutralizing French distrust and German resentment. This proposal was known as the Schuman Declaration, but the man who authored the plan and became the first president of the ECSC's High Authority was Jean Monnet, a former deputy secretary-general of the League of Nations who many consider to be the founding father of European integration. Schuman and Monnet were subsequently able to persuade Belgium, France, the FRG, Italy, Luxembourg and Holland of the benefits of the ECSC, but the attempt to win over Britain failed, and thus the original 'Six' came into being.

Even without the British, the founding countries of the ECSC continued to expand the scope of integration. Not all of their initiatives were successful.

Following the ECSC proposal, the French proposed the creation of a European Defence Community (EDC) as a means of nullifying the threat posed by West German rearmament. Ironically, although the treaty was negotiated and signed by the 'Six' in 1952, the French National Assembly then refused to ratify it. Thus, an early opportunity to move towards a common European security policy was missed and instead West German rearmament took place under the umbrella of the **North Atlantic Treaty Organization (NATO)** alliance.

In 1957, however, only three years after the collapse of the EDC, representatives from the six ECSC countries gathered in Rome to consider ambitious plans for deepening economic integration beyond coal and steel production. The result was two treaties: one founded the European Atomic Energy Community (EURATOM), and the other the EEC. Of these the latter was vastly more important, for it created the basic building blocks of modern integrated Europe. Like the future EU, the EEC was forged through a process of compromise that sought to meet the various states' interests. The French, for example, were far more protectionist than the Germans or the Dutch, but accepted the principle of a common market in return for a major role in atomic energy development, the establishment of a Common Agricultural Policy (CAP) and the association of colonial territories with the EEC on favourable terms (Belgium and France were the only ones of the Six that still had substantial colonial holdings in 1957). Meanwhile, the Italians, who were economically in the poorest state, received other incentives, most importantly free movement of labour and the creation of a European Investment Bank to promote regional development. Although the Rome Treaties were very much a result of a high-level poker game between national politicians, the end result was still impressive. When it entered into force on 1 January 1958, the EEC represented a common market of 167 million people, and its key countries, France and West Germany, had moved from bitter rivalry to the beginning of an integration process that would change European history.

see Chapter 9

North Atlantic Treaty Organization (NATO)
Established by the North Atlantic Treaty (4 April 1949) signed by Belgium, Canada, Denmark, France, Great Britain, Iceland, Italy, Luxembourg, the Netherlands, Norway, Portugal and the United States. Greece and Turkey entered the alliance in 1952 and the Federal Republic of Germany in 1955. Spain became a full member in 1982. In 1999 the Czech Republic, Hungary and Poland joined in the first post-Cold War expansion, increasing the membership to nineteen countries.

Widening and deepening in the shadow of the Cold War

Enlargement is a central part of the story of European economic integration, but it was by no means pre-ordained. For four decades after the Treaty of Rome the Cold War division of Europe set clear parameters as to how 'wide' Europe could become. Meanwhile, different notions about the direction and the nature of European integration, and particularly the degree to which it should be a political as well as an economic process, made a number of states reluctant to join the EEC. That some countries, particularly France, were bent on using the EEC to further their own nationalist agenda, rather than succumb to the loss of national sovereignty that true integration necessitated, cast an additional shadow over European integration in its first decades.

France's president from 1958 to 1969, Charles de Gaulle, symbolized this tendency. Although he disliked the federalist elements of the Rome Treaty, de

Gaulle did not challenge it directly. Instead, he sought to use the EEC as a means of advancing French power. EURATOM, for example, was quickly sidelined in favour of France's own nuclear programme. De Gaulle's efforts to portray France as the leader of a continental European bloc did little to further the integration process. Nor did his insistence on the centrality of the CAP, which granted significant subsidies to French farmers, endear him to his fellow Europeans. Eventually his intransigence led in 1965–66 to the 'Empty Chair' crisis, during which France boycotted the meetings of the Council of Ministers – the highest body and executive arm of the EEC – for a six-month period. The solution to what amounted to the first serious internal crisis within the EEC was the so-called Luxembourg Compromise of 1966 which, in essence, gave France a veto right over such key issues as agricultural policy. Following this compromise, the EEC was able to complete a customs union in 1968, earlier than the Rome Treaty had required. This, perhaps more than anything else, signified the emergence of the EEC as an important trading bloc with significant bargaining power on tariff and trade matters vis-à-vis the United States.

De Gaulle's dominance of French politics not only prevented any rapid moves towards further integration, but also acted as an obstacle to EEC enlargement. Concerned at the prospect of Europe's and France's relative loss of power vis-à-vis the United States, de Gaulle was determined to pursue a more independent line in foreign policy, where French political and military power would be supplemented by the vitality of Western European economic growth. Naturally, de Gaulle was jealous of any development that might threaten to undermine France's revival, and it was this that led him to oppose an enlargement that promised a substantial enhancement of the EEC's economic strength but a diminishing of French influence – the accession of Britain.

In the early to mid-1950s, with its empire and associated trade links still largely intact, Britain had been distinctly lukewarm about European integration. It recognized the latter's political potential for solving the German problem, but felt little need to become directly involved. However, by the late 1950s, with decolonization under way in South-East Asia, the Middle East and Africa, Britain looked again at the idea of expanding its trade links with Europe. Its first move was the creation of the European Free Trade Area (EFTA) in 1960. As the name implies, EFTA's purpose was to promote free trade among its member countries without any forging of institutional, systemic or political integration. With seven members (Austria, Denmark, Great Britain, Norway, Portugal, Sweden and Switzerland), EFTA was not inconsequential as a trading zone, but it was handicapped by the fact that less than a year into its existence, the largest EFTA member, Britain, applied for membership of the EEC. For the government of Harold Macmillan, the Outer Seven (as EFTA was called) had always essentially been a bargaining chip that was intended to obtain better conditions for entry into the Inner Six of the EEC.

De Gaulle, however, had no intention of allowing British membership of the EEC. The entry of such a sizeable political, economic and military Power clearly had the potential to clip France's wings. Moreover, de Gaulle was not convinced that Britain was sincere in its sudden conversion to the European ideal, believing that it would merely act as a 'Trojan horse' that would in reality do America's bidding. Thus in 1963 de Gaulle announced that France would veto British entry. In 1967, when the government of Harold Wilson put together a second bid for membership, de Gaulle declared himself still unconvinced and repeated the veto. It was only with de Gaulle gone from the scene that Britain, along with Denmark and Ireland, finally negotiated its way into the EEC in January 1973. Building on the foundations of the customs union established five years earlier, the EEC was now, with its three new members, clearly on its way to becoming a key player in the world economy. Thus, while the Americans may have officially promoted further integration and Britain's entry into the EEC, they were by 1973 beginning to rue the results of their sponsorship. Following the entry of the new members, *Time* magazine marked the event with the headline 'America's new rival', and for the next two years relations between Washington and the Western European capitals went through a difficult patch.

In the subsequent decade and a half the EEC continued its widening and deepening. The 1980s saw southern enlargement as Greece (1981), Portugal and Spain (both in 1986) became members. All three had moved from authoritarian to democratic governments prior to joining; thus the southern enlargements set a precedent: membership of the integrated European community became a means of solidifying democratic rule in new member countries. In the post-Cold War era, a variation of this argument would often be used to justify the entry of the former Soviet bloc countries into the EU.

The latest enlargements were significant, but it was the 'deepening' of European integration that was the truly distinctive feature in the new wave of integration. One important development was the push towards direct democracy. In 1979 the European Parliament (EP), which had started its life in 1952 as the Common Assembly of the ECSC, held its first direct election. Until then, the representatives of the national assemblies had selected the Parliament's members. Since 1979 the EP has grown in size every time new member states have been added. It has also gradually grown in importance by acquiring continent-wide legislative powers and can no longer be described as a mere 'talking shop'. Nevertheless, the EP's significance continues to be hampered by its sheer size (capped at 750 members in the twenty-first century), and the democratic deficit created by the geographical distance of its headquarters in Strasbourg from most voters. Nor does the constant decline in voter participation in EP elections (45 per cent in 2004) augur well for the success of this sort of deepening.

A second important development towards a 'deeper' Europe in the late 1970s was the creation of the European Monetary System (EMS) and the defining of the European Currency Unit (ECU). Although not a new idea, the EMS was pushed forward as a response to the uncertainties in global currency markets in the 1970s following the end of the post-war **Bretton Woods** system. Already in 1972 the EEC countries had agreed not to allow their currencies to fluctuate more than 2.25 per cent against each other and had created a European Monetary Co-operation Fund to help countries stay within this range. The EMS retained this agreement (with Italy being allowed 6 per cent fluctuations) by creating a basket of currencies known as the ECU. The 1979 agreement also created an exchange rate mechanism to help

Bretton Woods
The site of an inter-Allied conference held in 1944 to discuss the post-war international economic order. The conference led to the establishment of the IMF and the World Bank. In the post-war era the links between these two institutions, the establishment of GATT and the convertibility of the dollar into gold were known as the Bretton Woods system. After the dollar's devaluation in 1971 the world moved to a system of floating exchange rates.

keep fluctuations to the minimum and extended European credit facilities. All this amounted to the first step towards a common currency.

The next important step towards further integration was, undoubtedly, the passing of the Single European Act (SEA) in December 1985–January 1986. This constituted the first major revision of the Rome Treaty and established a single European market. In addition, the SEA also formalized the notion of European Political Co-operation (EPC) by extending the EEC's competencies into the foreign policy arena. Floated in various reports since the early 1970s, the adoption of the EPC, highly contested though it was and remains, signalled another important deepening of the EEC's *raison d'être*.

Notwithstanding the security and foreign policy aspects of the agreements, the SEA was ultimately a response to a contemporary dilemma. European economies had stagnated in the 1970s and this had given rise to the derogatory term 'euro-sclerosis'. To many, the heart of the problem was the fact that, despite the abolition of tariffs, a number of invisible barriers to internal EEC trade remained intact. Both business and political leaders noted the need to harmonize laws and remove policy discrepancies between the EEC countries; indeed, they listed no fewer than 300 specific issues that needed to be fixed. The basic argument of the French mastermind behind the SEA, Jacques Delors, was that Europe could only improve its competitiveness and escape stagnation by becoming a true common market.

However, only a few years after the passing of the SEA, the future of European integration became far less predictable. In 1989 the Berlin Wall came down, and this and other related events, such as the dissolution of the Soviet bloc and the disintegration of the USSR, inevitably had a profound effect on the path that the EEC would follow in the 1990s.

An ever-wider Europe and the conundrums of success

The end of the Cold War opened up new possibilities for both the widening and the deepening of European integration. At the time that the Berlin Wall came down, both the German chancellor, Helmut Kohl, and the French president, François Mitterrand, were committed to the cause of integration. Both, in particular, supported the idea that a single European currency was the obvious next step. Needless to say, however, bargaining and self-interest continued to play crucial roles. After 1989, Kohl needed French support to bring about German unification; Mitterrand, much like Robert Schuman with the creation of the ECSC in the early 1950s, wished to anchor an enlarged Germany into an integrated Europe and saw a common currency as a useful way of achieving this goal. The stage was therefore set for another dramatic step forward in the integration process, the Maastricht summit of 1992.

By creating a unique entity, the European Union, the 1992 Maastricht Treaty (or the Treaty on European Union, TEU) laid to rest most concerns about the

Plate 21.1 Paris, September 1992. German Chancellor Helmut Kohl, left, says goodbye to French President François Mitterrand, after their meeting at the Elysée Palace to discuss the construction of a European Union following the narrow French approval by referendum of the Maastricht Treaty. (Photo: Joel Robine/AFP/Getty Images)

revival of old national rivalries. It was divided into three so-called pillars: first, the European communities; second, common foreign and security policy; and, third, police and judicial co-operation in criminal matters. Among the most significant outcomes was the harmonization of monetary matters: the TEU provided for the creation of a common currency (the first euro coins and notes would be in circulation ten years after the Maastricht Treaty) and the European Central Bank. The Maastricht Treaty also enhanced the power of various supra-national European institutions (particularly the EP), introduced a social chapter and dropped 'Economic' from the title of the EEC, and thus became the founding contract of today's European Union (EU).

Like any treaty related to European integration, Maastricht was a compromise and it left few of those involved in the negotiations satisfied. The British, even after the staunchly anti-integrationist prime minister Margaret Thatcher had left the premiership in 1990, remained deeply sceptical. Her successor, John Major, insisted that Britain would not join the common currency and during the tough negotiations his continental counterparts eventually accepted this decision (Denmark followed Britain in also refusing to join the euro). In the end the treaty was ratified by all twelve member states of the EC, but the Danes had to hold a second referendum to reach that point, while French voters gave the treaty only a slim majority. In Britain, politicians did not dare to ask the public's view. Ratification was instead pushed through the House of Commons (the final vote in May 1993 was 292–112 in favour). In other key countries, such as Germany, there was little opposition in the legislature but much scepticism in the press.

Historic but unsatisfactory and unpopular, the Maastricht Treaty was followed by several further attempts to deepen European unity. In 1997 EU member states negotiated the Amsterdam Treaty, which stressed the need for a Europe-wide employment policy as well as a true common foreign and security policy. Perhaps most tellingly, the Amsterdam Treaty, which entered into force in 1999, aimed to enhance individual rights and freedoms while strengthening the powers of the European Parliament. Equally significant, the Treaty of Nice (signed in 2001 and in force two years later) fixed the relative voting powers of individual countries in the Council of the European Union, the highest decision-making body of the EU. It also enlarged the number of seats in the EP to reflect the forthcoming enlargement of the EU. These initiatives all reflected the biggest dilemma and irony for the EU as the twentieth century drew to a close. Never before had democracy been so widely accepted in Europe, but the citizens participating in that historic experiment felt increasingly alienated from the faceless institutional hybrid that the EU had become. Perhaps because of this, the role of national parliaments and national politics retained their significance and popularity (voting percentages were customarily much higher in national elections than European ones).

The scepticism of the multitude did not, however, stop the rapid widening of the EU. After the end of the Cold War Europe saw three significant enlargements: in 1995 (three countries), 2004 (ten) and 2007 (two). As a result, six decades after the Rome Treaty, in 2007 the EU consisted of twenty-seven member states. The Franco-German dominance that had characterized much of the history of the EEC was thus increasingly challenged by influential newcomers like Poland, while the EU's geographical balance shifted towards the east. In terms of population growth, the six nations that concluded the Rome Treaty in 1957 had a total combined population of 167 million. In 2007 the EU's population was 493 million, of which 'only' 215 million lived in the 'original Six'. Unlike in traditional states like China or India where population rises with a decrease in mortality rates, the EU's rapid population growth was mainly due to the external expansion that had taken place since the end of the Cold War. But in contrast to most cases of expansion in European history, the unique feature of EU expansion was its peaceful nature. Nations had voluntarily joined this new realm, and when doing so they accepted a number of economic, political and social contracts.

This presented no real problem during the first post-Cold War enlargement. The entry of Austria, Finland and Sweden into the EU in 1995 simply meant the arrival of three 'like-minded' countries (liberal democracies for several generations), whose citizens, in fact, enjoyed income levels above the average of the original twelve EU nations. In EU parlance, this meant that the three countries met the three so-called Copenhagen criteria for enlargement: that is, first, stability of democratic institutions; second, a functioning and competitive market economy; and, third, an ability and willingness to adapt to the obligations of EU membership. In fact, the refusal of such countries as Norway and Switzerland to join was in large part based on fears that membership would translate into a net

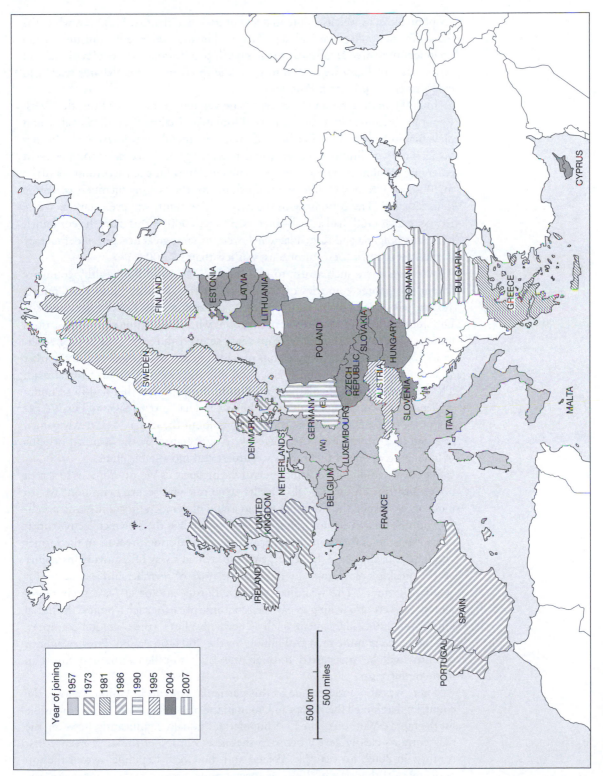

Map 21.1 EEC/EU enlargements

Year of joining
1957
1973
1981
1986
1990
1995
2004
2007

FINLAND
ESTONIA
LATVIA
LITHUANIA
SWEDEN
POLAND
SLOVAKIA
HUNGARY
ROMANIA
BULGARIA
GREECE
CYPRUS
DENMARK
GERMANY (E)
CZECH REPUBLIC
AUSTRIA
SLOVENIA
ITALY
MALTA
NETHERLANDS
GERMANY (W)
LUXEMBOURG
BELGIUM
FRANCE
UNITED KINGDOM
IRELAND
PORTUGAL
SPAIN

500 km
500 miles

economic loss, as well as a potential loss of national identity. However, while the Cold War neutrality that had kept Austria, Finland and Sweden out until 1989 no longer presented an obstacle to membership in 'Europe', issues of national and economic suitability were soon to be at the forefront in the debates related to enlargement into Eastern Europe.

In 2004, in the largest wave of expansion yet, ten countries, Cyprus, the Czech Republic, Estonia, Hungary, Latvia, Lithuania, Malta, Poland, Slovakia and Slovenia, joined the EU. The bulk of these new members were from the former Soviet bloc, with limited experience in democratic governance, and most possessed emerging economies. The average per capita income of the ten accession countries in 2004 was just over €9,000, while the figure for the existing members was more than €20,000. The contrast with the two 2007 entrants was even starker. While EU per capita GDP had actually increased to €26,000 by this date, the combined figure for Bulgaria and Romania, which were also not great beacons of democracy in the eyes of most West Europeans, was less than €9,000.

Why was there such a rush to join the EU? Why did the wealthy countries accept the poorer countries of Eastern and Central Europe into their midst? Where will enlargement end? Such big questions require complex answers. Different countries had different motivations when submitting their applications for accession to the EU, but it seems that the overriding rationale among applicants was twofold: EU membership provided access to a large, wealthy market and assurances against future intervention into their internal affairs from abroad. The last point was particularly significant to the countries that had lived under Soviet domination throughout the Cold War and had proved eager to join NATO in the 1990s. Concerns within these nations about the loss of their newly gained freedom to a faceless EU bureaucracy were outweighed by the assumed benefits of belonging to one of the world's wealthiest and most stable clubs.

The explanation for the willingness of the prosperous West Europeans to accept poor cousins from the East also has its economic and security components. To most of the former, the EU represents an island of democratic stability and a well-functioning market economy, but EU leaders also had their own collective threat perceptions, ones that were dramatically increased during the wars in the former Yugoslavia. In this sense, EU enlargement provided a way of removing instability on the outskirts of 'Europe' by holding the prize of membership as a carrot for 'good behaviour'. The wealthier Western Europeans (or at least their representatives) were also willing to pay the economic price for such a policy: the initial bill for the 2004 enlargement, such as new subsidies to the accession countries, was estimated at more than €40 billion for the 2004–06 period. Further billions of euros will be transferred through the EU's so-called structural funds in forthcoming years.

see Chapter 20

There was also another side to this particular equation. As noted above, the countries that joined the European Union in the new millennium were responsible for the rapid expansion of the EU's population. Equally significantly, however, the new entrants clearly gave a boost to the 'new' Europe of the early twenty-first century. In 2007, for example, Poland and the Czech Republic, two of the top performers of the 'class of 2004', enjoyed annual growth rates of approximately

6 per cent, which was double the EU's average. In addition, the accession of the new states provided some older members with access to a new labour force that contributed to economic growth, with Britain and Ireland in particular benefiting from the arrival of East European migrant workers.

This expansion of the EU into Eastern Europe, did not, however, do much to overcome one of the EU's central problems, its ability to take on a global role in the post-Cold War world. Perhaps the biggest challenge for the EU remains the need for a well-defined and commonly accepted interpretation of its Common Foreign and Security Policy (CFSP). Defined in the 1992 Maastricht Treaty as one of the three pillars of the EU, the CFSP has never worked well. The inability of the twelve, fifteen, twenty-five and now twenty-seven countries to co-ordinate their foreign policies is a well-documented fact. The French and the British, for example, continue to bicker over transatlantic relations as much as they did in the 1960s during the presidency of Charles de Gaulle. And it is difficult to imagine how states such as Finland and Portugal, or Malta and Denmark, could have similar security interests.

To be sure, there has intermittently been successful co-ordination, but it has tended to be confined to the economic arena. The EU countries have been increasingly successful in harmonizing their approach over issues of tariffs and trade, for example forming a cohesive group in the negotiations at the World Trade Organization. The EU is also the world's biggest donor of development aid. Originally concentrating on Africa, the EU has developed comprehensive policies for virtually all continents (save North America). In addition, the EU's external relations are characterized by a focus on humanitarian aid and the promotion of human rights. In the autumn of 2007, for example, the EU was quick to condemn human rights abuses and institute economic sanctions after the brutal crackdown by Burma's ruling military junta against widespread pro-democracy protests.

The EU does, however, lack unity and effectiveness when it comes to some of the most pressing international issues of the twenty-first century. It has worked closely with other countries and international organizations on issues like the environment, terrorism, international crime, drug trafficking and illegal immigration, but it lacks the type of collective capacity that may be needed to carry out military operations, an issue that has been on the table ever since the failure of the EDC in the early 1950s. As a result, on most large-scale security issues, such as the intervention in Kosovo in 1999 or Afghanistan after 2001, the EU has yielded to NATO; this, in turn, has naturally prolonged the European countries' reliance upon the United States in the security field.

An added, perhaps the most fundamental, problem is the sheer confusion about where the power lies when it comes to foreign and security policy. Since 1999 the EU has had a high representative for foreign and security policy, but there is also a commissioner for external relations, a Council of Foreign Ministers (in which all twenty-seven member states' foreign ministers meet regularly), as well as a large number of committees. Each country, naturally, has its own specific needs and interests, which further complicates the process of unified decision-making. In fact, although EU leaders agreed in 2004 to create the post of EU foreign minister, the plan remains on hold owing to the rejection by French and Dutch voters of the EU Constitutional Treaty in 2005.

In short, in the international arena the EU has yet to replace the dwindling influence of individual European Powers with something more substantial. National differences and bureaucratic confusion play a major role in explaining the paradox that one of the world's richest regions remains – sixty years after the Treaty of Rome that created the EEC – a virtual dwarf when it comes to global political influence.

The EEC/EU as inspiration: integration in Asia and the Americas

The success of European integration is not just evident in the fact that most of the former members of the Warsaw Pact aspired to membership after the end of the Cold War, for the EU's achievements have also inspired politicians and intellectuals outside Europe. As with the countries of Central and European Europe, what has interested its extra-European admirers has been the ability of integration to bring both political stability and economic growth. With decolonization and superpower rivalry in the Cold War having created profound and long-lasting instability, the potential of regional integration to deliver a respite from territorial disputes and from an unhealthy reliance on the superpowers for trade and security is undoubtedly beguiling.

The first indication that another region might step along the same road came in 1967 with the formation of ASEAN. The idea that South-East Asia might benefit from economic integration was not, however, new. As early as 1945 the British had used their paramount influence in the region to push for a multinational approach towards post-war reconstruction. This culminated in 1950 with the establishment of the Colombo Plan, in which the British Commonwealth and the United States offered economic aid to the newly independent states and colonies of South and South-East Asia. However, contrary to the pattern in Western Europe, where the Marshall Plan proved an important stimulus to economic integration, the Colombo Plan did little to encourage co-operation between the newly independent states. Moreover, integration was impossible in the light of the fact that the region was deeply divided about how to react to the Cold War. Indonesia and Burma, which had both experienced a turbulent journey to independence, were jealous of their newly acquired sovereignty and mistrustful of the West, and thus became enthusiastic advocates of neutralism. Meanwhile, the Philippines, with its close ties to Washington, and Thailand, with its fear of communist control of Indochina, became in 1954 members of the American-dominated **South-East Asian Treaty Organization (SEATO)**.

The first indigenous step towards economic integration came in July 1963 when Malaya, the Philippines and Thailand formed the Association of South-East Asia (ASA). Any further efforts to build on this platform were, however, soon frustrated by the controversy later that year over the creation of Malaysia, which

South-East Asia Treaty Organization (SEATO)
An alliance organized in 1954 by Australia, France, Great Britain, New Zealand, Pakistan, the Philippines, Thailand and the United States. SEATO was created after the Geneva conference on Indochina to prevent further communist gains in the region. However, it proved of little use in the Vietnam War and was disbanded in 1977.

see Chapters 10 and 12

was opposed by the Philippines diplomatically and Indonesia militarily. Two events in 1965–66 helped to break the logjam. First, the United States, in the face of the escalating war in Vietnam, tried to stabilize the region and isolate the communist bacillus by sponsoring the cause of regional economic development and encouraging Japanese capital investment. Second, the South-East Asian states suddenly found themselves in a position to take advantage of this encouragement because the most destabilizing and divisive politician in the region, President Sukarno of Indonesia, was removed from power. Sukarno's ousting and the rise to prominence of General Suharto provided a catalyst for profound change, for Indonesia now emerged as an anti-communist state that was willing to accept Malaysia's existence and to play a decisive part in developing the region. Accordingly, in August 1967 ASA metamorphosed into ASEAN, consisting of Malaysia, Singapore, Thailand, Indonesia and the Philippines.

see Chapter 12

At first ASEAN was a rather loose organization, which concentrated entirely on economic, social and cultural matters. Before too long, however, it was forced to extend its remit into the political field. The stimulus for this was the steady American de-escalation of its presence in South Vietnam. Fearing that this might encourage Soviet and Chinese machinations, in November 1971 the ASEAN states adopted the idea of regional neutralization and declared that South-East Asia was 'a zone of peace, freedom and neutrality'. ASEAN's move towards greater cohesion was then further cemented later in the decade by the Vietnamese invasion of Cambodia in 1978–79, which raised the prospect of a threat to Thai security. ASEAN's ability to talk for the region, its moves to encourage Western capital investment and its average annual economic growth rates of 6–9 per cent meant that it soon found international sponsors. The United States, with its animus towards Vietnam still running high, was willing after 1978 to support the organization's political pretensions, while Japan emerged at this point as its major trading partner and source of international aid, as well as the inspiration for the individual states' development of export-orientated economies.

see Chapter 14

However, while the organization did much to encourage trade and investment, it differed from the EEC in that it lacked any solid institutional base or any outright commitment to the ideal of greater integration and the formal pooling of sovereignty. It was only in 1994 that it finally launched the ASEAN Free Trade Area and it has never followed the EEC/EU's example in regulating agricultural production, allowing for the free movement of labour and introducing a parliament to oversee legislation. Moreover, while it began in the 1990s to espouse the cause of democracy, it has found it difficult to live up to this rhetoric owing to the arrival of new members such as Brunei Darussalam in 1984, Vietnam in 1995, the Lao People's Democratic Republic and Burma in 1997, and Cambodia in 1999.

Moving into the twenty-first century, ASEAN faced two key challenges: first, formulating a security response to the threat emanating from Jemaah Islamiyya (JI), a regional *jihadist* network with links to **al-Qaeda** (see Chapter 22); and second, Burma's lack of progress towards democracy. The authoritarian nature of Burma's military government became the focus of ASEAN discussions as Burma's turn to chair ASEAN in 2006 approached. Burma's military government and its poor human rights record were seen as detrimental to ASEAN interests. It was

al-Qaeda (Arabic: Base) Islamist umbrella organization established by Osama Bin Laden drawing upon the network of international *jihadists* established during the Afghan War to support the *mujahedeen*. Founded as early as 1988, al-Qaeda emerged into the public eye in 1990.

feared that under Burmese chairmanship ASEAN would lose vital trade and economic relations with Western countries which had levied sanctions against Burma's military regime. This would have damaged ASEAN's 'Vision 2020', which saw the organization playing a pivotal role in the international community. In an almost unprecedented fashion, given ASEAN's principle of non-interference in the domestic affairs of its member states, legislators from Malaysia, the Philippines and Singapore urged Burma to withdraw from the chairmanship. At the same time, in an attempt to keep this an 'internal issue', they rejected Western calls to suspend Burma's ASEAN membership. The chairmanship crisis was resolved in July 2005 when Burma's foreign minister requested a postponement so that Burma could focus on national reconciliation. Reconciliation, however, has remained elusive. In September and again in November 2007, pro-democracy demonstrators and Buddhist monks were brutally suppressed as they took to the streets in what was called the 'Saffron Revolution'. While ASEAN condemned the Burmese military government's crackdown and pressed for the release of pro-democracy leaders, it failed to take concrete steps to deal with Burma.

Thus ASEAN has remained rather limited in scope. However, its success both in the political and in the economic field has enabled it to provide a useful foundation for other attempts to develop new international fora. For instance, in the field of security, the rise of China under Deng Xiaoping's leadership led in 1993 to ASEAN seeking to reduce potential international tension by sponsoring the development of an ASEAN Regional Forum (ARF). This organization brings together the main Powers with interests in the region in the hope that a consensus on security issues can be found. In addition, from 1996 biennial conferences were established between the EU and ASEAN. Another regional development came in the economic field with the foundation in 1989 of an organization called Asia-Pacific Economic Co-operation (APEC), which was an Australian initiative with significant American and Japanese support. Again the organization existed primarily as a force that was designed to pave the way for greater trade liberalization, but, as it included the United States, the PRC, Russia and Japan, it also proved another useful forum for consultation and dialogue.

There has also been talk of ambitious plans to move beyond the establishment of regular ASEAN, ARF and APEC summit conferences and to attempt more directly to emulate the work of Schuman, Monnet and Delors. Most notably in December 2005 a summit meeting of Asian-Pacific Powers was held in Kuala Lumpur to investigate the possibility of moving towards the formation of an Asian Community. After a year in which PRC–Japanese relations had fallen to their lowest ebb since relations were opened in 1972, the idea of a move towards an EU-type organization that would overcome past hostilities echoing the reduction of Franco-German rivalry held great attraction. However, the diversity of political ideologies and practices in Asia, to say nothing of the strategic rivalries and huge discrepancies in economic power, made progress extremely difficult to achieve.

In the 1990s the Western Hemisphere also saw a movement towards free trade and regional integration, which were considered by many as the best long-term solutions to Latin America's economic difficulties. The principal and most ambitious attempt to bring about hemispheric integration was the **North**

American Free Trade Agreement (NAFTA). Signed in October 1992, NAFTA brought together the United States, Canada and Mexico into a trading bloc of 370 million people. The three countries pledged to eliminate trade barriers, duties and tariffs over the subsequent fifteen years. Its most substantial impact was on Mexico, for NAFTA opened up the country to American (and Canadian) investment. However, it also raised the spectre of companies moving south to take advantage of cheaper labour, and understandably, American and Canadian labour unions were NAFTA's most persistent foes. In the end, NAFTA did boost the growth of regional trade (American–Mexican trade, for example, doubled between 1993 and 1997, from $83 billion to $157 billion).

NAFTA was, in fact, probably most significant for Mexico. It allowed President Carlos Salinas to push through aggressive economic reforms of privatization and liberalization and, so it was hoped, to move away from the semi-authoritarian rule of the Institutional Revolutionary Party (PRI). Unfortunately for those dreaming of Mexico's 'democratization', Salinas was faced with a sudden explosion of guerrilla warfare when the Zapatista movement in the poor Chiapas region denounced and, in 1994, forcefully opposed both NAFTA and Salinas. The following year Mexico faced a currency crisis that could only be solved with an American-backed IMF bailout of $50 billion. Suddenly, Mexico looked like a Third World country in the midst of a political and economic crisis, rather than a fast-developing democratic partner in the NAFTA bloc. Yet by 1997 the internal stability as well as the economic state of Mexico began to improve, in large part as a result of the boost in the American economy. By the end of the century Mexico, Canada and the United States shared, albeit in differing degrees, in the boom of the late Clinton years. Yet it is worth noting that underneath the façade of prosperity lay a deep undercurrent of poverty: in Mexico, an estimated one-third of the population lived below the poverty line at the end of the millennium. In large part owing to continued discontent within Mexico, the July 2000 elections resulted in the final end of Mexico's one party-rule as the PRI, after seventy-one years, lost the presidency to Vicente Fox Quesada's centre-right National Action Party (PAN).

In the 1990s there was also much talk about extending NAFTA eventually to incorporate all of the Western Hemisphere (generally called WHFTA, the Western Hemisphere Free Trade Area). Many, including President Clinton, spoke of NAFTA as a mere starting point. With many economic analysts predicting a boom in the Latin American economies, the hopes of a hemispheric trading bloc dwarfing that of the European Union were high. Yet, by the end of the decade, there was neither a WHFTA nor an expansion of NAFTA. A number of political and economic obstacles help explain this. First, the Latin American countries, perhaps most significantly Brazil, were concerned that WHFTA might endanger their attempts to diversify their trade portfolios and lead to increased political dependency on the North. Second, NAFTA, unlike the European Union, had little to offer beyond removing trade barriers. There were no provisions for the free movement of people and no political superstructure. This point linked closely with the question of the nature of regimes to be allowed to join a prospective WHFTA. Should membership in a prospective WHFTA be based on political criteria (in the same way as in the EU)? If so, what should one make of Mexico's

North American Free Trade Agreement (NAFTA)
A 1992 accord between Canada, Mexico and the United States establishing a free-trade zone in North America from 1 January 1994. NAFTA immediately lifted tariffs on the majority of goods produced by the signatory nations. It also calls for the gradual elimination of barriers to cross-border investment and to the movement of goods and services between the three countries.

early membership, for as a *de facto* one-party state it hardly constituted a democracy. Last, one needs to stress the continued American reluctance to submit to any sort of supra-governmental authority. Thus, by the end of the 1990s, the talks about WHFTA (or the alternative Free Trade Area of the Americas, FTAA) were in deadlock, a situation made worse by an emerging economic crisis in Latin America that would soon plunge such countries as Argentina into a serious recession. Instead, the concrete results of the free trade movement in the Western Hemisphere were (in addition to NAFTA) limited to such smaller-scale regional free trade zones as the **Mercosur**, the Common Market of the South that linked Argentina, Brazil, Uruguay and Paraguay in 1991.

Mercosur
Or the Southern Cone Common Market. A Latin American trade organization established in 1991 to increase economic co-operation in the eastern part of South America. Full members include Argentina, Brazil, Paraguay and Uruguay. Bolivia and Chile are associate members. Mercosur's goals include the gradual elimination of tariffs between member states and harmonization of external duties.

Conclusion

'Europe will not be made all at once, or according to a single plan'; these words from Robert Schuman's famous declaration that in May 1950 launched the ECSC are symbolic of the nature of post-war European integration. Almost six decades later, building 'Europe' remains a work in process, lacking a clear single-minded direction. Neverthelees the emergence of the EU is an impressive achievement. By 2007 a grouping of previously antagonistic countries had somehow managed to form an entity that, in the end, did represent an island of stability in a perilous and rapidly changing world. The twenty-seven countries of the EU had previously often fought against each other, and even in the Cold War had formed such military (offensive or defensive) alliances as NATO and the Warsaw Pact. By 2007 they were co-operating, belonging to a community that accounted for about a fifth of the world's exports and imports, and more than 30 per cent of the global gross domestic product. While the future of the EU remains uncertain, further enlargements (to Croatia and possibly to Turkey) appeared more or less a certainty. Furthermore, the deepening of integration is similarly on the cards, despite the often negative attitude of the citizens of EU states. While lacking in the global clout reserved for more traditional nation-states like the United States, Russia or China, the EU is clearly an integral part of the global community in the early twenty-first century. Moreover, outside Europe the success of the EU has acted as an inspiration to politicians who have sought greater strength for their countries both economically and politically through regional unity and the pooling of sovereignty. These extra-European institutions have, however, achieved relatively limited success, which only helps to underline the impression that the EU has benefited from a number of distinct advantages that are difficult for others to emulate. The 'European experiment' rested, after all, on the need to overcome the trauma created by two disastrous wars and the threat posed by the Soviet Union. Moreover, it had the advantage that all of its members were committed to liberal democracy and the rule of law, as well as sharing a common culture. Built on these solid foundations, the EU has been able to widen and deepen in a continuous process of evolution, while its imitators, lacking the same base for consensus building, have not made much progress.

Where scholars disagree: realists, liberal inter-governmentalists, functionalists and federalists

The basic debate about European integration focuses on a simple question: how to explain the emergence of the EEC and EU? There are two broad ways of answering the question: by emphasizing the role of member (nation-)states or by stressing the impact of supra-national institutions. The answers reflect the cleavage between those who think that the creation of the common market has been the central outcome of the integration process and those who believe that it is the shared institutions, customs and laws that truly define the 'new Europe'.

Those who maintain that nation-states have and will remain the main movers of the process of integration are, in general, referred to as realists or neo-realists. Their key argument is that the decades of integration have not fundamentally changed the role of the nation-state as the prime actor in European international relations. States are simply pursuing their national interests in a changed context, as maintained by such authors as Kenneth Waltz and John Mearsheimer. Relatively close to the 'realists' are those scholars labelled as 'liberal inter-governmentalists'. Like the realists, they stress the role of individual states, but they also tend to emphasize the domestic political setting in EEC and EU member states as the key determinants of how these nations act within the inter-governmental playing field. A key practitioner of this school of thought is Andrew Moravcsik.

A third broad approach to explaining European integration is usually called functionalism or neo-functionalism. Building upon the theories of Ernst Haas and Leon Lindberg, such scholars explain the integration from the early 1950s to the present as a gradual spillover process. While the original ECSC was limited to two industrial sectors, the functionalists argue, various interest groups and political parties responded to problems in related sectors by pushing to enhance the competence and scope of the Community and the Union. The 'deepening' of integration, such as the move from a common market to a common currency, is often cited as a more recent case that 'proves' the neo-functionalists' argument. Among its most prominent representatives is Stanley Hoffman.

Lastly, there are the federalists. Authors like John Pinder generally maintain that the deepening of integration was not due to some spillover effect but was rather a reflection of the inability of individual governments to deal with a growing number of transnational issues – security, trade, environment – without close co-operation. The federalists also stress the idealistic aspects of the process of European integration, namely the fact that democratic governance is at the heart of the integration experience. Perhaps more than the analysts in other groups, the federalists are concerned about the so-called democratic deficit within the European Union. This seems like a legitimate concern, for if European integration is simply a modern expression of nationalism it is based upon shaky ground.

Recommended reading

Much has been written about European integration, but a great deal of it remains too detailed for a general audience. Perhaps the best general overviews are John Gillingham, *European Integration 1950–2003: Superstate or New Market Economy?* (Cambridge, 2003), John Pinder, *The European Union: A Very Short Introduction* (Oxford, 2007) and Pinder, *The Building of the European Union* (Oxford, 1999). Derek Urwin, *The Community of Europe: A History of European Integration since 1945* (London, 1994) offers a slightly dated survey of the history of integration, while Ben Rosamond (ed.), *Theories of European Integration* (London, 2000) offers an interesting contrast of the various ways in which scholars have explained the phenomenon of integration. For a magisterial account of Europe's post-war history, including integration, see Tony Judt, *Postwar: A History of Europe since 1945* (New York, 2005). Further examples of overviews include James Dean, *Ending Europe's Wars* (New York, 1994), James E. Goodby, *Europe Undivided* (Washington, DC, 1998), M. Emerson, *Redrawing the Map of Europe* (New York, 1998), Michael J. Brenner, *Multilateralism and Western Security* (New York, 1995), F. Cameron, *The Foreign and Security Policy of the European Union* (London, 1999), A. Mayhew, *Recreating Europe* (New York, 1998), Tom Buchanan, *Europe's Troubled Peace, 1945–2000* (Oxford, 2006) and M. A. Smith and G. Timmins, *Building a Bigger Europe* (Aldershot, 2000). A comprehensive collection of essays discussing the various aspects of the European Union is Helen Wallace and William Wallace (eds), *Policy Making in the European Union* (Oxford, 2000).

For the controversies over British entry into the EEC see N. Piers Ludlow, *Dealing with Britain: The Six and the First UK Application to the EEC* (Cambridge, 1997), James Ellison, *Threatening Europe: Britain and the Creation of the European Community, 1955–1958* (London, 2000) and Helen Parr, *British Policy towards the European Community: Harold Wilson and Britain's World Role, 1964–1967* (Aldershot, 2005). For the 'Empty Chair' crisis, see N. Piers Ludlow, *The European Community and the Crises of the 1960s: Negotiating the Gaullist Challenge.* (London, 2006). For the Maastricht Treaty see Cole Mazzucelli, *France and Germany at Maastricht: Politics and Negotiations to Create the European Union* (London, 1999).

The most detailed analyses of the EU's foreign policy include Paolo Foradori, *Managing a Multilevel Foreign Policy: The EU in International Affairs* (Lanham, MD, 2007), Cameron Fraser, *An Introduction to European Foreign Policy* (London, 2007), Neil Winn and Christopher Lord, *EU Foreign Policy beyond the Nation-State* (London, 2001) and Simon Nuttall, *European Foreign Policy* (Oxford, 2000). European integration in a global context is discussed in a number of books. See, for example, David Calleo, *Rethinking Europe's Future* (Princeton, NJ, 2001) and Gregory Treverton, *America, Germany, and the Future of Europe* (Princeton, NJ, 1992). There is no shortage of works on the development and impact of European integration. For an account exploring America's role in this development, see Geir Lundestad, *'Empire' by Integration* (New York, 1997). For an influential perspective on the transatlantic relationship, see Thomas Risse-

Kappen, *Cooperation among Democracies: The European Influence on US Foreign Policy* (Princeton, NJ, 1995).

For studies of ASEAN see Jurgen Haacke, *ASEAN's Diplomatic and Security Culture: Origins, Developments and Prospects* (London, 2003), David Jones, *ASEAN and East Asian International Relations: Regional Delusion* (Northampton, MA, 2006) and Shaun Narine, *Explaining ASEAN: Regionalism in Southeast Asia* (Boulder, CO, 2002). In regard to ASEAN's relations with Japan, see Sueo Sudo, *The Fukuda Doctrine and ASEAN* (Singapore, 1992). See also P. Korhonen, *Japan and Asia Pacific Integration: Pacific Romances 1968–1996* (London, 1998). On NAFTA and free trade see George Grayson, *The North American Free Trade Agreement* (Lanham, MD, 1995), Barry Bosworth *et al.*, *Coming Together? Mexico–US Relations* (Washington, DC, 1997) and Silvia Saborio, *The Premise and the Promise: Free Trade in the Americas* (New Brunswick, NJ, 1992).

CHAPTER TWENTY-TWO

The war on terror in a globalized world

Introduction

In 2001 Afghanistan, a state which had sunk back into isolation and relative obscurity following its high profile in the closing decade of the Cold War, suddenly became the focus of the world's attention. The reason for this was that the attacks on the World Trade Center in New York and the Pentagon in Washington on 11 September 2001 were quickly traced back to **al-Qaeda**, headed by Saudi-born Islamic militant Osama Bin Laden, who had been provided with sanctuary by Afghanistan's ruling **Taliban** movement. Determined to seize Bin Laden and destroy al-Qaeda, an American-led military campaign was launched to dislodge the Taliban. Together with the broader 'war on terror', which focused on cutting the logistical and financial links between Islamic militants, this resulted in the capture or arrest of hundreds of terrorist suspects (some of whom were sent to, of all places, the American base in Guantanamo Bay, Cuba). America's **NATO** allies, invoking Article 5 of the Alliance's charter for the first time in history, quickly lined up with the United States.

In the period following the events of 11 September 2001 the troubles with the 'war on terror' have proved manifold. In a few years the United States went from being the champion of a righteous cause to occupying a position where many in the world saw it as being the major source of much of the globe's problems. One reason for this was that the Bush administration's basic stance towards inter-

see Chapter 19

al-Qaeda (Arabic: Base) Islamist umbrella organization established by Osama Bin Laden drawing upon the network of international *jihadists* established during the Afghan War to support the *mujahedeen*. Founded as early as 1988, al-Qaeda emerged into the public eye in 1990.

national affairs was summed up in the immortal phrase of the president: 'you're with us or you're against us'. In other words, no grey zones were to be allowed as the United States and its willing allies went on a modern crusade to extinguish terrorism and spread democracy to the Middle East. Thus, the Bush administration, buoyed by an electorate craving action against what former US Secretary of Defense Donald Rumsfeld once characterized as 'evil-doers', brushed aside international organizations and those stressing the need for diplomacy and multilateralism.

Unfortunately, there were, by 2008, few signs that this largely unilateral effort to reshape global politics was succeeding and that the 'evil-doers' were approaching extinction. By this date the United States had more than 150,000 troops in Iraq and faced a chaotic situation that brought back memories of the débâcle in Vietnam, not least to American public opinion which began to turn against the war effort. Meanwhile Afghanistan was witnessing a resurgence of the Taliban, which in turn put the NATO alliance under strain, as many of its members were reluctant to commit troops to this distant and inhospitable battlefield. To be sure, there had been no further terrorist attacks on the United States, but other countries, including Britain and Spain, were the victims of indiscriminate bombings. Moreover, as the United States began to experience what looked like a much overdue economic downturn, its dominant global position was increasingly challenged not only by the economic rise of China, India and even a resurgent Russia, but also by the perception that it was wasting precious resources fighting an enemy that simply could not be defeated through military means.

From 9/11 to 'Iraqi Freedom'

The 11 September 2001 attacks fundamentally changed the American outlook on national and international security. While terrorism was not, of course, a new phenomenon, terrorist attacks on American targets up to this point had either been small scale or relatively unsuccessful. Moreover, when the United States had been a target, attacks had usually been on installations and personnel overseas, not strikes at the 'heart of America'. However, the destruction of the twin towers of the World Trade Center in the heart of New York City revealed the ability of small but dedicated terrorist groups using unconventional weapons and tactics to circumvent the most sophisticated security and defence technology in order to strike at America directly. The images of the collapsing twin towers shook the world to the core. Thus, it is not surprising that the Bush administration declared that the 'war on terror' – the 'first war of the twenty-first century' – was a struggle that had to be fought until complete victory was achieved no matter what the cost. Many even spoke of the 'war on terror' as a new Cold War, a new struggle between good and evil.

The trouble was, however, that whereas during the Cold War the front lines were seemingly clear and the sources of danger and insecurity relatively easily

Taliban (Arabic: students)
Term used to refer to the fundamentalist Muslim militia of Pashtun Afghans and Pakistanis that overthrew the Afghan ethnic coalition government of Ahmad Shah Masood in 1998.

North Atlantic Treaty Organization (NATO)
Established by the North Atlantic Treaty (4 April 1949) signed by Belgium, Canada, Denmark, France, Great Britain, Iceland, Italy, Luxembourg, the Netherlands, Norway, Portugal and the United States. Greece and Turkey entered the alliance in 1952 and the Federal Republic of Germany in 1955. Spain became a full member in 1982. In 1999 the Czech Republic, Hungary and Poland joined in the first post-Cold War expansion, increasing the membership to nineteen countries.

Plate 22.1 New York, 11 September 2001. Plane approaching one of the twin towers just before impact. (Photo: Carmen Taylor, AP/PA Photos)

weapons of mass destruction (WMD)
Commonly understood to be nuclear, chemical and biological weapons. The uses of bacteriological agents and chemicals in warfare pre-date the twentieth century, but nuclear weapons made their first appearance at the end of the Second World War. Of the three, nuclear bombs are the only weapons genuinely capable of the 'mass' destruction of life and property. The term WMD denotes the stigma associated with the development and use of these particular weapons, however, more than offering an accurate description of the scale of their destructive effects. Some experts suggest that chemical, biological and radiological weapons (dirty bombs) should in fact be described as 'weapons of mass terror'.

(although sometimes mistakenly) identified, this new conflict was not only unpredictable, but also essentially borderless and global. While destroying the Taliban stronghold in Afghanistan in the initial campaign of the 'war on terror' proved relatively easy, how to follow up this offensive was far from clear. The most obvious move was to call on friendly states around the world to clamp down on the dozens, if not hundreds, of terrorist organizations in operation and to act to deny them arms, money and any form of sanctuary. That still left, however, the problem of what to do about unfriendly states that either might directly, through overt or secret assistance, or indirectly, by creating regional instability, provide sustenance to terrorists.

Among those states perceived as unfriendly, the United States was most concerned about those that it believed were pursuing the acquisition of **weapons of mass destruction (WMD)**. This was in part because they were perceived as potentially representing a direct threat to American soil, but also because it was held that they might assist terrorist groups in gaining a WMD capability. Unnerved by the events of 11 September, the United States announced in December 2001 that it intended to withdraw from the 1972 Anti-Ballistic Missile Treaty so that it could build a new missile defence system capable of protecting itself from limited nuclear strikes by 'rogue states'. The Bush administration was not, however, thinking only of passive defence, for the president began to argue, in what eventually became known as the 'Bush Doctrine', that the United States reserved to itself the right to take pre-emptive action against potential security threats. In his 2002 State of the Union Address, he went further, accusing Iran, Iraq and North Korea of constituting an 'axis of evil' that presented a clear threat to the international community. The question then was against whom would pre-emption be used first.

Eventually in the autumn of 2002, the Bush administration singled out Iraq from among these pariah states as its main target. It accused Saddam Hussein, who was still reigning supreme despite twelve years of the economic sanctions that had been imposed after the 1990–91 Gulf War, of harbouring WMD and of seeking once again to achieve a nuclear capability. In fact, the Bush administration had been focusing on Iraq even before 11 September, for many among its senior personnel believed that the president's father, George H. W. Bush, had erred in 1991 when he failed to push on to Baghdad and overthrow the Saddam regime. The unfortunate result was that Saddam had been left in power as a constant thorn in the side of American interests in the Middle East. The terrorist attacks in September 2001, however, made the need for action even more pressing, for the removal of Saddam was now seen potentially as a panacea that might alleviate some of the reasons for America's unpopularity in the Middle East. One rationale for acting to remove Saddam was that the 'liberation' of Iraq might initiate a swing towards more democratic government in the region, which would, in turn, generate greater international political stability. In addition, it was felt that the introduction of democracy might produce states that were more receptive to the need for social and economic reform and thus able to address and blunt the frustrations that led people to support the radical Islamist groups. Another issue was the concern that as long as Iraq remained an unpredictable pariah state, then the United States had to maintain large military forces in Saudi Arabia. This was a problem because it allowed al-Qaeda to generate support by declaring that 'infidels' were defiling the country that contained Mecca.

In addition to the sense that the overthrow of Saddam might have positive benefits, there was a feeling that failure to act might only lead to a worsening of the situation. The problem from this perspective was that the sanctions regime that had been overseen by the **United Nations (UN)** since 1990 was coming under increasing international attack for being an ineffective and immoral instrument that hurt ordinary Iraqis while doing nothing to undermine Saddam. The prospect was thus looming into sight of UN sanctions ending and Saddam then being freed from their vice-like grip and being given the space to reactivate his WMD programmes. The combined effect of these considerations, allied to the fact that Bush had overwhelming domestic support for any action that might

see Chapter 20

see Chapter 19

United Nations (UN)
An international organization established after the Second World War to replace the League of Nations. Since its establishment in 1945, its membership has grown to 192 countries.

enhance American security, thus pushed the administration towards the fateful decision to invade Iraq. In October 2002 Bush requested and received the permission of both the House of Representatives and the Senate to use force against Iraq.

Document 22.1

The Bush Doctrine – Excerpts from the National Security Strategy of the United States, 22 September 2002

The United States possesses unprecedented – and unequaled – strength and influence in the world. Sustained by faith in the principles of liberty, and the value of a free society, this position comes with unparalleled responsibilities, obligations, and opportunity. The great strength of this nation must be used to promote a balance of power that favors freedom.

For most of the twentieth century, the world was divided by a great struggle over ideas: destructive totalitarian visions versus freedom and equality.

That great struggle is over. The militant visions of class, nation, and race which promised utopia and delivered misery have been defeated and discredited. America is now threatened less by conquering states than we are by failing ones. We are menaced less by fleets and armies than by catastrophic technologies in the hands of the embittered few. We must defeat these threats to our Nation, allies, and friends.

This is also a time of opportunity for America. We will work to translate this moment of influence into decades of peace, prosperity, and liberty. The US national security strategy will be based on a distinctly American internationalism that reflects the union of our values and our national interests. The aim of this strategy is to help make the world not just safer but better. Our goals on the path to progress are clear: political and economic freedom, peaceful relations with other states, and respect for human dignity.

And this path is not America's alone. It is open to all. To achieve these goals, the United States will:

- champion aspirations for human dignity;
- strengthen alliances to defeat global terrorism and work to prevent attacks against us and our friends;
- work with others to defuse regional conflicts;
- prevent our enemies from threatening us, our allies, and our friends, with weapons of mass destruction;
- ignite a new era of global economic growth through free markets and free trade;
- expand the circle of development by opening societies and building the infrastructure of democracy;
- develop agendas for cooperative action with other main centers of global power; and
- transform America's national security institutions to meet the challenges and opportunities of the twenty-first century.

Source: http://www.whitehouse.gov/nsc/nss.html

The United States did not, however, wish to launch the attacks on Iraq without support from the international community. Thus, Washington, acting under considerable pressure from Britain, took its case to the UN. By taking this route it was, however, putting itself in an awkward position, for if it desired a UN-sanctioned attack against Iraq, then it had to rest its case entirely on the argument that Saddam was clearly guilty of ignoring UN Security Council resolutions pertaining to WMD. It could not make reference to the additional motives for taking extreme action, such as the desire for 'regime change', for this would have been against the terms of the UN Charter. On 12 September 2002 President Bush made his initial case for the overthrow of Saddam Hussein in a speech to the UN Security Council in which he argued that Iraq, which had refused to co-operate with UN weapons inspectors since 1997, was continuing to develop WMD. However, he failed to obtain UN authorization to use force, for influential countries, including France and Germany, were sceptical of the American claims. As a result in November the UN Security Council hammered out a compromise: instead of an invasion, Security Council Resolution 1441 authorized further inspections and threatened 'serious consequences' for Iraq in case of non-compliance. Headed by the Swedish diplomat Hans Blix, the UN's new inspection team arrived in Baghdad on 18 November 2002.

Over the next four months the noose around Iraq tightened. American, British, Australian and selected other countries' troops began arriving in the Persian Gulf region; by mid-March 2003 they numbered about 200,000. In February 2003 Secretary of State Colin Powell made a strong effort to persuade the UN Security Council that authorization for disarming Iraq, which was a euphemism for invasion, was necessary. Powell presented evidence, much of which was later discredited, of an ongoing Iraqi chemical and biological weapons programme as well as outlining Saddam's supposed links to al-Qaeda and other terrorist organizations. The United States, supported by Britain and Spain, then submitted a resolution authorizing the use of force. Faced with a likely veto from France and Russia, the Americans later withdrew the resolution, but the preparations for invasion still went ahead, and on 17 March Bush publicly demanded that Saddam Hussein and his two sons leave Iraq within two days. They did not. However, the remaining UN weapons inspectors took the hint and exited the country.

On 20 March 2003 the American-led attack on Iraq – 'Operation Iraqi Freedom' – commenced despite massive European, and even domestic American, scepticism over the necessity and wisdom of such an undertaking. The military success of the invasion was unquestionable. On 9 April American forces entered Baghdad and on 15 April the invasion was officially deemed to have achieved its goals. On 1 May 2003 President Bush made this clear by giving his infamous 'Mission Accomplished' speech in which he asserted that combat operations were over. He spoke much too soon.

Backfire: Iraq, Afghanistan and the war on terror

Over the next few years members of the Bush administration continued to claim that developments in Iraq were heading in the right direction. Their main argument rested on the belief that after liberation the country was steadily moving towards adopting a democratic system of government. This focus on democracy was important not only because it chimed with American values, but also because it was discovered soon after the invasion that the main justification for the war,

THE WAR ON TERROR

the idea that Saddam Hussein possessed WMD, was wholly unsubstantiated. As no WMD could be found, it was necessary to find another reason for justifying the war, and the Bush administration, with the UN now sidelined, therefore put increasing stress on the idea that the overthrow of Saddam Hussein had created the conditions for establishing a democratic Iraq that could in turn act as a model for the greater Middle East region.

Initially, it did appear as though some progress was being made in this area. After about a year of rule by the so-called Coalition Occupation Authority, Iraq returned to being an independent state in June 2004. Following another transitional phase, a new Iraqi constitution was approved and this was then followed by the December 2005 parliamentary elections. People who had once been forced to engage in phoney exercises in representation manufactured by Saddam Hussein's **Ba'th** Party were now able to select candidates in real elections. An impressive 76.9 per cent of eligible Iraqis cast their vote and no fewer than twelve parties came to be represented in the new House of Representatives. All this was significant, but it took place against the background of an ever-worsening wave of violence that threatened to snuff out the stumbling efforts to create democracy and risked provoking the partition of the country.

The roots of violence were many, but two factors stand out. First, the United States was seen as attempting to impose its own political system on Iraq and its excessive influence was naturally resented. Second, there was the simple fact that if Iraq did become democratic then power would most likely be exercised by the **Shi'a** majority, leaving the **Sunni** minority, which had traditionally dominated the government, on the periphery. Not surprisingly Sunni militants, who included a number of Saddam loyalists, had no intention of being consigned to such a position and tried to derail the democratic process by taking up arms against both the Americans and the Shi'a. Unfortunately poor American decision-making only fanned the flames, for shortly after the occupation began the Iraqi army was disbanded and the Ba'th Party banned, thus providing a huge reservoir of disgruntled, unemployed men with military and political training for the growing insurrection. Worse still was that the existence of American targets and the chance to create hostility between Sunni and Shi'a proved an irresistible lure to al-Qaeda-linked operatives who began to engage in a series of high-profile and extremely bloody terrorist acts. With too few American troops stationed in Iraq to maintain order, by 2006 virtual civil war conditions existed as relentless terrorist attacks and fighting between Sunnis and Shi'as, fuelled by eager elements entering Iraq from the outside, threatened to tear the country apart.

In order to try to bring this situation under control, in 2007 the Bush administration increased troop levels by 20,000, thus bringing the overall size of the American force in Iraq to 150,000. Critics of this so-called 'surge' recalled similar episodes during the Vietnam War in the 1960s, when the addition of extra troops was supposed to turn the tide of the war. By the autumn of 2007 it did appear that the surge had led to a diminution of violent attacks. However, whether this would continue into the long term was most uncertain as the desire for revenge, sectarian hatred and the wish to obstruct any attempt at nation-building continued to motivate a variety of different insurgent groups. All that was clear

Ba'th (Arabic: Renaissance) The name given to the pan-Arab socialist party founded by Michel Aflaq and Salah Bitar in 1947. Its first congress was held in Damascus. It subsequently spread to Lebanon, Jordan and Iraq and eventually resulted in the establishment of two rival Ba'thist regimes, one in Syria since 1963 and one in Iraq 1968–2003.

Shi'a Islam
Muslim sect which emerged out of the struggle over the succession following the death of the Prophet Muhammad. Derived from Shi'a Ali (the Party of Ali) or those who supported the Prophet's son-in-law Ali's accession to the Caliphate. An estimated 15 per cent of Muslims are Shi'a. They are concentrated in the areas of Iran, Iraq and southern Lebanon, with smaller communities scattered throughout the Muslim world.

Sunni Islam
The main body of Muslims, who follow the path (*sunna*) of the Prophet Mohammed and the Quran and the *hadith*.

by October 2007 was that almost 4,000 US military personnel had died in Iraq, the great majority of them after major combat operations were supposedly finished.

For the Iraqis themselves accurate casualty figures were difficult to come by. Some surveys put the number as high as 1.2 million since March 2003; other estimates range from 20–30,000 to 600,000. The other measure that stood as a testimony to the horror of the civil war was the displacement of millions of Iraqis. By 2007 the United Nations High Commissioner for Refugees (UNHCR) reported that 2 million Iraqis had fled to neighbouring countries, while an almost equal number had been internally displaced. This amounted to 16 per cent of the Iraqi population, which meant that Iraq proportionally had more refugees than any other country in the world. In 2006 about 100,000 Iraqis fled to neighbouring Syria and Jordan each month, causing further political destabilization in an already fragile region. Most obviously from the perspective of the 'war on terror', such dislocation did little to persuade anyone that American policies were somehow making the world a safer place. Only one region of Iraq saw relatively little violence and this was the area inhabited predominantly by the Kurdish minority. However, even here there was growing evidence in 2007 that the Kurds were facing problems ahead, for their success was earning them the hostility of Turkey, which feared the possible effect on its own Kurdish minority. Iraq by the end of 2007 thus still faced a troubled future with little prospect of a return to peace.

In Afghanistan the situation was only slightly better. To be sure, a national government was in place, headed since 2002 by the seemingly popular Hamid Kharzai, and by 2007 'only' 445 Americans had been killed, in addition to a number of Britons, Canadians and other nationalities. Afghan casualties, while again difficult to calculate, were estimated to be somewhere between 50,000 and 100,000 since 2001. Afghanistan had produced the largest number of refugees of any single country before 2001; in 2002 1.8 million returned. Despite this, 3 million Afghans were still living outside the country in late 2007. While most of these had not been driven out of their homeland as a result of post-9/11 developments, their unwillingness to return was hardly a vote of confidence in the so-called 'Operation Enduring Freedom'.

The explanation for this lack of interest in returning to Afghanistan was twofold: escalating violence and limited economic opportunity. By 2003, less than two years after being ousted from power, the Taliban began a new insurgency. Sporadic attacks on coalition targets soon became endemic, causing an immense strain between the Afghan government on the one hand and the United States and its allies on the other. In 2007 President Kharzai publicly admitted that he had been seeking peace terms with the Taliban, a quest that proved unsuccessful. Meanwhile a number of NATO countries were making moves to reduce their presence in the country.

The resurgence of the Taliban was complemented by the resurgence of opium as the major cash crop in Afghanistan. Ironically, the Taliban had banned and effectively curtailed the Afghan drug trade when they were in power, but production dramatically increased soon after the US-led invasion began. By 2007 it amounted to more than 50 per cent of the country's gross domestic product. The coalition forces' efforts to attack production were either unsuccessful or even counter-productive, causing further violence over control of the crop. In the end, far from being a success, Afghanistan, which had been the first major front line in the war on terrorism, was suffering from an abundance of insurgents and warlords, both undermining the Kharzai government's fragile hold on power.

In sum, by 2007 the 'war on terror' was hardly going according to plan. Iraq had been described as a central front in this war, but many came to believe, by 2007, that America's presence there was having the exact opposite effect from what had been intended. Instead of becoming a 'poster child for democracy', Iraq had turned into a breeding and training ground for terrorists. In Afghanistan, which had too often been relegated to Iraq's shadow, the old protectors of Osama Bin Laden and al-Qaeda were far from finished. And, while the United States itself had not been hit by terrorist strikes since 2001, many other cities suffered severe blows, most notably London and Madrid. Even in the United States, where support for the invasion of Iraq and other policies had earlier been high, public opinion had turned sour. Fewer than 30 per cent of Americans polled in 2007 thought that the United States and its allies were winning the 'war on terror'. The problems, however, did not end there, for the United States had also to contend with the other members of the 'axis of evil'. And ironically, Iran and North Korea, the two countries that had shared this dubious honour with Iraq, actually did have something that the Iraqis, perhaps because an assiduous sanctions and inspection regime had made it impossible, did not: a realistic possibility of obtaining nuclear weapons.

The challenge of nuclear proliferation

The public justification for the invasion of Iraq, namely the removal of a regime bent on developing WMD, did apparently have an impact on a number of countries. For example, Libya, which had been headed by Colonel Muammar Gaddafi since 1969, announced in December 2003 that it was about to abandon its WMD programme. In May 2006 the United States duly 'rewarded' Libya by restoring diplomatic relations with the North African state (relations had been cut in 1980, after the State Department had placed Libya on a list of countries that support terrorism). Secretary of State Condoleezza Rice's statement on the occasion was revealing:

> We are taking these actions in recognition of Libya's continued commitment to its renunciation of terrorism and the excellent co-operation Libya has provided to the United States and other members of the international community in response to common global threats faced by the civilized world since September 11, 2001.
>
> (Cited at http://www.cnn.com/2006/US/05/15/libya/index.html)

This was a far cry from 1986 when the United States had bombed Libya in retaliation for its support for a series of terrorist acts.

The sudden transformation of Libya from an international pariah to a cooperative partner in the global war on terror stood in stark contrast to the lack of progress with Iran and North Korea. In the years following the invasion of Iraq both countries successfully defied international pressure to abandon their nuclear programmes, thus starkly revealing the limitations on American diplomatic and military power. In the case of North Korea the sheer impossibility of bringing coercive power to bear meant that the United States was forced to agree to give the former aid in return for an apparent suspension of its nuclear programme.

see Chapter 15

A North Korea with nuclear weapons was clearly dangerous, but at least Pyongyang was both strategically and ideologically isolated. The same was not true of Iran, a country that had severed its diplomatic relations with the United States following the 1979 Islamic revolution. Iran was located in an extremely important strategic position. It sat between the two 'war on terror' battlefields of Afghanistan and Iraq and was in range of two of America's most important allies, Israel and Saudi Arabia. Ideologically it saw itself as the champion of the Shi'a faith and had links with the Shi'a community in Iraq and with Hizb'allah in Lebanon. A nuclear-armed Iran thus had the potential to destabilize further an already fragile region. However, the other side of the picture was that, sharing borders with both Iraq and Afghanistan, the leaders of the Islamic Republic of Iran were understandably nervous about the sudden arrival of large numbers of American and other foreign troops near their territory.

see Chapter 19

Publicly Iran's official line was that its nuclear programme, which had been suspended throughout the 1980s, was not aimed at developing weapons. Thus, unlike North Korea, Iran did not leave the **NPT** and, indeed, it engaged in limited co-operation with the UN. Thus, in 2003, following reports that it was engaged in developing nuclear materials at previously non-disclosed facilities, it allowed inspectors from the International Atomic Energy Agency (IAEA), the UN's nuclear watchdog, into the country. However, despite such co-operation, Iran's nuclear programme continued to cause concern around the world, particularly in the United States. One reason for this was the fact that Iran was sitting on large oil reserves, which made external observers deeply suspicious of its claims that it needed to develop nuclear power for peaceful purposes.

Owing to the lack of diplomatic relations between Washington and Teheran, it was the so-called **EU** Three (Britain, France and Germany) that took the lead in negotiations with the Iranian government. However, after two long years of talks, the issue finally came to a head in August 2005 when the Iranians opened a uranium enrichment facility in Isfahan (300 miles south of Teheran). To ward off any escalation of the crisis the EU promptly offered economic and political concessions in return for shutting down the facility, but these were quickly rejected by the newly elected Iranian president, Mahmoud Ahmadinejad, an outspoken critic of the United States. Accordingly, in February 2006 the UN Security Council took up the Iranian nuclear weapons issue and began to discuss the imposition of sanctions.

Nuclear Non-Proliferation Treaty (NPT)
Proposed by the USSR and the United States in 1968, and subsequently approved by the UNGA, the treaty prohibits the proliferation of nuclear weaponry to 'new' countries. It has been ratified by more than 180 nations but has not prevented some states from either openly or secretly acquiring a nuclear weapons capability.

European Union (EU)
A political and economic community of nations formed in 1992 in Maastricht by the signing of the Treaty on European Union (TEU). In addition to the agreements of the European Community, the EU incorporated two inter-governmental – or supra-national – 'pillars' that tie the member states of the EU together: one dealing with common foreign and security policy, and the other with legal affairs. The number of member states of the EU has expanded from twelve in 1992 to twenty-seven in 2007.

However, despite the obvious international concern, by the autumn of 2007 the standoff remained essentially unchanged. In August 2007 Iran and the IAEA negotiated a deal in which the former agreed to a timetable to settle any outstanding issues arising from their nuclear programme, but continued to insist that it had no intention of developing weapons. The Americans and the other Western powers remained sceptical, but there was a division between the permanent members of the UN Security Council. While the Americans received firm support from Britain and, after the election of Nicolas Sarkozy in the spring of 2007, also from the French, this hardly sufficed, for Iran maintained good ties with Russia and China. In fact, the Iranian nuclear programme had benefited from both Russian technical assistance and purchases of Chinese material to help in the uranium enrichment process that is necessary to develop nuclear power. Beijing, in particular, viewed Iranian oil as crucial for its growing energy needs, while Moscow's relatively close links to Teheran were at least partly explained by Russia's increasingly muscular diplomacy in the years following 11 September 2001. The United States, already beleaguered in Iraq and Afghanistan, was in a difficult position: even tougher sanctions against Iran were opposed by Russia's president, Vladmir Putin, who, in October 2007, became the first Russian leader to visit Teheran since Stalin had gone there to meet with Churchill and Roosevelt in 1943.

In the end, the plain truth was that within a few years of the invasion of Iraq, the American ability to deal with what had been defined as a crucial aspect of its national security agenda, namely preventing unfriendly states from acquiring nuclear weapons, had been severely hampered. North Korea had apparently been successful in its nuclear blackmail. Iran remained defiant. President Ahmadinejad's speeches to the UN General Assembly in New York in October 2007 were notable for his references to 'arrogant powers' and his criticism of the continued American occupation of Iraq. He also flatly maintained that the Iranian nuclear issue was 'now closed'. The State Department immediately countered, saying that Ahmadinejad was the only one who thought that way, but it appeared that in 2007, with America's standing in the world severely diminished compared with just a few years earlier, the Iranians had no reason to be concerned about a potential attack. The once-confident 'hyperpower', as the former French foreign minister Hubert Vedrine described the United States, appeared to be in serious need of a fresh approach to its foreign policy.

America's conundrums: hyperpower humbled

By 2008 America's role in the world was at a crossroads. The explosion of scepticism and outright hatred that the Iraqi War and the subsequent occupation had wrought around the globe was worrying American foreign policy analysts. The United States had, some charged in the wake of the invasion of Iraq, become a 'rogue superpower'. Indeed, from 2003 to 2007 global opinion polls showed a steady erosion of goodwill for America around the world. Transatlantic relations were in crisis as many of its key NATO allies opposed the invasion and expressed their consternation over the subsequent occupation in no uncertain terms. Elsewhere, from South America to Africa and Asia, the Bush administration was condemned by popular opinion as well. Highly publicized disclosures of unsavoury American activity, such as the pictures and stories documenting the use of torture in the American-run Abu Ghraib prison in Iraq, played a substantial role in causing America to lose its ability to persuade other countries and peoples by using so-called 'soft power'.

The Americans themselves were apparently the last people to wake up to the realization that their country was perceived by many in the outside world as the twenty-first century's 'evil empire'. Abroad, the resounding victory of George W. Bush in the 2004 US presidential election only further inflamed the critics of Amerian foreign policy. The Democratic candidate, John Kerry, had, after all, made improving America's global standing an important part of his campaign. His defeat seemingly confirmed the continuation of the unilateralist policy of the incumbent president.

In the next few years, however, it became clear that the loss of friends and allies was neither as complete as many argued nor as completely ignored by the Bush administration as most assumed. Some key countries, most significantly Britain, remained steadfast in their support of the United States. Germany and France, perhaps the fiercest critics of the Iraq invasion, began to reconcile with the United States after new leaders assumed power (Angela Merkel in 2005 and Nicolas Sarkozy in 2007). As the news from Iraq continued to be bad, the heads of the most prominent supporters of the invasion and the 'war on terror' (save the president and the vice-president, Dick Cheney) began to roll. Most significantly, after the November 2006 mid-term Congressional elections in which the president's Republican Party suffered a major defeat, Bush ousted Secretary of Defense Donald Rumsfeld. Even before that, however, the administration had started rebuilding relations with European and Asian countries. The president also became a late convert to such multilateral issues as climate change; by September 2007 he was publicly making speeches about the need for a 'new approach' to tackle the global problem which he had, in earlier days, castigated as mere speculation. Bush's 'new diplomacy' is, however, unlikely to win many friends; that task will be left to his successor.

The troubles for America and its role in the world were, however, deeper than Iraq and the 'war on terror'. For the world of 2008 is far different from that predicted in 1991 when pundits talked of a post-Cold War world dominated by a lone American superpower. Terrorism and the American inability to rein in opposition in Iraq and Afghanistan were symptoms of the relative impotence of traditional forms of military power. Meanwhile the defiance of North Korea and Iran was a reminder of the relative impotence of diplomacy and economic sanctions in the modern world and the ability of countries, even small ones, to maintain their independent course even in a globalized world.

Challenges to American dominance of international relations were also emerging from other large nation-states. For example, the United States retained a substantial lead in its military capacities over its closest competitors, but such countries as China and Russia were rapidly moving towards modernization. The former, buoyed by decades of uninterrupted economic growth, was planning its first manned mission to the moon. The latter, encouraged by new-found prosperity based on significant profits from its ample reserves of energy sources (oil and natural gas), was planning an overhaul of its badly demoralized post-Cold War military forces. Neither country saw a world dominated by America as necessarily in its interest. In 2008 some analysts even saw worrying signs of a renewed cold war between the United States and Russia, or between the United States and China. In the end, the United States may well withstand any challenges to its dominant global role. However, as Americans geared up for the 2008 presidential campaign, the combination of uneven globalization and a 'war on terror' that ultimately lacked clear-cut front lines was eroding the 'unprecedented strength and influence' upon which the so-called Bush Doctrine had been based.

Al-Qaeda since 9/11

see Chapter 19

The 11 September 2001 attacks on the World Trade Center in New York and the Pentagon in Washington not only had a profound impact on the victim of the assault but also affected its instigator, al-Qaeda. The unparalleled success of the attacks propelled a hitherto fairly unknown organization into the public eye and on to the international political stage. This increased its popularity in many parts of the Muslim world and resulted in an increase in al-Qaeda recruitment as well as a proliferation of al-Qaeda-inspired Islamist organizations. The attacks also resulted in a heavy-handed US-led military and counter-terror response aimed at capturing Osama Bin Laden and destroying al-Qaeda. Both had the long-term effect of strengthening the organization.

The repeated media exposure of the images of the spectacular collapse of the two towers served as inspiration for like-minded Islamists and those who sought to join al-Qaeda. Not surprisingly, this resulted in similar attacks in other parts of the world by organizations with and without direct links. For instance, in October 2002 **Jemaah Islamiyya** (JI), which had links to al-Qaeda through one of its commanders, Hambali, carried out simultaneous suicide bombings on the island of Bali and in August 2003 bombed the Marriott Hotel in Jakarta. In March 2004 Islamists inspired by al-Qaeda attacked Madrid's commuter train network at rush hour, simultaneously bombing four stations three days before the Spanish elections. The Spanish judiciary was unable to establish a direct link with al-Qaeda. On 7 July 2005 a series of co-ordinated bomb attacks hit London's public transport system, with bombs exploding on three underground trains and one bus. Two weeks later, on 21 July, bombs were again placed on three underground trains and on one bus, but while all four detonators exploded none of the main explosive charges did. In September 2005, al-Qaeda claimed responsibility for the attacks in a video sent to al-Jazeera television station.

Jemaah Islamiyya (JI)
(Arabic: Islamic Community) Southeast Asian Islamist Organization established by Indonesians Abdullah Sunkar and Abu Bakar Ba'ashir in 1995. JI seeks to establish a Southeast Asian Islamic state encompassing Indonesia, Malaysia, Singapore, Brunei, southern Thailand and the southern Philippines through militant means.

While the 'strengthening' effect on al-Qaeda of the World Trade Center attacks was direct, the 'strengthening' effect of the US 'war on terror' was indirect and inadvertent. Indeed, initially, the 2001 US-led invasion of Afghanistan weakened al-Qaeda, for with the toppling of the Taliban government al-Qaeda lost its hosts and its territorial base. However, rather than this facilitating the capture of its leaders and the collapse of the organization, al-Qaeda adapted itself. It adopted a simpler cell-type structure and transformed itself into a more loosely knit network and above all into an idea. Indeed al-Qaeda became one of the most powerful ideas in the Muslim world as its leadership, Bin Laden and his deputy, Ayman Zawaheri, eluded even the most highly trained American 'special forces' units.

One of the key factors which led to a strengthening of al-Qaeda was the weakening of American counter-terror efforts as the US opened another front in 2003 with the invasion of Iraq. This operation diverted resources away from the real 'war on terror', leaving American forces overstretched and thus undermining continuing operations in Afghanistan. Moreover, the removal of Saddam Hussein's authoritarian regime opened up Iraq not just to democratic aspirations but also to Islamist and *jihadi* forces, including al-Qaeda operatives and al-Qaeda sympathizers. The civil war that followed provided a fertile breeding ground for radical Islamist ideas and territorial pockets for *jihadis*.

And last but certainly not least, the US 'war on terror', rather than isolating the extremists by cutting them off from their popular support base, funding and communication, increased Muslim solidarity as its heavy-handedness and lack of political nuance allowed it to be perceived as a 'war on Islam'. This too helped al-Qaeda to strengthen its organization. Thus it is not too surprising that in July 2007 the US government released a report stating that, despite many military campaigns and counter-terror operations against it, al-Qaeda had not only managed to regroup but was, in fact, now stronger than at any time since the 11 September attacks. Al-Qaeda had found refuge in the Afghan–Pakistani tribal border areas, which were *de facto* not under Pakistani state control. There, according to US intelligence, it was conducting training, planning operations and nurturing relations with its affiliates in the Middle East, North Africa and Europe. US intelligence also detected an upsurge in communications and an increased flow of money, raising the possibility of further attacks. Moreover, the continuing political instabilty that dogged Pakistan as President Musharaf laboured to stay in power did not suggest that al-Qaeda's territorial sanctuary was likely to be effectively challenged. If anything, the turmoil in Pakistan appeared to offer al-Qaeda a further breeding ground for new recruits and a promising arena for challenging American interests.

jihad
Struggle in the way of God. A fundamental tenet of Islam consisting of the Greater *jihad* which is above all a personal struggle to be a better Muslim and the Lesser *jihad* which is physical fighting.

The 'war on terror' in South-East Asia

The 'war on terror' was not, however, limited to the Middle East and what the world perceived as the heartland of the Muslim faith, for the rise of political Islam

535

also had repercussions for other regions less commonly associated with radical Islamic beliefs. This phenomenon was most evident in South-East Asia. On 12 October 2002 simultaneous car bombs exploded in the Sari Club and Paddy's Pub in the tourist area of Kuta on the island of Bali in Indonesia. The explosions killed 202 people, of whom 164 were foreign nationals. The bombings were attributed to Jemaah Islamiyya (JI), a transnational Islamist organization with links to al-Qaeda. Bali was targeted for two key reasons: first, it was a crucial economic pillar of the Indonesian Republic, a 'secular' state that JI sought to destroy; second, Kuta was an area frequented by Western tourists and thus a symbolic target.

The bombings shook up a hitherto complacent Indonesian government, which had previously denied the existence of JI. It placed formulating a response to JI on the top of the security agenda of the **Association of South-East Asian Nations (ASEAN)** because of JI's regional aims and structure. These aims are to establish a South-East Asian Islamic state encompassing Indonesia, Malaysia, Singapore, Brunei, the Philippines and Thailand, as well as purifying Islam within those countries. JI is structured hierarchically under an emir across four regions or *mantiqis*. *Mantiqi* I covers Singapore and Malaysia and its main function is economic. *Mantiqi* II covers Indonesia except for Sulawesi; this was designated as the arena of *jihad*. *Mantiqi* III covers Mindanao and Sulawesi and its purpose is training. *Mantiqi* IV covers Papua and Australia and its function is fundraising.

While ASEAN increased security and intelligence co-operation in order to deal with JI it was left up to the individual member states to devise their own counter-terror strategies. As a result there was no uniform approach. The Philippines, in whose southern territories most of JI's training camps were located, decided to confront JI militarily. The counter-terror efforts thus became integrated into the ongoing low-intensity conflict of the Manila government with the Moro Islamic Liberation Front. As a predominantly Christian country, the Philippines had no difficulty accepting American military aid, including troops. However, President Gloria Macagapal Arroyo made it very clear that in doing so the Philippines was not joining the global 'war on terror' but rather the United States was contributing to a local 'war on terror' that pre-dated the American effort by three decades. The aim of the military operations was the total destruction of JI's camps in order to remove its training capacity.

Singapore's counter-terror strategy revolved around the already existing Internal Security Act (ISA), which allowed for surveillance and arrests of terror suspects. The city-state's approach resulted from the discovery of a JI plan to attack US and Israeli targets in Singapore in December 2001. Increased surveillance and pre-emptive arrests were accompanied by a rethinking of non-Muslim–Muslim relations, increased efforts to include Singapore's Muslim minority more comprehensively in all aspects of life, and a conscious decision to reach out to the families of the arrested *jihadis* and to support them. Like Singapore, Malaysia based its strategy on its ISA. However, unlike Singapore, Malaysia had to balance counter-terror against the Muslim sensitivities of its own population and the government's own Islamic credentials. This was made somewhat easier by the fact that Malaysia had not been targeted directly by JI. Thus the country was able to focus on dismantling JI's front businesses and financial network and to arrest

see Chapter 19

Association of South-East Asian Nations (ASEAN) Organization founded in 1967 by Indonesia, Malaysia, the Philippines, Singapore and Thailand to provide a forum for regional economic co-operation. From 1979 it took on more of a political and security role. Membership increased with the accession of Brunei in 1984, Vietnam in 1995, Burma in 1997 and Cambodia in 1999.

suspected JI members, while at the same time vehemently condemning the US and the West for their involvement in Afghanistan and Iraq.

Indonesia faced the greatest obstacles in formulating a counter-terror strategy. The country had been heavily hit by the 1997 Asian financial crisis and was still in the process of its transition to democracy after the fall of Suharto in 1998. As part of this reform process the military's power had been reduced and any involvement of the army in counter-terrorism was ruled out because there were fears that the armed forces might use such a role in order to regain their old position. Similarly the idea of an ISA was rejected because it could be abused by the security sector. Counter-terror thus became the domain of the police, which was undergoing a 'civilianization' and reform process and whose capacity was limited in both resources and personnel. Moreover, like Malaysia, the Indonesian government had to tread carefully as it was a predominantly Muslim country with very vocal Islamist opposition groups. At the same time it had to act, as Indonesia was JI's arena of *jihad* and the country was thus faced with more violence than any other state. Indeed, as Indonesian investigators soon discovered, the Bali bombings were not the first JI attacks. They had been preceded by a car bomb attack on Jakarta's Istiqlal mosque in April 1999, a bomb attack on the residence of the Philippine ambassador in August 2000, a car bomb attack on the Jakarta stock exchange in September 2000, bomb attacks on eleven churches across the country on 24 December 2000 and on two churches in Jakarta in July 2001, another bomb attack on a church in November 2001, and a grenade attack near the US embassy warehouse in Jakarta in September 2002. Until the Bali bombings, these attacks were seen as unconnected and were attributed to elements disgruntled with the reform or political process. After the 2002 Bali bombings JI moved on to higher-profile targets. In August 2003 it bombed the Marriott Hotel in Jakarta, in September 2004 it bombed the Australian embassy in Jakarta, and in 2005 it struck Bali again.

The Indonesian government adopted what it called a 'soft' counter-terror approach. At the heart of this approach were intelligence gathering and arrests, followed by prosecution and trials, jail sentences and even death sentences. This was accompanied by an innovative de-radicalization programme through which the Indonesian police was able to gain further insight into the JI network as well as obtaining crucial intelligence, which allowed them to arrest operational commander Abu Dujana in 2006. It is to this arrest that Indonesia attributes the lack of JI activity in 2006 and 2007.

While Indonesia was criticized by the West for treading too softly, its counter-terror approach nevertheless produced results. Since 2002 more than 200 JI members have been arrested, including several of the organization's emirs and operational commanders. The primary impact upon JI was the disruption of its *mantiqi* structure and internal factionalization. Following the arrest and conviction, albeit for immigration offences, of JI co-founder Abu Bakar Ba'asyir, a split emerged between Ba'asyir's followers and a group of younger militants. The former wanted to open up the movement through the Majles Mujahedin Indonesia and to take advantage of the new post-Suharto openness to struggle politically for an Islamic state, while the latter wanted to step up the underground, military struggle. This factionalization has made it both easier and more difficult to deal with JI. On the one hand, intelligence has been forthcoming from JI members on the more radical elements. On the other hand, the disruption of the structure has meant that JI now mainly exists in cell form, which has made it more difficult to track down, infiltrate and dismantle.

Conclusion: where to next?

Although the debate over war against Iraq and the ongoing struggle against terrorism have commanded most headlines since 11 September 2001, a brief survey of the state of the world in the early twenty-first century does not necessarily lead to the conclusion that the most significant structural issue facing the globe revolves around the fate of dictators or terrorists. Terrorism and the threat of WMD are bound to remain a constant scourge in the search for a stable and secure world order in the new century but, as a few observers have noted, terrorism was but a symptom of a deeper conflict that was pitting the secular West (or, some argued, the Judaeo-Christian West) against the fundamentalist (or Islamic) East. The 'war on terror' would be, according to such logic, not only the first war of the twenty-first century, but one bound to escalate into a 'clash of civilizations', lending credence to a thesis first advanced by Samuel Huntington in 1993.

Not everyone agreed with such a pessimistic analysis; indeed, some pointed out that the state of the world was, in fact, better than ever before. As the American political scientist Michael Mandelbaum argued in late 2002, a triad of liberal ideas – peace, democracy and free markets – represented the true underpinnings of the world in the new century. None of the political ideas that had challenged democracy had been successful in the twentieth century, he argued. Communism and Nazism had both been defeated, the former by the powerful and mutually reinforcing combination of democratic ideals and the prosperity provided by free markets, and the latter by force of arms. Western ideas, developed in the nineteenth century and forcefully espoused by Woodrow Wilson in the aftermath of the First World War, had finally triumphed and were threatening to engulf even such countries as China. Peace, democracy and free markets, Mandelbaum maintains, are not only the 'American way' at the dawn of the twenty-first century, they are the global wave of the present and the future.

Is the world of the twenty-first century headed for a 'clash of civilizations' or a triumph of liberal ideas? Historians, by and large, are hesitant to make such judgements. For while it is easy to look at the past and explain how certain developments were seemingly 'inevitable', it is always hazardous to presume that one can predict the future with any precision. Yet it might be worthwhile, in closing, to consider the world of the early twenty-first century as compared with the world of the early 1900s.

To some extent, the early twenty-first-century world actually looks uncannily similar to the world a century earlier. Economically, despite the promise of the beneficial effects of **globalization**, the world remains unequal and polarized. On the one hand, what many writers call the 'core' countries of the West – those in North America and Western Europe, and Japan – experience levels of prosperity that would have been unimaginable a century earlier. On the other hand, the majority of the globe's population, who live in what had been dubbed the **Third World** during the Cold War and had belonged to various European empires before the Second World War, remain largely marginalized. While many Western observers hail free markets as the 'universally accepted' principle for the organization of economic life in the aftermath of the Cold War, the benefits of neo-liberalism are hardly evident to the unemployed in Brazil and Argentina, or the starving farmers in Sub-Saharan Africa. Moreover, while many in China may have benefited greatly from the transformation of their country's state-run economy, millions of others, particularly in rural areas, have plunged deeper into poverty. Similar developments can be observed in other communist or post-communist states (from Russia to Vietnam), as well as in the most populous democracy of the globe (India). In short, while free (or relatively free) markets offer the only broadly accepted principle for organizing economic life in the early twenty-first century, they have yet to offer a panacea. Much as it was in the early 1900s, and very much along similar geographical lines, the world's wealth and economic power remain unequally distributed.

Therein lies perhaps the greatest challenge for the new century. As the experience of the twentieth century showed, such unequal distribution of wealth and power, whether internal or international, could easily act as the catalyst for conflict and change. The great communist revolutions of the twentieth century, in Russia and China, were both made possible by the existence of large groups of disaffected people. **Nazi** Germany would hardly have emerged without the economic turmoil of the late 1920s. In contrast, the lack of war among the previously quarrelsome European powers after 1945 can, at least in part, be explained by the shared prosperity resulting from European integration. Whether such 'war-free zones' can be replicated elsewhere is an open question, but in areas lacking relative prosperity it appears unlikely.

The twentieth century was one of persistent change and intermittent conflict. It saw the rise and fall of Nazism and communism, the collapse of empires and a rapid increase in the number of independent states. It witnessed the development of the nuclear bomb but also the establishment of the first truly international organizations, the **League of Nations** and, in particular, the United Nations. It was a century that saw highly systematic and bureaucratized forms of genocide as exemplified by the **Holocaust** and ethnic cleansing in Bosnia and by the butchering of human lives in the killing fields of Cambodia or Rwanda. It saw the forced labour camps in Siberia, but also the virtual eradication of war from the European continent after 1945. Two world wars and countless other military conflicts killed millions around the globe, but the century was also an age of impressive innovations in every field of human endeavour, some of the most far-reaching in medicine, science and computer technology.

The twentieth century was, in short, an amalgam of human experience, a hybrid of disaster and triumph. It is likely that in this essential way the twenty-

---

globalization
The cultural, social and economic changes caused by the growth of international trade, the rapid transfer of investment capital and the development of high-speed global communications.

Third World
A collective term of French origin for those states that are part of neither the developed capitalist world nor the communist bloc. It includes the states of Latin America, Africa, the Middle East, South Asia and South-East Asia. Also referred to as 'the South' in contrast to the developed 'North'.

Nazis (or Nazi Party)
The abbreviation for the National Socialist German Workers Party (*Nationalsozialistische Deutsche Arbeiterpartei* (NSDAP)). It was founded in October 1918 as the German Workers Party by the German politician Anton Drexler to oppose both capitalism and Marxism. It took on its more notorious title in February 1920. One year later Hitler became the Nazi Party Führer (German: leader).

League of Nations
An international organization established in 1919 by the peace treaties that ended the First World War. Its purpose was to promote international peace through collective security and to organize conferences on economic and disarmament issues. It was formally dissolved in 1946.

Holocaust
The systematic mass murder of six million European Jews by the Nazis between 1939 and 1945.

first century, even as its specific characteristics are bound to be unique, will be very much like its predecessor.

Recommended reading

For general discussions on terrorism see Walter Reich, *Origins of Terrorism: Psychologies, Ideologies, Theologies, States of Mind* (Washington, DC, 1998), Bruce Hoffman, *Inside Terrorism* (New York, 2006), Mark Sageman, *Understanding Terror Networks* (Philadelphia, PA, 2004) and Fawaz A. Gerges, *The Far Enemy: Why Jihad went Global* (Cambridge, 2005). The literature on 9/11 is already a virtual subfield of its own. For a relatively sober collection of essays see Mary L. Dudziak (ed.), *September 11 in History: A Watershed Moment?* (Raleigh, VA, 2003).

On US foreign policy and the Bush Doctrine see Ivo H. Daalder and James M. Lindsay, *America Unbound: The Bush Revolution in Foreign Policy* (New York, 2005), Paul Pillar, *Terrorism and US Foreign Policy* (Washington, DC, 2004) and Ron Suskind, *The One Percent Doctrine: Deep inside America's Pursuit of its Enemies since 9/11* (New York, 2006). The trilogy by Bob Woodward offers an entertaining if not always fully reliable narrative account of the Bush administration's conduct of the war on terror: *Bush at War*, *Plan of Attack* and *State of Denial* (New York, 2002, 2004, 2006). David J. Rothkopf, *Running the World* (New York, 2006) places the decision-making in the Bush White House into a broader historical perspective. For another type of overview, focusing on the notion of empire and where America may be heading, see Niall Ferguson, *Colossus: The Price of America's Empire* (New York, 2004).

The literature on the invasion of Iraq is already vast. Among the most thought-provoking are Michael Gordon, *Cobra II: The Inside Story of the Invasion and Occupation of Iraq* (New York, 2007), Michael Isikoff and David Corn, *Hubris: The Inside Story of Spin, Scandal, and the Selling of the Iraq War* (New York, 2007), Thomas Ricks, *Fiasco: The American Military Adventure in Iraq* (London, 2006), Peter Galbraith, *The End of Iraq: How American Incompetence Created a War without End* (New York, 2007) and George Packer, *The Assassins' Gate: America in Iraq* (New York, 2007). As the titles of these works indicate, the war is not particularly popular with scholars and journalists.

The same is true of the first front line in the war on terror. Afghanistan is the focus of Nick B. Mills, *Karzai: The Failing American Intervention and the Struggle for Afghanistan* (New York, 2007) and Sonali Kolhatkar, James Ingalls and David Barsamian, *Bleeding Afghanistan: Washington, Warlords, and the Propaganda of Silence* (New York, 2006). A view from inside Afghanistan can be gleaned from Sarah Chayes, *The Punishment of Virtue: Inside Afghanistan after the Taliban* (New York, 2006) and Ann Jones, *Kabul in Winter: Without Peace in Afghanistan* (New York, 2007).

The issue of nuclear proliferation is dealt with extensively in Kurt M. Campbell, Robert Einhorn and Mitchell Reiss (eds), *The Nuclear Tipping Point: Why States*

Reconsider their Nuclear Choices (Washington, DC, 2004), Joseph Cirincione, *Bomb Scare: The History and Future of Nuclear Weapons* (New York, 2007) and Graham Allison, *Nuclear Terrorism: The Ultimate Preventable Catastrophe* (New York, 2005). An overall discussion of the potential threat of WMD is Joseph Cirincione, John B. Wolfstahl and Miriam Rajkumar, *Deadly Arsenals: Nuclear, Biological and Chemical Threats* (New York, 2005).

For the Iranian nuclear programme see Ali Ansari, *Confronting Iran: The Failure of American Policy and the Next Great Crisis in the Middle East* (New York, 2006), Shahram Chubin, *Iran's Nuclear Ambitions* (New York, 2006), Alireza Jafarzadeh, *The Iran Threat: President Ahmadinejad and the Coming Nuclear Crisis* (New York, 2007), Kenneth M. Pollack, *The Persian Puzzle: The Conflict between Iran and America* (New York, 2005) and Kenneth M. Timmerman, *Countdown to Crisis: The Coming Nuclear Showdown with Iran* (New York, 2006).

For readings on al-Qaeda and on the 'war on terror' in South-East Asia, see the recommended reading section in Chapter 19.

Glossary

Abyssinian War On 3 October 1935, the brutal conquest of Abyssinia by Italian troops launched from neighbouring Italian Eritrea began. It arose from Mussolini's desire to exercise the martial prowess of his Fascist regime and thereby further his revolution. The war was popular inside Italy as revenge for Italy's defeat at Adowa in 1896. Emperor Haile Selassie appealed to the League of Nations, but his small kingdom was abandoned to its fate. The war ended on 5 May 1936.

Afrikaners The white population in South Africa who are of Dutch descent, also known as Boers.

Aliyah (Hebrew: Ascent) The wave of Jewish immigration to Palestine and, later, to Israel.

Alliance for Progress The American assistance programme for Latin America begun in 1961, which called for an annual increase of 2.5 per cent in per capita income, the establishment of democratic governments, more equitable income distribution, land reform, and economic and social planning. Latin American countries (excluding Cuba) pledged $80 billion over ten years, while the United States pledged $20 billion. After a decade of mixed results, the Alliance was disbanded in 1973.

al-Qaeda (Arabic: Base) Islamist umbrella organization established by Osama Bin Laden, drawing upon the network of international *jihadists* established during the Afghan War to support the *mujahedeen*. Founded as early as 1988, al-Qaeda emerged into the public eye in 1990.

Anschluss The political union of Germany and Austria. *Anschluss* was specifically prohibited under the Versailles Treaty, but was carried out by Hitler in March 1938 without any resistance from the victors of the First World War.

Anti-Ballistic Missile (ABM) Treaty An agreement between the United States and the USSR signed on 26 May 1972, limiting the number of ABM deployment areas, launchers and interceptors. The United States withdrew from the treaty in 2002.

anti-Semitism A word which appeared in Europe around 1860. With it, the attack on Jews was based no longer on grounds of creed but on those of race. Its manifestations include pogroms in nineteenth-century Eastern Europe and the systematic murder of an estimated six million Jews by Nazi Germany between 1939 and 1945.

apartheid The Afrikaans word for racial segregation. Between 1948 and 1990 'apartheid' was the ideology of the Nationalist Party in South Africa.

appeasement A foreign policy designed to remove the sources of conflict in international affairs through negotiation. Since the outbreak of the Second World War, the word has taken on the pejorative meaning of the spineless and fruitless pursuit of peace through concessions to aggressors. In the 1930s, most British and French officials saw appeasement as a twin-track policy designed to remove the causes of conflict with Germany and Italy, while at the same time allowing for the buildup of sufficient military and financial power to bargain with the dictators from a position of strength.

Arab nationalism The belief that all Arabic-speakers form a nation that should be independent and united.

Arab Revolt Peasant uprising in Palestine between 1936 and 1939 characterized by strikes and civil disobedience during the first year and violence against the British and Zionists during the subsequent two years.

Article 9 Article in the Japanese constitution of 1947 barring the country from going to war and possessing armed forces. Later interpreted to mean that Japan still had the right to self-defence and could maintain armed forces designed with that purpose in mind.

Association of South-East Asian Nations (ASEAN) Organization founded in 1967 by Indonesia, Malaysia, the Philippines, Singapore and Thailand to provide a forum for regional economic co-operation. From 1979 it took on more of a political and security role. Membership increased with the accession of Brunei in 1984, Vietnam in 1995, Burma in 1997 and Cambodia in 1999.

Atlantic Charter A document signed by Franklin Roosevelt and Winston Churchill in August 1941 which committed the United States and Britain to support democracy, self-determination and the liberalization of international trade.

autarky A policy that aims at achieving national economic self-sufficiency. It is commonly associated with the economic programmes espoused by Germany, Italy and Japan in the 1930s and 1940s.

Axis A term coined originally by Mussolini in November 1936 to describe the relationship between Fascist Italy and Nazi Germany. The German–Italian Axis was reinforced by the so-called Pact of Steel signed by Rome and Berlin in May 1939. More broadly speaking, the term is often used (as in Chapter 8 of this book) to refer to the relationship between Germany, Italy and Japan. These three Powers were formally linked by the German–Japanese Anti-Comintern Pact of November 1936, which Italy signed one year later, and the Tripartite Pact of September 1940.

Bandung Afro-Asian Conference The conference of Asian and African states held in Bandung in Indonesia in 1955. Commonly seen as the first move towards the establishment of a Third World lobby in international politics.

Ba'th (Arabic: Renaissance) The name given to the pan-Arab socialist party founded by Michel Aflaq and Salah Bitar in 1947. Its first congress was held in Damascus. It subsequently spread to Lebanon, Jordan and Iraq and eventually resulted in the establishment of two rival Ba'thist regimes, one in Syria since 1963 and one in Iraq 1968–2003.

Bay of Pigs   The site on 17 April 1961 of an unsuccessful invasion of Cuba by Cuban exiles opposed to the Castro regime. It had the support of the American government and the CIA was heavily involved in its planning. By 20 April most exiles were either killed or captured. The failed invasion was the first major foreign policy act of the Kennedy administration and provoked anti-American demonstrations in Latin America and Europe and further embittered American–Cuban relations.

Black September   The confrontation between the Jordanian army and Palestinian guerrillas in Jordan in September 1970, as a result of which the PLO was expelled from Jordan and relocated its headquarters to Beirut, Lebanon.

Bolsheviks   Originally in 1903 a faction led by Lenin within the Russian Social Democratic Party, over time the Bolsheviks became a separate party and led the October 1917 revolution in Russia. After this 'Bolsheviks' was used as a shorthand to refer to the Soviet government and communists in general.

Bretton Woods   The site of an inter-Allied conference held in 1944 to discuss the post-war international economic order. The conference led to the establishment of the IMF and the World Bank. In the post-war era the links between these two institutions, the establishment of GATT and the convertibility of the dollar into gold were known as the Bretton Woods system. After the dollar's devaluation in 1971 the world moved to a system of floating exchange rates.

Brezhnev Doctrine   The 'doctrine' expounded by Leonid Brezhnev in November 1968 affirming the right of the Soviet Union to intervene in the affairs of communist countries in order to protect communism.

Caliphate   The office of the successor to the Prophet Muhammad in his political and social functions. The Caliphate was abolished by the Turkish president Mustafa Kemal Atatürk in 1924 after the dismemberment of the Ottoman Empire and the establishment of the Turkish Republic.

collective security   The principle of maintaining peace between states by mobilizing international opinion to condemn aggression. Commonly seen as one of the chief purposes of international organizations such as the League of Nations and the United Nations.

COMECON   The Council for Mutual Economic Assistance, a Soviet-dominated economic organization founded in 1949 to co-ordinate economic strategy and trade within the communist world.

Cominform   The Communist Information Bureau, organized in 1947 and dissolved in 1956. Dominated by the USSR, the Cominform attempted to re-establish the links between the European communist parties that had lapsed since the dissolution of the Comintern. The major event in the Cominform's history was when it expelled Yugoslavia in 1948.

Comintern   The Communist or Third International founded in Moscow in 1919 as an organization to direct and support the activities of communist parties outside Russia. It was abolished in 1943 in a short-lived effort by Stalin to reassure Britain and the United States that the Soviet Union no longer sought to export Marxism-Leninism.

Commonwealth, The   An organization of independent self-governing states linked by their common ties to the former British Empire.

Concert of Europe   The nineteenth-century European system of regulation of international affairs by the Great Powers. Although much of the historical literature argues that the system was successful in keeping the general peace of Europe because it was based on a 'balance of power', more recent work has stressed the importance of shared rules of conduct, values, goals and diplomatic practices in relations between the Great Powers.

Conference on Security and Co-operation in Europe (CSCE)   An agreement signed in Helsinki, Finland, in 1975, by thirty-five countries including the United States and the Soviet Union, which promoted human rights as well as co-operation in economic, social and cultural progress. It was succeeded in the 1990s by the Organization for Security and Co-operation in Europe, which has fifty-five members, including all European nations, all former republics of the Soviet Union, the United States and Canada.

Congo Crisis   The civil war that took place in the Congo (the former Belgian Congo) from 1960 to 1963. The crisis was caused largely by the attempt of the copper-rich province of Katanga to secede from the Congo. The secession was defeated eventually by a UN force, but in the process there were scares that the dilatory UN response would lead the Congolese government to turn to the Soviet Union for support.

Congress   Shorthand for the Indian National Congress, a nationalist party first formed in India in 1885. Congress played the most important role in bringing about Indian independence in 1947 and since then has been one of the major political parties in Indian politics.

containment   The term coined by George Kennan for the American, and broadly Western, policy towards the Soviet Union (and communism in general). The overall idea was to contain the USSR (that is, keep it within its current borders) with the hope that internal division, failure or political evolution might end the perceived threat from what was considered a chronically expansionist force.

Cultural Revolution   The movement initiated by Mao in 1966 to rid the CCP of 'revisionists' whom he accused of seeking to introduce the type of state capitalism that existed in the Soviet Union. The Cultural Revolution was at its height between 1966 and 1969, but did not end officially until Mao's death in 1976.

Danzig, Free City of (Polish: Gdansk)   A historically and commercially important port city on the Baltic Sea. In 1919, the Paris peacemakers made Danzig politically independent as a 'free city' under the League of Nations in order to give the new state of Poland free access to the sea. However, the vast majority of the city's inhabitants were Germans. The return of Danzig to German sovereignty was thus a key issue for German nationalists between the wars. Hitler exploited the Danzig question as a pretext for his attack on Poland in 1939.

decolonization   The process whereby an imperial power gives up its formal authority over its colonies.

Democratic People's Republic of Korea (DPRK)   The official name of North Korea. The DPRK came into existence in 1948 under the leadership of Kim Il-Sung.

Democratic Republic of Vietnam (DRV)   The official name of communist Vietnam; the DRV was initially proclaimed by Ho Chi Minh in 1945. Between 1954 and 1975 it comprised only the northern part of Vietnam (North Vietnam).

de-Stalinization   The policy, pursued in most communist states and among most communist groups after 1956, of eradicating the memory or influence of Stalin and Stalinism. Initiated by the Soviet Union under the guidance of Nikita Khrushchev.

détente   A term meaning the reduction of tensions between states. It is often used to refer to the superpower diplomacy that took place between the inauguration of Richard Nixon as the American president in 1969 and the Senate's refusal to ratify SALT II in 1980.

developmental state   A term coined by the political scientist Chalmers Johnson to refer to a state which plays a direct strategic role in planning the development of a capitalist economy. First used in relation to Japan, but subsequently utilized more broadly to refer to South Korea, Taiwan and the developing countries in South-East Asia.

Dominion   A completely self-governing colony which is freely associated with the mother country. Within the British Empire, the Dominions were Australia, Canada, the Irish Free State (1922–49), New Zealand and South Africa.

Dow Jones Industrial Average (DJIA)   The statistical tool used to measure the performance of the New York Stock Exchange.

Entente Cordiale   A phrase coined to describe the Anglo-French rapprochement that took place in 1904. Subsequently used as a shorthand for the Anglo-French relationship in the twentieth century.

European Coal and Steel Community (ECSC)   Established by the Treaty of Paris (1952) and also known as the Schuman Plan, after the French foreign minister, Robert Schuman, who proposed it in 1950. The member nations of the ECSC – Belgium, France, Italy, Luxembourg, the Netherlands and West Germany – pledged to pool their coal and steel resources by providing a unified market, lifting restrictions on imports and exports, and creating a unified labour market.

European Community (EC)   Formed in 1967 with the fusion of the European Economic Community (EEC, founded in 1957), the European Atomic Energy Community (EURATOM, also founded in 1957), and the European Coal and Steel Community (ECSC, founded in 1952). The EC contained many of the functions of the European Union (EU, founded in 1992). Unlike the later EU, the EC consisted primarily of economic agreements between member states.

European Economic Community (EEC) Established by the Treaty of Rome of 1957, the EEC became effective on 1 January 1958. Its initial members were Belgium, France, Italy, Luxembourg, the Netherlands and West Germany (now Germany); it was known informally as the Common Market. The EEC's aim was the eventual economic union of its member nations, ultimately leading to political union. It changed its name to the European Union in 1992.

European Union (EU)   A political and economic community of nations formed in 1992 in Maastricht by the signing of the Treaty on European Union (TEU).

In addition to the agreements of the European Community, the EU incorporated two inter-governmental – or supra-national – 'pillars' that tie the member states of the EU together: one dealing with common foreign and security policy, and the other with legal affairs. The number of member states of the EU has expanded from twelve in 1992 to twenty-seven in 2007.

Fatah   Palestinian guerrilla organization founded in 1957 in Kuwait by, among others, Yasser Arafat. It became the core of the PLO.

fedayeen (Arabic: guerrillas; suicide squads)   Originally associated with the Ismaili 'Assassins' in medieval history. After 1948 the term was used to describe Palestinian guerrilla groups.

Federal Republic of Germany (FRG)   The German state created in 1949 out of the former American, British and French occupation zones. Also known as West Germany. In 1990 the GDR merged into the FDR, thus ending the postwar partition of Germany.

Fidelistas   The name used for the Cuban revolutionaries under Fidel Castro's leadership. After a long guerrilla campaign the Fidelistas eventually toppled the Batista regime on 1 January 1959.

Final Solution (*Endlösung*)   The Nazi euphemism for the mass murder of European Jews.

fourteen points   A speech made by the American president Woodrow Wilson on 8 January 1918 in which he set out his vision of the post-war world. It included references to open diplomacy, self-determination and a post-war international organization.

Free French Forces   General Charles de Gaulle commanded an armoured division in the battle of France and then, briefly, held a junior post in Paul Reynaud's cabinet on the eve of France's defeat. In June 1940, in radio broadcasts from London, he called upon French people everywhere to join him in the struggle to free France from the Nazi occupation and, later, Marshal Pétain's Vichy regime. At first, the general's calls went largely unanswered. His abrasive, overbearing personality and his lack of diplomatic finesse ensured that his relationship with Roosevelt and Churchill was always rocky at best. By 1943, however, he had become the undisputed leader of the Free French movement, whose growing volunteer forces participated in Allied military operations in North Africa and the Middle East. In 1944, Free French Forces triumphantly participated in the liberation of France. The Allies recognized his administration as the French provisional government in October 1944, and de Gaulle, a national hero, was elected president in November 1945. He resigned shortly thereafter when the National Assembly refused to grant him American-style executive powers. He again served his country as president from 1958 to 1969.

Gang of Four   The radical group centred upon Mao's wife, Jiang Qing, that helped to initiate and perpetuate the Cultural Revolution. They were purged in 1976 following Mao's death, put on trial for treason and later executed.

General Agreement on Tariffs and Trade (GATT)   An international agreement arising out of the Bretton Woods conference covering tariff levels and codes of conduct for international trade. The progressive lowering of tariffs took place in a succession of negotiating rounds. In 1995 it passed its work on to the World Trade Organization.

Geneva Accords (July 1954)   The international agreement that provided for the withdrawal of the French and Viet Minh to either side of the 17th parallel pending reunification elections in 1956, and for the independence of Laos and Cambodia.

Geneva disarmament talks   Article 8 of the Covenant of the League of Nations committed its signatories to the lowest level of armament consistent with national security and the fulfilment of international obligations. It also called for a Preparatory Commission to meet to draft a disarmament convention. The Preparatory Commission did not meet until 1926, and the disarmament talks did not begin at Geneva until 1932. Britain and France differed markedly over how to proceed, while the Weimar government refused to accept anything short of equality under the new convention. With Hitler's chancellorship, the chances for general disarmament evaporated. The Geneva disarmament talks were formally suspended in June 1934.

German Democratic Republic (GDR)   The German state created in 1949 out of the former Soviet occupation zone. Also known as East Germany. The GDR more or less collapsed in 1989–90 and was merged into the FRG in 1990, thus ending the post-war partition of Germany.

glasnost (Russian: openness)   Initiated in 1985 by Gorbachev, *glasnost* refers to the public policy within the Soviet Union of openly and frankly discussing economic and political realities.

globalization   The cultural, social and economic changes caused by the growth of international trade, the rapid transfer of investment capital and the development of high-speed global communications.

Good Neighbor Policy   A diplomatic policy introduced in 1933 by President Franklin D. Roosevelt, which was designed to encourage friendly relations and mutual defence among the nations of the Western Hemisphere after decades of American military interventionism.

Great Leap Forward   The movement initiated by the CCP in 1958 to achieve rapid modernization in China through the construction of communes and the utilization of the masses for large-scale infrastructure projects.

Great Powers   Traditionally those states that were held capable of shared responsibility for the management of the international order by virtue of their military and economic influence.

Group of 7 (G-7)   The Group of 7 was the organization of the seven most advanced capitalist economies – the United States, Japan, Canada, Germany, France, Italy and Britain – founded in 1976. The G-7 held and continues to hold annual summit meetings where the leaders of these countries discuss economic and political issues.

Group of 77 (G-77)   An organization, originally of seventy-seven nations, that has lobbied at the United Nations for the need to equalize the terms of trade between the developed and developing worlds and to ease access to international aid from institutions such as the World Bank and the IMF.

Gulf of Tonkin Resolution   A resolution passed by the US Congress in August 1964 following alleged DRV attacks on American ships in the Gulf of Tonkin, which authorized the president to employ all necessary measures to repel attacks against American forces and to take all steps necessary for the defence of American allies in South-East Asia. Presidents Johnson and Richard M. Nixon used it to justify military action in South-East Asia. The measure was repealed by Congress in 1970.

Guomindang (GMD)   The Chinese Nationalist party founded in 1913 by Sun Yatsen. Under the control of Jiang Jieshi, it came to power in China in 1928 and initiated a modernization programme before leading the country into war against Japan in 1937. It lost control over mainland China in 1949 as a result of the communist victory in the civil war. From 1949 it controlled Taiwan, overseeing the island's 'economic miracle', until its electoral defeat in 2000.

hadith   The traditions collected by witnesses to the Prophet Muhammad's life at Medina. An estimated 7,000 were handed down through oral traditions, collected, edited and recorded by Bukhari (d. 807) and Muslim (d. 875).

Haganah (Hebrew: Defence)   Jewish underground organization established in 1920 following Arab riots and the British failure to defend the Jews. It became the core of the IDF in 1948.

Hamas   The acronym for *Harakat al-Muqawama al-Islamiyya* (Islamic Resistance Movement). Emerged during the first *intifada* in 1987 in the Gaza Strip.

Hashemites   The family of the Sharifs of Mecca who trace their descent to the Prophet Muhammad.

Hizb'allah (Arabic: Party of God)   Lebanese Shi'a Islamist group which emerged in reaction to the 1982 Israeli invasion of Lebanon. Its primary aim until the Israeli withdrawal in May 2000 was the liberation of southern Lebanon.

Ho Chi Minh trail   A network of jungle paths from North Vietnam through Laos and Cambodia into South Vietnam. Used as a military route by North Vietnam to send supplies and troops to the South.

Holocaust   The systematic mass murder of six million European Jews by the Nazis between 1939 and 1945.

import substitution   The process whereby a state attempts to achieve economic growth by raising protective tariffs to keep out imports and replacing them with indigenously produced goods.

indirect rule   The system whereby a colonial power delegates limited powers to indigenous institutions.

Institutional Revolutionary Party (PRI)   A Mexican political party established in 1929, which took its present name in 1946. Until the election of Vicente Fox Quesada in July 2000, all Mexican presidents and most officials belonged to the PRI.

Inter-American Development Bank   Organized in 1959 to foster the economic development of the Western Hemisphere. It is mainly funded by the United States.

inter-continental ballistic missile (ICBM)   Any supersonic missile that has a range of at least 6,500 kilometres and follows a ballistic trajectory after launching. The Soviet–American SALT I Agreements limited the number of ICBMs that each side could have.

intifada (Arabic: shaking off)   Name given to the Palestinian uprising against Israeli occupation which began on 9 December 1987 and lasted until the signing of the 1993 Oslo Accords between the PLO and Israel.

Irish Republican Army (IRA)   Militant Irish nationalist organization formed in 1919 as the military wing of Sinn Fein. The IRA's original aim was to establish an Irish Socialist Republic in all of Ireland. In 1969 the IRA split into the Official and Provisional IRA. The Provisionals or Provos carried out a militant campaign in Northern Ireland in order to expel the British. In 1994 the IRA called a ceasefire and Sinn Fein entered into negotiations that resulted in the 1998 Belfast Agreement which provided for power-sharing in Northern Ireland.

isolationism   The policy or doctrine of isolating one's country by avoiding foreign entanglements and responsibilities. Popular in the United States during the inter-war years.

Jemaah Islamiyya (JI) (Arabic: Islamic Community)   Southeast Asian Islamist Organization established by Indonesians Abdullah Sunkar and Abu Bakar Ba'ashir in 1995. JI seeks to establish a Southeast Asian Islamic state encompassing Indonesia, Malaysia, Singapore, Brunei, southern Thailand and the southern Philippines through militant means.

jihad   Struggle in the way of God. A fundamental tenet of Islam consisting of the Greater *jihad* which is above all a personal struggle to be a better Muslim and the Lesser *jihad* which is physical fighting.

Kashmir   Province in the north-west of the Indian subcontinent. Although mainly Muslim in population, the Hindu ruler in 1947 declared his allegiance to India. Pakistan reacted by seizing control of some of the province. Divided ever since by what is known as the Line of Control, Kashmir has been a perpetual sore in Indo-Pakistani relations. Terrorist campaigns by Islamic militants in the 1990s led the two countries to the brink of war on a number of occasions.

Kellogg–Briand Pact   Or more formally the 'International Treaty for the Renunciation of War as an Instrument of National Policy', 27 August 1928. It arose from a suggestion by the French prime minister, Aristide Briand, to the US secretary of state, Frank Kellogg, that the two states should agree to renounce war. At Kellogg's suggestion, other states were invited to join France and the United States in signing an agreement. In total, sixty-five did so. Manifestly a failure, the pact is often ridiculed as an empty gesture indicative of the idealistic internationalism of the inter-war years. In fact, Briand saw the treaty as a way to obtain some sort of moral American commitment to the preservation of the status quo.

Khalifat **Movement**   The protest movement that swept through the Islamic world from 1919 to 1923 in opposition to the harsh treatment meted out by the Christian powers to the Ottoman sultan, who as Caliph was one of the protectors of the faith.

Khmer Rouge   The Western name for the communist movement, led by Pol Pot, which came to power in Cambodia in 1975. The new government carried out a radical political programme that led to 1.5 million deaths. In 1979 it was overthrown by Vietnam, but continued to fight a guerrilla war campaign into the 1990s.

League of Nations An international organization established in 1919 by the peace treaties that ended the First World War. Its purpose was to promote international peace through collective security and to organize conferences on economic and disarmament issues. It was formally dissolved in 1946.

Lend-Lease With the Lend-Lease Act of March 1941, the US Congress empowered the president to lease or lend arms and supplies to any foreign government whose defence the administration considered essential to US national security. The programme, originally intended to rescue Britain, was eventually extended to more than thirty-eight states fighting the Tripartite Pact Powers.

Limited Test Ban Treaty An agreement signed by Britain, the Soviet Union and the United States in 1963, committing nations to halt atmospheric tests of nuclear weapons; by the end of 1963, ninety-six additional nations had signed the treaty.

Locarno treaties The series of treaties concluded at Locarno in Switzerland in October 1925. The most important was the Rhineland Pact, signed by France, Germany and Belgium and guaranteed by Britain and Italy, which affirmed the inviolability of the Franco-German and Belgo-German borders and the demilitarization of the Rhineland. In addition, Germany signed arbitration treaties with France, Belgium, Poland and Czechoslovakia.

McCarthyism General term for the practice in the United States of making accusations of pro-communist activity, in many instances unsupported by proof or based on slight, doubtful or irrelevant evidence. The term is derived from its most notorious practitioner, Republican Senator Joseph R. McCarthy of Wisconsin (1909–57).

Manchuria The three north-eastern provinces of China and home of the Manchu people. From 1932 to 1945, with the addition of Jehol province, it became the Japanese puppet state of Manchukuo.

mandates The colonial territories of Germany and the Ottoman Empire that were entrusted to Britain, France, Japan, Australia and South Africa under the supervision of a League of Nations Commission.

Marshall Plan Officially known as the European Recovery Programme (ERP). Initiated by American Secretary of State George C. Marshall's 5 June 1947 speech and administered by the Economic Co-operation Administration (ECA). Under the ERP the participating countries (Austria, Belgium, Denmark, France, Great Britain, Greece, Iceland, Italy, Luxembourg, the Netherlands, Norway, Sweden, Switzerland, Turkey and West Germany) received more than $12 billion between 1948 and 1951.

massive retaliation A strategy of military counter-attack adopted in the United States during the Eisenhower administration, whereby the United States threatened to react to any type of military offensive by the Soviets or the Chinese with the use of nuclear weapons. The strategy began to lose its credibility as the Soviets developed a substantial nuclear capability in the late 1950s.

Mein Kampf (German: *My Struggle*)   A semi-autobiographical book dictated by Adolf Hitler to his chauffeur and his personal secretary, Rudolf Hess, while he was serving a prison sentence for his part in the failed Munich beer hall *putsch* of 9 November 1923. It was published in 1925–26 in two volumes. Sales did not reach the hundreds of thousands until Hitler took power in 1933. It is a myth that the book was unread or ignored by foreign statesmen. It contained no detailed timetable for aggression; instead, *Mein Kampf* is a rambling exploration of Hitler's basic political and racial views.

Mercosur   Or the Southern Cone Common Market. A Latin American trade organization established in 1991 to increase economic co-operation in the eastern part of South America. Full members include Argentina, Brazil, Paraguay and Uruguay. Bolivia and Chile are associate members. Mercosur's goals include the gradual elimination of tariffs between member states and harmonization of external duties.

Ministry of International Trade and Industry (MITI)   The Japanese government ministry most closely associated with directing Japan's economic growth.

missile defence programme   Or missile defence initiative, or national missile defence. A futuristic plan to provide the United States (and possibly other countries) with a missile shield against potential attacks.

'modernization' theory   The idea that rapid economic development is achieved by a state going through a 'take-off' stage in which an entrepreneurial class and high investment in economic growth play a crucial part. The theory is closely associated with the Massachusetts Institute of Technology (MIT) economist Walt Rostow, who served in both the Kennedy and Johnson administrations.

Monroe Doctrine   The doctrine declared by President James Monroe in 1823 in which he announced that the United States would not tolerate intervention by the European Powers in the affairs of the Western Hemisphere.

mufti   A government-appointed Muslim religious official who pronounces usually on spiritual and social matters. The exception is the *mufti* of Jerusalem who also played a political role.

mujahedeen (Arabic: those who struggle in the way of God)   Term used for the Muslim guerrillas who fought against the Soviets in Afghanistan in 1979–89.

multiple independently targetable re-entry vehicle (MIRV)   A re-entry vehicle that breaks up into several nuclear warheads, each capable of reaching a different target. Not included in the SALT I agreements of 1972.

mutually assured destruction (MAD)   An American doctrine of reciprocal deterrence resting on the United States and Soviet Union each being able to inflict unacceptable damage on the other in retaliation for a nuclear attack.

naqba (Arabic: disaster)   Term for the Palestinian experience in the 1947–49 Arab–Israeli war, alluding to the Arab defeat and the Palestinian refugee situation.

National Liberation Front (NLF)   Established in 1960 as an umbrella organization for those opposing the rule of President Ngo Dinh Diem in South Vietnam. Supported by North Vietnam, the NLF played an important role in the Vietnam War throughout the 1960s.

Nazi New Order The German propaganda euphemism for the racial transformation and economic reordering of Europe to conform with the barbaric principles and criminal practices of German national socialism.

Nazis (or **Nazi Party**) The abbreviation for the National Socialist German Workers Party (*Nationalsozialistische Deutsche Arbeiterpartei* (NSDAP)). It was founded in October 1918 as the German Workers Party by the German politician Anton Drexler to oppose both capitalism and Marxism. It took on its more notorious title in February 1920. One year later Hitler became the Nazi Party Führer (German: leader).

neo-colonialism The process whereby a colonial power grants juridical independence to a colony, but nevertheless maintains *de facto* political and economic control.

neutralism The policy whereby a state publicly dissociates itself from becoming involved in Great Power conflicts. The first major advocate of the policy was Jawaharlal Nehru on behalf of post-independence India.

New Democracy The reformulation of Marxism-Leninism by Mao in the late 1930s and early 1940s in which he 'sinicized' communism and argued for the need for an alliance of classes, including both the proletariat and the peasantry, to bring about socialism.

New International Economic Order (NIEO) The proposal put forward by the Non-Aligned Movement and adopted by the UN in 1974 for major changes to be made to the international trading and financial order.

Non-Aligned Movement The organization founded in 1961 by a number of neutral states which called for a lowering of Cold War tensions and for greater attention to be paid to underdevelopment and to the eradication of imperialism.

non-alignment A state policy of avoiding involvement in 'Great Power conflicts', most notably the Cold War. It was first espoused by India on its becoming independent in 1947.

North American Free Trade Agreement (NAFTA) A 1992 accord between Canada, Mexico and the United States establishing a free-trade zone in North America from 1 January 1994. NAFTA immediately lifted tariffs on the majority of goods produced by the signatory nations. It also calls for the gradual elimination of barriers to cross-border investment and to the movement of goods and services between the three countries.

North Atlantic Treaty Organization (NATO) Established by the North Atlantic Treaty (4 April 1949) signed by Belgium, Canada, Denmark, France, Great Britain, Iceland, Italy, Luxembourg, the Netherlands, Norway, Portugal and the United States. Greece and Turkey entered the alliance in 1952 and the Federal Republic of Germany in 1955. Spain became a full member in 1982. In 1999 the Czech Republic, Hungary and Poland joined in the first post-Cold War expansion, increasing the membership to nineteen countries.

Nuclear Non-Proliferation Treaty (NPT) Proposed by the USSR and the United States in 1968, and subsequently approved by the UNGA, the treaty prohibits the proliferation of nuclear weaponry to 'new' countries. It has been ratified by more than 180 nations but has not prevented some states from either openly or secretly acquiring a nuclear weapons capability.

open door   The maintenance in a certain territory of equal commercial and industrial rights for the nationals of all countries. As a specific policy, it was first advanced by the United States in the late nineteenth century as a way of safeguarding American economic interests in China.

Organization of African Unity (OAU)   The organization of African states founded in Addis Ababa in 1963. It has upheld the territorial status quo in Africa and acted in the 1960s and 1970s as an important forum for attacks on colonialism. At the July 2002 Durban Summit the OAU was formally disbanded and became the African Union (AU).

Organization of American States (OAS)   An organization formed in 1948 for the purpose of co-ordinated action in economic, political and military matters. Its members include all countries in the Western Hemisphere.

Organization of Petroleum Exporting Countries (OPEC)   The organization founded in 1960 to represent the interests of the leading oil-producing states in the Third World.

Ostpolitik   The West German policy towards the Soviet Union and Eastern Europe in the 1960s and 1970s, which aimed at reducing tensions with the ultimate hope of negotiating the peaceful unification of Germany.

overseas Chinese   The descendants of the Chinese who immigrated to South-East Asia in the nineteenth and early twentieth centuries. They have tended to act as a merchant class and as such have stirred up a good deal of resentment among the indigenous people who envy their wealth and doubt their loyalty to their adopted countries.

Pacific War   The phrase usually used to refer to the Allied war against Japan from 1941 to 1945.

Palestine Liberation Organization (PLO)   Founded by Nasser in 1964, it comprises the Palestine National Council as its supreme body, the Palestine Executive Committee for everyday affairs, and the Palestine Liberation Army. Chaired initially by Ahmad Shuqairy and after the 1967 war by Yasser Arafat. In 1989, the PLO Central Council nominated Arafat as Palestinian president, with the PLO assuming the role of government in exile until the 1993 Oslo Accords.

pan-Africanism   The belief that Africans wherever they live share common cultural and spiritual values. Pan-Africanism was an important influence on the rise of nationalist movements in Africa in the first half of the twentieth century, but after decolonization its impact waned as the new states were reluctant to compromise their independence.

pan-Americanism   The movement towards commercial, social, economic, military and political co-operation among the nations of North, Central and South America.

pan-Arabism   Movement for Arab unity as manifested in the Fertile Crescent and Greater Syria schemes as well as attempted unification of Egypt, Syria and Libya.

pan-Asianism   The idea that Asia should free itself from Western imperialism and unite in a common effort to modernize. Espoused chiefly by Japan before 1945, but some Indian and Chinese nationalists were also attracted to the concept.

Paris Peace Accords   Signed on 27 January 1973, the Paris Agreements provided for a cease-fire in Vietnam, the withdrawal of remaining American troops and the return of American prisoners of war.

peaceful co-existence   An expression coined originally by Trotsky to describe the condition when there are pacific relations between states with differing social systems and competition takes place in fields other than war. The idea was vital to Soviet diplomacy, particularly after the death of Stalin.

People's Republic of China (PRC)   The official name of communist or mainland China. The PRC came into existence in 1949 under the leadership of Mao Zedong.

perestroika (Russian: restructuring) The term attached to the attempts (1985–91) by Mikhail Gorbachev to transform the command economy of the Soviet Union into a decentralized market-oriented economy. Industrial managers and local government and party officials were granted greater autonomy, and open elections were introduced in an attempt to democratize the Communist Party organization.

Platt Amendment   Introduced by Orville H. Platt, an American senator (1879–1905), the Platt Amendment to the Cuban Constitution stipulated the conditions for American intervention in Cuban affairs and permitted the United States to lease a naval base in Cuba (Guantanamo Bay). The United States subsequently intervened in Cuban affairs in 1906, 1912, 1917 and 1920. The Platt Amendment was abrogated in 1934, although the United States has retained its naval base in Guantanamo Bay.

Plaza Accord   The agreement reached by the G-5 (G-7 minus Canada and Italy) finance ministers at the Plaza Hotel in New York in 1985 to raise the value of the yen and the Deutschmark and to lower that of the dollar. The accord helped to lead to the Japanese 'bubble economy' of the late 1980s.

Popular Front   The Comintern policy announced in 1935 of encouraging communist parties to form coalitions with other socialist and non-socialist parties in order to provide a common front against fascism.

Prague Spring   A brief period of liberal reforms attempted by the government of Alexander Dubček in 1968. The period ended with the invasion by Soviet-led Warsaw Pact military forces.

Princely States   The states in British India that remained formally under the control of local rulers rather than direct British administration. They included states such as Hyderabad and Kashmir.

protectionism   The practice of regulating imports through high tariffs with the purpose of shielding domestic industries from foreign competition.

protectorates   Territories administered by an imperial state without full annexation taking place, and where delegated powers typically remain in the hands of a local ruler or rulers. Examples include French Morocco and the unfederated states in Malaya.

Red Guards   The students and workers who acted as the foot soldiers of the Chinese Cultural Revolution, 1966–69.

Reichstag   The lower house of the German parliament during the Wilhelmine and Weimar periods.

Republic of China (ROC)   The official name for the government of China in Taiwan.

Republic of Korea (ROK)   The official name of South Korea. The ROK came into existence in 1948 under the leadership of Syngman Rhee.

Republic of Vietnam (RVN)   The official name of South Vietnam until re-unification in 1975.

reverse course   The change of emphasis from democratization to economic reconstruction that the United States introduced in its occupation of Japan, 1947–49.

Rio Treaty (Inter-American Treaty of Reciprocal Assistance)   Signed on 2 September 1947, and originally ratified by all twenty-one American republics. Under the treaty, an armed attack or threat of aggression against a signatory nation, whether by a member nation or some other power, will be considered an attack against all.

Roosevelt Corollary (to the Monroe Doctrine)   Unveiled by President Theodore Roosevelt in 1904, the Roosevelt Corollary to the Monroe Doctrine asserted that the United States had the right to intervene in the affairs of an American republic threatened with seizure or intervention by a European country.

salafi   Pertaining to the good ancestral example and tradition of the Prophet Muhammad, his companions and the first four Caliphs.

Schlieffen Plan   The German pre-1914 plan for a pre-emptive military offensive against France, which would involve troops passing through neutral Belgium. It is named after the German army chief of staff, General Alfred von Schlieffen.

self-determination   The idea that each national group has the right to establish its own national state. It is most often associated with the tenets of Wilsonian internationalism and became a key driving force in the struggle to end imperialism.

shari'a   Islamic law which covers all aspects of life, not just religious practices.

Shi'a Islam   Muslim sect which emerged out of the struggle over the succession following the death of the Prophet Muhammad. Derived from Shi'a Ali (the Party of Ali) or those who supported the Prophet's son-in-law Ali's accession to the Caliphate. An estimated 15 per cent of Muslims are Shi'a. They are concentrated in the areas of Iran, Iraq and southern Lebanon, with smaller communities scattered throughout the Muslim world.

Sino-Soviet split   The process whereby China and the Soviet Union became alienated from each other in the late 1950s and early 1960s. It is often dated from 1956 and Khrushchev's speech to the twentieth congress of the CPSU, but this view has been challenged in recent years.

social Darwinism   A nineteenth-century theory, inspired by Charles Darwin's theory of evolution, which argued that the history of human society should be seen as 'the survival of the fittest'. Social Darwinism was the backbone of various theories of racial and especially 'white' supremacy.

Solidarity Movement   Polish independent trade union federation formed in September 1980, which, under Lech Walesa's leadership, soon posed a threat to Poland's communist government. In December 1981, the Polish government banned it and imprisoned most of its leaders. However, it persisted as an underground organization and played a major role in the negotiations that, in 1989, led to the end of communist rule in Poland.

South-East Asia Treaty Organization (SEATO)   An alliance organized in 1954 by Australia, France, Great Britain, New Zealand, Pakistan, the Philippines, Thailand and the United States. SEATO was created after the Geneva conference on Indochina to prevent further communist gains in the region. However, it proved of little use in the Vietnam War and was disbanded in 1977.

Spanish Civil War   Began on 18 July 1936 as an attempted right-wing military coup led by General Francisco Franco. The coup was launched with elite troops from Spanish Morocco to topple the recently elected socialist and anti-clerical Popular Front government. Franco's Nationalists failed to take Madrid, and the Republican government of President Azana remained in control of much of Spain. Both sides appealed for outside help to achieve victory. As a result, Spain became Europe's ideological battlefield. Nazi Germany and Fascist Italy intervened on the side of the Nationalists, while the Soviet Union sent aid to the Republicans. Britain and France tried to contain the war. The fighting dragged on for three terrible years, during which three-quarters of a million people perished. The civil war ended in April 1939. General Franco's dictatorship lasted until he died in 1975.

Strategic Arms Limitation Treaties (SALT I and II)   The agreements between the United States and the Soviet Union for the control of certain nuclear weapons, the first concluded in 1972 (SALT I) and the second drafted in 1979 (SALT II) but not ratified.

Strategic Arms Reduction Talks (START)   Begun in 1982, after the failed ratification of the SALT II Agreement, the START negotiations between the United States and the USSR led first to the 1987 Intermediate Nuclear Forces (INF) treaty to eliminate intermediate-range nuclear forces. In 1991 START I committed both sides to additional reductions in American and Soviet nuclear arsenals as well as on-site inspections. This was followed in 1993 by START II which called for a reduction in nuclear warheads by two-thirds by 2003. START also provided a framework for the nuclear disarmament of Ukraine, Belarus and Kazakhstan.

structural adjustment programme   The idea propagated by the World Bank from the end of the 1970s which linked the provision of development aid to Third World states to the latter committing themselves to balanced budgets, austerity programmes and the sale of nationalized industries and property.

submarine- (or sea-) launched ballistic missile (SLBM)   A ballistic missile designed for launch by a submarine (or surface ship).

Sudetenland   The geographical area in Bohemia mainly inhabited by ethnic Germans. In 1919 it was placed on the Czech side of the German–Czech border and in 1938 led to an international crisis ending in the infamous Munich Agreement.

Suez Crisis   The failed attempt by Britain and France in 1956 to take advantage of a war between Israel and Egypt by seizing control of the Suez Canal and bringing down the government of Gamal Abdel Nasser. It is often taken as a symbol of the collapse of European imperialism and the rise of the Third World.

Sunni Islam   The main body of Muslims, who follow the path (*sunna*) of the Prophet Mohammed and the Quran and the *hadith*.

Taliban (Arabic: students)   Term used to refer to the fundamentalist Muslim militia of Pashtun Afghans and Pakistanis that overthrew the Afghan ethnic coalition government of Ahmad Shah Masood in 1998.

Tet Offensive   The attack launched by the NLF in South Vietnam in late January and early February 1968, named after the country's most important holiday, the lunar new year. Although the offensive was not a military success for the NLF, it was a political and psychological victory as it dramatically contradicted optimistic claims by the American government that the war had already been won.

Third World   A collective term of French origin for those states that are part of neither the developed capitalist world nor the communist bloc. It includes the states of Latin America, Africa, the Middle East, South Asia and South-East Asia. Also referred to as 'the South' in contrast to the developed 'North'.

Tiananmen Square   The main square in Beijing where Mao declared the foundation of the PRC in October 1949 and where students protested against communist rule in the spring of 1989. The student movement was crushed on 3 June 1989 by units of the PLA.

total war   A war that uses all resources at a state's disposal including the complete mobilization of both the economy and society.

Tripartite Pact   A mutual aid treaty signed between Germany, Japan and Italy in Berlin on 27 September 1940. The pact was intended to deter the United States from interfering in the creation of a German new order in Europe and a Japanese new order in Asia. Article 3 of the pact as well as additional secret clauses were drafted that stated that the pact did not commit the parties to go to war on each other's behalf.

Truman Doctrine   The policy of American President Harry S. Truman, as advocated in his address to Congress on 12 March 1947, to provide military and economic aid to Greece and Turkey. Subsequently used to justify aid to any country perceived to be threatened by communism.

U-2 spy planes   An American high-altitude reconnaissance aircraft used to fly over Soviet and other hostile territories.

U-boat (English abbreviation of *Unterseeboot*)   A German submarine.

ulama   Clerics or Islamic scholars who are learned in theology and the *shari'a*.

unconditional surrender   A doctrine first articulated at Casablanca in January 1943 by President Roosevelt at the Anglo-American summit meeting. The view that there could be no negotiated peace with the Axis stemmed from the sharp moral distinction between the Grand Alliance and the Axis as expressed in documents such as the Atlantic Charter and the United National Declaration, as well as the desire on the part of the Allies not to repeat what they saw as the chief error of 1918–19 – that Germany had not been thoroughly beaten before the Versailles Treaty was imposed.

United Nations (UN)   An international organization established after the Second World War to replace the League of Nations. Since its establishment in 1945, its membership has grown to 192 countries.

Versailles Treaty   The treaty that ended the Allied state of hostilities with Germany in 1919. It included German territorial losses, disarmament, a so-called war guilt clause and a demand that reparations be paid to the victors.

Vichy France   The regime led by Marshal Pétain that surrendered to Hitler's Germany in June 1940 and subsequently controlled France until liberation in 1944.

Viet Minh   Vietnamese, communist-led organization whose forces fought against the Japanese and the French in Indochina. Headed by Ho Chi Minh, the Viet Minh was officially in existence from 1941 to 1951.

Vietnamization   President Nixon's policy of gradually withdrawing US ground troops from Vietnam while simultaneously building up the strength of the South Vietnamese armed forces. The policy was implemented starting in 1969 when there were more than half a million US troops in Vietnam; the programme of withdrawals was effectively completed in the autumn of 1972.

Warsaw Pact (Warsaw Treaty Organization)   An alliance set up in 1955 under a mutual defence treaty signed in Warsaw by Albania, Bulgaria, Czechoslovakia, East Germany, Hungary, Poland, Romania and the Soviet Union. The organization was the Soviet bloc's equivalent of NATO. Albania formally withdrew in 1968. The Warsaw Pact was dissolved in June 1991.

weapons of mass destruction (WMD)   Commonly understood to be nuclear, chemical and biological weapons. The uses of bacteriological agents and chemicals in warfare pre-date the twentieth century, but nuclear weapons made their first appearance at the end of the Second World War. Of the three, nuclear bombs are the only weapons genuinely capable of the 'mass' destruction of life and property. The term WMD denotes the stigma associated with the development and use of these particular weapons, however, more than offering an accurate description of the scale of their destructive effects. Some experts suggest that chemical, biological and radiological weapons (dirty bombs) should in fact be described as 'weapons of mass terror'.

Weimar Republic   The German parliamentary democracy that existed between November 1918 and January 1933. Attacked from both the Right and the Left of the political spectrum, it never won the loyalty of the majority of Germans.

Wilsonian internationalism   Woodrow Wilson's notion, outlined in his so-called fourteen points, of trying to create a new world society, which would be governed by the self-determination of peoples, be free from secret diplomacy and wars, and have an association of nations to maintain international justice.

yishuv (Hebrew: settlement)   The Jewish settlement in Palestine before the establishment of the State of Israel.

Young Plan   Name given to a financial scheme, worked out in 1929 by a committee chaired by the American businessman Owen D. Young, to reduce German reparations and arrange fresh credit for Germany. It was *informally* agreed by German, French and British delegates that reparations would be scaled back further if the former European Allies secured a reduction in debt repayments to the United States.

Young Turks   Name given to a group of young army officers who in 1908 pushed the Ottoman Empire towards reformist policies and a more overtly Turkish nationalist stance.

Zionism   Movement for the re-establishment of a Jewish state in Palestine. Theodor Herzl is conventionally seen as the founding father of political Zionism based on his 1896 book *Der Judenstaat*.

BIBLIOGRAPHY

Abuza, Z. (2006) *Militant Islam in Southeast Asia: Crucible of Terror*, New York.

Adamthwaite, A. (1995) *Grandeur and Misery: France's Bid for Power in Europe, 1914–1940*, London.

Akbar, M. J. (1989) *Nehru: The Making of India*, London.

Albright, D. E. (ed.) (1980) *Africa and International Communism*, London.

Alexander, M. (1990) 'The Fall of France 1940', *Journal of Strategic Studies*, vol. 13, pp. 10–44.

Alexander, M. (1992) *The Republic in Danger: General Maurice Gamelin and the Politics of French Defence, 1933–40,* New York.

Ali, T. (2000) *Masters of the Universe? NATO's Balkan Crusade*, New York.

Allison, G. T. (1999) *Essence of Decision: Explaining the Cuban Missile Crisis*, Cambridge.

Allison, G. T. (2005) *Nuclear Terrorism: The Ultimate Preventable Catastrophe*, New York.

al-Madfai, R. (1993) *Jordan, the United States and the Middle East Peace Process, 1974–1991*, Cambridge.

Aly, G. (1999) *'Final Solution': Nazi Population Policy and the Murder of European Jews*, London.

Ambrosius, L. E. (1991) *Wilsonian Statecraft: Theory and Practice of Liberal Internationalism during World War I*, Wilmington, DE.

Amos, J. W. (1980) *Palestinian Resistance: Organisation of a National Movement*, New York.

Amsden, A. (1989) *Asia's Next Giant: South Korea and Late Industrialization*, New York.

Anderson, D. L. (1991) *Trapped by Success: The Eisenhower Administration and Vietnam, 1953–1961*, New York.

Anderson, D. L. (ed.) (1993) *Shadow on the White House: Presidents and the Vietnam War, 1945–1975*, Lawrence, KS.

Anderson, M. (1993) *The Rise of Modern Diplomacy*, London.

Ang, C. G. (1997) *Vietnamese Communists' Relations with China and the Second Indochina Conflict, 1957–1962*, Jefferson, NC.

Ansari, A. (2002) *A History of Modern Iran since 1921*, New York.

Ansari, A. (2006) *Confronting Iran: The Failure of American Policy and the Next Great Crisis in the Middle East*, New York.

Antonius, G. (1938) *The Arab Awakening: The Story of the Arab National Movement*, London.

Armstrong, C. K. (2003) *The North Korean Revolution, 1945–1950*, Ithaca, NY.

Armstrong, D., Lloyd, L. and Redmond, J. (1982) *From Versailles to Maastricht: International Organisation in the Twentieth Century*, New York.

Armstrong, K. (2000) *Islam: A Short History*, London.

Armstrong, K. (2001) *Muhammad: Biography of the Prophet*, London.

Arnold, J. R. (1991) *The First Domino: Eisenhower, the Military, and America's Intervention in Vietnam*, New York.

Ash, T. G. (1990) *The Magic Lantern: The Revolution of 1989 Witnessed in Warsaw, Budapest, Berlin and Prague*, New York.

Ashrawi, H. (1995) *This Side of Peace: A Personal Account*, New York.

Atkins, G. P. (1989) *Latin America in the International Political System*, Boulder, CO.

Atkins, G. P. and Wilson, L. C. (1972) *The United States and the Trujillo Regime*, New Brunswick, NJ.

Austin, G. and Harris, S. (2001) *Japan and Greater China: Political Economy and Military Power in the Asian Century*, London.

Avineri, S. (1981) *The Making of Modern Zionism: The Intellectual Origins of the Jewish State*, New York.

Axtmann, R. (1998) *Globalization and Europe*, London.

Ayubi, N. (1991) *Political Islam: Religion and Politics in the Arab World*, London.

Badawi, A. A. (2006) *Islam Hadhari: A Model Approach for Development and Progress*, Petaling Jaya.

Baker, C., Johnson, G. and Seal, A. (eds) (1981) *Power, Profit and Politics: Essays on Imperialism, Nationalism and Change in Twentieth-Century India*, Cambridge.

Baker, R. S. (1922) *Woodrow Wilson and the World Settlement*, New York.

Balaban, O. (2005) *Interpreting Conflict: Israeli–Palestinian Negotiations at Camp David II and Beyond*, New York.

Ball, G. (1984) *Error and Betrayal in Lebanon: An Analysis of Israel's Invasion of Lebanon and the Implications for US–Israeli Relations*, Washington, DC.

Baram, A. and Rubin, B. (eds) (1993) *Iraq's Road to War*, New York.

Barber, J. (1999) *South Africa in the Twentieth Century*, Oxford.

Bardon, J. (1992) *A History of Ulster*, Belfast.

Barnhart, M. (1987) *Japan Prepares for Total War: The Search for Economic Security, 1919–1941*, Ithaca, NY.

Barnhart, M. (1995) *Japan and the World since 1868*, London.

Barnhart, M. (1996) 'The Origins of the Second World War in Asia and the Pacific: Synthesis Impossible?', *Diplomatic History*, vol. 20, pp. 241–60.

Barnouin, B. and Yu Changgen (1998) *Chinese Foreign Policy during the Cultural Revolution*, London.

Bar-On, M. (1994) *The Gates of Gaza: Israel's Road to Suez and Back, 1955–1957*, New York.

Bartlett, C. J. (1994) *The Global Conflict: The International Rivalry of the Great Powers, 1880–1990*, London.

Bartlett, C. J. (1996) *Peace, War and the European Powers, 1814–1914*, Basingstoke.

Barton, G. (2005) *Jemaah Islamiyah*, Singapore.

Bartov, O. (1992) *Hitler's Army: Soldiers, Nazis and the War in the Third Reich*, Oxford.

Baum, R. (1994) *Burying Mao: Chinese Politics in the Age of Deng Xiaoping*, Princeton, NJ.

Bayart, J.-F. (1993) *The State in Africa: The Politics of the Belly*, London.

Beale, H. K. (1956) *Theodore Roosevelt and the Rise of America to World Power*, Baltimore, MD.

Beasley, W. G. (1987) *Japanese Imperialism, 1894–1945*, Oxford.

Beasley, W. G. (1990) *The Rise of Modern Japan*, London.

Begin, M. (1951) *Revolt: Story of the Irgun*, New York.

Beisner, R. L. (1986) *From the Old Diplomacy to the New*, Arlington Heights, IL.

Bell, C. (1977) *The Diplomacy of Détente: The Kissinger Era*, Cambridge.

Bell, P. M. H. (1974) *A Certain Eventuality: Britain and the Fall of France*, Farnborough.

Bell, P. M. H. (1996) *France and Britain, 1900–1940: Entente and Estrangement*, London.

Bell, P. M. H. (1997) *The Origins of the Second World War in Europe*, London; 3rd edn, 2007.

Benjamin, J. R. (1990) *The United States and the Origins of the Cuban Revolution: An Empire of Liberty in an Age of National Liberation*, Princeton, NJ.

Bennett, A. (1999) *Condemned to Repetition: The Rise, Fall, and Reprise of Soviet-Russian Military Interventionism, 1973–1996*, New York.

Bennett, R. (1994) *Behind the Battle: Intelligence in the War with Germany*, London.

Berghahn, V. R. (2002) *America and the Intellectual Cold Wars in Europe*, Princeton, NJ.

Berman, B. and Lonsdale, J. (1992) *Unhappy Valley: Conflict in Kenya and Africa*, London.

Berman, L. (1982) *Planning a Tragedy: The Americanization of the War in Vietnam*, New York.

Berman, L. (1989) *Lyndon Johnson's War*, New York.

Berman, L. (2001) *No Honor, No Peace*, New York.

Bernhard, M. H. (1993) *The Origins of Democratization in Poland: Workers, Intellectuals, and Oppositional Politics, 1976–1980*, New York.

Beschloss, M. (1991) *Kennedy versus Khrushchev: The Crisis Years, 1960–1963*, New York.

Best, A. (1995) *Britain, Japan and Pearl Harbor: Avoiding War in East Asia, 1936–41*, London.

Best, A. (2002) *British Intelligence and the Japanese Challenge in Asia, 1914–1941*, Basingstoke.

Bethell, N. (1979) *The Palestine Triangle: The Struggle between the British, the Jews and the Arabs, 1935–1948*, London.

Betts, R. F. (1991) *France and Decolonization, 1900–1960*, Basingstoke.

Bew, P. (1994) *Ideology and the Irish Question: Ulster Unionism and Irish Nationalism, 1912–1916*, Oxford.

Billings-Yun, M. (1988) *Decision against War*, New York.

Bills, S. (1990) *Empire and Cold War: The Roots of US–Third World Antagonism, 1945–47*, Basingstoke.

Bischof, G. (1999) *Austria in the First Cold War, 1945–1955: The Leverage of the Weak*, London.

Bischof, G. and Dockrill, S. (eds) (2000) *Cold War Respite: The Geneva Summit of 1955*, Baton Rouge, LA.

Black, A. (2001) *The History of Islamic Political Thought: From the Prophet to the Present*, Edinburgh.

Blasier, C. (1986) *The Hovering Giant: US Responses to Revolutionary Change in Latin America*, Pittsburgh, PA.

Blasier, C. (1988) *The Giant's Rival: The USSR and Latin America*, Pittsburgh, PA.

Blatt, J. (1997) *The French Defeat of 1940: Reassessment*, Oxford.

Blight, J. G. and Welch, D. A. (1989) *On the Brink: Americans and Soviets Re-examine the Missile Crisis*, New York.

Boemeke, M. F., Feldman, G. D. and Glaser, E. (eds) (1998) *The Treaty of Versailles: A Reassessment after 75 Years*, Washington, DC.

Boog, H. *et al.* (eds) (1996) *Germany and the Second World War*, vol. III: *The Attack on the Soviet Union*, Oxford.

Borg, D. and Okamoto, S. (1973) *Pearl Harbor as History: Japanese–American Relations, 1931–1941*, New York.

Bose, S. and Jalal, A. (1998) *Modern South Asia: History, Culture, Political Economy*, London.

Bosworth, B. *et al.* (1997) *Coming Together? Mexico–US Relations*, Washington, DC.

Boutwell, J. D. (ed.) (1985) *The Nuclear Confrontation in Europe*, London.

Bowie, R. and Immerman, R. (1998) *Waging Peace*, New York.

Bowker, M. and Ross, C. (2000) *Russia after the Cold War*, New York.

Bowker, M. and Williams, P. (1988) *Superpower Détente: A Reappraisal*, New York.

Bowyer Bell, J. (1977) *Terror out of Zion: Irgun Zvai Leumi, LEHI and the Palestinian Underground, 1929–1949*, New York.

Boyce, D. G. (1992) *Ireland 1828–1923: From Ascendancy to Democracy*, Oxford.

Boyce, R. (1989) 'World War, World Depression: Some Economic Origins of the Second World War', in Boyce, R. and Robertson, E. M. (eds), *Paths to War*, Basingstoke.

Boyce, R. and Maiolo, J. A. (eds) (2003) *The Origins of World War Two: The Debate Continues*, Basingstoke.

Bradsher, H. S. (1999) *Afghan Communism and Soviet Intervention*, New York.

Brands, H. W. (1989) *The Specter of Neutralism: The United States and the Emergence of the Third World, 1947–1960*, New York.

Brands, H. W. (1992) *Bound to Empire: The United States and the Philippines 1890–1990*, New York.

Brands, H. W. (1999) *TR: The Last Romantic*, New York.

Brecher, M. (1980) *Decisions in Crisis: Israel 1967 and 1973*, Berkeley, CA.

Bregman, A. (2003) *A History of Israel*, Basingstoke.

Brenner, M. J. (1995) *Multilateralism and Western Security*, New York.

Brenner, M. J. (1998) *NATO and Collective Security*, New York.

Bridge, F. R. and Bullen, R. (2004) *The Great Powers and the European States System, 1815–1914*, second edition, London.

Brigham, R. (1999) *Guerrilla Diplomacy*, New York.

Brown, A. (1996) *The Gorbachev Factor*, Oxford.

Brown, J. (1989) *Gandhi: Prisoner of Hope*, New Haven, CT.

Brown, J. and Louis, W. R. (eds) (1999) *The Oxford History of the British Empire*, vol. IV: *The Twentieth Century*, Oxford.

Brown, L. C. (1996) *Imperial Legacy: The Ottoman Imprint on the Balkans and the Middle East*, New York.

Browning, C. (1992) *The Path to Genocide: Essays in the Launching of the Final Solution*, Cambridge.

Brzezinski, Z. (1967) *The Soviet Bloc*, Cambridge, MA.

Buchanan, T. (2006) *Europe's Troubled Peace, 1945–2000*, Oxford.

Buckley, R. (1992) *US–Japan Alliance Diplomacy, 1945–90*, New York.

Bull, H. (1977) *The Anarchical Society: A Study of Order in World Politics*, London.

Bulmer-Thomas, V. (1994) *The Economic History of Latin America since Independence*, Cambridge, MA.

Bundy, M. (1988) *Danger and Survival: Choices about the Bomb in the First Fifty Years*, New York.

Bundy, W. (1998) *A Tangled Web*, New York.

Burke, J. (2003) *Al-Qaeda: Chasing Shadows of Terror*, London.

Burke, J. P., Greenstein, F. I. *et al.* (1989) *How Presidents Test Reality: Decisions on Vietnam, 1954 and 1965*, New York.

Burr, W. (ed.) (1994) *The Berlin Crisis, 1958–1962*, Alexandria, VA.

Burr, W. (ed.) (1998) *The Kissinger Transcripts*, New York.

Butler, L. J. (2002) *Britain and Empire: Adjusting to a Post-Imperial World*, London.

Butow, R. (1974) *The John Doe Associates: Backdoor Diplomacy for Peace, 1941*, Stanford, CA.

Buttinger, J. (1977) *Vietnam: The Unforgettable Tragedy*, New York.

Buzo, A. (1999) *The Guerilla Dynasty: Politics and Leadership in the DPRK 1945–1994*, London.

Buzo, A. (2002) *The Making of Modern Korea*, London.

Buzzanco, R. (1996) *Masters of War: Military Dissent and Politics in the Vietnam Era*, Cambridge.

Cable, L. (1991) *Unholy Grail: The US and the Wars in Vietnam, 1965–8*, New York.

Cain, P. and Hopkins, A. (2002) *British Imperialism, 1688–2000*, London.

Calder, K. (1993) *Strategic Capitalism: Private Business and Public Purpose in Japan*, Princeton, NJ.

Calhoun, F. S. (1986) *Power and Principle: Armed Intervention in Wilsonian Foreign Policy*, Kent, OH.

Calleo, D. (1987) *Beyond American Hegemony*, New York.

Calleo, D. (2001) *Rethinking Europe's Future*, Princeton, NJ.

Calvocoressi, P. (1985) *Independent Africa and the World*, London.

Calvocoressi, P., Wint, G. and Pritchard, J. (1989) *Total War: The Causes and Course of the Second World War*, vol. II, London.

Cambridge History of China (1987 and 1990), vols 14 and 15, Cambridge.

Cameron, F. (1999) *The Foreign and Security Policy of the European Union*, London.

Campbell, K. J. (2007) *A Tale of Two Quagmires: Iraq, Vietnam, and the Hard Lessons of War*, New York.

Campbell, K. M., Einhorn, R. and Reiss, M. (eds) (2004) *The Nuclear Tipping Point: Why States Reconsider their Nuclear Choices*, Washington, DC.

Caplan, N. (1978) *Palestine Jewry and the Arab Question, 1917–1925*, London.

Caplan, N. (1983) *Futile Diplomacy*, vol. I: *Early Arab–Zionist Negotiation Attempts, 1913–1931*, London.

Caplan, N. (1986) *Futile Diplomacy*, vol. II: *Arab–Zionist Negotiations and the End of Mandate*, London.

Carlton, D. (2000) *Churchill and the Soviet Union*, New York.

Carothers, T. (1991) *In the Name of Democracy: US Policy toward Latin America in the Reagan Years*, Berkeley, CA.

Carpenter, T. G. and Bandow, D. (2004) *The Korean Conundrum: America's Troubled Relations with North and South Korea*, London.

Castle, T. (1993) *At War in the Shadow of Vietnam: United States Military Aid to the Royal Lao Government, 1955–75*, New York.

Cha, V. (1999) *Alignment despite Antagonism: The US–Korea–Japan Security Triangle*, Stanford, CA.

Cha, V. D. and Kang, D. C. (2005) *Nuclear North Korea: A Debate on Engagement Strategies*, New York.

Chafer, T. (2002) *The End of the Empire in French West Africa*, Oxford.

Chandler, D. P. (1991) *The Tragedy of Cambodian History: Politics, War and Revolution since 1945*, New Haven, CT.

Chandler, D. P. (1992) *Brother Number One: A Political Biography of Pol Pot*, Boulder, CO.

Chang, G. (1989) *Friends and Enemies: The United States, China and the Soviet Union*, Stanford, CA.

Chang, L. and Kornbluh, P. (eds) (1992) *The Cuban Missile Crisis*, New York.

Chanock, M. (1977) *Unconsummated Union: Britain, Rhodesia and South Africa, 1900–45*, London.

Charmley, J. (1995) *Churchill's Grand Alliance: The Anglo-American Special Relationship, 1940–1957*, New York.

Charters, D. A. (1989) *The British Army and Jewish Insurgency in Palestine, 1945–1947*, New York.

Chayes, S. (2006) *The Punishment of Virtue: Inside Afghanistan after the Taliban*, New York.

Che Man, W. K. (1990) *Muslim Separatism: The Moros of Southern Philippines and the Malays of Southern Thailand*, Singapore.

Chen Jian (1994) *China's Road to the Korean War: The Making of the Sino-American Confrontation*, New York.

Chen Jian (2001) *Mao's China and the Cold War*, Chapel Hill, NC.

Cheng Guan Ang (1997) *Vietnamese Communists' Relations with China and the Second Indochina Conflict, 1957–1962*, Jefferson, NC.

Christiansen, T. (1996) *Useful Adversaries: Grand Strategy, Domestic Mobilization and Sino-American Conflict, 1947–1958*, Princeton, NJ.

Christie, C. J. (1996) *A Modern History of Southeast Asia: Decolonization, Nationalism and Separatism*, London.

Chubin, S. (2006) *Iran's Nuclear Ambitions*, New York.

Cirincione, J. (2007) *Bomb Scare: The History and Future of Nuclear Weapons*, New York.

Cirincione, J., Wolfstahl, J. B. and Rajkumar, M. (2005) *Deadly Arsenals: Nuclear, Biological and Chemical Threats*, New York.

Clapham, C. (1988) *Transformation and Continuity in Revolutionary Ethiopia*, Cambridge.

Clapham, C. (1996) *Africa in the International System: The Politics of State Survival*, Cambridge.

Clark, I. (2002) *The Post-Cold War Order: The Spoils of Peace*, New York.

Clavin, P. (2000) *The Great Depression in Europe, 1929–39*, Basingstoke.

Clinton, B. (2004) *My Life*, New York.

Coatsworth, J. H. (1994) *Central America and the United States: The Clients and the Colossus*, New York.

Cobban, H. (1984) *The Palestine Liberation Organisation: People, Power, and Policies*, Cambridge.

Coble, P. (1991) *Facing Japan: Chinese Politics and Japanese Imperialism, 1931–1937*, Cambridge, MA.

Cogan, C. (1997) *Forced to Choose: France, the Atlantic Alliance and NATO*, Westport, CT.

Cohen, M. (1978) *Palestine – Retreat from the Mandate: The Making of British Policy, 1936–1945*, London.

Cohen, M. (1982) *Palestine and the Great Powers, 1945–1948*, Princeton, NJ.

Cohen, M. (1987) *Zion and State: Nation, Class and the Shaping of Modern Israel*, Oxford.

Cohen, W. (1980) 'Acheson, his Advisers, and China, 1949–50' in Borg, D. and Heinrichs, W. (eds) *Uncertain Years: Chinese–American Relations, 1947–1950*, New York.

Cohen, W. (1987) *Empire without Tears*, New York.

Cohen, W. (ed.) (1996) *Pacific Passage: The Study of American–East Asian Relations on the Eve of the Twenty-First Century*, New York.

Cohrs, P. O. (2006) *The Unfinished Peace after World War I: America, Britain and the Stabilisation of Europe, 1919–1932*, Cambridge.

Coker, C. (1985) *NATO, the Warsaw Pact and Africa*, Basingstoke.

Collin, R. (1985) *Theodore Roosevelt, Culture, Diplomacy, and Expansion*, Baton Rouge, LA.

Conboy, K. (2006) *Second Front: Inside Asia's Most Dangerous Terrorist Network*, Jakarta.

Connelly, M. (2002) *A Diplomatic Revolution: Algeria's Fight for Independence and the Origins of the Post-Cold War Era*, New York.

Connelly, M. (2006) 'To Inherit the Earth: Imagining World Population from the Yellow Peril to the Population Bomb', *Journal of Global History*, vol. 1, pp. 299–319.

Constable, P. and Valenzuela, A. (1991) *A Nation of Enemies: Chile under Pinochet*, Baltimore, MD.

Cooper, F. (2002) *Africa since the 1940s: The Past of the Present*, Cambridge.

Cooper, J. M. (1983) *The Warrior and the Priest*, Cambridge, MA.

Copper, J. (1999) *Taiwan: Nation-State or Province?*, Boulder, CO.

Cordesman, A. H. (2006) *Arab–Israeli Military Forces in an Era of Asymmetric War*, Westport, CT.

Costigliola, F. (1992) *France and the United States*, New York.

Cox, M. (1996) *US Foreign Policy after the Cold War*, London.

Cox, M. *et al.* (eds) (2000) *US Democracy Promotion*, New York.

Crockatt, R. (1995) *The Fifty Years War*, New York.

Crowley, J. B. (1966) *Japan's Quest for Autonomy: National Security and Foreign Policy, 1930–38*, Princeton, NJ.

Cullather, N. (1994) *Illusions of Influence: The Political Economy of United States–Philippines Relations, 1942–1960*, Stanford, CA.

Cumings, B. (1981 and 1990) *The Origins of the Korean War*, 2 vols, Princeton, NJ.

Cumings, B. (1997) *Korea's Place in the Sun: A Modern History*, New York.

Curtis, G. (1999) *The Logic of Japanese Politics: Leaders, Institutions, and the Limits of Change*, New York.

Daalder, I. H. and Lindsay, J. M. (2005) *America Unbound: The Bush Revolution in Foreign Policy*, New York.

Dallek, R. (1979) *Franklin D. Roosevelt and American Foreign Policy, 1932–1945*, Oxford.

Dallek, R. (2007) *Nixon and Kissinger*, New York.

Dalloz, J. (1990) *The War in Indochina, 1945–54*, New York.

Davenport, R. and Saunders, C. (2000) *South Africa: A Modern History*, Basingstoke.

Davidson, B. (1992) *The Black Man's Burden: Africa and the Curse of the Nation-State*, Oxford.

Davis, N. (1985) *The Last Two Years of Salvador Allende*, Ithaca, NY.

Dawisha, K. (1984) *The Kremlin and the Prague Spring*, Berkeley, CA.

Dayan, M. (1981) *Breakthrough: A Personal Account of the Egypt–Israel Peace Negotiations*, New York.

Dean, J. (1994) *Ending Europe's Wars*, New York.

Dear, I. C. B. and Foot, M. R. D. (eds) (1995) *The Oxford Companion to World War II*, Oxford.

Deighton, A. (1990) *The Impossible Peace: Britain, the Division of Germany, and the Origins of the Cold War*, New York.

de Witte, L. (2001) *The Assassination of Lumumba*, London.

Dibb, P. (1988) *The Soviet Union: The Incomplete Superpower*, Cambridge.

Dickinson, F. (1999) *War and National Reinvention: Japan in the Great War, 1914–1919*, Cambridge, MA.

Diefendorf, J. M. *et al.* (eds) (1993) *American Policy and the Reconstruction of West Germany*, New York.

Dilks, D. and Erickson, J. (eds) (1994) *Barbarossa: The Axis and the Allies*, Edinburgh.

Dinges, J. (1991) *Our Man in Panama: The Shrewd Rise and Brutal Fall of Manuel Noriega*, New York.

Diplomatic History (1997) Symposium on the 'Lost Chance' thesis, vol. 21, pp. 71–115.

Divine, R. A. (1969) *Roosevelt and World War II*, Baltimore, MD.

Dockrill, M. L. and Goold, J. D. (1981) *Peace without Promise: Britain and the Peace Conferences, 1919–1923*, London.

Dockrill, S. (1996) *Eisenhower's New Look National Security Policy*, New York.

Dominguez, J. (1989) *Making the World Safe for Revolution: Cuba's Foreign Policy*, Cambridge, MA.

Dower, J. (1986) *War without Mercy: Race and Power in the Pacific War*, New York.

Dower, J. (1999) *Embracing Defeat: Japan after World War II*, New York.

Drake, P. (ed.) (1994) *Money Doctors, Foreign Debts, and Economic Reforms in Latin America from the 1890s to the Present*, Wilmington, DE.

Drakulic, S. (1993) *The Balkan Express*, New York.

Dudziak, M. L. (ed.) (2003) *September 11 in History: A Watershed Moment?*, Raleigh, VA.

Duiker, W. J. (1981) *The Communist Road to Power in Vietnam*, Boulder, CO.

Duiker, W. J. (1986) *China and Vietnam: The Roots of Conflict*, Berkeley, CA.

Duiker, W. J. (1994) *US Containment Policy and the Conflict in Indochina*, Stanford, CA.

Duiker, W. J. (1995) *Sacred War: Nationalism and Revolution in a Divided Vietnam*, New York.

Duiker, W. J. (2000) *Ho Chi Minh*, New York.

Dunbabin, J. P. (1993) 'The League of Nations' Place in the International System', *History*, vol. 78, pp. 421–42.

Dunn, P. M. (1985) *The First Vietnam War*, London.

Dupuy, T. N. (1978) *Elusive Victory: The Arab–Israeli Wars, 1947–1974*, New York.

Dutton, D. (2001) *Neville Chamberlain*, London.

Duus, P. (ed.) (1988) *The Cambridge History of Japan*, vol. VI: *The Twentieth Century*, Cambridge.

Dyer, T. (1980) *Theodore Roosevelt and the Idea of Race*, Baton Rouge, LA.

Eastman, L. (1974) *The Abortive Revolution: China under Nationalist Rule, 1927–1937*, Cambridge, MA.

Edmonds, R. (1983) *Soviet Foreign Policy: The Brezhnev Years*, Ithaca, NY.

Edmonds, R. L. and Goldstein, S. (eds) (2001) *Taiwan in the Twentieth Century: A Retrospective View*, New York.

Effendy, B. (2001) *Islam and the State: The Transformation of Islamic Political Ideas and Practice in Indonesia*, Singapore.

Ehteshami, A. (1995) *After Khomeini: The Iranian Second Republic*, London.

Eisenberg, C. (1996) *Drawing the Line: The American Decision to Divide Germany*, New York.

Ekwe-Ekwe, H. (1990) *Conflict and Intervention in Africa: Nigeria, Angola, Zaire,* Basingstoke.

El-Gamasy, M. (1993) *The October War,* Cairo.

Ellison, J. (2000) *Threatening Europe: Britain and the Creation of the European Community, 1955–1958,* London.

Emerson, M. (1998) *Redrawing the Map of Europe,* New York.

Emmerson, D. K. (ed.) (1999) *Indonesia beyond Suharto: Polity, Economy, Society, Transition,* New York.

English, R. (2000) *Russia and the Idea of the West,* New York.

Esherick, J. W. *et al.* (eds) (2006) *The Chinese Cultural Revolution as History,* Stanford, CA.

Esposito, J. (ed.) (1990) *The Iranian Revolution: Its Global Impact,* Miami, FL.

Esposito, J. (ed.) (1997) *Political Islam: Revolution, Radicalism or Reform?,* Boulder, CO.

Esposito, J. (1999) *The Islamic Threat: Myth or Reality?* New York.

Evans, R. and von Strandmann, H. P. (1988) *The Coming of the First World War,* Oxford.

Evron, Y. (1987) *War and Intervention in Lebanon,* London.

Fage, J. D. (1995) *A History of Africa,* London.

Fairbank, J. (ed.) (1983 and 1986) *The Cambridge History of China,* vols XII and XIII: *The Republican Era, 1912–1949,* Cambridge.

Farsoun, S. K. and Aruri, N. H. (2006) *Palestine and the Palestinians: A Social and Political History,* Boulder, CO.

Fawcett, L. (1992) *Iran and the Cold War: The Azerbaijan Crisis of 1946,* New York.

Fawcett, L. and Sayigh, Y. (1999) (eds), *The Third World beyond the Cold War,* Oxford.

Ferguson, N. (1998) *The Pity of War,* London.

Ferguson, N. (2004) *Colossus: The Price of America's Empire,* New York.

Ferris, J. (1991) 'Ralph Bennett and the Study of Ultra', *Intelligence and National Security,* vol. 6, pp. 437–86.

Fieldhouse, D. K. (1973) *Economics and Empire, 1880–1914,* London.

Fieldhouse, D. K. (1986) *Black Africa 1945–80: Economic Decolonization and Arrested Development,* London.

Fieldhouse, D. K. (1999) *The West and the Third World,* Oxford.

Filtzer, D. (1993) *The Khrushchev Era: De-Stalinisation and the Limits of Reform in the USSR, 1953–1964,* Basingstoke.

Fink, C. (1984) *The Genoa Conference: European Diplomacy 1921–22,* Cambridge.

Fink, C. *et al.* (eds) (1991) *Genoa, Rapallo, and European Reconstruction in 1922,* Washington, DC.

Fischer, B. (1997) *The Reagan Reversal: Foreign Policy and the End of the Cold War,* Columbia, MO.

Fischer, F. (1967) *Germany's Aims in the First World War,* London.

Fitzpatrick, D. (1998) *The Two Irelands, 1912–1939,* Oxford.

Flamhaft, Z. (1996) *Israel on the Road to Peace: Accepting the Unacceptable,* Boulder, CO.

Flapan, S. (1987) *The Birth of Israel: Myths and Realities*, New York.

Fodor, N. (1990) *The Warsaw Treaty Organization*, New York.

Foot, R. (1990) *A Substitute for Victory: The Politics of Peacemaking at the Korean Armistice Talks*, Ithaca, NY.

Foot, R. (1997) *The Practice of Power: US Relations with China since 1949*, Oxford.

Foradori, P. (2007) *Managing a Multilevel Foreign Policy: The EU in International Affairs*, Lanham, MD.

Forrester, G. (ed.) (1999) *Post-Soeharto Indonesia: Renewal or Crisis?*, New York.

Forsberg, A. (2000) *America and the Japanese Miracle: The Cold War Context of Japan's Postwar Economic Revival, 1950–1960*, Chapel Hill, NC.

Francis, M. J. (1977) *The Limits of Hegemony*, Notre Dame, IN.

Fraser, C. (2007) *An Introduction to European Foreign Policy*, London.

Fraser, T. G. (1995) *The Arab–Israeli Conflict*, New York.

Freedman, L. (1981) *The Evolution of Nuclear Strategy*, New York.

Freedman, L. (1993) *The Gulf War 1990–1991: Diplomacy and War in the New World Order*, London.

Freedman, L. (2000) *Kennedy's Wars: Berlin, Cuba, Laos, and Vietnam*, Oxford.

Freund, B. (1998) *The Making of Contemporary Africa*, Basingstoke.

Frieser, K.-H. (2005) *The Blitzkrieg Legend: The 1940 Campaign in the West*, Annapolis, MD.

Fung, E. (1991) *The Diplomacy of Imperial Retreat: Britain's South China Policy, 1924–31*, Oxford.

Fursenko, A. and Naftali, T. (1997) *'One Hell of a Gamble': The Secret History of the Cuban Missile Crisis*, New York.

Gabriel, J. M. (1989) *American Conception of Neutrality after 1941*, New York.

Gabriel, R. (1984) *Operation Peace for Galilee: The Israel–PLO War in Lebanon*, New York.

Gaddis, J. L. (1982) *Strategies of Containment*, New York.

Gaddis, J. L. (1997) *We Now Know: Rethinking Cold War History*, New York.

Gaddis, J. L. (2006) *The Cold War: A New History*, New York.

Gaiduk, I. (1996) *The Soviet Union and the Vietnam War*, Chicago.

Galbraith, P. (2007) *The End of Iraq: How American Incompetence Created a War without End*, New York.

Gallagher, J. (1982) *The Decline, Revival and Fall of the British Empire*, Cambridge.

Gallagher, J., Johnson, G. and Seal, A. (eds) (1973) *Locality, Province and Nation: Essays on Indian Politics, 1870–1940*, Cambridge.

Ganin, Z. (1979) *Truman, American Jewry and Israel, 1945–1948*, New York.

Gardner, L. (1984) *Safe for Democracy*, New York.

Gardner, L. C. (1988) *Approaching Vietnam: From the Second World War through Dienbienphu*, New York.

Gardner, L. C. (1995) *Pay Any Price: Lyndon Johnson and the Wars for Vietnam*, Chicago.

Garthoff, R. L. (1994) *Détente and Confrontation*, Washington, DC.

Garthoff, R. L. (1994) *The Great Transition: American–Soviet Relations and the End of the Cold War*, Washington, DC.

Garver, J. (1982) *China's Decision for Rapprochement with the United States, 1968–1972*, Boulder, CO.

Garver, J. (1988) *Chinese–Soviet Relations 1937–1945: The Diplomacy of Chinese Nationalism*, New York.

Garver, J. (1993) *Foreign Relations of the People's Republic of China*, Englewood Cliffs, NJ.

Gati, C. (1986) *Hungary and the Soviet Bloc*, Durham, NC.

Gati, C. (2006) *Failed Illusions: Moscow, Washington, Budapest, and the 1956 Hungarian Revolt*, Stanford, CA.

Gelb, L. H. and Betts, R. K. (1979) *The Irony of Vietnam: The System Worked*, Washington, DC.

Gellman, I. F. (1979) *Good Neighbor Diplomacy*, Baltimore, MD.

Gelman, H. (1984) *The Brezhnev Politburo and the Decline of Détente*, Cambridge.

George, T. J. S. (1980) *Revolt in Mindanao: The Rise of Islam in Philippine Politics*, Kuala Lumpur.

Gerges, F. (1994) *The Superpowers and the Middle East: Regional and International Politics, 1955–1967*, Boulder, CO.

Gerges, F. (1999) *America and Political Islam: Clash of Cultures or Clash of Interests?*, Cambridge.

Gerges, F. (2005) *The Far Enemy: Why Jihad went Global*, Cambridge.

Gershovich, M. (2000) *French Military Rule in Morocco: Colonialism and its Consequences*, London.

Giacaman, G. and Lonning, D. J. (eds) (1998) *After Oslo: New Realities, Old Problems*, London.

Gibbs, D. N. (1992) *The Political Economy of Third World Intervention: Money, Mines and US Policy in the Congo*, Chicago.

Gieling, S. (1999) *Religion and War in Revolutionary Iran*, London.

Gifford, P. and Louis, W. R. (eds) (1982) *The Transfer of Power in Africa: Decolonization 1940–1960*, New Haven, CT.

Gifford, P. and Louis, W. R. (eds) (1988) *Decolonization and African Independence: The Transfers of Power 1960–1980*, New Haven, CT.

Gilbert, F. and Large, D. C. (1991) *The End of the European Era, 1890 to the Present*, 4th edn, New York.

Gilderhus, M. T. (1977) *Diplomacy and Revolution*, Tucson, AZ.

Gilks, A. (1992) *The Breakdown of the Sino-Vietnamese Alliance, 1970–1979*, Berkeley, CA.

Gillingham, J. (2003) *European Integration 1950–2003: Superstate or New Market Economy?*, Cambridge.

Gittings, J. (1968) *Survey of the Sino-Soviet Dispute*, London.

Gitz, B. (1992) *Armed Forces and Political Power in Eastern Europe*, New York.

Gleijeses, P. (1978) *The Dominican Crises: The 1965 Constitutionalist Revolt and American Intervention*, Baltimore, MD.

Gleijeses, P. (1991) *Shattered Hope: The Guatemalan Revolution and the United States, 1944–1954*, Princeton, NJ.

Gleijeses, P. (2002) *Conflicting Missions: Havana, Washington and Africa, 1959–1976*, Chapel Hill, NC.

Glenny, M. (1992) *The Fall of Yugoslavia*, New York.

Golan, G. (1988) *The Soviet Union and National Liberation Movements in the Third World*, London.

Golan, G. (1992) *Moscow and the Middle East: New Thinking on Regional Conflict*, New York.

Gold, T. (1986) *State and Society in the Taiwan Miracle*, Armonk, NY.

Goldgeier, J. (1994) *Leadership Style and Soviet Foreign Policy: Stalin, Khrushchev, Brezhnev, Gorbachev*, Baltimore, MD.

Goncharov, S., Lewis, J. and Xue Litai (1993) *Uncertain Partners: Stalin, Mao and the Korean War*, Stanford, CA.

Goodby, J. E. (1998) *Europe Undivided*, Washington, DC.

Gordon, A. (ed.) (1993) *Postwar Japan as History*, Berkeley, CA.

Gordon, M. (2007) *Cobra II: The Inside Story of the Invasion and Occupation of Iraq*, New York.

Gordon, P. (1995) *France, Germany and the Western Alliance*, Boulder, CO.

Gorny, Y. (1987) *Zionism and the Arabs, 1882–1948: A Study of Ideology*, New York.

Gorodetsky, G. (1999) *Grand Delusion: Stalin and the German Invasion of Russia*, London.

Gorodetsky, G., Chubarian, A. O. and Naveh, S. (eds) (2001) *The Soviet Union and the Outbreak of War, 1939–1941*, New Haven, CT.

Gorst, A. and Johnman, L. (1997) *The Suez Crisis*, London.

Gott, R. (2005) *Hugo Chavez and the Bolivarian Revolution*, New York.

Gowan, P. (1999) *Global Gamble*, New York.

Grandin, G. (2006) *Empire's Workshop: Latin America, the United States and the Rise of the New Imperialism*, New York.

Gray, J. (1990) *Rebellions and Revolutions: China from the 1880s to the 1990s*, Oxford.

Gray, W. G. (2007) *Germany's Cold War*, Chapel Hill, NC.

Grayson, G. (1995) *The North American Free Trade Agreement*, Lanham, MD.

Green, M. (1995) *Arming Japan: Defense Production, Alliance Politics and the Postwar Search for Autonomy*, New York.

Green, M. (2001) *Reluctant Realism: Japanese Foreign Policy in an Era of Uncertain Power*, Basingstoke.

Greenlees, D. and Garran, R. (2002) *Deliverance: The Inside Story of East Timor's Fight for Freedom*, St Leonards, NSW.

Greider, W. (1997) *One World, Ready or Not: The Manic Logic of Global Capitalism*, New York.

Gresh, A. (1985) *The PLO: The Struggle Within: Towards an Independent Palestinian State*, London.

Grow, M. (1981) *The Good Neighbor Policy in Paraguay*, Lawrence, KS.

Guimaraes, F. A. (1988) *The Origins of the Angolan Civil War: Foreign Intervention and Domestic Political Conflict*, Basingstoke.

Gunaratna, R. (2002) *Inside Al Qaeda: Global Network of Terror*, London.

Gunning, J. (2008) *Hamas in Politics: Democracy, Religion, Violence*, London.

Gutierrez, E. (2000) *Rebels, Warlords and Ulama: A Reader on Muslim Separatism and the War in the Southern Philippines*, Quezon City.

Gutman, R. (1987) *Banana Diplomacy*, New York.

Haacke, J. (2003) *ASEAN's Diplomatic and Sceurity Culture: Origins, Developments and Prospects*, London.

Hadari, Z. V. (1991) *Second Exodus: The Full Story of Jewish Illegal Immigration to Palestine, 1945–1948*, London.

Haggard, S. (1990) *Pathways from the Periphery: The Politics of Growth in the Newly Industrializing Countries*, Ithaca, NY.

Hakovirta, H. (1988) *East–West Conflict and European Neutrality*, Oxford.

Hall, R. C. (2000) *The Balkan Wars 1912–13: Prelude to the First World War*, London.

Halliday, F. (1986) *The Making of the Second Cold War*, New York.

Hammer, E. J. (1987) *A Death in November: America in Vietnam, 1963*, New York.

Hamzeh, Ahmed Nizar (2004) *In the Path of Hizbullah*, New York.

Hanhimäki, J. (1997a) *Containing Coexistence*, Kent, OH.

Hanhimäki, J. M. (1997b) *Scandinavia and the United States: An Insecure Friendship*, New York.

Hanhimäki, J. M. (2004) *The Flawed Architect: Henry Kissinger and American Foreign Policy*, New York.

Harbeson, J. and Rothchild, D. (eds) (2000) *Africa in World Politics: The African State in Flux*, Boulder, CO.

Harbutt, F. (1986) *The Iron Curtain: Churchill, America, and the Origins of the Cold War*, New York.

Harding, H. (1992) *A Fragile Relationship: The United States and China since 1972*, Washington, DC.

Harding, H. and Yuan Ming (eds) (1989) *Sino-American Relations 1945–1955: A Joint Assessment of a Critical Decade*, Wilmington, DE.

Hargreaves, J. (1996) *Decolonization in Africa*, London.

Harris, J. (2007) 'Encircled by Enemies: Stalin's Perceptions of the Capitalist World, 1919–1941', *Journal of Strategic Studies*, vol. 30, pp. 513–45.

Harrison, M. (ed.) (2000) *The Economics of World War II: Six Great Powers in International Comparison*, Cambridge.

Harrison, S. S. (2003) *Korean Endgame: A Strategy for Reunification and US Disengagement*, Princeton, NJ.

Hart, A. (1994) *Arafat: A Political Biography*, London.

Haslam, J. (1984) *The Soviet Union and the Struggle for Collective Security in Europe 1933–1939*, London.

Haslam, J. (1992) *The Soviet Union and the Threat from the East, 1933–41*, Basingstoke.

Haslam, J. (1997) 'Soviet–German Relations and the Origins of the Second World War: The Jury is Still Out', *Journal of Modern History*, vol. 69, pp. 785–97.

Haslam, J. (2005) *The Nixon Administration and the Death of Allende's Chile: A Case of Assisted Suicide*, London.

Hathaway, R. (1981) *Ambiguous Partnership: Britain and America, 1944–1947*, New York.

Havens, T. (1987) *Fire across the Sea: The Vietnam War and Japan, 1965–1975*, Princeton, NJ.

Healy, D. (1970) *US Expansionism*, Madison, WI.

Healy, D. (1989) *Drive to Hegemony: The United States in the Caribbean*, Madison, WI.

Hefner, R. W. (2000) *Civil Islam: Muslims and Democratisation in Indonesia*, Princeton, NJ.

Hefner, R. W. and Horvatich, P. (1997) *Islam in an Era of Nation-States: Politics and Religious Renewal in Muslim Southeast Asia*, Honolulu, HI.

Heikal, M. (1975) *The Road to Ramadan*, London.

Heikal, M. (1978) *The Sphinx and the Commissar: The Rise and Fall of Soviet Influence in the Middle East*, New York.

Heikal, M. (1986) *Cutting the Lion's Tail: Suez through Egyptian Eyes*, London.

Heikal, M. (1992) *Illusion of Triumph: An Arab View of the Gulf War*, London.

Heikal, M. (1996) *Secret Channels: The Inside Story of Arab–Israeli Peace Negotiations*, London.

Hein, L. (1996) 'Free-Floating Anxieties on the Pacific: Japan and the West Revisited', *Diplomatic History*, vol. 20, pp. 411–37.

Heinrichs, W. (1988) *Threshold of War: Franklin D. Roosevelt and American Entry into World War Two*, New York.

Heller, F. and Gillingham, J. (1996) *The United States and the Integration of Europe*, New York.

Heller, J. (2000) *Birth of Israel, 1945–1949: Ben Gurion and his Critics*, Gainesville, FL.

Hellmann, J. (1986) *American Myth and the Legacy of Vietnam*, New York.

Hennessy, T. (2000) *The Northern Ireland Peace Process: Ending the Troubles*, Dublin.

Herbst, J. (2000) *States and Power in Africa: Comparative Lessons in Authority and Control*, Princeton, NJ.

Herring, G. C. (1994) *LBJ and Vietnam: A Different Kind of War*, Austin, TX.

Herring, G. C. (1996) *America's Longest War*, New York.

Herwig, H. H. (1998) *The First World War: Germany and Austria-Hungary, 1914–1918*, London.

Herzog, C. (1982) *The Arab–Israeli Wars*, New York.

Herzog, C. (2003) *The War of Atonement: The Inside Story of the Yom Kippur War*, London.

Hess, G. R. (1987) *The United States' Emergence as a Southeast Asian Power, 1940–1950*, New York.

Hess, G. R. (1990) *Vietnam and the United States: Origins and Legacy of War*, Boston.

Hesse, B. J. (2001) *The United States, South Africa, and Africa*, Aldershot.

Higgins, T. (1987) *The Perfect Failure*, New York.

Hill, C. (1991) *Cabinet Decisions on Foreign Policy*, Cambridge.

Hilton, S. (1981) *Hitler's Secret War in South America, 1939–1945*, Baton Rouge, LA.

Hinsley, F. H. (1963) *Power and the Pursuit of Peace*, Cambridge.

Hitchcock, W. I. (1998) *France Restored*, Chapel Hill, NC.

Hixson, W. (1997) *Parting the Curtain*, Basingstoke.

Hodgkin, T. L. (1981) *Vietnam: The Revolutionary Path*, New York.

Hoffman, B. (2006) *Inside Terrorism*, New York

Hogan, M. (1987) *The Marshall Plan*, New York.

Hogan, M. (1998) *A Cross of Iron*, New York.

Holden, G. (1990) *The Warsaw Pact*, New York.

Holden, R. H. and Zolov, E. (2000) *Latin America and the United States*, New York.

Holland, R. (1985) *European Decolonization 1918–1981: An Introductory Survey*, Basingstoke.

Holloway, D. (1983) *The Soviet Union and the Nuclear Arms Race*, New Haven, CT.

Holloway, D. (1994) *Stalin and the Bomb: The Soviet Union and Atomic Energy, 1939–1956*, New Haven, CT.

Holm, H.-H. (1995) *Whose World Order? Uneven Globalization and the End of the Cold War*, Boulder, CO.

Hood, S. J. (1992) *Dragons Entangled: Indochina and the China–Vietnam War*, Armonk, NY.

Hook, G. and MacCormack, G. (2001) *Japan's Contested Constitution: Documents and Analysis*, London.

Hook, G., Dobson, H., Gilson, J. and Hughes, C. (2001) *Japan's International Relations: Politics, Economics and Security*, London.

Horn, R. C. (1982) *Soviet–Indian Relations: Issues and Influence*, New York.

Hourani, A. (1993) *Arabic Thought in the Liberal Age, 1798–1939*, Cambridge.

Howe, C. (1996) *The Origins of Japanese Trade Supremacy: Development and Technology in Asia from 1540 to the Pacific War*, London.

Hughes, C. (1997) *Taiwan and Chinese Nationalism: National Identity and Status in International Society*, London.

Hunt, M. (1980) 'Mao Tse-tung and the Issue of Accommodation with the United States, 1948–1950', in Borg, D. and Heinrichs, W. (eds) *Uncertain Years: Chinese–American Relations, 1947–1950*, New York.

Hunt, M. (1987) *Ideology and American Foreign Policy*, New Haven, CT.

Hunt, M. H. (1996a) *Lyndon Johnson's War: America's Cold War Crusade in Vietnam, 1945–1965*, New York.

Hunt, M. H. (1996b) *The Genesis of Chinese Communist Foreign Policy*, New York.

Huntington, S. (1996) *The Clash of Civilisations and the Remaking of the World Order*, London.

Hyland, W. G. (1999) *Clinton's World*, Westport, CT.

Iatrides, J. O. and Wrigley, L. (eds) (1995) *Greece at the Crossroads: The Civil War and its Legacy*, University Park, MD.

Iliffe, J. (1979) *A Modern History of Tanganyika*, Cambridge.

Iliffe, J. (1995) *Africans: The History of a Continent*, Cambridge.

Imlay, T. (1998) 'Allied Economic Intelligence and Strategy during the "Phoney War"', *Intelligence and National Security*, vol. 13, pp. 107–32.

Imlay, T. (2003) *Facing the Second World War: Strategy, Politics, and Economics in Britain and France, 1938–40*, Oxford.

Immerman, R. (1982) *The CIA in Guatemala*, Austin, TX.

Iriye, A. (1965) *After Imperialism: The Search for a New Order in the Far East, 1921–1931*, Cambridge, MA.

Iriye, A. (1987) *The Origins of the Second World War in Asia and the Pacific*, London.

Iriye, A. (1997) *Japan and the Wider World: From the Mid-Nineteenth Century to the Present*, London.

Isaacs, A. (1983) *Without Honor: Defeat in Vietnam and Cambodia*, Baltimore, MD.

Isacoff, J. B. (2006) *Writing the Arab–Israeli Conflict: Pragmatism and Historical Enquiry*, Lanham, MD.

Isikoff, M. and Corn, D. (2007) *Hubris: The Inside Story of Spin, Scandal, and the Selling of the Iraq War*, New York.

Ismael, T. (1994) *The Gulf War and the New World Order: International Relations in the Middle East*, Gainesville, FL.

Jaber, H. (1997) *Hezbollah: Born with a Vengeance*, New York.

Jackson, A. (1999) *Ireland 1798–1998*, Oxford.

Jackson, H. F. (1984) *From the Congo to Soweto: US Foreign Policy towards Africa since 1960*, New York.

Jackson, P. (2000) *France and the Nazi Menace: Intelligence and Policy-Making 1933–39*, Oxford.

Jacobson, J. (1972) *Locarno Diplomacy: Germany and the West, 1925–1929*, Princeton, NJ.

Jacobson, J. (1983) 'Strategies of French Foreign Policy after World War I', *Journal of Modern History*, vol. 55, pp. 78–95.

Jafarzadeh, A. (2007) *The Iran Threat: President Ahmadinejad and the Coming Nuclear Crisis*, New York.

Jaipul, R. (1987) *Non-Alignment: Origins, Growth and Potential for World Peace*, New Delhi.

Jankowski, J. and Gershoni, I. (eds) (1997) *Rethinking Nationalism in the Arab Middle East*, New York.

Jayal, A. (1985) *The Sole Spokesman: Jinnah, the Muslim League and the Demand for Pakistan*, Cambridge.

Jeffrey, R. (ed.) (1981) *Asia: The Winning of Independence*, London.

Johnson, C. (1982) *MITI and the Japanese Miracle: The Growth of Industrial Policy, 1925–1975*, Stanford, CA.

Johnson, J. J. (1990) *A Hemisphere Apart: The Foundations of United States Policy toward Latin America*, Baltimore, MD.

Joll, J. (1990) *Europe since 1870*, 4th edn, London.

Joll, J. (1992) *The Origins of the First World War*, 2nd edn, London.

Jones, A. (2007) *Kabul in Winter: Without Peace in Afghanistan*, New York.

Jones, C. (1981) *Soviet Influence in Eastern Europe*, New York.

Jones, D. (2006) *ASEAN and East Asian International Relations: Regional Delusion*, Northampton, MA.

Judt, T. (2005) *Postwar: A History of Europe since 1945*, New York.

Kahin, G. (1986) *Intervention*, New York.

Kaiser, W. (1996) *Using Europe, Abusing the Europeans: Britain and European Integration, 1945–1963*, New York.

Kalb, M. (1982) *The Congo Cables: The Cold War in Africa from Eisenhower to Kennedy*, New York.

Kamali, M. (1998) *Revolutionary Iran: Civil Society and State in the Modernization Process*, Brookfield, IL.

Kamel, I. (1986) *The Camp David Accords: A Testimony*, London.

Kamman, W. (1968) *A Search for Stability: United States Diplomacy toward Nicaragua*, Notre Dame, IN.

Kaplan, K. (1987) *The Short March: The Communist Takeover in Czechoslovakia, 1945–1948*, New York.

Kaplan, L. (1994) *NATO and the United States: The Enduring Alliance*, New York.

Karabell, Z. (1999) *Architects of Intervention: The United States, the Third World, and the Cold War, 1946–1962*, Baton Rouge, LA.

Karnow, S. (1983) *Vietnam: A History*, New York.

Karsh, E. (1988) *Neutrality and Small States*, London.

Kataoka, T. (1991) *The Price of Constitution: The Origin of Japan's Postwar Politics*, New York.

Katz, F. (1981) *The Secret War in Mexico*, Chicago.

Katzenstein, P. (1996) *Cultural Norms and National Security: Police and Military in Postwar Japan*, Ithaca, NY.

Keeton, E. (1985) 'Politics and Economics in Briand's German Policy, 1925–31', in Fink, C. (ed.), *German Nationalism and the European Response*, Norman, OK.

Keith, R. (1989) *The Diplomacy of Zhou Enlai*, New York.

Kennedy, P. (1988) *The Rise and Fall of the Great Powers: Economic Change and Military Conflict from 1500 to 2000*, London.

Kennedy, R. (2001) 'Woodrow Wilson, World War I and the American Conception of National Security', *Diplomatic History*, vol. 25, pp. 1–31.

Keogh, D. (1994) *Twentieth Century Ireland: Nation and State*, Dublin.

Kepel, G. (2002) *Jihad: The Trail of Political Islam*, London.

Kepel, G. (2005) *The Roots of Radical Islam*, London.

Keylor, W. (ed.) (1998) *The Legacy of the Great War: Peacemaking, 1919*, New York.

Keynes, J. M. (1919) *The Economic Consequences of the Peace*, London.

Khalaf, I. (1991) *Politics in Palestine: Arab Factionalism and Social Disintegration, 1939–1948*, Albany, NY.

Khalidi, R. (1997) *Palestinian Identity: The Construction of Modern National Consciousness*, New York.

Khalidi, R. (2006) *Iron Cage: The Story of the Palestinian Struggle for Statehood*, Boston, MA.

Khalidi, R. *et al.* (eds) (1991) *The Origins of Arab Nationalism*, New York.

Khalidi, W. (1992) *All that Remains: The Palestinian Villages Occupied and Depopulated by Israel in 1948*, Washington, DC.

Khashan, H. (2000) *Arabs at the Crossroads: Political Identity and Nationalism*, Gainesville, FL.

Khatab, S. (2006) *The Power of Sovereignty: The Political and Ideological Philosophy of Sayyid Qutb*, London.

Khomeini, Imam Ruhollah (1980) *Islam and Revolution: Writings and Declarations of Imam Khomeini*, Berkeley, CA.

Khroub, K. (2000) *Hamas: Political Thought and Practise*, Washington, DC.

Kiernan, B. (1985) *How Pol Pot Came to Power: A History of Communism in Kampuchea, 1930–1975*, London.

Kiernan, B. (1992) *The Pol Pot Regime: Race, Power, and Genocide in Cambodia under the Khmer Rouge, 1975–79*, London.

Kim, C. I. E. and Mortimore, D. E. (eds) (1977) *Korea's Response to Japan: The Colonial Period, 1910–1945*, Kalamazoo.

Kim, H.-A. (2003) *Korea's Development under Park Chung Hee: Rapid Industrialization, 1961–1979*, London.

Kimball, J. (1999) *Nixon's Vietnam War*, Lawrence, KS.

Kimball, W. F. (1969) *The Most Unsordid Act: Lend-Lease 1939–1941*, Baltimore, MD.

Kimball, W. F. (1991) *The Juggler: Franklin Roosevelt as Wartime Statesman*, Princeton, NJ.

Kimche, D. (1955) *The Secret Roads: The 'Illegal' Migration of a People, 1938–1948*, New York.

Kimmerling, B. and Migdal, J. S. (2003) *The Palestinian People: A History*, Cambridge, MA.

Kingsbury, D. (2000) *Guns and Ballot Boxes: East Timor's Vote for Independence*, Clayton, Victoria.

Kingsbury, R., Remenyi, J., McKay, J. and Hunt, J. (2004) *Key Issues in Development*, Basingstoke.

Kitchen, H. (ed.) (1987) *Angola, Mozambique and the West*, New York.

Kitchen, M. (1990) *A World in Flames: A Short History of the Second World War in Europe and Asia, 1939–45*, London.

Klare, M. (1999) *Rogue States and Nuclear Outlaws*, New York.

Klinghofer, A. J. (1998) *The International Dimension of Genocide in Rwanda*, Basingstoke.

Knox, M. (1982) *Mussolini Unleashed 1939–41*, Cambridge.

Knox, M. (2000a) *Common Destiny: Dictatorship, Foreign Policy and War in Fascist Italy and Nazi Germany*, Cambridge.

Knox, M. (2000b) *Hitler's Italian Ally*, Cambridge.

Koch, H. W. (1984) *The Origins of the First World War*, 2nd edn, London.

Kolb, E. (1988) *The Weimar Republic*, London.

Kolhatkar, S., Ingalls, J. and Barsamian, D. (2006) *Bleeding Afghanistan: Washington, Warlords, and the Propaganda of Silence*, New York.

Kolko, G. (1985) *Anatomy of a War: Vietnam, the United States, and the Modern Historical Experience*, New York.

Kolko, G. (1988) *Confronting the Third World: United States Foreign Policy, 1945–1980*, New York.

Kolko, G. and Kolko, J. (1972) *The Limits of Power*, New York.

Korbonski, A. and Fukuyama, F. (eds) (1987) *The Soviet Union and the Third World: The Last Three Decades*, Ithaca, NY.

Korhonen, P. (1998) *Japan and Asia Pacific Integration: Pacific Romances 1968–1996*, London.

Kornbluh, P. (ed.) (2005) *The Pinochet File*, New York.

Kotz, D. and Weir, F. (1997) *Revolution from Above: The Demise of the Soviet System*, London.

Kovrig, B. (1991) *Of Walls and Bridges: The United States and Eastern Europe*, Durham, NC.

Kozloff, N. (2006) *Hugo Chavez: Oil, Politics, and the Challenge to the US*, London.

Krasner, S. (1985) *Structural Conflict: The Third World against Global Liberalism*, Berkeley, CA.

Krüzel, J. and Haltzel, M. H. (1989) *Between the Blocs: Problems and Prospects for Europe's Neutral and Nonaligned Countries*, New York.

Krystyna, K. (1991) *The Establishment of Communist Rule in Poland, 1943–1948*, Berkeley, CA.

Kumaraswamy, P. R. (ed.) (2000) *Revisiting the Yom Kippur War*, Portland, OR.

Kuniholm, B. (1980) *The Origins of the Cold War in the Near East: Great Power Diplomacy in Iran, Turkey, and Greece*, Princeton, NJ.

Kyle, K. (1991) *Suez*, New York.

Lacqueur, W. (1972) *A History of Zionism: From the French Revolution to the Establishment of the State of Israel*, New York.

LaFeber, W. (1969) *The New Empire*, Ithaca, NY.

LaFeber, W. (1983) *Inevitable Revolutions: The United States in Central America*, New York.

LaFeber, W. (1989) *The American Age*, New York.

Laffan, M. (1983) *The Partition of Ireland, 1911–25*, Dundalk.

Lake, A. (1989) *Somoza Falling*, Boston.

Lamb, M. and Tarling, N. (2001) *From Versailles to Pearl Harbor: The Origins of the Second World War in Europe and Asia*, Basingstoke.

Lane, A. and Temperley, H. (eds) (1995) *The Rise and Fall of the Grand Alliance, 1941–1945*, Basingstoke.

Langer, W. L. (1951) *The Diplomacy of Imperialism*, New York.

Langhorne, R. (1981) *The Collapse of the Concert of Europe: International Politics, 1890–1914*, London.

Langley, L. D. (1980) *The United States and the Caribbean, 1900–1970*, Athens, GA.

Langley, L. D. (1982) *The United States and the Caribbean in the Twentieth Century*, Athens, GA.

Lankov, A. N. (2001) *From Stalin to Kim Il Sung: The Formation of North Korea, 1945–1960*, London.

Latham, M. E. (2000) *Modernization as Ideology: American Social Science and 'Nation Building' in the Kennedy Era*, Chapel Hill, NC.

Lawrence, B. (ed.) (2005) *Messages to the World: The Statements of Osama Bin Laden*, London.

Lebow, R. N. and Stein, J. G. (1994) *We All Lost the Cold War*, Cambridge.

Leffler, M. (1979) *The Elusive Quest: America's Pursuit of European Stability and French Security, 1919–1933*, Chapel Hill, NC.

Leffler, M. (1992) *A Preponderance of Power: National Security, the Truman Administration and the Cold War*, Stanford, CA.

Leffler, M. (2007) *For the Soul of Mankind: The United States, the Soviet Union, and the Cold War*, New York.

Leffler, M. and Painter, D. S. (eds) (1994) *The Origins of the Cold War*, New York.

Lentin, A. (1984) *Lloyd George and the Pre-history of Appeasement*, London.

Leogrande, W. (1998) *Our Own Backyard*, Chapel Hill, NC.

Leonhard, A. T. (ed.) (1988) *Neutrality: Changing Concepts and Practices*, Lanham, MD.

Lesch, A. M. (1979) *Arab Politics in Palestine, 1917–1939: The Frustration of a National Movement*, Ithaca, NY.

Lévesque, J. (1997) *The Enigma of 1989: The USSR and the Liberation of Eastern Europe*, Berkeley, CA.

Levine, A. J. (1995) *The United States and the Struggle for Southeast Asia, 1945–1975*, Westport, CT.

Levy, J. S., Christensen, T. J. and Trachtenberg, M. (1991) 'Mobilisation and Inadvertence in the July Crisis', *International Security*, vol. 16, pp. 189–203.

Lewin, R. (1982) *The American Magic: Codes, Cyphers, and the Defeat of Japan*, New York.

Lewinson, J. and de Onis, J. (1970) *The Alliance that Lost its Way: A Critical Report on the Alliance for Progress*, Chicago.

Li, N. and Cribb, R. (eds) (2003) *Imperial Japan and National Identities in Asia, 1895–1945*, London.

Lieber, R. J. (1997) *Eagle Adrift*, New York.

Lieberthal, K. (1995) *Governing China: From Revolution to Reform*, New York.

Light, M. (ed.) (1993) *Troubled Friendships: Moscow's Third World Ventures*, London.

Lincoln, J. and Ferris, E. (1981) *Latin American Foreign Policies: Global and Regional Dimensions*, Boulder, CO.

Lindeman, M. *et al.* (1993) *The Role of the United States in a Changing World: Choices for the 21st Century*, New York.

Link, A. S. (1979) *Woodrow Wilson, Revolution, War, and Peace*, Arlington Heights, IL.

Liow, J. (2006) *Muslim Resistance in Southern Thailand and Southern Philippines: Religion, Ideology, and Politics*, Washington, DC.

Litwak, R. S. (1984) *Détente and the Nixon Doctrine: American Foreign Policy and the Pursuit of Stability, 1969–1976*, Cambridge.

Liu, Xiaoyuan (1996) *A Partnership for Disorder: China, the United States and their Policies for the Postwar Disposition of the Japanese Empire, 1941–1945*, Cambridge.

Ljunggren, B. (1993) *The Challenge of Reform in Indochina*, Cambridge, MA.

Lockman, Z. and Beinin, J. (1989) *The Palestinian Uprising against Israeli Occupation*, London.

Logevall, F. (1999) *Choosing War*, Berkeley, CA.

Lomperis, T. J. (1996) *From People's War to People's Rule: Insurgency, Intervention, and the Lessons of Vietnam*, Chapel Hill, NC.

Longmire, R. A. (1989) *Soviet Relations with South-East Asia: An Historical Survey*, London.

Louis, W. R. (1977) *Imperialism at Bay: The United States and the Decolonization of the British Empire*, Oxford.

Louis, W. R. (1984) *The British Empire and the Middle East, 1945–1951: Arab Nationalism, the United States and Postwar Imperialism*, Oxford.

Louis, W. R. and Stookey, R. W. (1986) *The End of the Palestine Mandate*, Austin, TX.

Lowe, P. (1977) *Great Britain and the Origins of the Pacific War: A Study of British Policy in East Asia, 1937–1941*, Oxford.

Lowe, P. (1996) *The Origins of the Korean War*, London.

Lowe, P. (ed.) (1998) *The Vietnam War*, London.

Lowenthal, A. (1972) *The Dominican Intervention*, Cambridge, MA.

Lowry, B. (1996) *Armistice 1918*, Kent, OH.

Lucas, N. (1975) *The Modern History of Israel*, New York.

Ludlow, N. P. (1997) *Dealing with Britain: The Six and the First UK Application to the EEC*, Cambridge.

Ludlow, N. P. (2006) *The European Community and the Crises of the 1960s: Negotiating the Gaullist Challenge*, London.

Ludlow, N. P. (ed.) (2007) *European Integration and the Cold War: Ostpolitik, Westpolitik, 1965–1973*, London.

Lughod, I. A. (1987) *The Arab–Israeli Confrontation of June 1967: An Arab Perspective*, Evanston, IL.

Lukacs, J. (1976) *The Last European War, September 1939–December 1941*, New York.

Lukacs, J. (1994) *Five Days in London: May 1940*, London.

Lukes, I. and Goldstein, E. (eds) (1999) *The Munich Crisis, 1938: Prelude to World War II*, London.

Lundestad, G. (1975) *The American Non-Policy in Eastern Europe*, New York.

Lundestad, G. (1998a) *'Empire' by Integration: The United States and European Integration, 1945–1997*, New York.

Lundestad, G. (ed.) (1998b) *No End to Alliance*, New York.

Lyons, F. S. L. (1973) *Ireland since the Famine*, London.

McAdams, J. (1985) *East Germany and Détente: Building Authority after the Wall*, Cambridge.

McCann, F. D. (1973) *The Brazilian–American Alliance*, Princeton, NJ.

McCarthy, J. (2000) *The Ottoman Peoples and the End of Empire*, London.

McCauley, M. (1995) *The Origins of the Cold War*, 2nd edn, London.

McCormack, G. (2004) *Target North Korea: Pushing North Korea to the Brink of Nuclear Catastrophe*, Washington, DC.

McCormick, T. J. (1995) *America's Half Century*, Baltimore, MD.

MacDonald, C. (1981) *The United States, Britain and Appeasement 1936–1939*, London.

MacDonald, C. A. (1972) 'Economic Appeasement and the German "Moderates" 1937–1939', *Past and Present*, vol. 56, pp. 105–35.

McDougall, W. (1978) *France's Rhineland Diplomacy, 1914–1924: The Last Bid for a Balance of Power in Europe*, Princeton, NJ.

MacFarquhar, R. (1974–97) *The Origins of the Cultural Revolution*, 3 vols, New York.

Macfie, A. L. (1998) *The End of the Ottoman Empire, 1908–1923*, New York.

McGarry, J. (2001) *Northern Ireland and the Divided World: Post-Agreement Northern Ireland in Comparative Perspective*, Oxford.

McGlothlen, R. (1993) *Controlling the Waves: Dean Acheson and US Foreign Policy in Asia*, New York.

McGwire, M. (1991) *Perestroika and Soviet National Security*, Washington, DC.

McKenna, T. M. (1998) *Muslim Rulers and Rebels: Everyday Politics and Armed Separatism in the Southern Philippines*, Berkeley, CA.

McKercher, B. J. (1984) 'Austen Chamberlain's Control of British Foreign Policy, 1924–29', *International History Review*, vol. 6, pp. 570–91.

Mackerras, C., Taneja, P. and Young, G. (1998) *China since 1978*, London.

McMahon, R. (1981) *Colonialism and the Cold War: The United States and the Struggle for Indonesian Independence, 1945–1949*, Ithaca, NY.

McMahon, R. (1994) *Cold War on the Periphery: The United States, India and Pakistan*, New York.

McMahon, R. (1995) 'The Cold War in Asia: Towards a New Synthesis', in Hogan, M. (ed.), *America in the World: The Historiography of American Foreign Relations since 1941*, New York.

McMahon, R. (1999) *The Limits of Empire: The United States and Southeast Asia since World War II*, New York.

Macmillan, M. (2007) *Nixon and Mao*, New York.

Maghoori, R. (1981) *The Yom Kippur War*, Washington, DC.

Mahathir M. (1986) *The Challenge*, Subang Jaya.

Maier, C. S. (1997) *Dissolution: The Crisis of Communism and the End of East Germany*, Princeton, NJ.

Maiolo, J. A. (1998) *The Royal Navy and Nazi Germany: A Study in Appeasement and the Origins of the Second World War*, Basingstoke.

Maiolo, J. A. and Boyce, R. (eds) (2003) *The Origins of World War Two: The Debate Continues*, Basingstoke.

Maley, W. (ed.) (1998) *Fundamentalism Reborn? Afghanistan and the Taliban*, London.

Malley, R. (1996) *The Call from Algeria: Third Worldism, Revolution and the Turn to Islam*, Berkeley, CA.

Mallie, E. and McKittrick, D. (1996) *The Fight for Peace: The Secret Story behind the Irish Peace Process*, London.

Mamdani, M. (1996) *Citizen and Subject: Contemporary Africa and the Legacy of Late Colonialism*, Princeton, NJ.

Mamdani, M. (2001) *When Victims Became Killers: Colonialism, Nativism and the Genocide in Rwanda*, Princeton, NJ.

Mandel, N. J. (1976) *The Arabs and Zionism before World War I*, Berkeley, CA.

Mandelbaum, M. (1981) *The Nuclear Revolution*, Cambridge.

Mann, J. (1998) *About Face: A History of America's Curious Relationship with China: From Nixon to Clinton*, New York.

Manning, C. and Van Diermen, P. (eds) (2000) *Indonesia in Transition: Social Aspects of Reformasi and Crisis*, Singapore.

Maoz, M. (1995) *Syria and Israel: From War to Peacemaking*, Oxford.

Mardor, M. M. (1964) *Haganah*, New York.

Marks, S. (1978) 'The Myth of Reparations', *Central European History*, vol. 18, pp. 231–55.

Marks, S. (2003) *The Illusion of Peace: International Relations in Europe, 1918–1933*, 2nd edn, Basingstoke.

Marr, D. (1981) *Vietnamese Tradition on Trial, 1920–1945*, Berkeley, CA.

Marsden, P. (1998) *The Taliban: War, Religion and the New Order in Afghanistan*, London.

Marshall, B. (1997) *Willy Brandt: A Political Biography*, Cambridge.

Martel, G. (1991) 'The Meaning of Power: Rethinking the Decline and Fall of Great Britain', *International History Review*, vol. 13, pp. 662–94.

Martel, G. (ed.) (1992) *The Origins of the Second World War Reconsidered*, London.

Martin, E. (1994) *Kennedy and Latin America*, Lanham, MD.

Martin, I. (2001) *Self-Determination in East Timor: The United Nations, the Ballot, and International Intervention*, Boulder, CO.

Martin, M. A. (1994) *Cambodia: A Shattered Society*, Berkeley, CA.

Masalha, N. (1992) *Expulsion of the Palestinians: The Concept of 'Transfer' in Zionist Political Thought, 1882–1948*, London.

Mason, M. (1992) *American Multinationals and Japan: The Political Economy of Japanese Capital Controls, 1899–1980*, Cambridge, MA.

Mastanduno, M. (1992) *Economic Containment: CoCom and the Politics of East–West Trade*, Ithaca, NY.

Mastny, V. (1979) *Russia's Road to the Cold War: Diplomacy, Warfare, and the Politics of Communism, 1941–1945*, New York.

Mastny, V. (1996) *The Cold War and Soviet Insecurity*, New York.

Mastny, V. and Byrne, M. (eds) (2006) *A Cardboard Castle? An Inside History of the Warsaw Pact*, Budapest.

Matar, P. (1988) *The Mufti of Jerusalem: Al-Hajj Amin al-Husayni and the Palestinian National Movement*, New York.

Matlock, J. F. (1995) *Autopsy on an Empire: The American Ambassador's Account of the Collapse of the Soviet Union*, New York.

May, E. R. (1961) *The Imperial Democracy*, New York.

May, E. R. (2000) *Strange Victory: Hitler's Conquest of France*, London.

May, E. R. and Zelikow, P. (eds) (1997) *The Kennedy Tapes: Inside the White House during the Cuban Missile Crisis*, Cambridge.

Mayer, A. (1968) *Politics and Diplomacy of Peacemaking: Containment and Counterrevolution at Versailles*, London.

Mayer, A. J. (1964) *Wilson versus Lenin: Political Origins of the New Diplomacy, 1917–18*, New Haven, CT.

Mayhew, A. (1998) *Recreating Europe*, New York.

Mazower, M. (1998) *Dark Continent: Europe's Twentieth Century*, London.

Meisner, M. (1999) *Mao's China and After: A History of the People's Republic*, New York.

Meital, Y. (2006) *Peace in Tatters: Israel, Palestine and the Middle East*, Boulder, CO.

Mendelson, S. E. (1998) *Changing Course: Ideas, Politics, and the Soviet Withdrawal from Afghanistan*, Princeton, NJ.

Meredith, M. (2005) *The State of Africa: A History of Fifty Years of Independence*, London.

Merrill, D. (1990) *Bread and the Ballot: The United States and India's Economic Development, 1947–1963*, Chapel Hill, NC.

Metcalf, B. D. and Metcalf, T. R. (2002) *A Concise History of India*, Cambridge.

Mickelson, S. (1983) *The Word War: The Story of Radio Free Europe and Radio Liberty*, New York.

Migdal, J. S. (1980) *Palestinian Society and Politics*, Princeton, NJ.

Miller, D. (1999) *The Cold War: A Military History*, New York.

Miller, J. (1986) *The United States and Italy, 1945–1950*, Chapel Hill, NC.

Mills, N. B. (2007) *Karzai: The Failing American Intervention and the Struggle for Afghanistan*, New York.

Milner, A. (1994) *The Invention of Politics in Colonial Malaya*, Cambridge.

Milstein, U. (1997) *History of Israel's War of Independence*, Lanham, MD.

Milward, A. (1984) *The Reconstruction of Western Europe*, New York.

Milward, A. (1992) *The European Rescue of the Nation-State*, Berkeley, CA.

Mishal, S. (1986) *The PLO under Arafat: Between Gun and Olive Branch*, New Haven, CT.

Mishal, S. and Sela, A. (2000) *The Palestinian Hamas: Vision, Violence and Coexistence*, New York.

Mitchell, G. (1999) *Making Peace: The Inside Story of the Making of the Good Friday Agreement*, London.

Mitchell, N. (1996) 'The Venezuela Blockade, 1902–3', *Diplomatic History*, vol. 20, pp. 185–209.

Mitchell, N. (1999) *The Danger of Dreams: German and American Imperialism in Latin America*, Chapel Hill, NC.

Mitchell, R. P. (1969) *The Society of the Muslim Brothers*, London.

Moaddel, M. (1992) *Class, Politics, and Ideology in the Iranian Revolution*, New York.

Moaddel, M. and Talatoff, K. (eds) (1999) *Contemporary Debates in Islam: An Anthology of Modernist and Fundamentalist Thought*, New York.

Mohamedou, M. M. O. (2007) *Understanding Al-Qaeda: The Transformation of War*, London.

Moïse, E. E. (1996) *Tonkin Gulf and the Escalation of the Vietnam War*, Chapel Hill, NC.

Monroe, E. (1981) *Britain's Moment in the Middle East 1914–1971*, London.

Montgomery Watt, W. (1968) *Islamic Political Thought*, Edinburgh.

Moore, R. J. (1974) *The Crisis of Indian Unity, 1917–40*, Oxford.

Moore, R. J. (1983) *Escape from India: The Attlee Government and the Indian Problem*, Oxford.

Morley, J. W. (ed.) (1976) *Deterrent Diplomacy: Japan, Germany and the USSR, 1935–1940*, New York.

Morley, J. W. (ed.) (1980) *The Fateful Choice: Japan's Advance into Southeast Asia, 1939–1941*, New York.

Morley, J. W. (ed.) (1983) *The China Quagmire: Japan's Expansion on the Asian Continent, 1933–1941*, New York.

Morley, J. W. (ed.) (1984) *Japan Erupts: The London Naval Conference and the Manchurian Incident, 1928–32*, New York.

Morley, J. W. (ed.) (1994) *The Final Confrontation: Japan's Negotiations with the United States, 1941*, New York.

Morris, B. (1987) *The Birth of the Palestinian Refugee Problem, 1947–1949*, Cambridge.

Morris, B. (1993) *Israel's Border Wars, 1949–1956*, Oxford.

Morris, B. (1999) *Righteous Victims: A History of the Zionist–Arab Conflict*, New York.

Morris, S. J. (1999) *Why Vietnam Invaded Cambodia: Political Culture and the Causes of War*, Stanford, CA.

Mortimer, R. (1984) *The Third World Coalition in International Politics*, Boulder, CO.

Morton, W. F. (1980) *Tanaka Giichi and Japan's China Policy*, New York.

Moussalli, A. (1999) *Moderate and Radical Islamic Fundamentalists: The Quest for Modernity, Legitimacy, and the Islamic State*, Gainesville, FL.

Munch-Petersen, T. (1981) *The Strategy of the Phoney War: Britain, Sweden and the Iron Ore Question, 1939–1940*, Stockholm.

Munro, D. G. (1974) *The United States and the Caribbean Republics, 1921–1933*, Princeton, NJ.

Murray, W. J., Knox, M. and Bernstein, A. (eds) (1994) *The Making of Strategy: Rulers, States and War*, Cambridge.

Musallem, A. (2005) *From Secularism to Jihad: Sayyid Qutb and the Foundations of Radical Islamism*, Westport, CT.

Muslih, M. Y. (1988) *The Origins of Palestinian Nationalism*, New York.

Mutalib, H. (1990) *Islam and Ethnicity in Malay Politics*, Singapore.

Naim, T. M. (2000) *Rise of the Young Turks: Politics, the Military and the Ottoman Collapse*, London.

Naimark, N. (1997) *The Russians in Germany*, Cambridge, MA.

Narine, S. (2002) *Explaining ASEAN: Regionalism in Southeast Asia*, Boulder, CO.

Nash, P. (1997) *The Other Missiles of October*, Chapel Hill, NC.

Nathan, A. and Ross, R. (1997) *The Great Wall and the Empty Fortress: China's Search for Security*, New York.

Nelson, K. (1995) *The Making of Détente: Soviet–American Relations in the Shadow of Vietnam*, New York.

Neuhold, H. and Thalberg, H. (eds) (1984) *The European Neutrals in International Affairs*, Boulder, CO.

Neuman, I. and Westad, O. A. (1994) *The Soviet Union in Eastern Europe, 1945–1989*, Oslo.

Nevakivi, J. (ed.) (1993) *Neutrality in History*, Helsinki.

Newhouse, J. (1988) *War and Peace in the Nuclear Age*, New York.

Newman, J. M. (1992) *JFK and Vietnam: Deception, Intrigue, and the Struggle for Power*, New York.

Newton, S. (1996) *Profits of Peace: The Political Economy of Anglo-German Appeasement*, Oxford.

Nicolson, H. (1933) *Peacemaking, 1919*, London.

Ninkovich, F. (1995) *Germany and the United States: The Transformation of the German Question since 1945*, New York.

Nish, I. (1972) *Alliance in Decline: A Study in Anglo-Japanese Relations, 1908–1923*, London.

Nish, I. (1993) *Japan's Struggle with Internationalism: Japan, China and the League of Nations, 1931–3*, London.

Noer, T. J. (1985) *Cold War and Black Liberation: The United States and White Rule in Africa, 1948–1968*, Columbia, MO.

Norton, A. R. (2007) *Hezbollah: A Short History*, Princeton, NJ.

Nüsse, A. (2002) *Muslim Palestine: The Ideology of Hamas*, London.

Nuttall, S. (2000) *European Foreign Policy*, Oxford.

Nye, J. S. (1993) *Understanding International Conflicts: An Introduction to Theory and History*, London.

Oberdorfer, D. (1998) *The Two Koreas: A Contemporary History*, Reading.

O'Day, A. (1998) *Irish Home Rule, 1867–1921*, Manchester.

Offner, A. A. (2002) *Another Such Victory: Harry S. Truman and the Cold War*, Stanford, CA.

Ogata, S. (1988) *Normalization with China: A Comparative Study of US and Japanese Processes*, Berkeley, CA.

O'Halpin, E. (1987) *The Decline of the Union: British Government in Ireland, 1892–1920*, Dublin.

O'Hanlon, M. and Mochizuki, M. M. (2003) *Crisis on the Korean Peninsula*, New York.

Okimoto, D. (1989) *Between MITI and the Market: Japanese Industrial Policy for High Technology*, Stanford, CA.

Olson, J. S. and Roberts, R. (1996) *Where the Domino Fell: America and Vietnam, 1945–1990*, New York.

Oren, M. (2002) *Six Days of War: June 1967 and the Making of the Modern Middle East*, New York.

Ouimet, M. J. (2003) *The Rise and Fall of the Brezhnev Doctrine in Soviet Foreign Policy*, Chapel Hill, NC.

Overy, R. J. (1989) *The Road to War*, London.

Overy, R. J. (1995) *Why the Allies Won*, London.

Packard, G. (1966) *Protest in Tokyo*, Princeton, NJ.

Packer, G. (2007) *The Assassins' Gate: America in Iraq*, New York.

Painter, D. S. (1999) *The Cold War*, New York.

Papacosma, V. and Rubin, M. (eds) (1988) *Europe's Neutral and Nonaligned States: Between Nato and the Warsaw Pact*, Wilmington, DE.

Pappé, I. (1994) *The Making of the Arab–Israeli Conflict, 1947–1951*, London.

Pappé, I. (ed.) (1999) *The Israel/Palestine Question*, London.

Pappé, I. (2006) *Ethnic Cleansing of Palestine*, Oxford.

Park, H. O. (2005) *Two Dreams in One Bed: Empire, Social Life, and the Origins of the North Korean Revolution in Manchuria*, Durham, NC.

Parker, R. A. C. (1993) *Chamberlain and Appeasement: British Policy and the Coming of the Second World War*, Basingstoke.

Parker, R. A. C. (2001) *The Second World War: A Short History*, Oxford.

Parker, R. B. (ed.) (1996) *The Six Day War: A Retrospective*, Gainesville, FL.

Parker, R. B. (ed) (2001) *The October War: A Retrospective*, Gainesville, FL.

Parks, J. D. (1983) *Culture, Conflict and Coexistence: American–Soviet Cultural Relations, 1917–1958*, Jefferson, NC.

Parr, H. (2005) *British Policy towards the European Community: Harold Wilson and Britain's World Role, 1964–1967*, Aldershot.

Parsa, M. (1998) *Social Origins of the Iranian Revolution*, New Brunswick, NJ.

Patch, W. L. (1998) *Heinrich Brüning and the Dissolution of the Weimar Republic*, Cambridge.

Paterson, T. G. (1992) *On Every Front*, New York.

Paterson, T. G. (1994) *Contesting Castro: The United States and the Triumph of the Cuban Revolution*, New York.

Paterson, T. G., Clifford, J. G. and Hagan, K. J. (1999) *American Foreign Policy: A History since 1900*, New York.

Patman, R. (1990) *The Soviet Union in the Horn of Africa*, Cambridge.

Patterson, T. C. (1999) *Change and Development in the Twentieth Century*, Oxford.

Pearlman, W. (2003) *Occupied Voices: Stories of Everyday Life from the Second Intifada*, New York.

Pells, R. (1997) *Not Like Us*, New York.

Pepper, S. (1978) *The Civil War in China: The Political Struggle, 1945–1949*, Berkeley, CA.

Peres, S. (1995) *Battling for Peace: A Memoir*, London.

Peretz, D. (1990) *Intifada: The Palestinian Uprising*, Boulder, CO.

Peretz, D. (1996) *Library in a Book: The Arab–Israel Dispute*, New York.

Peters, J. (1996) *Pathways to Peace: The Multilateral Arab–Israeli Peace Talks*, London.

Petterson, D. (1999) *Inside Sudan: Political Islam, Conflict, and Catastrophe*, Boulder, CO.

Peukert, D. J. K. (1991) *The Weimar Republic*, London.

Phillips, A. (1989) *The Enigma of Colonialism: British Policy in West Africa*, London.

Pick, D. (1993) *War Machine: The Rationalisation of Slaughter in the Modern Age*, New Haven, CT.

Pillar, P. (2004) *Terrorism and US Foreign Policy*, Washington, DC.

Pinder, J. (1999) *The Building of the European Union*, Oxford.

Pinder, J. (2007) *The European Union: A Very Short Introduction*, Oxford.

Pittman, A. (1992) *From Ostpolitik to Reunification*, Cambridge.

Pleshakov, C. (2005) *Stalin's Folly: The Secret History of the German Invasion of Russia, June 1941*, London.

Pollack, K. M. (2005) *The Persian Puzzle: The Conflict between Iran and America*, New York.

Pollard, R. A. (1985) *Economic Security and the Origins of the Cold War*, New York.

Pons, S. (2002) *Stalin and the Inevitable War: Origins of the Total Security State in the USSR and the Outbreak of World War II in Europe*, London.

Porat, D. (1990) *The Blue and Yellow Stars of David: The Zionist Leadership in Palestine and the Holocaust, 1939–1945*, Cambridge.

Porath, Y. (1974) *The Emergence of the Palestinian Arab Nationalist Movement, 1918–1929*, London.

Porath, Y. (1977) *The Palestinian Arab National Movement 1929–1939: From Riots to Rebellion*, London.

Porter, B. (1996) *The Lion's Share: A Short History of British Imperialism 1850–1995*, London.

Posel, D. (1991) *The Making of Apartheid 1948–61: Conflict and Compromise*, Oxford.

Post, G., Jr (1993) *Dilemmas of Appeasement: British Deterrence and Defence, 1934–1937*, Ithaca, NY.

Pottier, J. (2002) *Re-Imagining Rwanda: Conflict, Survival and Disinformation in the Late Twentieth Century*, Cambridge.

Prange, G. (1981) *At Dawn We Slept: The Untold Story of Pearl Harbor*, New York.

Prazmowska, A. J. (2000) *Eastern Europe and the Origins of the Second World War*, Basingstoke.

Preston, A. (2006) *The War Council: McGeorge Bundy, the NSC, and Vietnam*, Cambridge, MA.

Price, R. (1991) *The Apartheid State in Crisis: Political Transformation in South Africa, 1975–1990*, London.

Prunier, G. (1995) *The Rwanda Crisis, 1959–1994: The History of a Genocide*, London.

Qassem, N. (2005) *Hizbullah: The Story from Within*, London.

Qing, S. (2006) *From Allies to Enemies: Visions of Modernity, Identity, and US–China Diplomacy, 1945–1960*, Cambridge, MA.

Quandt, W. (1986) *Camp David: Peace Making and Politics*, Washington, DC.

Qutb, S. (1990) *Milestones*, Indianapolis, IN.

Rabe, S. G. (1988) *Eisenhower and Latin America: The Foreign Policy of Anticommunism*, Chapel Hill, NC.

Rabe, S. G. (1999) *The Most Dangerous Area in the World*, Chapel Hill, NC.

Rabinovich, I. (1985) *The War for Lebanon, 1970–1985*, New York.

Rabinovich, I. (1998) *The Brink of Peace: The Israeli–Syrian Negotiations*, Princeton, NJ.

Ramakrishna, K. and Tan, S. S. (2003) *After Bali: The Threat of Terrorism in Southeast Asia*, Singapore.

Randall, S. J. (1977) *The Diplomacy of Modernization: Colombian–American Relations, 1920–1940*, Toronto.

Randall, V. and Theobald, R. (1998) *Political Change and Underdevelopment: A Critical Introduction to Third World Politics*, Basingstoke.

Rashid, A. (2000) *Taliban: The Story of the Afghan Warlords*, London.

Reich, B. (1985) *Israel: Land of Tradition and Conflict*, Boulder, CO.

Reich, B. (1995) (ed.) *Arab–Israeli Conflict and Conciliation: A Documentary History*, Westport, CT.

Reich, W. (1998) *Origins of Terrorism: Psychologies, Ideologies, Theologies, States of Mind*, Washington, DC.

Reinhart, T. (2006) *Road Map to Nowhere: Israel/Palestine since 2003*, London.

Reinharz, J. and Shapira, A. (eds) (1996) *Essential Papers on Zionism*, London.

Remme, T. (1994) *Britain and Regional Cooperation in Southeast Asia, 1945–49*, London.

Remnick, D. (1998) *Resurrection: The Struggle for a New Russia*, New York.

Reynolds, D. (1981) *The Creation of the Anglo-American Alliance 1937–1941: A Study in Competitive Co-operation*, London.

Reynolds, D. (1985) 'Churchill and Britain's Decision to Fight on in 1940', in Langhorne, R., (ed.), *Diplomacy and Intelligence during the Second World War*, Cambridge.

Reynolds, D. (1989) 'Power and Wealth in the Modern World', *Historical Journal*, vol. 32, pp. 475–87.

Reynolds, D. (1990) '1940: Fulcrum of the Twentieth Century', *International Affairs*, vol. 66, pp. 325–50.

Reynolds, D. (ed.) (1994) *The Origins of the Cold War in Europe*, New Haven, CT.

Reynolds, D. (2001) *From Munich to Pearl Harbor: Roosevelt's America and the Origins of the Second World War*, Chicago.

Reynolds, D., Kimball, W. F. and Chubarian, A. O. (eds) (1994) *Allies at War: The Soviet, American and British Experience, 1939–45*, London.

Rich, N. (1992) *Great Power Diplomacy, 1815–1914*, New York.

Richardson, B. (1997) *Japanese Democracy*, New Haven, CT.

Richter, J. G. (1994) *Khrushchev's Double Bind: International Pressures and Domestic Coalition Politics*, Baltimore, MD.

Ricklefs, M. (1999) *A History of Modern Indonesia*, London.

Ricks, T. (2006) *Fiasco: The American Military Adventure in Iraq*, London.

Risse-Kappen, T. (1995) *Cooperation among Democracies: The European Influence on US Foreign Policy*, Princeton, NJ.

Riste, O. (ed.) (1985) *Western Security: The Formative Years*, New York.

Robb, P. (2002) *A History of India*, Basingstoke.

Roberts, G. (1995) *The Soviet Union and the Origins of the Second World War*, London.

Roberts, P. (ed.) (2006) *Behind the Bamboo Curtain: China, Vietnam, and the Cold War*, Stanford, CA.

Robinson, M. (2007) *Korea's Twentieth Century Odyssey*, Honolulu, HI.

Robinson, R. (1972) 'Non-European Foundations of European Imperialism: Sketch for a Theory of Collaboration', in Owen, R. and Sutcliffe, R. (eds) *Studies in the Theory of Imperialism*, Harlow.

Robinson, T. and Shambaugh, D. (eds) (1994) *Chinese Foreign Policy: Theory and Practice*, Oxford.

Rochester, S. I. (1977) *American Liberal Disillusionment in the Wake of World War I*, University Park, PA.

Rodman, P. (1994) *More Precious than Peace: The Cold War and the Struggle for the Third World*, New York.

Rogan, E. and Shlaim, A. (eds) (2002) *War for Palestine: Rewriting the History of 1948*, Cambridge.

Rogers, W. D. (1967) *The Twilight Struggle: The Alliance for Progress and the Politics of Development in Latin America*, New York.

Roman, P. J. (1995) *Eisenhower and the Missile Gap*, Ithaca, NY.

Roper, J. and Dockrill, S. (2007) *Over Thirty Years: The United States and the Legacy of the Vietnam War*, London.

Rosati, J. A. (1991) *The Carter Administration's Quest for Global Community*, Columbia, SC.

Rosberg, C. and Jackson, R. H. (1982) *Personal Rule in Black Africa: Prince, Autocrat, Prophet, Tyrant*, Berkeley, CA.

Rosenberg, E. (1982) *Spreading the American Dream*, New York.

Ross, D. (2005) *Missing Peace: The Inside Story of the Fight for Middle East Peace*, New York.

Ross, R. (1995) *Negotiating Cooperation: US–China Relations, 1969–1989*, New York.

Ross, R. and Jiang Changbin (eds) (2001) *Re-examining the Cold War: US–China Diplomacy, 1954–1973*, Cambridge, MA.

Ross, R. S. (1988) *The Indochina Tangle,* New York.

Roth, J. (1988) *The Impact of the Six Day War: A Twenty Year Assessment,* Basingstoke.

Rothkopf, D. J. (2006) *Running the World*, New York.

Rotter, A. J. (1987) *The Path to Vietnam: The Origins of the American Commitment to Southeast Asia*, Ithaca, NY.

Rotter, A. J. (2000) *Comrades at Odds: The United States and India, 1947–1964*, Ithaca, NY.

Rowe, J. C. and Berg, R. (1991) *The Vietnam War and American Culture*, New York.

Roxborough, I. (1979) *Theories of Underdevelopment*, Basingstoke.

Roy, O. (1994) *The Failure of Political Islam*, London.

Roy, O. (2000) *Globalised Islam: Fundamentalism, De-territorialisation and the Search for a New Ummah*, London.

Ruane, K. (2000) *The Rise and Fall of the EDC: Anglo-American Relations and the Crisis of European Defence, 1950–1955*, New York.

Rubin, B. (1994) *Revolution until Victory?: The Politics and History of the PLO*, Cambridge.

Rubin, B. (2003a) *Political Islam: Critical Concepts in Islamic Studies*, London.

Rubin, B. (2003b) *Revolutionaries and Reformers: Contemporary Islamist Movements in the Middle East*, Albany, NY.

Rubinstein, M. (1999) *Taiwan: A New History*, New York.

Ruiz, R. (1980) *The Great Rebellion*, New York.

Rusbridger, J. and Nave, E. (1991) *Betrayal at Pearl Harbor: How Churchill Lured Roosevelt into War*, London.

Rust, W. J. (1985) *Kennedy in Vietnam*, New York.

Rystad, G. (1982) *Ambiguous Imperialism*, Stockholm.

Saad-Ghorayeb, A. (2001) *Hizbullah: Politics and Religion*, London.

Saaler, S. and Koschmann, J. V. (eds) (2007), *Pan-Asianism in Modern Japanese History: Colonialism, Regionalism and Borders*, London.

Saborio, S. (1992) *The Premise and the Promise: Free Trade in the Americas*, New Brunswick, NJ.

Sachar, H. (1979) *A History of Israel: From the Rise of Zionism to our Time*, New York.

Sageman, M. (2004) *Understanding Terror Networks*, Philadelphia, PA.

Said, E. (1995) *Peace and its Discontents: Gaza-Jericho, 1993–1995*, London.

Said, E. (2000) *The End of the Peace Process: Oslo and After*, London.

Sainsbury, K. (1985) *The Turning Point . . . The Moscow, Cairo and Teheran Conferences*, Oxford.

Sam'o, E. (1971) *The June 1967 Arab–Israeli War: Miscalculation or Conspiracy?*, Wilmette, IL.

Sarantakes, N. (2000) *Keystone: The American Occupation of Okinawa and US–Japanese Relations*, College Station, TX.

Savir, U. (1998) *The Process: 1,100 Days that Changed the Middle East*, New York.

Sayigh, Y. (1997) *Armed Struggle and the Search for State: The Palestinian National Movement, 1949–1993*, Oxford.

Sayigh, Y. and Shlaim, A. (eds) (1997) *The Cold War and the Middle East*, Oxford.

Schaller, M. (1985) *The American Occupation of Japan: The Origins of the Cold War in Asia*, New York.

Schaller, M. (1997) *Altered States: The United States and Japan since the Occupation*, New York.

Scheman, R. (ed.) (1988) *The Alliance for Progress: A Retrospective*, New York.

Schiff, Z. and Ya'ari, E. (1984) *Israel's Lebanon War*, London.

Schiff, Z. and Ya'ari, E. (1989) *Intifada: The Palestinian Uprising – Israel's Third Front*, London.

Schimd, A. (2002) *Korea between Empires, 1895–1919*, New York.

Schoenhals, M. (1996) *China's Cultural Revolution, 1960–1969: Not a Dinner Party*, London.

Schoonover, T. (1991) *The United States in Central America, 1860–1911: Episodes in Social Imperialism and Imperial Rivalry in the World System*, Durham, NC.

Schoultz, L. (1998) *Beneath the United States: A History of US Policy toward Latin America*, Cambridge, MA.

Schraeder, P. J. (1994) *United States Foreign Policy towards Africa: Incrementalism, Crisis and Change*, Cambridge.

Schram, S. (1989) *The Thought of Mao Zedong*, Cambridge.

Schroeder, P. W. (1976) 'Alliances, 1815–1945: Weapons of Power and Tools of Management', in Knorr, K., *Historical Problems of National Security*, Lawrence, KS.

Schroeder, P. W. (1986) 'The 19th-Century International System: Changes in Structure', *World Politics*, vol. 39, pp. 1–26.

Schroeder, P. W. (1992) 'Did the Vienna Settlement Rest on a Balance of Power?', *American Historical Review*, vol. 92, pp. 683–706.

Schuker, S. (1988) *American 'Reparations' to Germany, 1919–1933*, Princeton, NJ.

Schulze, K. E. (1998) *Israel's Covert Diplomacy in Lebanon*, Basingstoke.

Schulze, K. E. (1999) *The Arab–Israeli Conflict*, London.

Schulzinger, R. (1997) *A Time for War*, New York.

Schulzinger, R. (2006) *A Time for Peace: The Legacy of the Vietnam War*, New York.

Schwabe, K. (1985) *Woodrow Wilson, Revolutionary Germany and Peacemaking, 1918–1919*, Chapel Hill, NC.

Schwartz, T. A. (1991) *America's Germany*, Cambridge, MA.

Scott, J. (1998) *After the End: Making US Foreign Policy in the Post-Cold War World*, Durham, NC.

Seal, A. (1968) *The Emergence of Indian Nationalism: Competition and Collaboration in the Later Nineteenth Century*, Cambridge.

Segal, G. (1982) *The Great Power Triangle*, Basingstoke.

Seiler, J. (ed.) (1980) *Southern Africa since the Portuguese Coup*, Boulder, CO

Sexton, B. (1989) *Ireland and the Crown, 1922–36: The Governor Generalship of the Irish Free State*, Dublin.

Shambaugh, D. (ed.) (1995) *Deng Xiaoping: Portrait of a Chinese Statesman*, Oxford.

Shambrook, P. (1998) *French Imperialism in Syria*, Reading.

Shapir, G. (1989) *Land, Labor and the Origins of the Israeli–Palestinian Conflict, 1882–1914*, Cambridge.

Shapira, A. (1992) *Land and Power: The Zionist Resort to Force*, New York.

Sharp, A. (1991) *The Versailles Settlement: Peacemaking in Paris 1919*, Basingstoke.

Sharp, A. and Stone, G. (eds) (2000) *Anglo-French Relations in the Twentieth Century: Rivalry and Cooperation*, London.

Shawcross, W. (1987) *Sideshow: Kissinger, Nixon and the Destruction of Cambodia*, New York.

Sheehan, N. (1990) *A Bright Shining Lie*, London.

Sheng, M. (1997) *Battling Imperialism: Mao, Stalin and the United States*, Princeton, NJ.

Sher, G. (2006) *Israeli–Palestinian Negotiations 1999–2004: Within Reach*, New York.

Shimazu, N. (1998) *Japan, Race and Equality: The Racial Equality Proposal of 1919*, London.

Shipway, M. (1996) *The Road to War: France and Vietnam, 1944–1947*, Oxford.

Shiraishi, T. (1990) *An Age in Motion: Popular Radicalism in Java 1912–1926*, Ithaca, NY.

Shlaim, A. (1983) *The United States and the Berlin Blockade*, Berkeley, CA.

Shlaim, A. (1988) *Collusion across the Jordan: King Abdullah, the Zionist Movement, and the Partition of Palestine*, Oxford.

Shlaim, A. (1995) *War and Peace in the Middle East: A Concise History*, London.

Shlaim, A. (2000) *The Iron Wall: Israel and the Arab World*, London.

Short, A. (1975) *The Communist Insurrection in Malaya, 1948–60*, London.

Short, A. (1989) *The Origins of the Vietnam War*, London.

Sigal, L. (1997) *Disarming Strangers: Nuclear Diplomacy with North Korea*, Princeton, NJ.

Sigmund, P. (1993) *The United States and Democracy in Chile*, Baltimore, MD.

Simms, B. (2001) *Unfinest Hour: Britain and the Destruction of Bosnia*, London.

Simpson, H. R. (1994) *Dien Bien Phu: The Epic Battle America Forgot*, McLean, VA.

Singh, A. I. (1987) *The Origins of the Partition of India, 1936–1947*, Oxford.

Singh, A. I. (1993) *The Limits of British Influence: South Asia and the Anglo-American Relationship, 1947–56*, London.

Skidmore, D. (1996) *Reversing Course: Carter's Foreign Policy, Domestic Politics, and the Failure of Reform*, Nashville, TN.

Skidmore, T. E. and Smith, P. H. (2002) *Modern Latin America*, New York.

Slater, K. and Johns, A. L. (eds) (2006) *The Eisenhower Administration, the Third World and the Globalization of the Third World*, Lanham, MD.

Smith, C. D. (1996) *Palestine and the Arab–Israeli Conflict*, New York.

Smith, D. (1995) *Japan since 1945: The Rise of an Economic Superpower*, Basingstoke.

Smith, G. (1986) *Morality, Reason and Power*, New Haven, CT.

Smith, G. (1993) *The Last Years of the Monroe Doctrine*, New York.

Smith, M. A. and Timmins, G. (2000) *Building a Bigger Europe*, Aldershot.

Smith, P. A. (1984) *Palestine and the Palestinians, 1876–1983*, London.

Smith, P. H. (2000) *Talons of the Eagle: Dynamics of US–Latin American Relations*, New York.

Smith, P. J. (ed.) (2005) *Terrorism and Violence in Southeast Asia: Transnational Challenges to States and Regional Security*, Armonk, NY.

Smith, R. B. (1984–1990) *An International History of the Vietnam War*, 3 vols, New York.

Snyder, J. (1984) 'Civil–Military Relations and the Cult of the Offensive, 1914 and 1984', *International Security*, vol. 9, pp. 58–146.

Sodaro, M. J. (1991) *Moscow, Germany and the West: From Khrushchev to Gorbachev*, Ithaca, NY.

Solomon, R. (1999) *The Transformation of the World Economy*, Basingstoke.

Sparks, A. (1995) *Tomorrow is Another Country: The Inside Story of South Africa's Negotiated Revolution*, London.

Spector, R. H. (1984) *Eagle against the Sun: The American War with Japan*, London.

Spence, J. (1999) *The Search for Modern China*, New York.

Starr, F. (1983) *Red and Hot: The Fate of Jazz in the Soviet Union*, New York.

Stegemann, B. *et al.* (1991) *Germany and the Second World War*, vol. II: *Germany's Initial Conquests in Europe*, Oxford.

Stegewerns, D. (ed.) (2003), *Nationalism and Internationalism in Imperial Japan: Autonomy, Asian Brotherhood, or World Citizenship?*, London.

Stein, K. (1984) *The Land Question in Palestine, 1917–1939*, Chapel Hill, NC.

Steiner, Z. (2005) *The Lights that Failed: European International History 1919–1933*, Oxford.

Stent, A. (1981) *From Embargo to Ostpolitik*, New York.

Stevenson, D. (1982) *French War Aims against Germany, 1914–1919*, Oxford.

Stevenson, D. (1991) *The First World War and International Politics*, Oxford.

Stevenson, D. (1996) *Armaments and the Coming of War: Europe, 1904–1914*, Oxford.

Stevenson, D. (1997a) 'Militarization and Diplomacy in Europe before 1914', *International Security*, vol. 22, pp. 125–61.

Stevenson, D. (1997b) *The Outbreak of the First World War: 1914 in Perspective*, London.

Stevenson, D. (2004) *1914–18: The History of the First World War*, London.

Stevenson, R. (1985) *The Rise and Fall of Détente: Relaxations of Tension in US–Soviet Relations, 1953–1984*, New York.

Stewart, D. J. (2007) *Good Neighbourly Relations: Jordan, Israel and the 1994–2004 Peace Process*, London.

Stinnett, R. (2000) *Day of Deceit: The Truth about FDR and Pearl Harbor*, New York.

Stockwin, J. A. A. (1999) *Governing Japan: Divided Politics in a Major Economy*, Oxford.

Stokes, G. (1997) *The Walls Came Tumbling Down*, New York.

Stone, N. (1999) *Europe Transformed, 1878–1919*, Oxford.

Strachan, H. (2001) *The First World War: To Arms*, Oxford.

Stuart-Fox, M. (1997) *A History of Laos*, Cambridge.

Stueck, W. (1995) *The Korean War: An International History*, Princeton, NJ.

Sudo, S. (1992) *The Fukuda Doctrine and ASEAN*, Singapore.

Summers, H. G., Jr. (1981) *On Strategy: The Vietnam War in Context*, New York.

Sun, Youli (1993) *China and the Origins of the Pacific War, 1931–1941*, New York.

Suret-Canale, J. (1971) *French Colonialism in Tropical Africa, 1900–1945*, London.

Suri, J. (2003) *Power and Protest: Global Revolution and the Rise of Détente*, Cambridge, MA.

Suskind, R. (2006) *The One Percent Doctrine: Deep inside America's Pursuit of its Enemies since 9/11*, New York.

Swain, G. and Swain, N. (1993) *Eastern Europe since 1945*, Cambridge.

Szalontai, B. (2005) *Khrushchev versus Kim Il-sung: Soviet–DPRK Relations and the Roots of North Korean Despotism, 1953–1964*, Stanford, CA.

Tal, D. (2004) *War in Palestine, 1948: Strategy and Diplomacy*, London.

Tamari, S. and Zureik, E. (2001) *Reinterpreting the Historical Record: The Uses of Palestinian Refugee Archives for Social Science Research and Policy Analysis*, Jerusalem.

Tarling, N. (ed.) (1992) *The Cambridge History of Southeast Asia*, vol. II, Cambridge.

Taubman, W. (1982) *Stalin's American Policy*, New York.

Taylor, A. J. P. (1954) *Struggle for the Mastery of Europe, 1848–1914*, Oxford.

Taylor, A. J. P. (1961) *The Origins of the Second World War*, London.

Taylor, C. (1999) *Sacrifice as Terror: The Rwandan Genocide of 1994*, Oxford.

Taylor, W. P. N. (2007) *State, Lands and Rural Development in Mandate Palestine, 1920–1948*, Brighton.

Teiwes, F. (1999) *China's Road to Disaster: Mao, Central Politicians, and Provincial Leaders in the Unfolding of the Great Leap Forward, 1955–1959*, Armonk, NY.

Telhami, S. (1990) *Power and Leadership in International Bargaining: The Path to the Camp David Accords*, New York.

Tessler, M. (1994) *A History of the Israeli–Palestinian Conflict*, Bloomington, IN.

Thakur, R. and Thayer, C. (1992) *Soviet Relations with India and Vietnam*, New York.

Thayer, C. (1989) *War by Other Means: National Liberation and Revolution in Viet-Nam, 1954–60*, Cambridge, MA.

Thomas, M. (2000) *The French North African Crisis: Colonial Breakdown and Anglo-French Relations, 1945–62*, Basingstoke.

Thorne, C. (1972) *The Limits of Foreign Policy: The West, the League, and the Far Eastern Crisis of 1931–1933*, London.

Thornton, R. C. (1991) *The Carter Years: Toward a New Global Order*, New York.

Tibi, B. (1997) *Arab Nationalism: Between Islam and the Nation-State*, London.

Timmerman, K. M. (2006) *Countdown to Crisis: The Coming Nuclear Showdown with Iran*, New York.

Tiruneh, A. (1993) *The Ethiopian Revolution 1974–1987: A Transformation from an Aristocratic to a Totalitarian Autocracy*, Cambridge.

Todd, O. (1990) *Cruel April: The Fall of Saigon*, New York.

Tomlinson, B. (1979) *The Political Economy of the Raj, 1914–1947: The Economics of Decolonization in India*, London.

Tooze, A. (2006) *The Wages of Destruction: The Making and Breaking of the Nazi Economy*, London.

Tov, Y. B. S. (1994) *Israel and the Peace Process, 1977–1982: In Search of Legitimacy for Peace*, Albany, NY.

Trachtenberg, M. (1980) *Reparations in World Politics: France and European Economic Diplomacy, 1916–1923*, New York.

Trachtenberg, M. (1982) 'Versailles after Sixty Years', *Journal of Contemporary History*, vol. 17, pp. 487–506.

Trachtenberg, M. (1991) *History and Strategy*, Princeton, NJ.

Trachtenberg, M. (1999) *A Constructed Peace: The Making of the European Settlement*, Princeton, NJ.

Trask, D. F. (1981) *The War with Spain in 1898*, New York.

Treverton, G. (1992) *America, Germany, and the Future of Europe*, Princeton, NJ.

Troen, S. I. and Shemesh, M. (eds) (1990) *The Suez-Sinai Crisis 1956: Retrospective and Reappraisal*, London.

Trotter, A. (1975) *Britain and East Asia, 1933–1937*, Cambridge.

Tsuzuki, C. (2000) *The Pursuit of Power in Modern Japan 1825–1995*, Oxford.

Tuch, H. J. (1990) *Communicating with the World: US Public Diplomacy Overseas*, New York.

Tucker, N. (1983) *Patterns in the Dust: Chinese–American Relations and the Recognition Controversy, 1948–1950*, New York.

Tucker, R. W. and Hendrickson, D. C. (1992) *The Imperial Temptation*, New York.

Turley, W. S. (1986) *The Second Indochina War: A Short Political and Military History, 1954–1975*, Boulder, CO.

Turner, H. A. (1996) *Hitler's Thirty Days to Power*, London.

Tyler, P. (1999) *A Great Wall: Six Presidents and China*, New York.

Uldricks, T. J. (1979) 'Russia and Europe: Diplomacy, Revolution and Economic Development in the 1920s', *International History Review*, vol. 1, pp. 55–83.

Urwin, D. W. (1991) *The Community of Europe: A History of European Integration*, New York.

Utley, J. (1985) *Going to War with Japan, 1937–1941*, Knoxville, TN.

Van Evera, S. (1984) 'The Cult of the Offensive and the Origins of the First World War', *International Security*, vol. 9, pp. 58–146.

van Oudenaren, J. (1991) *European Détente: The Soviet Union and the West since 1953*, Durham, NC.

Vital, D. (1975) *The Origins of Zionism*, Oxford.

Vital, D. (1982) *Zionism: The Formative Years*, Oxford.

Vital, D. (1987) *Zionism: The Critical Phase*, Oxford.

Vogel, E., Yuan Ming and Tanaka, A. (eds) (2002) *The Golden Age of the US–China–Japan Triangle, 1972–1989*, Cambridge, MA.

Wachtel, A. (1998) *Making a Nation, Breaking a Nation*, Stanford, CA.

Wade, R. (1990) *Governing the Market: Economic Theory and the Role of Government in East Asian Industrialization*, Princeton, NJ.

Wagnleitner, R. (1994) *Coca-Colonization*, Chapel Hill, NC.

Wahl, N. and Paxton, R. (1994) *De Gaulle and the United States*, New York.

Walker, M. (1994) *The Cold War*, New York.

Walker, T. (ed.) (1987) *Reagan versus the Sandinistas*, Boulder, CO.

Walker, T. (1990) *Revolution and Counterrevolution in Nicaragua*, Boulder, CO.

Wall, I. (2001) *France, the United States and the Algerian War*, Berkeley, CA.

Wallace, H. and Wallace, W. (eds) (2000) *Policy Making in the European Union*, Oxford.

Walworth, A. (1986) *Wilson and the Peacemakers*, New York.

Wasserstein, B. (1978) *The British in Palestine: The Mandatory Government and the Arab–Jewish Conflict, 1917–1929*, London.

Watt, D. C. (1989) *How War Came: The Immediate Origins of the Second World War, 1938–39*, London.

Watts, R. S. (1990) *Saigon: The Final Days*, Boise, ID.

Wawro, G. (2000) *Warfare and Society in Europe, 1792–1914*, London.

Wedeman, A. (1987) *The East Wind Subsides: Chinese Foreign Policy and the Origins of the Cultural Revolution*, Washington, DC.

Wegner, B. (1997) *From Peace to War: Germany, Soviet Russia, and the World, 1939–1941*, Oxford.

Weinberg, G. L. (1970 and 1980) *The Foreign Policy of Hitler's Germany*, vol. I: *Diplomatic Revolution in Europe, 1933–36* and vol. II: *Starting World War II, 1937–39*, Chicago.

Weinberg, G. L. (1994) *A World in Arms: A Global History of World War II*, Cambridge.

Welfield, J. (1988) *An Empire in Eclipse: Japan in the Postwar American Alliance System*, Atlantic Highlands, NJ.

Wenger, A. (1997) *Living with Peril: Eisenhower, Kennedy, and Nuclear Weapons*, Lanham, MD.

Westad, O. A. (1993) *Cold War and Revolution: Soviet–American Rivalry and the Origins of the Chinese Civil War, 1944–1946*, New York.

Westad, O. A. (ed.) (1997) *The Fall of Détente: Soviet–American Relations during the Carter Years*, Oslo.

Westad, O. A. (ed.) (1999) *Brothers in Arms: The Rise and Fall of the Sino-Soviet Alliance, 1945–1963*, Stanford, CA.

Westad, O. A. (ed.) (2000) *Reviewing the Cold War*, London.

Westad, O. A. (2003) *Decisive Encounters: The Chinese Civil War, 1946–1950*, Stanford, CA.

Westad, O. A. (2005) *The Global Cold War: Third World Interventions and the Making of our Times*, Cambridge.

Westad, O. A. *et al.* (eds) (1994) *The Soviet Union in Eastern Europe, 1945–1989*, New York.

Westrate, B. (1992) *The Arab Bureau: British Policy in the Middle East, 1916–20*, University Park, PA.

Whitfield, S. (1991) *The Culture of the Cold War*, Baltimore, MD.

Wieck, R. (1992) *Ignorance Abroad: American Educational and Cultural Foreign Policy*, Westport, CT.

Wigley, P. G. (1977) *Canada and the Transition to Commonwealth: British–Canadian Relations, 1917–26*, Cambridge.

Wilbur, J. M. (1984) *The Nationalist Revolution in China, 1923–1928*, Cambridge.

Willetts, P. (1978) *The Non-Aligned Movement: The Origins of a Third World Alliance*, London.

Williams, M. (1990) *Third World Cooperation: The Group of 77 in UNCTAD*, London.

Williams, P. (2002) *Al Qaeda: Brotherhood of Terror*, Parsippany, NJ.

Wilson, E. M. (1979) *Decision on Palestine: How the US Came to Recognize Israel*, Stanford, CA.

Wilson, K. (1994) 'The Anglo-Japanese Alliance of August 1905 and Defending India: A Case of the Worst Scenario', *Journal of Imperial and Commonwealth History*, vol. 21, pp. 334–56.

Wilson, K. (ed.) (1995) *Decisions for War, 1914*, London.

Wilson, S. (2001) *The Manchurian Crisis and Japanese Society, 1931–33*, London.

Winand, P. (1993) *Eisenhower, Kennedy and the United States of Europe*, New York.

Winn, N. and Lord, C. (2001) *EU Foreign Policy beyond the Nation-State*, London.

Wohl, R. (1980) *The Generation of 1914*, London.

Wohlforth, W. C. (1993) *The Elusive Balance: Power and Perceptions during the Cold War*, Ithaca, NY.

Wohlstetter, R. (1962) *Pearl Harbor: Warning and Decision*, Stanford, CA.

Wolffson, M. (1987) *Israel: Polity, Society and Economy, 1882–1986*, Atlantic Highlands, NJ.

Woo, J. (1991) *Race to the Swift: State and Finance in Korean Industrialization*, New York.

Woo-Cumings, M. (ed.) (1999) *The Developmental State*, Ithaca, NY.

Woods, R. B. (1980) *The Roosevelt Foreign Policy Establishment and the 'Good Neighbor'*, Lawrence, KS.

Woodward, B. (2002) *Bush at War*, New York.

Woodward, B. (2004) *Plan of Attack*, New York

Woodward, B. (2006) *State of Denial*, New York.

Worden, N. (2000) *The Making of Modern South Africa*, Oxford.

Wright, J. (1995) 'Stresemann and Locarno', *Contemporary European History*, vol. 4, pp. 109–31.

Wright J. W., Jr (2002) *Structural Flaws in the Middle East Peace Process: Historical Contexts*, New York.

Wright, T. (2001) *Latin America in the Era of the Cuban Revolution*, Westport, CT.

Wyback, T. (1990) *Rock around the Bloc: A History of Rock Music in Eastern Europe and the Soviet Union*, New York.

Xu, G. (2005) *China and the Great War: China's Pursuit of a New National Identity and Internationalization*, Cambridge.

Young, C. (1994) *The African Colonial State in Comparative Perspective*, New Haven, CT.

Young, J. (1990) *France, the Cold War, and the Western Alliance, 1944–1949*, New York.

Young, J. W. (1993) *Britain and European Unity, 1945–1992*, New York.

Young, L. (1997) *Japan's Total Empire: Manchuria and the Culture of Wartime Imperialism*, Berkeley, CA.

Young, L. (1999) 'Japan at War: History Writing on the Crisis of the 1930s', in Martel, G. (ed.), *The Origins of the Second World War Reconsidered*, London.

Young, M. B. (1990) *The Vietnam Wars*, New York.

Young, R. J. (1996) *France and the Origins of the Second World War*, New York.

Young, W. K. (2005) *Transforming Korean Politics: Democracy, Reform and Culture*, Armonk, NY.

Youngs, T. (2001) *The Middle East Crisis: Camp David, the 'Al-Aqsa Intifada' and the Prospects for the Peace Process*, London.

Zagoria, D. S. (1962) *The Sino-Soviet Conflict, 1956–1961*, Princeton, NJ.

Zaloga, S. (1993) *Target America: The Soviet Union and the Strategic Arms Race, 1945–1964*, Novato, CA.

Zayatt, M. (2004) *The Road to Al-Qaeda: The Story of Bin Laden's Righthand Man*, London.

Zhai, Q. (2000) *China and the Vietnam Wars, 1950–1975*, Chapel Hill, NC.

Zhang, S.-G. (1992) *Deterrence and Strategic Culture: Chinese–American Confrontations, 1949–1958*, Ithaca, NY.

Zhang, S.-G. (1995) *Mao's Military Romanticism: China and the Korean War, 1950–1953*, Lawrence, KS.

Zubok, V. (2007) *A Failed Empire: The Soviet Union in the Cold War from Stalin to Gorbachev*, Chapel Hill, NC.

Zubok, V. and Pleshakov, C. (1996) *Inside the Kremlin's Cold War: From Stalin to Khrushchev*, Cambridge, MA.

Zweig, R. (1986) *Britain and Palestine during the Second World War*, Woodbridge, Suffolk.

Index

eBooks

eBooks – at www.eBookstore.tandf.co.uk

A library at your fingertips!

eBooks are electronic versions of printed books. You can store them on your PC/laptop or browse them online.

They have advantages for anyone needing rapid access to a wide variety of published, copyright information.

eBooks can help your research by enabling you to bookmark chapters, annotate text and use instant searches to find specific words or phrases. Several eBook files would fit on even a small laptop or PDA.

NEW: Save money by eSubscribing: cheap, online access to any eBook for as long as you need it.

Annual subscription packages

We now offer special low-cost bulk subscriptions to packages of eBooks in certain subject areas. These are available to libraries or to individuals.

For more information please contact webmaster.ebooks@tandf.co.uk

We're continually developing the eBook concept, so keep up to date by visiting the website.

www.eBookstore.tandf.co.uk